D0237999

STRATEGIC ASIA 2005-06

STRATEGIC ASIA 2005–06

MILITARY MODERNIZATION
in an Era of Uncertainty

Edited by

Ashley J. Tellis and Michael Wills

With contributions from

Stephen J. Blank, John H. Gill, Christopher W. Hughes,
Roy D. Kamphausen, Kimberly Marten, Michael O'Hanlon,
Dwight Perkins, Jonathan D. Pollack, Mitchell B. Reiss, David Shambaugh,
Sheldon W. Simon, Michael D. Swaine, and Hugh White

NBR THE NATIONAL BUREAU *of* ASIAN RESEARCH
Seattle and Washington, D.C.

THE NATIONAL BUREAU *of* ASIAN RESEARCH

Published in the United States of America by
The National Bureau of Asian Research, Seattle, WA and Washington, DC
www.nbr.org

Copyright © 2005 by The National Bureau of Asian Research

All rights reserved. No part of this publication may be reproduced, stored in a retrieval
system, or transmitted in any form or by any means, electronic, mechanical, photocopying,
recording, or otherwise, without prior permission of the publisher.

Preparation of this publication was supported in part by the U.S. Department of Energy under
Grant No. DE-FG52-03 SF22724. The views expressed in these papers are those of the authors,
and do not necessarily reflect the views of the Department of Energy.

NBR makes no warranties or representations regarding the accuracy of any map in this
volume. Depicted boundaries are meant as guidelines only and do not represent the views of
NBR or NBR's funders.

Publisher's Cataloging-In-Publication Data
(Prepared by The Donohue Group, Inc.)

Strategic Asia 2005-06 : military modernization in an era of uncertainty /
    edited by Ashley J. Tellis and Michael Wills ; with contributions from Stephen J. Blank
    ... [et al.]
        p. : ill., maps ; cm.
        Prepared in part under U. S. Dept. of Energy grant no. DE-FG52-03 SF22724.
        Includes bibliographical references and index.
        ISBN: 0-9713938-6-9

    1. Asia--Defenses. 2. Asia--Strategic aspects. 3. Asia--Military policy. 4. Asia--Re-
lations--United States. 5. United States--Relations--Asia. 6. National security--Asia. I.
Tellis, Ashley J. II. Wills, Michael, 1970- III. Blank, Stephen, 1950- IV. National Bureau
of Asian Research (U.S.)

UA830 .S77 2005
355/.03/5

Design and publishing services by The National Bureau of Asian Research

Cover design by Stefanie Choi

Printed in Canada

The paper used in this publication meets the minimum requirement of the American National
Standard for Information Sciences—Permanence of Paper for Printed Library Materials, ANSI
Z39.48-1992.

Contents

Strategic Asia: Regional Studies

security relations with the United States, China, Japan, India, and
Australia.

Strategic Asia: Special Studies

An examination of the development of Australian strategic policy
and defense capabilities since the end of the Vietnam War.

An analysis of the current security climate in Asia with regard
to nuclear weapons, incentives for their acquisition, and different
contingencies that may prompt nuclear proliferation.

An examination of whether China will be able to sustain high
rates of economic growth over the coming decades, with implications drawn for the Chinese defense budget.

An in-depth review of Taiwan's security environment and qualitative and quantitative efforts to modernize its military in the face
of growing threats from China.

Strategic Asia: Indicators

Preface

Richard J. Ellings

Military modernization is occurring across Asia, but nowhere is it more striking than in China. For the past decade China has been rapidly modernizing its military capabilities through a combination of indigenous development, foreign purchases, and major improvements in doctrine, education, and training. The results, impressive by any measure, have surprised most observers; one of the contributors to this volume describes China's achievements as a "mini-leap." That may be an understatement. Military planners of the People's Liberation Army (PLA) have focused primarily on capabilities designed both to pressure Taiwan and to counter third parties, especially the United States, in a cross-Strait conflict. Many of these capabilities are mobile and flexible, however, and thus could be utilized for other contingencies. And some military programs will, in time, provide China the capacity to project power well beyond Taiwan.

China's rise constitutes the most salient change in international relations thus far in the 21st century. Accordingly, Chinese defense modernization and economic and diplomatic achievements are "drivers" that alter security perceptions throughout Asia as well as across the Pacific. Taiwan and Japan, in varying degrees, are modernizing their militaries and changing their security calculations in order to balance China's new capabilities. China is vying for influence in Central Asia, and has taken an active role in the region through the Shanghai Cooperation Organization. Southeast Asian states and India are also watching China's rise, finding that Beijing's newfound power and strategic interests represent a complex balance of economic opportunities and increasing uncertainties. As the recent Department of Defense report on China's military modernization notes, the fact that China is developing capabilities and likely readying for scenarios beyond Taiwan poses implications for the United States and the rest of Asia.

Strategic Asia 2005–06: Military Modernization in an Era of Uncertainty is the fifth volume in a series of annual reports from NBR's Strategic Asia Program. Like its predecessors, *Military Modernization in an Era of Uncertainty* is an integrated set of original studies that aims to provide the most authoritative information and analysis possible on strategic issues affecting U.S. interests in Asia. A companion website makes the Strategic Asia books and their accompanying executive summaries available online. The website also provides access to the groundbreaking Strategic Asia database, which contains a wealth of indicators for Asian demographic, trade, and financial trends; measures of states' economic and military capabilities; and information on political and energy dynamics.

The National Bureau of Asian Research (NBR) developed the Strategic Asia Program in order to fulfill three goals: (1) to provide a comprehensive understanding of the strategic environment in Asia; (2) to look forward five years, and in some cases beyond, to contemplate the region's future; and (3) to establish a record of data and assessment that will assist those interested in understanding both Asia's changing strategic landscape and the implications for regional stability. In essence, the aim of the program is to help policymakers, strategists, and scholars comprehend this critical region, and in particular the rise of China.[1]

Over the past five years the series has addressed how Asia is increasingly functioning as a zone of strategic interaction, one with a rapidly changing balance of power. The first volume in the series, *Strategic Asia 2001–02: Power and Purpose*, provided a systematic assessment of the strategies and interactions of the largest and most significant Asian powers—China, Japan, South Korea, Russia, and India. *Strategic Asia 2002–03: Asian Aftershocks* examined the consequences of the September 11 terrorist attacks on the United States and Asia. The third volume, *Strategic Asia 2003–04: Fragility and Crisis*, examined the sources of vulnerability in the political and economic systems of key states as well as in regional security and economic institutions, with particular reference to structural weaknesses in the balance of power. *Strategic Asia 2004–05: Confronting Terrorism in the Pursuit of Power* last year explored the implications of the war on terrorism for ongoing political, economic, social, and strategic transformations.

---

[1] The Strategic Asia Program views "Asia" as constituting the entire eastern half of the Eurasian landmass and the arc of offshore islands in the western Pacific. This vast expanse can be pictured as an area centered on China and consisting of four distinct sub-regions arrayed clockwise around it: Northeast Asia (including the Russian Far East, the Korean Peninsula, and Japan), Southeast Asia (encompassing both its mainland and maritime components), South Asia (including India and Pakistan, and bordered to the west by Afghanistan), and Central Asia (comprised of Kazakhstan, Kyrgyzstan, Tajikistan, Turkmenistan, Uzbekistan, and southern Russia). The Strategic Asia Program also tracks significant developments across the Asia-Pacific to the United States and Canada.

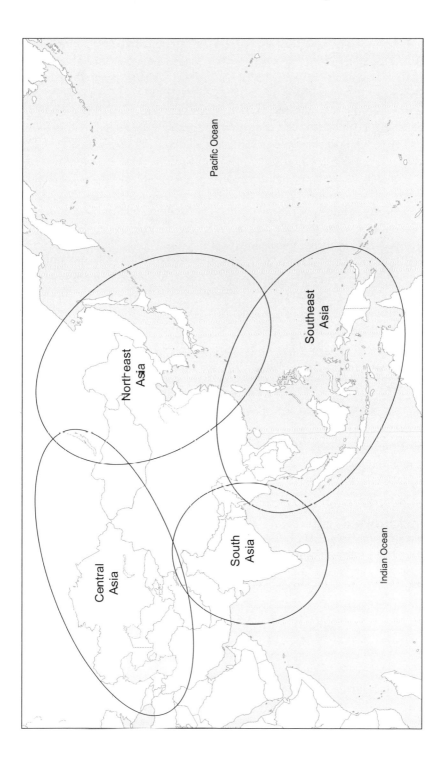

Following in the path of its predecessors, *Strategic Asia 2005–06: Military Modernization in an Era of Uncertainty* examines how the United States and the major Asian powers are transforming their defense capabilities in the context of their grand strategies. This assessment consists of a series of focused country, regional, and topical studies that address military modernization in response to significant developments in the region—China's rise as a regional power, the war on terrorism, changes in U.S. force posture, the revolution in military affairs, and local security dilemmas. Military modernization across Asia has been driven by the shifting priorities and changing security scenarios that have resulted from these dramatic events. Even as the United States undergoes its own force restructuring and military transformation, it remains the major actor in the region and the primary security guarantor for many of these countries. This year's volume identifies the strategic objectives of Asia's major powers and examines trends in the underlying balance of power, highlighting likely threats and opportunities that may arise in the next five years.

Strategic Asia 2005–06: Military Modernization in an Era of Uncertainty is designed to be the definitive reference volume that allows the reader to understand both the state and context of military modernization in Asia. The policy implications presented in each chapter flow directly from this objective. The volume sets out discussions of Asian countries' military capabilities, priorities, acquisitions, and defense transformations, all within larger analyses of their strategic objectives and perceptions of the regional security environment. The potential ramifications for the United States are assessed in the hope that identifying and examining the consequences of these strategies and military developments in the region will assist U.S. decisionmakers in their efforts to craft and strengthen U.S. policy toward Asia.

Acknowledgements

This year marks the Strategic Asia Program's fifth anniversary, and it is extremely gratifying to look back and see all that has been accomplished by the nearly 50 leading specialists who have written for the series. From the program's early conceptual origins in 1991, to our first planning meetings in Bellevue, Washington in the summer of 2000 involving the research team that contributed chapters to *Strategic Asia 2001–02: Power and Purpose*, through to this current volume, the program has developed into a sophisticated, forward-looking source of analysis and information for policymakers and academe. Presentations to public audiences and private briefings to government officials and members of Congress have been held every year to accompany the launch of each new volume, and have since expanded into regular events. Authors have frequently testified before committees of Congress. Since its inception in late 2001, the Strategic Asia website and database have provided an authoritative source, particularly for policymakers but also for students—the next generation of Asia specialists.

None of these achievements would have been possible without the wise advice and stewardship of the Strategic Asia Program's two Senior Advisors: General John Shalikashvili (ret.), former Chairman of the Joint Chiefs of Staff, and the program's founding research director Aaron Friedberg of Princeton University, whom we were very pleased to welcome back from leave following the conclusion of his government service as Deputy National Security Advisor to the Vice President. John and Aaron have been instrumental in shaping Strategic Asia, and I owe them an enormous debt of gratitude.

We were all delighted that Ashley Tellis elected to serve a second term as Research Director. His wisdom and fine judgment on the critical issues facing Asia and the United States have contributed immensely to the development of a policy-relevant research agenda, and, combined with his amicable personality, have also resulted in outstanding leadership of the research process. No less valuable have been the contributions of Program Director Michael Wills. Strategic Asia continues to develop and flourish as a result of Michael and Ashley's deft management and oversight. In their work, the directors have been assisted by Jessica Keough, who has managed many of the important day-to-day undertakings of the program—from the research planning meeting in March (held at the Sigur Center for Asian Studies at George Washington University), through the production of the book, to the organization of this year's presentation (at the Woodrow Wilson International Center for Scholars). NBR's new Editor, Andrew Marble, has superbly directed the review, editing, and production process for the volume, raising the standard of the book even higher. In this effort, he was ably assisted by Justin Jacobs and Jay Juntti. The technological aspects of the program, including the Strategic Asia website and database, are maintained through the remarkable dedication and expertise of Senior Programmer Erick Thompson and Programmer Ben Andrews.

The production of each Strategic Asia volume is a challenging task that depends on the work of many at NBR throughout the year. Graduate research fellows Peter Mattis and Evan Morrisey provided exceptional research assistance to the authors, compiled the appendix and indexed, and—along with Krista Goff, Michael Jones, and Jeremy Yellen—proofread the volume.

The outstanding work of this year's research team of scholars is the most important part of this process, and I would like to acknowledge the dedication and flexibility of the contributors in working to meet our exacting standards against tight deadlines. Thanks are also due to the many academic specialists and government analysts who assisted us this year with blind reviews of the draft chapters. Although remaining anonymous, they are by no means forgotten, and the high quality of this year's volume is in large part a result of their insightful comments and suggestions.

During this exciting period I have been extremely fortunate to be able to rely on the acumen and counsel of George Russell, NBR's Chairman, as well as the unfailing guidance of our Board of Directors. I also want to acknowledge with deep gratitude Brigitte Allen and Karolos Karnikis, Vice Presidents for Institutional Development and for Programs and Administration, respectively. Their valuable contributions are integral to the success of Strategic Asia and virtually everything we do at NBR. Lastly, I want to extend my deep gratitude to and acknowledgement of the Strategic Asia Program's sponsors—the Lynde and Harry Bradley Foundation, the Department of Energy, the GE Foundation, and the Henry M. Jackson Foundation. The generous support and commitment of these institutions have made all of our endeavors possible and encourage us to reach new heights.

Richard J. Ellings
President
The National Bureau of Asian Research
August 2005

STRATEGIC ASIA 2005–06

OVERVIEW

Executive Summary

This chapter overviews the strategic environment in Asia as it affects the military modernization efforts being undertaken by states in the region.

MAIN ARGUMENT:

Asian militaries are transforming their capabilities in order to cope with various kinds of strategic uncertainty. The defense transformation strategies followed by different Asian states reflect their specific threat environments, economic performance, security dilemmas, and national regime and state structures. This change has the potential to alter the region's strategic balance, and poses significant opportunities and challenges for both the U.S. and Asia.

POLICY IMPLICATIONS:

- Although a broad consensus exists across Asian states regarding the necessity of peace and political stability for the achievement of economic prosperity, a number of structural drivers, reinforced by internal considerations, are pushing states to invest in military modernization.

- China, India, Russia, Japan, and the U.S. are each qualitatively improving the force structure, warfighting capabilities, and deployed inventory of their armed forces. Most states are also increasing defense outlays and incorporating RMA components into their military modernization programs, with significant consequences for the regional balance of power.

- The U.S. will be called upon to maintain or even increase its role as regional security guarantor for a number of Asian states. This will require the U.S. to preserve its current military dominance, protect its existing alliances, and develop new ties to major states that are not allied or opposed to Washington. Not doing so would likely lead to military build-ups, increased tension, and even nuclear weapons proliferation.

- China will increasingly be the most important actor in Asia, both for other Asian countries as well as for the U.S. Many Asian powers are responding, at least in part, by developing military capabilities and outlaying defense expenditures as a safeguard against China's rise.

Military Modernization in Asia

Ashley J. Tellis

There is now a broad consensus that the Asian continent is poised to become the new center of gravity in global politics. From a historical perspective, this transformation is momentous in that—if present trends hold—for the first time since the beginning of modernity (circa 1500) the single largest concentration of global economic power will be found not in Europe or the Americas but rather in Asia. As the pioneering work of Angus Maddison has demonstrated, the Asian continent accounted for approximately 65% of the global product in 1500, in contrast to the 20% and .03% respective shares of Europe and the Americas. The era that followed saw the rise of colonialism, the emergence of revolutionary technical change, new patterns of global trade, and the phenomenon of major inter-state war. Asia's share of the global product declined precipitously during this new era, largely thanks to the fluctuating fortunes of key states such as China, Japan, and India. By 1950 Europe's share of the global product had risen to 29%, the Americas had claimed a hefty 38%, while the Asian portion of the total had fallen to only 18%.[1]

The end of World War II and the concomitant restructuring of the global system that followed ushered in new conditions that served to engender the recrudescence of Asia. The demise of the colonial order, the imperial (though contested) peace that was created and sustained by U.S. power, and the presence of purposive national elites in many Asian countries all combined to create the appropriate conditions for the success of specific national

---

Ashley J. Tellis is Senior Associate at the Carnegie Endowment for International Peace. He is Research Director of the Strategic Asia Program at NBR and co-editor of *Strategic Asia 2004–05: Confronting Terrorism in the Pursuit of Power*. He can be reached at <atellis@carnegieendowment.org>.

[1] Calculated from data in Angus Maddison, *The World Economy: A Millennial Perspective* (Paris: Development Centre of the Organisation for Economic Co-operation and Development, 2001), 261. Russia's contribution to the global output was excluded in these figures.

economic strategies that would produce sustained growth over time.[2] These economic strategies—which consisted of directed capitalism first witnessed in Japan and then in North and Southeast Asia, China, and India—paved the way for an explosion of national economic growth and an expansion of Asia's share in the global product. By 1998 Asia's share of global GNP had risen to about 37%, and most projections indicate that this proportion is likely to increase even further over the next decade and beyond. Lower growth in the labor force, reduced export performance, diminishing returns to capital, changes in demographic structure, and the maturation of the economy all suggest that national growth rates in several Asian states—in particular Japan, South Korea, and possibly China—are likely to decline in comparison to the latter half of the Cold War period. Asia's share of the global economy is, however, nevertheless likely to reach about 43% by 2025—and thus will constitute the largest locus of economic power worldwide.[3]

The current and prospective growth of the Asian economy will likely lead to larger military expenditures and different forms of military modernization. This expectation is based on the realist hypothesis that, since economic growth creates expanding national assets, all states embedded in a competitive system of international politics inevitably seek to protect these resources by increasing their military capabilities.[4] This crude causal relationship is qualified by a variety of factors, however, including a country's size, its geographical location, historical burdens, the salience of its immediate threats, regime character and state structure, and the structure of the larger regional or international system.[5]

Size is important because large states—whether in physical or economic terms—usually have immediate command over more resources than small states. Geographical location is likewise crucial, as strategically placed states must often allocate a relatively greater amount of military resources in order to protect their privileged position. Historical burdens become important when a state's experience of past threats, warfare, or defeat might motivate military investments. The salience of immediate threats is important for obvious reasons: the greater the security competition facing a state, the

[2] Ashley J. Tellis, "Smoke, Fire, and What to Do in Asia," *Policy Review*, no. 100 (April and May 2000), http://www.policyreview.org/apr00/tellis.html; and Ashley J. Tellis, et al., "Sources of Conflict in Asia," in *Sources of Conflict in the 21st Century: Regional Futures and U.S. Strategy*, ed. Zalmay Khalilzad and Ian O. Lesser (Santa Monica: RAND, 1998), 43–170.

[3] Norihisa Sakurai, "Growth Potential of Asian Economy," Central Research Institute of Electric Power Industry, annual research report, 2001, http://criepi.denken.or.jp/en/e_publication/a2001/01seika45.pdf.

[4] See the historical evidence as reviewed in Paul Kennedy, *The Rise and Fall of the Great Powers: Economic Change and Military Conflict from 1500 to 2000* (New York: Random House, 1987).

[5] Jasen Castillo, et al., *Military Expenditures and Economic Growth* (Santa Monica: RAND, 2001).

larger the incentives are to neutralize threats through military preparation, whether via internal balancing or external alliances. Regime character and state structure are critical because they determine how able a country is in accurately processing information concerning its external environment. These two variables also shape resource allocation for internal versus ex ternal defense, as well as condition outside perceptions of a country's fears, ambitions, and ideology. Finally, the structure of the larger regional or international system is important because it defines, in a Parsonian sense, the "system of action" within which a country must operate: the international structure describes the distribution of power, particularly the potential for alliances insofar as they either exacerbate or mitigate the security dilemmas facing any particular state.

Asia as a Cynosure for Military Modernization

All of the above factors are examined, explicitly or implicitly, in the various country and regional studies gathered in this volume on military modernization in Asia. Taken together, the chapters show that military modernization, as a response to uncertainty, remains alive and well throughout "Strategic Asia." The forms such modernization takes, the challenges it is oriented to address, and the urgency with which it is undertaken, however, reflect both the diversity of the region itself and the challenges peculiar to each of the "security complexes" of which Asia is composed.[6] If military expenditures are any indication, then defense spending by key actors in Strategic Asia's prism of focus suggests an upward trend positively correlated with each country's pattern of economic growth in the post-1990 period. This phenomenon is not surprising when viewed against the backdrop of their grand strategies: the military capabilities of the various Asian states in general and their modernization efforts in particular reveal that the Asian continent remains an arena of active high politics.

The sheer productivity of the continent ensures this outcome in the first instance. Apart from the United States, which is an Asian power by virtue of both its global preeminence and its security presence on the continent, the region hosts a concentration of major economic centers: Japan, China, South Korea, India, Australia, and important though lesser Southeast Asian states. The continuing growth of these centers, which is in large part due to foreign trade, strengthens their connectivity both with the United States and increasingly with one another. This dynamic of economic growth has result-

---

[6] For more on the term "security complexes," see Barry Buzan, *People, States and Fear: An Agenda for International Security Studies in the Post-Cold War Era* (Boulder: Lynne Rienner Publishers, 1991), 190 ff.

ed ineluctably in rising energy requirements, most of which cannot be satisfied domestically. As a result, almost every major Asian economic power has begun to look outward for dependable sources of energy; this in turn has led to a mix of competitive acquisition strategies that may require military components to assure their effectiveness.[7] The chapters on China, Japan, and India conclude that the protection of energy access constitutes one of the key drivers of military modernization among the large Asian states.

While the demands of sustaining economic growth may thus by themselves assure the continuing relevance of military instruments in Asia—at least for all the major powers and for many of the lesser states as well, the vitality of traditional inter-state politics in Asia further guarantees their prominence well into the foreseeable future.

First and foremost, the Asian continent remains the arena wherein the interests of three great powers—the United States, Russia, and China—actively intersect. Japan and India have also leveled claims for similar recognition through their expressed desire for permanent United Nations Security Council membership. At the moment, peaceful relations exist between all five of these states. Whether such a state of tranquility can last in perpetuity, however, is unclear. China and India are rising powers both haunted by historical humiliations and intent on securing their rightful place in the emerging international order. As a result, the two countries are extraordinarily sensitive to issues of sovereignty and status, and both face secessionist (or potential secessionist) movements. Not surprisingly, then, Beijing and New Delhi have also embarked on major programs of military modernization in a bid to consolidate existing capabilities while simultaneously developing new competencies. In this volume, David Shambaugh's chapter on China and John Gill's chapter on India document the multiple dimensions of this phenomenon.

While both China and India constitute conspicuous examples of rising Asian powers, the challenge of integrating the former into the international system is, for multiple reasons, likely to be far more difficult than integrating the latter. First, Chinese efforts to resolve the "secessionist threat" posed by Taiwan (which Beijing—despite having no physical control over the island— regards as an inalienable part of China) puts China into potential conflict with the United States. As "long cycle" theorists of international politics have persuasively pointed out, systemic wars often arise not so much because rising states mount direct attacks on a hegemon, but rather because such states happen to attack either key allies of the existing hegemon or important neu-

---

[7] Thomas P.M. Barnett, "Asia's Energy Future: The Military-Market Link," in *Globalization and Maritime Power*, ed. Sam J. Tangredi (Washington D.C.: National Defense University Press, 2003), 189–200.

trals.[8] Such regional conflicts often degenerate into systemic struggles that conclude only when the existing hegemon—which enters the fray initially to protect an embattled ally or neutral—has effectively arrested the threatening shift in the future balance of power.[9]

Second, China (unlike India) historically presided over a unique system of regional hierarchy where its primacy was acknowledged (even when its power was challenged) by the surrounding states.[10] If the current Chinese effort at accumulating national power is successful, Beijing is likely to pursue some facsimile of that same historical order that served China's power and status so well. The prospect of such an outcome, which could eventually include an effort to marginalize the United States in Asia, has already spurred both the United States and regional powers (such as Japan and India) to carefully scrutinize China's emerging military capabilities. Michael O'Hanlon, Christopher Hughes, and John Gill each expand on this point in their respective chapters on U.S., Japanese, and Indian military modernization. That Taiwan is particularly concerned about China's political objectives should not come as a surprise. In their chapter on Taiwan's military modernization, Michael Swaine and Roy Kamphausen note, however, that Taipei's pressing security concerns have, partly for reasons of domestic politics and partly because of sclerotic bureaucratic processes, not translated into an entirely coherent military acquisition and force structure response. Even in Southeast Asia where, as Sheldon Simon points out in his chapter, military modernization is driven more by internal rather than by external security drivers, concern about China's strategic trajectory remains strong. Key Southeast Asian states not only desire a continued U.S. presence to balance China, but given their interests as trading states may also be willing to countenance an Indian and Japanese naval presence designed specifically to protect the sea lines of communication so vital to their national security.

Concerns regarding China's growing power and future trajectory are felt keenly even in Russia, a country that has contributed more to the modernization of Beijing's military capabilities than any other. Moscow's assistance to Beijing—which stems from an effort to sustain Russia's military-industrial complex until the national economy can stabilize—carries grave risks, however. As Stephen Blank notes in his chapter, though Russia fears "the rise of China and Beijing's attendant enhanced ability to project power into Central Asia, Korea, and Taiwan," Moscow appears unable to "compete

---

[8] The *locus classicus* of long cycle theory remains George Modelski, *Long Cycles in World Politics* (Seattle: University of Washington Press, 1987).

[9] See Michael D. Swaine and Ashley J. Tellis, *Interpreting China's Grand Strategy: Past, Present, and Future* (Santa Monica: Rand, 2000), 182–229.

[10] John K. Fairbanks, ed., *The Chinese World Order* (Cambridge: Harvard University Press, 1968).

with China's booming wealth and power. Many Russian scholars fear that Russia has no strategy toward China (or Asia in general), let alone one to deal with urgent threats like the nuclearization of North Korea. Thus Russia risks dependence upon China."

Thus concerns about the future of Beijing's growing power are present in all the major states along China's periphery. If Beijing decides to pursue a policy of actively asserting Chinese centrality in the Asian security order at some future point in time, conflict with the United States and possibly with other regional entities would almost certainly follow. Cognizant of this prospect, Beijing has in recent years adopted "a kinder, gentler turn" in its grand strategy.[11] This change is designed both to allay the fears of the international community and preempt the rise of balancing coalitions against China. Despite these efforts, fears that China might increasingly assert itself in line with its growing economic power have already evoked suspicion—occasionally bordering on mistrust—in the United States and Asia. This problem is exacerbated by other issues involving trade, currency arrangements, border disputes, and the extent of Beijing's military modernization. Although both U.S. and Asian policymakers politely welcome China as an emerging power into the international community, there is a palpable sense of uncertainty—and a subliminal disquiet—concerning China's future interests and behavior.

The prospect that China may be able to sustain such rapid growth some time into the future only strengthens concerns regarding Beijing's long-term intentions. Dwight Perkins' special study in this volume on the future of China's growth captures two dimensions of this issue. He notes that despite significant weakness in the financial system, severe environmental degradation, and the challenges posed by large-scale rural to urban migration, Chinese economic growth is likely to be sustained "for at least the next decade" as long as exogenous problems such as Taiwan can be successfully avoided. This in turn implies that Beijing's military spending and technological modernization will likely continue to rise (as it has since 1996) in real terms. Such a continued increase will probably exacerbate anxiety over Chinese military capabilities that are now prevalent in the United States, Japan, India, Russia, and some Southeast Asian states. Since high rates of economic growth are essential for China's political stability, however, and since protectionist responses in the United States to this growth would only exacerbate the already high bilateral tensions, Perkins prudently concludes that the United States (and its European allies) should not assist Beijing's de-

---

[11] Ashley J. Tellis, "China's Grand Strategy," IISS *Strategic Comments* 10, no. 9 (November 2004), http://www.carnegieendowment.org/publications/index.cfm?fa=view&id=16178.

fense modernization efforts. Outside of this lone strategy, there is little these Western countries can do to prevent rising Chinese military expenditures.

Finally, the authoritarian character of China's domestic regime makes Beijing the object of suspicion in the United States as well as in many other countries. Beijing has been gradually accumulating sophisticated military capabilities, first in the realm of hardware but equally and perhaps more importantly in the area of integration, which includes advances made in manpower quality, organization, doctrine, tactics, training, education, maintenance, logistics, and infrastructure. That such a powerful, non-democratic regime is improving its military capabilities in this way has strengthened concerns regarding the future of Chinese power in a way that does not carry over comparably to a democratic state like India. U.S. Secretary of State Condoleezza Rice conveyed these anxieties carefully when she stated:

> ... China's internal evolution is still undetermined. And as we look at issues of religious freedom, issues of human rights, as we look to the relationship between Taiwan and China, we see that there are matters of concern that still might take a bad turn, and so our policies have to be aimed at trying to [make] the most of our opportunities to mitigate against that circumstance in those cases.
>
> ... We want a confident China that can play an increasing role [in the region]. It is nonetheless a good thing that China plays that role in the context of democratic alliances like the United States and Japan that bring not just [strength], economic and other strengths, but bring democratic values to the core of this region. So, as we look to China's life, I really do believe that the U.S.-Japan relationship, the U.S.-South Korean relationship, the U.S.-Indian relationship, all are important in creating an environment in which China is more likely to play a positive role than a negative role. These alliances are not against China; they are alliances that are devoted to a stable security and political and economic and, indeed, values-based relationships that put China in the context of those relationships, and a different path to development than if China were simply untethered, simply operating without that strategic context.[12]

Exacerbating such fears are China's relatively faster economic growth and larger concentration of capabilities relative to India. Moreover, the fact that many of the military instruments now being acquired primarily for employment against Taiwan have great utility beyond this contingency (i.e., can be used to support a regional dominance role) and the fact that the Communist regime in Beijing has had a history of ruthlessly employing force against its own subjects, only makes the nature of the Chinese state a critical variable with respect to integrating that country into the global order.

---

[12] Secretary of State Condoleezza Rice, "Remarks at Sophia University," Tokyo, March 19, 2005, http://www.state.gov/secretary/rm/2005/43655.htm.

The integration of the region's rising powers has a direct bearing on military modernization in Asia. Managing the evolution of other established states, however, also affects stability in different ways. One example is Russia, which—though possessing enormous nuclear capabilities, a significant military-industrial complex, and large natural resources—must come to terms with its own weakness. While Moscow is no doubt attempting comprehensive modernization, Stephen Blank's chapter concludes that "summing up Russia's overall strategic environment, defense reforms, and defense economy, the unavoidable conclusion is that Russia—much like the USSR—remains trapped on a 'treadmill of reforms.'"

North Korea embodies even more complicated problems. The last Stalinist regime on earth oversees a totalitarian political structure, a brittle and decaying economy, a large and capable—though currently stagnant—conventional military force, and new nuclear capabilities of uncertain magnitude. In his survey of the Koreas in this volume, Jonathan Pollack reminds readers, however, that although there have been repeated predictions of its demise, the Democratic People's Republic of Korea (DPRK) has demonstrated "grim resilience and a knack for exploiting external aid and economic ties." South Korea, a loyal U.S. ally throughout the Cold War, now appears to have reached a strategic crossroads. Seoul struggles to accommodate a competitive but failing North, while South Korea's democratic efflorescence appears to be leading the nation away from the United States and back into China's sphere of influence—where it has historically resided across the centuries. Pollack's essay urges U.S. policymakers to recognize the fact that the ROK "no longer describes the DPRK as the ROK's 'major enemy,'" but more importantly, that South Korean leaders presently believe that their country "cannot achieve its full power potential in the absence of normal relations with the North and more equitable ties with the United States." This quest for equitable ties, Pollack warns, portends "a major redefinition of ROK national interests and a parallel commitment to pursue policies independent of the United States."

A comparable dynamic may be underway in Australia, another traditional ally of the United States. In his special study on Australian strategic policy in this volume, Hugh White cautions that, at least as far as the rise of China is concerned, Canberra's attitudes now differ greatly from those of Washington. White notes that Canberra has identified one of its interests as preventing the emergence of Chinese hegemony in Asia, and is investing in maritime capabilities that will allow it to support the United States in the Western Pacific over coming decades. As in many other Asian states, however, China's economic influence has begun to change political calculations even in Australia, and White accordingly warns that "Australia will not support a U.S. approach that forces its allies to choose between the United States and China."

While Australia has not yet articulated a definitive approach to China, Japan is clearly moving in a more decisive direction. This is partly due to Japan's physical proximity to China, the ongoing difficulties in Sino-Japanese relations, and the historical rivalry between the two countries. Continuing a strategic shift dating back to the 1980s, Japan appears to be slowly but surely stepping out of its atypical postwar straitjacket of being an economic strength married to military weakness. The prospect of such a new role for Japan not only evokes mixed feelings around the Asian periphery but also holds significant implications for the larger balance of power. As Christopher Hughes observes in his chapter, an "increasing emphasis on military modernization will provide a route for Japan to achieve its long-debated, more proactive and 'normal' role in regional and global security, and one closely identified with expanded U.S.-Japan alliance cooperation." He cautions, however, that "Japanese policymakers—as is the case with other 'normal' key allies—will remain mindful of entrapment, and will thus seek to maintain their 'double hedge' against both exclusive reliance on military power and the U.S.-Japan alliance as a security guarantee." The various Southeast Asian states remain engrossed in managing domestic problems even as they sustain impressive rates of economic growth, manage the threats of terrorism and interethnic rivalries, and attempt to positively engage China through economic interdependency. Viewed in this context, Sheldon Simon concludes that "by maintaining an ongoing air and naval presence in the region, the United States can both assist Southeast Asian states with external balancing vis-à-vis China and support anti-piracy, maritime, and anti-terrorism efforts."

In the greater South Asian region, Pakistan—a critical battlefront in the global war on terrorism—remains in the process of an ongoing internal transformation, one which unfortunately has not yet been thorough or successful enough. As John Gill's contribution points out, this failure is in part due to Islamabad's continued support of *jihadi* insurgents who operate in Indian Kashmir and elsewhere as "a low-cost means of occupying and demoralizing Indian ground forces." This strategy has not only "come to threaten Pakistan itself," but also other countries around globe—as the recent terrorist activities in London and elsewhere have demonstrated. Further west, Iran continues to be ruled by Islamist clerics. After years of economic stagnation, rising oil prices have recently granted Tehran a reprieve. If the current discussions with the EU-3 (France, Germany, and the United Kingdom) fail to produce a satisfactory outcome, however, Iran will likely continue along the path toward development of a nuclear weapons capability. Mitchell Reiss's contribution on "Patterns of Future Nuclear

Proliferation in Asia" notes, however, that "Tehran's nuclear program is not nearly as advanced as Pyongyang's," which "may make it relatively easier to dismantle facilities—such as uranium enrichment and plutonium separation facilities—that present the greatest proliferation risks. In short, in Iran's case there is time for diplomacy to work."

Finally, to the north of Iran lies the cluster of post-Soviet Central Asian states that have historically been—and are again today—objects of a Great Game. In her survey of the region, Kimberly Marten observes that these states remain locked in the crisis of transition that defined their existence since their separation from the Soviet Union: the effort to consolidate democratic institutions and market economies continues amidst authoritarian efforts to maintain power, an ongoing (and justified) war on terrorism and religious extremism (which various regional political leaders unfortunately exploit to discredit their legitimate opposition), and the presence of rampant corruption and suffocating state dominance of the national economy. Against this backdrop, the Central Asian states—much like their counterparts in Southeast Asia—view the rise of China as merely one more challenge to overcome alongside such others as defeating Islamist opposition groups, the acquisition of "defense-related external support to be used as a domestic political resource; improving defense against external threats, including border disputes among states in the region; and the use of defense support as a means of competition between the external great powers."

These diverse realities condition military modernization in Asia in complex ways. They suggest beyond a doubt that military instruments are in no danger of becoming irrelevant in Asia and, given the significant security competition and interstate disputes that define the continental landscape, will continue to remain crucial. Many interstate disputes in Asia stem from historical legacies, including the status of Taiwan, China's boundary disagreements with India, competing claims in the South China Sea, the rivalry between India and Pakistan, Japan's territorial disputes with Russia, and the challenges of Korean unification. In this context, issues revolving around Taiwan, Korea, and the Indian subcontinent remain the most important contingencies likely to further intensify military modernization well into the foreseeable future. Interstate disputes, including those between local entities and the United States, also drive the perennial interest in weapons of mass destruction (WMD). The cases of North Korea and Iran (both emerging nuclear powers) and China (an established nuclear power) are clear examples. As Gaurav Kampani succinctly stated in last year's Strategic Asia volume:

> Three out of the world's four remaining states suspected of possessing chemical weapons are in Asia, and all of the states with biological weapons programs are Asian as well. Similarly, five of the current eight nuclear weapon powers

are located on the continent, which is also home to the two other countries widely suspected of pursuing nuclear weapons programs—North Korea and Iran. Within Asia, new demand for WMD is concentrated in three subregions: the Korean Peninsula, South Asia, and the Middle East. North Korea's ruined economy has left the Kim Jong Il regime with few assets other than WMD and ballistic missiles to trade with the outside world. In South Asia, recurrent Indo-Pakistani crises over Jammu and Kashmir have led most observers to conclude that the region is perhaps the likeliest site for a future nuclear exchange. The Middle East has a history of autocratic governance, political violence, and WMD use in both intrastate and interstate conflict. The region's problems with Islamism, sectarian religious conflicts, high population growth, economic stagnation, and popular disaffection with ruling regimes conjure up nightmare scenarios of political instability, revolution, civil war, failed states, and WMD terrorism. The intersection of mass destruction capabilities and the rise of religious extremism, political disaffection, economic disarray, and deep interstate and intrastate conflicts make Asia the most disaster-prone region in the world.[13]

While Kampani's judgments are sobering, Mitchell Reiss's essay emphasizes that "the United States will likely remain the key actor in preventing [further] nuclear proliferation in the region but this will require significant time and resources." This responsibility would require Washington to pay attention to the reinvigoration of international institutions and regimes that manage proliferation—such as the International Atomic Energy Agency (IAEA), Nuclear Non-Proliferation Treaty (NPT), and the U.S. Cooperative Threat Reduction (Nunn-Lugar) program. It is equally important to stress, however, that what will determine the success or failure of all international nonproliferation efforts is not merely upholding certain universal rules but preserving the potency of U.S. power, especially its military instruments. Accordingly, Reiss persuasively concludes that, because the temptations for countries to pursue WMD ambitions (especially nuclear programs) will endure for a variety of reasons, the United States ought to adopt a broader, more strategic approach that is more in tune with the interests of Washington's friends and allies in Asia while continuing to maintain the requisite deterrence capabilities necessary to assure the success of this strategy. The most recent innovations in both U.S. policy (such as the Bush administration's recent agreement on civil nuclear cooperation with India) and in U.S. nuclear strategy (as exemplified by the Nuclear Posture Review) ought to be viewed in this light.[14]

---

[13] Gaurav Kampani, "WMD Diffusion in Asia: Heading Towards Disaster?" in *Strategic Asia 2004–05: Confronting Terrorism in the Pursuit of Power*, ed. Ashley J. Tellis and Michael Wills (Seattle: The National Bureau of Asian Research, 2004), 381–82.

[14] For details, see The White House, "Joint Statement Between President George W. Bush and Prime Minister Manmohan Singh," July 18, 2005, http://www.whitehouse.gov/news/releases/2005/07/20050718-6.html; and Department of Defense, "Special Briefing on the Nuclear Posture Review," January 9, 2002, http://www.defenselink.mil/transcripts/2002/t01092002_t0109npr.html.

The complexity of the security environment in Asia explains the emphasis on, and variation in, military modernization in the region. These structural drivers behind military modernization in Asia are reinforced, moreover, by internal drivers, which include bureaucratic politics, the presence of product champions within various domestic political systems, interest groups with a stake in continued military modernization, and the co-existence of different ideologies, many of which advocate and justify the need for strong national military capabilities. Despite the presence of all these variables, however, a remarkable consensus obtains throughout the continent that political stability and the absence of war are essential for the successful conclusion of Asia's current economic transition. Whether by allowing for the completion of ongoing domestic reforms, raising trade intensity as a function of GNP, or increasing participation in regional economic bodies so as to raise growth levels and secure larger shares of the global product, national leaders and elites in all of the major Asian states (China, Japan, South Korea, India, Russia, and Australia) remain preoccupied with enhancing economic performance. In order to reach such ambitious goals, a long peace is essential. Consequently, all the Asian countries agree that— barring any grave provocation or threat—recourse to military action is undesirable. Thus most, if not all, states seek to avoid disturbing the territorial status quo. Even where revisionist activities are underway—mostly notably in Taiwan with respect to China and Pakistan vis-à-vis India—they take the form of political activism and terrorism rather than concerted challenges involving overt military action.

Despite the strong conviction of various national leaders that peace is indispensable for the successful culmination of their economic renewal efforts, Asian countries continue with defense inventory expansion, upgrade, and diversification. The fact that military modernization persists in the major regional states alongside a robust commitment to economic development suggests that the most consequential players in Asia have reached at least three preliminary conclusions (insofar as such modernization is driven at least as much by structural as by bureaucratic interests). First, they do not perceive military modernization to be in any way subversive of larger economic aims. Second, there is sufficient strategic uncertainty in the future security environment that Asian leaders feel the need—despite a fervent commitment to economic renewal—to acquire the relevant military capabilities. Third, national leaders are not convinced that the current surge in economic activity and the accompanying growth in economic interdependence witnessed all around Asia provide sufficient guarantees for the spread of peace and prosperity in the foreseeable future—or at least a peace secure enough so as to obviate the need for military modernization in the interim.

Asian Military Modernization in this Volume

This volume, titled *Strategic Asia 2005-06: Military Modernization in an Era of Uncertainty*, reexamines a theme—namely military capabilities of various Asian states as seen in the context of their grand strategies—that was first explored five years ago in the inaugural work, *Strategic Asia 2001-02: Power and Purpose*. The continuing ferment in Asia provides ample justification for revisiting the nature and patterns of military modernization in the continent, and particularly in the specific geographic areas of interest to the Strategic Asia Program. For the purposes of this volume, the definition of military modernization is deliberately broad and inclusive. As there is no single universally understood or accepted concept of military modernization, this volume focuses on the improvement of military capabilities. Military modernization is thus defined as the relevant upgrade or improvement of existing military capabilities through the acquisition of new imported or indigenously developed weapons systems and supporting assets, the incorporation of new doctrines, the creation of new organizational structures, and the institutionalization of new manpower management and combat training regimes. The chapters in this volume all suggest that varied and diverse activities in the areas listed above are underway in each of the countries or regions covered by the Strategic Asia Program. A focused and systematic analysis of these activities is worthwhile for at least three specific reasons.

First, Asian economic growth has picked up considerably following the financial hiccups of the late 1990s, and the region has now returned to its role as the engine of global economic growth. Not surprisingly, Asian defense budgets are therefore rising once again, and the region is probably the largest arms market in the world—the Asia-Pacific region alone acquired more than $150 billion worth of arms between 1990 and 2002. Some of the world's most prolific arms buyers are located in this region, including Taiwan, Japan, Australia, China, South Korea, and India. Richard Bitzinger has called attention to the steadily rising defense budgets in the region:

> Military expenditures in the Asia Pacific market grew by nearly 27 percent in real terms over the past decade, and an extra $126 billion was added to regional defense budgets between 1992 and 2002. India's defense budget has doubled since the early 1990s, for example, while Chinese military expenditures increased by more than 140 percent in just the past six years (1997-2003).[15]

---

[15] For a superb overview of this issue, see Richard A. Bitzinger, "The Asia-Pacific Arms Market: Emerging Capabilities, Emerging Concerns," *Asia-Pacific Security Studies* 3, no. 2 (March 2004). This and the following paragraph draw extensively from Bitzinger's paper.

A multitude of evidence suggests that all the major countries in the Asia-Pacific region (with the lone exception of Thailand) increased their overall defense spending during the decade from 1992–2002. Even taking into account the 1997 Asian financial crisis, the remaining states were at least able keep their military budgets above their 1992 levels (See **Figure 1**). The purchases that the various Asian states are making, the integration of these new capabilities, and the strategic and operational purposes behind these new acquisitions are therefore worthy of sustained examination.

Most informed observers conclude that rising regional military expenditures—and the concomitant trend in rising arms imports—are unlikely to abate any time soon. China, Japan, South Korea, Taiwan, India, and Australia have all unveiled multibillion-dollar military modernization programs that will be implemented in the coming decade. Chinese defense spending will likely continue to grow at double-digit rates for some time to come. South Korea intends to invest more than $17 billion in modernizing its armed forces from 2003 to 2007. Taiwan will spend more than $20 billion over the next decade on new military equipment, including eight diesel-electric submarines, antisubmarine warfare (ASW) aircraft, and an anti-ballistic missile system. For three consecutive years now, India has announced double-digit increases in defense spending. After a hiatus of many years, Pakistan has increased defense expenditures by more than 15 percent in its national budget for 2005–06. Japan, Malaysia, and Singapore have also recently committed to major increases in defense expenditures over the next few years. Uncertainties in the future strategic environment appear to be the common ingredient underlying this phenomenon. As one industry analyst has described the situation:

> One aspect of Asian defense is [that] it is very difficult to know what the future threat will look like. Procurement has to be based on a variety of scenarios and allow for a variety of potential opponents equipped with a variety of potential systems. It is difficult to determine where the next 10 years will go. The one thing that is certain is that air dominance remains absolutely the most important thing.[16]

Second, the current geopolitical environment in Asia is changing in ways that are likely to have global consequences over the long term. China's ascent to great power status has so far proceeded more or less successfully. China has managed to sustain relatively high rates of economic growth for close to thirty years now, and continues to pursue accelerated military modernization across both the nuclear and conventional realms. This modern-

---

[16] Richard Aboulafia, senior analyst, Teal Group, cited in Amy Bickers, "Asia: Military Spending," *GlobalSecurity.org*, March 6, 2000, http://www.globalsecurity.org/wmd/library/news/china/2000/-000306-prc1.htm.

Figure 1. Asian Defense Expenditures by Region

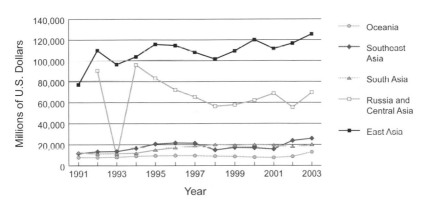

Source: International Institute for Strategic Studies, *The Military Balance*, (London: Oxford University Press, various years).

ization, though motivated immediately by Beijing's desire to deter Taiwan independence, could, in the words of the Pentagon's most recent report on China's military modernization, "provide China with a force capable of prosecuting a range of military operations in Asia—well beyond Taiwan potentially posing a credible threat to modern militaries operating in the region."[17] According to the U.S. Department of Defense, the character, extent, and pace of China's military modernization are already "such as to put regional military balances at risk" and have significant implications for the Asian continent as a whole.[18] Furthermore, Japan, India, and Russia (among others) have already begun to respond in both overt and subtle ways to the growth of Chinese military power.

Partly in anticipation of the rise of China, the United States is implementing plans to revamp its global basing strategy. Such a development will carry major implications for Washington's capacity to project power in Asia and thereby sustain current (and prospective) U.S. alliances in the region. The structural principles motivating this new basing strategy transcend China, however, and are rooted in the larger obligations associated with the maintenance of U.S. global primacy. In order to accomplish these aims, Washington intends to maintain a ring of permanent military hubs on the U.S. mainland and overseas territories (such as Guam) as well as in closely allied countries (such as the United Kingdom and Japan). Many of the major

---

[17] Department of Defense, "The Military Power of the People's Republic of China, 2005," annual report to Congress, 13.

[18] Ibid.

bases on which the United States had relied in the past, however—such as those in Saudi Arabia, Turkey, Germany, and South Korea—are slated to be replaced by dozens of spartan "forward operating bases" and "forward operating locations." These so-called "lily pads," which will be located throughout southern Europe, the Middle East, and Asia, will be maintained by small, permanent support units. Taken together, these "lilies across a pond" will be the base of operations for highly sophisticated and flexible U.S. and coalition units that will deploy with maximum speed into trouble spots lying along a vast "arc of instability" running from the Andean region in the Southern Hemisphere through North Africa to the Middle East and into and around Southeast Asia.[19] In Asia, the challenges of dealing with a wide gamut of contingencies—ranging from the defeat of Islamist terrorism to the rise of China—have compelled Washington to supplement traditional U.S. bases in Northeast Asia with new access arrangements and facilities in Central and Southeast Asia (extending as far east as Guam). These new facilities will likely become a new hub for the deployment of U.S. long-range bombers, an Air Force fighter wing, refueling aircraft, long-range unmanned air vehicles (UAV), an aircraft carrier, and additional nuclear attack submarines. Examining how these developments condition the grand strategic choices of various Asian states—including the prospects for new alliances and other forms of security cooperation, options for developing national deterrents involving WMD, as well as all the more usual alternatives involving conventional military modernization—remain an object of great interest to this volume.

Third, the revolution in military affairs (RMA), first dramatized during the 1991 Gulf War and further reflected in the U.S. military's performance in both Afghanistan since 2001 and Iraq since 2003, has changed the conception of modern warfare. If the promise of the RMA is to be realized, however, new generations of weaponry and concomitant doctrinal, organizational, and training innovations must follow the growth in networked information technologies. While the United States remains the leading proponent of the incorporation of the RMA within its military force structure, defense transformation is not, and will never be, an enduring monopoly of the United States.[20] The major changes currently transforming both technology and the character of conflict almost certainly ensure that various competitors—such as the large, well-endowed, and resource-advantaged states in Asia—will likely absorb RMA technologies into their military forces. This

---

[19] Vernon Loeb, "New Bases Reflect Shift in Military: Smaller Facilities Sought for Quick Strikes," *Washington Post*, June 9, 2003.

[20] Andrew F. Krepinevich, "Defense Transformation," testimony before the United States Senate Committee on Armed Services, April 9, 2002, 3.

may occur either in a straightforward emulative way or, in some instances, in an asymmetric fashion intended to obstruct the United States from successfully prosecuting its own operational objectives.

The Bush administration's emphasis on defense transformation is undoubtedly linked to the preservation of U.S. primacy. The strategic objective in this instance is to create capabilities that are "strong enough to dissuade potential adversaries from pursuing a military build-up in hopes of surpassing, or equaling, the power of the United States."[21] At a more prosaic level, however, defense transformation is aimed at resolving critical operational problems that confront the exercise of U.S. power—in particular, the challenge of protecting the homeland while simultaneously preserving the capacity to engage in unhindered power projection operations worldwide. The United States must meet these twin objectives in the face of global terrorism, a significant number of states armed with WMD and long-range delivery systems, and several regional competitors in possession of both capable military forces and ingenious ways of employing military instruments. In order to overcome these challenges, the United States is exploiting the emerging RMA to address what the 2001 Quadrennial Defense Review termed "critical operational goals."[22] These goals include the protection of critical bases of operation both at home and abroad through the use of both conventional forces and the deployment of extended air and missile defenses; combating chemical, biological, radiological, nuclear, and high-explosive weapons and their delivery systems; prevailing in offensive and defensive information warfare; projecting and sustaining U.S. forces in an anti-access/area-denial environment (A2/AD) and defeating A2/AD threats; denying enemies sanctuary from U.S. attack; preserving U.S. capabilities to operate effectively in a competitive outer space environment; and leveraging information technologies and innovative operational concepts in order to develop a truly interoperable, joint command, control, communications, computers and intelligence, surveillance, and reconnaissance (C4ISR) architecture.[23]

As Michael O'Hanlon notes in his chapter on the United States, the necessity of mastering these operational challenges underscores both the enduring and the novel challenges confronting U.S. defense policy. The relatively unchanging dimensions of U.S. defense policy writ large consist of the need to protect allies, prepare to fight and win major wars, deter adversaries, and reassure neutrals. If the United States is to successfully implement its grand strategy, Washington must successfully attain these goals within the

---

[21] The White House, "The National Security Strategy of the United States of America," September 2002, 30.

[22] Department of Defense, "Quadrennial Defense Review Report," September 30, 2001, 30.

[23] Department of Defense, "Quadrennial Defense Review Report."

context of a rapidly changing technological environment, the prospect of new geopolitical threats in Asia, and the diffusion of leading-edge weapon systems used either symmetrically or asymmetrically to strike at the heart of U.S. vulnerabilities.

Against this backdrop, the U.S. effort to protect the military foundations of its primacy in tandem with the autonomous spread of technology itself have combined to create incentives for various Asian states to acquire RMA technologies. How much any particular Asian state is willing to invest in incorporating such resources, however, depends greatly on its specific threat environment and resource base. Because defense transformation is an expensive proposition, only countries with high-performing economies and in the midst of serious security dilemmas can afford to embark on such investments. Even if these two variables are present, the likelihood of new defense transformation being disruptive (as all military revolutions inevitably are) implies that even those Asian candidates best positioned to exploit the RMA are likely to tread warily. In every instance, the challenges of managing the organizational disruption caused by the introduction of new technology, the burdens of marrying new systems with the legacy components already in place, and the difficulties of retraining operators familiar only with older systems all combine to make even the most appropriate candidate recipients particularly cautious regarding investments in defense transformation.[24] This volume will examine whether various Asian states are attempting to incorporate transformational capabilities in their military forces, and if so, how concertedly and to what operational-tactical ends.

No other issue illustrates the tremendous diversity of the Asian continent as much as the question of how various Asian states are pursuing defense transformation. Such transformation is understood here as encompassing the pervasive presence of seamlessly networked C4ISR, precision weapons, and suitable delivery platforms, all of which allow the exploitation of shared situational awareness enabling the prosecution of more accurate engagements at standoff ranges with speed and agility that utilize jointness and interoperability.[25] When read synoptically, the chapters in this volume offer evidence that suggests the following broad generalizations. Russia probably remains the only Asian state capable of developing the technical accoutrements necessary to sustain defense transformation on a major scale and in all warfighting arms through internal means alone. Nevertheless, failures in Russia's national economy, disrepair in the Russian military, and the

---

[24] Richard A. Bitzinger, "Challenges to Transforming Asian-Pacific Militaries," *Asia-Pacific Security Studies* 3, no. 8 (October 2004): 1–4.

[25] The definition is based on Richard A. Bitzinger, "Defense Transformation and the Asia Pacific: Implications for Regional Militaries," *Asia-Pacific Security Studies* 3, no. 7 (October 2004): 2.

lack of urgent demand from the armed forces for RMA technologies (due mostly to resource management and leadership deficits) effectively ensure that Russia—from whence the concept of the military-technical revolution initially originated—will be unable to field a transformed military force any time in the near future.[26]

The major Asian powers—China, Japan, and India—lie in the next tier. Of the three, Japan possesses the most technologically sophisticated armed forces and enjoys the best access to transformation instruments produced by the United States. The Japanese force structure is still relatively unbalanced, however, and, while RMA elements are likely to increasingly appear in Japanese naval and air warfare capabilities, their effectiveness will not be fully realized so long as these war-fighting arms are not intended to service the complete panoply of offensive missions. China and India undoubtedly remain deeply interested in acquiring transformative military capabilities, yet confront problems different from those facing Japan. Although both China and India possess large and competent militaries, they continue to face significant resource constraints. These budgetary limitations ensure that any transformative technologies that these two states acquire—most probably through import—will likely be niche capabilities slated for integration into pre-existing military organizations and oriented toward accomplishing traditional operational tasks more effectively. Of the two states, however, India is the farthest along in implementing organizational restructuring to exploit the advent of new military technologies. As a result of the lessons learned from recent subcontinental crises, the Indian Army—which is the country's dominant combat arm—is currently in the midst of implementing its most significant organizational restructuring in modern history. Particularly where China is concerned, many transformative capabilities that are likely to be acquired by Beijing in the years ahead will probably be employed to service various kinds of asymmetric strategies that collectively have been labeled "the assassin's mace,"[27] because among the three major Asian powers China alone is faced with task of parrying various regional competitors while also directly competing with powers greater than itself such as the United States.

Australia, Singapore, South Korea, and Taiwan appear to be at varying stages of incorporating defense transformation into their military modernization programs. Australia and Singapore have seemingly made the most progress in this regard. Despite great disparity in size, they are similar in

---

[26] For a superb review, see Stephen Blank, "Preconditions for a Russian RMA: Can Russia Make the Transition?" *National Security Studies Quarterly* 6, no. 2 (Spring 2000): 1–27.

[27] U.S.-China Security Review Commission, "The National Security Implications of the Economic Relationship Between the United States and China," report to Congress, July 2002, 8.

one key respect: as both states have relatively small armed forces, their task of revolutionary modernization is far more tractable in comparison to the challenges facing the larger Asian states. Both Australia and Singapore have invested heavily in intelligence, surveillance, and reconnaissance capabilities, with Australia having benefited additionally from its connectivity with the U.S. global intelligence collection system. Both have also sought to increase the effectiveness of their relatively small forces by acquiring various precision weapons delivered by multiple means. Though South Korea and Taiwan have ambitious plans for incorporating similar capabilities, this task will likely require at least another decade to be completed.[28]

Further down the chain of military modernization are a large number of countries—Indonesia, Malaysia, Thailand, the Philippines, Vietnam, Pakistan, Kazakhstan, Kyrgyzstan, Tajikistan, Turkmenistan, Uzbekistan, and Afghanistan—that are confronted by various sorts of security demands yet lack the resources to contemplate defense transformation in any meaningful way. Of the countries in this category, Pakistan has come closest to introducing modern—though hardly transformative—military technologies in its armed forces. Islamabad faces a strategic environment that it believes justifies the acquisition of the best weapons money can buy. Pakistan's armed forces are professional and competent, and its national economic performance has improved in recent years. Pakistan still faces serious resource constraints, however, and must contend with unresolved issues of limited access to the best sources of military technology. Consequently, implementation of leading-edge military technologies in Pakistan's armed forces is likely to be marginal in the foreseeable future. North Korea, a country in parlous economic circumstances, is certain to continue its current strategy of trading the newest information-based RMA for the fruits of an older RMA, namely nuclear weapons. While conventional military modernization will probably endure in focused areas, Pyongyang is—so long as North Korea's relationship with the United States does not improve—likely to seek regime security through nuclear arms.

By contrast, many of the Southeast Asian nations will make modest forays into the RMA through the acquisition of several discrete components, including precision-guided munitions, small numbers of advanced combat aircraft, and improved command, control, and communications systems. One scholar has described this effort as "modernization-plus," a term that implies a process of general, evolutionary, and incremental improvement rather than true disruptive innovation.[29] In the Central Asian states and in

---

[28] Bitzinger, "Defense Transformation and the Asia Pacific," 1–4.

[29] Bitzinger, "Transforming Asian-Pacific Militaries," 1–4.

Afghanistan, however, defense acquisition—to say nothing of defense transformation—is today virtually stagnant. All of these states remain focused
on either rebuilding the personnel cadre of their armed forces or struggling
to maintain military professionalism. These two modest goals are attempted mostly through increased linkages with the military forces of the major
powers that are either present in or abutting their national borders.

The diverse nature of military modernization in Asia reflects the complexity of the region as well as the multitude of security dilemmas visible in
its sub-regions. In light of these two undercurrents, each of the country and
regional chapters in this book broadly follows the following methodology.

Each chapter first establishes the strategic context by examining how
certain strategic realities—such as the ongoing rise of China; the continuing
war on terrorism; anticipated changes in U.S. regional presence, force posture, and political-military capabilities; RMA and defense transformation
issues; local security dilemmas; and the threat perceptions arising from the
nuclear capabilities of neighboring states—are affecting military modernization programs. The grand strategic dimension examined in each chapter
seeks to provide the geopolitical framework for understanding a particular
country's strategic choices and how the leadership views the employment
of various political strategies—such as alliances, internal balancing, and
WMD—along with the military instruments to support those strategies as
solutions to that state's security problems.

Each chapter then focuses on the military modernization occurring
within the country or region itself. The discussions here center on analyzing, where appropriate, defense budget statistics; the size, configuration, and
intended capabilities of the armed forces; and the character of civil-military relations. The nature of the military modernization that is occurring
within the country or region is then examined, and the author provides an
overview of the technologies (especially transformational and asymmetric
capabilities) currently being acquired, and assesses whether changes in military strategy, organizations, and doctrine are occurring in tandem. To the
extent possible, the chapters also describe any debates that may be occurring within the country/region, with the ultimate intent of assessing what
changes in military capacity are sought—or are likely to obtain—as a result
of the modernization activities described.

Finally, each chapter assesses the political and strategic implications of
the ongoing military modernization in each sub-region as well as on the region as a whole. Particular attention is paid to assessing whether the military
modernization in question has the potential to change the local balance of
power; whether it changes the country's capacity to achieve certain political
goals that previously lay beyond its reach; whether it alters the country's mil-

itary capacity with respect to the United States either locally, regionally, or globally; or if the changes in military capacity hold the potential of assisting the United States with respect to achieving certain local, regional, or global goals. Finally, each chapter evaluates the general implications for stability in the region or the continent writ large.

The special studies in this volume differ from this general template in that each uses a methodology appropriate to the subject. Viewed in its totality, however, the volume seeks to become a summary reference that places the ongoing military modernization in Asia in a larger strategic context.

Evaluating Asian Military Modernization

The presently robust defense expenditure programs in many important regional states in Asia will, over time, result in significant qualitative improvements in national capabilities. The technological components of many military inventories in the region will be upgraded with sophisticated systems that were beyond the reach of many countries as recently as a decade ago. Such systems include:

- new mobile ballistic and cruise missiles (both anti-ship and land-attack)

- imaging satellites

- advanced satellite launch vehicles

- access to GPS/GLONASS, differential GPS, and other terminal guidance systems as well as access to new sophisticated civilian imagery systems like SPOT and IKONOS

- advanced sensor technologies capable of long-range, all-weather, battlefield target detection and acquisition, including UAVs

- advanced battlefield fire-management systems and advanced fire systems such as artillery and rockets capable of delivering a variety of highly lethal, long-range, guided munitions

- long-range transportation in the form of air and sealift capabilities

- air-to-air refueling platforms

- advanced combat aircraft equipped with active air-to-air missiles, advanced air-to-ground munitions, and secure tactical communications

- special mission platforms that include electronic counter measures (ECM), suppression of enemy air defenses (SEAD), reconnaissance, and airborne warning and control systems (AWACS)

- aircraft carriers; nuclear and advanced diesel-electric submarines equipped with air independent propulsion

- modern mine warfare systems

- more generally, the progressive (if piecemeal) introduction of C4ISR, automated planning, and battle management systems that will increase the effectiveness and capabilities of any discrete component beyond its individual capacity

Evaluating the impact and likely consequences of this military modernization is a complex and difficult task. In many cases, it is difficult to discern the precise capabilities of the technologies now entering service in many Asian states. Though various specialized means of intelligence collection are likely over time to uncover the technical parameters of these systems, the contribution such capabilities will make to the military effectiveness of these countries promises to remain a subject of perpetual debate. Finally, the crucial policy question of whether the United States ought to be concerned with the changing character of military technology in particular—and of military modernization more generally—on the Asian continent will remain an issue that not only animates ongoing planning exercises such as the forthcoming Quadrennial Defense Review but also U.S. grand strategy more broadly. No single volume can pretend to answer these complex questions definitively. This overview will conclude, then, not with a comprehensive prescription for how Washington should approach emerging patterns of military modernization in Asia, but rather with a conceptual framework useful for the debate of this issue.

Ongoing military modernization in Asia poses challenges for regional stability that cannot be understood without reference to specific U.S. geopolitical objectives in the continent. Jonathan Pollack best summarized these objectives in an early post-Cold War essay, "The United States in East Asia," in which he described the goals of U.S. strategy in Asia as "holding the ring."[30] This phrase is best understood as a metaphor describing the condition of strategic stability that results when no regional state has either the military capabilities or the political intentions to seriously harm one another, yet an external power that does possess such capabilities, such as the

---

[30] Jonathan D. Pollack, "The United States in East Asia," in *Asia's International Role in the Post-Cold War Era*, International Institute for Strategic Studies, Adelphi Paper, no. 275, 1993, 69–82.

United States, lacks incentives to abuse them because it superintends the continent and safeguards the peace in order to protect a larger political and economic good. This holding-the-ring strategy thus capitalizes on America's geographical distance—but not its absence—from Asia. While assuming the role of a non-threatening, engaged external protector, the United States simultaneously seeks to prevent any regional competitors from pursuing blatantly revisionist goals or acquiring military capabilities that would make the U.S. task to protect the stability of the region more difficult.

The fact that the United States formally offers security guarantees to many Asian states, engages in strategic partnerships with non-allied but friendly regional states, and maintains forward-deployed and forward-operating military forces in Asia are all critical to the strategy of holding the ring for both reasons of "insurance" and "investment."[31] The insurance aspect of the strategy aims at preventing any single power or consortium of powers achieving dominance over the Asian continent.[32] Toward this end, the superior war-fighting capability of the U.S. military serves as a reminder to would-be challengers that attempts at hegemonic dominance would be extremely costly and ultimately unfruitful. In case a prospective challenger should fail to accurately interpret this message, U.S. forward-deployed and forward-operating forces also serve a second function by ensuring the safety of local allies and bolstering the resilience of regional states.

The investment aspect of the strategy aims to bear the costs of maintaining region-wide order so that local states do not fritter away resources in competitive attempts at maintaining security.[33] In the absence of such tangible U.S. protection, every regional state would have to rely exclusively on its own capabilities in order to ensure its safety. Because each state would be forced to engage in security competition (where the benefits accruing from an international division of labor do not exist) rather than economic competition (where specialization according to comparative advantage serves to continually expand the international production-possibility frontier), this in turn would inevitably lead to the destruction or appreciable weakening of the Asian "economic miracle." Allocating resources to security maintenance would not only retard the processes of wealth production that have been underway in Asia since the end of World War II, but would also result in a diminution of the growth and prosperity of the United States. U.S. forward-

---

[31] Ibid., 79 ff.

[32] Jonathan D. Pollack and James A. Winnefeld, *U.S. Strategic Alternatives in a Changing Pacific* (Santa Monica: RAND, 1990), 6–9.

[33] This argument relies on some minimal version of the "hegemonic stability" theory associated with political realism. For an elaboration, see Robert Gilpin, *The Political Economy of International Relations* (Princeton: Princeton University Press, 1987), 85–92.

deployed and forward-operating forces serve, therefore, to obviate destructive local security competition and create the preconditions for continued prosperity in the region. This, by extension, ensures the continued economic well-being of the United States.

The question of how military modernization affects political stability in Asia should be considered against the backdrop of the above strategic objectives. The relationship between these two variables can be stated thus: continental stability would be enhanced if no Asian state possessed the kind of military technology that could seriously (1) threaten the territorial integrity of another local state, (2) threaten the ability of the United States to defend a local state, or (3) impede the ability of the United States to either operate within the region or to reinforce its already existing capabilities along the Asian rimland. Obviously, any military technology acquired by any regional state will have an impact on these three criteria to some degree or another. It would be presumptuous, however, to imagine that Washington could prevent various Asian states from acquiring military technology on the grounds that all technologies affect the above calculus. In an environment where multiple weapons producers exist, where indigenous production capabilities are not inconsequential, and where the search for national autonomy is strong, a strategy of "broad spectrum" technology denial would be both impossible to sustain and would ultimately be self-defeating.[34]

Consequently, there is need for a more sensitive approach, relative to the three criteria defined above, to the issue of military modernization and stability. This approach ought to be grounded in a triangular judgment based on three separate, though related, clusters of questions. The first set of questions centers on the issue of political aims and is based on the presumption that revisionist states, irrespective of their military capacity, pose especially problematic challenges to stability. Accordingly, the following queries should guide any assessment of military modernization in Asia. Which Asian countries, if any, have oriented their national military modernization toward the pursuit of revisionist goals with regard to a neighboring state? Does this reorientation involve attempts to impede the ability of the United States to either defend the threatened state or operate within the relevant geographic areas necessary to defend that state? Finally, what are the political goals, ambitions, and nature of the regime in the revisionist state, and what are the relevant circumstances that account for its dissatisfaction with the prevailing status quo? Several countries, *prima facie*, would meet the criterion laid out in the opening query: China vis-à-vis Taiwan, North Korea vis-à-vis South Korea, Iran vis-à-vis the Gulf States and perhaps Saudi Arabia, and Pakistan

---

[34] See the discussion in Michael Moodie, "Beyond Proliferation: The Challenge of Technology Diffusion," *Washington Quarterly* 18, no. 2, (Spring 1995): 183–202.

vis-à-vis India. When the two other derivative issues are considered, however, only China, North Korea, and Iran possibly both aim to impede the United States from assisting various protectees and also maintain ongoing military modernization programs oriented toward constraining U.S. freedom of action in this regard.

The second set of questions that must be answered in regard to judging the effects of Asian military modernization on regional stability refers to the nature of the technology itself—specifically how the quality, number, and technical characteristics of various coercive instruments possessed by different states directly affect regional threat perceptions. In the late 1980s, the U.S. Department of Defense made a concerted effort to identify the types of military technology acquisitions that should be considered problematic. In 1990, Henry D. Sokolski, then Deputy Assistant Secretary for Nonproliferation Policy, disclosed a broad U.S. policy framework initially devised by Henry S. Rowen, who was then Assistant Secretary of Defense for International Security Affairs.[35] The Rowen framework argued that any particular regional military technology acquisition should be considered destabilizing if (1) it enabled the possessor to inflict high-leverage strategic harm against the United States or its allies, (2) the United States lacked effective defenses against this capability or if prevailing U.S. defenses were too difficult or cumbersome to employ, or (3) the very acquisition of such capabilities changed the perceived balance of power in the region.

These three provisos were intended to provide a more sensitive definition of which military technology acquisitions are likely to prove problematic (i.e., have the potential to impede U.S. strategic objectives). As Sokolski aptly summarized, each of these litmus tests were intended to identify the kinds of technologies that "could enable [other] states to threaten war-winning or victory-denying results against the United States or its friends ..."[36] Given the compact nature of these formulations, it is important to elaborate further on these three provisos and examine how they approach the problem of identifying destabilizing military technology acquisitions.

The first proviso argues that military technologies capable of inflicting "high-leverage strategic harm" are of particular concern. High-leverage harm as used here should not be understood merely as a proxy for high-technology weaponry. Rather, the phrase is meant to capture the kind of prohibitively costly or simply unacceptable damage that the acquisition of

---

[35] Henry D. Sokolski, "Proliferation and Regional Security in the 1990s," testimony and prepared statement, U.S. Senate, Committee on Governmental Affairs, 101st Congress, 2nd Session, October 9, 1990, 28–41, 65–88.

[36] Henry Sokolski, "Fighting Proliferation with Intelligence," *Orbis* 38, no. 2 (Spring 1994): 249.

any specific technology could inflict on the United States.[37] Shifting the focus from the level of technology *per se* to the type of warfighting outputs that the technology could potentially obtain is critical to this concept. This shift in emphasis implies that a large variety of military instruments—ranging from relatively sophisticated technologies (WMD combined with advanced delivery systems) to more primitive capabilities (mine-warfare systems and cheap, accurate, and plentiful sea-based cruise missiles)—could be equally problematic, depending on their potential to frustrate U.S. military capabilities (or those of U.S. allies) in specific operational contexts.

Appearing deceptively obvious at first, the second proviso is actually somewhat more complicated. This proviso asserts that technology acquisitions lacking an effective and useable U.S. countermeasure are to be treated as intrinsically destabilizing. This is due to the fact that such acquisitions could be used to prosecute certain strategic, operational, or tactical objectives with complete immunity from U.S. counteraction. The proliferation of certain kinds of aviation stealth technologies would be the most obvious example of destabilizing technological acquisitions within this category. Other pertinent examples might include advanced diesel-electric submarines and advanced mine warfare systems. These technologies would be problematic not because the United States does not possess adequate defenses against such threats, but rather because combating such threats in certain operational environments would be a cumbersome, time-consuming process without any guarantee of ultimate success. Furthermore, the prosecution of such operations could very likely result in substantial and perhaps unacceptable losses to U.S. forces.

The third proviso is based upon the Hobbesian insight that "Reputation of power is Power; because it draweth with it the adhaerence of those that need protection."[38] This argument holds that, because certain military technologies embody such palpable awe both in the public imagination and in the calculations of policymaking elites, the political significance of such weapons could easily overwhelm their operational merit.[39] As a result, acquisition of such weapons by a regional state could cause dramatic shifts in the perceived balance of power, which would in turn precipitate local political realignments that would make the attainment of U.S. regional stra-

---

[37] This argument is elaborated at some length in Henry Sokolski, "Nonapocalyptic Proliferation: A New Strategic Threat?" *Washington Quarterly* 17, no. 2 (Spring 1994): 115–28.

[38] Thomas Hobbes, *Leviathan*, ed. C. B. Macpherson (Harmondsworth: Penguin Books, 1986), 150.

[39] This characteristic captures what Brad Roberts calls "leveraging technologies," which he describes as "technologies creating military capabilities of strategic consequence, which is to say capabilities that operate fundamentally on the perceptions of choice by the leaders of targeted nations." See Brad Roberts, "From Nonproliferation to Antiproliferation," *International Security* 18, no. 1 (Summer 1993): 148–49.

tegic objectives highly problematic. A sudden acquisition of WMD and associated delivery capabilities is one such example. Similarly, the acquisition of aircraft carriers, advanced nuclear submarines, dedicated amphibious forces, or accurate ballistic or land-attack cruise missiles are also unnerving because they signify potential transformations in maritime or continental power projection capabilities. The resulting sense of vulnerability in the region could lead to temptations on the part of the local states to "bandwagon" with a rising power—to the detriment of larger U.S. and allied interests.

When Asian military modernization is judged upon the merits of technology, it is clear that many of the weapons systems meeting Sokolski's provisos will increasingly make appearances in different quadrants of the Asian landmass. All the major Asian powers—China, Russia, Japan, India, South Korea, Australia, and even the more advanced Southeast Asian states—will possess various military systems that are capable of inflicting "high-leverage strategic harm," are effective against different U.S. defenses, and will enhance their strategic reputation within the region and beyond. Fortunately, many of these states are friends and allies of the United States; thus, their growing technological sophistication is unlikely to raise serious political concerns in Washington. The steadily increasing sophistication of these same militaries suggests, however, that at a purely technological level, the operating environment facing U.S. forces in and around Asia is likely to grow increasingly complex over time. Similarly, as certain geopolitically startling technologies (e.g., nuclear weapons) begin to gradually appear, critical portions of the Asian landmass may even become wholly immune to the successful application of U.S. military power.[40] In light of these trends, ongoing transformations in the U.S. armed services, including basing and deployment patterns abroad, may need to be accelerated in order to protect Washington's ability to implement its current holding-the-ring strategy in Asia.

The third cluster of questions concerning defense modernization and stability is related to military effectiveness. Since technology alone remains only one element of combat capacity, judgments regarding the possible adverse regional impact of a state's military modernization must include not only an assessment of what coercive capabilities it is acquiring, but also a considered appraisal of whether these capabilities have been effectively integrated into the state's military forces. The enhancement of military capabilities and warfighting effectiveness require not only new hardware but also the development of integrative dimensions—manpower, organization, doctrine, tactics, training, education, intelligence, logistics, maintenance, and infrastructure—that enable a combat force to utilize its new technology and

---

[40] Paul Bracken, *Fire in the East: The Rise of Asian Military Power and the Second Nuclear Age* (New York: HarperCollins, 1999).

other supporting resources effectively. Hence, the third cluster of queries focuses on understanding the nature of a country's warfighting competencies in ground, sea, and air environments.

Figures 2–4 depict what a progressive increase in warfighting capabilities in each dimension would look like.[41] **Figure 2** maps an array of ground combat proficiency along a spectrum ranging from irregular infantry operations all the way up to knowledge-based warfare. Naval force competencies are structured in an analogous manner, with coastal defense and mining representing the most primitive naval warfighting competency at one end, and comprehensive sea control at the other. In the spectrum of air warfare capabilities, airspace sovereignty defense is the most primitive form of air capabilities, and suppression of critical mobile targets (CMT) and information dominance—whereby a force relies on information imbalances to paralyze adversaries and dominate the battlespace—are at the high end.

Military effectiveness can thus be arrayed along a spectrum of increasing complexity, with each realm of operations (ground, naval, and air) containing internal domains separated by different thresholds of technology and integrative capacity. This notion permits the military competencies of a country to be located on a schematic map. This map in turn allows for the depiction of a state's relative capabilities both at a given point in time and in comparison to a select group of peers. In such a context, technology and integrative capacity are essentially economizing abstractions that include many varieties of strategic resources as well as the conversion capability possessed by the state.[42] Prudent appraisals of military effectiveness in Asia would therefore also require answers to the following queries:

- What is the quality of the doctrine, training, and organization governing the operations of the relevant combat arms in the country concerned?

- Does the state maintain the requisite schools, infrastructure, logistics, and maintenance capabilities necessary to support the newly acquired technologies effectively?

- Are state intelligence organizations sufficiently skilled to assess developments occurring abroad, and are they influential enough at home so as to be able to shape the manpower, organization, tactics, and training of its own armed forces?

---

[41] These figures are based on research carried out by Jeffery A. Isaacson and his colleagues at RAND in the 1990s. The framework is detailed in Ashley J. Tellis, Janice Bially, Christopher Layne, and Melissa McPherson, *Measuring National Power in the Postindustrial Age* (Santa Monica: RAND, 2000), 133–76.

[42] Ibid.

Depending on the answers to these and other queries, it is possible to assess a state's present and potential ability to engage in various kinds of complex military operations. Identifying such capacities, however, does not allow predictions regarding likely victory in a war between two countries because victory is invariably contingent upon a wide variety of factors. Mapping military capabilities, therefore, merely enables a qualitative judgment concerning force competence in a variety of combat operations without in any way implying an ironclad relationship between high competency and certain victory.

The analysis found in this volume and elsewhere permits the following summary of military competencies in some of the key Asian states. Where ground combat is concerned, for example, most observers would agree that, because the old Soviet army possessed both the relevant range of technologies and the integrative capacity identified in **Figure 2**, the USSR was entirely capable of prosecuting full combined arms operations. Though the Russian Army today may possess many of the relevant technologies, its integrative capacity has suffered greatly; Russia will thus be unlikely to emulate its Soviet predecessor. The Chinese People's Liberation Army (PLA), by contrast, is likely capable of basic combined arms operations; Beijing's ultimate military modernization plans are, however, oriented more toward acquiring the capabilities necessary for coordinated deep attack. The North and South Korean armies and the Indian and Pakistani armies—which combined make up the majority of land forces in Asia—are also placed similarly. The ground forces of the Central Asian states today would most likely be capable of little beyond elementary combined arms.

In terms of naval warfare (see **Figure 3**), the Japanese navy specializes in anti-submarine warfare, primarily through surface and organic air assets and, secondarily, through submarines. Its effective surface fleet and land-based strike aircraft, however, enable the navy to competently conduct a range of activities from mine countermeasures warfare to naval strike operations that would produce a modicum of sea control. In the realm of naval strike operations, Australia's navy is comparable to that of Japan. Due to the Indian navy's long experience with aircraft carriers, New Delhi commands both naval strike capabilities as well as limited air control. Its emerging capabilities will likely permit both limited sea control and deep strike capabilities in the near future. The Chinese People's Liberation Army Navy (PLAN) is currently most proficient in anti-surface warfare, but is developing mine and anti-submarine warfare proficiency as well. Likewise, the best navies of the Southeast Asian states (such as Singapore) would be judged to be most proficient in anti-surface warfare and naval strike warfare as conducted either by surface ships or land-based aircraft.

Figure 2. Ground Force Capabilities Spectrum

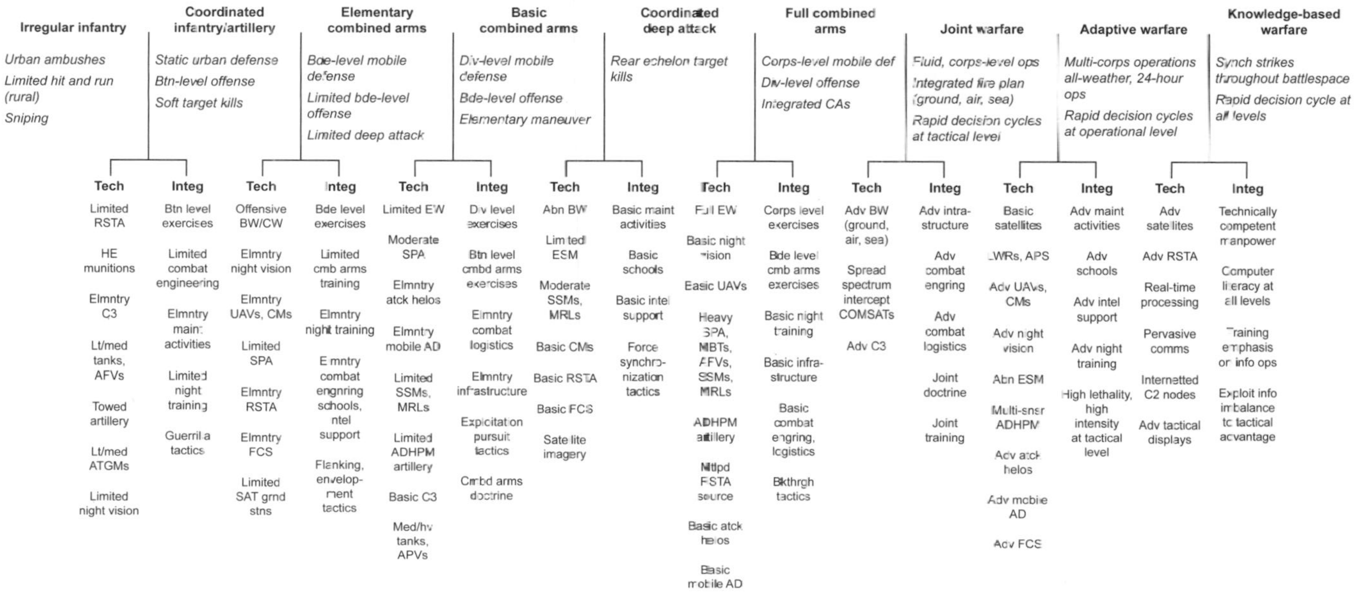

Irregular infantry
Urban ambushes
Limited hit and run (rural)
Sniping

Tech	Integ
Limited RSTA	Btn level exercises
HE munitions	Limited combat engineering
Elmntry C3	Elmntry maint activities
Lt/med tanks, AFVs	Limited night training
Towed artillery	Guerrila tactics
Lt/med ATGMs	
Limited night vision	

Coordinated infantry/artillery
Static urban defense
Btn-level offense
Soft target kills

Tech	Integ
Offensive BW/CW	Btn level exercises
Elmntry night vision	Limited combat engineering
Elmntry UAVs, CMs	Elmntry maint activities
Limited SPA	Limited night training
Elmntry RSTA	Guerrila tactics
Elmntry FCS	
Limited SAT grnd stns	

Elementary combined arms
Bde-level mobile defense
Limited bde-level offense
Limited deep attack

Tech	Integ
Limited EW	Bde level exercises
Moderate SPA	Limited cmb arms training
Elmntry attck helos	Elmntry night training
Elmntry mobile AD	E mntry combat schools, ntel support
Limited SSMs, MRLs	Flanking, envelopment tactics
Limited ADHPM artillery	
Basic C3	
Med/hv tanks, APVs	

Basic combined arms
Div-level mobile defense
Bde-level offense
Elementary maneuver

Tech	Integ
Limited EW	Div level exercises
Moderate SPA	Btn level cmbd arms exercises
Elmntry attck helos	Elmntry combat logistics
Elmntry mobile AD	Elmntry infrastructure
Limited SSMs, MRLs	Exploitation pursuit tactics
Limited ADHPM artillery	Cmb'd arms doctrine
Basic C3	
Med/hv tanks, APVs	

Coordinated deep attack
Rear echelon target kills

Tech	Integ
Atn BW	Basic maint activities
Limited ESM	Basic schools
Moderate SSMs, MRLs	Basic intel support
Basic CMs	Force synchro-nization tactics
Basic RSTA	
Basic FCS	
Satellite imagery	

Full combined arms
Corps-level mobile def
Div-level offense
Integrated CAs

Tech	Integ
Full EW	Corps level exercises
Basic night vision	Bde level cmb arms exercises
Easic UAVs	Basic night training
Heavy SPA, MBTs, AFVs, SSMs, MRLs	Basic infra-structure
ADHPM artillery	Basic combat engring, logistics
Mltrpd F-STA source	Blthrgh tactics
Basic attck helos	
Basic mobile AD	

Joint warfare
Fluid, corps-level ops
Integrated fire plan (ground, air, sea)
Rapid decision cycles at tactical level

Tech	Integ
Adv BW (ground, air, sea)	Adv intra-structure
Spread spectrum intercapt COMSATs	Adv combat engring
Adv C3	Adv combat logistics
	Joint doctrine
	Joint training

Adaptive warfare
Multi-corps operations all-weather, 24-hour ops
Rapid decision cycles at operational level

Tech	Integ
Basic satellites	Adv maint activities
WRs, APS	Adv schools
Adv UAVs, CMs	Adv intel support
Adv night vision	Adv night training
Atn ESM	High lethality, high intensity at tactical level
Multi-snsr ADHPM	
Adv attck helos	
Adv mobile AD	
Adv FCS	

Knowledge-based warfare
Synch strikes throughout battlespace
Rapid decision cycle at all levels

Tech	Integ
Adv satellites	Technically competent m'anpower
Adv RSTA	Computer literacy at all levels
Real-time processing	"training emphasis or info ops
Pervasive comms	Exploit info im balance tc tactical advantage
Intermated C2 nodes	
Adv tactical displays	

Source: Ashley J. Tellis et al., *Measuring National Power in the Postindustrial Age* (Santa Monica, CA: RAND, 2000).

Figure 3. Naval Warfare Capabilities Spectrum

Coastal defense mining	Coastal anti-surface warfare	Anti-surface warfare		Anti-submarine warfare (submarine)	Naval strike	Multi-mission air control	Sea control
		Anti-air warfare (surface) / Conterming / Naval gun fire support	Anti-surface warfare (submarine) / Anti-submarine warfare (surface/organic air)		Limited air control	Limited sea control / Deep strike	

Coastal defense mining
- Tech: Patrol craft, RPGs, Small caliber guns, LOS targeting, Coastal CMs, ASMs, SAMs

Coastal anti-surface warfare
- Integ: Commercial navigation skills, Limited military training, Indep ops

Anti-surface warfare — Anti-air warfare (surface) / Conterming / Naval gun fire support
- Tech: Corvettes, FFs, DDs, Mine warfare ships, Medium caliber guns, Elmntry radars, Elmntry naval CMs, ASMs, SAMs
- Integ: Elmntry ship handling skills, Elmntry DC, FC, AAW training, SAGs, Elmntry maint activities, Elmntry logistics, Elmntry infrastructure

Anti-surface warfare (submarine)
- Tech: Elmntry subs, Elmntry sonars, Elmntry torps
- Integ: Sub school, Basic ship handling skills, Basic DC training, Basic FC training

Anti-surface warfare (submarine) — organic air
- Tech: Embd helos, Basic sonars, Elmntry data links
- Integ: Cmb ASW ops, Basic ASW training (large subs), Elmntry fleet exercises, Elmntry intel support, Oceano-graphy

Anti-submarine warfare (surface/organic air)
- Tech: Basic subs, Adv sonars, Basic torps

Anti-submarine warfare (submarine)
- Integ: Passive sonar training, Adv FC training, Adv ship handling skills, Basic maint activities, Basic logistics, Basic infra-structure
- Tech: Basic carrier, Basic carrier CGs, DDGs, FFG, Basic radar, Basic naval CM, ASMs, SAM, Basic data links, Secure comms, Satellite imagery

Naval strike — Limited air control
- Integ: Carrier ops, Flight training (at sea), Basic fleet exercises, Basic AAW training, CWC equiv, Basic intel support
- Tech: Adv carrier, Adv carrier, Nuc, UNREP ships, Basic satellite, Adv radars, CMs, ASMs, SAMs, Adv data links

Multi-mission air control — Limited sea control / Deep strike
- Integ: Adv fleet exercises, Joint exercises, Adv DC, AAW training, Adv maint activities, Adv logistics, Adv infra-structure, UNREP training, Adv intel support
- Tech: Adv satellites, Adv OTH RSTA, Real-time processing, Pervasive comms, Internetted C2 nodes, Adv tactical displays

Sea control
- Integ: Technically competent manpower, Computer literacy at all levels, Training emphasis on info ops, Exploit info imbalance to tactical advantage

Source: Ashley J. Tellis et al., *Measuring National Power in the Postindustrial Age* (Santa Monica, CA: RAND, 2000).

Figure 4. Air Warfare Capabilities Spectrum

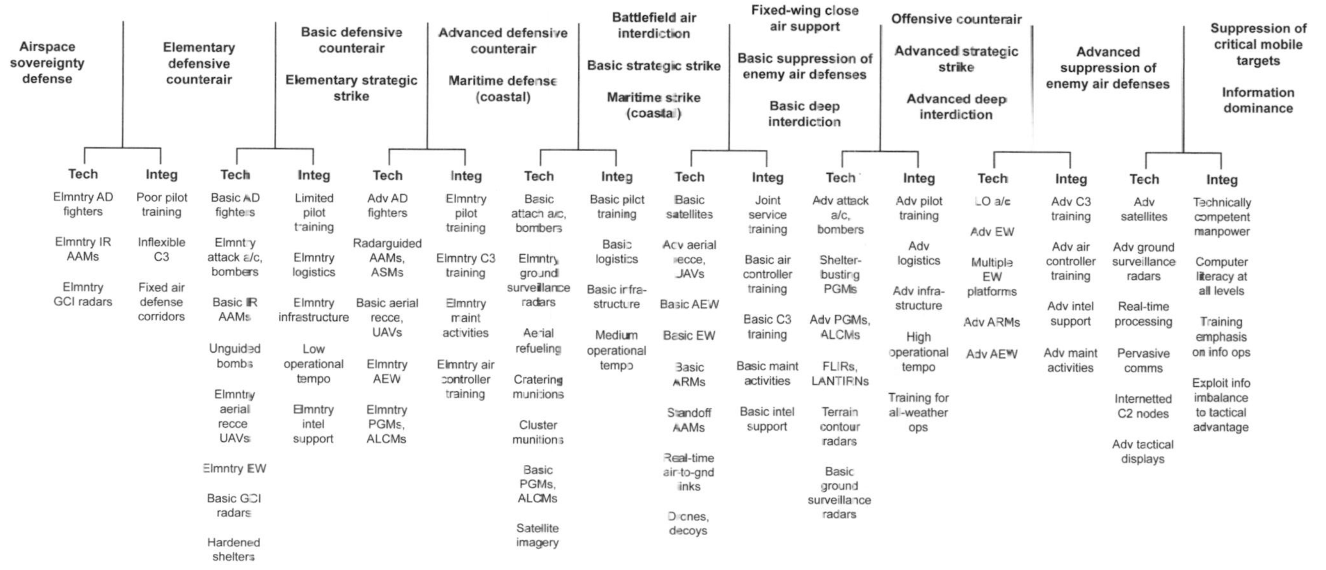

Source: Ashley J. Tellis et al., *Measuring National Power in the Postindustrial Age* (Santa Monica, CA: RAND, 2000).

In terms of air power (see **Figure 4**), the current capabilities of the Japanese air force allow the implementation of advanced defensive counterair operations, maritime strike, basic strategic strike, basic SEAD, and basic deep interdiction. The Australian air force possesses similar competencies. In comparison, the Chinese People's Liberation Army Air Force (PLAAF) possesses lower-order competencies that are mostly in basic defensive counterair, though increasingly in advanced defensive counterair, maritime strike, and battlefield air interdiction operations. Compared to the PLAAF, the Indian air force has exhibited greater competency in a wider range of air operations, including advanced defensive counterair, maritime strike, battlefield air interdiction operations, basic SEAD, and basic deep interdiction. Pakistan's air force, by contrast, commands the integrative capacity for more extensive warfighting competencies than its technology permits, which by all accounts is optimized primarily for basic defensive counterair and elementary strategic strike. Russia's air force possesses the technology to support a wide range of combat activities, including offensive counterair, advanced strategic strike, and advanced deep interdiction operations; whether Russia's current integrative capacity today has kept pace with its technology base is, however, unknown.

Any useful appraisal of Asian military modernization, and especially the resulting consequences for strategic stability, moves beyond the realm of brute facts and into the arena of nuanced judgment. In this regard, policymakers have to triangulate the nature of a state's political aims (including history, the character of the regime, and the underlying reason for various political pursuits), the nature of the military technology acquired or likely to be acquired (including the ability to inflict "high-leverage strategic harm"), and the likely combat effectiveness of a state's military forces in different warfighting dimensions. Systematic analysis of these three broad realms invariably leads to a focus on the large and consequential powers of Asia—namely China, Russia, Japan, India, and to a lesser extent South Korea and Australia. While other states will acquire different types of sophisticated military capabilities over time, only the large and consequential powers are likely to incorporate such capacities in both breadth and depth within their armed services. Consequently, military modernization in these countries is likely to receive the lion's share of attention both within Asia and in the United States.

From Washington's perspective, however, Beijing will continue to dominate the agenda. Of all the Asian states discussed above, only China remains a rapidly growing power in pursuit of both strategic goals that are potentially incompatible with those of the United States and various "war-winning" or "victory-denying" military technologies that could make an appearance in any serious confrontation with the United States. China's deliberate emphasis on asymmetric strategies aimed against the United States is only likely to deepen U.S. anxieties. The emerging Sino-U.S. strategic relationship thus bears some uncanny resemblances to the years between the first and second world wars. Then, as now, the principal actors in the political drama were struggling to resolve certain pressing strategic problems of vital interest to their national security. Germany, for instance, sought recognition of its rising power in the face of English predominance, while China today seeks both legitimation of its growing strength and the prevention of potential secessionism in the face of a U.S. dominance capable of undermining both goals. Then, as now, the rising power sought to use familiar weapons in unfamiliar ways in order to resolve operational dilemmas that were critical to the successful exercise of force. By combining an extant technology (the tank) in a novel way with infantry and airpower, Germany was able to successfully implement blitzkrieg and thereby obviate the attrition warfare that stymied its ambitions during World War I. Similarly, China today has sought to utilize an old weapon (the conventionally armed ballistic missile) in novel ways so as to develop not only a mass raid capability with the potential to overwhelm or paralyze regional adversaries and achieve precision kill effects when used against either static land targets, but, even more ambitiously, highly mobile platforms such as U.S. aircraft carriers. Chinese success in this last endeavor would mark the first time a country anywhere in the world has developed ballistic missiles capable of interdicting a mobile sea-based platform. Such an innovation would have grave consequences for the survivability of U.S. forward-operating forces in Asia.

One might hope that the presence of nuclear weapons, the reality of economic interdependence, and the gradual global efflorescence of democratic ideals would all help to prevent a catastrophic meltdown of the sort witnessed in World War II. There are, however, continuing suspicions both in Washington (concerning China's eventual political aims and the objectives of its military modernization) and in Beijing (the same with respect to the United States) that are likely to fuel anticipatory responses on both sides that have the potential to disturb the geopolitical environment further. Consequently, although the growth of Chinese military power may be inexorable and even natural given Beijing's ascendant economic trajectory, the security dilemmas exacerbated by this expansion both within Asia and with respect to the United States are certain to shape the dynamics of military modernization throughout the Asian continent for many years to come.

STRATEGIC ASIA 2005–06

COUNTRY STUDIES

Executive Summary

This paper examines whether U.S. military modernization will enable the U.S. to meet threats to its national security interests that are most likely to arise in Asia.

MAIN ARGUMENT:
Despite both geostrategic upheaval (e.g., the rise of China, the nuclearization of North Korea, and the reach of Al Qaeda and affiliates into Asia) and hype over changing U.S. defense policy (e.g., Bush administration revolutions and the RMA), many attributes of U.S. military power are changing only slowly, and most U.S. interests are changing little in Asia. The U.S. remains focused on protecting its security and trade interests and those of its allies, as well as reducing incentives for countries to acquire weapons of mass destruction and engage in conflict with other states.

POLICY IMPLICATIONS:
- The U.S. would benefit from continuing to prepare for several relatively unchanging military conflict scenarios. Traditional military infrastructure—weaponry, force structure, basing arrangements, and key allies—should thus not be sacrificed in an overzealous belief in the power of rapid defense transformation.

- The Korean Peninsula, the Taiwan Strait, and South Asia are the three areas in the region most likely to require focused U.S. attention.

- In order to maximize U.S. ability to meet these and any other challenges in the region, the United States would benefit from:

  - Maintaining a wide range of military capabilities, including higher-tech "transformative" assets but also large numbers of infantry forces

  - Operating a wide range of military bases

  - Maintaining a network of allies and other partners that can assist the United States with forward missions, provide bases and protection of bases, and confer political legitimacy to U.S. military operations

U.S. Military Modernization: Implications for U.S. Policy in Asia

Michael O'Hanlon

Is the United States capable of meeting threats to U.S. security interests that are most likely to arise in Asia? In trying to answer this question, one must bear in mind the fact that events and issues originating from outside Asia color U.S. policy toward that region. U.S. military modernization, for example, is determined by both general technological innovations as well as the Pentagon's generic R&D budget—which are in turn shaped not just by Asia-Pacific concerns but also by the general desire to maintain global dominance across a wide array of warfighting scenarios and capabilities.[1] While China may constitute one key motivator for U.S. military investment, there are certainly a host of others. Additional drivers of U.S. military modernization include developments in the Middle East and Persian Gulf regions, the war against terrorism, and Washington's desire to stay ahead of both Russia and China in technological and military modernization efforts. New military technologies then become available for use in the Asia-Pacific region even if they were designed for and motivated by issues in other regions. In sum, U.S. military policy is influenced by both efforts to reinforce U.S. global primacy and consideration of concrete regional scenarios.

An analysis of U.S. security capabilities in Asia thus requires an examination of three interrelated issues. The first concerns how the United States both defines its interests (whether globally or in the Asian context) and identifies possible challenges to these interests. Given that policymaking requires the matching of interests with capabilities, the second task is then to

Michael O'Hanlon is Senior Fellow in Foreign Policy Studies at the Brookings Institution, a visiting lecturer at Princeton University, and a member of the International Institute for Strategic Studies and the Council on Foreign Relations. He can be reached at <mohanlon@brookings.edu>.

[1] See Department of Defense, *Quadrennial Defense Review Report* (Washington, D.C.: Department of Defense, 2001), 12.

evaluate recent evolutions in general U.S. security doctrine and defense posture, including how these changes have affected U.S. posture in Asia. This examination of both interests and capabilities provides the foundation for a third and final step: an evaluation of whether current U.S. doctrine and defense posture will allow Washington to manage the various challenges to its security interests that are likely to emerge in Asia. These three dimensions—interests, capabilities, and likely future regional scenarios—are respectively taken up in the first three sections of this chapter.

The main arguments are as follows. In terms of U.S. interests, Asia is currently undergoing a period of geostrategic upheaval characterized by the war against terrorism, the rise of China, and North Korea's development of a de facto nuclear arsenal. Despite these changes, the main theme of the chapter is that much actually remains constant in Asia. In broad, theoretical terms, Washington remains intent on preserving a favorable preponderance of power in Asia for both the United States as well as its close allies. In more specific terms, the United States is focused on minimizing the threat of conflict among states, ensuring free and open trade, reducing the incentives for countries to acquire weapons of mass destruction (WMD), protecting allies, and dissuading other countries from engaging in military competition with the United States.

In terms of capabilities, this chapter argues that, despite much commentary about defense revolutions, there is also much more continuity than change in terms of both U.S. defense doctrine and posture. This consistency is especially true for the global U.S. military presence and defense arrangements. Bush administration policies have modified, rather than redesigned, the U.S. approaches to such issues as warfighting strategy, military size, major base locations, and the balance of military capabilities. Similarly, U.S. defense posture in Asia—particularly with regard to troop deployments and alliances—has changed little.

Though continuity is the overarching theme of this chapter, a number of changes are also afoot. First, U.S. military capabilities have shifted southward in Asia, and with a greater focus on Taiwan and Southeast Asia and a relatively reduced emphasis on Korea. Second, the Pentagon is increasingly intent on preparing U.S. forces for a broader range of scenarios than in the past. These include possible missions involving Taiwan, counterterrorism operations, and stabilization missions in South or Southeast Asia. To sum up, at the broadest level, the U.S. military presence in Asia resembles its Cold War structure; yet a number of significant additions and modifications are now occurring within that relatively stable architecture.

The chapter concludes by examining some policies that would transform the current force posture and alliance management approach and improve U.S. defense capabilities in Asia. The three main recommendations are as follows: (1) develop a wide range of military capabilities, including higher-tech "transformative" assets, but also maintain large U.S. and allied infantry forces in the region; (2) prioritize the maintenance of a wide range of military bases; and (3) continue to foster relationships with allies and other partners for military assistance with forward missions, base access and protection, and political legitimacy in Asia.

Challenges to U.S. Strategic Interests in Asia

U.S. Global and Regional Interests

The United States has a wide range of security interests. Stated most broadly, U.S. policymakers prefer to influence the international environment before vital threats develop. The current consensus holds that in a world of WMD and apocalyptic terror, the United States cannot always wait, as President Bush stated, for threats to "gather" before doing something about them. Additionally, Washington has learned that upholding an international system of market-oriented trading economies—populated by as many democracies as possible—is the best way to promote U.S. values and protect material and security essentials. U.S. presidents ever since World War II have promoted this philosophy.

Given such interests, the United States pursues what many would describe as hegemony or primacy—but one of a different type of primacy than great powers have practiced in the past. While admittedly still to some extent competing with other countries (in particular non-market, non-democratic countries that have hostile relations with the United States or its allies) the United States employs a largely cooperative approach toward international relations. Indeed, the U.S.-led alliance system—despite the tensions surrounding the 2003 decision to invade Iraq—is still the most powerful and cohesive in history, with some 70 security partners around the world. Nevertheless, foreign policy is still based upon a desire for dominance in certain spheres that, in the eyes of many scholars and analysts, would qualify as hegemonic.

From the perspective of what might be termed a defensive realist framework (patterned after Kennan's famous five centers of global economic strength of the last century),[2] the United States has an interest in ensuring that major powers—such as China, Japan, Russia, and India—are not

---

[2] George Kennan, *Memoirs: 1925–1950* (Boston and Toronto: Little, Brown and Company, 1967), 359.

aligned against it. This is not to say that the United States requires close alliances with all of these countries, but rather that Washington must pay careful attention to developments in these countries and ensure that strong anti-U.S. alliances not take form among them.

Since the end of the Cold War, however, a more assertive form of realism has increasingly replaced Kennan's defensive realism in U.S. political debates. Rather than merely preventing the coalescence of threatening constellations of power opposing the United States, this school of thought argues that Washington should seek to ensure U.S. primacy. Though partly one of nuance and degree, the distinction is nonetheless important.

Neither Kennanesque realism nor assertive realism, however, can fully explain current U.S. foreign policy. The United States also harbors important economic goals that are dependent upon an open global economic system in general and reliable access to the major resources of and shipping lanes around the Persian Gulf and East Asian littoral in particular. Additional security interests focus on maintaining peace among the major powers, the nonproliferation of WMD, and the defeat of *jihadist* terror. Washington must also be concerned about whether China can handle the challenges of a growing population and economy without bringing on massive social unrest domestically, major local and global environmental degradation, and disruptive usage of key natural resources such as petroleum and ocean fishery beds.[3]

The United States holds a general interest in the prevention of regional warfare, particularly among Asia's larger powers. These interests are not only motivated by humanitarian concerns, but also by the desire to prevent disruptions to global commerce and the likely exacerbation in tensions and possibility of arms races that could result in the aftermath of a regional war. In addition, wars often propagate extremist politics, a particularly alarming prospect in an era of jihadist terror and WMD proliferation. Asia is so economically dynamic that any movement toward extremist politics or arms races could lead to a more challenging threat environment. In sum, increased military capabilities as a result of regional dissension or instability—even if initially localized—could cast broader shadows across the region as a whole.[4] Just as hegemonic competition and deteriorating relations among the major powers of early 20th century Europe ultimately affected not only those

---

[3] National Intelligence Council, *Mapping the Global Future: Report of the National Intelligence Council's 2020 Project* (Washington, D.C.: Government Printing Office, December 2004), 47–51, 62.

[4] Department of Defense, *Quadrennial Defense Review Report*, 4; and Ashley J. Tellis, Chung Min Lee, James Mulvenon, Courtney Purrington, and Michael D. Swaine, "Sources of Conflict in Asia," in *Sources of Conflict in the 21st Century*, ed. Zalmay Khalilzad and Ian O. Lesser (Santa Monica, CA: RAND, 1998), 52–59.

countries but the entire world, war and military buildups in Asia would have significant consequences for the United States and its allies.

Finally, it is worth adding a note that no form of realism tends to fully capture the character of American foreign policy, which has for a century been partially motivated by Wilsonian normative concerns. The United States has not simply been content to protect itself, but has often attempted to shape the world. Washington's historical decision to do so was not the result of idealism but rather of the bitter experiences of two world wars in the 20th century, which taught the United States that isolationism could not stand as a viable national security policy. This outlook led to a somewhat messianic streak in U.S. foreign policy that for decades has promoted global democracy and economic prosperity. President Bush's second inaugural address, which placed a high emphasis on the spread of "freedom," is thus very much in the U.S. tradition of Presidents Wilson, Roosevelt, Truman, Kennedy, Reagan, and Clinton.

To sum up, U.S. interests in Asia include the protection of democratic countries, the dependability and safety of shipping lanes and commercial networks, halting the proliferation of WMD, eliminating global terrorism, and ensuring that densely populated territories remain stable. Though most of these objectives relate to the protection of U.S. prosperity and security, they often have a values-based element as well.

Challenges to U.S. Interests in Asia

Asia is currently a region of many uncertainties. The Bush administration has spoken positively of the People's Republic of China (PRC), stating in the 2002 *National Security Strategy* that the United States "welcome[s] the emergence of a strong, peaceful, and prosperous China." The administration also believes, however, that China's avowed peaceful ascent cannot be taken for granted, and that the lack of democratization or political liberalization in China may portend bumpy Sino-U.S. relations in the future, and may even lead to PRC aggression.[5] Note also that Washington is unsure whether relations with Beijing will improve or worsen, and cannot easily estimate the odds of possible war over Taiwan. President Bush's advisors once spoke of China as a strategic rival, the president himself has declared his firm commitment to defend Taiwan, and Secretary Rumsfeld has expressed alarm regarding the pace and nature of China's defense buildup.[6] Partly in consid-

---

[5] President George W. Bush, "National Security Strategy of the United States," September 2002, ch. 8.

[6] Matt Kelley, "In China Remarks, Rumsfeld Continues to Push for Change," *Boston Globe*, June 5, 2005.

eration of the above factors, Tokyo and Washington have recently stated that the U.S.-Japan alliance would take seriously any conflict over Taiwan.

Nor can Washington predict a peaceful resolution to the current nuclear crisis with North Korea. Similarly, Washington is uncertain whether other countries in Asia will tolerate the presence on their soil of terrorist organizations determined to attack the United States. Likewise, Washington must attempt to lessen the remarkable degree of animosity toward the United States that has arisen in most Muslim countries (particularly in the Arab world). Further worries demand focused attention: nuclear-armed Pakistan could face serious domestic instability or engage in war with nuclear-armed India, and Iran might obtain nuclear weapons that would allow Tehran to threaten Israel or another country, which would thereby endanger Persian Gulf shipping. Finally, a more general anti-U.S. coalition could form in response to perceived U.S. unilateralism. The likelihood of this last scenario occurring seems quite low, however. Despite criticisms of recent U.S. policy, no ally has severed its security relationship with the United States, and there is continued demand to join U.S.-led alliance systems.

U.S. Defense Posture: An Era of Transformation?

Although some fear U.S. military strength, the United States is far from omnipotent. Past eras when major powers could easily conquer distant lands are gone. In today's world, the United States can be said to possess, in Posen's terms, command of the commons—i.e., air, oceans, and space—but to have trouble contending with many conflicts on land, particularly against irregular resistance fighters.[7] This section will thus examine how Washington views the U.S. security environment and how it is seeking to transform U.S. capabilities in order to meet the demands of being the world's only superpower at the start of the 21st century. The section closes with a discussion of how these changes have begun to affect U.S. defense posture in Asia.

A key argument of this section is that continuity rather than change characterizes both U.S. defense doctrine and posture. The Bush administration's foreign policy has made frequent headlines, and two distinguished scholars have spoken of the "Bush revolution" in American foreign policy;[8] yet if the focus is limited to a broad military presence and defense arrangements, continuity in policy is strikingly apparent. On matters ranging from

---

[7] Barry Posen, "Command of the Commons: The Military Foundation of U.S. Hegemony," *International Security* 28, no. 1 (Summer 2003): 5–46; for a related argument, see Michael O'Hanlon, *Technological Change and the Future of Warfare* (Washington, D.C.: Brookings, 2000), 106–67.

[8] Ivo H. Daalder and James M. Lindsay, *America Unbound: The Bush Revolution in Foreign* Policy (Washington, D.C.: Brookings, 2003).

warfighting strategy and the size of the military to the locations of major bases and the relative balance of capabilities from various military services, Bush administration policies have constituted modifications, rather than wholesale changes, to previous U.S. approaches.

U.S. Defense Spending

The U.S. national security budget has grown to nearly $450 billion in 2006; this figure does not include the additional costs of operations in Iraq or Afghanistan (which presently average about $75 billion a year), and does not count the activities that fall under the Department of Homeland Security budget. This is nearly a 50 percent increase in the nominal budget since the Clinton presidency (and about a one-third increase as measured in real-dollar, inflation-adjusted terms). Even taking inflation into account, the budget exceeds average Cold War levels.

Judging whether U.S. defense spending is high or low depends, however, on the measure. By comparison with other countries, of course, this budget is obviously enormous. According to the Stockholm International Peace Research Institute, the United States accounted for roughly 47 percent of all global military spending in 2004.[9] Relative to the size of the U.S. economy, by contrast, the 4 percent of GDP that military expenditures consume appear more moderate—being less than the levels under the Reagan, Ford, and Carter administrations, and only half of typical Cold War outlays.

The rationale for a large U.S. defense budget is fairly clear. Washington maintains security partnerships with more than 70 countries (including the other 25 members of NATO, all of the Rio Pact countries in Latin America, several allies in the Western Pacific, and roughly a dozen countries in the Persian Gulf/Mideast region). Alone among the world's powers, the United States structures its forces so as to project substantial amounts of military power at a rapid speed over great distances, and maintains such forces in these regions for long periods of time.[10] The United States undergirds a collective security system that helps many countries feel secure to the point where they do not engage in arms races with neighbors, launch preemptive wars of their own, or develop nuclear weapons.

Given these commitments, the U.S. defense budget will likely continue to grow faster than inflation alone would necessitate. Weapons purchased

---

[9] Any specific estimate is somewhat imprecise given uncertainty over true military spending by China and several other countries. See Stockholm International Peace Research Institute (SIPRI), "The 15 Major Spenders in 2004," military expenditure database, http://www.sipri.org.contents/milap/milex/mex_major_spenders.pdf.

[10] Michael E. O'Hanlon, *Expanding Global Military Capacity for Humanitarian Intervention* (Washington, D.C.: Brookings, 2003), 56–57.

largely in the Reagan years are nearing the end of their life cycles and will have to be replaced more quickly than has been the case in the past fifteen years. Meanwhile, the cost per weapon continues to climb. Historically, weapons costs increase 2–3 percent per year in real, inflation-adjusted terms; the same is true in the operations and support accounts. For example, the Department of Defense's (DoD) medical costs almost doubled in real terms between 1988 and 2003, to just under $30 billion.[11] Military compensation, now comparable with civilian jobs requiring similar experience and education, must remain competitive in order to maintain a high-quality all-volunteer force.[12]

Congress will continue to make the case for increased expenditure in the size and cost of U.S. ground forces. The Iraq mission and other responsibilities continue to place enormous strain on the U.S. army and marine forces. As such, upward movement of the U.S. defense budget will continue, although the expected growth looks barely inadequate to U.S. defense planners charged with addressing the looming needs of the armed forces.

Doctrinal Change?

Since the early 1990s, U.S. defense planners have fielded armed forces designed to fight and win two full-scale wars at once. The Bush administration adjusted this requirement in 2001 arguing that only one of the victories needed to be both immediate and permit, if necessary, the occupation of the enemy's country. The new force planning framework was described as a "1-4-2-1" Framework.[13] Under this conception U.S. military capabilities would be designed to defend the homeland, maintain a presence and deterrence capabilities in four theaters, fight up to two wars at a time, and be capable of winning one of them overwhelmingly (including the overthrow of an enemy government and the occupation of its territory).[14]

More notable than the change in terminology (i.e., from "two major regional contingencies" to "1-4-2-1") is the continuing emphasis on retaining a two-war capability. This criterion indicates a need for the United States to

---

[11] Allison Percy, *Growth in Medical Spending by the Department of Defense* (Washington, D.C.: Congressional Budget Office, 2003), 1–2.

[12] See Amy Belasco, *Paying for Military Readiness and Upkeep: Trends in Operation and Maintenance Spending* (Washington, D.C.: Congressional Budget Office, 1997), 5; and Lane Pierrot, *Budgeting for Defense: Maintaining Today's Forces* (Washington, D.C.: Congressional Budget Office, 2000), 18–23.

[13] See General Richard B. Myers, Chairman of the Joint Chiefs of Staff, posture statement before the Senate Armed Services Committee, 108th Congress, February 3, 2004; and Department of Defense, *Quadrennial Defense Review Report*.

[14] General Richard Myers, *National Military Strategy of the United States, 2004* (Washington, D.C.: Department of Defense, 2004), 18.

be able to fight one war without letting its guard down elsewhere. In addition, the perceived need to prepare for other, smaller contingencies was also incorporated into U.S. military planning in the 1990s.

Given ongoing U.S. commitments both in Iraq and for the war against terrorism, the purported two-war capability is today on somewhat shaky ground. The United States would currently be hard pressed to conduct an additional major operation. In extreme circumstances, however, the United States still has options. Note, for instance, that most air force and navy assets are available for possible crises. Moreover, in a true emergency, the army and marine forces could still muster several divisions. These units would not be rested, would possess considerable amounts of inoperable equipment, would be low in ammunition stocks, and could take several months to deploy to the battlefield; these forces could still operate, nonetheless, at perhaps 50 to 80 percent of full effectiveness.

The Bush administration is best known not for its two-war force structure, but for its doctrine of preemption. This doctrine, codified in the 2002 *National Security Strategy of the United States*, is better described as a policy of preventive war. It emphasizes that in a world where extremist states armed with WMD and terrorist organizations are numerous, the United States cannot wait for dangers to "gather" before taking action against them. Many U.S. leaders have contemplated preemptive options in the past, including President Clinton in 1994, when his administration examined options for destroying North Korea's nuclear infrastructure.[15] Being diplomatically costly, militarily difficult, and politically contentious, preventive or preemptive strikes are unlikely, however, to occur with any frequency.

Troop Size

The U.S. military establishment has scaled down in size by about one-third since the Cold War ended. Active-duty personnel currently number 1.4 million. Additionally, there are about one million reservists, of whom 150,000–200,000 have been activated in recent years.[16] The U.S. active-duty force is not particularly large, being about half the size of China's military and only modestly larger than the armed forces of India, Russia, or North

---

[15] See Michael O'Hanlon and Mike Mochizuki, *Crisis on the Korean Peninsula: How to Deal with a Nuclear North Korea* (New York: McGraw-Hill, 2003), 1–55.

[16] Department of Defense, "National Guard and Reserve Mobilized as of February 25, 2004," February 25, 2004, http://www.defenselink.mil/releases/2004/nr20040225-0366.html. Mobilized Army reservists at that time totaled approximately 155,000, Air Force 18,400, Marine Corps 5,400, Navy 2,300, and Coast Guard 1,600.

Korea. U.S. advantages lie in quality, technology, training, global presence, and rapid deployability.[17]

There is considerable consensus in U.S. politics regarding the size of U.S. military forces. The 2001 *Quadrennial Defense Review* (QDR) retained the active-duty troop levels of about 1.4 million maintained during the Clinton administration. Despite the current debate concerning whether the size of the army and marine corps are large enough for the demands of the missions in Iraq and Afghanistan, current proposals would only increase U.S. active-duty strength by about 3–5 percent. The 2001 QDR also retained most of the existing agenda for weapons modernization and added new initiatives in areas such as missile defense, advanced satellites, and unmanned aerial vehicles (UAV).

Defense Revolutions and Transformations?

The Bush administration believes, as does much of the U.S. defense community, that a revolution in military affairs (RMA) is underway. The promise of the RMA lies in the hope that further advances in precision munitions, real-time data dissemination, and other modern technologies can—if combined with appropriate war-fighting doctrines and organization—transform warfare. The unprecedented pace of technological change, many observers hold, will sharply alter the size and composition of U.S. military forces.[18]

With regard to the Asia theater, this revolution might be expected to allow a greater role for airpower in any future Korean war than would have been previously expected; more to the point, looking toward the longer-term future, the RMA could work to preserve U.S. technological dominance over China and perhaps even allow for the defense of Taiwan or other U.S. regional interests without the need for frequent access to forward bases.

Proponents of the RMA thesis can be divided into several camps.[19] One emphasizes those areas of technology where revolutionary progress is undoubtedly occurring, most notably in computer technology and associated systems such as robotics and communications, and suggests that the United States must emphasize such progress in future modernization efforts. This "computers-first" school of thought prioritizes purchases of precision-strike weapons, UAVs (and perhaps similar vehicles for land or water), automated data processing, and targeting and communications grids that allow the

---

[17] Department of Defense, "Active Duty Military Personnel Strengths by Regional Area and By Country (309A)," December 31, 2004, http://web1.whs.osd.mil/mmid/military/history/hst1204.pdf.

[18] See, most notably, Admiral William A. Owens with Ed Offley, *Lifting the Fog of War* (New York: Farrar, Straus, and Giroux, 2000).

[19] See Michael O'Hanlon, *Technological Change and the Future of Warfare* (Washington, D.C.: Brookings, 2000), 1–31.

quick sharing of information on the locations of enemy assets. Supporters of this RMA approach sometimes raise the concept of network-centric warfare, noting the stunning success of small numbers of U.S. special forces working in conjunction with U.S. airpower and Afghan resistance forces in the war to overthrow the Taliban. A more ambitious school of thought speaks of "dominant battlespace knowledge," where rapid advances can occur not only in computers and electronics but also sensor technology, thus making the battlefield "transparent" to U.S. forces.[20] Unfortunately for the proponents of this view, sensor technology is not advancing as fast as hoped, as was reflected most recently in the difficulties locating insurgents and their weaponry in Iraq. A third school of thought, the "global reach" community, argues that weapons such as long-range bombers, space systems, and much lighter and more transportable ground forces can usher in the day of rapid and accurate intercontinental strikes, thereby largely eliminating the need for overseas basing.[21] The overall thesis of this last school of thought—though not without its merits—is also highly suspect.

The Bush administration does not exclusively subscribe to any one of these camps. Rather, the administration's major transformational programs span the gamut from "school one" systems (better computers and communications systems, as well as attempts to develop UAVs, etc.), "school two" systems (with an emphasis on space-based radar constellation), to "school three" concepts (which includes the army's Future Combat System and the Marine Corps V-22 Osprey tilt-rotor aircraft). Though there are merits to all three systems, one must be realistic regarding the near term prospects of achieving technological breakthroughs worthy of major investment decisions. Other weapons platforms—such as the F-22 and Joint Strike Fighter, the *Virginia*-class submarine, the littoral combat ship, and the Aegis destroyer—are intended as much to obviate existing or possible future vulnerabilities in U.S. weapons systems as to develop radically new types of capabilities (they thus might be lumped together under a fourth school of RMA thought, the "vulnerability school").[22] In sum, the Pentagon's use of RMA and transformation terminology encompasses many different types of efforts, some much more practical and feasible than others.

---

[20] See for example, Stuart E. Johnson and Martin C. Libicki, eds., *Dominant Battlespace Knowledge* (Washington, D.C.: National Defense University Press, 1996).

[21] See for example, David A. Ochmanek et al., *To Find and Not to Yield: How Advances in Information and Firepower Can Transform Theater Warfare* (Santa Monica, CA: RAND, 1998); and Daniel Goure and Stephen A. Cambone, "The Coming of Age of Air and Space Power," in *Air and Space Power in the New Millennium*, ed. Daniel Goure and Christopher M. Szara (Washington, D.C.: Center for Strategic and International Studies, 1997), 1–47.

[22] Department of Defense, "President Bush's FY 2006 Defense Budget," February 2005, http://www.dod.mil/news/Feb2005/d20050207budget.pdf.

There are several reasons why the first and fourth elements of RMA thought—the computers-first and the vulnerability schools—are more compelling than the other two. Though currently making rapid advances, military technology may not outpace advances of the past half-century. Adherents of the "revolution" thesis invoke "Moore's law," which holds that the number of transistors on a semiconductor chip will double every 18–24 months. Though this assessment may be accurate with respect to the computer revolution, it would be a mistake to extrapolate from this trend in computer chips to predict equally rapid progress in entirely different realms of technology.[23] Advances in electronics and computers do not necessarily imply comparably rapid changes in the basic functioning of tanks, ships, aircraft, rockets, explosives, and energy sources. Moreover, modernization of these latter types of major platforms is extremely expensive.

Some point to Afghanistan and Iraq as evidence that the defense revolution is, or should be, mostly focused in the area of air capabilities. Yet the main pillars of success in these regional operations included traditional ground-force capabilities as much as high technology, especially in terms of the air campaign.

The Afghan conflict, while pathbreaking in the use by the United States of high technology such as GPS-guided bombs, Predator UAVs, and special forces, did not invalidate all past concepts of warfare. The Northern Alliance and other Afghan units were needed on the ground to help defeat the Taliban and Al Qaeda. In addition, by relying too much on airpower and local allies, U.S. forces failed to achieve key objectives in and around Tora Bora. Finally, stabilizing Afghanistan effectively would have required considerably more ground forces—if not during main combat operations, then after.[24]

The U.S.-led coalition's key assets in Iraq—new technology and traditional skills—resulted in a remarkable fusion of capabilities. In terms of equipment, of particular note were the all-weather reconnaissance systems, all-weather bombs, and modern communications networks that were developed in the last decade. The competence of U.S. and British troops and their commanders, and the excellence of their doctrine and training were, however, equally striking. Indeed, traditional equipment such as tanks and the old-fashioned skills of infantry soldiers were very important, and urban combat operations were, on the whole, executed admirably. In fact, the difficulty of stabilizing Iraq in the aftermath of the invasion has likely underscored the

---

[23] National Defense Panel, "Transforming Defense: National Security in the 21st Century," December 1997, 7–8; and Michael O'Hanlon, *Technological Change and the Future of Warfare* (Washington, D.C.: Brookings, 2000), 32–105.

[24] Biddle, *Afghanistan and the Future of Warfare*, 43–58.

need for traditional infantry, intelligence, and armored capabilities as much as "shock and awe" high-tech capabilities.

Though U.S. defense planners should continue to pursue new technological opportunities, the above examples highlight some limitations of the defense revolution hypothesis. Existing Pentagon programs seem to suggest that important recent progress will continue in a number of more traditional areas, including the development of new types of precision-strike weapons that work in bad weather or at night (e.g. increasingly accurate GPS-guided munitions such as the JDAM), obtaining targeting information more quickly and continuously (via platforms such as the JSTARS aircraft and a host of unmanned planes like Predator and Global Hawk), getting targeting information quickly to those who launch such weapons (through communications networks such as the Link 16 program and the Aegis Navy network), and gradually increasing the types of platforms, some manned and some unmanned, that can gather information more frequently (such as the littoral combat ship and unmanned underwater vehicles). Among other constraints, however, army divisions will remain cumbersome and difficult to transport, the utility of aircraft in the urban battlefield will remain constrained, sensors searching for WMD or other key military-related technologies will have to move close to their quarry in order to find such materials in a timely and reliable manner, while quiet submarines and mines will remain very hard to detect (with enemy assets in these two areas constantly improving), and finding insurgents within a local population will continue to elude technological quick-fixes.[25]

Missile Defense and Space Systems

Of all the systems in development as part of the U.S. defense transformation, missile defense is of particular importance to Asia, especially in light of North Korean and Chinese ballistic missile capabilities. The Bush administration has nearly doubled funding for missile defense to the current level of about $9 billion per year, which constitutes a significant increase over the Clinton-era levels of about $5 billion per year (which, in turn, were roughly comparable to average levels during the Reagan and first Bush administrations).[26]

The Pentagon is deploying several interceptors capable of shooting down long-range warheads. The first was installed in July 2004,[27] and by

---

[25] O'Hanlon, *Technological Change and the Future of Warfare*, 32–142.

[26] James M. Lindsay and Michael E. O'Hanlon, *Defending America: The Case for Limited National Missile Defense* (Washington, D.C.: Brookings, 2001), 6.

[27] Associated Press, "Missile Interceptor Installed in Alaska," *Los Angeles Times*, July 23, 2004.

the end of 2005 a total of twenty interceptors will be stationed on land (in Alaska and California) and an additional ten at sea. Radars—used to detect incoming missiles and track their warheads—are located on land and at sea, with a number of existing sensors undergoing improvements and others being built anew.[28] Over time, more interceptors are due to be added at various sites both in the United States and at sea, including a shorter-range land-based interceptor known as THAAD and quite possibly multiple-warhead defensive missiles to improve the original system based in Alaska and California. New development might also include sea-based interceptors, an airborne platform using a laser (which would add more defensive firepower), and land-based interceptors designed to shoot down an enemy rocket in its boost phase (and deployed overseas near possible launch points). Ultimately, an additional site might be built in eastern Europe.[29]

Given current threats and available technologies, no space-based weapons are included in this architecture.[30] Plans are underway, however, for improved sensor networks, including two new satellite constellations that will detect missile launches and track warheads.[31]

U.S. missile defense programs are far from mature. Yet even if the technology is rushed and the deployment timelines are partly political (particularly for the midcourse system based in Alaska and California), the deployment of an interim missile defense capability appears logical. Because the United States currently lacks a missile defense capability, even an imperfect system is arguably better than the status quo that does not provide a credible defense against the long-range missile threat from North Korea. North Korea surprised the U.S. intelligence community in 1998 with a partially successful test of a three-stage rocket. Whether Pyongyang could repeat this provocative feat—or even field a workable missile—remains in doubt. Some will argue that North Korea would never strike the United States with a long-range missile, as such a move would ensure the regime's demise. Pyongyang might, however, feel more emboldened to provoke security crises and attempt to extort benefits from the United States and its neighbors if North Korea possessed a long-range missile. In the event that war again breaks out on the Korean Peninsula, a nuclear-armed North Korean regime on the verge of collapse could fire missiles at a U.S., Japanese, or South Korean city.

---

[28] Tony Cappacio, "Lockheed Upgrading Destroyers to Monitor North Korea," *Bloomberg.com*, July 15, 2004.

[29] Jonathan S. Landay, "U.S. Ponders Antimissile Site in Eastern Europe," *Miami Herald*, June 28, 2004.

[30] Gopal Ratnam, "No Missile Defense Shield in Space, For Now: Kadish," *DefenseNews.com*, March 23, 2004.

[31] Missile Defense Agency, "Press Release: Fiscal Year 2005 Budget Estimates," February 18, 2004, http://www.acq.osd.mil/bmdo/bmdolink/html/guide.html.

Despite the above strategic rationales for missile defense, some sense of perspective is in order. First and foremost, these systems are extremely expensive. Future budgets may very likely be cut somewhat, and programs delayed or scaled back; indeed, the 2006 budget reflects reductions relative to what had originally been planned for that year.

A scaled-back missile defense program will face several options. Such a program might limit the scale of any deployment of the main midcourse system to 50–100 interceptors—enough to deal with the more plausible threat of a North Korean attack but insufficient to handle a concerted Russian, and possibly even Chinese, attack. In addition, the multitude of missile defense programs could be scaled back somewhat. The navy's lower-tier missile defense system was already eliminated following mediocre performance. Depending on the future progress of the technologies, it may become necessary to cancel another system as well; possible candidates include the airborne laser, which is experiencing significant development problems, or (if ABL turns out to work well) a kinetic-energy boost-phase interceptor program.[32] Another set of concerns relates to space-based assets. Certain expensive technologies that are designed to enhance the performance of missile defense systems—most notably the planned STSS constellation of low-orbit tracking satellites—might be canceled.[33]

Current Defense Posture in Asia

How are these broad changes affecting Asia? This analysis will examine two key areas: troop deployments and allies.

Troop deployments. There has been considerable continuity in troop deployments in East Asia. Admittedly, the Bush administration has not felt obliged to retain the 1995 Nye Initiative's floor of about 100,000 U.S. military personnel in the region, and is relocating and reducing many U.S. forces in Korea south of the Han River and out of Seoul.[34] There is a good deal of

---

[32] Gopal Ratnam, "Technical and Budget Issues May Ground Airborne Laser," *Space News*, July 12, 2004, 6.

[33] This leads naturally to the question of weapons in space. Although some in the Bush administration favor space-based missile defenses as well as dedicated antisatellite programs, such programs are very expensive, technologically challenging, of limited relevance to immediate security challenges, and politically controversial. See Michael O'Hanlon, *Neither Star Wars Nor Sanctuary: Constraining the Military Uses of Space* (Washington, D.C.: Brookings, 2004). Other space programs are relatively noncontroversial and will probably be pursued. Greater hardening against attack for U.S. military satellites makes sense, for example, as does improved ability to deal with jamming (especially for GPS systems). See Bill Gertz, "Signal Jamming a Factor in Future Wars, General Says," *Washington Times*, July 16, 2004, 10.

[34] General Richard Myers stated that "During the FY 2004 budget cycle, Congress voiced concern over the Department's overseas basing plans. Since then, our global posture strategy has matured. We are now in the process of detailed consultation with our allies and members of Congress." See Myers, posture statement, 33.

new language, many new acronyms, and much discussion regarding how the changing security environment necessitates major adjustments to U.S. defense posture. Yet the actual cuts in Asia will change overall force numbers there by only slightly more than 10 percent—much less than the 25 percent reduction in the immediate aftermath of the Cold War, and far less than the reductions in U.S. deployments in Europe during the same time period. Moreover, in Korea, where the most notable shifts are occurring, the changes are justified at least as much in terms of force reduction in congested urban areas (which would reduce friction with South Koreans) as in carrying out a new strategy.[35] The United States will maintain major air and naval hubs in Japan, including an aircraft carrier and associated escort ships at Yokosuka near Tokyo; the Kadena Air Force base, which houses fighters, transport, and reconnaissance aircraft; and marine facilities for the 31st Marine Expeditionary Unit and 3rd Marine Division on Okinawa. The United States will also retain tactical aircraft in Korea, a military headquarters, and one of the two brigades normally based there.

The United States has partially compensated for force reductions by basing at least three more submarines in Guam.[36] These changes built upon Clinton administration increases in equipment prepositioned on Guam and Korea by up to 50 percent, and fast sealift by comparable proportions.[37] On balance, the overall magnitude of changes is modest, encompassing a geographic shift southward and an operational shift toward longer-range platforms capable of operating throughout the region (instead of being effectively anchored to the Korean Peninsula).

Allies. The state of U.S. alliances in Asia has changed only moderately during the Bush presidency. Tokyo has drawn even closer to Washington, but the movement to strengthen the alliance, gradually normalize Japan's role within it, and bring Taiwan within its sphere of influence was already well underway in the 1990s.[38] Moreover, while Japan's contributions in Afghanistan and Iraq have been significant, it is easy to overstate such aid. For example, the approximately 500 Japanese troops in Iraq must be protected by NATO forces in order to ensure they do not get into difficult firefights

---

[35] Douglas J. Feith, *Strengthening U.S. Global Defense Posture: Report to Congress*, Department of Defense, September 2004, 12.

[36] Eric J. Labs, *Increasing the Mission Capability of the Attack Submarine Force* (Washington, D.C.: Congressional Budget Office, 2002), 10.

[37] Rachel Schmidt, *Moving U.S. Forces: Options for Strategic Mobility* (Washington, D.C.: Congressional Budget Office, 1997); and Michael O'Hanlon, "Clinton's Strong Defense Legacy," *Foreign Affairs* 82, no. 6 (November-December 2003): 126–34.

[38] Mike M. Mochizuki, "U.S. Strategy in the Asia-Pacific: Alliances and Coalitions, Wheels and Webs," in *The Okinawa Question and the U.S.-Japan Alliance*, ed. Akikazu Hashimoto, Mike Mochizuki, and Kurayoshi Takara (Washington, D.C.: The George Washington University, 2005), 27.

(which raises the question of whether the Japanese forces are a net asset or a liability). The relationship with South Korea is troubled, largely due to differing views over policies toward North Korea as well as over the possibility of having to reorient the alliance to hedge against an ascendant China in the near future. Seoul has, however, sent 3,500 troops to Iraq in part as assistance to the United States (without the types of constraints placed by Tokyo on the Japanese Self-Defense Forces). Counterterrorism cooperation with the Philippines has strengthened the U.S.-Philippine relationship, but the Philippines' contribution to the Iraq mission was minimal and short-lived. The U.S.-Australian relationship remains strong, and Canberra made substantial contributions to the U.S.-led military efforts in Afghanistan and Iraq. Australia's growing economic ties with China, however, make Canberra more reluctant to side clearly with Washington in any possible dispute over Taiwan.[39]

One can debate at length the relative importance of these and other developments in various U.S. alliances in Asia. On balance, however, there does not appear to be an overarching trend. The systemic strain of relations witnessed in some important relationships is not present in U.S. relationships in Asia. Yet at the same time, China's improving diplomacy and strengthening economy have increased the interest of countries such as Korea and Australia in maintaining good relations with both the United States and China. In addition, multilateral security mechanisms have not progressed far enough so as to represent a significant alternative to the bilateral alliance structures that remain dominant throughout the region.

In short, despite a slightly greater emphasis on Taiwan contingencies and counterterror missions in recent years, speculation of major defense reforms has proven empty, and U.S. military posture in Asia under the Bush administration has remained strikingly consistent. Less by choice than by strategic necessity, the Bush administration has not revolutionized U.S. interests and role in the greater Asia-Pacific.

The United States in Asia: Future Prospects

Continuity will therefore continue to characterize much of U.S. security policy toward Asia. Notable changes—such as the above-noted basing changes as well as the new policy of dispatching Navy ships overseas quickly in times of crisis as a means of forgoing a constant forward presence—are not radical. Nevertheless, some second-order changes must be implement-

---

[39] See James A. Kelly, "George W. Bush and Asia: An Assessment," in *George W. Bush and East Asia: A First Term Assessment*, ed. Robert M. Hathaway and Wilson Lee, (Washington, D.C.: Woodrow Wilson Center for Scholars, 2005), 15–30.

ed within specific plans and preparations. Policymakers will still face major challenges simply to maintain U.S. interests and the overall role of the United States in Asia.

The immediate challenges confronting U.S. defense planning involve managing the current strains on the military, particularly in Iraq, while keeping the defense budget within bounds. These tasks are difficult, and occupy the bulk of U.S. defense planning today. U.S. defense strategists must, however, begin to consider an appropriate guiding defense framework once the intense period of the Iraq operation is over. Whether through defense transformation or changing force posture in Asia, the reshaping of U.S. armed forces should not ignore the wide range of possible and quite demanding scenarios in Asia capable of threatening U.S. security. At least two conflict scenarios are quite plausible: conflict against North Korea or in the Taiwan Strait. Each could involve 200,000 or more U.S. troops for significant periods of time. Several other possible contingencies, some of which may fester for years, could involve 30,000–50,000 U.S. troops at a time. Readying for these potential scenarios would require a force structure at least as large as the current one—particularly since two of these contingencies could occur at the same time. An examination of three of these plausible contingencies will allow a better appreciation of the demands that could be placed on the U.S. military.

Conflict on the Korean Peninsula

Many analysts at the Pentagon have long believed that a surprise North Korean attack on South Korea could achieve important successes—including the capture of Seoul—before U.S. reinforcements could arrive in sufficient numbers.[40] In light of continued improvements in South Korean and U.S. capabilities, combined with gradual atrophy of the North Korean military, however, allied prospects for successfully defending South Korea are actually quite good. Still, Washington cannot neglect Korea. If the United States and its allies grow acutely worried that North Korea might sell nuclear materials abroad, or if they decided that Pyongyang must be prevented from developing a large nuclear arsenal, an escalating crisis over nuclear weapons could lead to war. Likewise, Pyongyang may miscalculate the leverage of its nuclear capabilities and push brinkmanship to a dangerous level.

At the operational level, South Korea worries perennially about a DPRK surprise attack, although North Korea's severely degraded conventional

---

[40] Pentagon models reportedly estimate about 50,000 U.S. and 500,000 South Korean military casualties during the first three months of war. See Don Oberdorfer, "A Minute to Midnight," *Newsweek*, October 20, 1997, 18.

force capabilities, combined with South Korea's much improved posture and changing political attitudes in Seoul, make this scenario of far less concern than in earlier decades.

On the other hand, might the ROK and the United States employ pre-emptive force against North Korea based on the precedent of the campaign in Iraq? This possibility seems very unlikely for a number of strategic and political reasons. First, because so many North Korean weapons are positioned within striking distance of Seoul, even a well-timed surprise attack led by the United States could not prevent a barrage of missile and artillery rounds from landing in Seoul.[41] Second, many North Korean military and political headquarters are deep underground, which makes a "shock and awe" type of air campaign very difficult.[42] Third, because there are no easy approaches to Pyongyang similar to the open desert used by coalition forces to reach Baghdad in March and April 2003, enemy harassment of supply lines could prove to be a pervasive problem. Fourth, North Korea's military, with a total active-duty force of around one million, is much larger than the military in Iraq.[43] Fifth, North Korean troops are reportedly more indoctrinated by their leadership—and hence more dedicated to their nation's defense—than were Iraqi forces.[44] Finally, though North Korea's ability to mount its suspected nuclear weapons on missiles remains in doubt, the possibility still exists that Pyongyang could utilize one or more nuclear weapons in response to an invasion.

In either case, a decisive victory in Korea would therefore likely require hundreds of thousands of U.S. troops in addition to the large ROK armed forces. There is little reason to worry that U.S. forces today, though overstretched as they are in Iraq, could not deter conflict on the Korean Peninsula. Moreover, improvements in both South Korea's military and U.S. airpower give the alliance a robust defensive capability regardless of the level

---

[41] North Korea has about 500 artillery tubes within range of Seoul. Each could fire one or more rounds a minute at the South Korean capital over an extended period of time. Unless virtually all of their locations were known in advance, a typical North Korean weapon would still be able to fire several shots before being destroyed.

[42] Given the degree to which the country is cut off from outsiders, U.S. special forces would also have a harder time infiltrating North Korea and locating sites for aerial attack than in Iraq.

[43] Moreover, three-fourths of Iraq's troops were thought unlikely to fight hard before the war began; few make a similar assumption about North Korea's military. See "Lessons from the Iraq War: Strategy and Planning," *Strategic Comments* 9, no. 3 (May 2003).

[44] Such ideas have reportedly been investigated with regard to North Korea, and Pyongyang is surely aware of this. Similar conclusions follow for North Korea's top military and political leadership, which would probably fight on even if Kim Jong Il were targeted and killed in a "decapitation attack" of the type attempted against Saddam Hussein at the beginning of Operation Iraqi Freedom. See Thom Shanker, "Lessons from Iraq Include How to Scare North Korean Leader," *New York Times*, May 12, 2003.

of U.S. ground reinforcements. An actual invasion by the North could, however, prove to be extremely difficult.

One final scenario involves the collapse of the Kim Jong Il regime; coalition forces make mention of a "Plan 5029" (in contrast to the traditional war plan, which is designated with a 5027), which is designed to handle just such a contingency. Admittedly, the consequences of a governmental collapse in North Korea are impossible to predict. If command and control broke down very quickly within DPRK ranks and mass surrenders occurred at the unit level, such a war could be over quickly. As argued above, however, North Korean morale and commitment appear reasonably strong, which suggests that U.S. and ROK forces may need to fight their way to Pyongyang. One key question concerns the role that China might play in helping to stabilize the northern reaches of the DPRK. While many in the Combined Forces Command would likely resist Beijing's participation, such an idea might be workable provided that China limited its role to dealing with the refugee problem (for example, by helping establish camps within the DPRK so that millions of refugees would not need to enter China). In addition, Beijing, like Washington, would have to clearly commit to follow Seoul's directives promptly and unconditionally following the conclusion of hostilities, and withdraw forces if and when asked.

A China-Taiwan War

It seems extremely unlikely, now or anytime in the foreseeable future, that the PRC could seize Taiwan by means of an amphibious assault. China's strategic lift is inadequate, modern U.S. and Taiwanese sensors prevent the chance of a surprise attack, and precision weapons make it harder than ever for large transports (such as ships and airplanes) that are required for a major assault to successfully reach enemy shores.[45] While the Pentagon argued in 2004 that China could probably invade Taiwan in the absence of third-party intervention, the 2005 report did not repeat this assertion.[46]

---

[45] See Bill Gertz, "Admiral Says Taiwan Invasion Would Fail," Washington Times, March 8, 2000, A5; Harold Brown, Joseph W. Prueher, and Adam Segal, eds., Chinese Military Power (New York: Council on Foreign Relations, 2003), 27–28; Tony Capaccio, "China Has Boosted Military, U.S. General Says," Bloomberg.com, January 13, 2004; David Shambaugh, Modernizing China's Military (Berkeley, CA: University of California Press, 2002), 328–30; and Michael O'Hanlon, Defense Policy Choices for the Bush Administration, 2nd ed, (Washington, D.C.: Brookings, 2002), 154–203. The Pentagon is somewhat more worried about the invasion option but does not disagree with the assertion that it would be very challenging (largely because of lift constraints) and probably not China's preferred option. See Department of Defense, "The Military Power of the People's Republic of China, 2004," annual report to Congress, 46–52; and Michael D. Swaine and Ashley J. Tellis, Interpreting China's Grand Strategy (Santa Monica, CA: RAND, 2000), 167.

[46] Department of Defense, "The Military Power of the People's Republic of China, 2005," 42.

Beijing could use limited military force in order to pressure Taipei to accept terms for a political settlement highly favorable to Beijing. Two scenarios are of particular interest: a missile attack designed to terrorize or coerce Taiwan and a blockade.

A missile attack by China against Taiwan poses several challenges to Beijing. As of 2005, the PRC has some 700 ballistic missiles deployed near Taiwan.[47] Though the M-9 and M-11 missiles can reach Taiwan, neither traditionally possessed sufficient accuracy to strike military assets using conventional explosives. If China exhausted the bulk of its (relatively inaccurate) missile inventory to temporarily slow operations at a port or airfield, intimidation would have little of its intended effect. As China improves the quality of its missile guidance, however, its capacity for precision strikes would grow proportionately.

Until that point is reached, perhaps the most troubling coercive scenario from a Taiwanese and U.S. perspective is a blockade (perhaps done in conjunction with cyberattacks or a few missile strikes). Rather than relying on sheer terror and intimidation, a blockade would take aim at Taiwan's economy and attempt to impoverish the island for an indefinite period of time. Though unlikely to truly cut Taiwan off from the outside world, a blockade could certainly exact attrition from commercial ships trading with Taiwan as well as Taiwanese military forces attempting to break the blockade. This in turn would drive up the costs of insuring any vessels that continued to carry goods to and from Taiwan. Though China could not in all likelihood quarantine Taiwan, even an imperfect, "leaky blockade" could still sink enough commercial ships to put an effective halt to trade with Taiwan.[48] Should Beijing convince enough commercial shippers not to risk trips to Taiwan, China could effectively begin to strangle the island. Beijing might then be able to force a compromise deal that secures Taiwan's capitulation.[49]

U.S. military intervention would be necessary in order to protect Taiwan and its economy against such a blockade. U.S. forward basing need not be designed to maintain a war-winning capability in the Taiwan Strait at all times, but over a period of weeks or months U.S. assistance in the Taiwan

---

[47] Department of Defense, "The Military Power of the People's Republic of China, 2005," 45.

[48] Michael A. Glosny, "Mines Against Taiwan: A Military Analysis of a PRC Blockade," *Breakthroughs* 12, no. 1 (Spring 2003): 31–40.

[49] For example, Beijing might demand reaffirmation of the one-China principle and some degree of political fealty from Taiwan while permitting the island to retain autonomous rule and finances, and perhaps some armed forces. Moreover, whether Taipei could be coerced in this way or not, China might believe it could—and hence try such a coercive use of force in response to future behavior from Taipei that it finds unacceptable. For a somewhat similar assessment, see Richard A. Bitzinger and Bates Gill, *Gearing Up for High-Tech Warfare?: Chinese and Taiwanese Defense Modernization and Implications for Military Confrontation Across the Taiwan Strait, 1995–2005* (Washington, D.C.: Center for Strategic and Budgetary Assessments, 1996), 44–45.

Strait could prove pivotal. U.S. antisubmarine operations could presumably be set up to maintain a safe shipping lane east of Taiwan and near Taiwanese ports. To carry that mission out, the United States, together with Taiwan, would need to establish air superiority over the Taiwan Strait, protect ships against Chinese submarine attack, and cope with the threat of mines.

This author has estimated that the United States would need a force exceeding 100,000 personnel in order to help break the Chinese blockade.[50] Such an operation would require few if any ground forces, but call upon perhaps 25–50 percent more naval capabilities than commonly assumed for a major theater conflict. Depending on the availability of bases in Guam and Japan (and possibly Taiwan), substantial numbers of Air Force combat capabilities, reconnaissance capabilities, and personnel could be utilized.

The outcome of such an engagement would almost assuredly favor the United States and Taiwan (assuming no nuclear escalation). There is, however, debate concerning the likely losses that would result in the process. Some have argued that a dozen or more U.S. ships could be sunk, chiefly by a Chinese submarine force that is adding at least eight modern vessels in the coming years.[51]

Preventing Nuclear Catastrophe in South Asia

A failed Pakistani state ranks high on the list of military scenarios that would involve the vital interests of the United States. The combination of Islamist extremists and nuclear weapons in Pakistan is extremely worrisome; were parts of Pakistan's nuclear arsenal to fall into the wrong hands, Al Qaeda could conceivably gain access to a nuclear device. Another quite worrisome South Asia scenario concerns the Indo-Pakistani crisis, which could lead to war over Kashmir between the two nuclear-armed states.[52] This scenario illustrates the types of stabilization missions that Washington must stay attentive to in future U.S. force planning for the region.

Given Islamabad's relatively pro-Western and secular officer corps, the Pakistani collapse scenario appears unlikely.[53] On the other hand, Pakistani intelligence services, which supported the Taliban and have condoned if not abetted Islamist militants in Kashmir, are less dependable. Moreover, the country as a whole is sufficiently infiltrated by terrorist groups, as the at-

---

[50] O'Hanlon, *Defense Policy Choices*, 154–203.

[51] Lyle Goldstein and William Murray, "Undersea Dragons: China's Maturing Submarine Force," *International Security* 28, no. 4 (Spring 2004): 161–96.

[52] Sumit Ganguly, *Conflict Unending: India-Pakistan Tensions Since 1947* (New York: Columbia University Press, 2001).

[53] Stephen Philip Cohen, *The Idea of Pakistan* (Washington, D.C.: Brookings, 2004), 97–130.

tempted assassinations against President Musharraf can attest, that this terrifying scenario of civil chaos cannot be entirely dismissed.[54]

Were Pakistan to spiral into chaos, the United States, among others, would face very difficult choices. Surgical strikes designed to destroy the nuclear weapons before extremists could obtain them would likely fail. Not only is Washington unaware of the location of Pakistani nuclear weapons, but any Pakistani government in power at the time would prove unlikely to countenance such a move, even under duress.

If surgical strikes or commando-style raids were not possible, the only remaining option might be to try and restore order before the extremists could seize the weapons. The United States and other outside powers might, for example, respond to a request by the Pakistani government to help restore order. Given the immense political embarrassment associated with requesting such outside help, however, such a request might not be made until the state was already near collapse. The international community could help to suppress an insurrection, offer to police Pakistan's borders in an attempt to prevent the smuggling of nuclear weapons, or provide technical support to the Pakistani armed forces in order to combat the insurrection. In light of the potentially dire consequences, the United States would literally have to do anything it could to prevent nuclear weapons from falling into the wrong hands.

Should stabilization efforts prove necessary, the scale of the undertaking would be breathtaking. Pakistan is a very large country, with a population of just under 150 million—six times that of Iraq. Pakistan's land area is roughly twice the size of Iraq and its perimeter is about 50 percent longer. Stabilizing a country of this size could easily require several times as many troops as the Iraq mission—possibly numbering even one million. Of course, an international force would be assembled, but the U.S. share of this total could easily exceed 50,000–100,000 ground forces.[55]

In an armed conflict between Pakistan and India over Kashmir, the United States would likely not clearly support one state over the other. There are, however, other ways in which foreign forces might become involved. If India and Pakistan approached—or even crossed—the threshold of nuclear

---

[54] International Crisis Group, *Unfulfilled Promises: Pakistan's Failure to Tackle Extremism* (Brussels, 2004).

[55] Some fraction of Pakistan's security forces would presumably remain intact, able, and willing to help defend their country. Pakistan's military consists of 550,000 army troops, 70,000 uniformed personnel in the air force and navy, another 510,000 reservists, and almost 300,000 gendarmes and Interior Ministry troops. See International Institute for Strategic Studies, *The Military Balance 2003-2004* (London: Oxford University Press, 2003), 140–42. If, however, some substantial fraction of the military broke off from the main body—perhaps a quarter to a third—and were assisted by extremist militias, it is quite possible that the international community would need to deploy 100,000 to 200,000 troops in order to ensure a quick restoration of order.

weapons use, New Delhi and Islamabad might consider the previously un-thinkable: pleading for help from the international community. While this scenario is unlikely in view of India's adamant objections to international in-volvement in the Kashmir issue, such an approach cannot be dismissed en-tirely under conditions when all-out nuclear war was seen as the only alter-native on the subcontinent. Since Kashmir is about twice the size of Bosnia in terms of population and half the size of Iraq in terms of both population and land mass, initial stabilization forces would have to be in the general range of 100,000, with the U.S. contribution perhaps 30,000–50,000.

Conclusion

Careful consideration of the above scenarios leads to three main con-clusions. First, the United States and its allies must retain a wide range of military capabilities, including higher-tech "transformative" assets as well as large numbers of infantry forces. Plausible future scenarios in the Asia-Pacific include high-intensity air and naval battles with China over Taiwan, a more classic ground-air confrontation with North Korea, and a large-scale stabilization mission that includes special force operations and counterin-surgency forces in South Asia. Moreover, defense transformation will not produce radical changes in military capabilities anytime soon, which means that the requirement for a wide range of assets will remain. The United States appears to possess adequate capabilities to handle these contingen-cies at present—or at least to handle one at a time, though any mission re-quiring large numbers of U.S. ground forces would clearly be much more difficult during a time when large numbers of U.S. forces remain in Iraq. Moreover, even if U.S. capabilities are generally adequate at present, major vulnerabilities (including susceptibility to missile strikes or artillery bar-rages in Korea) remain that could lead to large numbers of casualties in any war. Furthermore, the military capabilities of some U.S. adversaries could become much more significant in coming years, particularly China's pre-cision-strike systems, submarines, airpower, and other weapons platforms. Though these considerations do not require the United States to develop any specific weapon system, they do provide a strong rationale for further efforts in the construction of missile defenses, stealthier ships, aircraft capable of operating from shorter runways, space systems capable of maintaining U.S. dominance in the "reconnaissance-strike" arena, and other efforts associ-ated with the concept of defense revolution or transformation in the current U.S. debate.

Second, the United States will continue to require the use of a wide range of military bases in Asia, and Washington should place a premium on maintaining diversity in such arrangements. Given the great distances necessary in transporting military forces from the United States to the Western Pacific, such facilities will continue to claim paramount importance. Those who argue that defense transformation will radically reduce the need for overseas bases do not make a convincing case.

Third, U.S. allies and other partners can assist in such important areas as providing military aid with forward missions, offering the use of bases and (protecting those bases), and for political legitimacy. Despite recent developments in the region, only U.S. bases in Japan appear to retain widespread utility for the most serious and plausible scenarios in the region, bases in countries such as South Korea and facilities in Australia are either too circumscribed in potential utility or too remote. Even though Washington has made progress both in Japan's willingness to deploy troops abroad as well as the Philippines' willingness to tighten military ties with the United States, only Australia and South Korea—and to a lesser extent some Southeast and South Asian states—appear to be prepared to deploy substantial military capabilities in support of the United States.

Executive Summary

This chapter analyzes the direct and contextual factors driving Chinese military modernization efforts, evaluates the current capabilities and development trajectories of the People's Liberation Army (PLA), and assesses the likely impact that an increasingly modern Chinese military will have on Asian regional security.

MAIN ARGUMENT:

Although Chinese modernization has accelerated and improved in pace and scope at a surprising rate, this should not be misconstrued to mean that the PLA can transform itself into a first-class military with global reach over the next decade. The PLA's regional reach will, however, steadily improve—and consequently will alter the balance of power in Asia.

POLICY IMPLICATIONS:

- China's military modernization is shaped not only by the military dimensions of the Taiwan issue, but also by a number of other *contextual drivers* (i.e., China's desire to become a global power, the regional security environment, the U.S. military footprint around Asia, and growing energy needs) and *direct drivers* (i.e., China's military budget, domestic politics, military doctrine and defense policy, and effects of the military-industrial complex).

- China's aspirations and plans for its military modernization program are on par for a nation of China's location, size, wealth, national interests, and global role.

China's Military Modernization: Making Steady and Surprising Progress

David Shambaugh

This chapter explores the state of China's military modernization program in 2005, assesses how much progress the People's Liberation Army (PLA) has made in recent years, discusses the drivers of the program, elucidates its principal trends and trajectories, identifies important indicators to monitor in the future, and notes important policy implications for the United States.

There are two main types of drivers that shape China's military modernization program: *contextual* and *direct*. Contextual drivers include a range of external factors in China's national security environment that shape China's threat perceptions, strategic outlook, and contingency planning. Direct drivers include a range of financial, political, and technological factors more internal to China. These contextual and direct drivers are thus respectively the focus of the first two sections of the chapter.

Sections three and four overview PLA capabilities. Section three is an inventory of PLA forces and weapons capabilities, while section four offers a net assessment of the current state of China's military modernization program by evaluating progress made, as well as deficiencies and challenges ahead. A concluding section identifies indicators to watch in assessing future progress in China's military modernization and offers implications for U.S. policy.

David Shambaugh is Professor of Political Science & International Affairs at The George Washington University, where he also directs the China Policy Program. In addition, he is a nonresident Senior Fellow in the Foreign Policy Studies Program and the Center for Northeast Asian Policy Studies at The Brookings Institution. He can be reached at <shambaug@gwu.edu>.

The author wishes to thank Dennis Blasko, Paul H.B. Godwin, and Eric McVadon for their excellent comments and suggestions on previous drafts, and Peter Mattis for his research assistance

Contextual Drivers of China's Military Modernization

Taiwan

Preventing Taiwan independence (and concomitantly bringing about "reunification" with the mainland) is one of China's highest priorities. For the PLA this translates into a military mission, if so ordered, of forcibly preventing Taiwan independence. As the 2004 Defense White Paper boldly warned: "Should the Taiwan authorities go so far as to make a reckless attempt that constitutes a major incident of 'Taiwan independence', the Chinese people and armed forces will resolutely and thoroughly crush it at any cost."[1] In actuality, preparing for a series of potential conflict scenarios with Taiwan (and the United States) is the nearest-term catalyst for defense resource allocations and military preparations, and is driving a number of decisions regarding weapons procurements and deployments, training and readiness, and other elements of the PLA's order of battle. These preparations include attaining the capabilities to perform the following military tasks:

- launch precision strikes against high-value command, control, and political targets

- using special operation forces, undertake sabotage attacks against key military and civilian infrastructure targets on Taiwan and adjacent islands

- ground Taiwan's air force by saturating airfields, runways, and aircraft shelters with ballistic or cruise missiles

- "deafen and blind" Taiwan's command, control, communications, and intelligence infrastructure through a combination of missile strikes and electronic and information warfare attacks (including, perhaps, atmospheric electromagnetic pulse [EMP] detonations)

- bottleneck/blockade Taiwan's navy in ports at Tsoying, Su'ao, Keelung, and Kaohsiung, which would also effectively blockade civilian shipping in and out of the latter two ports, thus stifling the island's merchandise trade and energy imports

- take control of the airspace over Taiwan and the entire Taiwan Strait in order to launch amphibious landings and air-drops of paratroopers or airborne troops

---

[1] Information Office of the State Council, *China's National Defense in 2004*, 4, http://news.xinhuanet. com/english/2004-12/27/content_2384679.htm.

- create a *cordon sanitaire* around Taiwan to force the U.S. Navy to base operations at a distance

- interdict the logistical supply lines of U.S. forces in the western Pacific

- attack U.S. carrier strike groups (possibly with ballistic missiles)

- deter or prevent U.S. (and Taiwan) forces from attacking targets on mainland China

One can trace much of recent PLA procurement, deployments, and training to attaining this range of capabilities. Following the 1995–96 Taiwan Strait crises, the Chinese military performed "after-action assessments" and discovered that, at the time, PLA capabilities against Taiwan were, in fact, quite limited. The ballistic missile option existed for the purpose of taking out military targets, terrorizing the civilian population, and destabilizing the economy, but PLA offensive strike capabilities in these other areas were very limited or non-existent. Nor were ballistic missile deployments sufficient in number or accuracy to fulfill all of the PLA's missions: ground Taiwan's air force, knock out other high-value targets, and keep American aircraft carrier strike groups at bay.

Today the PLA is increasingly capable of carrying out this wider spectrum of coercion or warfighting. Since 1996 the Chinese military has worked very assiduously to attain this broader range of deterrence, compellence, and attack capabilities. In just about every area noted, the PLA has, in this author's estimation, now achieved sufficient capabilities to prosecute a broad-gauged campaign across a horizontal spectrum of contingencies and up a vertical hierarchy of "thresholds." Attaining sufficient numbers of "boots on the ground" to successfully occupy Taiwan (via amphibious landings and air-drops) remains the greatest difficulty, but the PLA has attained sufficient capabilities in virtually every other category. To be sure, occupation is likely the PLA's last priority should conflict erupt. A much more probable strategy would consist of launching quick "saturation strikes" over the course of 48–72 hours in order to compel Taiwan to surrender and/or negotiate before the United States could arrive in force.

Yet China's military modernization cannot be explained by Taiwan contingencies alone. There are five other broader and longer-term considerations that underlie and shape decisions and directions in China's military modernization program.

Becoming a Global Power

The second contextual driver is China's desire to become a global power. China is increasingly such a power in economic and political/diplomatic terms, but—with the exception of possessing intercontinental ballistic missiles (ICBM)—has no global military capabilities. Nor is there any indication that Beijing is seeking to develop such capabilities. With the exception of certain naval programs, resources are simply not being allocated to building power projection systems that would give the PLA out-of-area capabilities. While evidence of such an aspiration is lacking at present, over time China could quite possibly seek to develop a more global military position—yet aspiration does not readily translate into capability. Moreover, Beijing's worldview would need to undergo dramatic transformation in order to justify such an offensive posture. That said, there are three areas where China's aspirations to become a global power are already influencing Beijing's military modernization efforts.

The first is in military diplomacy. The PLA is increasingly involved in various forms of military exchanges with foreign militaries. These exchanges have included the dispatch of high-level military delegations to over 60 countries, the hosting of 130 delegations from over 70 nations, and the dispatch of PLA military attachés to over 100 nations in 2003–04.[2] In addition, the PLA sends its officers abroad for training and hosts foreign officers at the National Defense University in Beijing. Military diplomacy also includes ship visits by the PLA Navy (PLAN). In 2004 the PLAN sent a *Luhai*-class destroyer and two support ships on an around-the-world voyage of military diplomacy, and PLAN destroyers increasingly call on ports throughout Asia and the Middle East. Military diplomacy also involves combined naval exercises. While having a practical dimension, such exercises should be viewed first and foremost as confidence-building measures. Since 2004 the PLAN has begun to undertake naval search-and-rescue exercises with foreign navies (including, to date, those of France, India, Pakistan, Vietnam, and the United Kingdom), and since 2003 PLA ground forces have undertaken cross-border counterterrorism exercises with China's Shanghai Cooperation Organization (SCO) partners. In August 2005 China and Russia undertook unprecedented combined exercises, which included the dispatch of 3,000 Russian soldiers to Chinese territory. These global activities in military diplomacy require investment in personnel, ships, and training (although not in classic power projection terms); hence the PLA has been actively developing these resources.

---

[2] Information Office of the State Council, *China's National Defense in 2004*, 32.

The second form of China's global military presence is an increased participation in peacekeeping operations (PKO) sponsored by the United Nations (UN). China dispatched an engineering battalion to Cambodia in the early 1980s as well as military observers to other PKOs since 1990. Only in the past few years, however, has China begun to deploy PLA personnel for peacekeeping and peace enforcement operations. The PLA has provided the majority of Chinese deployments, but these have been supplemented by police from the Ministry of Public Security as well as health workers, which in 2005 were deployed in Afghanistan, East Timor, Haiti, Indonesia, Kosovo, and Liberia. In addition to these units, PLA engineering and medical units are presently deployed in the Congo and Liberia, and in 2004 China participated in twelve out of seventeen PKOs in Africa.[3] China has been increasing its PKO contributions in recent years (1,026 participants in twelve PKOs as of May 2005),[4] a development commensurate with a broader realization in Beijing that China, as a permanent member of the UN Security Council, should do more to shoulder its global responsibilities. Because this undertaking is of symbolic importance to China, PLA forces must therefore be prepared to undertake such missions at any time.

Increasing military transparency is the third example of how global responsibilities are beginning to shape the PLA. Many foreign observers consider Chinese military transparency to be an oxymoron, as the PLA has lagged far behind global and regional standards. This too is beginning to change, however. Beijing has increasingly invited foreign military attachés and visiting military delegations to observe PLA exercises inside China. While many of these events continue to have a "set piece" quality to them, foreign observers have been allowed since 2003 to observe training operations of an increased scale and complexity.[5] These operations have included ground force, marine, mechanized, amphibious, special operations, counterterrorism, combined arms, and joint force exercises.

China has also now published four defense white papers. Each has been progressively more open and more detailed. To be sure, China still has some way to go before it releases the level of information commonplace in other nation's white papers. The information that Beijing provides is also considerably less than what can be found in the International Institute of Strategic Studies' (IISS) annual *The Military Balance*, Stockholm International Peace

---

[3] Information Office of the State Council, *China's National Defense in 2004*; and Bates Gill, "China's Evolving Role in Global Governance," Stiftüng Wissenschaft ünd Politik, April 2005, http://www.tfpd.org/pdf/Gill.ChinaPaper.Apr2005.pdf.

[4] See United Nations, "Monthly Summary of Contributors of Military and Civilian Police Personnel," http://www.un.org/Depts/dpko/dpko/contributors/.

[5] Author's discussions with U.S., British, Singaporean, and Swiss military attachés in Beijing, 2004–05. The author is also indebted to Dennis Blasko on this point.

Research Institute's (SIPRI) annual yearbook, or a host of other intergovernmental, governmental, and nongovernmental assessments and databases. Nonetheless, over time China's defense white papers have become more and more revealing. The most recent paper, published in December 2004, includes an unprecedented amount of information on PLA doctrine, expenditure, mobilization, and defense industries.

Thus, while these three examples do not exemplify growing Chinese global military muscle, they nonetheless are examples of how the PLA is being affected by China's international roles and responsibilities. Each can be expected to continue to grow and improve in coming years.

The Regional Security Environment

A third contextual driver of PLA modernization is the regional security environment that China faces. There are several operative dimensions to consider.

The first is the fact that most of China's regional relationships—with the important exceptions of Japan, North Korea, and Taiwan—have never been better. China has, in both bilateral and multilateral fora, proactively and positively engaged neighbors all along its periphery in recent years. This engagement has earned Beijing considerable praise from governments around the region, the international media, and scholars—and has captured the attention of the U.S. government as well.[6] Some analysts believe that China's peripheral engagement is producing fundamental changes in the regional order.[7] Relations with the member states of the Association of Southeast Asian Nations (ASEAN) are particularly sound, but China has also succeeded in reversing formerly antagonistic relationships—such as those with India, South Korea, and Vietnam—into much more positive and productive interactions. In addition, China has become much more deeply

---

[6] See Robert Sutter, *The Rise of China in Asia* (Lanham, MD: Roman & Littlefield, 2005); Kokubun Ryosei and Wang Jisi, eds., *The Rise of China and a Changing East Asian Order* (Tokyo: Japan Center for International Exchange, 2004); Jane Perlez, "The Charm from Beijing: China Strives to Keep Its Backyard Tranquil," *New York Times*, October 8, 2003; Jane Perlez, "Asian Leaders Find China a More Cordial Neighbor: Beijing's Soaring Economy Weakens U.S. Sway," *New York Times*, October 18, 2003; Jane Perlez, "As U.S. Influence Wanes, A New Asian Community," *New York Times*, November 4, 2004; "China's More Nuanced Diplomacy," *New York Times*, October 14, 2003; Philip Pan, "China's Improving Image Challenges U.S. in Asia," *Washington Post*, November 15, 2003; and Michael Vatikiotis and Murray Hiebert, "How China Is Building an Empire," *Far Eastern Economic Review*, November 20, 2003.

[7] See David Shambaugh, ed., *Power Shift: China and Asia's New Dynamics* (Berkeley and London: University of California Press, 2005); David Shambaugh "China Engages Asia: Reshaping the Regional Order," *International Security* 29, no. 3 (Winter 2004–05): 64–99; David C. Kang, "Getting Asia Wrong: The Need for New Analytical Frameworks," *International Security* 27, no. 4 (Spring 2003): 57–85; and Morton Abramowitz and Stephen Bosworth, "Adjusting to the New Asia," *Foreign Affairs* 82, no. 4 (July-August 2003): 119–31.

involved in Asian multilateral institutions, regimes, and dialogue groupings. These bilateral and multilateral efforts have been successful in changing the perceptions that many Asians have of China from malign to benign. Taken together, China's regional engagement has been a positive stabilizing force in the Asian region—this has had a reciprocal positive impact on China's own security and threat perceptions.

Nonetheless, not all is calm around China's periphery, and potential instabilities are having an impact on PLA thinking and on the military's modernization program. The potential for Taiwan independence still ranks highest in Beijing's national security calculations. The North Korean nuclear program and potential for instability on the Korean Peninsula is also a pressing concern. China's strained political relationship with Japan, the 2005 U.S.-Japan Security "2+2 Joint Statement" (which explicitly includes Taiwan as a matter of mutual security concern),[8] Japan's desire to play a broader role in regional maritime security, and the two nation's contested maritime disputes are a third set of worries for China.

All three of these regional security concerns have a direct impact on China's military modernization program: they determine contingency planning, training and exercises, the shape of the force structure, deployment of troops and equipment, and allocation of financial and other resources.

The U.S. Military Footprint Around China

Three aspects of U.S. behavior have a major impact on China's national security calculus and military modernization program:

- the architecture of U.S. bilateral alliances, non-allied security partnerships, and multilateral military training around China's periphery

- the deployment of U.S forces around China's periphery

- rhetoric about China and its military modernization program, from U.S. officials and commentators

While conceptually distinct, the first two factors can be considered together insofar as the second is largely a consequence of the first.

For half a century, the United States has maintained bilateral security alliances with five Asian countries: Australia, Japan, the Philippines, South Korea, and Thailand.[9] These five alliances have been the architectural anchor

---

[8] See U.S. Department of State, "Joint Statement of U.S.-Japan Security Consultative Committee," February 19, 2005, http://www.state.gov/r/pa/prs/ps/2005/42490.htm.

[9] Technically, the alliance with Australia is a tripartite one including New Zealand (ANZUS), although Wellington's participation has been dormant for more than 25 years.

of regional security and stability in East Asia since at least the U.S. withdrawal from Vietnam in 1975. In the case of Japan and South Korea, the United States deploys 77,000 soldiers on the ground (45,000 in Japan and 32,000 in South Korea) and an additional 16,000 at sea (with most ships homeported at Yokuska and Sasebo, Japan). While being reduced in line with the U.S. Global Defense Posture Review (GDPR) and Quadrennial Defense Review (QDR),[10] these numbers still constitute both a substantial deployment and a tangible commitment to the alliances. Additionally, approximately 124,000 U.S. forces are deployed under the Pacific Command (PACOM) in Hawaii, Alaska, and the west coast of the continental United States.[11] PACOM has been a favored command under Secretary of Defense Donald Rumsfeld, and there has been a substantial reorganization and considerable buildup of U.S. forces under its purview.

These alliances and forward forces figure prominently in China's regional security calculus as they are deployed right on China's doorstep and could easily be used to intervene in a Taiwan or Korean contingency. Moreover, U.S. Navy and surveillance aircraft (such as the EP-3) regularly patrol along China's coastline and through the Taiwan Strait. China has had to live with this presence for many years. While the United States and its five allies profess that these alliances are not aimed at China, many Chinese view them in this light.

What gives Beijing greater pause are two more recent developments. One is the increased deployments of U.S. forces elsewhere around China's periphery (as depicted in **Map 1**)—including Guam and other islands in the southwest Pacific, Diego Garcia in the Indian Ocean, Central Asia, and Afghanistan and Iraq. A second development is enhanced security partnerships (sometimes dubbed "Cooperative Security Locations" by Pentagon planners) between the United States on the one hand, and India, Mongolia, Pakistan, and Singapore on the other.

U.S. deployments to these locations have been stimulated not only by the wars in Afghanistan and Iraq, but also by the Pentagon's reassessment, in light of the "capability-based" planning mandated by the GDPR and QDR, of the U.S. military's global footprint.[12] Since 2001 the U.S. has deployed some 25,000 troops in or near Afghanistan, 150,000 in Iraq, and variable

---

[10] See "America's Alliances in East Asia: Purposes and Prospects," IISS *Strategic Comments* 11, no. 3 (May 2005).

[11] International Institute for Strategic Studies, *The Military Balance 2004–2005* (London: Oxford University Press, 2004), 31.

[12] See Evan Medeiros, "The U.S. Global Defense Posture Review and Implications for the Security Architecture in the Asia-Pacific Region" (paper presented at the Waldbröhl Transatlantic Dialogue on Asian Security, Berlin, December 11, 2004).

Map 1. U.S. Troop Deployments Around China

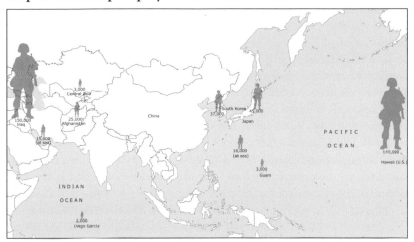

Sources: "America's Alliances in East Asia: Purposes and Prospects," IISS *Strategic Comments* 11, no. 3 (May 2005); International Institute for Strategic Studies, *The Military Balance 2004–2005* (London: University of Oxford Press, 2004); Michael O'Hanlon, *Defense Strategy for the Post-Saddam Era* (Washington, D.C.: Brookings Institution Press, 2005); and Robert Kaplan, "How We Would Fight China," *Atlantic Monthly*, June 2005.

numbers in Central Asia (principally in Kyrgyzstan and Uzbekistan).[13] In July 2005 China joined other SCO members in calling for a specific time-table for withdrawal of U.S. forces from these countries.[14]

Meanwhile, Washington has also initiated a major buildup of U.S. forces in Guam and Diego Garcia.[15] Although all of these bases would be useful in both East Asian and Persian Gulf contingencies, some commentators be-lieve that they serve a single long-term mission: to contain China.[16]

Guam in particular is being built up into a forward base of major sig-nificance. The forces deployed there are directly relevant to China and other potential contingencies in the Taiwan Strait or Korean Peninsula, but can also be used for deployments to the Indian Ocean, Persian Gulf, and the broader Middle East. Andersen Air Force Base on Guam is home to the 13th Air Force command, which includes growing numbers of B-1, B-2, and B-52

---

[13] Michael O'Hanlon, *Defense Strategy for the Post-Saddam Era* (Washington, D.C.: Brookings Insti-tution Press, 2005), 60.

[14] See Wang Xiaoyu, "Can the U.S. Military Really Withdraw from Central Asia?" *Zhongguo qingnian bao*, July 18, 2005 (trans. FBIS, July 18, 2005).

[15] The former is in the southern Marianna Islands, and the latter is a British territory in the Indian Ocean.

[16] See, for example, Robert Kaplan, "How We Would Fight China," *Atlantic Monthly*, June 2005; and Richard Halloran, "Checking the Threat That Could be China," *Japan Times*, June 12, 2005.

strategic bombers; C-17 Globemaster long-range transports; Global Hawk and E-2 Hawkeye reconnaissance aircraft; F/A-18 Hornet fighters; in-flight refueling tankers; and other aircraft.[17] Guam is now home to a growing number of *Los Angeles*-class nuclear attack submarines and a growing number of surface combatants. The United States is also considering homeporting an aircraft carrier battle group there. The Third Marine Expeditionary Force is being relocated from Okinawa to Guam.

These U.S. military deployments supplement a series of security partnerships that the United States has developed in recent years with India, Mongolia, Pakistan, and Singapore.[18] In each case, the United States undertakes combined exercises, shares intelligence, sells weapons, provides training, and—in the case of Singapore—routinely uses naval and logistical facilities. Many of these militaries (particularly the navies) also participate in U.S.-led multilateral exercises such as Rim of the Pacific (RIMPAC).

These enhanced U.S. strategic relationships and military deployments have (with the exception of Singapore) all developed in the post-September 11 era. When the five bilateral alliances in Asia mentioned earlier are also taken into consideration, some Chinese analysts now argue that China is effectively encircled by a string of U.S. defense relationships and forces. This de facto military encirclement of China is a central factor in Beijing's defense planning.

The final element of the U.S. military posture affecting Chinese thinking and planning are statements by U.S. officials concerning China's military modernization program. While the steady drumbeat of commentary among American pundits has done much to convince many Chinese of U.S. hostile intent, statements of concern regarding China's military modernization made by U.S. officials further impact Chinese calculations.[19] In recent months, the directors of both the Central Intelligence Agency (CIA) and Defense Intelligence Agency (DIA) have given testimony before Congress that has called attention to the progress being made in China's military modernization program.[20] More recently, at the 2005 annual IISS Shangri-la Dialogue in Singapore, Secretary of Defense Rumsfeld also made note of

---

[17] Kaplan, "How We Would Fight China."

[18] Even Malaysia and Indonesia have quietly enhanced ties with the U.S. military.

[19] For example, see Robert Kaplan's sensationally titled article in note 16.

[20] Porter J. Goss, Vice-Admiral Lowell E. Jacoby et al., "Current and Projected National Security Threats to the United States," statement before the Senate Intelligence Committee, http://intelligence.senate.gov/ 0502hrg/050216/witness.htm.

China's increased military budgets, arms purchases, and deployments, and questioned the need for these changes if China was not threatened.[21]

Taken together, these three elements of the U.S. defense posture in Asia—alliances and security partnerships, military deployments, and rhetoric—all serve as an important contextual driver for Chinese security calculations and defense planning.

Growing Energy Needs

A final factor shaping China's military modernization program (albeit over the longer term) is China's increased demand for energy. As China's economy has continued to grow at an astonishing pace, the country's appetite for all forms of energy has increased concomitantly. China was the source of 40% of the world's oil demand between 2000–04. At present rates of consumption this could grow to 50% by 2010, and 80% by 2025 (15–20 million barrels per day).[22] Today China consumes 6.4 million barrels of crude oil per day, having surpassed Japan in 2003 as the world's second largest consumer behind the United States. As a result, Beijing has been signing deals worldwide to increase and diversify China's access to oil, natural gas, nuclear power, and other energy sources. These partnerships include a $15 billion deal with Australia that was inked in 2004, a $70 billion deal struck with Iran in 2005, and an unsuccessful $18.5 billion bid to buy a controlling share of the U.S. energy company Unocal. China's foreign policy is increasingly shaped by the nation's demand for energy inputs.

The implications of this rising energy demand for China's military are twofold. First, military modernization (particularly of the naval and air forces) means that the PLA's own consumption needs will increase. Second, ensuring a regular flow of energy imports into China will increasingly become the responsibility of the Chinese military. As a result, the PLAN may increasingly feel the need to patrol the sea lines of communication (SLOCs) not only of East Asia but even through the Indian Ocean to the Persian Gulf. The Strait of Malacca—through which 25% of global commerce and 50% of world oil exports pass—will be a particularly important strategic asset that China will need to keep open. In 2004 approximately one-third of all

---

[21] Donald Rumsfeld, "Remarks to the International Institute for Strategic Studies Shangri-la Dialogue," Singapore, June 4, 2005, http;//dod.mil/transcripts/2005/tr20050604-secdef3002.html. The irony of U.S. military posture arrayed around China apparently did not dawn on Rumsfeld.

[22] For various projections of China's future oil demand and consumption, see Department of Defense, "The Military Power of the People's Republic of China 2005," annual report to Congress, 10, http://www.defenselink.mil/news/Jul2005/d20050719china.pdf.

of China's imported oil passed through the Strait of Malacca.[23] Little wonder then that Chinese President Hu Jintao has reportedly referred to China's "Malacca dilemma."[24]

In maintaining open SLOCs through the East Asian littoral, Malacca Strait, and Indian Ocean, China thus shares a strategic commonality with other East Asian states, India, and the United States. In the event of a conflict, Beijing fears that the United States would seize control of the SLOCs upon which China depends. This concern, in turn, may drive the PLAN to develop its own SLOC protection capacity. For China, any actual move to seize the above-mentioned SLOCs would be militarily suicidal; the distances are so great that sustaining the necessary defenses would drain the PLAN of most of its resources.[25]

Direct Drivers of China's Military Modernization

Though these are the broad factors shaping China's military modernization program, they are only contextual considerations. While certain contingencies—particularly regarding Taiwan and the United States—do drive budgets, deployments, and allocation of resources, they are more in the realm of what the PLA requires rather than what the PLA actually receives. In order to determine the latter, four direct drivers must also be considered: money, technology, politics, and doctrine. This section will examine each in turn.

The Military Budget

Estimating the Chinese military budget is one of the great conundrums of studying the PLA. Even the PLA is probably unsure of how much money the Chinese military has at its disposal. This is in part because the PLA has long had sources of revenue beyond what has been officially allocated by the state (including commercial earnings, in-kind subsidies and revenue-sharing practices, and monies secretly buried in other state budgets). Thus there has been a discrepancy between the PLA's official budget and actual revenue. The official defense budget is, however, becoming increasingly accurate due to the following developments: the 1998 commercial divestiture order (which banned the PLA and other internal security services from en-

---

[23] Gordon Feller, "China's Rising Demand for Oil and Pipelines Has Worldwide Implications," *Pipeline and Gas Journal*, May 2005, http://www.undergroundinfo.com/PGJ/pgj_archive/May%2005/05-05%20ss%20china%20rising.pdf.

[24] Author's interview with a foreign policy specialist, Shanghai, June 21, 2005.

[25] I am indebted to Paul Godwin for his analysis of this problem.

gaging in business activities), the introduction of the zero-based budgeting (ZBB) and accounting system in 2001, and the continual decline in off-budget hidden allocations since 2000. Within three to five years, the margin of discrepancy will be negligible.

This trend has not, however, precluded widely variant and—in the author's view—grossly exaggerated estimates of Chinese military spending. Estimates by Western experts range from 1.4 to 12 times the official budget. At the lower end of the spectrum, a team of Rand Corporation specialists undertook a very careful, disaggregated "bottom-up" review and concluded in 2005 that China's total defense expenditures (based on 2003 data) were "between 1.4–1.7 times the official number."[26] The author's own earlier estimates, based on 2000 data, were that the actual amount was slightly over two times the official budget,[27] but due to commercial divestiture, ZBB, and the effort to bring more defense expenditures online, I would now concur with the recent Rand estimate. A Council on Foreign Relations (CFR) task force, composed of many of the leading PLA experts in the United States, concluded in 2003 that total defense spending was two to three times the official figure.[28] IISS estimates (also using 2003 data) that China's military spending was 2.5 times the official figure.[29] At the higher end of the spectrum, other nongovernmental studies, using purchasing power parity (PPP) calculations, have produced estimates ranging up to twelve times the official budget.[30]

U.S. government estimates have consistently been higher than most nongovernmental estimates (PPP estimates notwithstanding). In its initial report to Congress on Chinese military power in 2002, the Department of Defense (DoD) claimed that China's military spending was four times higher than the official figure (approximately $85 billion). This estimate was inexplicably scaled back in the 2003 report to three times as large (approximately $95 billion), while the 2004 report provided a range of three to four times larger (approximately $80–106 billion). In the most recent report, released in July 2005, DoD continued to scale back earlier estimates by claiming that China's military spending was two to three times higher than the official budget of RMB 247.7 billion ($30 billion) for 2005–06 (resulting in an ac-

[26] Keith Crane, Roger Cliff, Evan Medeiros, James Mulvenon, and William Overholt, *Modernizing China's Military: Opportunities and Constraints* (Santa Monica: RAND, 2005), xx and 133.

[27] David Shambaugh, *Modernizing China's Military: Progress, Problems, and Prospects* (Berkeley and London: University of California Press, 2002), 223.

[28] Harold Brown and Joseph Preuher, eds., *Chinese Military Power* (New York: Council on Foreign Relations, 2003), 57.

[29] IISS, *The Military Balance 2004–2005*, 322.

[30] See Charles Wolf, Jr., *Asian Economic Trends and Their Security Implications* (Santa Monica: Rand Corporation, 2000).

tual budget of $60–90 billion).[31] In none of these reports, however, does the Pentagon explicate its empirical base or methodology for arriving at these estimates. These official estimates are therefore quite unlike most nongovernmental estimates, which at least draw on internal Chinese materials and statistics and attempt to disaggregate and reconstruct the component parts of China's military revenue base and expenditures. Without a much more detailed explanation of its methodologies, the Pentagon estimates open themselves to controversy and raise further questions.

For its part, the Chinese government only complicates matters by steadfastly claiming that China's officially announced budget is the accurate figure (these claims are disingenuous given that internal Chinese sources themselves admit to, and detail, off-budget revenues to the PLA). Chinese commentators regularly denounce foreign estimates as fabricated exaggerations that are politically motivated and are maliciously intended to spread the "China threat theory." Moreover, until 2003 official Chinese sources refused to provide any detailed breakdown of defense expenditure. The last two defense white papers have stated, however, that defense expenditure is divided roughly into thirds between human resources, operations, and equipment.[32] If this is the case, then PLA personnel costs are less than most modern militaries, while operations costs are relatively high (particularly for a military that does not deploy abroad). What is clear from official Chinese budget data is that the costs have been increasing steadily at double-digit rates since 1989—by an average of 14.5% per year. At this rate of increase, the official budget doubles in real terms about once every five years. Moreover, these increases have come largely in an inflation-free, or even deflationary, fiscal environment. This growth is evident in **Table 1** and **Figure 1**.

Although there is no doubt that the PLA is receiving an increasing piece of a growing pie, there are two other considerations to take into account. The first is that military spending had been severely depressed until the 1990s. Second, as a percentage of GDP and total government expenditure—what economists describe as the "defense burden"—military spending remains modest (approximately 1.6% and 8.5% respectively over the same period). These allocations also support a very large defense establishment of currently 2.25 million active-duty soldiers with attendant large military bureaucracies.[33] Despite these caveats, China's military spending is growing both

---

[31] Department of Defense, "The Military Power of the People's Republic of China 2005."

[32] *China's National Defense in 2004*, 14.

[33] This figure does not include the estimated 1.5 million in the People's Armed Police and approximately 800,000 reservists. An unknown number of uniformed PLA civilians (*wenzhi ganbu*) are included in the 2.25 million active duty figures. I am indebted to Dennis Blasko on this point. See also IISS, *The Military Balance 2004–2005*, 170, 173.

Table 1. Official Chinese Defense Expenditures 1988–2005

Year	Official defense expenditure (billions of Yuan)	Percentage increase
1988	21.8	4.0
1989	25.2	20.2
1990	29.0	15.1
1991	32.5	12.1
1992	37.0	13.8
1993	43.2	16.8
1994	52.0	20.4
1995	63.7	22.5
1996	72.0	13.0
1997	81.3	12.9
1998	93.5	15.0
1999	107.7	15.2
2000	121.3	12.6
2001	141.0	16.2
2002	170.8	13.5
2003	190.9	11.8
2004	211.7	10.9
2006	247.7	17.0

Figure 1. Official Chinese Military Expenditures 1988–2005

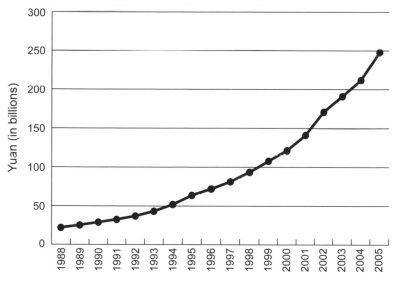

rapidly and in a sustained fashion precisely at a time when there is no pressing external threat to China. This alone fuels perceptions on the part of some of China's neighbors that Beijing is actively pursuing a military buildup.

Can this level of funding be sustained? China could probably shoulder such outlays, but at the likely cost of an increased percentage of central government expenditures (CGE), increased deficit financing, and growing "guns vs. butter" tensions. Now that increases in China's defense spending have been more or less fixed in the 12–14% range in recent years, such de facto "indexing" will be difficult to decrease without substantial opposition from the military. The PLA has come to expect a certain level of funding, and the civilian leaders have given the PLA leaders little reason to doubt continued support.

How can the government continue such outlays? In recent years, this has been done through deficit financing, which has been rising steadily and can be anticipated as the principal source of future defense spending increases. Another major consideration is that claims on central government spending by other civilian sectors (health, education, welfare, environment, public safety, etc.)—all of which have badly atrophied and been starved for state funds—are only going to increase.[34] Such demands are natural and, as China makes the transition from a developing country to a newly industrialized one, should be expected to increase. While the funds will likely continue to flow to the military at current percentage levels, skeptical voices inside China may begin to question the need for such levels of expenditure.

Domestic Politics

How Chinese leaders view both the PLA and the importance of the military modernization program is a second direct driver. At present, the Hu Jintao-Wen Jiabao leadership seems to be adopting the politically wise strategy of placing the same priority on both the PLA and military modernization as did their predecessors Jiang Zemin and Zhu Rongji. Politically Hu and Wen are wise to do so, as no Chinese leader can survive without the support of the PLA, although this factor has become less and less important in recent years as civil-military relations have become more institutionalized and the military itself has become more professional.[35] In the post-Mao era, the military has exercised progressively less political influence within the senior levels of the Chinese Communist Party (CCP), and military represen-

---

[34] Crane et al., *Modernizing China's Military: Opportunities and Constraints.*

[35] See Andrew Scobell, "China's Evolving Civil-Military Relations: Creeping *Guojiahua*," *Armed Forces and Society* 31, no. 2 (Winter 2005): 227–44; David Shambaugh, "Civil-Military Relations in China: Party-Army or National Army?" *Copenhagen Papers in Asian Studies*, Fall 2002; and Shambaugh, *Modernizing China's Military*, ch. 2.

tation on the Politburo and Central Committee today is at an all-time low. Even within the new PLA High Command, authority is derived primarily from bureaucratic position in the military institutional hierarchy.[36] Under such conditions of increasing civil-military bifurcation, there is little chance that the PLA could stage a political coup d'etat—unless there was a complete breakdown of CCP authority and social stability, in which case the military would likely intervene to restore social order and protect the integrity of the nation-state.

For his part, Hu Jintao has moved very cautiously and prudently in dealing with the PLA. After assuming the party leadership and state presidency at the Sixteenth Party Congress in October 2002, Hu continued to serve in the shadow of Jiang Zemin as Vice-Chairman of the Central Military Commission (CMC). Then, in September 2004 at the Fourth Plenum of the Sixteenth Central Committee, Hu succeeded Jiang as chairman of the party CMC (he subsequently became head of the state CMC in March 2005). Hu now holds the trifecta of top party, state, and military positions, and is regarded as China's undisputed "commander-in-chief." Authority and power do flow from official position in China, but they also derive from personal connections (*guanxi*) and, increasingly, from professional competence. Hu commands loyalty from the PLA simply by virtue of his official positions, but still has to prove himself on these other two scores. Although Hu has served on the CMC since 1992, and thus has become a familiar face to the senior military brass, it is unclear whether he will be more proactive in cultivating PLA loyalties and constituencies.[37] The PLA, like other bureaucracies and groups in China today, is a political constituency that requires time, effort, and cultivation from the country's political leaders. Hu could, as Jiang Zemin did in a similar position in 1989–90, tour all seven military regions, meet with all of the major PLA departments and services, and give a series of speeches declaring his support for various sub-constituencies within the PLA.

The onus of juggling any "guns vs. butter" pressures will land on the shoulders of Premier Wen Jiabao and Finance Minister Xiang Huaicheng, rather than on Hu. Since 2000 the Ministry of Finance become the decisive actor and arbiter in the military budget process. While neither Wen nor Xiang hold any military portfolio, both must approve the annual military budget and balance military financial requirements against other competing

---

[36] See David Shambaugh, "The Changing of the Guard: China's New Military Leadership," in *The New Chinese Leadership: Challenges and Opportunities After the 16th Party Congress*, ed. Yun-han Chu, Chih-cheng Lo, and Ramon H. Myers (Cambridge: Cambridge University Press, 2004).

[37] This process is detailed in David Shambaugh, "China's Commander-in-Chief: Jiang Zemin and the PLA," in *China's Military Modernization*, ed. C. Dennison Lane et al. (Routledge: Kegan Paul, 1996).

domestic demands. This task is likely to become increasingly difficult over time.

Military Doctrine and Defense Policy

The defense policy and warfighting doctrine of the PLA is another immediate driver of military modernization. Though closely related, these two factors are somewhat different in orientation and content.

All modern militaries operate according to doctrinal dictates. Training regimens, financial allocations, weapons procurement decisions, and a broad range of other considerations are determined by the operative military doctrine. In the case of the PLA, contemporary doctrine is designed to prepare the military force to fight and win what China terms a "limited war under high technology and information conditions." This is the latest stage in evolving PLA doctrine. Since its inception, PLA doctrine has evolved through five principal stages: People's War (1935–79), People's War Under Modern Conditions (1979–85), Limited War (1985–91), Limited War Under High Technology Conditions (1991–2004), and Limited War Under High Technology and Information Conditions (2005–). The evolution to the most recent stage reflects PLA appreciation of the role of information warfare on the modern battlefield. This recognition grew out of what the PLA not only witnessed in the two Iraq wars, but also has studied, more broadly, concerning the Revolution in Military Affairs (RMA).

China's current official defense policy incorporates this recognition and is termed "the Revolution in Military Affairs with Chinese Characteristics."[38] According to China's December 2004 Defense White Paper, this RMA includes the following component parts: "reducing the PLA by 200,000; strengthening the Navy, Air Force, and Second Artillery Force; speeding up 'informationalization'; accelerating the modernization of weaponry and equipment; implementing the 'strategic project for talented people'; intensifying joint training; deepening logistics reform; innovating political work; and governing the armed forces strictly and according to law."[39]

These are, in fact, the principal component parts of the entire PLA modernization program at present, and reflect a level of transparency about what the Chinese military is trying to accomplish. This list of priorities makes abundantly clear that the PLA is placing an emphasis on "software" rather than "hardware." The PLA has absorbed a crucial lesson from studying the U.S., North Atlantic Treaty Organization (NATO), Russian, Israeli, and other leading militaries: modern weapons alone do not make for a modern

---

[38] *China's National Defense in 2004*, 4.

[39] Ibid., 5–12.

military. In other words, modernization requires professionalization. This, in turn, requires a number of capabilities that can be classified as "software": educated forces, tight discipline, a non-commissioned officer (NCO) corps, a streamlined force structure, a ready reserve corps, rigorous training, rapid deployment and transport, mobility and jointness in campaign operations, sophisticated intelligence and reconnaissance, digitized command and control ("total battlefield awareness"), regularized professional military education, an efficient and rational budgeting system, a centralized logistics system, and a competitive and high-tech military-industrial complex.

These capabilities are the keys to becoming a modern military. The PLA has fully absorbed each of these lessons and has been moving to implement all of these reforms in recent years.[40] Accordingly, the PLA has been emphasizing acquisition of these "software" capabilities rather than devoting the bulk of its attention and resources to building and buying large amounts of advanced "hardware." Having recognized this priority, what is the current state of PLA weaponry? The answer requires an examination of the final direct driver of China's military modernization program: the country's defense industries.

The Military-Industrial Complex

Though China has purchased a significant number of weapons systems from Russia (see **Table 2** below), the PLA is ultimately dependent on China's military-industrial complex (CMIC). While the CMIC indigenously produces the full panoply of weapons systems for the PLA ground forces, air force, navy, and missile forces, its qualitative record to date has been mostly unsatisfactory. Ballistic missiles have always been the important exception to this rule—China mastered this technology in the 1960s and has already produced the full gamut of short- and intermediate-range ballistic missiles (SRBM and IRBM) as well as ICBMs. During the 1980s the CMIC began to produce high quality surface-to-air and surface-to-surface missiles, and more recently land attack cruise missiles (LACM).

With this important exception of missiles, the CMIC has largely failed to produce modern or near state-of-the art weaponry. Therefore, until recently, most foreign PLA experts judged the CMIC to be twenty or more years behind the state-of-the-art.[41] There have been numerous problems and impediments—innovative, economic, political, bureaucratic, and techno-

---

[40] See Shambaugh, *Modernizing China's Military*, chs. 3–5; and Dennis Blasko, *The Chinese Army Today* (London: Routledge, forthcoming).

[41] See, for example, Brown and Preuher, eds., *Chinese Military Power*.

Table 2. Principal Weapons Systems Supplied by Russia

System	Type	Quantity	Purchase/Delivery Dates
Su-30MK2 Flanker	Maritime strike fighter	28	2004
Su-30MKK Flanker	Multi-role ground attack fighter	38	1999–2000
Su-27UBK Flanker	Ground attack fighter	40	2000–01
Su-27 Flanker	Multi-role fighter, ground attack	72	1992–95 (200 Su-27SK models now under co-production in China, known as the J-11)
Kilo SSK	Diesel attack submarine	5	1995–96 (7 more on order, due for delivery in 2007)
Sovremenny	Guided missile destroyer	2	2002 (two more on order, due for delivery in 2005-2006)
A-50 Mainstay	Airborne early warning and control	~6	2000
SS-N-22 Sunburn	Ship-to-ship missile	24	1998–2000
SS-N-27 Sizzler	Ship-to-ship missile	?	2005–06
SS-N-27B (for the 8 new Kilos)	Ship-to-ship missile	?	2005–06
AL-31FN	Fighter aircraft engine (for F-10)	?	2002–04
Ka-28 Helix	Naval helicopter	12	1998–2000
Mi-17 (and variants)	Transport helicopter	264	1991–2004
Il-76 Candid	Transport aircraft	20	1997–2002
IL-78 Midas	Transport and refueling aircraft	?	2005
Kr-1/YJ-91	Air-to-surface/sea missile	?	1997
SA-20	Surface-air missile	?	2003–04 (?)
SA-10 (S-300)	Surface-air missile	~30	1990–92

Sources: Estimates are based primarily on data provided in IISS, *The Military Balance* and *SIPRI Yearbook*, various years; and Department of Defense, *The Military Power of the People's Republic of China 2005*.

logical in nature—that have constrained the CMIC over time.[42] Since 2001–02, however, this situation has begun to change.[43] As we will see below, the

---

[42] See Shambaugh, *Modernizing China's Military*, ch. 6.

[43] See, for example, "Chinese Defense Industry: Chinese Puzzle," *Jane's Defense Weekly*, January 21, 2004; and Evan S. Medeiros, "Analyzing China's Defense Industries and the Implications for Chinese Military Modernization," RAND Testimony, February 2004.

CMIC is beginning to produce tanks, planes, ships, and other weapons for the PLA arsenal that are approaching certain European or Russian standards (although the gap between Chinese and U.S. weaponry is actually widening).

Why has the CMIC apparently begun to turn the corner and produce weaponry nearer to the top standards? According to one new study, the CMIC has employed a strategy of three main elements to improve its qualitative products.[44] The first is selective modernization, a process in which resources are concentrated in areas of Chinese industrial strength and comparative advantage, particularly in electronics needed for C4ISR,[45] guidance systems, both information and electronic warfare (IW and EW), and precision-strike weapons. The second is civil-military integration, which provides incentives to the more sophisticated and well-developed civilian sector to "spin-on" its expertise and knowledge to the defense sector. The third is exploiting foreign technology by attempting to acquire advanced defense technologies directly from suppliers like Russia, Israel, or Brazil, or indirectly through dual-use technology imports from Europe and the United States.

Two other reforms merit mention. The first has involved bureaucratic/institutional reorganization. One major initiative included both the creation of the PLA General Armaments Department in 1998 to supervise and reorganize the CMIC, and the simultaneous relegation of the Commission on Science, Technology, and Industry for National Defense (COSTIND) to the State Council in order to oversee what are essentially defense industries that had been converted to civilian production. While previous reorganizations had all failed to turn the CMIC around, this one seems to have at last produced some results.

The other factor has been the gradual attempt to introduce market mechanisms—specifically contract bidding—into the military-industrial procurement process. Previously, the CMIC had been a classic state-owned enterprise, replete with heavy subsidies, government ownership, quota-driven production targets, and other features of state socialism. Since about 2004 real efforts—although still experimental and limited—have been made to rectify these impediments and bring market incentives to the CMIC.[46]

These reforms, taken together, have begun to produce a qualitative change for the better in some parts of the CMIC—most notably in ship-

---

[44] The following discussion derives from Crane et al., *Modernizing China's Military*, xx–xxii and 154–75.

[45] C4ISR refers to "Command, Control, Communications, Computers, Intelligence, Surveillance and Reconnaissance."

[46] Crane et al., *Modernizing China's Military*, 175; and Xinhua, "New Public Companies Gain Limited Access to Military Industry," June 13, 2005.

building, information technology, and to a lesser extent in the aviation industry. These advances will be explored in more detail in the next section, which examines the PLA's weapons capabilities.

PLA Capabilities

This chapter has thus far concentrated on the factors and inputs that are determining China's military modernization program. These factors and inputs have been the focus in part because the parameters of PLA capabilities are fairly well known and can be summarized rather succinctly, and in part because it is more analytically important to identify the variables that are shaping and driving the program. Knowing the weapons systems inventory of a military is only of limited value—more important is to understand the strategy, doctrine, politics, perceptions, contingencies, technologies, manpower, training, logistics, and other "software" factors that shape the use of force. In the final calculation, how a military fights and wages war depends more on the latter factors than on the former. Still, the following summary of the hardware capabilities of the PLA today is useful.[47]

The Ground Forces

Given that they are embedded within the General Staff Department, China's ground forces are technically not a separate service within the PLA. They still constitute, however, the numerical bulk of PLA forces—i.e., 1.6 million out of a total active duty force of 2.25 million.[48] Of these, somewhere between 35–50% of the ground forces are at full strength and readiness, and are ready to deploy for combat (this likewise means that half or more are not ready for deployment).[49] Fully half of ground force deployments (approximately 800,000) remain concentrated in north, northeast, and eastern China. In an attempt to reduce costs, improve readiness, and eliminate redundancies, the ground forces have undergone a substantial streamlining and downsizing in recent years. Group Armies (comprised of between 30,000–65,000 troops) remain the center of the main force deployments, but in an attempt to downsize to the division and brigade levels (with approximately 12,000–15,000 personnel), they are undergoing structural changes. This streamlining is intended to improve mobility, jointness, and combined-

---

[47] Unless otherwise noted, the following information derives from IISS, *The Military Balance 2004– 2005*; and Department of Defense, "The Military Power of the People's Republic of China 2005." Numbers of equipment are based on *The Military Balance*, and are the most up-to-date possible.

[48] For the best study of the ground forces, see Dennis Blasko, *The Chinese Army Today*.

[49] See the discussion in Shambaugh, *Modernizing China's Military*, 154.

arms capabilities. A substantial increase in transport helicopters has also contributed to the rapid reaction capabilities of the ground forces. The education levels of ground force officers and conscripts has also increased, with new respective targets of college and high school equivalency having been set as a goal to be achieved by the end of 2005. Importantly, a NCO corps has also been established. While the ground forces have received lesser priority relative to other services in recent years, they remain the backbone of the PLA.

The PLA ground forces field a full range of equipment, including tanks, armored personnel carriers, artillery, surface-to-surface and surface-to-air missiles, and helicopters and unmanned aerial vehicles. While the numbers of inventory are large, the quality remains very uneven and much of the hardware remains antiquated. For example, of the 7,580 main battle tanks, 6,300 are of 1950s–1980s vintage. The remaining 1,280 are composed of the T-96 through T-99 series, which have fairly advanced fire control systems, laser range-finders, all-weather computerized control, hardened composite armor, and an engine with improved speed and power-to-weight ratio. The ground forces also possess a huge number of towed artillery (14,000), anti-tank weapons (7,200), air defense guns (7,700), and other conventional land systems.

The Air Forces

The PLA Air Force (PLAAF) best exemplifies two long-standing and principal deficiencies in the PLA: high quantity but low quality, and a desire for an advanced domestic defense industrial base but continuing reliance on foreign suppliers.[50] The inability to indigenously design and build modern attack aircraft has been a chronic and perpetual problem for the PLA. Yet, over the past decade, the second of these deficiencies has helped to alleviate the first. For example transfers of Su-27 and Su-30 fighters from Russia have provided the PLAAF with modern fourth-generation aircraft. This, in turn, has both provided the PLAAF with a serious strike capability against Taiwan and has permitted the PLAAF to retire large numbers of antiquated aircraft. In only the last five years, the PLAAF has retired approximately 4,000 fighters (primarily Korean War and 1960s vintage versions of Soviet MiGs). The PLAAF still deploys approximately 350 J-6 and 300 Q-5 fighters (both modeled on the MiG-19) and 650 upgraded and modified versions of

---

[50] For the best study of the Chinese air force (although now somewhat dated), see Kenneth W. Allen, Glenn Krumel, and Jonathan D. Pollack, *China's Air Force Enters the 21st Century* (Santa Monica: RAND, 1995).

the MiG-21 (designated the J-7II series), which entered the Soviet air force around 1970.

The rest of the fighter inventory are third- and fourth- generation aircraft that have entered the fleet over the past fifteen years. These include approximately 184 aircraft of various versions of the J-8 (J-8, J-8IIA, J-8IIB, J-8IID, J-8E), an indigenously manufactured plane that first went into production in large numbers in 1992. The PLAAF's most advanced fighters are the 78 Su-27s sold by Russia (now also being co-produced in Shenyang) and the 76 Su-30 fighter-bombers. Since 2003 the indigenously built J-10 has also begun production following two full decades of manufacturing difficulties. This aircraft is powered by a Russian AL-31-FN engine, has Israeli avionics (from the aborted Lavi program), and has an airframe cloned from the U.S. F-16 A/B. Another new fighter, dubbed the J-11, is the domestically assembled version of the Russian Su-27SK (being produced in Shenyang). The FB-7, an all-weather medium-range fighter-bomber, is also under development. In addition, the PLAAF flies approximately 100 helicopters, 513 transports, 10 tankers, 180 bombers (all of old Soviet design but many with upgraded capabilities), 290 reconnaissance aircraft, and 200 trainers.[51]

The PLAAF's interest in acquiring force-multiplier capabilities—particularly airborne command and control systems and in-flight refueling—is another recent development. There is now evidence that the PLAAF possesses these capabilities, although in both cases such capability is very limited.[52] The air force has acquired and adapted AWAC aircraft from Russia, and is also building its own indigenous version. The PLAAF is also known to possess in-flight refueling tankers ever since such aircraft were first seen overflying the 50th anniversary of the PRC parade in 1999, but to date no foreigners have witnessed the PLAAF actually undertaking this complicated maneuver. Apparently, though, limited numbers of tankers and fighters have now mastered this procedure, and the Chinese military media claimed in 2005 that some J-8II aircraft were, for the first time, successfully refueled over the East China Sea.[53]

Thus, like the rest of the PLA, the PLAAF is in transition from dated to more modern equipment. Yet, more than other PLA services, the Air Force has been severely handicapped by the problems afflicting China's indigenous defense industries. What the PLAAF lacks in quality, it attempts to make up

---

[51] Note that the PLA ground forces have their own helicopters.

[52] Photographs of a converted Russian IL-76 transport AWAC-type aircraft have circulated on the Internet. See "KJ-2000 Mainstay," http://mil.jschina.com.cn/huitong/y-8x_sh-5_a-50i.htm.

[53] "Chinese Air Force Successfully Performs Aerial Refueling Over Sea," *Beijing zhongguo wang*, April 25, 2005, cited in Kenneth Allen, "Reforms in the PLA Air Force," Jamestown Foundation, *China Brief* 5, no. 15 (July 5, 2005), http://www.jamestown.org/publications_details.php?volume_id=408&issue_ id=3390&article.id=2369972.

in quantity (despite mothballing large numbers of aircraft in recent years). Unless and until China can sort out its production handicaps, however, the PLAAF will remain dependent on foreign sources of supply for its most advanced aircraft.

Missile Forces

If military aircraft production has a longstanding legacy of problems and failures, then China's missile forces (dubbed the Second Artillery) have been a shining success story.[54] This has been brought about by a combination of circumstance (in particular, Nikita Khrushchev's 1959 decision to discontinue support for China's atomic weapons development and delivery programs), skill (i.e., the knowledge of Chinese scientists), sustained resources, and political protection. For five decades China's military-industrial complex has been producing a wide range of ballistic missiles, including the conventional and nuclear warheads deployed on them.

Today the missile forces include 30 or more ICBMs (DF-5/5A, DF-31 and DF-41 [both in testing], DF-41), 110 or more IRBMs (DF-3/3A, DF-4, DF-21/21A), and around 700 SRBMs (DF-7, DF-11/11A, DF-15). Deployment of the ICBMs and IRBMs are dispersed throughout the country, while the bulk of SRBMs are deployed on the eastern seaboard within range of Taiwan. The DIA estimates that China's total force of SRBMs is between 650–730, and is increasing at a rate of 75–120 per year.[55] The PLAN also has deployed one *Xia*-class nuclear submarine with approximately 12 JL-1 ICBMs, and has successfully flight-tested a new longer-range and more accurate JL-2 version (which will eventually be deployed in the Type 094 nuclear-powered ballistic missile submarine, now under construction). Moreover, in recent years a priority has been placed on making the missile forces more mobile (and therefore harder to detect), solid-fueled (and thus much quicker to launch), and possessing smaller, more accurate, and more potent warheads.

Taken together, the Second Artillery possesses the full spectrum of offensive missile forces as well as a bona fide second-strike nuclear deterrent. Of special interest is the imminent prospect of deploying SRBMs or medium-range ballistic missiles (MRBM) with the accuracy and warhead maneuverability to threaten ships at sea at ranges of more than 1,000 kilometers.

---

[54] For the best study of China's missile forces, see Mark Stokes, *China's Strategic Modernization: Implications for the United States* (Carlisle, PA: U.S. Army War College Strategic Studies Institute, 1999).

[55] Department of Defense, "The Military Power of the People's Republic of China 2005," 29. The report specifically cites these as DIA estimates.

The PLA has recently supplemented its strengths in ballistic missiles by adding a cruise missile capability to its inventory. While air- and sea-launched cruise missiles have been in the PLA's arsenal for a number of years and more advanced versions have been recently transferred from Russia, China is now building its own LACMs. These have been undergoing tests, and can be expected to be deployed soon (if not already) within range of Taiwan. Development of these missiles would significantly complicate the island's defense even further and give the PLA a new accurate strike capability. Modeled on the existing sea-launched C-801 and C-802 (which were cloned from the French *Exocet*), the new LACMs add another key dimension to the modernizing PLA. Longer-range LACMs, with the ability to reach Okinawa and the accuracy of precision weapons, are expected soon.

The Naval Forces

The PLAN has probably been the highest priority service for modernization in recent years.[56] This has been the case for three principal reasons: due to the military demands of contending with a Taiwan contingency, because of the desire to eventually establish a blue water presence throughout the western Pacific and Indian Ocean, and due to the attributes of China's shipbuilding industry. Additionally, Russia has helped to supply not only key destroyers and submarines but also the best supersonic anti-ship cruise missiles available in the world. Thus, broad military doctrine together with specific warfighting scenarios and industrial capacity have all combined to make the PLAN a favored service.

Today the PLAN deploys 64 principal surface combatants, approximately 331 coastal patrol craft, 34 mine warfare vessels, 50 amphibious landing ships, 160 or more support ships, and 69 submarines.[57] Like the PLAAF, most of the surface warships (destroyers and frigates) are 20–30 years old and have been retrofitted and upgraded over time. Though a limited number of these vessels can be considered blue-water capable, the vast majority constitute a coastal force that operates in brown and green water. The most advanced destroyers are clearly the two Russian *Sovremenny*-class guided missile destroyers that were deployed in 2000–01. Each carries eight SS-N-22 "Sunburn" sea-skimming anti-ship missiles, which are among the most advanced in the world. The Sunburns were designed specifically to penetrate the defenses of U.S. Navy Aegis destroyers and aircraft carrier battle groups.

---

[56] For the best study of the Chinese navy, see Bernard Cole, *The Great Wall at Sea: China's Navy Enters the 21st Century* (Annapolis, MD: Naval Institute Press, 2001).

[57] There is a discrepancy in the estimated number of submarines in the PLAN. IISS identifies 69 in *The Military Balance 2004–2005*, while the 2005 DoD report identifies 55. Similarly, IISS lists 50 amphibious landing ships while DoD lists 40 "medium and heavy amphibious lift vessels."

China has ordered two more *Sovremennys* from Russia, which are due for delivery in late 2005 or early 2006.

The PLAN has also commissioned two new *Luhai*-class guided missile destroyers, the *Shenzhen* and the *Yantai*. These indigenously produced ships are a smorgasbord of imported armaments and equipment, including Ukrainian gas turbine engines, German electrical systems, French radars, Russian sonars, Russian helicopters, and Italian torpedoes. They also incorporate stealth-like features on the bridge similar to the French *Lafayette*-class frigates. The PLAN also possesses two Type 052 *Luhu*-class destroyers, which are composed of a similar set of hybrid systems. Several new, modern destroyers are in sea trials or under construction, including what is called China's "Aegis-equivalent." In addition to these vessels, the rest of the PLAN's 57 surface combatants are older, retrofitted *Luda*-class destroyers modeled on the 1950s-era Soviet *Kotlin*-class design, and *Jiangwei*- and *Jianghu*-class frigates. The PLAN also possesses more than three hundred coastal patrol craft, a large number of logistical supply ships, and more than thirty mine warfare vessels.

Last, but not least, the PLAN has a substantial and diverse submarine force. Many of the known submarines in the fleet are old *Romeo*- and *Ming*-class, which are slow, noisy, and easy targets for modern anti-submarine warfare. The PLAN has, however, embarked on a substantial buying and building program in recent years. The navy bought four *Kilo*-class attack submarines (which is a conventional, diesel-powered vessel or SSK) from Russia during the mid-1990s and has eight more on order (with one delivered and others due for delivery by 2007). While the PLAN has experienced some maintenance problems with these submarines, the *Kilos* are quiet, relatively fast, well-armed, and can stay submerged for significant periods of time. Perhaps as important has been the very capable and adequately quiet *Song*-, *Yuan*-, and *Jin*- (Types 093 and 094) class submarines, all of which were developed domestically. The first *Song*-class submarine was launched in 1994 and, after some difficulties, has now gone into serial production; more than eight have been commissioned.[58] The appearance of the *Yuan*-class attack submarine (SSK) surprised analysts when photos appeared on the Internet in July 2004, but it is unknown whether this submarine has passed sea trials and gone into production yet. This SSK may have an advanced form of air-independent propulsion that would permit both longer periods of submersion and higher speeds. The Type 093 and 094 programs (dubbed the *Jin*-class) have been known for some time. The nuclear-powered (SSN) 093 was first launched in December 2002, continues to undergo

---

[58] Lyle Goldstein and William Murray, "China Emerges as a Maritime Power," *Jane's Intelligence Review*, October 2004.

sea trials, and (according to the U.S. DoD) will enter service in 2005.[59] The 093 is expected to replace the five *Han*-class SSNs. The 094 will not only be nuclear-powered but will also be armed with nuclear ballistic missiles. Development is not as far along as the 093, but two or three are thought to be under construction.[60] Each will carry sixteen 8,000 kilometer-range JL-2 sea-launched ballistic missiles (SLBM).

In sum, the PLAN is making some significant advances, and China's shipbuilding industry has demonstrated the capacity to build at a rapid rate. Still, only 10 percent of China's shipbuilding is for military purposes.[61] Nonetheless, construction and deployments at such a quick pace will give the PLAN expanded reach and presence in the western Pacific over the next few years.

Keeping China's Military Modernization in Perspective: A Net Assessment

So where does this leave our understanding of China's military modernization program? Like virtually everything else in China today, military modernization is a mixed picture and a moving target. Estimating the capabilities of the Chinese military is—more than most aspects of contemporary China—often prone to exaggeration and hyperbole in the U.S. media. Academic analysts, on the other hand, tend to emphasize the problem areas facing the PLA. U.S. government intelligence analyses seem to frequently fall in between these two. Although previous DoD annual reports on the military power of China were often alarmist and prone to reporting selective capabilities, the 2005 report is a much more judicious, balanced, empirical, and descriptive assessment (in spite of Beijing's quick and critical denouncement).[62] The following net assessment is the best judgment of this author, a non-governmental observer.

Fifteen years of sustained double-digit growth in Beijing's defense budget, continual downsizing and streamlining, doctrinal evolution, improved logistics, intensified training, and a variety of new weapons systems have all allowed the PLA to demonstrate new competencies and capabilities in 2005. Despite this accelerated progress, however, the PLA still exhibits numerous deficiencies (both in relative and absolute terms), and one must be careful

---

[59] Department of Defense, "The Military Power of the People's Republic of China 2005."

[60] Goldstein and Murray, "China Emerges as a Maritime Power."

[61] Xinhua, "Building Aircraft Carrier in Shanghai Denied," June 16, 2005, http://news.xinhuanet. com/ english/2005-06/16/content_3094231.htm.

[62] Department of Defense, "The Military Power of the People's Republic of China 2005."

not to overstate Chinese military capabilities. The PLA is certainly capable of defending China's continental territory from invasion, and now also possesses a substantially enhanced (compared with 5–10 years ago) range of coercive capabilities against Taiwan—including EW and IW capacities, naval blockade competence, air interdiction and dominance capabilities, improved sea and air denial assets, and increased ballistic and cruise missile deployments.

When viewed in a broader regional or global context, however, the PLA still has very limited or non-existent capabilities. The PLA has exhibited little evidence of attempting to acquire a power projection capability. Note, for instance, that the PLA has not built any aircraft carriers,[63] lacks a single intercontinental bomber, possesses only a very small fleet of in-flight refueling tankers (and has yet to fully master the skill of in-flight refueling) and airborne command and control aircraft, has only a small number of truly blue-water capable surface combatants, does not possess a single military base abroad, has no space-based global network of command and control, and lacks other elements that one would expect to find in a nation trying seriously to develop a power projection capability or become a global military power. A close reading of Chinese military doctrinal manuals gives little, if any, evidence that power projection beyond China's immediate periphery is a priority. Even if there is no attempt to develop any sort of a global military capability, the PLA's regional reach in Asia also remains restricted. China's mobile SRBMs could be redeployed away from the Taiwan theater to other border areas,[64] even though this was not the original intent behind their production and deployment. More to the point, there is no evidence of assertive PLA attempts to develop force multiplier capacities.

To be sure, as new weapons systems have come on stream and continued reforms of the force structure have been phased in, significant progress has been made in recent years (particularly since 2001–02). As a result, there is no doubt that the PLA today is significantly improved over a decade ago. Advancements in some sectors have been even more than incremental improvements. Qualitative advances have been made, new systems have been deployed and important new ones are under development, the fighting capacity of all services has increased, and—perhaps above all—the command, control, and interoperability of PLA forces have all improved. PLA forces are now undertaking certain types of exercises and are displaying certain ca-

---

[63] IISS claims that China has a program, begun in 1994 and designated Project 9935, to build three carriers, but provides no empirical data in support of this assertion. See IISS, *The Military Balance 2004–2005*, 161.

[64] This point is made in Department of Defense, "The Military Power of the People's Republic of China 2005," 12.

pabilities that many foreign analysts and intelligence agencies did not think likely only a few years ago.

While acknowledging the above enhancements, the PLA's broader capabilities must be kept in perspective. Although the military modernization program has developed steadily—with financial resources continually increasing at an average rate of 14.5% per year over the past sixteen years, depicting such modernization as a "crash program" or "buildup" would be inaccurate. Beijing still allocates less than 2% of GDP and less than 10% of CGE for China's official defense budget. The United States today spends more than 5% of GDP on defense (not including intelligence and other national and homeland security-related funding), while at the height of the Cold War the Soviet Union allocated between 50–60% of its CGE on the military. Perhaps with the exception of ballistic missile production, China does not appear to have embarked on any such accelerated or crash program of weapons production. Even China's weapons purchases from Russia, which have averaged approximately $2.2 billion per year over the past five years,[65] remain very modest both in terms of both financial outlays (Saudi Arabia bought approximately five times that amount in 2003)[66] and total numbers of platforms imported.

Moreover, the vast majority of the PLA's inventory of ground, naval, and air assets still remain a decade or more behind the international state-of-the-art, and, in many areas, the gap is actually widening (due to advances in U.S. and NATO systems). China's naval surface fleet is still classified as green water, capable only of patrolling China's coastline rather than the open ocean. The PLAAF is similarly dated (note that only 15% of its total fighter force includes fourth-generation interceptors).[67] While the PLA's newest conventional forces are approaching world standards (e.g., the T-98A and T-99 main battle tanks), the bulk of the ground forces' firepower still lags behind NATO, Russian, or even Japanese systems.

In comparing the quality of China's weapons systems regionally, however, the gap is not so great. The best of the PLAN's surface combatants compare well with those from any regional navy (the newer destroyers are even comparable to Japan's),[68] and the best of the PLAAF's fighters are roughly equivalent to those of Australia, Japan, Singapore, South Korea, Taiwan, and Thailand. The numbers of PLA air, ground, and naval weapons platforms

---

[65] Stockholm International Peace Research Institute, "Imported Weapons to China, 1989–2004," http://www.sipri.org/contents/armstrad/TIV_imp_CHI_89-04.pdf.

[66] "Arms Deliveries to Developing Nations: Leading Recipients in 2003," in *The Military Balance 2004–2005*, 359 (see table 40).

[67] 78 Su-27/J-11s and 78 Su-30s. See *The Military Balance 2004–2005*, 172.

[68] I am grateful to Rear Admiral (ret.) Eric McVadon on this point.

certainly dwarf those of any regional military. This is an important factor to consider in any potential regional conflict scenario involving China. Despite large numbers of retired systems in recent years (the PLAAF has been reduced from approximately 5,000 to 1,000 fighters since the late-1990s), the PLA can still bring to bear a substantial force and wave-upon-wave of attacks against any adversary. If necessary, mothballed weapons can likewise be refurbished and mobilized as necessary.

A net assessment of PLA capabilities and progress in China's military modernization program in 2005 must conclude that the proverbial glass of water is simultaneously half full and half-empty—yet the volume is rising. Only three or five years ago, such an assessment would have likely concluded that the glass was only one-quarter or one-third full. Thus, the PLA has made a mini-leap forward over the past three or so years. This is particularly the case with respect to IW and EW, LACMs, joint training, fourth-generation fighters, surface combatants (particularly the acquisition of the *Sovremenny*), and *Kilo* submarines. When the 093 and 094 submarines are fully deployed, China's submarine fleet will be quite advanced.

This assessment is also cognizant of the various bureaucratic, financial, industrial, and technological impediments confronting China's military-industrial complex, as well as the important fact that China remains essentially cut off from importing weapons or defense technologies from Western countries. Despite an arms "embargo" on China, in 2003 the European Union (EU) licensed €460 million (approximately $418 million) in sales of military-related equipment (not actual weapons systems) to China.[69] Thus, the European Union Code of Conduct for Armed Exports is not air-tight, and licenses for sales are still being issued.[70] If and when the EU "embargo" is lifted (likely in 2006), the EU has pledged that licenses will exceed neither the "quality or the quantity" of recent years.[71] EU officials have further signaled that a revised, strengthened, and legally binding code will be put in place in order to carefully monitor and regulate such sales.[72] Even if this were the case, most of the EU's arguments in favor of lifting the embargo seem specious to the United States, and there is indeed good reason to suspect that a new regulatory regime would not substantially limit defense

---

[69] See European Council, *Sixth Annual Report on the Implementation of the Code of Conduct*, November 11, 2004, http://www.sipri.org/contents/expcon/codereport6.pdf.

[70] Despite approving licenses for €460 million worth of equipment, EU officials claim that only €30 million in sales were actually made and transferred to China. Author's interview with European Council official, Paris, July 8, 2005.

[71] See Council of the European Union, "Presidency Conclusions," December 16–17, 2004, http://ue.eu.int/ueDocs/cms_Data/docs/pressData/en/ec/83201.pdf.

[72] Author's discussions with EU officials, Berlin, April 2005; Washington, May 2005; and Brussels, July 2005.

technology transfers to the PLA (though it is unlikely that EU states would sell end-use weapons to China).[73]

Meanwhile, Washington continues to enforce a total embargo on arms sales and defense technology transfers to Beijing, and there is little prospect that this embargo will be relaxed or lifted anytime soon. Thus, even with limited access to military-related technologies from Europe, China's only real foreign source of advanced weapons and defense technologies remains Russia and, to a much lesser extent, Israel and Brazil. In the case of Israel, Washington has stepped up its pressure on Tel Aviv to restrict such sales to the PLA.[74] China certainly does not like being dependent on foreign sources of supply, but it is a de facto admission of the inability of China's defense industries to produce systems of a global standard.

Without access to Western sources of supply, it would appear that the pace and scope of PLA modernization has been negatively affected. The PLA is modernizing, but the lack of access to advanced Western systems does substantially affect both the speed and scale of this modernization. As **Table 2** makes clear, Russia has been the only major supplier of entire end-use weapons platforms to the Chinese military.

By purchasing these systems from Russia, China has sought to address the PLA's most pressing needs and deficiencies. Weapons systems acquired from Russia are precisely those that China's own defense industries have proven unable to produce indigenously; they are also the systems that would be utilized in any contingency involving Taiwan and the United States. By using Russia to fill these "niche needs," China's own defense industries have been able to concentrate their resources on a wide range of other less-sophisticated systems. Additional, improved weapons systems from Russia can be anticipated in the future, perhaps including Su-35 fighters, multi-role destroyers, and non-nuclear *Amur*-class attack submarines.[75] Yet importation of this advanced equipment from Russia does not necessarily mean that the PLA has the operational capability to use such high-tech imports. As CIA Director Porter Goss recently stated to the U.S. Senate Intelligence Committee: "The PLA must overcome significant integration challenges to turn these new, advanced and disparate weapons systems into improved capa-

---

[73] See David Shambaugh, "Lifting the European Arms Embargo on China: An American Perspective," Stiftüng Wissenschaft ünd Politik, http://www.tfpd.org/pdf/Shambaugh.ChinaPaper.Apr2005.pdf.

[74] See Scott Wilson, "Israel Set to End China Arms Deal Under U.S. Pressure," *Washington Post*, June 27, 2005; Sharon Weinberger, "New Technology Transfers to China on Hold, Pentagon Official Confirm," *Defense Daily*, June 16, 2005; Arye O'Sullivan, "Defense Ministry Confessing All to U.S. Over China Sales," *Jerusalem Post*, June 13, 2005; and Ze'ev Schiff, "Israel Bows to U.S. Pressure, Will Curb Defense Exports," *Ha'aretz*, June 26, 2005.

[75] *Moscow Agentstvo Voyennykh Novostey* [Interfax Military News Agency], "Russia May Provide China with High-Tech Weapons" (trans. FBIS, June 23, 2005).

bilities. Beijing also faces technical and operational difficulties in numerous areas."[76]

Outlook: Indicators to Monitor and Policy Implications

China's military modernization program will continue to make steady, but uneven, progress. Many of these advances will continue to be incremental, and thus will only periodically catch the eye of foreign intelligence agencies and analysts. Some progress will represent more noteworthy advances and may surprise analysts, such as when a new system undergoes flight tests or sea trials. Significant advances require both sustained investment and trial and error. Many of the new systems entering the force structure at present are the result of years of development. Investment alone, however, is not enough. As noted above, due to both domestic impediments and very limited access to international technology inputs, China's military-industrial complex has been handicapped for a very long time. These obstacles must be overcome if Beijing is to break the PLA's dependency on foreign sources of supply.

Which indicators should analysts watch for when monitoring progress in China's military modernization program over the coming years? The 2003 CFR task force report listed 21 key indicators that were divided into five main categories: C4ISR, joint operations, precision strikes, combat support, and training.[77] As these benchmarks remain germane today, **Table 3** reviews progress made in each main category first by listing the indicators where progress has been made, then highlighting those lacking any real advances.

The CFR task force also set forth thirteen other indicators that would suggest incremental trajectory had changed significantly. These indicators are reproduced in **Table 4**. Note that none of these indicators have experienced significant change.

The CFR indicators provide useful benchmarks by which to take the measure of PLA development and China's military modernization program now and in the years to come. Few, if any, PLA watchers anticipated the kind of progress we have witnessed in such a short period of time in the aforementioned areas. This is indeed testimony that Chinese military modernization is accelerating and improving in both pace and scope. Yet, all of these capabilities are incremental in nature. Although many of them have

---

[76] These comments were made during a discussion of Russian arms transfers to China. See Porter J. Goss, "Current and Projected National Security Threats to the United States," statement before Senate Intelligence Committee, February 16, 2005, http://intelligence.senate.gov/0502hrg/ 050216/ witness.htm.

[77] Brown and Preuher, eds., *Chinese Military Power*, 65–68.

Table 3. Progress of PLA Modernization

	Indicator	Degree of progress
C4ISR	• Acquisition of AWACs • Development and use of unmanned aerial vehicles • Development of Chinese information operations able to degrade U.S. intelligence, surveillance, and reconnaissance systems	Limited but real progress has been made in the last two years
	• Launch and maintenance of C4ISR satellites	Progress is uncertain
Joint operations	• Development of better air defense capabilities, including integration of more advanced surface-to-air missiles like the SA-10	Progress has been made
	• The ability to coordinate and execute multi-service and joint operations in the various battle space dimensions • The reorganization (or abolition) of China's seven military regions, that would quickly enable the establishment of joint war zone commands • Improvements in communications architectures that enable war zone commanders to coordinate the movements and actions of major units across current military region boundaries • An increase in the number of command post exercises in which officers from different military regions and services practice joint command-and-control activities	Little or no evidence of significant progress
Precision strikes	• Improvement in targeting technologies, especially over-the-horizon targeting • Development and use of precision-guided munitions (PGMs) • Training with anti-ship missiles by the PLAAF or PLAN Air Force • Development of decoys, penetration aids, and other counters to missile defense measures	Progress has been made—though unquantifiable
	• Development of stealthy, long-range cruise missiles • Increased ability to use U.S., European, or future indigenous GPS systems to improve accuracy of SRBMs and other munitions	No evidence of progress
Combat support	• Improvements in the joint logistics system • Development of in-flight refueling and airborne command-and-control capabilities • Moderate increase in airlift ability • Moderate increase in sealift capabilities	Progress has been made
Training	• Increases in the frequency of training missions with the Su-27, Su-30, and other advanced aircraft; in the numbers of pilot hours of training in advanced fighters; and in the sortie rates that can be generated with these aircraft • Improved execution of training exercises that involve joint ground and air units	Modest progress has been made

Table 4. Other Indicators of Progress in PLA Modernization

Indicator	Degree of progress
• A crash program to build more amphibious ships • Rapid expansion of the marine force • Significant efforts to expand both airborne and airlift capabilities • A dramatic increase in the submarine force, particularly the 094 SSBN program • Major increases in ICBM production and deployments • A formal change in China's "no first use" (NFU) nuclear doctrine • Combat training in the use of nuclear or other unconventional weapons • Serious efforts to acquire one or more aircraft carriers • The development of a proven capacity to conduct ballistic missile attacks against ships • A proven ability to disable U.S. space assets.	No significant change
• Expanded acquisition of SU-27s and SU-30s and expanded operation of these aircraft over water • The assignment of senior PLAN and PLAAF officers to senior PLA posts • Greater attention to a blue-water naval capability	Some progress

been developed faster than anticipated, they are not dramatic or "leapfrog" developments.

In brief, the PLA has been steadily modernizing and making surprising progress in select areas. Compounded over time—particularly at the surprising rates of progress over the past two to three years, this modernization process will, within ten to fifteen years, transform the PLA into a fairly modern military, yet one that is still limited to a regional reach (notwithstanding ICBMs and SLBMs). Thus, the PLA has transitioned from being a third- to a second-tier military power, but still has a very long way to go before it can be described as a military of first-class global standard.

Policy Implications

Other chapters in this edition of *Strategic Asia* assess the impact of China's military modernization on Asia. They offer evidence that Australia, India, Japan, and Taiwan are responding to China's growing military muscle, while these and some Southeast Asian states may be strategically hedging against China by tightening their military ties to the United States.

Clearly, the United States is also taking development of the PLA's capabilities seriously. This is evident not only in the DoD's *Annual Report to Congress on the Military Power of the People's Republic of China*, but also in other DoD documents such as the *Quadrennial Defense Review, Nuclear Posture Review*, and the *Global Defense Posture Review*. China's growing military capabilities figure centrally in all of these key U.S. military guidance documents. U.S. concern is also clearly reflected in the regional redeployments of U.S. forces and equipment currently underway. While it would be incorrect to attribute all of these recent moves by the Pentagon, or even a majority of them, to the "China factor," growing PLA capabilities and U.S. allied defense responsibilities are clearly important considerations driving some of these redeployments.

All Asian nations and the United States must wrestle with the reality of a more modern Chinese military. This trend will continue, and may even accelerate in certain categories of military power. China will possess a modern military—the only real questions are when and to what ends will it be put? In some areas, capabilities have already been achieved in modern, near state-of-the-art capabilities (new generations of guided and ballistic missiles, fighters, destroyers, submarines, tanks, and EW). In many other categories, the CMIC is making incremental advances that, over time, should close the technological gaps. Yet, in other areas, the PLA continues to lag considerably behind modern capabilities (C4ISR and power projection). Thus, the answer to the question of "when" very much depends on the category of capability in question. The PLA does not suddenly arrive one day at the stage of "modernization" *in toto*—rather, as is already evident, certain sectors are attained before others, while some lag perennially behind.

The answer to the "to what ends" question is more complicated. This very much depends on perceptions. Some view the PLA's acquisition of any power projection capability as threatening and destabilizing simply by virtue of being a new capability that China had not previously possessed. A variant of this line of thinking wonders why China should even try to develop modern military capabilities if it did not intend to use them.

An alternative view offers a more sanguine assessment of PLA modernization and the development of power projection capability—that it is natural for a continental nation of China's size, level of development, and national security interests to build and possess the full range of modern military capabilities. Why is it unnatural, for instance, that the PLAN should possess the capability to patrol at least several hundred nautical miles out around its periphery and even to protect SLOCs beyond Asia in order to ensure maritime trade and energy shipping? Or for the PLAAF to possess the capability to loiter its fighters over the East or South China Seas, or to (safely) shadow foreign reconnaissance aircraft that try to spy on its territory from international airspace? Or for China to develop a robust and defendable second-strike deterrent capability against nuclear attack? Or for China to develop its own military satellites or anti-satellite weapons, in the event that Beijing has to fight a war against an enemy that possesses both? Why is it unnatural for China to buy weapons and defense technologies abroad that it cannot produce domestically? And why is it unnatural for China to prepare for a range of possible military contingencies to prevent what Beijing considers to be part of China's sovereign territory (Taiwan) from proclaiming independence? If viewed from these perspectives, acquiring these capabilities seems quite natural indeed.

The answer to the question of whether China's military modernization is natural or not thus depends very much on the metric applied. In the end, however, the key question does not concern military capabilities, but rather intentions and limitations. The subject of intentions is, of course, elusive—but it is why the first two sections of this chapter discussed contextual and direct factors affecting China's military modernization program and strategic outlook. There are several factors acting as deterrent effects on Beijing's intentions: the strategic landscape and regional security architecture around China, the interdependence produced by globalization, the horrendous potential economic and social costs of a conflict to China, and the increasing number of constraining confidence-building measures that Beijing has entered into with China's neighbors.

While the scope and pace of China's military modernization process can be slowed from the outside (e.g., via arms embargoes), it cannot be stopped. For those accustomed to a weak China and a weak Chinese military, this new reality will not be easy to accept, but it is one with which all must come to terms. The PLA's regional reach will steadily improve—and consequently will alter the balance of power in Asia.

Executive Summary

This chapter analyzes changes in Japan's security strategy, the modernization of JSDF capabilities, and the upgrading of the U.S.-Japan alliance in the
post-Cold War and post-September 11 periods.

MAIN ARGUMENT:

Japan is moving along a long-term trajectory to assume a "normal" security
role, as evidenced by (1) the JSDF's acquisition of enhanced power projection capabilities and (2) the gradual strengthening of the U.S.-Japan alliance
to play a more effective part in both regional and global security.

POLICY IMPLICATIONS:

- Japan is becoming a more reliable ally that will seek to support U.S. regional and global strategies in the post-September 11 period.

- Like all "normal" allies, Japan is, however, continuing to hedge against
over-dependence on its alliance with the U.S. Not only will Japan continue
to impose limits on the degree of its military cooperation with the U.S.
over such issues as Taiwan and Iran, but it will also explore UN-centered
security options.

- As a more "normal" ally seeking reciprocity in alliance ties, Japan will also
be more demanding over base issues in Okinawa, seek more equal treatment in decisionmaking within the alliance, and expect support for its
UN Security Council bid.

- This "normal" ally behavior notwithstanding, Japan's increasing military
integration with and dependence upon the U.S.—especially when combined with rising concerns regarding China and North Korea—indicate
that, ultimately, Japan will see little alternative but to continue to strength-
en the bilateral alliance relationship.

Japanese Military Modernization: In Search of a "Normal" Security Role

Christopher W. Hughes

Japan's grand strategy, security policy, and military doctrine and capabilities have undergone a significant round of change over the last ten years, and have recently begun yet another round of major transformation. The first cycle of military modernization began in the mid-1990s when Japan moved to revise both its National Defense Program Outline (NDPO) and the Japan-U.S. Guidelines for Defense Cooperation. These efforts upgraded both Japan's national military capabilities and the functions of the U.S.-Japan alliance to respond more effectively to regional security contingencies. In the aftermath of September 11, Japan has already dispatched the Japan Self-Defense Forces (JSDF) in support of many U.S. global security initiatives.

In late 2004, moreover, Japan took initial steps toward a second cycle of military modernization and upgrading of the U.S.-Japan alliance. As part of this effort, Japan undertook a second revision of the NDPO (now renamed the National Defense Program Guidelines [NDPG]), released a new Mid-Term Defense Program (MTDP) in December 2004, and is now committed to a Defense Policy Review Initiative (DPRI) with the United States over the future course of alliance cooperation. This new cycle will set the overall trajectory for Japan's security policy over the next decade and will potentially encompass changes far beyond those of the first cycle. Increasing emphasis on military modernization will provide a route for Japan to achieve its long-debated, more proactive and "normal" role in regional and global security, and one closely identified with expanded U.S.-Japan alliance cooperation.

Christopher Hughes is Senior Research Fellow and Deputy Director at the Centre for the Study of Globalization and Regionalization, University of Warwick, U.K. He can be reached at <c.w.hughes@warwick.ac.uk>.

This process of military modernization and adjustments to both security policy and the alliance relationship will not, however, always progress smoothly. First, Japan is seeking more reciprocity within the alliance by seeking to assert greater leverage over the strategic orientation of the United States. Second, while venturing to push outwards the potential envelope of alliance cooperation beyond traditional geographical and functional confines, Japan's policymakers will remain cautious and selective about the actual level of commitment to overseas military operations. The military support proffered to the United States will still be based upon careful calculation of Japan's perceived national interests. Japanese policymakers—as is the case with other "normal" key allies—will remain mindful of entrapment, and will thus seek to maintain their "double hedge" against both exclusive reliance on military power and the U.S.-Japan alliance as a security guarantee.

Nevertheless, even as Japan attempts to exploit these hedging options, Japanese policymakers will find it progressively harder both to exercise such options and to resist the logic of tighter and expanded U.S.-led alliance cooperation. Japan's very enactment of hedging strategies has created legal, political, and military-operational precedents that engender momentum and expectations on both sides for the continued expansion of alliance cooperation. At the same time, Japan's declining defense production capabilities along with its participation in ballistic missile defense (BMD) will further tighten U.S.-Japan alliance cooperation. Moreover, Japan's room to hedge against reliance on the United States will be continually eroded by the structural pressures manifested in the perceived threats from North Korea and China. Japan's next decade of security planning, initiated in 2005–06 is, therefore, likely to be characterized by Japan's re-emergence as a more "normal" power, but one that will continue to fulfill this security role chiefly through the mechanism of the bilateral alliance.

This chapter is divided into four main sections. The first overviews the past trajectory of Japan's comprehensive security policy and the U.S.-Japan alliance, and investigates the regional and global drivers modifying each. The second section overviews Japan's two cycles of security policy and alliance change. The third examines how Japan has sought to modernize its military in order to support Japan's emergent global security role via the strengthened U.S.-Japan alliance. A final section considers the implications of Japan's shifting security policy for regional stability and the global strategy of the United States.

Japan's Comprehensive Security Policy: Origins and Pressure to Change

Japan's Comprehensive Security Policy

The grand strategy that Japan adopted at the end of World War II was one that involved the pursuit of a comprehensive security policy. Resulting from Japan's wartime defeat, anti-militaristic norms, and constitutional prohibitions, this strategy has consisted of both military and non-military (i.e., economic and diplomatic) components. Japan's policymakers—in the guise of the Ministry of Foreign Affairs (MOFA), Japan Defense Agency (JDA), and governing Liberal Democratic Party (LDP)—have in large part entrusted the military component of the nation's security to the U.S.-Japan security treaty. This treaty is based in part on the strategic bargain of accepting U.S. military protection in return for Japan's provision of bases to facilitate U.S. power projection in East Asia. Japan's reliance on the U.S. military guarantee has always been tempered, however, by Japanese hedging against the dual alliance dilemmas of abandonment and, most especially, entrapment in U.S. regional and global military strategy.[1] Japan's security role in East Asia and beyond in the postwar period has thus been based on a U.S.-Japan alliance cooperation that is complementary but asymmetrical.[2]

Japan's postwar security policy has traditionally been predicated upon both individual national self-defense and the non-exercise of the right to collective self-defense; Japan has, for instance, prohibited itself from defending its U.S. security treaty partner outside Japanese territory. Throughout the Cold War period, Japan also chose to emphasize military cooperation with the United States under the security treaty in line with Article 5 (the immediate defense of Japan) rather than Article 6 (the maintenance of international peace and security in the Far East). Moreover, fear of entrapment has been the motivation behind Japan's avoidance of integrating JSDF capabilities and missions with those of the U.S. military. This was true even in the latter stages of the Cold War when Tokyo, hoping to counter the USSR's ability to threaten the airspace and sea lanes around Japan, embarked on a qualitative and quantitative build-up of JSDF capabilities that served to

---

[1] For the alliance dilemma, see Glen H. Snyder, "The Security Dilemma in Alliance Politics," *World Politics* 36, no. 4 (July 1984): 461–95; for specific application to the case of Japan, see Thomas J. Christensen, "China, the U.S.-Japan Alliance and the Security Dilemma in East Asia," *International Security* 23, no. 4 (Spring 1999): 49–80.

[2] Paul S. Giarra and Akihisa Nagashima, "Managing the New U.S.-Japan Security Alliance: Enhancing Structures and Mechanism to Address Post-Cold War Requirements," in *The U.S.-Japan Alliance: Past, Present and Future*, ed. Michael J. Green and Patrick M. Cronin (New York: Council on Foreign Relations Press, 1999), 98.

support overall U.S. strategy in Northeast Asia.[3] Consequently, Japan's military security role during the Cold War was geographically restricted to the area immediately surrounding Japan, and limited functionally to providing a defensive "shield" to support the U.S. offensive "sword" in Northeast Asia. Any Japanese contribution to wider regional security was effected indirectly through the mechanism of the bilateral alliance and general support for the U.S. presence in East Asia.

Under Japan's comprehensive security policy, both economic power and diplomacy have been the primary means not only to compensate for military deficiencies but also to further hedge against overreliance on military power and the U.S.-Japan alliance. Japanese policymakers in the postwar period have viewed economic power and diplomatic engagement (often taking the form of official development assistance [ODA] and the promotion of economic interdependency) as key tools for countering the rise of potential military security threats such as those related to China and North Korea.[4] In addition, Japan views economic insecurity and non-traditional security concerns as important issues in their own right within a comprehensive security agenda. Hence, Japan has played an important role in articulating conceptions of "human security" and in providing financial assistance for the East Asian states to deal with social, health, and food security problems resulting from the financial crises of 1997–98.[5] This active commitment to comprehensive security was demonstrated most recently by Japan's response to the Asian tsunami of 2004, when Tokyo disbursed $500 million in emergency grant aid and dispatched Japan Disaster Relief Teams (JDRT) and the JSDF to Sumatra for humanitarian relief operations.

Drivers of Security Policy Change

Since the end of the Cold War, however, Japan's grand strategy and comprehensive security policy have undergone important changes in response to a shifting international environment. The most immediate security threat that has confronted Japan is that of North Korea. Japanese security anxieties have focused on the North's potential development of nuclear weapons, anxieties compounded by the "Taepodong-1 shock" of August 1998 when the North test-fired a missile over Japanese airspace. Japanese policymak-

---

[3] Christopher W. Hughes and Akiko Fukushima, "U.S.-Japan Security Relations—Toward Bilateralism Plus?" in *Beyond Bilateralism: U.S.-Japan Relations in the New Asia-Pacific*, ed. Ellis S. Krauss and T. J. Pempel (Stanford: Stanford University Press, 2004), 61–63.

[4] Reinhard Drifte, *Japan's Security Relations with China Since 1989: From Balancing to Bandwagoning?* (London: Routedge, 2003), 133–39.

[5] Bert Edström, "Japan's Foreign Policy and Human Security," *Japan Forum* 15, no. 2 (2003): 209–25; and Hughes, *Japan's Security Agenda*, 208–18.

ers have been similarly concerned about incursions into Japanese waters by North Korean spy ships, as well as the risks of North Korean guerrilla attacks upon key facilities such as nuclear power installations on the Sea of Japan coast.

If North Korea represents the most immediate threat to Japan's security, then China poses the greatest challenge for Japan's security over the medium to long terms. Japan has been concerned about the modernization of China's conventional and nuclear forces since the early 1990s. These concerns focus not on China's military modernization *per se*, but upon signs that China is now willing to project military power beyond its borders. Beijing could use its small blue-water surface, submarine, and amphibious naval capacities to assert China's territorial claims to the South China Sea and thereby disrupt Japan's sea lines of communication (SLOC).[6] China's constant dispatch of both "research ships" and warships into Japan's exclusive economic zone (EEZ) around the disputed Senkaku Islands are viewed by many in Japan as evidence of aggressive intent.[7] Japan's concerns about China were heightened when a Chinese nuclear-powered submarine passed through Japanese territorial waters on November 10, 2004. Bilateral frictions have continued over China's natural gas exploration activities (begun in early 2005) in an East China Sea oil field abutting Japan's EEZ claim. Sino-Japanese ties have continued to deteriorate thus far in 2005, with renewed tensions over the correct representation of Japan's colonial past in Japanese history textbooks.[8]

Meanwhile, Japan-China security relations have been further complicated since the mid-1990s by both the Taiwan issue and Sino-U.S. strategic competition. Japan viewed the 1995–96 Taiwan Strait crises—including China's intimidation of Taiwan through the test-firing of ballistic missiles—as additional indicators of Chinese aggression. Specifically, Japan is worried about China's willingness to project military power in pursuit of its national interests, to possibly challenge the United States militarily in the region over the longer term, and to even use ballistic missiles to strike against U.S. bases in Japan and against rear area support facilities provided by Japan in the event of a full-blown conflict resulting from any Taiwanese move to declare independence. Japanese security planners also fear that in a Taiwan Strait

---

[6] Lyle Goldstein and William Murray, "Undersea Dragons: China's Maturing Submarine Force," *International Security* 8, no. 4 (Spring 2004): 161–96.

[7] Task Force on Foreign Relations for the Prime Minister, "Basic Strategies for Japan's Foreign Policy in the 21st Century New Era, New Vision, New Diplomacy," November 28, 2002, http://www.kantei.go.jp/jp/kakugikettei/2002/1128tf.html#2-2.

[8] Denny Roy, "The Sources and Limits of Sino-Japanese Tensions," *Survival* 47, no. 2 (Summer 2005): 196–205.

crisis China might attempt to seize offshore islands, such as parts of Okinawa Prefecture, in order to disrupt U.S.-Japan military cooperation.[9]

Beyond the region, Japan has similarly been presented with a new series of security challenges that demand a new set of responses. Japan's reaction to the 1990–91 Gulf War eventually took the form of underwriting the war financially to the tune of $13 billion; this dollar diplomacy was the subject of U.S. and international criticism and first made Japanese policymakers aware of the need to dispatch the JSDF in support of international responses to major post-Cold War security crises.[10] In the wake of September 11, Japan has been made aware of the threat of transnational terrorism and the need to support the efforts of its U.S. ally—and the international community in general—to expunge this threat. Japanese policymakers have also been in accord with their U.S. counterparts both on the need to halt the horizontal proliferation of weapons of mass destruction (WMD) and on the possible threat of the vertical proliferation of WMD to terrorist groups.

Japan's preferred role in responding to this post-Cold War and post-September 11 security agenda is clearly a non-military one. Japan has continued to rely on diplomatic efforts as the main means to deal with North Korea. The summits that Prime Minister Koizumi Junichiro initiated with the North in September 2002 and May 2004 were designed both to clear away domestic obstacles to the resumption of normalization negotiations and to demonstrate to the United States the need to persist with diplomacy in order to avoid an unwanted conflict on the Korean Peninsula.[11] Japan has also been working with South Korea to nudge Washington back toward negotiations with Pyongyang, and has been supportive of the Six Party Talks process. Similarly, Japanese policymakers are continuing their efforts to engage China economically and diplomatically, with both sides moving to ensure that bilateral tensions over historical and territorial issues do not spiral out of control. For instance, on April 24, 2005 Prime Minister Koizumi and President Hu Jintao agreed to meet on the sidelines of the Asia-Africa Summit in an attempt to patch up ties.

Nevertheless, Japanese policymakers are increasingly aware of the limits of economic and diplomatic engagement in dealing with these regional challenges. Japan's ability to engage the North has been severely hampered by domestic anti-North Korean feeling over the fate of Japanese abductees, the

---

[9] "Defense Paper Assumes China Invasion of Japan," *Japan Times Online*, May 15, 2004, http://www.japantimes.co.jp/cgi-bin/getarticle.pl5?nn20040515b6.htm.

[10] Kitaoka Shinichi, Yamazaki Masakazu, and Watanabe Taizo, "Wangan Senso to wa Nani Datta Ka: Nihon Tenkanten o Furikaeru" [What Was the Gulf War: Reflecting on Japan's Turning Point], *Gaiko Foramu*, no. 158 (September 2001): 28–37.

[11] Yakushiji Katsuyuki, *Gaimusho: Gaikoryoku Kyoka e no Michi* [The Ministry of Foreign Affairs: The Path to Strengthening Diplomatic Power] (Tokyo: Iwanami Shinsho, 2003), 14–22.

increasingly hard-line stance that Washington is taking toward the North, and the North's own nuclear brinkmanship. Despite attempts to keep open the door to engagement, Japan now acknowledges the need to line up more closely with U.S. efforts to apply military pressure upon North Korea over the nuclear issue.

Japanese policymakers have in recent years also shown signs of declining confidence in their ability to use economic and diplomatic means to manage China's rise.[12] Indeed, Japanese aid and economic engagement have played a large part in bringing China into the regional community in a relatively peaceful manner, and Japan's economic recovery has increasingly piggy-backed on China's economic expansion. Both Japan's perceived economic decline relative to China and the possible resulting asymmetric economic interdependency in favor of China over the longer term have, however, engendered concerns amongst Japanese policymakers that China may be emboldened to challenge Japanese economic and diplomatic interests in East Asia. Japanese policymakers are already concerned that China, through its free trade area (FTA) proposals, has begun to overtake Japan in the economic leadership of Southeast Asia. Japanese policymakers also feel they have fewer economic tools available either to engage China bilaterally or to balance Beijing's influence in the region. Japan has been forced to cut its overall ODA budget by around 30 percent from 1997 to 2004 (although some increases may be planned for fiscal year 2006), and Tokyo may cease loans (totaling around 3 trillion yen between 1980 and 2003) to China by 2008.[13] Recognizing that ODA may now not be the most effective means available with which to countervail the rise of China, Japan is increasingly obliged to look instead to military power and U.S.-Japan alliance ties.

Japan has taken similar lessons from both the "war on terrorism" and the Iraq war. True, Japan has sought a role in the Afghan conflict and in Iraq that emphasizes the use of economic power, post-conflict reconstruction, and state-building. Moreover, Japanese policymakers have strong reservations concerning such issues as the utility of military power in bringing about a resolution to the multi-causal phenomenon of terrorism in Afghanistan and elsewhere in the Muslim world, the linkages between Al Qaeda and Iraq, and the ability of the United States to reconstruct and stabilize postwar Iraq.[14] Nonetheless, Japan has perceived that September 11, the war on terrorism, and the Iraq war have presented demands for an enhanced military response in support of the United States and the international com-

---

[12] Michael J. Green, *Japan's Reluctant Realism: Foreign Policy Challenges in an Era of Uncertain Power* (New York: Palgrave, 2001), 77–109.

[13] "Nihon no ODA Gaku" [Japan's ODA Total], *Nihon Keizai Shimbun*, April 18, 2004, 8.

[14] Hughes, *Japan's Re-emergence*, 46–47.

munity. Tokyo needs to provide such support in part because these issues are tests of the political and military strength of U.S.-Japan alliance ties, but also because transnational terrorism and WMD in other contexts represent genuine threats to Japan's own security.[15]

Two Cycles of Security Policy Change: Strengthening Regional and Global Roles

As examined above, Japan in the post-Cold War period has been forced into the realization that its current comprehensive security approach is inadequate to respond to extant regional and global security challenges. Japanese policymakers have thus sought to change national security policy to allow for an expanded military role in the region and beyond.

Cycle One

The first wave of security policy change began in the mid-1990s and was primarily focused on the U.S.-Japan alliance's regional security functions, which have also been the essential basis of Japan's postwar security policy. Tokyo's recognition of the inadequacy of the alliance, including Japan's role within it, as a mechanism to respond to regional security challenges was initially triggered by the North Korean nuclear crisis of 1994–95. During the crisis, Japan faced U.S. requests for active support in the event of an actual conflict on the Korean Peninsula. Japanese policymakers were unable to respond effectively, however, due to their previous reluctance to consider Article 6-type cooperation for regional contingencies under the bilateral security treaty. The alliance's lack of military operability induced a crisis of confidence in the bilateral relationship and raised fears that the United States might abandon Japan as an unreliable ally.[16]

Looking to shore up the postwar strategic bargain with the United States, Japanese policymakers undertook initiatives to revise Japan's military doctrine and to redefine the alliance. In November 1995 Japan issued a revised NDPO, the document that sets out Japan's military doctrine alongside the necessary force structure. Significantly, the document stressed the need for stronger U.S.-Japan alliance cooperation and inserted a new clause to state that if a situation impacting national peace and security should arise in

---

[15] Argument as presented in Kamiya Matake, "Naze Jieitai o Iraq ni Hakken Suru no Ka?" [Why are the JSDF going to Iraq?], *Gaiko Foramu*, no. 188 (March 2004): 24–28.

[16] Yoichi Funabashi, *Alliance Adrift* (New York: Council On Foreign Relations Press, 1999), 280–95; and Christopher W. Hughes, *Japan's Economic Power and Security: Japan and North Korea* (London: Routledge, 1999), 93–97.

areas surrounding Japan (*shuhen*), then Japan should seek to deal with the situation in cooperation with the UN and via U.S.-Japan security arrangements. In April 1996 Japan and the United States issued a "Joint Declaration on Security" that opened the way for a revision (which took place between 1996 and 1997) of the original 1978 Japan-U.S. Guidelines for Defense Cooperation. The revised guidelines specified for the first time the extent of Japanese logistical support for the United States in the event of a regional contingency (*shuhen jitai*), and thereby switched the agreed emphasis of alliance cooperation from Article 5 to Article 6 of the security treaty.

Japan's focus on an expanded security role during this first cycle has not, however, been based exclusively on the U.S.-Japan alliance, nor has it been limited entirely to regional issues. Japan's failure to respond to U.S. and international expectations for JSDF dispatch during the Gulf War of 1990–91 led Japan to pass the June 1992 International Peace Cooperation Law (IPCL), which in turn allowed JSDF dispatch on any non-combat reconstruction UN peacekeeping operation (PKO). Japan to date has taken part in UN PKOs in Cambodia (1992–93), Mozambique (1993–95), Rwanda (1994), the Golan Heights (1996–), and East Timor (2002–04). In 2002 Japan also "unfroze" provisions in the IPCL in order to allow JSDF participation in "core" UN PKO, including the monitoring of ceasefires, collection of weapons, and exchange of prisoners. In the meantime, Japan has indicated further possibilities for cooperation with UN military activities through the Anti-Terrorism Special Measures Law (ATSML) and Iraqi reconstruction law. Even though these laws are clearly intended to boost U.S.-Japan alliance cooperation on a global scale, the predication of JSDF dispatch on UN resolutions opens up future avenues for Japan to dispatch the JSDF in line with the principle of collective security rather than collective self-defense.[17]

Another portent of its expanding military role was Japan's response to the Indian Ocean tsunami in late 2004. The JSDF used its dispatch on this non-combat humanitarian mission under the International Disaster Relief Law (which, involving 1,500 personnel, was its largest overseas mission ever) to test its joint and combined operation capabilities. Maritime Self Defense Force (MSDF) ships en route to return to Japan after service as part of the U.S.-led coalition in the Indian Ocean under the ATSML were first diverted to the vicinity of Thailand for relief assistance immediately following the tsunami. Then in January 2005 an MSDF flotilla, including an *Osumi*-class

---

[17] Collective security is seen to differ from collective self-defence in that the latter is an inherent right under the UN Charter that can be exercised without UN approval, whereas the former right must be sanctioned by the UN. Japanese policymakers have argued that the preamble of the Constitution, which states Japan's duty to cooperate with international society (equated with the UN), should provide Japan with the constitutional right to take part in collective security. For a fuller explanation, see Hughes and Fukushima, "U.S.-Japan Security Relations," 69–70.

transport, was dispatched to Sumatra. This flotilla carried five GSDF helicopters and twenty GSDF trucks, and acted as a "floating camp" for joint MSDF and GSDF operations.[18]

One must note, however, that though this first cycle of modernization has included important shifts in Japanese security policy, Japan has continued to hedge on its military commitments. For instance, in the revised Guidelines for Defense Cooperation, Japan stressed that the activation of the guidelines is predicated upon the concept of "situational need" rather than strict geographical demarcations, which introduces an element of strategic ambiguity as to whether the scope of the revised guidelines covers Taiwan. The constitutional and legal firewalls that Tokyo has enacted predicating JSDF dispatch to support U.S.-led coalitions in Afghanistan and Iraq on UN resolutions possibly limit the range of support that Tokyo is prepared to offer Washington. Moreover, Japan has restricted the expansion of JSDF activities regionally and globally to non-combat missions, and left intact its constitutional prohibition on the exercise of collective self-defense.[19]

Cycle Two

Japan's second cycle of policy change was spurred in response to changing overall U.S. global strategy needs. The Bush administration has, especially since September 11, been seeking to activate its regional alliances to function for global security. The United States emphasized this shift in the *Quadrennial Defense Review Report* of September 2001, the *National Security Strategy* of September 2002, and the *National Defense Strategy* of March 2005. The White House now supports a move from "threat-based" regional alliances to "capabilities-based" global alliances that are capable of constructing flexible coalitions with interoperable military assets for missions in the "arc of instability" stretching from the Middle East to Southeast Asia.[20] In addition, the Global Posture Review (GPR) of 2004 made clear that bases provided by regional alliances should be integrated into the U.S. strategy for the "surging" and global deployment of its forward forces.

Japanese policymakers have faced pressure to respond to these changes in U.S. strategy and the international security environment. This need has,

---

[18] "Kaijikan, Rikuji Shukueiji ni" [MSDF, a Base for the GSDF], *Asahi Shimbun*, February 2, 2005, 29.

[19] Hughes, *Japan's Re-emergence*, 131–33.

[20] Department of Defense, *Quadrennial Defense Review Report* (Washington, D.C., 2001), 25–27; The White House, *The National Security Strategy of The United States of America* (Washington, D.C., 2002), 22–24; Department of Defense, *The National Defense Strategy of The United States of America* (Washington, D.C., 2005), 12, 15, 17; and Yoko Iwama, "The New Shape of the U.S. Alliance System," *Gaiko Forum: Japanese Perspectives of Foreign Affairs* 4, no. 1 (Spring 2004): 28–29.

moreover, been intertwined with the ongoing and wider debate in Japan regarding the next steps in Japanese security policy. This reinvigorated domestic policy debate on security in the postwar period is still subject to a variety of divisions, but there has been an increasing convergence of mainstream opinion in favor of a more proactive, or "normal," military role for Japan.

There exists no objective standard in Japan, or indeed in any other state, for measuring the alleged status of a "normal" state.[21] At one extreme are the Japanese rightists and Gaullists who argue that Japan can only be "normal" by acting both more autonomously in relation to the United States and more assertive militarily against China and North Korea. At the other end of the continuum, the leftists and pacifists argue that real "normality" lies in renouncing military-centered approaches to security and the bilateral alliance. Most MOFA, JDA, and LDP policymakers, however, hold that the pathway toward the "normalization" of Japanese security policy is the incremental and cautious expanding of national military capabilities and responsibilities within the framework of a strengthened U.S.-Japan alliance. The Komeito, the LDP's coalition partner, similarly supports the U.S.-Japan alliance, but emphasizes the maintenance of restrictions on the exercise of Japanese military power and enhanced multilateral cooperation. The principal opposition party, the Democratic Party of Japan (DPJ), is in favor of maintaining the U.S.-Japan alliance, although it proposes that far greater weight should be given to a UN-centered security policy and the promotion of regional multilateral frameworks for security dialogue and cooperation. Moreover, all elements of the policymaking community recognize that there are opportunities for Japan to play an expanded role in UN PKOs.

Japan's debate concerning a more proactive military security role has also been reflected in proposals for constitutional revision. Following five years of deliberation, the National Diet's House of Representatives and House of Councilors released separate reports on constitutional revision in April 2005. The House of Representatives reported a consensus that Article 9 of the constitution should be revised in such a way that the first clause, the renunciation of the right to belligerency, should be kept in place, but that in the second clause Japan's right to self-defense and the constitutionality of the JSDF should be explicitly acknowledged.[22] The House of Councilors failed to agree on revisions to Article 9, and neither of the houses was able to reach a consensus on revisions relating to the exercise of the right of collective self-

---

[21] For a detailed summary of these debates see Mike M. Mochizuki, "American and Japanese Strategic Debates: The Need for a New Synthesis," in *Toward a True Alliance: Restructuring U.S.-Japan Security Relations*, ed. Mike M. Mochizuki (Washington D.C.: Brookings Institution Press, 1997), 59–62; and Hughes, *Japan's Re-emergence*, 49–59.

[22] "Shugiin Kempo Chosa Saishu Hokoku" [House of Representatives Final Report on the Constitution], *Yomiuri Shimbun*, April 16, 2005, 13.

defense—although they both agreed that Japan should engage more actively in international security cooperation. In this sense, many of the changes debated in the Diet reports were proposals only for *de jure* confirmation of the *de facto* realities of Japan's security policy. Nonetheless, these reports are important in initiating forthcoming Diet debates on constitutional revision. Moreover, there may be more radical proposals to come. For instance, in an intra-party report on constitutional revision, the LDP in the same month avoided proposals for the recognition of the right of collective self-defense within the Constitution itself, but did advocate that this right and the specific conditions for its exercise should be acknowledged in a Basic Security Law to be passed at the same time as any revisions.[23]

Despite the above debate, Japanese policymakers have still managed to draw a number of clear and long-term policy lessons from shifts in U.S. military strategy. In order both to remain indispensable as an ally and to maintain political and strategic influence over the United States, Japan needs to move beyond the changes made in alliance cooperation in the mid-1990s and the immediate post-September 11 period, and further strengthen the alliance to respond to both regional and global security contingencies.

As one step, Japan has begun participating in U.S.-led multinational coalitions, including the dispatch of the JSDF to support the Afghan campaign and Iraqi reconstruction. Moreover, Tokyo has become cognizant of Washington's expectations that U.S. regional alliances should function to support global security operations, as evidenced by specific GPR proposals relating to Japan since 2004. In the GPR the United States initially proposed to Japan that the 5th U.S. Air Force (USAF) Command at Yokota Air Base in Tokyo should be integrated with the command operations of the 13th USAF headquartered in Guam, a key base for long-range bombers and tanker aircraft often deployed in the Middle East. A second proposal was for the command functions of the U.S. Army I Corps, a rapid deployment force covering the Asia-Pacific, to be relocated from the U.S. state of Washington to Army Camp Zama in the Japanese prefecture of Kanagawa. The clear ramification of these base realignments was that Japan would serve essentially as a frontline U.S. command post for the Asia-Pacific and beyond, and that the increased concentration of command functions in Japan would also tighten military cooperation between U.S. forces and the JSDF.[24]

The Anti-Terrorism Special Measures Law (ATSML) passed through the National Diet in October has enabled the dispatch of JSDF units to the

---

[23] "Jimin Shinkempoho Kisoi Yoko" [LDP New Constitution Proposals Committee Outline], *Asahi Shimbun*, April 5, 2005, 1.

[24] "Rikuji to no Kankei Kyoka" [Strengthening Relations with the GSDF], *Asahi Shimbun*, December 8, 2004, 2.

Indian Ocean area to provide logistical support to U.S. and multinational coalition forces engaged in Afghanistan.[25] In July 2003 Japan then passed a Law Concerning Special Measures on Humanitarian and Reconstruction Assistance (LCSMHRA, or Iraq reconstruction law) that has enabled the dispatch of JSDF on non-combat reconstruction activities in the southern city of Samawah. Japan has predicated these laws and JSDF "out-of-area" dispatches upon linkages to relevant UN resolutions, and thus these security activities are strictly outside the geographical and functional scope of the U.S.-Japan security alliance. Nevertheless, the principal impetus behind the ATSML and Iraqi reconstruction law has centered on Japanese attempts to strengthen the range of U.S.-Japan alliance activities outside East Asia.

Meeting Changing Security Policy Needs via Military Modernization

In order to implement the strengthened alliance cooperation allowed for by this new shift in policy described above, Japan is now seeking to acquire both new doctrine and more interoperable JSDF capabilities. These changes are being undertaken with an eye toward expanding military activities alongside the United States and in U.S.-led multinational coalitions on a global scale. The goal is also to find a means within the U.S.-Japan security treaty to provide the United States with bases for regional and global deployments.[26]

NDPG and MTDP Revision: Pursuing Power Projection

Japan began this round of military modernization, which was timed to match its cycle of security policy change, with the issuance in October of the final report of the Prime Minister's Council on Security and Defense Capabilities, known as the "Araki Report" (after its chairman Araki Hiroshi). This panel—consisting of a range of business figures, academics, and former bureaucrats and JSDF officers—was notable in calling for an "Integrated Security Strategy" for Japan that would mandate a two-pronged approach for the JSDF: (1) the traditional function of preventing direct threats from hav-

---

[25] Paul Midford, "Japan's Response to Terror: Dispatching the SDF to the Arabian Sea," *Asian Survey* 43, no. 2 (April 2003): 331–33.

[26] Morimoto Satoshi, "Nichibei Domei no Shorai to Nihon no Sentaku" [The Future of the U.S.-Japan Alliance and Japan's Choices], *Gaiko Foramu* 5, no. 1 (January 2005): 46.

ing an impact on Japan and (2) a new emphasis on international cooperation outside Japan's own territory to prevent the rise of security threats.[27]

The Araki Report was followed in December 2004 with the release of the revised NDPG and the simultaneous release of a new MTDP for 2005–09. The NDPG followed the 1995 NDPO in stressing Japan's regional security concerns and the importance of the U.S.-Japan alliance in responding to these issues. The NDPG guidelines moved beyond its predecessor, however, by outlining a range of new threats to Japan, including ballistic missile attacks, guerrilla and special operations attacks, incursions into its territorial waters, and chemical and biological warfare. These concerns are a clear reflection of recent perceived regional threats from North Korea and China. The NDPG actually went further than the 1995 NDPO by not only identifying North Korea specifically as a destabilizing factor in East Asia, but also by identifying for the first time concerns about China's impact on regional security, although the latter was couched in the oblique language of needing to "remain attentive" to China's future military modernization.[28] The NDPG also went beyond the 1995 NDPO in its new emphasis upon global—as opposed to regional—security interests. The report stated that "the region spreading from the Middle East to East Asia is critical to Japan," thereby mapping Japan's own security interests onto those of the United States along the "arc of instability." The report also focused upon the need for Japan to engage actively in "international peace cooperation" activities through the dispatch of the JSDF to support UN and U.S.-led multinational operations.[29]

In order for Japan to fulfill these regional and global responsibilities, the NDPG and MTDP advocated that the JSDF should seek to establish "multifunctional, flexible, and effective" forces. These forces should be characterized by mobility and rapid-reaction; enhanced joint command and control, including the capability to undertake joint operations amongst the three services of the GSDF, MSDF, and ASDF; increased interoperability with UN and U.S. forces; and the utilization of state-of-the-art intelligence and military technologies. In terms of specific JSDF organization and hardware, the MTDP has stressed a quantitative build-down from Japan's Cold War-style forces. These forces have been characterized by large tank (Type-74 main battle tanks), interceptor (E-2C early warning aircraft and F-15 fighters), and anti-submarine warfare forces (destroyers, minesweepers, and P-3C

---

[27] The Council on Security and Defense Capabilities, "The Council on Security and Defence Capabilities Report: Japan's Visions for Future Security and Defense Capabilities," October 2004, 4–5, http://www.kantei.go.jp/jp/singi/ampobouei/dai13/13siryou.pdf.

[28] *National Defense Program Guideline FY 2005*, 2–3, http://www.jda.go.jp.

[29] Ibid., 9.

Table 1. Comparison between the Organization and Primary Equipment Scales of 1976 and 1996 NDPOs and 2004 NDPG

		1976 NDPO	1996 NDPO	2004 NDPG
GSDF	GSDF personnel	180,000	160,000	155,000
	Regular personnel		145,000	148,000
	Reserve personnel		15,000	7,000
	Major units			
	Regionally deployed	12 divisions 2 combined brigades	8 divisions 6 brigades	8 divisions 6 brigades
	Mobile operations	1 armored division 1 airborne brigade 1 helicopter brigade	1 armored division 1 airborne brigade 1 helicopter brigade	1 armored division central readiness group
	Ground-to-air missile units	8 anti-aircraft artillery groups	8 anti-aircraft artillery groups	8 anti-aircraft artillery groups
	Main equipment			
	Battle tanks	approx. 1,200	approx. 900	approx. 600
	Artillery	approx. 1,000	approx. 900	approx. 600
MSDF	**Major units**			
	Destroyers (mobile operations)	4 flotillas	4 flotillas	4 flotillas
	Destroyers (regional district)	10 divisions	7 divisions	5 divisions
	Submarines	6 divisions	6 divisions	4 divisions
	Minesweepers	2 flotillas	1 flotilla	1 flotilla
	Land-based patrol aircraft	16 squadrons	13 squadrons	9 squadrons
	Main equipment			
	Destroyers	approx. 60	approx. 50	47
	Submarines	16	16	16
	Combat aircraft	approx. 220	approx. 170	approx. 150
ASDF	**Major units**			
	Aircraft control and warning units	28 groups 1 squadron	8 groups 21 squadrons (1 early-warning)	8 groups 20 squadrons
	Interceptors	10 squadrons	9 squadrons	12 squadrons
	Support fighters	3 squadrons	3 squadrons	
	Air reconnaissance	1 squadron	1 squadron	1 squadron
	Air transport	3 squadrons	3 squadrons	3 squadrons
	Ground-to-air missile units	6 groups	6 groups	6 groups
	Main equipment			
	Combat aircraft	approx. 400	approx. 400	approx. 350
	of which fighters	approx. 350	approx. 300	approx. 260

Source: Bōeichōhen, *Bōei Hakusho* (Tokyo, Ōkurashō Insatsukyoku, 1995), 312, 321; and *National Defense Program Guideline FY 2005*, http://www.jda.go.jp.

patrol aircraft). Their mission has traditionally been to repel a Soviet land invasion, to protect U.S. air and naval forces in the immediate vicinity of Japan, and to help protect Japan's own SLOCs up to a range of 1,000 nautical miles. Now, the MTDP is seeking to switch to a lighter and qualitatively strengthened JSDF, which would be capable of greater power projection and expeditionary capabilities.

In line with the NDPG and MTDP, the GSDF is seeking to convert itself into a mobile force for overseas operations. This change entails the loss of approximately one-third of its main battle tanks and artillery (see **Table 1**), although the army will continue to introduce the highly sophisticated M-90 tank, the AH-64D *Longbow Apache* anti-tank and ground-attack helicopter, the UH-60JA *Apache* helicopter, the CH-47JA transport helicopter, and upgraded *Hawk* surface-to-air-missiles. The GSDF will also establish such new entities as a Central Readiness Group to coordinate nationwide mobile operations and special tasks, a rapid reaction force with access to its own helicopter transports, and a special unit to train personnel for dispatch overseas. Japan's ground forces will seek to acquire an expanded role in dealing with domestic terrorism, guerrilla incursions, and nuclear, biological, and chemical warfare.

Though set to lose another seven of its Cold War destroyer force, the MSDF power projection capabilities will, however, be boosted by the continued procurement of three *Osumi*-class transport ships, with flat decks for the landing of transport helicopters and an integral rear dock for the operation of hovercraft capable of landing tanks. The MSDF justifies these ships as necessary for GSDF UN PKOs and other international operations in support of peace, and two of the class have already been deployed to East Timor, Iraq, and Sumatra. The MSDF also has plans to construct four new DDH (Destroyer-Helicopter) ships, each mounting four helicopters. The displacement of the DDH, combined with their end-to-end flat tops and below-deck hangars, has raised suspicions that these ships could be suitable for use as mini-aircraft carriers. The MSDF is also seeking the indigenous development of a P-X replacement for its P-3C patrol and surveillance aircraft (although Japan might opt for purchasing the U.S. Multimission Maritime Aircraft). The MSDF's procurement from the United States of an off-the-shelf ballistic missile defense (BMD) system, mounted on a total of six Aegis war fighting system (AWS)-equipped *Kongo*-class destroyers, will further add to Japan's defensive power projection capabilities by providing a sea-mobile asset potentially capable of projecting an interoperable missile shield in support of its U.S. ally in contingencies in East Asia and beyond.

The ASDF's defensive (and potentially offensive) power projection capabilities are to be strengthened through the continued procurement of the

F-2 interceptor (although in smaller numbers than originally hoped for), and a C-X replacement for its C-1 transports, which will serve as the principal means of air transport for a GSDF rapid reaction force to regional contingencies and beyond. The ASDF will also procure four Boeing-KC767 tanker aircraft and, for the first time, an in-flight refueling capability; such power projection capabilities would potentially allow sorties overseas. In addition, the ASDF is believed to be looking to the next MTDP to replace its aging F-4 fighter-bomber with a version of the F-35 JSF, again increasing potential interoperability with the United States and the likely ability to operate across East Asia and even out-of-area. For BMD, the ASDF will deploy three batteries of Patriot Advanced Capability-3 (PAC III), and upgrade its Base Air Defense Ground Environment (BADGE) command and control system as the principal coordinator of Japanese air defense in the event of a missile attack.

Japan's defense planners have further plans for the JSDF to embark on its own revolution in military affairs (RMA) and U.S.-style "force transformation." Japan is eyeing additional capabilities not yet in the MTDP, with the GSDF interested in the indigenous development of unmanned aerial vehicles (UAV) for coastal battlefield surveillance, the MSDF in *Tomahawk* cruise missiles to strike against enemy missile bases, and the ASDF in joint direct attack munitions (JDAM) and airborne electronic jamming equipment, again making for the potential capability to strike enemy missile bases in combination with the new in-flight refueling assets.[30] In an attempt to integrate previously disparate JSDF intelligence gathering assets, Japan upgraded its intelligence capabilities through the establishment of the Japan Defense Intelligence Headquarters (JDIH) in 1997. From 1998 onwards, Tokyo has sought to deploy four indigenously produced intelligence satellites—two optical and two with synthetic aperture radar (SAR). These satellites have already proved of some use in monitoring North Korea's missile bases.[31] Japan is seeking to leverage these potential and existing assets through the promotion for the first time of joint JSDF operations. Japan has created a Common Operating Environment (COE) and a Defense Information Infrastructure (DII) designed to enable information sharing among the JSDF's three separate command and control systems. A new Central Command and Control System (CCS) has also been put in place to ensure a more

---

[30] *Midterm Defense Program (FY 2005–2009)*, 5, http://www.jda.go.jp; "UAVs Mulled," *Japan Times Online*, May 3, 2005, http://www.japantimes.co.jp/cgi-bin/makeprfy.pl5?nn20050503a3.htm; and "Senshu Boei ga Henshitsu" [The Changing Nature of Exclusively Defense Oriented Defense], *Asahi Shimbun*, December 4, 2004, 3.

[31] They lack the resolution capabilities of those of the United States, however, and Japan still remains dependent on crucial infra-red satellite surveillance from the United States for the detection of actual missile launches and the early-warning necessary to operate any BMD system.

comprehensive overview of military operations. Japan is also set to replace the current Joint Staff Council (JSC) with a new Joint Staff Organization (JSO) in early 2006. In the past, the three service chiefs of staff have reported individually to the Director General of the JDA. Now, however, the Chief of the JSO, drawn from one of the three JSDF services, will become the principal military advisor to the Director General, thereby centralizing decision-making and promoting the capability for joint tri-service operations.[32]

Continuing Domestic Obstacles to Modernization

Japan can thus be seen to have embarked on a major program of military modernization, marked in particular by an emphasis on power projection, amphibious capabilities, force transformation, and improved command and control. This new expansion should enable Japan to perform an expanded role in regional and global security. Nevertheless, important limitations have also been imposed on this NDPG revision and military modernization. Firstly, the Japanese defense establishment has been afflicted by organizational inertia. For instance, the GSDF has insisted on holding on to its core system of divisions and brigades responsible for the defense of designated regions in Japan and possessing their own independent tactical military capabilities; greater sharing of capabilities across units, for instance, might have made for more flexible forces.[33]

Secondly, the JDA faced considerable budgetary restrictions in the run-up to the release of the NDPG. The Ministry of Finance (MOF) refused JDA requests for a 1 percent increase in defense expenditure to pay for the costs of BMD, and proposed instead GSDF cuts of up to 40,000 personnel and 50 percent of its tank force, around 50 percent of the MSDF's destroyer force, and a third of the ASDF's fighter force.[34] The JDA has been forced to accept a 1 percent decrease in defense spending for 2005–06; the agency still managed, however, to secure a compromise with MOF for smaller cuts in GSDF personnel and cuts in tank and destroyer forces, and remains confident that it can fund BMD through financial mechanisms to roll over costs. Hence, even though Japan is attempting to limit its overall defense costs, the shift to qualitatively improved and lighter forces (including even big ticket

---

[32] Boeichohen, *Boei Hakusho* [Defense of Japan White Paper] (Tokyo: Zaimusho Insatsukyoku, 2004), 331–33.

[33] "Arata na Kyoi e Sokuo Jushi" [An Emphasis on Rapid Reaction to New Threats], *Asahi Shimbun*, December 11, 2004, 4.

[34] "Boeihigen Nerai Dokujian: Shinboeitako e Zaimusho" [An Independent Plan for Reductions in Defence Spending; MOF on the New NDPG], *Asahi Shimbun*, November 11, 2004, 3; and David Fouse, "Japan's FY 2005 National Defense Program Outline: New Concepts, Old Compromises," *Asia-Pacific Security Studies* 4, no. 3 (March 2005): 3.

items like BMD) should make an enhanced military role more affordable and practicable.

Thirdly, Japan's defense plans have been constrained by political pressures. The GSDF has reportedly requested that the MTDP should include the acquisition of surface-to-surface missiles as a means to defend Japan's offshore islands, possibly envisaging a Chinese threat to parts of Okinawa Prefecture. The Komeito vetoed this plan, however, suspecting that the 300-kilometer range of these missiles signaled an intent to move toward acquiring a missile capability to strike directly against North Korean missile bases.[35] Similarly, Komeito opposition was instrumental in blocking possible plans for Japan to lift its ban on the export of arms. The LDP's Defense Policy Subcommittee had advocated many changes: the lifting of Japan's blanket ban on exports that had been in place since 1976, the imposition instead of an arms licensing export system that would enable joint development and production with other developed states, and the sale of civilian-converted surplus equipment and military items to states not involved in conflicts or not under a UN arms embargo.[36] The lifting of the ban had been seen by many—including defense planners, the Ministry of Economy, Trade, and Industry (METI), and defense contractors—as an essential means of preserving Japan's indigenous military production capacity in an era of shrinking defense budgets, spiraling production costs, and increasing dependency on U.S. imports of key technologies such as BMD.[37] The Komeito, though, was prepared to accept only the export of arms technology to the United States for the purposes of joint BMD research and development, for fear that otherwise Japanese weapons would be exported to conflict zones.

Strengthening the Alliance: GPR, Base Realignments, and DPRI

Having revised its military doctrines and capabilities, Japan has now embarked on the next step in "normalizing" its security policy to deal with regional and global challenges: the further upgrading of U.S.-Japan alliance functions. Japan initially attempted to evade U.S. GPR proposals in 2004. MOFA officials stated that these would be "difficult to accept" (*ukeire wa*

---

[35] "Kenkyu Chakushu Miokuri: Choshatei Yudodan" [Research Plan Shelved: Long Range Guided Missile], *Asahi Shimbun*, December 8, 2004, 3.

[36] Defense Policy Subcommittee, National Defense Division Policy Research Council, Liberal Democratic Party, "Recommendations on Japan's New Defense Policy—Toward a Safer and More Secure Japan and the World," March 30, 2003, 15, http://www.jimin.jp/jimin/main/seisaku.html.

[37] "Kensho Buki Yushutsu Sangensoku Kanwa: Kokubozoku, Zaikai ga Kenin" [Investigation of Loosening the Restrictions on Arms Exports: The Defence Tribe and Business World Are Hauled Back], *Asahi Shimbun*, December 11, 2004, 4.

konnan).[38] They were cognizant that the relocation and integration of command functions of the U.S. Army and USAF would make overly explicit the functioning of U.S. bases in Japan for contingencies in the Middle East and beyond, and thus be seen to exceed the existing interpretations of the geographical and functional limits of the U.S.-Japan security treaty in East Asia. Japanese policymakers have long acknowledged that the United States has utilized its bases in Japan for the deployment of forces outside the scope of the Far East, as the Iraq war and the deployment of U.S. Marine Corps units from Okinawa clearly demonstrate. Japan has, however, officially maintained that these forces are first deployed out of Japan to an area in the Far East and then redeployed to the Middle East, thus meaning that they are not direct deployments under Article 6 of the security treaty.

Tokyo has been persuaded of the need to address in a more direct and comprehensive fashion the issue of U.S. force realignments, and to do so in a matter that strengthens the deterrent functions of the alliance whilst reducing the burden on the citizens of Okinawa.[39] This has come about for two main reasons: (1) recognition of the United States' clear intent to make these regional bases function for Washington's global security strategy and (2) concern about the domestic political damage inflicted by the renewed controversy over U.S. bases in Okinawa from late 2004 onwards. Meanwhile, the United States has come to some recognitions of its own. First, Washington may not have sufficiently consulted with Tokyo in the run-up to the GPR. Second, the United States has emphasized the exigencies of military operability over the political value of its force presence for the solidity of the alliance. Finally, the activation of the DPRI since late 2004 calls for a broader dialogue on the overall future functions of the alliance.

As of June 2005, Japan and the United States appear to have made significant progress on the principles of force realignments and the GPR. Japanese policymakers, while opposed to any security treaty revision for domestic political reasons, have shown a propensity to once again stretch the definitions of the security treaty in order to reconcile it with GPR expectations. By November 2004 Japan had formulated the basic position of being prepared to accept U.S. force dispositions with expanded "out-of-area" command functions as long as these could be demonstrated to in some way contribute to Japan's own security and the security of the Far East in line

---

[38] "Kyokuto Joko no Seiyaku Kanwa" [Loosening of Restrictions on the Far East Clause], *Asahi Shimbun*, November 12, 2004, 1.

[39] "Beigun Saihen: Yokushiryoku Iji shi Futankeigen" [U.S. Force Realignments: Maintaining Deterrence Power and Reducing Burdens], *Nihon Keizai Shimbun*, January 11, 2005, 2.

with Article 6 of the security treaty.[40] More specifically, Japanese policymakers pointed out that this basic position means that U.S. command centers and base usage cannot be countenanced in cases where they are judged, firstly, to have no relationship whatsoever to the Far East, and, secondly, where their activities outside of the Far East would deplete their ability to contribute to the security of this area.[41] By adopting this stance Japan has adhered to the letter of Article 6 and has retained a hedging option to place restrictions on U.S. activities; Japan has, however, also clearly moved the interpretational goalposts to enable the potential expansion of U.S.-Japan alliance cooperation. Consequently, in the final base realignments Japan will likely accept the relocation of U.S. Army I Corps function to Camp Zama. On the other hand, though, Japan has put forward a counterproposal regarding USAF command functions. Tokyo has requested that Washington essentially leave intact the 5th USAF Command at Yokota. Instead, Japan will move its ASDF command functions from Fuchu City to Yokota in order to establish a joint-use facility for the two countries. This request represents a success for Japan in that Tokyo has managed to limit U.S. redeployment of expanded command functions to Japan while maintaining the U.S. presence (with the USAF establishing an additional new War Fighting Headquarters in Hawaii). The joint use facility at Yokota is also an indication of strengthened bilateral cooperation in other ways, since Japan's intention is to promote the integration of ASDF and U.S. functions at Yokota for the purposes of BMD command and control.

Japan and the United States have found more contentious the issue of base realignments on Okinawa, and in particular the Futenma issue. Japan's official plan has been to relocate Futenma's functions to a new facility built on reclaimed land in the Henoko district, and the prefectural government and Nago City voted in 1999 to accept this plan. Japan's government has embarked on an environmental survey of the proposed site since September 2004, but progress on relocation has been halted by the prefectural government's insistence on limiting the usage of the air strip to fifteen years, a measure unacceptable to U.S. forces. In the meantime, a number of force realignment proposals have been passed back and forth between both sides since 2004. For example, in March 2005 a proposal was considered to redistribute Futenma's various functions. This would include moving both its tanker aircraft to the USMC Iwankuni base in Yamaguchi Prefecture on Honshu and its helicopter units to the USAF base at Kadena either to USMC

---

[40] Author's interview with Deputy Director-General, North American Affairs Bureau, Japan Ministry of Foreign Affairs, Tokyo, April 6, 2005.

[41] "Kyokuto Joko no Seiyaku Kanwa" [Loosening of Restrictions on the Far East Clause], *Asahi Shimbun*, November 12, 2004, 1.

Camps Hansen and Schwab or to ASDF facilities. MOFA has mainly persisted with its official line of relocation to Henoko, given that this proposal has city and prefectural approval, and given the potential opposition from other parts of Okinawa and the mainland to accepting the relocation of U.S. forces. As of June 2005, however, MOFA has been under pressure from the Prime Minister's Office to reconsider the Kadena option as a means to break the impasse over Futenma.[42] Given the misperceptions on both sides, Tokyo and Washington are likely to encounter continued difficulties over base realignments: the United States tends to stress military operability issues, whereas for Japan such issues are somewhat secondary to the issue of tackling domestic sentiment over basing burdens.

Japan's ability to reach an agreement over the Okinawa bases will be crucial for cementing the foundations of bilateral military cooperation, and for enabling Japan and the United States to push ahead with their future plans for security cooperation. This is evident from the Joint Statement of the Japan-U.S. Security Consultative Committee (SCC), or "2-Plus-2" meeting, on February 19, 2005.[43] The SCC statement drew considerable media attention due to its perceived focus upon China and identification of Taiwan as a "common strategic objective" for the alliance. The SCC statement is certainly significant in stressing the strengthened functions of the alliance for regional security, and represents a slightly more forthcoming statement than the revised guidelines concerning Taiwan's position as an object of alliance cooperation. The SSC statement has arguably been more significant, however, in indicating the intentions of U.S. and Japanese policymakers to use the latest cycle of alliance planning in order to upgrade cooperation for regional and global security objectives. The SCC statement gave equal prominence to "global common strategic objectives," including dealing with terrorism, limiting WMD, and bilateral cooperation in Afghanistan and Iraq. The statement also praised the revised NDPG and Japan's moves to respond to new threats, and stressed the need for greater U.S.-Japan military interoperability to deal with a variety of contingencies. The SCC statement's stress on countering threats, such as terrorism, that do not respect regional demarcations is a clear sign that Japan and the United States are creating greater leeway for the stretching of security treaty interpretations and for allowing the U.S.-Japan alliance to function in an increasingly global manner.

Japan and the United States are expected to follow the February SCC statement with another statement in mid to late 2005 that will move beyond

---

[42] "Kadena-osa e no Togo Kento" [Investigation of Integration Inside Kadena], *Sankei Shimbun*, April 13, 2005, 1.

[43] "Joint Statement U.S.-Japan Security Consultative Committee," Washington D.C., February 19, 2005, http://www.mofa.go.jp/region/n-america/us/security/scc/joint0502.html.

stressing the broadened principles of alliance cooperation to actually outlining specific military divisions of labor both regionally and globally. In
particular, Washington is prodding Tokyo to specify not only the types of
logistical support that Japan will provide in contingencies, but also to name
the actual airstrips, harbors, and civilian facilities and to draw up detailed
plans for their usage. This may then be followed by a new Japan-U.S. Joint
Declaration on Security that will supersede that of 1996 by emphasizing a
shift toward strengthened regional and global alliance functions. In order
to facilitate greater military cooperation for global contingencies, Japan and
the United States may move in late 2005 and early 2006 to once more revise
the Defense Guidelines. Due, however, to the domestic political difficulties
involved in revision and a desire to avoid any repeat of the protracted Diet
debates of the first revision, Japanese policymakers may seek only partial
revision—instead of a wholesale overhaul—on key areas such as logistical
support and BMD.[44]

Ballistic Missile Defense

Japan's engagement with BMD is potentially the most significant step
in forcing the pace of Tokyo's military modernization plans and strengthening the U.S.-Japan alliance. Japan decided in December 2003 to purchase an
off-the-shelf PAC-III and the Navy Theatre Wide Defense (NTWD) (in current U.S. terminology the Sea-Base Midcourse System [SMD] and Terminal
Defense Segment [TDS], respectively). This, along with continued joint research with the United States into NTWD interceptor missile technologies,
makes Japan the first U.S. security treaty partner to actively sign on to missile defense programs. Japan plans to deploy its first BMD capabilities on an
MSDF AWS-equipped destroyer by 2007, and on all six of its destroyers by
2011. The upgraded interceptor missiles for a PAC-III system are slated for
acquisition by 2007. The JDA estimates the total cost of deployment at $4.6
billion, and in June 2005 the United States was reported to have requested
that Japan invest $545 million in joint research on interceptor missile tech-
nologies.[45]

In order to operate the BMD system, Japan has already begun to implement a range of adjustments to its military doctrines and capabilities.
In February 2005 the government submitted to the Diet a bill for revisions

[44] Author's interview with Deputy Director-General, North American Affairs Bureau, Japan Ministry
of Foreign Affairs, Tokyo, April 6, 2005.

[45] "U.S. Asks Japan for $545 Million for Missile Defense Report," *DefenseNews.com*, http://www.
defensenews.com/story.php?F=925972&C=asiapac; International Institute for Strategic Studies,
"Japan's Push for Missile Defence: Benefits, Costs and Prospects," *IISS Strategic Comments* 9, no. 8
(October 2003); 1.

to the SDF Law that enables the Director General of the JDA to mobilize the JSDF to launch BMD interceptors against incoming missiles only with the approval of the Prime Minister (rather than in consultation with the Cabinet's National Security Council as mandated under the present law). In other situations, when there is no time to consult even with the Prime Minister, the Director General is entitled to mobilize JSDF interceptor launches in accordance with pre-planned scenarios.[46] The revised SDF Law is a necessary recognition that BMD systems can work only on the basis of short reaction times and by devolving control to military planners and commanders. For Japan this law constitutes a radical step toward reducing the strength of Cabinet-level civilian control over the JSDF in the postwar period.

Japan's BMD system may also necessitate the greater integration of Japanese and U.S. military forces and strategy. To operate BMD effectively, Japan will need to rely on U.S. infrared early warning satellite information, and to link for the first time JSDF command and control systems with those of the United States. Tokyo may be hoping to slightly lessen this dependency by developing—in cooperation with the United States—Infrared Search and Tracking (IRST) early warning sensors mounted on P-3Cs, a system that could undergo testing in September 2005.[47] Japanese dependency will be further reinforced by the fact that it is reliant on U.S. black-boxed technology for its first off-the-shelf systems. In seeking to deploy BMD in a time-frame similar to the United States, Tokyo made the decision to purchase its first BMD systems from the United States under the Foreign Military Sales (FMS) program without first negotiating a licensed production agreement. Japan now faces a uphill battle to secure any production rights for Japanese defense contractors—although in July 2005 Mitsubishi Heavy Industries may at least have achieved licensed production from Lockheed-Martin for the PAC-III.[48]

In acquiring a weapons system dependent on active U.S. cooperation to function properly, Japan will thus have to gear its entire strategic orientation even further to accommodate the United States.[49] Japan's declared intention

---

[46] Boeicho [JDA], *Boeicho Secchiho nado no Ichibu o Kaisei Suru Horitsuan Kankei Shiryo* [Documentation Relating to the Bill for the Partial Revision of the Defence Agency Establishment Law] (Tokyo: Boeicho, 2005), 11–13.

[47] Kawakami Takashi and Jimbo Ken, "Dando Misairu Boei to Nichibei Domei" [BMD and the U.S. Japan Alliance], in *Misairu Boei: Atarashii Kokusasi Anzen Hosho no Kozu*, ed. Morimoto Satoshi (Tokyo: JIIA, 2002), 278–79.

[48] "MD no Shogeki: Yunyu ni Konwaku Boei Sangyo" [Missile Defense Shock: Defense Contractors at a Loss over Imports], *Asahi Shimbun*, November 15, 2004, 1; and "Raisensu Seisan" [Licensed Production], *Asahi Shimbun*, July 20, 2005, 4.

[49] Matusmura Masahiro, *Nichibei Domei to Gunji Gijutsu* (Tokyo: Keiso Shobo, 1999), 135-48.

is to operate a BMD system on the basis of "independent judgment."[50] The U.S. expectation is, however, that Japan will deploy the system to defend U.S. bases in Japan in the event of a regional contingency (such as Taiwan). This plan will necessitate closer tactical planning between the JSDF and U.S. forces. In addition, Japan may in the future face pressure from the United States to deploy Japan's highly mobile and interoperable BMD assets in support of U.S. forces; whether this assistance was required in East Asia or in other regions, such requests would be in line with the new purport of alliance planning for global contingencies. Finally, BMD may also challenge Japan's non-exercise of collective self-defense given that these systems demand the freer, and possibly two-way, flow of military information between U.S. and Japanese command and control systems. Such communication is largely prohibited by current Japanese interpretations of collective self-defense.[51] If BMD obliges Japan to breach its prohibition on collective self-defense, more radical bilateral military cooperation may then occur in other alliance contexts—including combat support for the United States in a range of theaters falling outside the scope of the existing security treaty (such as the Middle East).

Implications for Regional and Global Security

Japan's military modernization has taken the form of enhanced JSDF interoperability and power projection capabilities, and has been planned in tandem with the strengthening of the U.S.-Japan alliance in order to deal with regional and global security issues. This modernization is allowing Tokyo to assume a more proactive and "normal" security role in the post-Cold War, and especially post September 11, world.

Japan's growing capabilities to undertake an expanded military role, and to do so alongside the United States (as showcased in the Asian tsunami), have important ramifications for security in East Asia, including the U.S. presence in the region. It is now possible to envisage the emergence of a more interoperable U.S.-Japan alliance, encompassing even stronger mutually reinforcing "sword" and "shield" functions, one that works to perpetuate U.S. military dominance across East Asia. Japan's continued strengths in anti-submarine warfare and minesweeping are represented by MSDF destroyer, minesweeping, and P-3C/P-X forces, all of which give Tokyo the ca-

---

[50] "Statement by the Chief Cabinet Secretary: Introduction of Ballistic Missile Defense System and Other Measures," December 19, 2003, http://www.kantei.go.jp/foreign/tyokan/2003/1219danwa_e.html.

[51] Hughes, *Japan's Re-emergence*, 112–14; and Morimoto Satoshi, "BMD to Nihon no Boeiei Seisaku" [BMD and Japan's Security Policy], in *Misairu Boei*, 308–9.

pability to dominate—through the ASDF's F-2 and in-flight refueling—the airspace around Japan and beyond. These capabilities should enable Tokyo to provide an effective defensive shield against any potential adversary, while at the same time enabling the United States to concentrate on projecting offensive power should a regional contingency arise.

Japan's improved military capabilities and the strengthened U.S.-Japan alliance will certainly assist U.S. efforts in the short term to deter China in a conflict involving Taiwan. At the very least, Japan possesses the legal frameworks and operational experience necessary to provide logistical support for the United States, the capabilities to prevent Chinese air and amphibious forces from assaulting Japanese territory, and, in the not-too-distant future, the capability to defend U.S. bases in Japan from Chinese missile attacks. Expanding U.S.-Japan alliance ties may, however, exacerbate Sino-U.S. and Sino-Japanese tensions and increase Japan's fear of entrapment in U.S. strategy toward China.

A strengthened U.S.-Japan alliance will also deter North Korea and reassure Japan about U.S. security guarantees in the event that the North demonstrates nuclear weapons capability. Most importantly, if the United States remains intent on containing or rolling back Pyongyang's nuclear program, Tokyo will have no need to discuss independent acquisition of a nuclear deterrent. Japan will, however, remain apprehensive concerning the possibility that the United States might harness the strengthened alliance as a means to exert pressure on North Korea without the prospect of dialogue—and thereby drag Japan into a possible confrontation with North Korea.

Meanwhile, Japan's strengthened power projection capabilities and alliance with the United States should also provide Tokyo with the confidence to engage other security partners in the region. Japan will probably continue to expand cooperation with South Korea in areas such as maritime safety and diplomatic cooperation toward North Korea. Nonetheless, as demonstrated by tensions between Japan and South Korea over the disputed Takeshima Islands, there remain clear limits to the extent of military cooperation between these two U.S. allies. Japan may instead show more military activism in Southeast Asia in combating piracy. Tokyo has attempted to launch a number of important anti-piracy initiatives via the ASEAN+3 process, and the Japan Coast Guard (JCG) has, since 2001, embarked on bilateral exercises and patrols with Singapore, the Philippines, Thailand, Malaysia, Indonesia, and Brunei. In a move that would seem to hint at an MSDF role in anti-piracy, former JDA Director General Ishiba Shigeru floated the idea in 2005 of Ocean Peacekeeping Operations. Indeed, many ASEAN states are receptive to enhanced Japanese naval cooperation as a means to counterbalance China's growing presence.[52]

Most intriguing of all, though, are the implications of Japan's changing military capabilities and the objectives of alliance cooperation for global security. Japan has already shown a degree of willingness to stretch alliance cooperation in humanitarian and non-combat logistical and reconstruction missions as far as the Indian Ocean and the Middle East. Japan's growing capabilities in amphibious and air-lift operations, deployment of rapid-reaction style forces, and mobile BMD systems (represented by its *Osumi*-class transports, DDH-class, AWS-equipped destroyers, and C-1/C-X transports) make Japan a potentially ideal partner to provide logistical and defensive support for U.S. war-fighting operations in the Indian Ocean and the Middle East. The JSDF has in fact already gained some valuable experience in operating with the United States and other states in a multinational environment through the establishment of a coordinating liaison headquarters alongside that of the United States at the Thai military base of U-Tapao.

Exactly how far Japan is willing to go in projecting power to the Middle East in support of the United States has yet to be tested. The revised NDPG's emphasis on security interests that correspond with those of the United States in the "arc of instability" is, however, one indication that Japan is contemplating an expanded security role covering the Middle East. Furthermore, Japan is not only showing a preparedness to stretch the geographical and functional scope of its military role in support of the United States, but is also beginning to work more closely within U.S.-led multinational coalitions for global contingencies. In supporting the Afghan campaign, Japan has worked to refuel coalition ships from the United Kingdom, Germany, France, Italy, and Australia, and has used amphibious capabilities to transport Thai army equipment to the Indian Ocean. JSDF officers have been stationed at U.S. Central Command at Tampa, Florida since 2001, and the JSDF in Iraq has accepted military protection from Dutch forces, and (as of mid-2005) from UK and Australian forces.[53] In October 2004, the JCG—with support from MSDF aircraft—also hosted a Proliferation Security Initiative interdiction exercise in Sagami Bay, south of Tokyo.[54] Thus Japan now appears to be an ally with greater interoperable capabilities and experience

---

[52] Minister of State for Defense Shigeru Ishiba, speech, IISS Asia Security Conference Singapore, June 5, 2004, http://www.iiss.org/newsite/shangri-la-speeches.php?itemID=36.

[53] "Kiro no Saizensen Jieitai 50nen: Yushi Rengo Mura" [The Crossroads Frontline, The JSDF's Fiftieth Year: Coalitions of the Willing Village], *Asahi Shimbun*, March 24, 2004, 1; and Purnendra Jain and John Bruni, "Japan, Australia and the United States: Little NATO or Shadow Alliance" *International Relations of the Asia-Pacific* 4, no. 2 (2004): 278–81.

[54] "PSI Godo Kunren, Nihon Tate ni" [PSI Combined Drill, Two Pillared], *Asahi Shimbun*, October 11, 2004, 2.

intent on supporting U.S. "coalitions of the willing." Such observations reinforce the impression that the U.S.-Japan alliance is indeed moving toward becoming a global alliance that provides not only bases but also boots on the ground.

There are, however, some major limitations and obstacles confronting Japan's military normalization and the continued strengthening of the U.S.-Japan alliance. Japan is not pursuing unconditional expanded alliance cooperation with the United States, and Tokyo clearly maintains concerns about abandonment and entrapment. In order to hedge against dependency on the alliance, Japan will continue to foster a certain degree of defense autonomy. Japanese policymakers will, for instance, continue to maintain indigenous defense production capabilities in order to avoid the risks of being left defenseless in the event of a breakdown of the alliance.[55] Japan will, however, find the maintenance of such indigenous capacities to be difficult, particularly in light of Tokyo's decision to buy off-the-shelf BMD technologies from the United States. Japan will also be reluctant to break the ban on collective self-defense. The LDP may be increasingly in favor of such a move, though MOFA—as can be seen from the cases of the ATSML and Iraq Reconstruction Law—is fighting a stubborn rearguard action to sustain constitutional divisions between different contexts of alliance cooperation so as to prevent entrapment and preserve anti-militaristic principles. Japanese policymakers might even be able to find a way to circumvent the problems that BMD poses for collective self-defense. Their argument is that because BMD is a purely defensive system the use of BMD is akin to raising a shield to deflect a blow, and that the use of such systems does not actually constitute a use of force in violation of constitutional interpretations.

Despite the ingenuity of Japanese policymakers, pressure is clearly growing from the United States and from within domestic political circles to breach the ban. For example, Richard Armitage, then Deputy Secretary of State, attempted in July 2004 to link Japan's interest in a UN Security Council seat with Tokyo's exercise of the right to collective self-defense.[56] Moreover, the degree to which the United States and Japan can resolve GPR, Okinawa, and other base-related issues will be crucial for the future of alliance cooperation. Futenma's relocation is a nagging and debilitating political thorn in the side of the alliance, and the resolution of this sensitive issue is crucial. Japan's list of the particular bases and facilities that it would be willing to

---

[55] Richard J. Samuels, *Rich Nation, Strong Army: National Security and the Transformation of Japan* (Cornell: Cornell University Press, 1994), 31.

[56] Although under political pressure he was later forced to retract these remarks. See "Armitage Now Has No Problem With Article 9: Okada," *Japan Times Online*, July 31, 2004, http://www.japantimes.co.jp/cgi-bin/getarticle.pl5?nn20040731a7.htm.

provide to the United States in any revision of the Defense Guidelines is also likely to be a lengthy process that will frustrate U.S. policymakers looking for quicker responses.[57] Finally, as part of base burden reduction, Japan is looking for further decreases in the Host Nation Support (HNS) budget that currently covers close to 100 percent of the costs of U.S. facilities in Japan.[58] The bilateral Special Measures Agreement will expire in 2006, and in any new agreement Japan will seek to continue annual cuts of around 1 percent in utility costs.[59]

U.S.-Japan alliance ties will also face tests over major regional and global strategic questions. Tokyo prefers that Washington work with Beijing to maintain the status quo over Taiwan, and U.S. policymakers should not take for granted that Japan—despite the 2-Plus-2 statement of February 2005— will support the United States militarily over Taiwan in anything other than the most extreme instances of Chinese aggression. Japan will continue to support the United States in Iraq, though Tokyo is now looking to withdraw the JSDF non-combat mission by December 2005. U.S.-Japan relations will, however, remain discordant over Iran. Tokyo continues to urge Tehran to halt its nuclear program, but Japan's oil interests in the Azadegan oil field mean that Tokyo is unlikely to support Washington in any attempt to militarily coerce Iran.[60]

Finally, U.S.-Japan alliance relations may experience difficulties over Japan's new and assertive push since late 2004 for a permanent seat on the UN Security Council (UNSC). Tokyo expects reciprocal and active U.S. support for its bid. The United States has indicated officially that it supports a permanent UNSC seat for Japan, and as of mid-2005 Japan even seems willing to drop its initial demands for veto rights in order to accord with the United States' preferred plans for UNSC reform. If the United States does not appear to actively campaign on Japan's part in UNSC negotiations and

---

[57] The February 2+2 statement indicating that a plan for realigning specific facilities could be produced within a matter of months, and the United States had hoped to conclude the plan by June 2005. Japan is now indicating, however, that it would only be ready for a mid-term general review report by July 2005 at the earliest due to its need to consult with local authorities about base realignments. For more, see "Beigun Saihen: Seifu, Jimoto e Itsu Dachin" [U.S. Military Realignments: Government and Local Authorities, When to Break the Deadlock], *Asahi Shimbun*, July 20, 2005, 4.

[58] This figure does not include the salaries of U.S. personnel. See Maeda Tetsuo, *Zainichi Beigun Kichi no Shushi Kessan* [The Balance Sheet for U.S. Bases in Japan] (Tokyo: Chikuma Shinsho, 2000), 162–65.

[59] MOF is, however, eager both for further cuts and to reduce the standard five-year time period of the agreement in order to review costs more frequently. "Japan Aims to Shorten Pact for Sharing U.S. Military Costs," *Japan Times Online*, May 3, 2005, http://www.japantimes.co.jp/cgi-bin/makeprfy.pl5?20050512f3.htm.

[60] Eric Heginbotham and Richard J. Samuels, "Japan," in *Strategic Asia 2002–03: Asian Aftershocks*, ed. Richard J. Ellings and Aaron L. Friedberg (Seattle: The National Bureau of Asian Research, 2004), 118–19.

passively allows China to veto Japan's entry, then this will raise perceptions of U.S. perfidiousness in Japanese eyes. If, on the other hand, Japan were to secure a seat on the UN Security Council, then Japan might be inclined to place its JSDF assets increasingly at the disposal of UN-led PKOs in areas such as Darfur in the Sudan, rather than the current trend of JSDF coopera- tion with U.S.-led coalitions (and subsequently weaker UN legitimization). In this instance, the extent of U.S.-Japan alliance cooperation outside the range of the security treaty in East Asia, and the rationale for the future so- lidity of the alliance in general, might be more questionable.

Based on deep-rooted current trends, however, Japan is likely to contin- ue on the path of tighter and expanded alliance cooperation with the United States. Japan's UNSC-centered security option at present seems unlikely to succeed, and looming regional concerns about North Korea and China, in tandem with the recognition of terrorism and WMD as global concerns, will continue to push Japan and the United States closer together. Japan's policymakers will largely be committed to this trend, even as they attempt, like all "normal" U.S. allies, to control the pace of these trends and to avoid unnecessary scenarios of entrapment. Japan's modernization of its security policy, military doctrines, and JSDF capabilities will only serve to reinforce the range of possibilities for bilateral alliance cooperation. In all likelihood, though, the international strategic environment and military-technological demands of the alliance mean that the odds are stacked against Japan re- taining sufficient room to hedge against or significantly influence U.S. secu- rity behavior. Japanese policymakers will thus be obliged not only to create more potential avenues for cooperation with the United States, but also to increasingly exercise such options by responding to regional and global con- tingencies. In turn, Japan's re-emergence as a more normal military power will also raise questions for the overall balance of its comprehensive security policy. The shift toward an emphasis on military alliance cooperation with the United States may impose important opportunity costs on Japan's ability to pursue non-military approaches to a security—including human secu- rity—agenda.

Executive Summary

This chapter assesses the main factors that will shape the security strategies and defense capabilities of North and South Korea in the next five years, particularly the potential for major shifts in the military confrontation between the two.

MAIN ARGUMENT:
Due to changing strategic priorities, the ground force standoff that has long dominated peninsular security will decline in relevance over the next five years. In order to compensate for North Korea's economic vulnerabilities, Pyongyang will increasingly focus on deterrence and longer-range strike capabilities. Seoul will pursue deterrence and defense capabilities even as it moves toward political accommodation with Pyongyang and develops a more regionally oriented defense policy.

POLICY IMPLICATIONS:
- Policies toward North Korea should not be premised on the expectation of regime collapse, even if this possibility cannot be precluded.

- Pyongyang is shifting to a more asymmetric military strategy in an attempt to enhance North Korea's economic power while simultaneously favoring the defense sector. This shift will greatly complicate efforts to constrain or dismantle North Korea's strategic capabilities in exchange for security assurances and economic assistance extended to Pyongyang.

- South Korea is seeking to develop capabilities that will diminish potential vulnerabilities to North Korean attack, but without automatically assuming adversarial relations with the North. Seoul will be increasingly unwilling, however, to undertake major long-term defense investments based on a predominantly threat-based military strategy.

- Both Koreas are seeking to increase their political-military autonomy from external powers. Meaningful threat reduction is indispensable for non-adversarial relations between North and South, but Seoul may settle for far less. This could pose acute risks to the U.S.-ROK alliance in future years.

The Strategic Futures and Military Capabilities of the Two Koreas

Jonathan D. Pollack

This chapter compares the security strategies and military capabilities of North and South Korea, and in particular explores the potential for change in the peninsular and in the regional balance during the next five years. The two sides are attempting to develop increased military lethality and reach, and thereby diminish their long-standing reliance on manpower-dominated approaches. Despite the fact that newly emergent military capabilities would better enable Seoul to prosecute a threat-based strategy toward North Korea, there are signs that the Republic of Korea (ROK) is moving away from such a strategy. The Democratic People's Republic of Korea (DPRK) continues to deem its military capabilities essential to the longer-term viability of the North Korean system, but Pyongyang also recognizes that the budgetary, manpower, and industrial claims of its armed forces relative to the economy as a whole exceed those of any other state in the world. The DPRK experienced acute economic privation and industrial decline during the 1990s, which led to major reductions in defense industrial production. Pyongyang's ability to acquire higher-end weapons systems from abroad has also diminished greatly.

To compensate for its diminishing conventional capabilities, North Korea is pursuing an asymmetric strategy aimed at enhancing its ability to strike civilian and military targets at longer range, focusing particular attention on self-propelled artillery, multiple rocket launchers, and—most

Jonathan D. Pollack is Professor of Asian and Pacific Studies at the Naval War College. His research focuses on East Asian security, politics, and military development, with particular attention to China, the Korean Peninsula, and U.S. foreign policy and defense strategy. He can be reached at <jonathan.pollack@nwc.navy.mil>.

The judgments in this paper are the author's own, and should not be attributed to the Naval War College, the Department of Defense, or the U.S. government.

importantly—ballistic missiles. North Korea is also relying more on its special forces, which can be introduced into combat zones by stealthier means. Asymmetric capabilities enable the DPRK to reach beyond its borders without necessitating large-scale movement of military personnel and equipment that would impose acute burdens on the North Korean economy. The missile program is one of the major achievements of the North Korean military's R&D sector. North Korea also claims to possess an unspecified number of nuclear weapons, though the size of this inventory and Pyongyang's delivery capabilities both remain highly uncertain. The DPRK views missile and nuclear capabilities not only as integral to regime security and survival, but also as the chief source of its negotiating leverage. Missile sales have also proved to be a lucrative export for North Korea. Only a profound internal political realignment and outside promises of extensive economic and security compensation would convince Pyongyang to relinquish these assets. Under prevailing circumstances, such prospects remain highly unlikely.

The ROK is likewise confronting major choices and dilemmas in its security strategy. Three factors are shaping South Korea's emergent security calculus: major changes in U.S. military strategy, Seoul's desire for increased autonomy within the U.S.-ROK alliance, and the ROK's political accommodation with the DPRK. By the end of 2008, approximately 12,500 U.S. military personnel will have been withdrawn from the ROK; South Korean forces are thus expected to fulfill roles previously assumed by the U.S. military. U.S. defense strategy will rely increasingly on the ability to project power quickly in a major crisis rather than maintain fully manned units on the peninsula. These shifts underscore the ROK's enhanced role in peninsular deterrence and defense. In political terms, the ROK is pursuing a strategy of reassurance and conflict reduction toward the North that will differentiate Seoul's defense policies from those long favored by U.S. security planners. In military terms, however, South Korea is developing more potent assets that could be directed against North Korea should the DPRK initiate major hostilities against the ROK.

South Korean defense planners have also put forward highly ambitious goals for military modernization that posit the development of a more regionally oriented force. These objectives are, however, unlikely to be fulfilled in accordance with the mid-term defense plan for 2005–09. ROK security planners envision a high-technology force more balanced across the service branches, thereby diminishing the long-standing dominance of the ground forces. Seoul is also seeking to enhance the ROK's capabilities in areas previously overseen by U.S. forces, most notably surveillance, reconnaissance, and early warning. Such a transformation depends, however, upon optimistic projections of future economic growth as well as heightened domestic priority for national defense. Moreover, even as North Korea's capacity to strike targets in South Korea continues to grow, South Korea's political leadership seems intent on threat reduction, military confidence-building, and increased economic ties with the DPRK. Despite Pyongyang's claim in February 2005 that North Korea possesses an unspecified number of nuclear weapons, the ROK's revised strategic judgment has not shifted. Senior South Korean defense officials assert the need for a "cooperative self-reliant defense posture," but remain elliptical about the focus of security planning should peninsular integration intensify or military tensions escalate.

Officially, both Seoul and Pyongyang no longer deem the other its main adversary. Pyongyang asserts that deterrence and retaliation against a prospective U.S. unilateral attack constitutes the DPRK's primary security pre occupation, which in turn necessitates both a nuclear deterrent and missile capability. Any military response undertaken by North Korea would, however, focus heavily on targets in the ROK—irrespective of whether Seoul was deemed responsible for the initiation of hostilities. Because Pyongyang is unlikely to consent to formally negotiated reductions in military strength, substantial amounts of aged, possibly non-operable equipment languish in the DPRK inventory. Over time, this will likely reinforce North Korea's increased emphasis on deterrence and on long-range strike capabilities. Relevant questions for the future are thus threefold: (1) whether political changes in inter-Korean relations will render the degraded legacy forces largely irrelevant, (2) the rate at which longer-range, more lethal capabilities are introduced into the inventories of North and South, and (3) how these first two developments refashion U.S. security requirements in Northeast Asia. Even as the United States remains deeply involved in peninsular defense planning, however, longer-term trends suggest a more offshore U.S. role, with the respective capabilities and political-military orientations of the two Koreas increasingly defining peninsular security.

This paper is divided into four main sections. The first section explores the security orientations of the two Koreas. The second examines the primary political and strategic uncertainties confronting the ROK and the DPRK. The third section assesses the options, tradeoffs, and implications of defense modernization in both states. The fourth section weighs the potential policy consequences of the future strategies and capabilities of North and South Korea.

The Strategic Directions of the Two Koreas

The military confrontation between the two Koreas represents the longest-running drama of the Cold War and, along with the division of China and Taiwan, the most acute potential crisis in East Asian international politics. In the final week of June 1950, two events fixed the strategic geography of Northeast Asia: North Korea's invasion of South Korea, and the resulting decision of the United States both to intervene on behalf of the ROK and to forestall the impending assault on Taiwan by Chinese forces. The historical demarcations that resulted from these events remain intact today.

The separation of the two Koreas, however, has proven more pervasive and enduring than the conflict between China and Taiwan. Economic and social contacts across the Taiwan Strait have surged even in the midst of heightened political and military tensions, but the military legacy of the Korean confrontation remains almost entirely undisturbed. Unlike East and West Germany, which experienced nearly two decades of quasi-normal relations prior to unification, the two Koreas continue to inhabit separate worlds. Interactions between the two governments remain uneven but are increasing, and senior South Korean officials express growing optimism over the possibility of greater strategic understanding between the two leaderships.[1] Military-to-military contacts have also increased significantly in recent years.[2] Inter-Korean ties remain weighted disproportionately in Pyongyang's favor, however, with the DPRK receiving ample political and economic compensation from the ROK without any equivalent reciprocity to the South. Even as the ROK has attempted to reduce military tensions and proffer increased economic assistance to the North, the DPRK has greatly enhanced its *songun* ("military first") ideology, which emphasizes the central role of the Korean People's Army (KPA) in sustaining the regime.[3] Pyongyang's renewed pursuit of a nuclear weapons capability also reflects the military's predominance within the North Korean system. This pursuit culminated in Pyongyang's February 2005 claim to possess an unspecified number of nuclear weapons.[4]

---

[1] Ministry of Unification, *Peace and Prosperity—White Paper on Korean Unification 2005* (Seoul: Ministry of Unification, 2005).

[2] For a chronology of inter-Korean military talks during 2000–04, consult Ministry of National Defense, *Defense White Paper—2004* (Seoul: Ministry of National Defense, 2005), 297–99.

[3] For a discerning review of the development of this concept and of Kim Jong Il's close identification with it, consult Byung Chul Koh, "'Military First Politics' and Building A 'Powerful and Prosperous Nation' in North Korea," Northeast Asia Peace and Security Network, April 14, 2005.

[4] For the official announcement claiming to have manufactured an unspecified number of nuclear weapons, see DPRK Ministry of Foreign Affairs, Korean Central Broadcasting System, statement, Pyongyang, February 10, 2005.

The military forces on the Korean Peninsula constitute the largest concentration of conventional capabilities anywhere in the world, and thus the peninsula is arguably the most dangerous flashpoint in global politics. The International Institute for Strategic Studies (IISS) has graphically captured the reality of the deployments proximate to Korea's demilitarized zone (DMZ):

> The DMZ is approximately 4 km wide and 250 km long ... More than one million troops and 20,000 armoured vehicles and artillery pieces—plus more than one million landmines and numerous fortified positions—are packed into a small area surrounding the DMZ. Furthermore, there is little "strategic depth" between the DMZ and the capital cities of Pyongyang (about 125 km north of the DMZ) and Seoul (approximately 40 km south of the DMZ). As a comparison, forces on either side of the DMZ are more densely concentrated than were those of the Warsaw Pact and the North Atlantic Treaty Organization in Central Europe during the Cold War.[5]

The ROK political leadership believes that engagement and reconciliation with Pyongyang offers the most cost-effective means for avoiding armed conflict or acute instability. However, DPRK military strategy and forces remain pervasively threat driven, with the United States (not the ROK) viewed as the primary threat. DPRK military doctrine (dating mostly from earlier decades) emphasizes blitzkrieg warfare and surprise attack; even if U.S. forces deployed in the ROK were a principal target, the actual hostilities would be heavily concentrated on the southern half of the peninsula. Some recent North Korean documents suggest heightened attention to war mobilization across various stages of potential conflict, based on the premise that North Korea would be attacked first.[6] Pyongyang asserts that its nuclear and missile programs are designed for deterrence and retaliation against a possible U.S. preemptive or preventive strike, and argues that the United States must offer explicit security assurances before North Korea would forego its strategic programs. The DPRK deems nuclear capabilities essential to its autonomy and national security, as well as a potential source of negotiating leverage.

By contrast, the ROK has advocated a more robust, diversified defense capability that (somewhat paradoxically) is devoid of a principal enemy (or of any enemy at all). Formal pronouncements by both states do not necessarily represent irreducible security perceptions, but they can serve as

---

[5] International Institute for Strategic Studies (IISS), *North Korea's Weapons Programmes—A Net Assessment* (London: International Institute for Strategic Studies, January 2004), 85.

[6] For a distillation of these wartime plans based on several confidential documents, see "Classified Document on Kim Jong Il's Wartime Guidelines Obtained," *Seoul Kyonghyang Sinmun*, January 5, 2004. The documents, purportedly issued directly by Kim Jong Il, date from April 2003, a month after the United States launched the invasion of Iraq.

baselines for assessing the feasibility and consequences of different national strategies.

Despite the protracted impasse over North Korea's nuclear weapons capabilities, political dynamics on the Korean Peninsula are in the throes of major change. Three factors highlight the possibilities for significant change: (1) the sustainability of the half-century military rivalry between North and South Korea, (2) shifting estimates of external threat in both Koreas, and (3) the ROK's pursuit of accommodation with the DPRK. Because the ROK leadership is intent on removing many of the ideological and institutional vestiges of military rule, major departures in South Korea's internal politics are also key factors in ROK calculations. It is therefore imperative to assess how the two Koreas conceptualize their strategic futures, the assumptions on which these judgments are based, and the prospects of either North or South Korea achieving its security goals.

The DPRK's Policy Options

North Korea is among a handful of surviving Stalinist systems, characterized by pervasive government control over the polity and economy. Pyongyang has long justified central planning and economic growth with the precepts of *juche*, a doctrine nominally premised on self-sufficiency, including (but not limited to) military self-sufficiency. This ideology, however—including the mythology surrounding it—obscures the DPRK's enduring dependence on external benefactors for aid, technology, and security. The end of the Cold War was a crucial turning point for North Korea. The loss of major Soviet subsidies combined with China's insistence, since the early 1990s, that payments for oil and food be tendered in hard currency sent North Korea's economy (in particular the industrial economy) into a precipitous decline.[7] Widespread crop failures and a resultant famine exacerbated these problems and led to the collapse of the central distribution system in the early and mid-1990s. Some modest stabilization and recovery has occurred since 1999, but the deeper systemic crisis persists.[8] In domestic propaganda, North Korea heralds itself an exemplar of economic devel-

---

[7] International Crisis Group, "North Korea: Can the Iron Fist Accept the Invisible Hand?" Asia Report, no. 96, April 25, 2005, 3–4. China has in recent years, however, selectively resumed direct grant aid to the North.

[8] For North Korea's GDP trends between 1990–2003, consult the National Accounts Aggregate Data Base of the United Nations Statistics Division. This data indicates a drop from 36.458 billion won in 1990 to 11.17 billion won in 1995, with GDP in the range of 22–24 billion won ever since. Data released by the Bank of Korea based on a somewhat different measure (gross national income, or GNI) suggest no acute drop in economic performance until 1997, when GNI declined from 21.4 billion won to 17.7 billion won, to a low point of 12.6 billion won in 1998, with GNI in 2003 reaching 18.4 billion won. Consult **Table 2**.

opment; whether the DPRK can achieve a modicum of economic recovery without undermining political control, however, remains to be seen.

Having long rejected major trade relations with the capitalist world, the DPRK remains almost entirely isolated from prevailing trends in the global economy (though Pyongyang contends that it now seeks such ties). In view of the profound decline of the North Korean system, it is very difficult to imagine a significant near- to mid-term economic transformation. Though Pyongyang occasionally publicizes selective changes, these do not portend a comprehensive shift in external economic relations. North Korea's foreign trade has, however, increased appreciably since the late 1990s and now encompasses growing imports from China, South Korea's involvement in industrial projects in North Korea, and earnings from tourist activities.[9] Large-scale food aid and energy assistance has helped compensate for acute shortfalls in domestic production.[10] The DPRK also engages in illicit economic activities that generate substantial foreign exchange earnings, much of which is channeled into North Korea's defense budget.[11] Increased encouragement of private commerce—especially in consumer goods and foodstuffs—is beginning to supplement the broken central distribution system, and some observers believe that market-based activity will increasingly dominate the internal economy. But Pyongyang continues to exhibit a profound wariness toward the outside world. The North Korean leadership fears that opening the sluice gates to external influence would undermine its grip on power as well as diminish the regime's control over the activities of foreign entities and non-governmental organizations operating within the country.

The abiding strategic concern of the North Korean leadership is regime survival, which is defined as the maintenance of power in the hands of Kim

---

[9] According to the Korea Trade-Investment Promotion Agency (KOTRA), North Korea's foreign trade in 2004 reached $3.55 billion, its highest level since 1991. Two-way trade with China (the DPRK's largest trading partner) reached $1.38 billion, a year-to-year increase of nearly 40 percent. South Korea was the North's second leading trading partner, with two-way trade of $697 million. See Sohn Suk-joo, "North Korea's Foreign Trade Volume Increases," *Vantage Point*, June 2005, 12.

[10] Mark E. Manyin, "U.S. Assistance to North Korea," Congressional Research Service, RL31785, April 26, 2005. The study also reviews the contributions of other countries and non-governmental organizations.

[11] Raphael F. Perl, "Drug Trafficking and North Korea: Issues for U.S. Policy," Congressional Research Service, RL32167, December 3, 2003; and Michael Horowitz, "Who's Behind That Curtain? Unveiling Potential Leverage over Pyongyang," *Washington Quarterly* 28, no. 1 (Winter 2004–05): 32–35. According to Horowitz, "upper level estimates from U.S. military analysts in South Korea placed North Korea's income from weapons exports at about $560 million in 2001, representing almost 2 percent of the country's total legitimate economy." U.S. efforts to constrict these weapons sales have in all likelihood appreciably reduced the amounts of DPRK weapons export earnings in recent years, though detailed estimates are not available. For a revealing account of the role of military trading companies in international commerce, consult Juliette Morillot and Dorian Malovic, *Evadés de Corée du Nord* [Escapees from North Korea] (Paris: Belfond/Presses de la Cite, 2004), 201–10.

Jong Il, the deflection of external pressures or outright threats to the well being and security of the DPRK, and the prevention of a breakdown in central political control. The leadership has grappled with these interconnected issues for the past decade, and the military has played an increasingly pivotal role. Through grim resilience and a knack for exploiting external aid and economic ties, the North Korean system has avoided the meltdown widely anticipated by external analysts since the early 1990s. Ever since his ascension to the nation's top leadership following the death of his father in 1994, Kim Jong Il has steadily increased his identification with and dependence upon the KPA. In order to substantiate his claims to unchallenged power, Kim requires a loyal political and institutional base.[12] But his dependence on the military also reflects practical needs—the military's sheer size and organizational reach make the KPA and its subordinate institutions integral to the day-to-day operation of the North Korean system.[13] In addition to controlling defense procurement, the KPA provides substantial manpower for a wide range of critical infrastructural tasks, including agricultural production, land reclamation, road building, housing projects, construction of power plants, and mining activity.[14] The army is thus a contributor to national security and to economic development, which enables the KPA to justify its extraordinary claims on budgetary and manpower resources. The relationship between Kim Jong Il and the KPA leadership is highly symbiotic; systemic continuity necessarily assumes ongoing mutual dependence between Kim and the North Korean armed forces.

The ROK's Quest for Policy Autonomy

The strategic directions of the ROK are profoundly different from those of the DPRK. Rejecting autarky, the ROK has since the 1960s transformed itself from a predominantly agrarian society into a major industrial and trading power, and has formed a close military alliance with the

---

[12] For a characteristic statement endorsing the "military first" policy, see "Let the Whole Party, The Entire Army, and All the People Single-Heartedly Unite and More Highly Display the Might of Military-First," *Nodong Sinmun, Choson Inmingun, and Ch'ongnyon Chonwi,* joint New Year's Day editorial in Pyongyang Korean Central Broadcasting Station, January 1, 2005 (trans. FBIS).

[13] According to the IISS, the North Korean armed forces experienced modest growth in absolute numbers during 2004. The institute estimates total active forces at 1,106,000 personnel, 4,700,000 committed to reserve duties, and an additional 189,000 assigned to public security. The DPRK's total population is estimated in the range of 22–23 million; in proportional terms, this military manpower level exceeds that of any other state in the world. See *The Military Balance, 2004–2005* (London: Oxford University Press, 2004), 178–79. The new version of the ROK defense white paper credits the DPRK with higher numbers: total active duty strength of 1,170,000, and a more inclusive definition of reserve forces that likely includes paramilitary organizations, totaling 7,700,000. By this estimate, the total of active and reserve forces comprises nearly 40 percent of the population of North Korea. See Ministry of National Defense, *Defense White Paper—2004,* 289.

[14] All these activities are noted in Koh, "Military First Politics."

United States. According to the Organization for Economic Cooperation and Development (OECD), South Korea's GDP in 2004 amounted to $679.7 billion at prevailing exchange rates, thereby ranking the ROK as the world's tenth largest economy.[15] South Korea's history of one-man rule and military domination of internal politics have given way to a democratic, if still highly personalized, political order. The maturation and expansion of the country's industrial and technological base have transformed South Korea into an emergent power of increasing international consequence. Seoul seeks an international role commensurate with the ROK's economic and political accomplishments. Though periodic tensions with Japan concerning disputed maritime claims and festering ROK resentments over Tokyo's brutal occupation of the peninsula during the first half of the 20th century continue to bedevil Korean-Japanese bilateral relations, Seoul is firmly anchored to all of its neighbors save the DPRK. Economic, political, and security ties with China—the ROK's former adversary and erstwhile ally of North Korea— have experienced especially dramatic development in recent years, and Beijing is now ranked as Seoul's leading trade partner. There is also a growing convergence in strategic perspectives between the two leaderships, and ROK public opinion toward China is increasingly positive.[16]

These trends underscore the profound asymmetries in the power positions and longer term trajectories of the two Koreas. According to every relevant measure of national power other than aggregate military capabilities, South Korea dominates North Korea by ever-wider margins. The ROK's gross national income (GNI) is 33 times larger than that of the DPRK; its per capita GNI is 15.5 times greater; ROK foreign trade surpasses that of North Korea by nearly 156 times; and South Korea's literate, prosperous, and highly educated population is slightly more than double that of North Korea.[17] Although the DPRK armed forces numerically exceed the ROK in most categories of weapons as well as in aggregate manpower, North Korea's outmoded equipment and diminished training time have eroded its previous conventional advantage (see **Table 1**).[18] Moreover, given the resources that South Korea is committing to weapons acquisition and to defense innovation (in particular higher-end air and naval systems and sophisticated

---

[15] Organization for Economic Cooperation and Development, "Main Economic Indicators," July 2005, 265.

[16] See Jonathan D. Pollack and Mitchell B. Reiss, "South Korea: The Tyranny of Geography and the Vexations of History," in *The Nuclear Tipping Point—Why States Reconsider Their Nuclear Choices*, ed. Kurt M. Campbell, Robert J. Einhorn, and Mitchell B. Reiss (Washington, D.C.: Brookings Institution Press, 2004), 274–77.

[17] Ministry of National Defense, *Defense White Paper—2004*, 288.

[18] For a detailed review of the conventional balance, consult IISS, *North Korea's Weapons Programmes*, 85–99.

Table 1. Military Capabilities of South and North Korea

Classification				South Korea	North Korea
Troops (peacetime)			Total	681,000	1,170,000
			Army	550,000	1,000,000
			Navy	67,000	60,000
			Air Force	64,000	110,000
Principal force capabilities	Army	Unit	Corps	13 (including the Army Aviation Operations)	19 (including the Artillery Corps, Missile Guidance Bureau and Light Infantry Instruction Guidance Bureau)
			Divisions	49	75
			Mobile brigades	9*	69 (about 10 guidance brigades not included)
		Equipment	Tanks	2,300	3,700
			Armored vehicles	2,400	2,100
			Field artillery	5,100	8,700
			MRLS	200	4,600
			Surface-to-surface guided weapons	30 (launchers)	60 (launchers)
	Navy	Surface ships	Warships	120	430
			Landing vessels	10	260
			Mine warfare ships	10	30
			Support vessels	20	30
	Air Force	Equipment	Fighters	530	830
			Special aircraft	70 (including naval aircraft)	30
			Support aircraft	200	520
			Helicopters	690 (all three services)	320
Reserved troops				3,040,000	7,700,000 (Reserve Military Training Units, Worker and Peasant Red Guard Units, and Red Youth Guards)

* The naval troops of the South include 27,000 troops of the Marine Corps. The equipment of its army (divisions and brigades) represents the combined equipment of the Army and Marine Corps. The field artillery of the North does not include infantry regiment class 76.2mm guns.

Source: Ministry of National Defense, *Defense White Paper—2004* (Seoul: Ministry of National Defense, 2005), 289.

intelligence and surveillance capabilities), none of these trends seem likely to be reversed in the near- to mid-term future.[19]

Despite extraordinary successes, the ROK chafes under two fundamental political frustrations: the unwillingness of North Korea to accord South Korea unambiguous political legitimacy, and the asymmetrical U.S. military presence on the peninsula, which retains full command and control (except in certain limited contexts) over U.S. and ROK military forces. This limited sovereignty is increasingly unacceptable to growing portions of the population, and the ROK leadership is debating how to increase South Korea's political autonomy.[20] Seoul views these two questions as interrelated. Both are deemed legacies of the division of the peninsula and of the divergent ideological and developmental paths of the two Koreas. Former ROK president Kim Dae-jung and current president Roh Moo-hyun have placed high priority on redefining the ROK's security strategy. Both leaders believe that the ROK cannot achieve its full power potential in the absence of normal relations with the North and more equitable ties with the United States. They have therefore made relations with the North a centerpiece of their respective policy agendas.

These issues have proven highly contentious both within South Korea as well as between Seoul and Washington. Presidents Kim and Roh have advocated two largely indistinguishable policies toward North Korea: Kim's "sunshine policy" and Roh's "policy of peace and prosperity." Both leaders assume that accommodation with Pyongyang will yield normal or at least quasi-normal relations with the DPRK, thus reducing the risks of severe instability. In support of these accommodation policies, some ROK leaders have, over the past few years, undertaken measures that have been highly unsettling even to advocates of engagement with Pyongyang. For example, in order to garner Kim an invitation to Pyongyang in June 2000 (the first-ever meeting between the leaders of North and South Korea), Kim Dae-jung's aides purportedly arranged for the transfer of at least $200 million into North Korean bank accounts.[21] In addition to the North-South summit, the DPRK has also benefited from substantial international assistance—assistance that numerous analysts deem essential to the survival of the North Korean system. According to an April 2005 study, between 1995 and 2004 more than $3.2 billion in commercial and governmental cash payments

---

[19] For a compilation of recent and pending ROK foreign acquisitions and domestic weapons programs, consult IISS, *The Military Balance, 2004–2005*, 329.

[20] Pollack and Reiss, "South Korea: The Tyranny of Geography and the Vexations of History," 266–70.

[21] Some estimates range as high as $500 million.

passed from the ROK to the DPRK (see **Table 2**). Total U.S. aid to the DPRK during the same period totaled more than $1.1 billion (see **Table 3**).

Seoul's engagement strategy has also had significant implications for ROK defense policy. Despite the DPRK's withdrawal from the Treaty on the Non-Proliferation of Nuclear Weapons (NPT) in January 2003 and its February 2005 claim to possess an unspecified number of nuclear weapons, Seoul has continued its policy of accommodation with Pyongyang. The ROK military leadership also conforms closely to policies enunciated by the civilian leadership. After a three-year hiatus, the Ministry of Defense (MND) released a new defense white paper in early 2005. Though the document reviews North Korea's military activities, and continues to regard North Korea as an ongoing threat,[22] it no longer describes the DPRK as the ROK's "major enemy." Thus defense policymakers characterize credible deterrence of North Korea as a primary security goal, while paramount policy objectives include reassurance of the North and a diminished threat environment. Caught between political pressures from civilian leaders, public opinion that is far less supportive of military expenditure, and demands from U.S. officials who expect the ROK military to fulfill responsibilities long assumed by U.S. forces, South Korea's military leaders are traversing multiple political minefields.

The Looming Uncertainties

Three principal considerations will shape the future military options and capabilities of the two Koreas as well as the resources both will allocate to national defense: (1) North Korea's political-economic prospects, (2) the sustainability of the U.S.-ROK security alliance, and (3) the consequences of both these issues for inter-Korean relations.

Prospects for the North Korean System

Since the fall of the Soviet Union, research and policy circles have continuously debated the longer-term viability of North Korea. Numerous other studies have posited predictions concerning the peninsula's future

---

[22] Ministry of National Defense, *Defense White Paper—2004*, 36–46. The document does explicitly make reference to the North Korean military threat, but it downplays threat-based planning to an unusual degree. The predominant tone of the white paper is geared toward cooperative security. For an extended discussion of the changes in the ROK's declaratory defense policy toward the North, consult National Institute of Defense Studies, *East Asian Strategic Review—2005* (Tokyo: The Japan Times, June 2005), 82–85, 87–90.

Table 2. South Korean Governmental Expenditures on Engaging North Korea, 1995–2004 (US$ million)

Expenditure Category	1995	1996	1997	1998	1999	2000	2001	2002	2003	2004	Total
KEDO	1.8	8.9	3.0	6.5	6.4	308.9	271.1	288.7	333.0	137.1	1,365.2
Food aid	240.0	2.9	23.1	11.0	…	93.4	17.3	120.4	122.2	164.6	794.9
Fertilizer	…	…	…	…	28.5	83.4	49.5	66.6	70.1	89.8	387.9
Road & rail links	…	…	…	…	…	12.9	69.6	53.5	94.1	55.8	285.9
Payment to DPRK for 2000 summit	…	…	…	…	…	200.0	…	…	…	…	200
Mt. Kumgang tour	…	…	…	…	…	…	34.8	45.9	5.1	6.8	90.6
Aid to ROK businesses	…	…	…	…	…	0.4	0.8	2.2	10.7	11.9	26.1
Kaesung industrial complex	…	…	…	…	…	…	…	…	…	21.8	21.8
Family reunions	…	…	…	…	0.4	…	1.0	1.6	2.5	2.8	10.7
Other	…	…	5.3	3.6	…	5.0	9.1	7.9	12.8	54.8	98.7
Total value	241.8	11.9	31.4	21.2	35.3	706.5	453.2	584.9	650.4	545.4	3,281.8

Source: Mark E. Manyin, "U.S. Assistance to North Korea," CRS Report to Congress, Congressional Research Service, RL31785, April 26, 2005, 31.

Table 3. U.S. Assistance to North Korea, FY 1995–2004 (US$ million)

Assistance Type	1995	1996	1997	1998	1999	2000	2001	2002	2003	2004	Total
Food aid	…	8.3	52.4	72.9	222.1	74.3	102.8	82.4	25.5	55.3	695.8
KEDO assistance	9.5	22.0	25.0	50.0	65.1	64.4	74.9	90.5	3.7	…	405.1
Medical supplies	0.2	…	5.0	…	…	…	…	…	…	0.2	5.4
Total	9.7	30.3	82.4	122.9	287.2	138.7	177.6	172.9	29.2	55.3	1,106.2

Source: Mark E. Manyin, "U.S. Assistance to North Korea," CRS Report to Congress, Congressional Research Service, RL31785, April 26, 2005, 31.

(all focusing on the fate of North Korea).[23] Most writings suggest variants of four different outcomes: (1) incremental reform that would result in accommodation between the two Koreas and presumably lead to longer-term unification, (2) a violent end to the North Korean system resulting from severe internal disequilibrium or outright military conflict, (3) "virtual unification," in which Seoul appeases Pyongyang in order to stave off collapse of the DPRK and prevent acute instability on the peninsula, and (4) a reinvigorated DPRK that proves capable of strengthening North Korea's economy while maintaining a highly robust military. In oversimplified terms, the ROK political leadership prefers the first scenario. The second scenario is the staple nightmare of Seoul and Beijing. Leading U.S. policy-makers fear the third scenario. The declared objective of the DPRK is to bring about the fourth scenario.

The above scenarios posit very divergent potential outcomes, and would necessitate starkly different U.S. and ROK policy responses. The ROK leadership favors the gradualist scenario, but Seoul is often criticized for its idealized assumptions and commitment to open-ended political and economic support for the DPRK. The collapse or regime change scenario—favored by various U.S. analysts and policy-makers—is faulted for its inattention to the larger consequences of a systemic meltdown, especially in light of North Korea's presumed nuclear capabilities. The appeasement scenario implies that good money must continue to chase after bad, and thus sustains a system that many observers believe would otherwise collapse of its own weight. The recovery scenario has received the least attention, both because it constitutes the goal of the DPRK leadership and because many deem it implausible. Regardless of these different potential outcomes, the available historical record reveals a besieged, paranoid leadership deeply suspicious of the malign intentions of all external powers.[24] The question confronting the international community is: how does North Korea get from here to

---

[23] For relevant examples, see David Reese, *The Prospects for North Korea's Survival* (London: IISS, November 1998); Jonathan D. Pollack and Chung Min Lee, *Preparing for Korean Unification—Scenarios and Implications* (Santa Monica, CA: RAND, 1999); Henry D. Sokolski, ed., *Planning for a Peaceful Korea* (Carlisle, PA: Strategic Studies Institute, February 2001); National Intelligence Council and Federal Research Division, *North Korea's Engagement: Perspectives, Outlook, and Implications* (Washington, D.C.: Library of Congress, May 2001); and Nicholas Eberstadt, "Korean Scenarios: Alternative Futures for the Korean Peninsula," in *Strategic Asia 2004–05: Confronting Terrorism in the Pursuit of Power*, ed. Ashley J. Tellis and Michael Wills (Seattle: The National Bureau of Asian Research, 2004), 427–55.

[24] Newly available archival materials highlight these acute fears; see The George Washington University, "The History of North Korean Attitudes toward Nuclear Weapons and Efforts to Acquire Nuclear Capability," Cold War International History Project, e-dossier, May 17, 2005; and Robert S. Litwak and Kathryn Weathersby, "The Kims' Obsession: Archives Show Their Quest to Preserve the Regime," NAPSNET Special Report 05-54A, June 30, 2005.

there, adapt to the modern world, and emerge as a more normal but still autonomous state?

Though some analysts anticipate the outright collapse of the North Korean system, this is a remote possibility, not least because China and South Korea remain unprepared to curtail their economic support for the North.[25] The leadership in Pyongyang seeks above all to preserve the system; toward that end, the state is permitting citizens to pursue alternatives to the largely inoperative central distribution system. Power preservation, as distinct from an intrinsic attachment to reform, has thus become the DPRK's prevailing leadership strategy. Though this does not preclude the development of a more competent class of managers and planners, their numbers and political weight should not be overstated. The KPA is ensconced atop the system, and remains the most powerful and reliable instrument of state power. Military strength is therefore seen as indispensable to national security as well as to the internal viability of the system and enables the DPRK leadership to pursue both goals in a somewhat straddled fashion. In January 2005, a major editorial observed:

> The national defense industry is the foundation of the nation's military and economic strength. We should strengthen in every way the self-reliant national defense industry which we built from scratch and have hardened...We should supply everything necessary for the national defense industry on a priority basis as required by the party's economic construction line in the military-first era.[26]

This approach underlies both the basic assumptions of the senior leaders and the priority they accord military modernization. Unlike the starkly different futures posited under the reform, collapse, and life support scenarios, the most likely outcome appears to be regime continuity fostered by constrained adaptation. A two-pronged strategy that combines economic renewal and national defense could, however, lead to contradictions that the leadership is unwilling and perhaps unable to reconcile.

---

[25] One recent assessment (drawing on interviews with specialists in China and the ROK) states: "Trade with and assistance from China is believed to account for up to 80 percent of North Korea's essentials and the bulk of its consumer goods." See International Crisis Group, *North Korea: Can the Iron Fist Accept the Invisible Hand?*, 7.

[26] "Let the Whole Party, the Entire Army, and All the People Single-heartedly Unite and More Highly Display the Might of Military-first," *Nodong Sinmun, Choson Inmingun, and Ch'ongnyon Chonwi,* January 1, 2005 (trans. FBIS).

The U.S.-Korea Alliance in Upheaval

Despite major achievements, the U.S-Korean alliance has had a tumultuous and conflict-ridden history.[27] Many of these tensions reflect the inherent asymmetries in the alliance—Washington has been the far more dominant actor over the decades. In recent years, South Korea has sought a larger role in formulating the alliance's purpose and direction. The democratization and demilitarization of South Korean internal politics has brought this more assertive posture to the forefront. Washington, for its part, seems much less inclined to uphold established U.S. security equities on the peninsula, especially now that competing military requirements (particularly in the Greater Middle East) increasingly preoccupy U.S. defense planners. The lack of agreement between Seoul and Washington over how to approach the renewed nuclear tensions with Pyongyang has reinforced these tendencies. Further sharpening these differences has been the Bush administration's determination to redefine U.S. global military strategy and to rethink the open-ended, largely static U.S. defense deployments in South Korea and other Cold War locales.

Following protracted and often contentious negotiations, Seoul and Washington reached agreement during 2003–04 on some of the largest changes in bilateral security ties in decades.[28] These changes encompass: (1) the redeployment of U.S. forces from their forward positions near the 38th Parallel to new positions mostly well south of the Han River, (2) the reassignment in August 2004 of the 2nd Infantry Division's 2nd Combat Brigade and the cumulative withdrawal (to be completed by the end of 2008) of 12,500 U.S. forces from Korea since the start of the Bush administration, (3) the shift of U.S. military headquarters from Seoul to Osan (with the ROK incurring most of the costs associated with the in-country redeployments), and (4) South Korea's assumption of numerous defense functions previously held by U.S. forces, a shift that will require South Korean forces to purchase new equipment and master new skills.

The looming shifts in strategy run even deeper. The U.S. view holds that neither country should devote major resources to a replay of the Korean War. U.S. strategists contend that North Korea would employ missiles, long-range artillery, and special forces to bypass traditional invasion corridors and instead concentrate on high-value targets throughout the southern half

---

[27] For a superb account, consult Don Oberdorfer, *The Two Koreas—A Contemporary History* (New York: Basic Books, 2001).

[28] This section draws heavily on "American Forces in South Korea—The End of an Era?" IISS *Strategic Comments*, July 2003; "U.S. Troop Withdrawals from South Korea—Beginnings of the End for the Alliance?" IISS *Strategic Comments*, June 2004; and "America's Alliances in East Asia—Purposes and Prospects," IISS *Strategic Comments*, May 2005.

of the peninsula. The redeployment of U.S. forces is therefore designed to limit the potential vulnerability of U.S. troops in a renewed conflict. U.S. planners also calculate that ROK forces in possession of newly mastered, modern U.S. technologies and operational concepts will be able to neutralize North Korean offensive capabilities. In order for this scenario to be viable, U.S. military leaders assume that ROK forces will procure high-technology equipment at an accelerated rate during the transitional period, including major new capabilities in ground and air defense, counter-battery fire, and airborne early warning. U.S. officials also assert that they will commit $11 billion over the coming half-decade to upgrade U.S. forces on the peninsula, though this figure likely derives from pre-existing modernization plans rather than any significant new budgetary commitments. The Pentagon also seems intent on developing more generic regional capabilities within its Korea-based forces by building U.S. bases into sea and air hubs for unspecified contingencies outside the peninsula.

These looming shifts have greatly discomfited ROK officials for two reasons. First, such changes mean that U.S. forces would be increasingly committed to non-peninsular missions. Second, many policymakers in South Korea believe that the United States would use its realigned bases as part of an attempt to envelop Seoul in contingency planning against China—a goal that the ROK leadership deems wholly contrary to its long-term interests. Seoul is equally concerned over more coercive U.S. approaches designed to contain North Korea's nuclear weapons and missile activities. These activities focus particularly on ballistic missile defense, interdiction of weapons-related cargo, and constriction of the DPRK's economic and financial activities. In the eyes of South Korean policymakers, Washington has taken these steps in a unilateral fashion, thereby eroding the sense of shared purpose in U.S.-ROK security relations.

In response to these developments, President Roh Moo-hyun has advocated the concept of a "balancer role" that would elevate the position of the ROK in Northeast Asian geopolitics. Roh believes that this balancer role would inhibit the possibilities of future major power conflict by constraining any prospect of U.S. unilateral actions on the peninsula. Roh's speech to the South Korean Air Force Academy graduation in March 2005 also offered a vision of a self-reliant future for the ROK military. Although voicing continued support for security collaboration with the United States, the fundamental thrust of his remarks diverged profoundly from existing alliance norms:

> We now have sufficient power to defend ourselves … Now the goal of our armed forces is to defend the peace and prosperity of not only the Korean peninsula but of Northeast Asia … [by] forging a security cooperative structure … We

need to possess a self-reliant defense capability along with such cooperation. Within the next 10 years, we will develop, on our own, into a self-reliant armed force with independent operational command ... Recently, various concerns have been voiced in some circles about the expansion of the USFK's role. This is what you would call an issue of "strategic flexibility." However ... our people will not become embroiled in conflicts in Northeast Asia without our consent. This is something that we must maintain as an uncompromising, firm principle under all circumstances.[29]

These views portend a major redefinition of ROK national interests and a parallel commitment to pursue policies independent of the United States.[30] Though it is premature to predict the end of the alliance, there is no question that U.S. and ROK policy trajectories are increasingly divergent. Seoul is seeking to place itself between Washington and the two defining contingencies in Northeast Asia (i.e., Korea and the Taiwan Strait) rather than maintain unequivocal identification with U.S. policy. Any future attempts by Seoul to inhibit U.S. military actions—especially in relation to a major crisis on the peninsula—could place the alliance at acute risk. This tension between the United States and the ROK has not escaped Pyongyang's notice. With neither Washington nor Seoul engaged in deeper mutual conversation concerning their respective strategic goals, the long-term stability and durability of the alliance can no longer be assumed. Amidst danger, uncertainty, and potential instability, both North and South Korea confront the possibility of strategic futures sharply at odds with the past.

The Implications of Alternative Futures

The trajectories of national power in the two Koreas have long been highly divergent, but the disparities have never been greater than they are at present. By every relevant measure, the ROK has emerged victorious in economic, political, and diplomatic competition. But North Korea continues to punch above its weight, enabling Pyongyang to operate on the margins of the international system and exploit opportunities to maneuver amidst the competing objectives and interests of different powers. South Korea's mas-

---

[29] President Roh Moo-hyun, speech, 53rd Air Force Academy Graduation and Commissioning Ceremony, Seoul, March 8, 2005, http://www.president.go.kr. As noted by a senior presidential aide who declined to be identified, "We understand the U.S. global strategy for employment of rapid deployment forces. It is acceptable if the United States moves some of its forces to Iraq or any other conflict areas on condition that the troop redeployment does not have a critical effect on the Korean peninsula. However, such a U.S. troop redeployment should be restricted if it involves regional conflicts in Northeast Asia." See Yonhap News Agency, March 8, 2005, http://www.yonhapnews.net/Engservices/3000000000.html.

[30] For a more fully elaborated version of a "balancer" strategy, see Secretariat of the ROK National Security Council, "Theory on Balancer in Northeast Asia, a Strategy to Become a Respected State in Northeast Asia, a Strategy To Become a Respected State of International Cooperation," April 27, 2005, http://www.president.go.kr.

sive power advantage has not always been matched by comparable political agility. To a significant extent, the debate in South Korea over North Korean policy, rather than representing a considered assessment of the benefits and risks of alternative courses of action, more often revisits the ROK's own tumultuous history. In the midst of the discordant, contradictory impulses of ROK policy, leaders in Seoul have, however, posed some fundamental questions regarding the longer-term trajectory of the nation:

- Under what circumstances might change occur in North Korea, and how can South Korean policy encourage such change?

- Are various scenarios of North Korea's future as starkly different as policy advocates imagine them, or do mechanistic renderings of the future obscure a more complex picture?

- Are Seoul's interests best served by a continued threat-based strategy toward Pyongyang, or do more feasible and cost-effective approaches exist?

- Can the ROK balance political accommodation with the DPRK while maintaining a transformed ROK military capable of counteracting North Korea's asymmetric capabilities?

- What are the implications of any of the above shifts for the longer-term viability of the U.S.-ROK alliance?

To consider these questions, this chapter will turn to the underpinnings of national security in North and South Korea, and explore how the military capabilities of both states will shape security on the Korean Peninsula.

The Military Capabilities of North and South Korea

This section reviews the technological, material, and doctrinal factors influencing the security strategies of the two Koreas, and explores how these changes might affect their respective military capabilities in the next half-decade. Though the changing defense postures of North and South Korea reflect military options that are more cost effective, they also entail shifts in threat perception. In relative terms, the DPRK remains the world's most militarized state. Nevertheless, the degradation of DPRK conventional capabilities over the past fifteen years, the army's increasing responsibilities for regime survival, and the commitment of regular and reserve forces to various non-military tasks have all recalibrated the roles and missions of the KPA. North Korea's forces remain heavily forward deployed and their absolute numbers are staggering. As characterized in the ROK defense white paper, "major combat units consist of more than 170 divisions and brigades, including 80 infantry divisions and brigades ... 30 artillery brigades, 10 tank brigades and 7 tank regiments, 20 mechanized brigades, and 25 special warfare brigades." The white paper also estimates that approximately 70 percent of North Korea's ground forces remain deployed south of the Pyongyang-Wonsan Line, with most less than 100 km from the 38th Parallel.[31]

Foreign analysts have often viewed this deployment pattern as evidence of an offensive war posture. Judgments regarding these forces and the operational plans associated with them are necessarily speculative, however, and data on readiness and training is highly incomplete. The available writings on North Korean military strategy date principally from the 1960s, and place preponderant emphasis on surprise attack and a quick decisive war that would incapacitate the ROK prior to the arrival of major U.S. reinforcements.[32] Though long enshrined as official doctrine, these writings bear only a remote connection to extant political-military realities, and do not reflect the sustained enhancement of South Korea's power, the pervasive decline of the DPRK, and the profound shifts in U.S. military doctrine and war-fighting capabilities (particularly in the precision use of air power). It is thus likely that the KPA is formulating plans for a wider variety of missions, including the defense of North Korea in the event of an attack.

North Korea's repeated warnings of an impending U.S. attack are often dismissed as largely delusional. Yet North Korea's use of force across the decades has been highly discriminate, carefully calibrated, and well short of total war. Actions likely to trigger a U.S. military response have been scrupulously avoided for many years, though Pyongyang has been prepared to undertake appreciable risks in selected contexts. As one specialist has observed: "The North Korean leaders have been neither crazy, nor are they military geniuses. Simply put, they have been highly rational and moderately successful high-risk takers with idiosyncratic political intentions."[33] Future war scenarios will therefore increasingly emphasize deep strike capabilities geared toward deterrent, defensive, or offensive purposes. Little is known regarding North Korean targeting doctrine, however, and estimates on the numbers, deployment patterns, and armaments of various missile systems

---

[31] Ministry of National Defense, *Defense White Paper—2004*, 41.

[32] For a detailed overview, consult James M. Minnich, *The North Korean People's Army—Origins and Current Tactics* (Annapolis, MD: Naval Institute Press, 2005).

[33] Narushige Michishita, "Calculated Adventurism: North Korea's Military-Diplomatic Campaigns, 1966–2000" (doctoral dissertation, John Hopkins University, May 2003), 13.

are also highly uncertain.[34] Despite the questionable reliability and accuracy of North Korean ballistic missiles, the DPRK's capability to reach deep into ROK territory (as well as Japan) is now an integral part of DPRK strategy, and constitutes a more credible threat than its increasingly obsolescent conventional forces. This shift in strategy indicates a significant recalibration of influence within the North Korean military system in accordance with appreciable change in the presumed value of various military capabilities. These developments highlight Kim Jong Il's ever increasing dependence on the KPA as well as a parallel belief that an asymmetrical strategy will free up resources vital to the rejuvenation of North Korea's tattered economy.

The ROK is also departing from past strategies, but is doing so for reasons very different than the DPRK. Seoul hopes to develop a far more responsive, technologically advanced military. For three decades, South Korean leaders have advocated a more self-reliant defense posture, and Washington increasingly argues that Seoul should fulfill predominant responsibility for its own security. South Korea's desire to break free from undue subordination to U.S. power lacks, however, a forthright acknowledgment of the costs and consequences of this strategic goal. Though South Korea may be approaching fuller sovereignty, the fulfillment of this aspiration may not yield the status and security that many anticipate—especially if the United States becomes a less committed partner. At the same time, South Korea's impressive scientific, technological, and industrial capabilities are only partially focused on military modernization goals. Thus both Koreas confront fundamental questions in future defense strategy. It remains to be seen whether their respective aspirations toward strategic autonomy will prove commensurate in the face of security challenges and available resources. Heightened national security efforts in both states could also complicate prospects for non-adversarial relations.

Prospects for Defense Industry Innovation in the North

North Korea is attempting to maintain a self-sufficient defense industry capable of meeting the full range of its long-term military requirements. In the 1960s and 1970s, when North Korea experienced rapid economic growth, the DPRK developed a largely autonomous military-industrial system. This enabled Pyongyang to manufacture tanks, artillery, submarines, and ultimately ballistic missiles. In the past, North Korea also reportedly assembled a limited number of fighter aircraft. The DPRK's capacity for defense innovation, however, remains highly circumscribed. Efforts to acquire

---

[34] For a careful review of the available data on North Korean missile development, consult IISS, *North Korea's Weapons Programmes*, 63–83.

technologies from abroad are presumably directed at areas where North Korea's indigenous skills remain quite modest: advanced electronics and metallurgy, information and communications technology, and related national defense priorities. How realistic, however, are Pyongyang's options for technological development?

Any effort to measure North Korea's capacity for defense innovation inevitably confronts severe data problems. The DPRK limits information on defense expenditure to a single figure in the annual budget that is announced at the Supreme People's Assembly, the nominal legislative body. Information on the size and location of North Korea's military production facilities remains sparse, and many facilities are presumably located underground. Any effective analysis of the North Korean military must therefore focus on output measures such as known military deployments and order of battle data. Though useful, these estimates exhibit a somewhat "layered" provenance. It is impossible to determine whether these estimates largely repeat previous intelligence judgments without evaluating the relevance of earlier findings in light of North Korea's economic decline in the 1990s. Meaningfully disaggregating different military capabilities within this larger picture is also a difficult task. The lack of information regarding the location of North Korea's nuclear activities compounds these issues: under prevailing conditions, the DPRK has no incentives to reveal information beyond what it disclosed while still a party to the NPT and a member of the International Atomic Energy Agency (IAEA).[35]

North Korea's defense capabilities and industrial potential reflect the DPRK economic system as a whole. DPRK defense industries embody numerous manifestations of the "dual economy" phenomenon evident in the Soviet Union and China during the Cold War. As an exporter of various conventional weapons systems and a large number of ballistic missiles, North Korea has been able to sustain various production programs, possibly subsidize specific R&D projects, and acquire high priority foreign technologies. The acute contraction of North Korea's economy over the past decade and a half, however, has also had an appreciable effect on the defense sector. During the 1980s, most estimates of the percentage of North Korea's GNP devoted to defense were in the range of 25–30 percent. If national income declined in the 1990s to nearly half its previous size, then sustaining defense expenditures at previous levels would have required 50 percent of GNP to be devoted to the military. No estimate of North Korea's defense burden approaches this level, and a commitment this substantial (even if the non-defense functions of the North Korean military are acknowledged) de-

---

[35] For a detailed appraisal of the history of the nuclear program, consult IISS, *North Korea's Weapons Programmes*, 27–48.

fies comprehension.[36] Although the defense sector may not have contracted at nearly the rate of the economy as a whole, it has had to operate with far fewer funds. Official budgetary data reveals significant declines in the DPRK defense budget during the late 1990s. According to these statistics, North Korean defense expenditures dropped from $2.08 billion in 1991 to $1.33 billion in 1998. North Korea's total announced budget since the latter half of the 1990s further suggests a halving of government expenditures compared to the first half of the decade (see **Table 4** below), although total expenditures and defense expenses again increased markedly in 2004 and 2005.[37]

Despite continued production in selected areas of defense equipment, various indicators suggest a major slowdown of most conventional procurement programs during the past decade. Estimates of the North Korean order of battle over the past ten years indicate only marginal augmentations to the existing inventory of conventional weapons.[38] Similarly, the only known acquisitions of foreign defense hardware were 5 Mi-17 helicopters from Russia in 1998, 30 Mig-21 fighter aircraft delivered from Kazakhstan in 2000, and an additional 10 Mig-21 fighter aircraft delivered by Russia in 2000.[39] The limits on these transactions (presumably from surplus weapons inventories) indicate acute shortages in the foreign exchange required for major purchases, and a reluctance on the part of foreign suppliers to make more advanced systems available to North Korea. More than likely, Pyongyang also realizes that additional acquisitions of outmoded military hardware and continued production of anything other than relatively advanced, up-to-date equipment will do little to narrow the growing gap in the conventional capabilities of North and South Korea, and even less to provide a credible military capability in the event of a U.S. attack. U.S. military commanders, however, have not acknowledged any significant degradation of the DPRK's military capabilities during its decade of acute economic decline, and in selected areas even assert that North Korea continues to augment its capabilities. As

---

[36] ROK government estimates of the North's defense expenditure have varied remarkably little since the early 1990s, which begs the question of whether independent estimates have been undertaken. As a consequence, this data offers the highest estimates of North Korea's defense expenditure relative to GNI, peaking at 37.9 percent in 1998. See **Table 4**.

[37] On April 12, 2005, the DPRK Minister of Finance announced defense budget increases of 15.6% and 15.9% respectively for 2004 and 2005, "with a view to bolstering the People's Army, developing the defense industry, and implementing to the letter the Party's policy of placing all the people under arms and turning the whole country into a fortress." See KCNA News Agency, BBC Monitoring, April 12, 2005. The year on year increase in revenues was estimated at 5.7% and 15% respectively, with defense expenditures for 2004 thus experiencing a significant increase relative to total governmental revenues. See Sohn Suk-joo, "Economic Programs and State Budget for 2005," *Vantage Point*, May 2005, 8, 10.

[38] See the annual issues of IISS' *The Military Balance*.

[39] These transactions are noted in the arms transfer tables in *The Military Balance, 2004–2005*, 329.

Table 4. North Korea's Annual Military Expenditures, 1991–2003 (US$ billion)

	GNI (as per ROK's Bank of Korea)	Total budget (official)	Military Expenditure	Ratio of military expenditure to GNI (%)	Ratio of military expenditure to total budget (%)
1991	22.9	17.2	5.1 (2.1)	22.4	29.9 (12.1)
1992	21.1	18.5	5.5 (2.1)	26.3	30.0 (11.4)
1993	20.5	18.7	5.6 (2.2)	27.2	30.0 (11.4)
1994	21.2	19.2	5.8 (2.2)	27.2	30.0 (11.5)
1995	22.3	20.8	6.2	28.0	30.0
1996	21.4	...	5.8	27.0	...
1997	17.7	9.1	4.8	27.0	52.0
1998	12.6	9.1	4.8 (1.3)	37.9	52.0 (14.6)
1999	15.8	9.2	4.8 (1.4)	30.0	51.0 (14.6)
2000	16.8	9.6	5.0 (1.4)	29.8	52.0 (14.3)
2001	15.7	9.8	5.0 (1.4)	31.8	51.0 (14.4)
2002	17.0	10.0	5.0 (1.5)	29.4	50.0 (14.9)
2003	18.4	11.3	5.0 (1.8)	27.2	44.4 (15.8)

Note: Figures in parenthesis represent military expenditures announced officially by North Korea. Military expenditures from 1995–97 are estimated at the average ratio of 27% to GNP.

Source: Ministry of National Defense, *Defense White Paper—2004* (Seoul: Ministry of National Defense, 2005), 288.

noted by Gen. Leon LaPorte, Commander of U.S. Forces Korea (USFK), DPRK forces:

> continue to improve their command, control, communications and intelligence systems, harden and bury their facilities, improve lines of communication, disperse forces, and improve camouflage, concealment, and deception measures. These efforts increase the survivability of North Korean combat power, and complicate our attack warning capability.[40]

South Korean military analysts contest these judgments. According to Chaiki Song, a leading ROK specialist on North Korea's defense economy, the North Korean economy shrank on average by 4.5% between 1990 and 2002, and total economic production in 2002 was at 45% of the 1990 baseline. He concludes that the downturn in the military economy has been somewhat less than in the economy as a whole (64% of the pre-crisis level), citing military expenditures as two-thirds of previous levels. Song sees an

---

[40] Gen. Leon J. LaPorte, Commander, United Nations Command; and Commander, Republic of Korea-United States Combined Forces Command and United States Forces Korea, testimony before the Armed Services Committee, United States Senate, March 13, 2003, 10.

"overall decline" in North Korea's ground force capabilities, and describes naval and air force capabilities as "stagnant." Though concluding that the accelerated military buildup that took place during the latter half of the 1980s has since slowed appreciably, Song acknowledges increases in North Korea's production of long-range and self-propelled artillery, multiple-rocket launchers, and ballistic missiles.[41] This production underscores the DPRK's increasing reliance on asymmetric military capabilities that are designed to attack critical targets at longer range rather than rely on large-scale conventional assaults in the early stages of a conflict (such as in the early stages of the Korean War).

North Korean defense policy will therefore emphasize weapons systems and defense technologies in the areas where the DPRK has demonstrated success in research, development, and production; they will similarly focus on areas that are capable of conferring meaningful strategic advantage. Ballistic missiles head this list, particularly since such capabilities do not require major manpower commitments to field them (though they do necessitate major allocations of technical personnel and integration of highly disparate technologies during the development process). North Korea's pursuit of such capabilities stretches back more than thirty years.[42] Efforts to exploit foreign technologies, system development, adaptive R&D solutions, operational deployment, and weapons export have all yielded impressive results. According to Joseph Bermudez Jr., by the end of 1999 total production of the Hwasong 5 and 6 missiles (based on Scud B and C derivatives first deployed in 1988, with ranges of 300–500 km) stood between 600 to 1,000, of which 300–500 were sold abroad and 300–600 remained in North Korea's operational inventory.[43] Production estimates of the Nodong missile (with a range of 1,300 km) are less certain. The ROK defense white paper dates the Nodong's initial operational deployment to 1998; IISS estimates suggest that current deployments could range between 40 to 200 (including reserves).[44] At least several dozen of these missiles have also been exported to preferred customers, most notably Pakistan and Iran. Though the reliability and accuracy of these missiles remain open to question, they give North Korea the

---

[41] Chaiki Song, "A Decade of Economic Crisis in North Korea: Impacts on the Military," KIDA Paper, no. 3, Korea Institute for Defense Analyses, October 2003. This paper is a summary of a more comprehensive research report, which was not available during the preparation of this study.

[42] For an excellent overview, see Joseph S. Bermudez Jr., "A History of Ballistic Missile Development in the DPRK," Monterey Institute of International Studies, Center for Nonproliferation Studies, Occasional Paper, no. 2, 1999. For additional details, consult IISS, *North Korea's Weapons Programmes*, 63–83; and Nuclear Threat Initiative, "North Korea Profile-Missile Overview," http://www.nti.org/e_research/profiles/nk/missile/index.html.

[43] Bermudez, "A History of Ballistic Missile Development in the DPRK," 16.

[44] Ministry of National Defense, *Defense White Paper—2004*, 290; and IISS, *North Korea's Weapons Programmes*, 73.

theoretical capability to reach targets throughout South Korea (in the case of the Hwasong 5 and 6) and Japan (in the case of the Nodong). Both types of missiles are fired from mobile launchers, with concealment enhancing survivability. Reaching U.S. bases and facilities elsewhere in the West Pacific would require the deployment of longer-range missiles that thus far have remained notional capabilities—though U.S. officials contend that such missiles are undergoing active development. Nonetheless, debate continues over whether North Korea has the ability to arm a ballistic missile with a nuclear warhead, or possesses long-range ballistic missiles capable of reaching U.S. territory (in particular the continental United States).[45]

Although the latter two issues command understandable attention by U.S. officials, the answers to such questions matter far less in a peninsular or regional context. The ability to reach major targets anywhere on the peninsula and in Japan provides North Korea with a military reach that conventional forces alone cannot provide. This enables Pyongyang to put high value targets (including U.S. bases in Korea and in Japan) at prospective risk. Further efforts to enhance the accuracy, reliability, and survivability of different systems (including advances in solid fuel missiles) reinforce the capability of the DPRK to undertake actions across a spectrum of potential contingencies. But the relationship between inherent capabilities (in particular the use of ballistic missiles, including those potentially armed with chemical weapons or biological agents) and strategic effects is seldom clearcut.[46] The requirements of deterrence can thus be viewed very differently on opposite sides of the military divide.

North Korea has striven to attain a clear preponderance of military power, but has wound up creating much uncertainty concerning the extent of its capabilities, in particular Pyongyang's nuclear potential and likely weapons inventory.[47] Although Pyongyang's February 2005 declaration removes some of the ambiguity regarding its nuclear claims, the statement resolves little regarding the true extent of either North Korea's programs

---

[45] For a searing critique of U.S. intelligence estimates, see Greg Thielmann, "Rumsfeld Reprise? The Missile Report That Foretold the Iraq Intelligence Controversy," *Arms Control Today*, July-August 2003, 3–8. In April 2005 testimony to the Senate Armed Services Committee, Vice Admiral Lowell Jacoby, Director of the Defense Intelligence Agency, initially agreed with a query from Sen. Hillary Clinton that North Korea "has the ability to arm a missile with a nuclear device." A subsequent clarification from a DIA spokesman claimed that this capability remained hypothetical, rather than a confirmed judgment by the intelligence community. See Bradley Graham and Glenn Kessler, "N. Korean Nuclear Advance Is Cited," *Washington Post*, April 29, 2005.

[46] For an especially subtle treatment of this issue in relation to the North's chemical weapons program and biological weapons potential, consult IISS, *North Korea's Weapons Programmes*, 49–62.

[47] Jonathan D. Pollack, "North Korea's Nuclear Weapons Activities—Assessing Knowns and Unknowns" (unpublished paper, Naval War College, December 2004); and Robert S. Norris and Hans M. Kristensen, "North Korea's Nuclear Program, 2005," *Bulletin of the Atomic Scientists*, May-June 2005, 64–67.

or the degree to which such weapons might be operationalized. Even as Pyongyang insists that a nuclear capability is vital to its security, the DPRK leadership asserts (at least for purposes of presentation) that this capability remains negotiable. The actual circumstances under which the DPRK would relinquish any of the weapons in its possession remains a matter of conjecture. Without a credible denuclearization agreement, however, the DPRK's nuclear competence (and longer-term potential for a more viable strategic capability) will likely increase over time. This would presumably invalidate the ROK's belief that DPRK nuclear weapons potential should not preclude the steady progression of inter-Korean relations. Such an outcome would vindicate Pyongyang and expose an essential yet often unspoken risk in South Korea's accommodation strategy. In the absence of meaningful, verifiable threat reduction, the ROK would simultaneously place its security at significantly increased risk as well as possibly jeopardize the U.S-ROK alliance. Notwithstanding the ROK's keen desire to open its doors to the DPRK, Seoul must ensure that Pyongyang's commitment to a non-nuclear peninsula is not an empty slogan. Though this is not a challenge that South Korea alone can confront, Seoul's conduct toward Pyongyang could appreciably shape longer-term outcomes.

ROK Plans for a More Technology-Intensive Force

The ROK has also articulated ambitious goals for defense modernization. These modernization objectives are intended to deter potential threats from North Korea while also advancing "a cooperative self-reliant defense." An essentially conservative military ethos has, under the U.S. security umbrella, dominated ROK military development for decades. This era is now drawing to a close. With Seoul less tethered to the alliance with Washington, South Korean defense planners are examining the possible security requirements in a less predictable world. A clear contradiction exists between the political premises of President Roh's "balancer" strategy and the operational characteristics of the force that defense planners are trying to build under the Mid-Term Defense Plan (2005–09). The spectrum of desired capabilities would greatly extend the reach and sophistication of ROK forces. As outlined in **Table 5**, the investment strategies of South Korea's MND for the coming half-decade posit a shift from limited capabilities in electronic warfare and C4I (command, control, communications, computers, and intelligence), maneuver and strike, coastal defense and maritime operations, and air-to-air combat and air defense, to strategic surveillance and early warning, expansion of deep battle capabilities, major sea lines of communication (SLOC) protection, and extended range air operations. The immediate implications of such a shift would greatly enhance ROK deterrence, defense, and war-fighting capabilities in relation to the DPRK, and would supplant U.S. capabilities being withdrawn between now and 2008. Recent or impending acquisitions include K1A1 tanks, self-propelled artillery, mobile rocket launchers, and counter-battery radars. In their totality, such force improvements would make the ROK a far more potent military force within a regional context. Pending acquisitions would greatly extend South Korea's strategic reach across a wide spectrum of capabilities. Some of the proposed weapons systems purchases include, most notably, AWACS aircraft, military satellites, advanced naval platforms (including the KDX destroyer, additional submarine purchases, and high-speed vessels), and acquisition and integration of F-15K fighters and aerial refueling capabilities. The above acquisitions would constitute the building blocks of a more autonomous and potent military force with conventional capabilities that vastly outstrip any augmentations that the KPA might envisage.

The immediate issue for ROK planners, however, is whether their reach will exceed their grasp. As argued by Ronald Mangum, a retired senior U.S. officer with ample command experience in the ROK, the South Korean armed forces must do far more than simply purchase new weapons systems. ROK forces must instead utilize such measures as the creation of a joint headquarters to achieve a degree of integration and doctrinal innovation heretofore lacking. If self-reliance is to be more than an empty slogan, then the ROK must also be prepared to undertake large-scale expenditures. As Mangum has observed, "While the government responds to public pressures to increase Korean military self-reliance, it seldom addresses the cost of achieving self-reliance."[48] Whether ROK planners have defined a realistic modernization program is a question that will be explored in the next section.

Budgetary Implications of ROK Military Modernization

The ROK MND periodically announces the major goals of ROK defense modernization, and recent attention has focused on high priority weapons development and acquisition targets. With the Blue House's articulation of a new national security strategy and the MND's release of a new defense white paper, it is possible to assess the feasibility of various projections. Like many defense establishments, the ROK military has relied on highly optimistic economic growth projections to provide additional government revenue

---

[48] Ronald S. Mangum, "Joint Force Training: Key to ROK Military Transformation," *Korean Journal of Defense Analysis* 16, no. 1 (Spring 2004): 119, 124. From 2000–03, General Mangum served as Commanding-General, United States Special Operations Command Korea.

Table 5: The ROK's Force Improvement Plan (2005–09)

Capability	Current level	Midterm target	Major weapons systems
C4I/Electronic warfare	Tactical surveillance and early warning capabilities	Establishment of strategic surveillance and early warning capabilities	*AWACS *Mid- and high-altitude reconnaissance UAVs *Military satellite communication, etc.
Maneuver/ Strike	Limited deep battle capabilities	Extension of deep battle capabilities	*K1A1 tanks *K-9 self-propelled artillery *MLRS *Counter-battery radars
Maritime/ Landing	Limited costal/ near sea maritime operation capabilities	Protection of major SLOCs in coastal/ near sea areas	*4,000/7,000-ton destroyers *Large-sized transport vessels *1,800-ton submarines *400-ton high-speed vessels, etc
Air/ Air defense	Limited air operation capabilities	Expansion of the scope of air operations	*Airborne tankers *F-15K fighters

*Next-generation guided munitions, etc.

Source: Ministry of National Defense, *Defense White Paper—2004* (Seoul: Ministry of National Defense, 2005), 168.

for defense modernization. This was pointedly evident in the high-growth era of the mid- to late 1990s, until the Asian financial crisis necessitated a sharp curtailment of numerous modernization plans, particularly in the acquisition of higher-end naval and air capabilities. The prodigious costs of advanced systems from abroad drove some of these reductions, which included the downsizing of various impending transactions or stretching out acquisition cycles (in some cases by nearly a decade). (See **Table 6**)

Even taking into consideration these modified plans, the ROK's midterm national defense goals are highly ambitious, at least with reference to the pace at which new capabilities are projected for introduction into the South Korean armed forces. This judgment reflects three considerations: overly optimistic projections of economic growth, unrealistic expectations of enhanced budgetary priority to defense modernization, and insufficient consideration of the costs associated with the relocation of U.S. forces on the peninsula (including corollary expenditures in the assumption of responsibilities previously assumed by U.S. forces). Though these points do not render modernization goals irrelevant, they do suggest that any transition

Table 6: ROK Weapons Procurement Goals (Original and Revised)

Weapon	Original plan		After adjustment		Remarks
	Date	Units	Date	Units	
F-15K fighters	1999–2003	120	2002–09	40	
AWACS	1998–2004	4	2004–12	4	AEWAC of Boeing E-737 and IAI Elta G-550 are candidates.
SAM-X	1991–97	128	2005–12	46	PAC-III surface-to-air guarded missile is being considered. The MND denied the procurement was connected with the U.S. missile defense system.
Aerial refueling tankers	2003–05	5	2009–15	4	
Short range surface-to-air missiles	1998–2007	160	1999–2010	120	
KDX-III	1999–2008	3	2001–12	3	Aegis-equipped destroyers. Hyundai Heavy Industries had its tender accepted in Aug 2004 for the construction of the first of the class to be delivered toward the end of 2008.

Source: National Institute for Defense Studies, *East Asian Strategic Review—2005* (Tokyo: The Japan Times, June 2005), 82.

in the defense force will likely prove more protracted than defense policy makers are ready to acknowledge.

Some relevant examples, drawn primarily from the ROK's 2004 defense white paper, highlight these looming gaps. The document states that realization of the defense plan assumes "a stable rate" of at least a 3% allocation of GNP to national defense "from the mid to long-term perspective."[49] The Defense Ministry projects total defense costs between 2005 and 2008 at approximately 99 trillion won, or slightly less than $100 billion at currently prevailing exchange rates. These projected costs assume annual defense growth of approximately 11% and defense expenditures of 3.2% of GDP by

[49] Ministry of National Defense, *Defense White Paper—2004*, 217.

2008.[50] Funds allocated for force investment and force improvement are projected to increase to nearly 40% of the total defense budget by the final year of the plan, as increasing portions are allocated to the navy and air force and a diminishing share to the army.[51]

These projections, however, assume enhanced economic growth and increased priority to defense expenditure, neither of which is substantiated by prevailing trends. To meet anticipated modernization goals, MND has posited real economic growth requirements of 5% and nominal growth requirements of approximately 8% on an annual basis, with military budget increases ranging between 9.9% and 11%.[52] However, defense budget increases since 2000, though significant, have not reached double digits.[53] Economic growth is also lagging well behind the ROK military's expectations, meaning that the requirements for defense modernization in percentage terms would have to increase appreciably. The Bank of Korea, for example, has reported economic growth in the first half of 2005 at 3%, the lowest figure since the financial crisis.[54] In absolute terms, Korea's GDP has continued to increase significantly, but in relative terms the ratio of defense expenditure to GDP has dropped steadily over the past quarter century, from a high of 6% in 1980 to 5.3% in 1985, 4.4% in 1990, 3.3% in 1995, and 2.8% in 2000.[55] Thus, the stated goal of apportioning at least 3% of GDP to national defense seems increasingly questionable.

South Korean defense policymakers have neither attempted to reconcile these discrepancies nor explain how the ROK plans to make do with less. If past practices are followed, further slippage in the delivery schedules of specific weapons systems and reductions in specific purchases should be expected. Reductions in the size of the ground forces will also be a pivotal consideration, though such steps entail enormous political sensitivities, es-

---

[50] Ministry of National Defense, *Defense White Paper—2004*, 101.

[51] The 2005 defense budget projects the breakdown across services as follows: 32.1% for the Army; 26.0% for the Navy; 22.4% for the Air Force, and 19.5% for other military organizations. See Juhyun Park, "Medium-Term Expenditure Framework and Year 2005 Defense Budget," Korea Institute for Defense Analysis, KIDA Paper, no. 9, March 2005, 6–7.

[52] The lesser percentage derives from an earlier assessment of the FY 2004–08 budget plan noted in Park, "Medium-Term Expenditure Framework and Year 2005 Defense Budget," 5; the higher figure is cited in the Ministry of National Defense, *Defense White Paper—2004*, 101.

[53] The increases in recent years have been 5.0% (2000), 6.3% (2001), 6.3% (2002), 7.0% (2003), 8.1% (2004), and 9.9% (2005). See Ministry of National Defense, *Defense White Paper—2004*, 323.

[54] Florence Lowe-Lee, "Economic Trends," *Korea Insight*, August 2005, 2.

[55] Ministry of National Defense, *Defense White Paper—2004*, 215.

pecially given looming U.S. force withdrawals.[56] ROK planners are therefore placing a premium on the introduction of high-technology systems as a substitute for more manpower-intensive strategies. Seoul also hopes to reform South Korea's defense acquisition process, presumably by eliminating various redundancies and, more importantly, by curtailing corruption endemic to the system. In addition, the ROK aspires to greatly expand exports of defense products and services, though these targets also seem ambitious, if not altogether out of reach.[57]

South Korea has set ambitious goals for the mid- and longer-term, hoping to move the ROK to the ranks of advanced military powers in coming decades. This process is likely to take longer than Seoul imagines, though it is possible that a major attenuation of the U.S.-ROK alliance will spur South Korea to accelerate the pursuit of this objective. At the same time, acquisition of higher-performance aircraft and more advanced naval platforms may also compel the ROK to revisit assumptions that posit the persistence of the North Korean threat. Might possession and successful incorporation of advanced battle management and intelligence capabilities, in combination with F-15K fighters and short-range missile assets, lead ROK planners to lean toward deep-strike operations against North Korea, rather than rely predominantly on deterrence and defense? Or could Seoul's efforts to reconcile with Pyongyang achieve such momentum that it becomes inconceivable for the ROK to plan seriously for war with the DPRK? Indeed, would such a counter-offensive capability be acceptable to ROK political leaders who are intent on reassuring Pyongyang at every turn? Though these are questions for the longer term, in all likelihood they continue to quietly animate defense deliberations in Seoul.

For ROK policymakers, fundamental questions persist regarding the force that South Korea hopes to build in future years. The ROK must also determine whether it can draw fully on U.S. defense technology for South Korea's own modernization plans, or whether the ROK must further diversify its technological and industrial ties by dealing with the European Union, Russia, and other prospective suppliers, as well as pursuing indig-

---

[56] A major reform of the ROK armed forces, which will purportedly recommend cuts in ground forces, is in preparation. According to press reports, a report entailing necessary reform measures will be submitted to the National Assembly in the fall of 2005. The report will also encompass measures to reduce the number of MND posts reserved for serving and retired officers, while increasing the number of civilian positions. See Jung Sung-ki, "S. Korea to Cut Troops," *Korea Times*, April 29, 2005.

[57] Military exports have expanded significantly in recent years, though with uneven year-to-year performance. According to the MND, exports between 2000 and 2004 have amounted to approximately $55 million, $237 million, $14 million, $240 million, and $418 million, respectively. The target goal for 2015 is annual sales of $1 billion. See Ministry of National Defense, *Defense White Paper—2004*, 177–78.

enous technological development. The defense white paper, for example, asserts that the ROK will "join the ranks of industrialized nations by acquiring core technologies necessary to attain advanced weaponry-related R&D by 2010 and securing capabilities to independently develop sophisticated future weapons systems by 2020." The sweep of these ambitions, however, is matched principally by their lack of specificity.[58] Further questions revolve around the ability to recruit and train a more technologically proficient officer corps during an era when the uniformed military no longer enjoys pride of place within the system. In addition, the ROK must balance the need to prudently prepare for deterrence and defense against the North without incurring such costs and commitments that little is left for a more future-oriented defense force. These issues will not be resolved anytime soon.

Weighing the Policy Consequences

The two Koreas appear to be on the cusp of a historic change that, in conjunction with ongoing shifts in the U.S. military presence on the peninsula, will redefine U.S. security policies in Northeast Asia more profoundly than at any time since the formative years of the Cold War. The Korean Peninsula will become increasingly "Koreanized," and the United States will progressively become more distanced from its dominant security role on the peninsula. Indeed, the largest changes in the near-term peninsular balance will concern U.S. troop withdrawals and redeployments rather than any prospective shifts in the order of battle between Seoul and Pyongyang. Though significant U.S. command, intelligence, logistics, and air assets will remain in place five years from now, the era of heavy U.S. ground-based deployments is drawing to a close. Barring resolution of the nuclear weapons impasse or the dissolution of the North Korean state, the United States will primarily focus its goals on deterrence and defense against any prospective nuclear and missile threats that North Korea might pose, and detection and interdiction of any prospective transfers of WMD-related technology and delivery systems that Pyongyang might attempt. Such missions do not require an appreciable U.S. military presence on the peninsula. If anything, they suggest a future U.S. strategy based primarily on maritime deployments (including ballistic missile defense) and long-range air power. Deterrence and defense on the peninsula would be largely in the hands of South Korea, which has long aspired to such a role.

But toward what end will the ROK pursue such objectives? In the preferred U.S. scenario, ROK defense planning would remain predominantly

---

[58] Ministry of National Defense, *Defense White Paper—2004*, 169.

peninsular in scope, and geared toward fulfilling missions long assumed by U.S. forces. Seoul's modernization priorities in part address the ongoing need to counter North Korean forces, but South Korea is also looking beyond an explicit North Korean threat. The political leadership in Seoul has defined an alternative strategic course that would not only diminish the possibilities of conflict between North and South Korea, but would also simultaneously inhibit the United States from undertaking any unilateral military action against the DPRK. Though it is possible to envisage a successor leadership to Roh Moo-hyun that is more wary of engagement with the North and intent on restoring a highly interdependent alliance with Washington, the present analysis does not posit such an outcome.

Seoul's efforts to diminish tensions include the implementation of direct contacts with the North Korean military. The ROK has entered into general-level officer talks with the DPRK that are focused principally on confidence-building measures as a means both to reduce the risks of accidental or inadvertent conflict (especially naval clashes) and to facilitate communication between the two sides.[59] These contacts, however, do not at present address the disposition of military forces, in particular those with an inherent capability to reach deeply into either state's territory. Thus a primary liability of a confidence-building strategy is that it presumes open-ended accommodation with Pyongyang without regard for the DPRK's capability to pose a direct threat to the security of both the ROK and Japan. Equally telling, the military-to-military talks have accelerated ever since the DPRK claimed its status as a nuclear weapons state. Although Pyongyang has reiterated its ultimate willingness to forego nuclear weapons capabilities, this pledge is contingent upon a "non-hostile" U.S. policy; taken to its logical conclusion, this would in effect invalidate the premises of any continuing U.S. security commitment to the ROK. If Seoul were prepared to enter into a longer-term accommodation with Pyongyang without credible resolution of North Korea's nuclear weapons activities, the longer-term prospects for sustaining the U.S.-ROK alliance are indeed bleak.

Inescapably, however, the ROK finds itself addressing the continued abnormality of a divided peninsula. Despite their geographic contiguity and common language and culture, the two Koreas represent two very different systems. Such profoundly different histories and strategic orientations over the past half century will make reintegration an immeasurably difficult prospect. Even now, as the ROK seeks to define a common identity with its northern neighbor and as the DPRK seeks to depict Seoul's long-time U.S. ally as the primary threat to North Korea's security and well-being, the

---

[59] For a summary of the results of the inter-Korean military talks to date, consult Ministry of Unification, *Peace and Prosperity—White Paper on Korean Unification 2005*, 32–36.

power trajectories of the two systems continue to diverge. The sheer concentration of military power on both sides of the 38th Parallel, however, begs the issue of whether the respective political needs of both states will enable either to circumvent their inescapable connectedness. The more extreme of the potential outcomes on the peninsula (e.g., war or regime collapse) would again envelop both Koreas in a shared fate; the benign if still distant prospect of large-scale economic and political integration would be comparably intertwining. But absent these possibilities on opposite ends of the political-military spectrum, North and South Korea still operate largely in parallel political universes even as both necessarily view the other as a point of reference and comparison.

From a political perspective, the concept of a peninsular military balance has lost much of its past meaning. Neither state any longer conceptualizes its military requirements exclusively in relation to the other. Pyongyang's defining priority is to legitimate the leadership's claims to unchallenged power, to organize its military power to support the resuscitation of the economic system, and to deter overt threats to the future of the system. In terms of military capabilities, North Korea will continue to hold South Korea hostage, but this is more to prevent overt U.S. coercion of the DPRK rather than preparation for war against its neighbor. Should North Korea ultimately prove capable of partially regaining its economic footing, it is possible (depending on political outcomes in South Korea and the future growth of ROK military power) that Pyongyang might renew a more overtly adversarial stance toward Seoul. But as long as the imperatives of national survival seem so pressing, and as long as South Korea remains singularly intent on accommodation with the North, this outcome seems unlikely.

Though South Korea's emergent strategic vision seeks to transcend the half century-long confrontation with North Korea, this vision includes appreciable risks to its long-term interests. Leaders in Seoul deem the DPRK's conventional capabilities as a carryover of the Cold War and characterize Pyongyang's pursuit of strategic weapons as a reflection of its vulnerabilities and fears; they thus ignore the inherent coercive potential of these capabilities. Both positions reflect the desire of South Korean policymakers to dismantle much of the national security state associated with the ROK's earlier decades of development. These positions leave several fundamental questions unaddressed, however. One such question is whether Seoul should choose to ignore Pyongyang's nuclear weapons claims. The ROK leadership has advocated an optimistic, almost idealized rendering of the peninsula's future. Seoul hopes to preclude the possibility of war, and is convinced that South Korean validation, compensation, and reassurance of the North will ultimately prompt reciprocal steps on the part of Pyongyang. If the ROK no longer accepts the logic of threat-based planning in relation to the DPRK, how does it justify its proposed transition to a far more potent military force? Putting aside this future-oriented vision, does the persistence of a diversified DPRK military threat ultimately make it impossible for the ROK to sustain its initiatives toward Pyongyang? Or does Seoul simply persist in its present course in spite of threats from Pyongyang and the risks to the U.S-ROK alliance? There are at present no answers to these questions; both Koreas instead uneasily eye a future that neither can foresee or fully control.

Executive Summary

This chapter examines military modernization in Russia and draws implications for Russia's defense strategy in Asia.

MAIN ARGUMENT:
Despite rising defense outlays, the Russian military is still an archaic, dysfunctional, and inefficient organization. Russia is therefore unlikely to effect military modernization that is capable of fulfilling Moscow's overly ambitious aims.

POLICY IMPLICATIONS:
- Absent major governmental, economic, social, and defense reforms, Russian influence in Eurasia (including East Asia) will continue to wane, and demographic and health crises will interact with each other to generate more defense crises in the future.

- If major reform does not occur, Russia will lack effective allies and partners, be unable to compete against U.S. primacy in global affairs, and gradually cede its influence in Eurasia to a rising China.

- U.S. defense and security cooperation with Russia is possible only in selected and limited areas (e.g., peacekeeping). In order for defense and security cooperation to succeed over the long term, Washington must exert constant pressure on Moscow to democratize.

- Because there is no guarantee that Putin's policies will survive his administration, Russia will likely move in a different direction after he leaves office—hence Moscow is still an unpredictable strategic partner.

Potemkin's Treadmill: Russian Military Modernization

Stephen J. Blank

Modernization, not reform, characterizes defense policy in Russia today. Defense Minister Sergei Ivanov defines modernization as policies that strengthen the combat capacity as well as the command and control (C2) structures of the armed forces.[1] Reforms thus entail the reorganization of force structures as well as the defense economy—a purely bureaucratic and technological orientation that derives from Soviet and Tsarist practice. This study focuses on modernization as defined by Defense Minister Ivanov, which entails neither civil-military issues, strategy, or operations. Although true defense reform—understood as a comprehensive reform of the entire defense and state structure, beginning with the president and embracing all aspects of the military (*voyennaya reforma*)—is not occurring in Russia, modernization and reform of the armed forces (*reforma vooruzhennykh sil'*) is finally taking place. The modernization and reforms currently underway, however, eschew political, constitutional, or democratizing reforms and serve to buttress President Vladimir Putin's authoritarian regime.

Since 2003 Ivanov and Putin have subordinated the General Staff to the Ministry of Defense (MOD), unified all force structures under one territorial command and control structure, and comprehensively transformed Russia's

Stephen J. Blank is Professor of Russian National Security Studies at the Strategic Studies Institute of the U.S. Army War College. Dr. Blank has been Associate Professor of National Security Affairs at the Strategic Studies Institute since 1989. He can be reached at <Stephen.Blank@us.army.mil>.

The views expressed here do not in any way represent those of the U.S. Army, Defense Department, or the U.S. government.

[1] "Interview with Minister of Defense Sergei Ivanov," *Argumenty i Fakty*, no. 13, March 30, 2005, 3.

overall state structure.[2] To what extent does this military modernization go beyond mere cosmetic change? Defense reform, if interpreted as the ongoing reorganization of force and bureaucratic structures and the revision of strategy and threat assessment, still falls short.

This assessment is based upon a consideration of the strategic environment within which Moscow must operate. The failure of the General Staff until at least 2004 to provide adequate guidance concerning the nature of threats and of contemporary war, the inability to overcome the Soviet legacy in the defense economy and the attendant economic crisis in the defense sector, and the failure to adopt a modern professional army in place of conscription must all be viewed within the greater strategic context. Although defense spending is growing at a high rate, it cannot begin to cover the present size of the armed forces, and further cuts will be necessary. Similarly, the same regression to Soviet and Tsarist habits evident in Russia's politics and economics is also taking place in the areas of the defense economy and conscription.

Russia continues to suffer from a glaring disparity between Moscow's self-proclaimed ambitions and the leadership's actual capabilities. Moscow still aspires to a great power role for Russia—despite the fact that it cannot afford this role either economically or militarily. Indeed, Russia's capacity for power projection, while undergoing reform, still does not stretch beyond the old Soviet boundaries. Thus Moscow must still rely on the threat of nuclear retaliation and—though refusing to admit it—the support of strangers (e.g., the United States) in order to address threats beyond Russia's borders. The failure to address conscripiton and reform of the defense sector leaves Moscow not only with a political and command structure akin to that of late Tsarism, but also a defense economy that still bears a close resemblance to its dysfunctional and sub-optimal Soviet predecessor. In summing up Russia's overall strategic environment, defense reforms, and defense economy, the unavoidable conclusion is that Russia—much like the USSR—remains trapped on a "treadmill of reforms."[3]

---

[2] Irina Isakova, *Russian Governance in the Twenty-First Century: Geo-Strategy, Geopolitics and Governance* (London: Frank Cass Publishers, 2004); Carolina Vendil Pallin, *Defense Decision Making and Russian Military Reform: The Oblomov Approach* (Stockholm: Swedish Defense Research Establishment FOI, forthcoming, cited with the consent of the author); and Denis Trifonov, "Russian Defence Reform: Reversing Decline," *Jane's Defence Weekly*, June 8, 2005, http://www.4janes.com/subscribe/jdw/doc.

[3] Gertrude Schroeder Greenslade, "The Soviet Economy on a Treadmill of 'Reforms'," in *The Soviet Economy in a Time of Change*, Joint Economic Committee, U.S. Congress (Washington, D.C.: GPO, 1979), 312–66; and Gertrude Schroeder Greenslade, "Soviet Economic 'Reform' Decrees: More Steps on the Treadmill," in *The Soviet Economy in the 1980s: Problems and Prospects*, Joint Economic Committee, U.S. Congress (Washington, D.C.: GPO, 1989), I, 79–84.

Russia's Strategic Environment

The concentration and centralization of political power in the hands of Putin and Ivanov are reflected in the defense reforms currently in motion in Russia. These defense reforms are, in turn, characteristic of Putin's power vertical, the Tsarist-Soviet ideal that bureaucratic reforms can create a perfectly rationalized governmental machine, and dirigiste policies intended to renovate Russia's weapons base and economy through 2020. Russian and foreign observers tend to agree that Russia's future depends as much upon a successful reform of the military and state structures as it does on geopolitical dexterity.[4]

Based on the above it is easy to despair over Russian military-political modernization. Despite ongoing reforms, Russian officials acknowledge that Moscow's policies remain militarily, administratively, and economically ineffective. In 2002 Chief of Staff General Anatoly Kvashnin announced that the state of the army was "beyond critical."[5] In 2004 Ivanov warned that failure to raise conscription levels could trigger the collapse of the army (which was unprepared for battle in the first place).[6]

The fighting in Chechnya also exhibits the central government's incompetent military leadership; disorganized and uncoordinated command structure; poorly-trained, demoralized, and corrupt soldiers; and outdated equipment.[7] No standardized basis for national security policymaking or democratic control exists: there is no parliamentary accountability over all of Russia's competing multiple militaries, no guarantees of the rights of soldiers and officers, and no executive accountability to the Parliament and the Duma's prerogative to monitor the defense budget of and policy implementation within Russia's multiple militaries. Meanwhile corruption, crime, and economic militarization are increasingly pervasive.[8] During a one week

---

[4] Charles Morrison, ed., *Asia Pacific Security Outlook 2004* (Tokyo: Japan Center for International Exchange, 2005), 161.

[5] *Moscow Agentstvo Voyennykh Novostey* (trans. Foreign Broadcast Information Service [FBIS], May 30, 2002).

[6] RIA Novosti, "Russian Defense Minister Voices Concern About Army Draft," October 1, 2004; Anne C. Aldis and Roger N. McDermott, eds., *Russian Military Reform 1992–2002* (London: Frank Cass Publishers, 2003); Steven E. Miller and Dmitri Trenin, eds., *The Russian Military: Power and Purpose* (Cambridge, MA: MIT Press, 2004); Alexander Golts and Tonya Putnam, "State Militarism and Its Legacies: Why Military Reform Has Failed in Russia," *International Security* 29, no. 2 (Fall 2004): 121–59; and Aleksandr' Golts, *Armiya Rossii: 11 Poteryannykh Let* [Russia's Army: 11 Lost Years] (Moscow: Zakharov, 2004).

[7] Mark Kramer, "Guerrilla Warfare, Counterinsurgency, and Terrorism in the North Caucasus: The Military Dimensions of the Russian-Chechen Conflict," *Europe-Asia Studies* 57, no. 2 (March 2005): 209–90; and Mark Kramer, "The Perils of Counterinsurgency: Russia's War in Chechnya," *International Security* 29, no. 3 (Winter 2004–05): 5–63.

[8] The term "economic militarization" is used here to describe policies that allocate an excessive portion of the economy to the defense sector.

period in June 2005 alone, 46 soldiers—the size of an entire platoon—died in non-combat situations. Several soldiers were shot by their own comrades in an attempt to halt drunken and violent rampages, eight committed suicide, and two others attempted suicide but failed.[9] The abiding military crisis both reflects and contributes to the state's ongoing crisis. Thus a number of Russian military analysts now argue that Putin should scrap Russia's entire military structure and rebuild it from scratch.[10]

This *cri de coeur* reflects a generation of strategic failure to realize any real military reform, to develop a sustainable military system, or to overcome persisting social pathologies concerning an army that strikes fear into the society it supposedly protects and yet cannot defend the homeland itself.[11] This failure resides mainly in the fact that the Russian state remains a government ruled by men—not laws, one that eerily resembles the equally dysfunctional late Tsarist system.[12] The central leadership in Moscow still aspires to defend Russian territory and interests, however, and believes that war remains a constant strategic reality that the state must master in order to survive.[13]

Although Russia currently faces the most benign threat environment in the nation's history, military modernization is occuring under inauspicious strategic circumstances. Russia must meet these challenges and avoid future strife with the United States, Europe, and China, as well as with multiple terrorist groups. Yet, for various reasons, Moscow seems unable to make lasting gains with Washington, Brussels, or Beijing. Russian officials and analysts postulate multiplying threats, claiming that these outside powers threaten Russia's very integrity through encirclement, attack, or even state disintegration.[14] This threat inflation—which includes internal, external, and trans-

---

[9] Andrew Osborn, "Conscripts Face Hell of Life in Russian Army," *New Zealand Herald*, June 17, 2005, http://www.nzherald.nz/index.

[10] The author heard repeated statements to this effect at the annual occurrence on Russian defense policy hosted by the U.S. Naval Postgraduate School in Monterey, California in 2002, as well as from the Russian participants in this conference since then.

[11] Natalia Kalashnikova, "Society Is Afraid of Our Army," May 11, 2005, http://www.mosnews.com; "Interview with Sergei Ivanov," *Rossiyskaya Gazeta*, May 4, 2005 (trans. FBIS, May 4, 2005); and RIA Novosti, "Press Conference With State Duma Committee for Defense Chairman Viktor Zavarzin," March 11, 2005.

[12] Peter Baker and Susan Glasser, *Kremlin Rising: Vladimir Putin's Russia and the End of Revolution* (New York : Scribner's, 2005), 417; Steven Rosefield, *Russia in the 21st Century: the Prodigal Superpower* (Cambridge: Cambridge University Press, 2004); and Stefan Hedlund, *Russian Path Dependence* (London: Routledge, 2005).

[13] Defense Minister Sergei Ivanov, "Russia's Armed Forces and Its Geopolitical Priorities," address, Moscow, February 3, 2004 (trans. FBIS, February 3, 2004).

[14] Associated Press, "Russia At Risk of Collapsing, Putin Says," April 18, 2005.

national threats—inhibits development of a comprehensive and effective defense policy.[15]

Current threats to Russia, as perceived by Moscow, include the collapse and slow recovery of the state and economy, European integration that largely excludes Russia, the revolution in military affairs (RMA), and U.S. global primacy.[16] Other threats include the rise of China and Beijing's attendant enhanced ability to project power into Central Asia, Korea, and Taiwan, as well as the rise of transnational terrorist groups who threaten vital Russian interests in the Caucasus or Central Asia. Moreover, there is some alarm in Moscow that the United States will increasingly resort to war without approval of the United Nations (UN) or other organizations, and that Washington's withdrawal from the Anti-Ballistic Missile Treaty (ABM) portends diminished strategic stability and a lowered threshold for the use of nuclear weapons during times of war.[17] Moscow also insists that Russia is a pole of an allegedly multipolar order and claims to have an independent foreign policy; Moscow cannot, however, afford to build bases at home for its troops in Georgia. A more preposterous and unsustainable imperialism is hard to imagine.

Consequently Russia lacks reliable allies. Even its partners evince discernible suspicions and reservations concerning Russian policy. While Russian security depends in many ways upon the kindness of strangers, Moscow consistently manages to estrange potential partners, thus further heightening Russia's perceived insecurity and ever multiplying threats. No military—especially one under such stress as Russia's—could easily frame rational strategic priorities under those conditions. Russia's prolonged economic crisis makes it easy to see why strategic and doctrinal pronouncements possess little policy relevance. Moscow responded to the growing trend of formulating Russia's defense policy on the basis of a macrostrategic framework by restoring the dysfunctional Tsarist model of governmental structure. Despite significant economic growth since 1998, industrial investment is still sorely lacking. Russia also faces catastrophic imbalances of investment and a collapsing infrastructure, while analysts warn that it risks becoming a Third World state excessively dependent on domestic energy

---

[15] Defense Minister Sergei B. Ivanov, "The World in the 21st Century: Addressing New Threats and Challenges," lecture, Council on Foreign Relations, New York, January 13, 2005, http://www.cfr.org; Defense Minister Sergei Ivanov, keynote address, International Institute for Strategic Studies, London, July 13, 2004; and Kremlin International News Broadcast, "Press Conference With First Deputy Chief of the Armed Forces General Staff, Yuri Baluevsky," February 19, 2004.

[16] U.S. global primacy includes Washington's ability to project high-tech military power into an expanded NATO as well as states in the former Soviet Union.

[17] Kremlin International News Broadcast, "Press Conference."

supplies.[18] Russia is also unable to compete with China's booming wealth and power. Many Russian scholars fear that Russia has no strategy toward China (or Asia in general), let alone one to deal with urgent threats like the nuclearization of North Korea. Thus Russia risks dependence upon China.[19]

Meanwhile, U.S. influence intrudes ever more along Russia's borders. Many Western countries now articulate a global "good governance paradigm" that measures a state's legitimacy and sovereignty by its level of democratization. Moscow thus faces constant pressure to modify Russian policies in strategic sectors such as energy and its political-military system so as to adopt the laws of these organizations and democratize itself.[20] Furthermore, the Paris Peace Treaty of 1990 and the Organization for Security and Co-Operation in Europe's (OSCE) 1991 Moscow Declaration—both of which are foundation documents of today's world order—state that democratic norms and the observation of these norms by the states party to those agreements are "matters of direct and legitimate concern to all participating States and do not belong exclusively to the internal affairs of the state concerned."[21] Because the legal, military, and political institutions of these participating states derive legitimacy from these documents, Russia's regressive state system risks being branded not only as ineffectual, but illegitimate as well.

Moscow resents, regresses, and resists this standard. The full gamut of Western power—political, economic, and military—both pressures and attracts Russia's neighboring states to democratize in ways that challenge Russia's perceived prerogative and imperial pretenses. Though many Russian elites believe this multi-dimensional pressure threatens Russia's integrity and the state itself,[22] Moscow's only response appears to be a vacillation between embracing China and regressing further into the archaic, autarchic, Muscovite paradigm that, while incapable of restoring Russia's international preeminence, will aggravate Moscow's vulnerabilities and lead Russia toward a strategic dead end.

---

[18] "Moscow Warns on Impact of Slowing Investment," *Financial Times*, March 30, 2005, 5.

[19] Author's personal observation, comments by Russian scholars (conference, "Russian Strategic Perspectives in Asia," Carnegie Endowment's Moscow center, March 16–17, 2005).

[20] Such laws include the European Union's Copenhagen criteria, NATO enlargement requirements, and civil-military institutional relationships under the Partnership for Peace.

[21] Phillip Bobbitt, *The Shield of Achilles: War, Peace, and the Course of History* (New York: Alfred A. Knopf, 2002), 634–38.

[22] E.G. Vyacheslav Nikonov, "Putin's Strategy," *Nezavisimaya Gazeta*, December 22, 2004.

Russia and the Challenges of Contemporary War

Russia unilaterally confronts the requirements of contemporary war by resurrecting an essentially autarchic defense industry within the old Soviet borders.[23] Though supposedly welcoming foreign investment in defense firms, Moscow actually fears and often impedes such investment.[24] Moreover, Russia's military-political leadership evinces great difficulty in fulfilling contemporary warfare's strategic requirements or in devising an effective policymaking and C2 organization.

Although Russian thinkers once theorized insightfully about future warfare, they now have trouble confronting this topic either theoretically or practically. Traditional Soviet defense planners began by defining the nature and location of a threat and then, based on that assessment, would force doctrine and policy into procuring the required military capabilities. Yet without a structured doctrinal process, Russia's military leaders today find themselves unable to follow old Soviet practice or even to devise a credible defense policy. Though seen in other countries as well, this phenomenon represents a failure of strategic leadership with profound implications for competition with more flexible militaries.

Numerous reasons account for this failure. First, many military leaders still regard the North Atlantic Treaty Organization (NATO) or the United States as Russia's chief adversary, and fixate upon a conventional theater war against these two enemies. This narrow fixation results in an obsessive desire to retain an obsolete and insufficient capability to mobilize the entire country against such a contingency.[25] Second, Russian military analysts conduct very little study on contemporary warfare—in particular guerrilla warfare—and are apparently uninterested in further research on these subjects.[26] Third, Russia's computerization has lagged for a generation.[27] Fourth, unreformed officer corps and military leaders refuse to grasp or evaluate budgets in proper economic terms, resulting in constrained budgets that preclude innovation and major investments. Fifth, while funding shortfalls remain a critical factor in derailing reform, failure to control the military establishment and

[23] Federal News Service, "Remarks By Defense Minister Sergei B. Ivanov Discussing the State of the Russian Military at the General Staff Academy," December 13, 2004.

[24] Lyuba Pronina, "Private Defense Firms Warned," *Moscow Times*, July 11, 2003, 5; and Alexander Golts, "Arming the World: Russia's Lethal Weapons," *Moscow News*, February 23–March 1, 2005.

[25] Russian Ministry of Defense, *Aktual'nye Zadachi Razvitie Vooruzhennykh Sil' Rossiiskoi Federatsii* [Urgent Tasks of the Development of the Armed Forces of the Russian Federation], Moscow, 2003; and Pronina, "Private Defense Firms Warned," 5.

[26] *Izvestiya* (Moscow), March 5, 2004, (trans. FBIS, March 5, 2004).

[27] Rear-Admiral V.V. Biryukov, "Problemy Upravleniya Informatizatsiei VS RF" [Problems of Administering the Informatization of the Armed Force of the Russian Federation], *Voyennaya Mysl'*, no. 4 (July-August, 1999): 36–41.

its spending has been a glaring, if not crucial, issue. Although Ivanov introduced a treasury board intended to make defense spending more transparent to the state, waste, ineffectual state control over finances, mismanagement, and corruption remain rampant, and legal or parliamentary accountability are non-existent.[28] Sixth, the lack of both effective democratic control and of civilian management and accountability allows the military to run its own affairs independently, thereby further inhibiting reform.

Thus Russia's military leadership is averse to innovation, detached from strategic reality, and unable to grasp the realities of contemporary warfare. Although Putin and his subordinates have claimed victory in the war in Chechnya, in both 2004 and 2005 Moscow sent an additional 5,000 reinforcements (for a current total of 85,000) to the region to counter not only the terrorists but also the paramilitaries of Russia's client government. These forces have exhibited a lack of both coordination and skill in numerous counter-terrorist operations during 2002–04.[29] Even if Moscow is capable of postulating a theoretical model of contemporary warfare—as was the case in the 2003 White Paper, Russian military leaders cannot implement military policies that fulfill this model.[30] Western attachés who regularly deal with the General Staff and the MOD find them hidebound, opposed to integration with the West, and unable or unwilling to reform and learn from foreign armies.[31]

Not surprisingly, military leaders in Russia have had difficulty coming to terms with contemporary warfare and seek to prepare for every possible contingency. In 2003 former Deputy Chief of Staff General (ret.) V.L. Manilov, then First Deputy Chairman of the Federation Council Defense and Security Committee, stated that Moscow did not even possess a national grand strategy that clearly delineated national interests, national security, or a methodology for decisionmaking.[32] Lacking a conceptual means for categorizing national interests and threats coherently, Russian planners inevitably see dangers everywhere. Consequently, Russian troops are ordered to perform traditional tasks and priority missions; these include defending Russian (Soviet) territorial boundaries, preventing and deterring attacks on Russia, and maintaining strategic stability. Soldiers must also participate di-

---

[28] Golts, *Armiya Rossii*; Golts and Putnam, "State Militarism and Its Legacies," 121–59; and Trifonov, "Russian Defence Reform."

[29] Kramer, "Military Dimensions of the Russian-Chechen Conflict," 209–90; and Kramer, "Russia's War in Chechnya," 5–63.

[30] Russian Ministry of Defense, "Development of the Armed Forces of the Russian Federation."

[31] Author's conversations with Western attachés and members of the Moscow NATO office, Moscow, March 2004.

[32] Anatoliy Antipov, "The Foundation For Re-arming Strengthens," *Krasnaya Zvezda*, February 7, 2003 (trans. FBIS, February 7, 2003).

rectly in promoting Russia's economic and political interests and conduct peacetime operations including peace operations sanctioned by the UN or the Commonwealth of Independent States (CIS). Ivanov frequently claims that Russia is optimizing its military structures and increasing the size of its ready reserves in order to meet these goals. The fact that Russia's forces must prepare for conventional, unconventional, anti-terrorist, and peace operations puts a strain on the military's preparedness, operational planning, and procurement. Moreover, Ivanov and the General Staff argue that Russian forces are capable of handling two simultaneous regional or local wars—a palpably false assertion, given the results in Chechnya.[33] As a result, multiple threats continue to bedevil coherent planning and policymaking. In 2003 Baluevsky stated that, because the General Staff could not decide whether "the enemy" was NATO or some other actor, Russia could not cooperate with NATO.[34] Thus the General Staff abdicated its main task of forecasting the nature of modern warfare.

This abdication came about not least because of the political infighting between the MOD, led by Marshal Igor Sergeyev and then Ivanov, and the General Staff, led by Kvashnin—a fight ultimately resulting in Kvashnin's fall in July, 2004. Kvashnin and Ivanov fought for power and over virtually every defense policy issue, revealing Moscow's inability to forge or control defense policy. Kvashnin and his acolytes promised quick victory in Chechnya, insisting that it was the template of all future threats and that force structure and state allocations must respond to the Chechen model above every other contingency. The General Staff has also successfully thwarted every attempt to abolish conscription and professionalize the armed forces; indeed, Ivanov clearly wants to increase conscription.[35] To thwart potential rivals, Kvashnin initiated several bizarre and misguided force restructurings that subsequently had to be reversed at a substantial cost. Kvashnin likewise sought to undermine and replace both Sergeyev and Ivanov, all while instituting a chaotic defense policy. This rivalry engendered a "dual power" in the formulation of defense policy, a phenomenon which is not only anathema to Russian political leaders but also a telling sign of incoherent defense planning. In a January 2004 speech, Ivanov excoriated the General Staff for bogging itself down in inappropriate tactical studies and administrative functions that prevented the Staff from defining a "clear and generalized type of modern war and armed conflict." Ivanov also indicted the General Staff for insuffi-

---

[33] Ivanov, keynote address, July 13, 2004.

[34] Yuriy Baluyevskiy, "I Consider It Inhumane To Report Losses," *Moskovskiy Komsomolets*, January 9, 2003 (trans. FBIS, January 9, 2003).

[35] Golts, *Armiya Rossii*.

cient study of contemporary wars, an unhealthy fixation on Chechnya, and insufficiently prepared command and control systems.[36]

Ivanov followed these criticisms by consolidating and subordinating power structures—most notably the General Staff—to the MOD. Nonetheless, Baluevsky continues to argue that any war, even a localized armed conflict, could lead the world to the brink of global nuclear war; Russian forces are thus obliged to train and prepare for all possible contingencies.[37] These remarks reflect a continuing preference to train for major theater and even intercontinental nuclear wars against the United States and NATO rather than contribute to and engage in anti-terrorist missions. Finally, material self-interest also predisposes many officers to retain a large number of conscript soldiers whom commanders feel free to treat like serfs. Officers frequently take bribes and compel soldiers to engage in forced labor or even criminal activities (e.g., salary theft).

The Defense Economy

Economic militarization still afflicts the state and the economy. While the current regime strives for economic stimulation, the true purpose is the revival of Russia's status as a great Eurasian power. Putin responded to the crisis in the defense sector by recentralizing the sector. Although rising defense expenditures take up the majority of the state budget, the defense sector still consumes vast amounts of unaccounted for and unaccountable funds. Vladimir Mukhin has written that:

> According to the roughest estimates, over one-half of the country's budget will come under the new military-industrial control. Solely in respect of direct allocation around $16 billion will officially pass through the Russian Federation Defense Ministry-controlled Federal Agency for the Defense Order and Federal Agency for Military-Technical Cooperation in 2004 (according to economic Development and Trade Ministry data, 341.2 billion rubles will be removed from the defense order and R 150 billion from the arms business). Expenditure on special construction and military reform, as well as on defense industry administration must be put into this category. *However, Comptroller's Office audits of the military department regularly reveal the nontargeted use of vast resources.*[38] (emphasis added)

In addition to the Federal Agency for Special Construction, Ivanov's ministry now includes the Russian Federation Federal Service for Military-

---

[36] Defense Minister Sergei Ivanov, speech, Academy of Military Sciences, January 24, 2004 (trans. FBIS, January 24, 2004).

[37] Kremlin International News Broadcast, "Press Conference."

[38] Vladimir Mukhin, "One-Half of Budget Entrusted to Sergei Ivanov: Defense Ministry Becomes Key Department," *Nezavisimaya Gazeta*, March 11, 2004 (trans. FBIS, March 11, 2004).

Technical Cooperation, Federal Service for the Defense Order, and the Federal Service for Technical and Export Control (all of which have been transformed from committees under the Russian Federation Defense Ministry). The Defense Ministry will also control the Federal Agency for Atomic Energy, which is a part of the new Ministry of Industry and Energy. The Russian Federal Railroad Troops Service, disbanded by presidential edict, has also passed to the ministry's control—a move which added 100,000 railroad troops to the MOD's rolls. The Defense Ministry's oversight functions extend to the administrations for munitions, shipbuilding, and conventional weapon, guidance, and control systems; all of these functions were reestablished within the Industry and Energy Ministry in place of the analogous agencies that have been abolished.[39] Thus the Defense Ministry acquired control of the entire defense industry complex.[40] Rosaviakosmos, the Russian Air and Space Agency, was divided between the Space Agency and the aviation sector which became part of the Federal Industry Agency with the other four liquidated agencies.

Insiders in the defense industry hailed these moves as a restoration that would encourage formation of a state-led, vertically integrated defense industrial complex capable of producing modern weapons and technology.[41] Moscow also hoped to concentrate the complex in large blocs controlled or at least directed by the state, thereby eliminating uncompetitive enterprises. Putin even appointed high-ranking state officials as the directors of several firms. Nonetheless, 25–40 percent of the 1,700 defense firms still in operation are bankrupt. Though the number of defense firms is far more than needed or sustainable,[42] Moscow refuses to allow private industry to run this sector lest the uncompetitive firms fail. First Deputy Minister of Industry, Science, and Technology Alexander Brindikov stated that even inefficient production capabilities must be retained for future contingencies lest the state forgo potential wartime requirements.[43]

---

[39] Mukhin, "Defense Ministry Becomes Key Department"; and Viktor Myasnikov, Vladimir Mukhin, and Vladislav Kramer, "Security Offices Weigh In Heavily: The Defense Ministry Grew by 10 Percent and the Defense Industry Got Its Own Mini Ministry," *Nezavisimoye Voyennoye Obozreniye*, March 12, 2004 (trans. FBIS, March 12, 2004).

[40] The four agencies of the complex—the Russian Conventional Arms Agency (RAV), the Russian Agency for control Systems (RASU), Rossudostroyeniye (Russian Shipbuilding Agency, and Rosboyepripasy (Russian Munitions Agency)—were disbanded.

[41] Andrei Shoumikhin, *Modernization of the Armed Forces in Russia: Goals and Problems* (Fairfax, VA: National Institute for Public Policy, 2004), 3–4.

[42] Vitaliy Vitebskiy, "Program Fulfilled Only By A Third," *Nezavisimoye Voyennoye Obozreniye*, July 28, 2000 (trans. FBIS, July 28, 2000); and Vitaly Shlykov, "The Economics of Defense in Russia and the Legacy of Structural Militarization," in *The Russian Military*, ed. Miller and Trenin, 160.

[43] Pronina, "Private Defense Firms Warned," 5.

Consequently, even though the state spends 187 billion rubles on defense contracts, the volume of defense production is negligible. Evidently the state wishes to retain immediate production capabilities for everything from Kalashnikovs to intercontinental ballistic missiles (ICBM), and so must allocate resources to every enterprise accordingly. This configuration results in small production runs or mere retrofitting of existing systems. Stalin's market-defying logic and total war mobilization philosophy still prevail in elite policy circles, while Russian arms exports—upon which the defense industry depends—are hitting a ceiling. This development is in turn forcing the defense industry to consider selling nuclear-capable systems that could potentially exacerbate existing proliferation threats facing Russia.[44] Moreover, there have not been any visible improvements in procurements. Current reforms aim to replace all existing conventional weaponry by 2020–25.

Meanwhile, Moscow is focusing on upgrading existing systems by incrementally adding new technologies, particularly by adding to the information component of weapons through 2015. As these reforms begin to be set in motion, priority will be placed on funding research and development both for new weapons and for maintaining open production lines and capabilities for existing weapons until 2015. In order to preserve production capabilities during this interval, the defense industry should begin introducing new weapons that allow upgrades, hardware development, procurement, and repairs to reach 50–60 percent of annual defense spending by 2015.[45]

In order to increase exports, Putin merged Russia's arms exporters—competition among whom knocked down the price of exports—into one group under his direct authority, and gave operational control to the MOD. Putin has also implemented plans to cut over 600,000 mostly administrative jobs in the defense industry by 2006, a move that will possibly necessitate the shutdown of factories and even entire design groups. The aerospace and shipbuilding industries in particular will be drastically concentrated into state-controlled holding companies. The government will likely unite the existing 1,700 defense enterprises under some 35–40 giant holding companies under state control. Those firms engaged in exports will constitute the resulting leading nuclei. Three key groups of firms will supply finished hardware such as aircraft, submarines, and tanks, as well as weapons sys-

---

[44] Golts, "Arming the World."

[45] Jan Leijonhielm, Jenny Clevstrom, Per-Olov Nilsson, and Wilhelm Unge, *Den Ryska Miliartenkisa Resurbasen* [The Russian Miliary-Technical Base] (Stockholm: Totalforsvaretsforskininginstitut, 2002), Executive Summary, 8, http://www.foi.se; and General Alexei Mikhailovich Moskovskiy, "Confidence in Tomorrow," *Voyennyi-Promyshlennyi Kuryer*, March 10, 2004 (trans. FBIS, March 10, 2004).

tems, engines, generators, and maintenance systems for those platforms.[46] In 2001–02 the production capabilities of many of these plants were at a mere 5–7 percent of capacity; their level has since risen to approximately 15–25 percent of capacity.

Nonetheless, external observers and elite officials alike agree that defense industrial policy has failed, has barely met the needs of the military, or has not been implemented at all. These critiques underscore the state's inability to make the neo-Soviet and neo-Tsarist model work under present conditions.[47] The Strategy and Technology Analysis Center (STAC) found that arms sale funds frequently never even reached the defense industry complex (whose survival is based almost exclusively on exports). Even though state funding has supposedly increased sharply since 1999, the defense sector still will not receive state funds this year because the state administration system remains broken. Deputy Director of STAC Konstantin Makiyenko found that, because the state administration reforms of 2004 abolished defense agencies, defense enterprises did not have to report their true economic and financial condition. The government is thus probably unaware of the defense sector's real situation. Even Makiyenko's figures are incomplete, insomuch as they do not reflect classified producers of strategic weapons.[48]

In 2003 Ivanov stated that "Units have only 70–85 percent of the required armament in working order, and the figure is less than 20 percent for up to date models." He also denounced what he saw as "inexpedient acquisitions."[49] This is not a surprising outcome. Though defense spending from 1999–2003 more than doubled in real terms, readiness did not improve. Since the military sets its own funding priorities independent of any real civilian oversight, funding disappears into untraceable "black holes." In 2002, for example, 79 billion rubles were allocated for 340 different types of military equipment. Orders frequently went for a single item rather than for serial production. The MOD's annual expenditures that pay for this piecework contain no guarantees of large-scale weapons production. Neverthless, Russia's 2002 armament program again failed to specify procurement priorities.[50]

---

[46] Stephen Blank, "The Material-Technical Foundations of Russian Military Power," *Ankara Papers*, no. 7, 2003.

[47] Moskovskiy, "Confidence in Tomorrow."

[48] Alexei Nikolsky, "The Starving Military-Industrial Complex," *Vedomosti*, June 9, 2005 (trans. FBIS, June 9, 2005).

[49] Yuliya Kalinina "The Army Armored Train Brought Out of the Siding," *Moskovskiy Komsomolets*, November 19, 2003 (trans. FBIS, November 19, 2003).

[50] Golts and Putnam, "State Militarism and Its Legacies," 132–33.

The federal budget for 2005 raises spending on defense and security forces by 30 percent from 2004, and mandates the following procurements:

Three battalions of T-90 tanks (90 vehicles in total), three battalions of armored transport vehicles (again 90 machines), the first battery of the Iskander-M operational-tactical missile complex (consisting of two launcher units), two warships, two TU-160 "Blackjack" strategic bombers (one new one to be refitted), seven modernized SU-17SM multi-role fighter jets, seven ballistic missiles (four Topol-M silo-based rockets and three on mobile launchers), nine military satellites, and seven booster rockets. In short, the budget calls for the purchase of about 300 individual weapons and pieces of military hardware, at a total cost of 188 billion rubles ($6.8 billion).[51]

The budget also includes provisions for two surface warships, nine defense satellites for intelligence and communication, and seven upgraded Su-27SM fighters to engage ground targets. The modernized Su-25 fighter will also engage ground targets, and 50 MI-24 attack helicopters will obtain night vision equipment. Russia will also add 12 satellites to the Global Orbiting Navigation Satellite System by 2010, bringing the total number to 24.

This neo-Soviet system naturally revives Soviet economic symptoms, substitutes plans and reports for actual execution, systematicallly obfuscates or falsifies statistics, and engenders an uncompetitive, wasteful, and inherently inflationary defense economy. The Ministry of Economic Development and Trade announced that inflation in 2004 was 12 percent instead of the actual 29 percent. When metal prices rose by much more than this in 2003–04, the increase led to procurement failures and eventual costs of 50–55 billion rubles for the year 2003.[52] Military producers had to absorb the difference, and many state orders went unfulfilled. Military modernization occurs in a strategic and economic vacuum that is unable either to sustain such projects or to impose credible, hard budgetary and policy constraints. The neo-Soviet system currently in place predictably invites efforts to deceive the state, to overcharge the government for inferior or non-existent projects, and to replicate many Soviet pathologies.

Defense modernization still entails excessive economic and political costs. These include preserving or transforming Soviet structural militarization to meet current challenges but without clear strategic guidance as to the priority threat or threats. This Soviet-like restoration will not likely be able to fulfill Russia's weapons plans by 2010 or 2015, modernize the defense economy, or overcome the legacy of structural militarization. As of 2004, according to Moskovskiy, the defense industry only met 10–15 percent of

---

[51] Viktor Litovkin, "Weapons by Numbers," *Russia Profile* 2, no. 3 (April 2005): 13.

[52] Andrey Garavskiy, "Monopolist Conspiracy against Defense Industry," *Krasnaya Zvezda*, April 27, 2004 (trans. FBIS, April 27, 2004).

military needs.[53] Ivanov similarly complained that the defense industry wants bailouts from the state (rather than to compete in the market) and sell products on that basis. He conceded that Russia still lives off the Soviet heritage.[54]

The systematic obfuscation of economic statistics also precludes any clarity concerning the extent of the economy's militarization or an accurate understanding of defense spending. Estimates vary significantly. The International Institute for Strategic Studies (IISS) in London observes that, by using the regime's formal budgetary statistics, Russian defense spending through 2002 amounts to about 2.5–3 percent of annual GDP.[55] These findings omit, however, the widespread reliance on falsified statistics, extra-budgetary allocations, budget add-ons (such as those decreed at the end of 2004), funds under the control of the General Staff for non-military purposes, regional and local spending on the military, and non-cash transactions.[56] United Kingdom (UK) Ministry of Defense analyst Christopher Hill has estimated that actual spending in 2000 was 143 billion rubles (in 2000 prices)—a significant rise from 1999, with actual defense spending being almost double the official budget.[57] In 2001 Hill found that defense spending reached $50 billion, while IISS estimated spending at $57 billion (both figures in constant 2000 prices). In 2001 Moscow announced that the government would reorient the balance of spending to an even 50–50 ratio between conventional and nuclear weapons by 2011. Whether this is actually occurring, however, is unclear. Although defense spending has risen greatly since 2001, there is no reason to assume either less opacity or a reduced defense burden has occurred in the past four years.

Hill's calculations also assumed that the military accounts for one-third to one-half of all expenditures on scientific research. Official statements suggest, however, that such an estimate is unduly conservative. As of 2001 defense spending probably accounted for 5 percent of GNP—a high proportion by NATO standards. Hill and Sutcliffe later argued in 2004 that defense spending remained in the range of 4.5–5 percent of GDP, that much defense spending remains off the budget or "extra-budgetary," and that actual spending on defense (by NATO standards of measurement) is 480 billion rubles.

---

[53] Moskovskiy, "Confidence in Tomorrow."

[54] "Interview with Sergei Ivanov," *Rossiyskaya Gazeta.*

[55] Rosefielde, *Russia in the 21st Century*, 96–97.

[56] Ibid.; and Peter J. Sutcliffe and Chris Hill, "An Economic Analysis of Russian Military Reform Proposals: Ambition and Reality," in *Russian Military Reform 1992–2002*, ed. Aldis and McDermott, 284–85.

[57] Christopher J. Hill, "Russian Defense Spending," in *Russia's Uncertain Economic Future*, ed. John P. Hardt (Armonk, NY: M.E. Sharpe & Co., Inc., 2003), 161–82.

They also found that Russia probably cannot reach official conscription or weapons procurement targets by 2010.[58] Ivanov's latest reforms, described below, confirm that insight.

The above analysis suggests that, with the exception of relatively few exports, most weapons production is worthless. If exports are hitting a ceiling, then a genuine crisis cannot be far behind.[59] Reports of new systems being introduced into the armed forces do not accurately or completely depict the truth, especially since few analyses take into consideration inflation, systematic mendacity, or real costs. In fact, the weapons program for 2001–10 essentially entails either replacing existing but worn out systems or incrementally adding to them—and not introducing groundbreaking technologies or breakthroughs in system integration. Even these incremental improvements, however, are failing. New deliveries are infrequent and in such small numbers as to have only a limited impact;[60] certainly the forces in Chechnya do not benefit from these deliveries.[61] Evidently new air, air defense, naval, and nuclear systems are being introduced, albeit not as fast as Moscow would like. Only in 2004 did the air force begin receiving the Su-27 that had been sold years earlier to China and India. Although Putin has struggled to revive the defense industrial sector, both officials and specialists agree that he has apparently failed.[62]

Moscow's state plan has promoted the idea of reorienting defense production so as to leap ahead to the next generation of weapons by 2020. For 2001–10 the government has given priority to new fifth-generation aircraft, air defenses, ships, space, command and control technologies, and nuclear missiles. Funding increases will chiefly be allocated to new sea-launched strategic missiles, cruise missiles, a fifth-generation fighter jet, new IFVs, tanks, and APCs.[63] Baluevsky has claimed that production-ready weapons, such as the sea-based Bulava nuclear missile and Iskander anti-aircraft cruise missile, represent the first new generation.[64] Remarks made by senior lead-

---

[58] Hill, "Russian Defense Spending"; and Sutcliffe and Hill, "Russian Military Reform Proposals," 284–95.

[59] Golts, *Armiya Rossii*, 171–75.

[60] Leijonhielm, Clevstrom, Nilsson, and Unge, *The Russian Military-Technical Base*, 8; and Moskovskiy, "Confidence in Tomorrow."

[61] Kramer, "Russia's War in Chechnya," 5–63; and Kramer, "Military Dimensions of the Russian-Chechen Conflict," 209–90.

[62] Golts, *Armiya Rossii*, 171–75; Sutcliffe and Hill, "Russian Military Reform Proposals," 284–85; Shlykov, "Economics of Defense in Russia," 160–82; and Moskovskiy, "Confidence in Tomorrow."

[63] Igor Ivanov, "Rearmament," *Current Digest of the Post-Soviet Press* 53, no. 1 (January 31, 2001): 13–14.

[64] Andrei Lebedev, "Yuri Baluevsky: The Russian Military Has a Chance to Straighten its Spine," *Izvestiya*, March 2, 2005, 11.

ers regarding Russia's possession of unique new missiles capable of evading detection by foreign missile defense systems may also refer to these same missiles and/or may include hypersonic, land-based, Topol-M nuclear missiles.[65] Other sources also confirm a priority investment in air defense weapons, new nuclear weapons, command and control equipment, and space and reconnaissance systems.[66]

These reports largely conform both to Deputy Defense Minister Nikolai Mikhailov's 2001 remarks concerning the future direction of R&D and procurement and to Richard Staar's findings in 1999–2000. The neo-Stalinist autarchic ideology of key actors holds that, since most high-tech research occurs in the defense industry, defense production is the locomotive of economic recovery. Mikhailov has stated that, in light of the fact that the military regularly consumes S&T products, the military can use such products to fulfill any combat mission only as long as they make maximal use of domestic scientific and engineering capabilities. Accordingly, the notion that this sector is the "permanently operating" (a classic Stalinist neologism) catalyst of technological recovery is utterly false and misleading.[67] Still, Mikhailov has conceded that Russia lags behind in computers and technology exports, and risks falling even further behind in the future. He then outlined a comprehensive program of military-technological modernization designed, in true Stalinist "storming" style, to restore Russia to an internationally competitive level by 2005–10.

Mikhailov insisted upon the priority of systems for terrestrial and sea reconnaissance; information support for troops; automated control systems and weaponry combat control systems; precision strike systems for land, sea, and air; modern global and theater navigation systems; optical and radio detection and ranging, as well as means for information processing; and other new munitions. He outlined the key areas where Russia must make improvements in domestic production in order to meet the rising threat from the United States. These include space and missile engineering to build Topol-Ms and missile defenses, a new generation of space apparatuses "for various targeting procedures," aeronautical engineering for new fighter planes, anti-air or air defense engineering, fourth- and fifth-generation submarine missile cruisers, heavy aircraft-carrying cruisers, precision guided missiles tanks, C2 systems for ground forces, and locally-built highly-integrated mi-

---

[65] Kremlin International News Broadcast, "Press Conference."

[66] Sergei Ptichkin, "New Weapons Will Not Appear Soon," *Rossiyskaya Gazeta*, August 8, 2002 (trans. FBIS, August 8, 2002).

[67] Igor Ivanov, "Rearmament," 13–14; Sergei Putilov, "Army to Buy 'Wonder Weapons," *Current Digest of the Post-Soviet Press* 53, no. 1 (January 31, 2001): 13; and interview with Russian Control Systems Agency General Director Vladimir Simonov, *Krasnaya Zvezda*, December 19, 2001 (trans. FBIS, December 19, 2001).

cro-processors, supercomputers, and neuroprocessors.[68] Staar suggests that future defense spending will feature major increases in aerospace systems; microelectronics; electro-optical systems; new strategic, tactical, and miniature nuclear weapons; the first *Borey*-class nuclear submarines armed with the new SS-NX-28 sea-launched ballistic missile (SLBM [Bulava]); various naval systems; and command, control, communications, and intelligence (C3I) technologies for both information warfare and nuclear C3I.[69]

While force development in the navy would need to double in order to complete new ships by 2008, prospects for even minimal development are bleak. Despite the imminent appearance of new, smaller ships, the navy—according to its sponsors—risks collapse.[70] Meanwhile, Moscow has initiated substantial modernization and upgrades on the Caspian Flotilla. A 2002 report described the fleet's growing power projection capabilities, which includes new ships, amphibious aircraft, patrol ship helicopters, new airfields at Kaspiisk, and a brigade of marines.[71]

According to Staar, Russia has also spent large sums on the research of directed energy weapons: lasers, microwave radiation emitters, particle-beam generators using subatomic particles to destroy targets at the speed of light, a new mass plasma weapon that could ionize the atmosphere and destroy incoming missiles and enemy aircraft, anti-stealth radar, indigenous stealthy air-launched cruise missiles (ALCM), newly tested anti-aircraft and anti-missile systems (e.g., the S-400, with a range of 250 miles), and a plasma coating to make fifth-generation aircraft invisible. Until these weapons are ready Russia must continue upgrading existing systems.[72] These programs reflect emerging Russian views of the future of warfare as characterized not only by high-tech, electronic, precision-strike air and airborne operations, but also by efforts to disorganize C2 systems.[73]

The Russian defense industry may remain competitive in traditionally strong sectors such as nuclear, laser, and space satellite technology; excessive dependence upon the state and structural militarization, however, makes this sector inherently dysfunctional. Even without considering a host of issues—manpower, professionalization of the armed forces, underinvestment

[68] Vitebskiy, "Program Fulfilled Only By A Third."

[69] Richard Staar, "A Russian Rearmament Wish List," *Orbis* 43, no. 4 (Fall 1999): 605–12; and Richard Staar, "Funding Russia's Rearmament," *Perspective* 10, no. 1 (September-October 1999): 1–2, 8–10.

[70] Radio Free Europe Radio Liberty Newsline, June 1, 2004.

[71] Igor Torbakov, "Russia to Flex Military Muscle in the Caspian With an Eye on Future Energy Exports," *Eurasia Insight*, July 31, 2002, http://www.eurasianet.org.

[72] Staar, "Russian Rearmament Wish List," 605–12; and Staar, "Funding Russia's Rearmament," 1–2, 9–10.

[73] Leijonhielm, Clevstrom, Nilsson, and Unge, *The Russian Miliary-Technical Base*, 11.

in education and science, lack of force organization, and the catastrophic state of its infrastructure—Russia may still be falling behind in cutting-edge, innovative technologies relevant to future warfare. As a result, despite Putin's misconceived efforts to overcome these problems through a reassertion of state control, the defense industry remains in crisis. Undoubtedly this crisis will provoke further reforms. Ivanov is now urging defense industries—and not the government—to fund R&D on their own, and give weapons to the military because defense orders have grown substantially and production has begun to revive. This will supposedly eliminate "dead souls" who produce nothing on the state's ledgers and put the onus of genuine weapon production on the defense industry, frequently resulting in the production of what are essentially Soviet-era weapons masquerading as new ones.[74] Though the success or failure of new reforms is uncertain, there is no doubt that the current crisis in the defense economy is intertwined with the abiding crisis within the state.

Nuclear Forces and Strategy

Lacking adequate conventional capabilities sufficient for the defense of the nation's enormous resources and borders, Russia's nuclear forces must be ready for any kind of conflict—including intercontinental nuclear war. Indeed, there is a direct relationship between local anti-terrorist wars and each step in the chain of esclation to nuclear war, particularly as Russia must threaten nuclear war in order to deter conventional opponents.[75] Thus Ivanov stated in 2004 that "Russian leaders regard the maintenance of fighting ability and readiness of strategic forces as their top priority task."[76] Deterrence is a cornerstone of Russian doctrine and strategy, and includes a readiness to preempt enemies with the threat of nuclear strikes, a move designed to control intrawar escalation and compel de-escalation. Policymakers also cite the growing likelihood that the use of nuclear weapons in war may become a policy guideline.[77] A 2000 doctrine and security concept proclaimed Moscow's intention to strike first with nuclear weapons across a range of conventional contingencies. Subsequent official statements (e.g., Ivanov's 2003 white paper) reiterate that point.[78] Moscow has

[74] Vitaly Shlykov, "The Defense Minister's Attack on the Defense Industry," *Izvestiya*, March 3, 2005, 4.

[75] Russian Ministry of Defense, "Development of the Armed Forces of the Russian Federation."

[76] Ivanov, keynote address, July 13, 2004.

[77] Ibid.; and Ivanov, "Russia's Armed Forces and Its Geopolitical Priorities."

[78] Russian Ministry of Defense, "Development of the Armed Forces of the Russian Federation."

repeatedly declared a willingness to deter even smaller-scale conventional attacks against key installations or allies (i.e., extended deterrence) with nuclear weapons. Indeed, Russian analysts and officials observed in 1999 that NATO's invasion of Kosovo instigated doctrine writers to add scenarios for the use of tactical nuclear weapons against purely conventional attacks.[79] In December 1999, following published doctrinal statements, Colonel General Vladimir Yakovlev, the commander-in-chief of Russia's nuclear forces, stated that "Russia, for objective reasons, is forced to lower the threshold for using nuclear weapons, extend the nuclear deterrent to smaller-scale conflicts and openly warn potential opponents about this."[80]

Yarkolev's "objective reasons" include Russia's financial crises (which have meant that rocket forces receive about half the needed funds), the depletion and incomplete recovery of Russia's conventional weapons and forces, and the emergence of regional powers armed with missiles and nuclear technology. In the meantime, Russia will continue to replace old missiles with new Topol-M ICBMs.[81] Such a posture logically implies the need both to maintain and even extend the lifespan of Russia's existing nuclear arsenal and at the same time to procure new weapons. This logic directly contradicted Kvashnin's position that deprecated nuclear or high-end conventional threats, and ultimately led to a new policy stressing greater nuclear procurement than initially advocated. Up until that point, Russia's military community had undergone a bruising debate over nuclear weapons. The issue became such a hot topic following not only Kvashnin's efforts in 2000 to gut Sergeyev's nuclear program, but also by Washington's decision to leave the ABM treaty, a move which opened up the possibility that the United States might develop new nuclear weapons.

Specifically the 2000 Security Concept stated that the armed forces must exercise deterrence that would prevent nuclear and conventional aggression against Russia and its allies (presumably CIS members): "Nuclear weapons should be capable of inflicting the desired extent of damage against any aggressor state or coalition of states in any conditions and circumstances." The report also declared that the use of nuclear weapons would become possible "in the event or need to repulse armed aggression, if all other measures of resolving the crisis situation have been exhausted and proven ineffective."[82]

Nuclear weapons are, therefore, an effective deterrent for the many contingencies along the spectrum of conflict that could threaten Russia. Such

---

[79] Author's conversations with Russian officers and analysts, Helsinki and Moscow, June 1999.

[80] Martin Nesirsky, "Russia Says Threshold Lower for Nuclear Weapons," Reuters, December 17, 1999.

[81] Ibid.

[82] As translated by FBIS, January 14, 2000.

weapons are also warfighting instruments available for use against numerous threats that could arise out of actual conflict scenarios. The Security Concept's use of phrases such as "aggression on any scale, nuclear or otherwise" and "to the desired extent of damage" imply that the use of nuclear weapons may be tailored to the particular threat at hand. Thus the Security Concept appears to declare the concept of limited nuclear war as Moscow's official war strategy against a variety of contingencies, and it further reflects Russian interest in using tactical nuclear weapons as actual warfighting weapons.[83] Key officials have confirmed that limited nuclear war is Russia's officially acknowledged strategy for many different contingencies.[84] This strategy also reflects Moscow's bizarre, unsettling, and unprecedented belief that Russia—despite forty years of Soviet experience to the contrary—would be able to control escalation and nuclear war as long as Russia was the initiator. Meanwhile, even as current procurement numbers fall, Russia is relying on new, mobile, and survivable nuclear weapons.

Consequently, qualitative improvement at reduced numbers characterizes nuclear force modernization in Russia. Moscow produces between four to seven new Topol-M ICBMs (SS-27Ms) per year, a number of Bulava sea-based nuclear missiles, and new nuclear submarines (SSBN) in spite of the constant delays in producing the *Borey*-class submarine. This modernization, prompted by Washington's withdrawal from the ABM treaty and Russia's ensuing departure from the START-2 treaty, allows Moscow to extend the life of its SS-18 and SS-19 ICBMs, and even to MIRV them.[85] This development saves Moscow money, and the mobility of the Topol greatly enhances Russia's first- and second-strike deterrent capability—possibly at lower nuclear thresholds than before. Similarly, the Bulava and possibly the Topol-M are allegedly being outfitted with missile warheads that fulfill Sergeyev's call for "gliding" nuclear weapons capable of eluding any missile defense system.[86] The above developments apparently are Moscow's "asymmetric" reply to Washington's moves to enhance its missile defense program,

---

[83] As translated by FBIS, January 14, 2000; Gunnar Arbman and Charles Thornton, *Russia's Tactical and Nuclear Weapons Part I: Background and Policy Issues* (Stockholm: Swedish Defense Research Agency, 2003); and Gunnar Arbman and Charles Thornton, *Russia's Tactical and Nuclear Weapons Part II: Technical Issues and Policy Recommendations* (Stockholm: Swedish Defense Research Agency, 2005).

[84] Arbman and Thornton, *Russia's Tactical and Nuclear Weapons Part II*.

[85] Rose Gottemoeller, "Nuclear Weapons in Current Russian Policy," in *The Russian Military: Power and Purpose*, ed. Miller and Trenin, 183–216; and Frank Umbach, "Nuclear vs Conventional Forces: Implications for Russia's Future Military Reform," in *Russian Military Reform 1992–2002*, ed. Aldis and McDermott, 77–98.

[86] Yevgeny Vladimirovich Myasnikov, *High Precision Weapons and the Strategic Balance* (Moscow: Internet Center for Arms Control Energy and Environmental Studies under MFTI, November 2000 [trans. FBIS, November 1, 2000]).

consider a new generation of so-called bunker buster and low-yield nuclear weapons, and withdraw from the ABM treaty.[87]

Moscow has also rebuilt a credible warfighting nuclear arsenal from still serviceable Tu-160 and Tu-95 bombers obtained from Ukraine, old and new SLBMs and ICBMs, and several thousand tactical nuclear weapons.[88] Outperforming previous ICBMs by 50–100 percent in terms of combat preparedness and by 100–150 percent in precision, the Topol-M is much cheaper to produce and maintain.[89] Moscow can reduce its strategic nuclear forces down to ten to twelve divisions (or perhaps even further) by 2016–20 (including old and new missiles). Another factor facilitating reduction of the nuclear arsenal is the improved precision and lethality of new conventional missiles. As older systems are gradually phased out, procurement of new systems at reduced quantities will continue through at least 2015, thus giving Moscow at least 1,000–1,500 usable nuclear weapons by the time the Moscow Treaty expires in 2012 (a number less than the 2,200 allowed by the treaty).[90] Even so, the modernization of Russia's nuclear forces, albeit necessary, is not sufficient to meet conventional military threats.

Conventional Forces

Though conforming with Putin and Ivanov's overall centralization of power by "optimizing" the bureaucracy, reforms of the MOD are also driven by budgetary exigencies. Thus it remains unclear whether or not these reforms are succeeding. Reforms began within the MOD itself in order to reduce the power of the conservatives (in particular their access to Ivanov). The treasury board supposedly provides Ivanov and his team more insight into and control over defense spending. Officials believe that, as defense spending rises, financial controls over implementing the budget will also tighten. They have also stated that Ivanov still seeks a central and coordinated procurement process and is hiring an external auditor to research the costs of major weapons systems. The MOD will also introduce a uniform tender format for all armed services and non-MOD security agencies that will procure weapons at fixed prices and tighten suppliers' quality control, requirements, and delivery schedules. These changes are not likely to be rap-

---

87 Kremlin International News Broadcast, "Press Conference."

88 No reliable estimates of the precise number or nature exist.

89 Gottemoeller, "Nuclear Weapons in Current Russian Policy," 183–98; Umbach, "Nuclear vs Conventional Forces," 77–98; and Igor Plugatarev, "Topol-M Ousts Molodets and Voeovda Systems," *Nezavisimoye Voyennoye Obozreniye*, no. 3, January 28–February 3, 2005, 1.

90 Plugatarev, "Topol-M Ousts Molodets and Voeovda Systems"; and Myasnikov, *High Precision Weapons and the Strategic Balance*.

id, however. A lawyer with the MOD's atomic energy agency has stated that the lack of transparency inside the procurement system serves the interests of both ministry personnel and contractors.[91]

Similarly, stripping the General Staff of virtually all of its administrative capabilities and transferring them to the MOD effectively centralizes control in that ministry. In August 2004 Putin signed a classified decree that confirmed the ministry as the sole elaborator and implementer of defense policy. The decree cut staff by 20 percent and capped central ministerial personnel at 10,350. The Defense Minister's staff under Lt. General Andrei Chobotov (Ivanov's protégé), a 350-man monitoring and evaluation unit, is now the MOD's key nerve center for monitoring compliance with policy, assessing policy and intelligence options, supervising media relations, and coordinating civilian agencies under the MOD. The General Staff, GRU Chief, and service and district chiefs all report to Ivanov. Nevertheless, Ivanov and his five deputy defense ministers have not improved genuine democratic or civilian control, accountability, or effectiveness. Major General Pavel Zolotarev, former Chief of the General Staff's Information and Analysis Center, charges that despite the changes and reshuffling that are passed off as reform, work continues as before—including in the General Staff.[92]

Force structure has also undergone significant transformation. Russia's nuclear forces (RSVN) have been downgraded from a branch to an arm of the armed forces, and their space assets (the Missile Space Defense Troops and Military Space Command) now form a new arm of troops (the Space Command). This structure has given Russia three branches: Ground Forces, the Navy, and the Air (and Air Defense) Forces. Within the Ground Forces, permanent readiness formations and units received priority and the Main Command of the Ground Forces has been restored. The Volga and Ural Military Districts merged into a Volga-Ural Military Districts with responsibility for Central Asia, units of the Caucasus were to undergo further development, and central command structures would undergo further "optimization."[93]

The demands made by Ivanov and Putin for continuing reform stem from their dissatisfaction with the level of preparedness; the military's lack of professionalism and strenuous opposition to reforms based on further force reductions; the priority threat of local wars like Iraq, the Caucasus and Central Asia; and the need for affordable, truly joint, highly mobile, and more professional forces led by a unified and single command structure that

---

[91] Trifonov, "Russian Defence Reform"; and Pallin, *Russian Military Reform*, 173–74.

[92] Pallin, *Russian Military Reform*; Vadim Solovyov, "Staff Reshuffles Completed at the Defense Ministry," *Nezavisimaya Gazeta*, November 19, 2004.

[93] Pallin, *Russian Military Reform*, 173–74.

places all of Russia's troops under the MOD.[94] Forces will be based on the approximately ten to sixteen permanent readiness divisions and four main fleets, in addition to the Caspian Flotilla that ideally will become increasingly professionalized and fully equipped. To realize this program, increased training and exercises have attempted to create unified, joint, professional forces under centralized control, capable of confronting all domestic and international threats.[95]

This vision obviously rejects much of the Soviet tradition and even goes much further. Ivanov typically denied reports of cutting the six military districts into four regional commands, the formation of a special forces arm of the MOD, and the cutting of another 250,000–300,000 (if not more) troops from the military; his actual goal is probably a force of between 500,000–750,000 men by 2010. Other aims likely include the creation of a new rapid reaction and/or special purpose force and deployment system.[96] Ivanov also overcame the resistance of the General Staff to creating a peacekeeping brigade interoperable with NATO and the UN (i.e., one having English language proficiency), and capable of performing missions within Russia.[97]

Since the military budget is still unable to meet Russia's defense needs, Moscow must cut more manpower from district bureaucracies and commands if Russia is to be able to afford high-tech weapons and professionalization. Reducing manpower and reassigning ex-soldiers to the Ministry of Interior's Internal Forces (VVMVD) saves money and reorients force structures to meet the more likely domestic (as opposed to external) threats. Such a realignment would mean that the armed forces would increasingly resemble a domestic gendarmerie that manages internal threats as foreign threats decrease.[98] Although undoing the VVMVD's 2001 reform plan calling for large-scale cuts, this change fulfills Ivanov and Kvashnin's shared aim of unifying all forces within a single territorial formation under the centralized control of one commander (although Kvashnin saw himself as that commander).

Ivanov is also forming rapid reaction and anti-terrorist forces. In 2003 the General Staff raised the issue of rapid reaction forces (SBR) that would be based in two districts. The first includes Leningrad, Moscow, North

---

[94] These forces include the Ministry of Interior's Internal Forces and those of the Federal Security Bureau (FSB), the successor to the KGB.

[95] Isakova, *Russian Governance in the Twenty-First Century*, 232–69; Trifonov, "Russian Defence Reform"; and Pallin, *Russian Military Reform*, 174–79.

[96] Vladimir Urban, "VV Epokhi Vladimira Vladimirovicha" [The Ministry of Interior's Forces in the Epoch of Vladimir Vladimirovich], *Moskovskie Novosti*, May 27, 2005.

[97] FBIS Report, "Russia: Profile of 15th Peacekeeping Brigade," February 17, 2005.

[98] Urban, "The Ministry of Interior's Forces."

Caucasus, and Volga-Ural; the second includes Siberia and the Far East. These forces will comprise the airborne troops, naval infantry, and permanent readiness tank and motorized-rifle formations of the ground troops. Building this force would require ending the duplication whereby each district contains two to four permanent readiness formations capable only of performing tactical missions. A truly joint rapid reaction force could become the basis for the combined-arms formation of an operational-scale army SBR.[99] After the 2004 Beslan catastrophe, reinforced mechanized infantry companies having 30-minute readiness were also organized. These companies are appointed for a month and conduct special anti-terrorist missions.[100] This new force emerged from maneuvers in the Far East in 2004, when marines and airborne troops were airlifted from the Northern Fleet and Pskov. Not having a permanent staff, this new force will come together only for specific missions, and its creation probably also entails reducing the RSVN to 8-10 divisions.[101]

This force structure is developing precisely because Russia can no longer maintain major army groups along its borders. Russia requires additional SBR units that are truly joint, fully equipped, and under a single command. These rapid reaction forces can be airlifted to operational zones to assist other security forces. There the MOD will apparently form a newly created special operation force (or Spetsnaz) from Spetsnaz brigades under the defense minister's direct control.[102] These forces will have air, marine, and ground components, and conduct peace support and counterterrorist operations.[103]

Moscow previously cut the VVMVD by at least 20,000 men, tripled its funding, and re-emphasized combat training. By 2005 Moscow intends to further reduce this command by 33,000 men. By reorganizing these troops into five regional commands and two main departments, as well as by shifting operational-purpose units to a brigade-battalion structure (including the VVMVD's Special Forces), Moscow has also restructured these forces to conform with MOD rapid reaction and special force groupings.[104] The Ground Forces will constitute the bulk of these combined forces in regional

[99] General Vyacheslav V. Zherebtov, "On Possible Ways of Developing Russian Armed Forces," *Voyennaya Mysl'*, December 15, 2003 (trans. FBIS, December 15, 2003).

[100] Alexei Ventslovsky, "The 58th Army in the Hot Place," *Krasnaya Zvezda*, March 18, 2005.

[101] Alexander Mikhailov, "3.1 Special Reduction Forces," *Russkii Kurier*, March 30, 2005, 2.

[102] Viktor Litovkin, "Spetsnaz To Be Reorganized," RIA Novosti, March 22, 2005.

[103] Ibid.; and Alexander Mikhailov, "3.1 Special Reduction Forces," 2.

[104] RIA Novosti, March 26, 2004 (trans. FBIS, March 26, 2004); *Agenstvo Voyennykh Novostey*, March 18, 2004 (trans. FBIS, March 18, 2004); and *Agenstvo Voyennykh Novostey*, February 19, 2004 (trans. FBIS, February 19, 2004).

and larger-scale wars. Both C2 and artillery forces must therefore also undergo reorganization to build reconnaissance-fire complexes and train these permanent readiness forces and their various forms of artillery support.[105] In the Air Defense and Navy forces, however, there are problems greater than a simple lack of readiness.

Although the roles that airpower and air defenses play in modern war are clearly growing, these services see themselves as embattled. As capital intensive services, they will likely be among the first victims of future reform. Numerous articles have attacked Kvashnin and Boris Yeltsin (and by implication Ivanov and Putin) for leaving Russia undefended against aerial attack and for making false claims about the Air Force and Air Defense's ability to repulse all conceivable attacks on Russia.[106] These articles frequently claim that the Air Force and Air Defense Forces were "blindsided" by impending reductions in size, and have even warned that the latter might collapse altogether.[107] Polemics also continue over the merits or demerits of Kvashnin's effort to unify the Air and Air Defense Forces in 1997–98, as well as Ivanov's subsequent separation of the Space Forces from the Air Defense Forces—another decision that could supposedly trigger the latter's collapse.[108]

Russia still cannot, short of invoking the nuclear option, defend itself against an aerial or space attack. Air Force Chief of Staff General Boris Cheltsov lamented the underfunding of the two services and admitted that fighter pilots averaged only 20–25 percent of the necessary flight time in 2004. Increases in flight time are not envisaged for 2005, as fuel limits have reduced combat training. In response Cheltsov has stated that the Air Force:

> possesses sufficient potential to fulfill tasks of repelling aggression on a local or regional scale using both conventional and nuclear weapons. Its command system provides command and control of strategic aviation nuclear forces and general-purpose forces.[109]

While increasingly accepting the priority of local or regional wars and the importance of joint force packages (comprising air and ground assets), Russian leaders still cannot create such forces. The Air and Air Defense

[105] Major General Sergei Bogatinov, "The Gods of War Aren't Surrendering Positions," *Armeyskiy Sbornik*, November 1, 2003 (trans. FBIS, November 1, 2003).

[106] Andrei Shoumikhin, "Russian Efforts to Improve Air and Space Defense," National Institute for Public Policy, May 2004, http://www.nipp.org/Adobe/Regional%20Web/May%2004%20webpage.pdf.

[107] Aleksandr Babakin, "Numbers Are Cut—Tears Are Shed. Air Force and Submarine Fleet Deemed Most Unnecessary in Ministry of Defense, *Nezavisimaya Gazeta*, October 12, 2004.

[108] Shoumikhin, "Russian Efforts to Improve Air and Space Defense."

[109] "Merger Affects Russian Air Defense Capabilities-General," *Mosnews.com*, May 13, 2005.

Forces, despite requiring enormous capital investments, must undergo further reorganization, reduction, and thus delay while undergoing re-equipping.[110] Officers are leaving at high rates, creating the possibility of a future shortage.[111]

The Navy's situation is equally desperate. Although Russia builds corvettes and frigates, massive decommissioning of SSBNs and of ships built in 1970–85 has already begun. Navy commanders have frequently yet fruitlessly argued for a global navy and the large-scale missions associated with such a navy. Exercises are targeted at countering threats of piracy and terrorism, not theater conventional or nuclear war. Russian commanders and analysts claim that, despite statements by Ivanov and others promising additional support for the Navy, not one new ship will enter service in 2005. Although new ships might begin to enter service by 2015, naval commanders—whether wedded to an illusory strategic mission or simply the notion of a large navy—constantly demand more money in support of a naval ministry. They claim that by 2020 or 2030 the navy will either contain only 50 warships or will be defunct.[112]

Kuroyedov recently reported that, if the navy conducts judicious repairs, the current number of ships can be maintained through 2020. New smaller ships must be built, however, as ships cannot be endlessly repaired. Meanwhile new multi purpose ships are being constructed that combine anti-submarine and missile ships.[113] If the new reforms described above occur, their impact on the Navy may, however, further disrupt existing and future projects. Therefore the Navy's future is as clouded as that of the Air and Air Defense Forces. The global mission is clearly unrealistic, and Russia will be hard pressed to build enough ships even to provide combat stability to the SSBNs supposedly slated to become the primary leg of the country's strategic nuclear forces.

Defense Reform and Professionalization

Despite the aforementioned reforms of the armed forces, the real challenge lies in the professionalization of the military. Only real professionalization can create well-educated, technologically capable forces with high morale and discipline. Much of the officer corps is a criminal class, or at

---

[110] Mikhail Khodarenok, "Possibilities of a Preventive Strike," *Voyenno-Promyshlennyi Kuryer*, no. 15, December 17–23, 2003, 1, 6.

[111] *Agenstvo Voyennykh Novostey*, April 29, 2004 (trans. FBIS, April 29, 2004).

[112] RIA Novosti, "Russia to Get New Battleships," May 24, 2005; and "Navy Chief Says Russia Can Be Left With 50 Warships by 2020," *Kommersant*, February 7, 2005.

[113] RIA Novosti, "Constructing Multi-Purpose Surface Ships," May 10, 2005.

least tolerates anomic and criminal behavior. Continuing military serfdom undermines officer corps professionalization, corrupts the entire state, and erodes the legitimacy and social status of the armed forces. In addition, the accompanying lack of accountability and of the rule of law in the military reinforces and parallels these same conditions throughout Russian society.

With the support of Putin, the military has, meanwhile, stonewalled all efforts at reform. Though Putin and Ivanov have repeatedly stated that by 2008 the professionalization of some 133,000–150,000 men would be completed (mostly in the permanent readiness forces), such a goal is unlikely to adequately address the crisis. Even such a modest goal as this, however, has been thwarted by the military. For example, Ivanov announced that, since professionals make better soldiers than conscripts, these future professionals would be sent to "hot spots" such as Chechnya. On March 25, 2005 General Aleksandr Baranov, commander-in-chief of the North Caucasus Military District, reiterated that there are no plans to enlist native residents of Chechnya to serve on a contract basis in Russian military subunits. On April 7, however, Secretary of the Chechen Security Council Rudnik Dudayev announced the resumption of a draft in Chechnya. Draftees will supposedly only serve in Chechnya, and will join the Russian Army's 42nd Division (or the VVMVD) and Chechen Emergency Situations forces.

In Ingushetia, letters from soldiers and press reports point to another version of this tactic. The 503rd Regiment is moving to contract service; lacking sufficient contract personnel conscripts, however, the regiment must sign service contracts. Hence the regiment is exchanging one form of military serfdom for another, suggesting a deliberate state program designed to meet the required quota for "professionals." For example, the 42nd Division (supposedly composed of Chechens) will reportedly become a contract unit. In actuality, this division's contract service personnel are composed of recruits that have already been conscripted (in 2004), and were forced to sign these contracts *ex post facto*. After their officers told them they had no legal recourse, desperate soldiers in the 503rd Regiment threatened to escape. Indeed, soldiers are often told that if they do not sign, or if they break the contract, they either will not be paid or must remit their wages to commmanders as a bribe.

Moreover, in April 2005 governors and ministers became responsible for activities linked to conscription. By obligating these officials "to fulfill the plan," Moscow has thus revived the Tsarist-Soviet practice of collective responsibility. In addition to recruiting 157,000 conscripts, governors must also find 42,000 "volunteers." Once signing their military oath, conscripts are reportedly given contracts and paid a monthly wage of 15,000 rubles. It is thus unsurprising to hear numerous complaints from the Russian military regarding the low quality of recruits and the unabated, organized thievery of resources supposedly earmarked for reconstruction in Chechnya and throughout the North Caucasus.[114] That this brutality, criminality, lawlessness, and enserfment masquerades as contracted service only underscores the urgency of subjecting the entire military establishment—from Putin on down—to comprehensive accountability to the law and the Duma.

Such serfdom is not confined to hapless soldiers; the regime also seeks to enserf officers and even high-ranking officials. In order to address the shortage of officers created by mass officer desertion, Duma member Andrei Golovatyuk proposed legislation empowering the state to force officers who "violate" the terms of their contract (by resigning after five years) to pay the state 130,000 rubles. The MOD supports this move and Ivanov reportedly issued a secret decree in 2004 rejecting the applications of young officers to leave the service. Golovatyuk also proposed to take *quitrent* (fixed rent paid in commutation of services) from cadets expelled from military schools for slow progress. Not surprisingly a Russian newspaper commented that "the Duma proposes to implement serfdom in the Army."[115] Furthermore, since conscripts will only serve one year (as opposed to two years, as is currently the case), more conscripts will be called up—effectively doubling the reserve mobilization base. Baluevsky admits that recent exercises designed to train joint forces also portend the return of a system of general mobilization of civilians.[116] As conscription in Russia equates more or less to state serfdom, attempts to invigorate that system, make the army and VVMVD a domestic gendarmerie, and create a new Spetsnaz accountable only to Ivanov and Putin are all steps that have an obvious anti-democratic—even sinister—significance. Atop the state, as Peter Baker and Susan Glasser report, holdovers from Yeltsin's time (such as Finance Minister Alexei Kudrin and Economic Development and Trade Minister German Gref) are literally not allowed to leave their posts. Fearing Kremlin reprisals, they are mere show ministers retained for the express purpose of mollifying Western observers and maintaining a pretense of reform, all the while taking the domestic blame for mishandled social reforms.[117]

[114] Stephen Blank, "Bait and Switch: Moscow's Shell Game in Chechnya," *Eurasia Daily Monitor*, April 14, 2005.

[115] This quote appeared in the *Nezavisimoye Voyennoye Obozreniye* [Independent Military Review], as cited in Blank, "Moscow's Shell Game in Chechnya."

[116] "Chief of Russia's General Staff Speaks About Current Challenges," *Krasnaya Zvezda*, November 6, 2004 (trans. FBIS, November 6, 2004).

[117] Baker and Glasser, *Vladimir Putin's Russia*, 374.

Conclusion

Genuine defense reform in Russia—i.e., the institution of legal account-ability for everyone from Putin on down, imposition of stiff penalties for military crimes, and the abolition of the nexus of autocracy, serfdom, law-lessness, lack of human rights, state militarism, and imperialism—is not possible under the current government. A reform of force structures along the outlines sketched above will undoubtedly continue into the foreseeable future. This reform will continue, however, under the lengthening shadow of the war in Chechnya, a war that to a considerable degree drives those force reforms. That war has even spread beyond Chechnya into the North Caucasus. This reality suggests that Moscow has articulated no clear concept of, or strategy for, achieving victory.

Yet Moscow continues to throw money at these problems in a futile attempt to fill the gaping chasm between Russia's ambitions and actual ca-pabilities. Meanwhile, the leadership continues to cut Russia's armed forces and insists on retaining a powerful nuclear deterrent. Thus Russian defense policy is simultaneously comprised of greatly increased spending, fruitless and incomplete efforts at reform of the defense economy, continued reliance on a smaller though still robust nuclear arsenal, and an effort to downsize and restructure the conventional forces for new missions like counterter-rorism and power projection inside the old Soviet borders. Moscow also proposes increasing partnership in NATO peacekeeping operations, but Russia's political and military leadership remain instinctively opposed to such a partnership. While desperately needing genuine partners and al-lies, Moscow also fears and spurns them more often than not. Though these moves may allow Russia to create a force that can project effective unilateral military power across the extent of post-Soviet geographical territory, such force projection remains as yet an unproven and probably unsustainable hope.

As long as the defense economy fails to deliver modern weapons to the armed forces, and as long as conscription remains, Moscow probably cannot develop the kind of conventional power to which it aspires. Hence Moscow will be forced to rely ever more on nuclear deterrence or on partnerships with other powers in order to secure Russia's interests. Inherently both im-perial and sub-optimizing, the dysfunctional state system compounds the nation's problems and generates demands for power and status impossible to satisfy. Moreover, even if Ivanov's reforms succeed to a measurable de-gree, the force that is emerging looks optimized primarily both for domes-tic counterinsurgency and for power projection to the CIS rather than for defense of the state against external attack. Even though there is no current external threat, will this system prove flexible enough to meet such a challenge in the future?

In the meantime, given the wholly dysfunctional defense economy and archaic political and command structrure, can Russia actually meet its pressing internal security challenges through a reliance on these mechanisms? Some benefits may accrue from the reorganization of the services or in procuring newer weapons. Leaving the foundations of autocracy and neo-Tsarism intact, however, exposes Russia to new threats—such as demographic and health crises—that Moscow will be unable to address.

The state, economy, and armed forces in Russia remain mired both in a neo-Tsarist autocracy and in the vaunted power vertical that merges Putin's farcical cult of personality with the official cult of the Orthodox Church. Unfortunately, the official nationalism of Nicholas I and the personality cult cultivated by Stalin—both of which Putin has sought to revive—lead either to permanent crisis or to a disastrous dead end. After Nicholas I died, a contemporary historian wrote that his reign was all a mistake. Genuine defense reform is a template for, and integral part of, any future hope for Russia; Putin and his colleagues, however, are resolutely barring that gate to the future. Future historians may thus similarly observe that Putin's reign was likewise a mistake.

STRATEGIC ASIA 2005–06

REGIONAL STUDIES

Executive Summary

This chapter examines military modernization in post-Soviet Central Asia (Kazakhstan, Kyrgyzstan, Tajikistan, Turkmenistan, and Uzbekistan) and Afghanistan.

MAIN ARGUMENT:

- Military modernization in the countries of Central Asia is much more dependent on officer corps retraining and professionalization than on hardware upgrade. Furthermore, each country is dependent on external support from the great powers interested in the region (i.e., the U.S., Russia, and China) for military modernization.

- State leaders often overplay the Islamist threat to outsiders, and use outside resources as a means to suppress populist opposition movements that do not threaten international security. Foreign security support, both political and financial, can thus serve to bolster weak regimes lacking domestic legitimacy. Security-related funding can also become an asset in domestic political competition as factions in the elite vie for control over contracts.

POLICY IMPLICATIONS:

Russia and China's continued military interest in the region, American distrust of neighboring Iran, and the potential to diversify sources of U.S. and allied petroleum imports mean that Washington will likely continue to make the region a high security priority. The U.S. should, however, bear in mind the following points:

- Some major security concerns in the region, such as the opium trade supporting warlords in Afghanistan, cannot be successfully addressed by military modernization alone.

- Military aid and other forms of security support may have the unintended consequence of strengthening authoritarian regimes while reducing human rights accountability and democratic advancement.

Central Asia: Military Modernization and the Great Game

Kimberly Marten

Analytical generalizations concerning military modernization across the five states of post-Soviet Central Asia are difficult to make, and even harder when neighboring Afghanistan is considered. Defense force sizes and capabilities differ substantially across the region, and the domestic political and foreign alliance patterns influencing military developments in these states vary. This chapter will argue, however, that two common political factors best define the processes of military modernization in Central Asia.

First, most major military developments in the region (with the partial exceptions of Kazakhstan and Turkmenistan, both of which are involved in Caspian Sea resource competition) are not geared toward changing the power balance between individual states, or even toward enhancing state defense self-sufficiency. Instead, military "modernization" centers on developing long-term military relationships with outsiders, especially the three great powers with an interest in the region: the United States, Russia, and China. These relationships include everything from foreign military training programs to weapons sales, and include the stationing of foreign forces and bases on Central Asian territory.

These foreign defense relationships serve several purposes. Each Central Asian state wants to improve its defense capabilities in order to deal with the threat posed by Islamist militants and terrorists, yet none is wealthy enough to do this effectively on its own. There is no question that insurgency

Kimberly Marten is Professor of Political Science at Barnard College, Columbia University. She is a member of the Council on Foreign Relations, and the Program on New Approaches to Russian Security at the Center for the Strategic and International Studies. She can be reached at <km2225@columbia.edu>.

The author is grateful to Peter Mattis for collecting data and analyzing hardware developments in the region.

and terrorism continue to constitute a formidable threat; the availability of outside help is therefore beneficial. Yet the threat of Islamist attack is often overblown by leaders who, out of self-interest, tend to paint all political opposition in Islamist terms. Defense relationships with outside powers serve non-military purposes as well, and are used by these leaders as a source of support—in the absence of domestic legitimacy—to buoy their regimes. In post-Soviet Central Asia, state leaders use external support to demonstrate to their citizens that powerful outsiders appreciate their country's participation in the war on terrorism. This ongoing war is likewise justification for human rights abuses by police forces throughout the region. In addition, some forms of external support, including foreign base contracts, are used as a financial reserve to pay off domestic regime supporters.

The second element characteristic of Central Asia and Afghanistan is the fact that military modernization in these countries is happening gradually at best, and for the most part is not centered on hardware acquisition. Instead, improved defense capabilities center on the professionalization of armed services personnel. Kazakhstan, Kyrgyzstan, Tajikistan, Turkmenistan, and Uzbekistan all have forces bearing the strong stamp of their Soviet legacies. When they were republics of the USSR, the Central Asian territories were not the preferred recruiting grounds for the national officer corps; the elite were dominated by Russians and other ethnic Slavs. This legacy has meant that creating a competent and professional national officer corps— which is crucial for instilling discipline as well as for combat efficiency—has been a formidable challenge for each Central Asian state in the post-Cold War period.

This chapter has two major sections. The first examines four sets of interests that motivate military modernization throughout the region: improving defense against Islamist opposition; gaining defense-related external support to be used as a domestic political resource; improving defense against external threats, including border disputes among states in the region; and the use of defense support as a means of competition between the external great powers. The second section examines current military developments in each of the six Central Asian states. A conclusion then outlines a set of policy implications for the United States in Central Asia.

The Four Drivers of Military Modernization

Defense Against Islamist Opposition

Central Asian states seek military assistance to shore up their defenses against threats of Islamist terrorism and insurgency, despite the dubious nature of these threats. It remains unclear how grave the Islamist threat is in the region. Yet since similar fears of violent Islamist extremism are shared by the United States in its war on Al Qaeda and terrorism, Russia in its ongoing civil war in Chechnya, and China in its attempts to control unrest among the Uighur minority population in Xinjiang, these great powers have all provided continuous regional military support in recent years.

Central Asian leaders tend to portray the Islamist threat as something that originates within neighboring states but then feeds off of domestic unruliness. This means that the concept of "defense" blurs the line between military and police functions. As **Table 1** reveals, in four of the post-Soviet Central Asian states, the domestic security or interior ministry forces almost rival the army in size. Turkmenistan lacks a separately designated internal security force, but military, law and order, and border protection troops are all seen as serving the common purpose of state defense.[1] Military troops often work in the civilian economy as well, further blurring the line between army and non-army activities.[2] Throughout post-Soviet Central Asia, peaceful opposition forces are quashed in the name of state defense, especially when they have some sort of association with Islam. Torture is routine. Some military and police assistance (such as that coming from the United States, the North Atlantic Treaty Organization [NATO], and the Organization for Security and Cooperation in Europe) is explicitly geared toward developing democratic professional norms among Central Asian officers. The fact, however, that defense budgets are fungible and that leaders can tout the assistance as a sign of support and legitimacy for their regimes abroad, raises uncomfortable dilemmas for many Western countries. This was demonstrated most recently by the fact that some Uzbek units used in the murderous Andijan crackdown of May 2005 may have received American military training, a possibility that has raised concerns among both elected officials and administrators in the United States.[3]

---

[1] Turkmen TV First Channel (Ashgabat), "Turkmen Leader Praises Law-Enforcement Agencies' Work in 2004," December 30, 2004 (as reported by the BBC news service).

[2] Victor Panov, "Turkmenia's Army Marks 13th Birthday," RIA Novosti (Moscow), January 27, 2005.

[3] Ann Scott Tyson and Robin Wright, "Crackdown Muddies U.S.-Uzbek Relations," *Washington Post*, June 4, 2005.

Table 1. Central Asian Military Structures, 2004

Country	Number and distribution of military personnel
Kazakhstan	Army: 46,800 Paramilitary (including Border Protection Forces, Internal Security Troops, Presidential and Government Guards): 34,500 Air Force (including Air Defense): 19,000
Uzbekistan	Army: 40,000 Paramilitary (including Internal Security Troops and National Guard): Approx. 18–20,000 Air Force: Approx. 10–15,000 Foreign forces present: • U.S. troops participating in *Operation Enduring Freedom*, centered at base in Khanabad: 1,000
Kyrgyzstan	Army: 8,500 Paramilitary (including Border Guards and National Guard): 5,000 Air Force (including Air Defense): 4,000 Foreign forces present: • approx. 865 U.S. and allied troops at military base at Manas • approx. 700 Russian troops at military base in Kant
Tajikistan	Army: 7,600 Paramilitary (Border Guards/Interior Ministry): 5,300 Foreign forces present: • Russian Border Guards (Russian officers, Tajik conscripts): 12,000 • Russian Army: 7,800 • Allied troops participating in *Operation Enduring Freedom*: 100
Turkmenistan	Army: 21,000 Navy: 700 Air Force (including Air Defense): 4,300
Afghanistan	Army: approx. 60–70,000 Border guards: approx. 12,000 Air force: approx. 8,000 Foreign forces present: • 19,500 U.S. and allied troops in *Operation Enduring Freedom* • 6,500 NATO and other troops in ISAF

Source: Compiled from International Institute for Strategic Studies, *The Military Balance*, 2004–05 (London: Oxford University Press, 2004), 141–60.

While post-Soviet Central Asian leaders may overplay the Islamist card for financial and political gain, the threat has a genuine core. The Islamic Movement of Uzbekistan (IMU), which has strong links to Al Qaeda, carried out violent incursions in the region in the late 1990s. While the IMU leadership cadre was largely destroyed when the movement fought against U.S. forces during *Operation Enduring Freedom* (OEF) in Afghanistan in late 2001, there were signs of a resurgence by 2003.[4] In addition, the avowedly peaceful Hizb-ut-Tahrir (HT) group, which calls for the non-violent, democratic overthrow of secular Central Asian regimes and their replacement by a regional caliphate, may be spawning splinter groups that reject non-vio-

---

[4] David C. Isby, "The Terrorist Threat in Central Asia: Resurgence and Adaptation," *Jamestown Foundation Terrorism Monitor* 2, no. 5 (March 11, 2004).

lence and attract HT followers to more brutal causes.[5] In recent years, HT members in Denmark, the United Kingdom, and Australia have distributed pamphlets and held rallies that advocate anti-Semitic violence, causing Jewish advocacy groups to call for surveillance of HT activities.

The present confusion over what role Islamist groups are playing in fomenting violence—and the violent response of governments to even peaceful protest activity—was revealed most starkly in the unrest in Uzbekistan in May 2005.[6] Uzbekistan faced a real threat of armed insurgency in the Ferghana Valley city of Andijan, where attacks on a prison, an army base, and various state offices seemed designed to undercut state control over its territory. Yet many analysts believe that Uzbekistan's inhumane treatment of its impoverished citizenry, along with its unwillingness to tolerate peaceful political protest, set the conditions for these attacks to occur and in general make the threat of popular violence a self-fulfilling prophecy. There is little question that the state's reaction to the events in Andijan will leave the government even more subject to the rage of its citizenry in the future.

These intertwined strands of state defense and authoritarian regime defense together provide an important motive for state military modernization across the region. The fact that the Uzbek protestors in Andijan were able to obtain weapons by raiding an Uzbek military base reinforces the need to professionalize the army; higher quality troops would have defended their armaments better.[7] A month later, it was reported that Kazakh military and police troops were engaged in exercises designed to use firearms against crowds of protestors, and at least one Kazakh senator expressed concern about the consequences of such action.[8]

These situations create difficult choices for Washington. Just days before the Andijan protests began, the United States reportedly sent terrorist suspects from around the world to Uzbekistan for interrogation and detention by that government. The more than $500 million in security assistance that the Pentagon gave Uzbek President Islam Karimov effectively replaced the aid withdrawn by the Department of State in response to the country's human rights violations.[9] While the violence in Andijan was ongoing, Gen. John P. Abizaid, Commander of U.S. CENTCOM forces, stated that the U.S.

---

[5] Ahmed Rashid, *Jihad: The Rise of Militant Islam in Central Asia* (New Haven: Yale University Press, 2002), 132–36.

[6] See C.J. Chivers, "Rights Group Calls Deadly Uzbek Crackdown a 'Massacre,'" *New York Times*, June 8, 2004.

[7] Interfax-Kazakhstan News Agency (Almaty), "Uzbek Events Show Professionals Should Serve in Army—Kazakh Minister," May 17, 2005 (as reported by the BBC news service).

[8] Gaziza Baituova, "Kazak Security Forces Bracing for Trouble," Institute of War and Peace Reporting, *Reporting Central Asia*, no. 386, June 2005, http://www.iwpr.org.

[9] Don Van Natta, Jr., "U.S. Recruits a Rough Ally to Be a Jailer," *New York Times*, May 1, 2005.

military base at Khanabad, Uzbekistan was somewhat limiting the scale of its activities. Yet he emphasized that this was because of "a potential change in the security situation" and "to reduce ... levels of vulnerability" for U.S. forces, not in retribution against Karimov's actions.[10] In June 2005 Washington revealed that it was negotiating a contract with Tashkent to give Washington long-term control of that base.[11]

Then in July, both Uzbekistan and Kyrgyzstan suddenly announced that they were reconsidering whether or not to terminate the U.S. military base presence in their countries. These announcements followed a declaration by the Shanghai Cooperation Organization (SCO) (a regional defense cooperative that includes Kazakhstan, Kyrgyzstan, Tajikistan, Uzbekistan, Russia, and China) stating that since the war in Afghanistan had been won, the U.S. military presence in the region should be withdrawn. Chairman of the U.S. Joint Chiefs of Staff Gen. Richard B. Myers argued that Russian and Chinese pressure was instrumental in Tashkent's and Bishkek's announcements.[12] Yet there is no doubt that Uzbek President Ismail Karimov was unhappy with American calls for an outside investigation into the Andijan events. Defense against terrorism, especially when supported by outside assistance, is a two-edged sword that can have uncomfortable consequences for U.S. democracy assistance in the region.

Defense as a Domestic Political Resource

Central Asian states have a second major motive to seek international security support, and one which has no basis in real security interests. Government corruption is endemic throughout Central Asia, and "the state" is often more a cash cow to be milked by familial- or clan-based patronage networks than a bulwark for protecting citizens. As ruling regimes try to keep opposition political parties from rising and the opposition tries to buy support, state resources (including foreign funds intended for security spending) become tools for factional political advancement.

The dominance of patronage networks was evident most recently in the disappointing finale to the so-called "Tulip Revolution" in Kyrgyzstan in March and April 2005. The widespread street demonstrations that led to the overthrow of the ruling Askar Akayev regime in Bishkek had roots in the popular outrage over election fraud, corruption, and the country's en-

---

[10] Gen. John P. Abizaid, roundtable press briefing transcript, May 18, 2005, http://www.centcom.mil/CENTCOMNews/transcripts/0518%20abizaid%20roundtable%20final.doc.

[11] Tyson and Wright, "Crackdown Muddies U.S.-Uzbek Relations."

[12] Eric Schmitt, "Rumsfeld Stop in Kyrgyzstan Aims to Keep Access to Base," *New York Times*, July 26, 2005.

demic poverty. Observers hoped that Kyrgyzstan would follow Georgia and Ukraine along the path toward populist democratization. Yet the conflict in Kyrgyzstan quickly devolved into a battle between existing political elites for the reins of economic control, and pitted Akayev against familiar opposition figures.[13]

In mid-May the two leading contenders in Kyrgyzstan's July 2005 presidential election announced plans to join forces, purportedly for the sake of stability in the country. Revealingly, Kurmanbek Bakiyev—the man who was elected president in a landslide vote—represents the dominant clans in the south of the country, while his prime minister, Felix Kulov, represents the dominant clans of the north. As other observers have noted, pacts between oligarchic clans are what maintains stability throughout Central Asia.[14] The "revolution" in Kyrgyzstan quickly became an opportunity for a new set of economically dominant factions to replace the old, with no real prospect for deep reform.

State corruption may appear irrelevant to the security interests of outside states that are providing military assistance to Central Asia. Opposition leaders in Kyrgyzstan were quick to announce that the state's stewardship of the U.S. air base in Manas and the Russian air base at Kant near Bishkek (officially re-established in 2003 as an apparent counter to the U.S. presence) would remain unchanged. Yet foreign military support plays a key role in the ability of these regimes to hand out favors, and often hence becomes a pawn in domestic political games.

President Akayev, for example, was widely known to be corrupt, and to hand out state-supported business favors to his family. Among the prizes were contracts with the U.S. Department of Defense for aviation fuel, landing fees, and parking and land lease payments at Manas, the primary re-supply point for OEF activities in Afghanistan.[15] The complex business structure of various airport activities involves both Kyrgyz and U.S. contractors. Until the fall of the Akayev regime, there were two companies that monopolized the provision of fuel and other airport-related contracts involving the base. The first was Manas International, the airport service firm whose ownership was controlled by Akayev's son; the second was Aalam Service, the fuel con-

---

[13] Craig S. Smith, "Kyrgyzstan's Shining Hour Ticks Away and Turns Out To Be a Plain, Old Coup," *New York Times*, April 3, 2005.

[14] Kathleen Collins, "The Logic of Clan Politics: Evidence from the Central Asian Trajectories," *World Politics* 56, no. 2 (January 2004): 224–61.

[15] See, for instance, Alexander Cooley, "Depoliticizing Manas: The Domestic Consequences of the U.S. Military Presence in Kyrgyzstan," Program on New Approaches to Russian Security, *Policy Memo*, no. 362, February 2005, http://www.csis.org/ruseura/ponars/policymemos/pm_index.cfm.

tractor controlled by Akayev's son-in-law.[16] The fuel contract alone was reportedly worth $25 million per year.[17] Recent investigations by Kyrgyzstan's new leaders into Akayev's corrupt activities appear to be designed to grab control of his old property for the "reformists" and their families.[18] Moreover, a struggle over fuel provisions at the airport is a part of this power grab. U.S. security expenditures in Kyrgyzstan are still subject to widespread corruption that has deleterious consequences on transparency and democratic accountability in the country.

U.S. foreign military assistance to Kyrgyzstan is not subject to such blatant corruption since the payments go directly to U.S. sources. Nonetheless, there are rumors that some foreign-supplied military equipment delivered to Bishkek was never used by Kyrgyz forces, but was instead resold by Kyrgyz officials for private gain. Foreign military assistance is not directly connected to the U.S. base presence. Such aid began with International Military Education and Training (IMET) support in 1994, and continued with Foreign Military Financing (FMF) in 1997—before Manas was even established. The base alone therefore does not determine the outlines of either the U.S.-Kyrgyz defense relationship or U.S. assistance for Kyrgyzstan's military modernization. Yet given the crucial role that the Manas base fulfills in the ongoing war on terrorism, it is not surprising that U.S. FMF agreements increased from $1 million in 2000 to almost $11 million in 2002 (the year the base contract was first signed), and continued at around $4 million per year thereafter.[19] Direct U.S. military assistance plays a substantial role in Kyrgyzstan—where the overall state budget revenues are estimated to be only $431 million per year[20]—and is clearly tied to other political objectives related to U.S. security contracting in the country. One of the primary means Central Asian leaders can use to bring about military modernization in their countries is the solicitation of cash and budgetary replacement items from outside players. This relieves the government of the need to use state taxes to pay for security requirements and provides opportunities to pay off political supporters as well as to stuff the private coffers of state bureaucrats.

---

[16] Interfax (Moscow), "Kyrgyz Fuel Suppliers Threaten to Paralyze Manas Airport," April 27, 2005 (as reported by the BBC news service).

[17] Cooley, "Depoliticizing Manas."

[18] Kabar News Agency (Bishkek), "World Bank Slates Kyrgyz Team Probing Akayev Property," May 9, 2005 (as reported by the BBC news service).

[19] U.S. Defense Security Operation Agency, *Foreign Military Sales, Foreign Military Construction Sales and Military Assistance Facts as of September 30, 2003* (see table 42-3), http://www.dsca.mil.

[20] U.S. Central Intelligence Agency, *World Factbook*, http://www.cia.gov.

Defense Against External Threats

While military modernization in Central Asia may be motivated mainly by threats from insurgencies and opposition or by mere political gain, there are some traditional security motives as well. Border delineation disputes have long bedeviled the Central Asian states (especially Kyrgyzstan and Uzbekistan). These disputes have largely been defused through negotiation, however, even though many remain unresolved. For example, Uzbekistan agreed in 2004 to de-mine its border with Kyrgyzstan, after having laid mines five years earlier in an attempt to prevent IMU rebels from crossing back into the country following incursions into Kyrgyz territory.[21] Yet in January 2005 Uzbek authorities bulldozed homes straddling the border with Kazakhstan, despite apparently successful negotiations on the issue.[22] Outside powers are encouraging the negotiation process, as is evident through U.S. Agency for International Development conflict resolution assistance to local villages.[23] China's decision to seek regional stability in pursuit of its own trade interests has also aided peaceful conflict resolution, and has led Beijing to resolve border disputes with its Central Asian neighbors.[24] Land-based border disputes do not appear to be spawning any new regional arms races.

Nonetheless, two states—Kazakhstan and Turkmenistan—harbor very real security concerns over border demarcation issues in the waters of the oil- (and caviar-) rich Caspian Sea. In 2003 Russia, Azerbaijan, and Kazakhstan signed a trilateral agreement that divided their respective sea-bed territories along national boundary lines while at the same time allowing each of them free access to surface waters. Since Iran's share of the sea-bed would be the smallest, however, Tehran has refused to assent to the proposed division and instead suggested a more equal division among coastal countries. In 2001 Iran sent a navy ship into the disputed waters and fired on an Azerbaijani boat, an act of aggression that nearly led to the militarization of the dispute. Turkmenistan accepts the post-Soviet rule of division in principle, but disagrees with Azerbaijan on how to define the sea-bed line between

[21] Yuri Yegotov, "Uzbekistan Agrees to Remove Minefields along Its Border with Kyrgyzstan," *Eurasia Daily Monitor* 1, no. 41 (June 29, 2004).

[22] Igor Rotar, "Uzbekistan Bulldozes Settlements along Border with Kazakhstan," *Eurasia Daily Monitor* 2, no. 9 (January 13, 2005).

[23] Barbara Junisbai, "Focus on USAID: Controlling Conflict in Central Asia," *Foreign Service Journal*, September 2002, 47–50, http://www.usaid.gov/locations/europe_eurasia/car/ctrl_conf_in_ car. html.

[24] Matthew Oresman, "Beyond the Battle of Talas: China's Reemergence in Central Asia," in *In the Tracks of Tamerlane: Central Asia's Path to the 21st Century*, ed. Daniel L. Burghart and Theresa Sabonis-Helf (Washington, D.C.: National Defense University Press, 2004), 401–24.

them.[25] While viewing the disagreement with Azerbaijan as a security issue requiring a defensive buildup, Ashgabat is simultaneously seeking support from outside investors for project development in the disputed territory.[26] Kazakhstan continues to balance Russian and U.S. military assistance while reforming its Caspian border defenses, and talks about building a navy in spite of slow progress in military modernization.[27] In contrast to Kazakhstan, Turkmenistan's President Saparmurat Niyazov, with his flamboyant, totalitarian, and paranoid personality cult, is pursuing an autarkic defense capability that will leave him independent of the great powers and capable of maintaining total non-alignment and neutrality. Hence Caspian security concerns do play a role in some Central Asian military modernization decisions.

Defense and the Great Game

Each of the external powers has mixed motives in the Caspian and Central Asian regions. On the one hand, as noted above, the United States, Russia, and China share an interest in combating terrorism, and are trying to improve Central Asia's terrorism response capabilities so that Islamist extremists cannot establish bases for training purposes or political gain. On the other hand, each of the outside powers is also trying to keep the Central Asian states out of one another's spheres of influence. This probably explains why Russia re-established its Soviet-era air base in Kyrgyzstan in 2003 only a few miles down the road from the U.S. air base established at Manas in 2002. This likely also explains why Russia was so eager to establish a long-term military base in Dushanbe in 2004 (transferring 7,000 troops from its 201st motorized rifle division, the largest foreign deployment of Russian forces).[28] In May 2005 Kyrgyz and Russian authorities reportedly began negotiations for a second Russian military base in Osh, near the border with Uzbekistan. These negotiations may have been motivated by the recent unrest in nearby Andijan.[29]

---

[25] Liz Fuller, "Analysis: Still No Decision on Caspian Sea," Radio Free Europe/Radio Liberty, February 2, 2005, http://www.rferl.org/featuresarticle/2005/02/45ebd366-d8e2-454c-a3db-be99e9d0269d.html.

[26] Roger McDermott, "Turkmenistan Seeks Stronger Military," Eurasia Daily Monitor 2, no. 24 (February 3, 2005).

[27] Roger McDermott, "Kazakhstan's Military Reform Creeps Forward," Eurasia Daily Monitor 1, no. 71 (August 11, 2004).

[28] Vladimir Socor, "Russian Army Base in Tajikistan Legalized; Border Troops to Withdraw," Eurasia Daily Monitor 1, no. 108 (October 19, 2004).

[29] Bagila Bukharbayeva, "Kyrgyzstan May Host 2nd Russia Army Base," Associated Press Online, May 24, 2005.

Russia has tried to revive its historical influence in the region by means of the Collective Security Treaty Organization (CSTO) of the Commonwealth of Independent States (CIS). The CIS has, however, remained primarily a consultative body, and Moscow's efforts to create real multilateral military organization have not been successful.[30] Russia has established a Collective Rapid Deployment Force (CRDF) (headquartered in Bishkek) that, by including battalions from Kazakhstan, Kyrgyzstan, and Tajikistan, may serve as a means for military-to-military training and institutional influence. In April 2005 the CRDF reportedly held command-staff exercises in Tajikistan that were designed to hone responses to any potential popular uprising stemming from an armed incursion from across the border.[31]

While the United States and Russia are the chief external powers in the region, China has attempted to increase its military influence as well, in particular through extensive joint training and military assistance cooperation with Kyrgyzstan. As noted above, China is also participating alongside Russia in the SCO. SCO members have joined forces to fight the "three evils" of drug trafficking, arms trafficking, and illegal migration, as well as the three forces of terrorism, separatism, and extremism.[32] In late May 2005, following the violence in Andijan, Beijing praised Uzbek President Karimov for his "crackdown on the three forces."[33] The SCO has established a permanent Regional Antiterrorist Structure (RATS) in Tashkent designed to share intelligence and liaise with a parallel CIS Antiterrorist Center in Bishkek.[34] The Chinese government is expected to base at least a small number of its security personnel at RATS,[35] thereby giving China a permanent presence in Central Asia. The ongoing rivalry between Kazakhstan and Uzbekistan, however—which includes allegations over the harboring of terrorists—makes true regional cooperation difficult. The Central Asia Nuclear Weapon Free Zone treaty, originally finalized in 2002 and revised and ready for signing in

---

[30] Roger McDermott, "Security in Central Asia Moves Closer to Moscow's Orbit," *Eurasia Daily Monitor* 2, no. 34 (February 17, 2005).

[31] The source emphasized that current instability in Kyrgyzstan was not what spawned the scenario. Ivan Safronov, "Bishkek As In the Days of Frunze: CIS Military Training in Counterrevolutionary Struggle," *Kommersant*, April 4, 2005 (as reported by the BBC news service).

[32] Mariam Arunova and Vladimir Goriunkov, "The Shanghai Cooperation Organization: An Analysis of Its Sustainability and Development," *Central Asia and the Caucasus*, no. 6, December 31, 2004, 120–24.

[33] C.J. Chivers, "China Backs Uzbek, Splitting with U.S. on Crackdown," *New York Times*, May 25, 2005.

[34] Roger McDermott, "SCO Summit in Tashkent: Breakthrough in Practical Cooperation," *Eurasia Daily Monitor* 1, no. 33 (June 17, 2004).

[35] Oresman, "China's Reemergence," 416.

July 2005, may be a lone exception.[36] This treaty ensures that Central Asia will never again become a testing or deployment ground for Russian nuclear weapons on the model of Soviet-era Kazakhstan.

As the multitude of SCO goals makes clear, Russia and China have domestic political concerns that extend to Central Asia. Moscow wants to protect ethnic Russian minorities living abroad in Central Asia, and keep a close eye on the activities of ethnic Chechen refugees living in Kazakhstan and Kyrgyzstan. Moscow fears these refugees may play a role in Russia's ongoing civil war, including related terrorist attacks within Russia. China has a similar parallel concern about the ethnic Uighur minority population living in Kazakhstan and Kyrgyzstan, and is also attuned to issues surrounding its own migrant trader population throughout the region. Ethnic Russians were targeted by some of those participating in the unrest in Kyrgyzstan in spring 2005, and Chinese traders were also targeted by looters at that time.

India has also recently become involved in Central Asia. In 2002 New Delhi first began to establish a foreign military presence in Tajikistan by reconstructing the Ayni air base next to the Afghan border that was destroyed in Tajikistan's civil war, and also by providing antiterrorism and air-defense training to the Tajik military.[37] In 2005 India signed a series of agreements with Uzbekistan that included mention of cooperation on defense and antiterrorism, and Tashkent continued to supply India with Il-78 refueling aircraft in a joint deal with the Russian Ilyushin Design Bureau.[38] New Delhi's efforts are partly due to an association that India has long believed to exist between Pakistan and Afghanistan; this historical suspicion makes the recent Taliban resurgence especially worrisome. Growing regional inroads from China—India's other major military rival—point to more general geostrategic concerns. India cannot afford to sit on the sidelines of this new "Great Game," and indeed has recently negotiated with Russia to ensure that Moscow and New Delhi's actions in the region do not conflict.[39] India also seeks the votes of Central Asian leaders in the General Assembly for its bid to gain a permanent seat on the United Nations Security Council.

Access to and control over petroleum resources—including both oil fields and oil and gas pipelines—define the parameters of the new Great Game in Central Asia. Although a major concern in the long-term security

---

[36] ITAR-TASS News Agency (Moscow), "Central Asian Countries Approve Treaty on Nuclear Free Zones," February 9, 2005.

[37] Ramtanu Maitra, "India and Russia Have Much to Lose," *Asia Times Online*, November 26, 2003.

[38] Stephen Blank, "Ties Strengthen Between Tashkent and New Delhi," *Eurasia Daily Monitor* 2, no. 69 (April 8, 2005).

[39] Roger McDermott, "Russia and India Explore Cooperation in Central Asia," *Eurasia Daily Monitor* 1, no. 141 (December 7, 2004).

calculations of all the interested external powers (including neighbors such as Turkey and Iran), the competition for petroleum resources does not seem to have translated into direct outside support for local military development in Central Asia. Most immediate foreign military sales appear to have little association with the region's oil and gas reserves; Turkmenistan, discussed below, constitutes the sole exception. This dynamic may change, however, with Kazakhstan's stated intention to build its own Caspian Sea navy, and Astana's decision to seek outside support from the United States, Russia, and Turkey for this undertaking. As of yet, no new equipment has been purchased or manufactured to further this goal, but should Astana do so, it will mean that Kazakhstan is willing to ally with outsiders for the explicit purpose of protecting its petroleum resources.

The Central Asian Militaries

Table 1 above reveals two striking tendencies in the basic structural outlines of each Central Asian state's military organization in 2004. First, the internal ministry and other paramilitary forces are disproportionately larger than the regular army in Kazakhstan, Kyrgyzstan, Tajikistan, and Uzbekistan. This is in part a legacy from Soviet times. More than a simple organizational legacy, however, such structures also reflect the approach of these countries to the perceived threat of domestic and foreign Islamist insurgencies. Second, with the exception of Kazakhstan and Turkmenistan, each state hosts a significant presence of foreign forces. While the threat of Islamist insurgency or terrorism appears to justify the presence of these troops, there are surely other geopolitical motives as well.

In terms of military equipment, post-Soviet Central Asia has continued to rely on Soviet-era hardware, upgrading to newer Russian-made equipment only when available and decommissioning obsolete items as necessary. Immediately following independence in 1991 (or, in the case of Tajikistan, after the end of the civil war in 1997), there was a concerted effort to increase the size and capabilities of military forces across Central Asia. In recent years, however, increases in the quantity and quality of military equipment have been modest at best.[40] The next section will discuss military developments in each of the Central Asian states.

---

[40] All of the numerical data, unless otherwise noted, is from the International Institute for Strategic Studies *Military Balance* yearly compilations.

Kazakhstan

Post-Soviet Central Asia's geographically largest state also maintains the largest military forces, and Kazakhstan's leaders have consistently stated that an increased capacity to defend the Caspian Sea region is a high priority. Indeed, by implementing a new regional and branch command structure to improve efficiency, and making progress in efforts to move to a contract-based recruitment system, Astana has achieved some success in restructuring forces inherited from Soviet times. Pilot training time has also increased drastically. Yet outside of Kazakhstan's well-known decision to become a nuclear-free state by removing its Soviet-era intercontinental ballistic missiles and bombers, few drastic changes have been made in the weapons base. By reaching a deal allowing Moscow continued use of the Baikonur space launch facilities and other testing ranges in Kazakhstan, Astana in turn received not only Russian military training for over a thousand Kazakh officers, but also heavily discounted deals on Russian aircraft, helicopters, and anti-aircraft systems.[41] In the late 1990s, Kazakhstan placed some of its older aircraft into storage and purchased 19 MiG-29 and 11 MiG-31 advanced fighters, in addition to 14 Su-25 and 14 Su-27 fighter-ground attack aircraft.

Kazakhstan's army has seen few changes to its weapons systems in recent years. The number of main battle tanks increased from 624 in 1995 to 930 in 2004, but the same T-62 and T-72 systems are still in use. Similar patterns are evident in Kazakhstan's arsenal of reconnaissance vehicles, armored personnel carriers, and artillery. Yet despite this weapons continuity across the years, the army has managed to cooperate closely with the United States and Washington's NATO allies. In 2004, with the aim of strengthening U.S.-Kazakh relations, Kazakhstan deployed a 27-member, all-Muslim engineering unit from its peacekeeping battalion to Iraq (KAZBAT) for de-mining and water purification missions. Such cooperation built upon ongoing military cooperation with Washington, which included the use of Kazakh airspace and emergency airfield landing rights for OEF operations in Afghanistan, as well as the signing in September 2003 of a bilateral agreement that highlights military interoperability as a key platform.[42] Interoperability for peacekeeping operations with NATO has been a goal of the Kazakh army since the mid-1990s, when its forces first participated in a failed effort to

---

[41] Lt. Col. William Lahue, "Security Assistance in Kazakhstan: Building a Partnership for the Future," *Defense Institute of Security Assistance Management Journal* (Fall 2002-Winter 2003): 6–18.

[42] Roger McDermott, "Abizaid Visit Highlights Kazakh Role in Iraq," *Eurasia Daily Monitor* 1, no. 67 (August 5, 2004).

develop a multilateral Central Asian Peacekeeping Battalion under NATO's Partnership for Peace (PFP) program.[43]

In recompense for ongoing cooperation, U.S. Secretary of Defense Donald Rumsfeld signed an agreement in 2004 providing Kazakhstan with $12 million over five years, with the express purpose of assisting with military exercises and military base refurbishment.[44] The United States provides IMET assistance to support the training of non-commissioned officers, and has also provided ammunition, advanced military vehicles (HMMWVs), body armor, and communications equipment to Kazakhstan. The United States sees oil-wealthy Kazakhstan as a potential market for future defense industrial sales growth.

Support has also come from other NATO members. Turkey signed a five-year military cooperation plan with Kazakhstan in 2004 that includes construction of a Caspian Sea diver training center,[45] and in June 2004 the United Kingdom's BAE Systems corporation won a tender to upgrade Kazakh air defenses.[46] In April 2005 Kazakh Defense Minister Gen. Mukhtar Altynbayev announced that Kazakhstan would scrap its use of dangerous Soviet-era ammunition and begin to manufacture NATO-compatible ammunition for its forces.[47]

Although reaching out to the United States and NATO, President Nursultan Nazarbayev has likewise attempted to integrate Kazakhstan's forces into the Russian-led CSTO, and has accepted military education assistance from India as well.[48] Mere weeks after the BAE Systems deal was reached, Astana announced that Russian firms would also participate in the air-defense upgrade contract.[49]

Some analysts posit Kazakhstan's recent drift toward Russia as being a direct result of Georgia's "Rose Revolution" in November 2003, when the specter of populist democratization began to haunt Central Asia's authori

[43] Roger N. McDermott, "Enhancing Kazakhstan's Peacekeeping Capabilities: Interoperability and Regional Cooperation," *Central Asia and the Caucasus*, no. 2, April 30, 2004, 70–82.

[44] John D. Banusiewicz, "Rumsfeld Visits Kazakhstan for Talks on Strengthening Relationship," American Forces Press Service, February 25, 2004, http://www.defense.gov/news/Feb2004/ n02252004_200402251.html.

[45] McDermott, "Kazakhstan's Peacekeeping Capabilities," 75.

[46] Roger McDermott, "Kazakhstan's Air Defense Deal with UK Signals Shift," *Eurasia Daily Monitor* 1, no. 34 (June 18, 2004).

[47] Roger McDermott, "Kazakhstan Moves Closer toward Future NATO Integration," *Eurasia Daily Monitor* 2, no. 84 (April 29, 2005).

[48] McDermott, "Kazakhstan's Military Reform Creeps Forward."

[49] Roger McDermott, "Kazakhstan's Western Military Cooperation Sparks Tensions with Russia," *Eurasia Daily Monitor* 1, no. 50 (July 13, 2004).

tarian rulers.[50] The September 2004 parliamentary elections in Kazakhstan, which conferred an overwhelming majority on the pro-Nazarbayev Fatherland Party, were widely believed to be rigged. Kazakhstan's opposition forces have shown increasing signs of unrest in recent months, and the December 2006 presidential election looms on the horizon. U.S. support for democratization throughout the region may lead Nazarbayev to doubt U.S. support for the continuation of his regime, and could even push him closer to Moscow.

Astana's vacillation between the United States and NATO on the one side and Russia and the CSTO on the other may well have political gain—rather than military modernization—as its primary motive. For all of Astana's stated desire to modernize and improve its armed forces, Kazakhstan still spends only 1 percent of its GDP on the military.[51] President Nazarbayev has toyed for years with the notion of building an indigenous navy consisting of 25 combat ships to be supplied by domestic factories working in tandem with the United States, Turkey, and Russia;[52] there is no evidence as of yet to suggest that any such plans are underway.

Kazakhstan's military modernization difficulties appear to be due in large part to staffing inefficiency and the challenge of adapting Soviet-era procedures to the expectations of modern military assistance contracting.[53] Increased attention to these issues by the United States could make Astana a key future partner for Washington.

Kyrgyzstan

Kyrgyzstan is a small country with a small army and, unlike most of petroleum-rich Central Asia, has few natural resources worth defending (save, perhaps, the Kumtar gold mine). While Kyrgyzstan is, like the rest of Central Asia, strategically located and potentially threatened by an Islamist insurgency, its mountainous terrain and landlocked territory make it a less interesting geopolitical target than some of its neighbors. Because Kyrgyzstan's majority Muslim population has not historically been drawn to fundamentalist extremism, the country has not constituted fertile ground for outside terrorist groups.

Since the collapse of the Soviet Union, Kyrgyzstan's persistent domestic political troubles have often brought more international attention to the

---

[50] Stephen Blank, "Kazakhstan's Foreign Policy in a Time of Turmoil," *Eurasia Insight*, April 27, 2005.

[51] McDermott, "Kazakhstan's Military Reform Creeps Forward."

[52] Altynbsary Sakenov, "A Reliable Shield," *Ekspress-K* (Kazakhstan), March 24, 2004 (as reported by the BBC news service, April 14, 2004).

[53] Lahue, "Security Assistance in Kazakhstan."

country than would otherwise be expected. President Askar Akayev was initially looked upon favorably in many Western countries as the only Central Asian leader seemingly taking his country on the path toward liberal democracy and, as a result, succeeded in garnering large amounts of international development assistance. When Akayev began to adopt clearly authoritarian ruling methods in the late 1990s, his regime became both increasingly illiberal and corrupt. Nevertheless, the strategic location of the Bishkek airport coupled with Kyrgyzstan's friendly relationship with NATO's Partnership for Peace (PFP) program made Kyrgyzstan an attractive partner for OEF in Afghanistan.

In March 2005 many Western countries hoped that the populist ouster of Akayev's regime would lead Kyrgyzstan onto similar democratic pathways in the mold of Georgia in 2003 and Ukraine in 2004. Yet while the July 2005 presidential elections were generally perceived to be free and fair, the pre-election maneuverings among supposedly competing parties to present voters with only one dominant choice were disappointing. It appears that President Bakiyev will continue to play the United States and NATO on the one side against Russia and the CSTO on the other. The clearest evidence of such an approach over the years can be found in Bishkek's unusual willingness to allow both U.S. and Russian airbases to operate near the capital. Claiming that U.S. agents were fomenting popular unrest in the country, the Akayev regime in February 2005 reportedly refused a request from the United States to allow AWACS reconnaissance planes to be deployed at the Manas base.[54] The willingness to consider allowing Russia to open a second Russian base at Osh appears to indicate that Kyrgyzstan may currently be tilting in favor of Russia, although the future of the U.S. basing relationship remains uncertain.

Kyrgyzstan's troop levels and army and air force equipment have remained fairly constant over the past decade. Kyrgyzstan relies on weaponry inherited from its Soviet past, including T-72 tanks and aging MiG-21 aircraft. Bishkek's major military hardware purchases—light weapons, optics, body armor, and armored vehicle spare parts—are still supplied by Russian firms.[55] Russia has also provided border control communications equipment to Kyrgyzstan,[56] and agreed to modernize the Kyrgyz-manufactured com-

---

[54] Agence France-Presse, "Kyrgyzstan Rejects U.S. Request to Host Reconnaissance Planes," February 15, 2005.

[55] Roger McDermott, "Kyrgyzstan As Consumer of Security Assistance," *Eurasia Daily Monitor* 1, no. 29 (June 11, 2004).

[56] RIA News Agency (Moscow), "Russia to Lend Military Aid to Kyrgyzstan," May 8, 2002 (as reported by the BBC news service).

ponent of the combined CIS air defense system.[57] Russia still maintains a communications center and an anti-submarine test facility on Kyrgyz territory.[58] As in the case of Kazakhstan, however, Kyrgyzstan has also accepted military assistance from other foreign sources. U.S. IMET program assistance includes modern computer and communications equipment that are used for military education and training,[59] as well as special forces training for counterinsurgency operations.[60] The overall levels of U.S. military assistance increased dramatically after September 11. Turkey also supplies some military assistance to the country.[61] Leading Kyrgyz political figures have also asked NATO to donate the outdated military equipment of other PFP members to Bishkek.[62] In addition, China provided Kyrgyzstan with $1.2 million in military assistance in 2003.[63]

Kyrgyzstan's military is generally seen as weak and ineffective. Its vulnerabilities were dramatically displayed in 1999 when IMU insurgents made incursions into the country through the mountains on the Tajik border and forced Bishkek to request air support from Uzbekistan (which then mistakenly bombed a Kyrgyz village). Inclement winter weather—and not the Kyrgyz military—eventually forced the IMU insurgents to withdraw. Poorly-coordinated and ill-equipped Kyrgyz forces were unable to fight off the insurgents by themselves. The continued Russian military presence in Kyrgyzstan is valued precisely for this reason. This time period also saw the advent of military assistance from China. More recently in March 2005, when protestors began taking over regional administration buildings throughout the south, authorities were unable to react for several days; crowds even seized airports in order to prevent troop reinforcements from being flown in. U.S. assistance programs emphasizing human rights training for Interior Ministry troops may well have facilitated these popular opposition forces. Unlike the harsh methods utilized in the brutal crackdown a mere two months later in Uzbekistan, Kyrgyz troops managed—at least temporarily—to evict

---

[57] William D. O'Malley and Roger N. McDermott, "Kyrgyzstan's Security Tightrope: Balancing its Relations with Moscow and Washington," *Journal of Slavic Military Studies* 3, no. 16 (September 2003), reprinted by the Ft. Leavenworth Foreign Military Studies Office, http://fmso.leavenworth. army.mil/ documents/Kyrgystan/Kyrgystan.htm.

[58] O'Malley and McDermott, "Kyrgyzstan's Security Tightrope."

[59] Kyrgyz Television First Channel (Bishkek), "Kyrgyz Military School Receives Aid from USA," May 4, 2005 (as reported by the BBC news service).

[60] O'Malley and McDermott, "Kyrgyzstan's Security Tightrope."

[61] Anatolia News Agency (Ankara), "Turkey to Continue Military Aid to Kyrgyzstan," April 19, 2005 (as reported by the BBC news service).

[62] Interfax/AVN Military News (Moscow), "Kyrgyz Speaker Asks NATO for Arms Becoming 'Unnecessary' After Modernization," October 19, 2004 (as reported by the BBC news service).

[63] Merat Yermukanov, "Global and Regional Aspects of Sino-Kyrgyz Cooperation," *CEF Quarterly,* China-Eurasia Forum, October 2004, http://www.chinaeurasia.org/newsletter.html.

protestors from the administrative buildings in Osh and Jalalabad without firing their weapons. While the protestors resisted and some were injured in the ensuing melee, there were no reported deaths.[64] When the protestors proved too strong and retook the buildings the next day, the Kyrgyz troops withdrew rather than foment more violence. Eventually the security troops deserted the regime, even holding a military parade when opposition forces took Osh.[65]

Tajikistan

Tajikistan has the smallest army in Central Asia and, despite plans to procure Mi-8 and Mi-24 helicopters and Su-25 fighters from Belarus, no existing air force. Like its neighbors, Tajikistan relies on Soviet era weapons stocks, including 45 T-72 battle tanks. The presence of the new Russian 201st Motorized Rifle Division base near Dushanbe, as well as a supporting Russian air base at Ayni, constitute the bulk of Tajikistan's external defense. The Russian air base in neighboring Kyrgyzstan is integrated into the country's air defense system,[66] and one battalion of the 201st (alongside one Tajik, one Kazakh, and one Kyrgyz battalion) is earmarked for the joint CSTO Rapid Deployment Forces.[67] As noted above, the Rubezh-2005 CSTO exercises were conducted in Tajikistan in spring 2005, and used air defense assets and Rapid Deployment Forces in a scenario designed to "repel the attacks of large gangs that infiltrate Tajik territory."[68]

Though negotiations to establish a new Russian military base were ultimately successful (and thus formalized a virtually permanent Russian presence), many sensitive issues prolonged the process. Dushanbe harbored concerns regarding Russia's continued dominance over Tajikistan's security since the end of its civil war in 1997, and wanted Moscow to pay rent for the use of the facilities; Moscow refused. The final deal was reached when Russia agreed to write off $242 million of Tajikistan's $300 million debt in return for a 49-year essentially cost-free lease on the base, an anti-missile warning sys-

[64] ITAR-TASS News Agency (Moscow), "No Arms Used against Protestors in Kyrgyz South," March 20, 2005 (as reported by the BBC news service).

[65] Kyrgyz Television First Channel, "Kyrgyz in South Celebrate New Leadership with Army Parade," March 27, 2005 (as reported by the BBC news service).

[66] RIA Novosti, "Russian Military Base Set up in Tajikistan," April 5, 2005.

[67] Vladimir Socor, "Russian Army Base in Tajikistan Legalized, Border Troops to Withdraw," Eurasia Daily Monitor 1, no. 108 (October 19, 2004).

[68] RIA Novosti, "Russian Military Base Set up in Tajikistan."

tem at Nurek, and the accompanying Okno anti-missile system. Russia also agreed to pay for the training of Tajik officers in Russian military schools.[69]

As part of the same deal, Russian border troops currently deployed on Tajikistan's border with Afghanistan are increasingly turning assets and responsibilities over to their Tajik counterparts. As a result, in the past year alone the Tajik army has increased in size from 6,000 to roughly 7,600 troops. Nonetheless, the 201st will likely retain at least some of Russia's border control operations in Tajikistan, particularly given the deficiencies of Tajik border forces.[70] While concerns have been raised that Tajikistan's capacity to defend against drug trafficking and Islamist incursions from Afghanistan will weaken, such fears are not necessarily warranted. Russia has a vested interest in preserving Tajikistan as a buffer state against Islamist unrest that might otherwise overrun its Central Asian backyard. A Russian military presence in Tajikistan is also useful to Moscow as a way to keep an eye on U.S. activities in Afghanistan. Russian officers themselves have long been rumored to be major participants in the cross-border trafficking of Afghanistan's opium.

As in the case of its neighbors, Tajikistan has sought and accepted military assistance from multiple external sources, despite the strong Russian presence on its territory. India signed a military-technical agreement with Dushanbe in fall 2004, which followed an earlier deal to upgrade the Ayni air base used by Russian forces.[71] The Indian Air Force is slated to use Ayni for training Tajik air forces, and views the foreign base as an opportunity to extend its strategic reach.[72] The United States provided $2.3 million in military assistance in 2004, once again largely focused on training and professionalization of the officer corps and NCOs.[73] China sent a military delegation for negotiations to Dushanbe in late 2004, and the two countries are actively considering ways to broaden Tajikistan's participation in the SCO.[74] Nonetheless, of all the Central Asian states, Tajikistan remains the most dependent on military support from Russia for its survival.

---

[69] Kambiz Arman, "Russia and Tajikistan: Friends Again," *Eurasia Insight*, October 28, 2004; Socor, "Russian Army Base in Tajikistan Legalized."

[70] Bruce Pannier, "Central Asia: Tajiks Begin Taking over Guard Duties from Russians on Southern Border," Radio Free Europe, November 15, 2004.

[71] Interfax/AVN Military News Agency, "Tajik-Hosted Russian Air Squadron to be Relocated," April 14, 2005 (as reported by the BBC news service).

[72] "First Foreign Military Base by Year-End," *Deccan Herald*, October 19, 2004.

[73] Roger McDermott, "Tajikistan Diversifies its Security Assistance," *Eurasia Daily Monitor* 1, no. 90 (September 22, 2004).

[74] Roger McDermott, "Tajikistan and Uzbekistan Look Beyond U.S. Security Assistance," *Eurasia Daily Monitor* 2, no. 4 (January 6, 2005).

Turkmenistan

According to the most reliable data available (see **Table 1**), the armed forces of Turkmenistan are four to five times smaller than the number touted by Turkmen President Niyazov in public speeches.[75] Part of this discrepancy may be due to the definition of "active military service," which in Turkmenistan includes draftees working in the civilian economy.[76] The inflated figures also fit, however, with the overall tendency of the Turkmenbashi ("Head of the Turkmen") to exaggerate his own status in the world order. Much like other world leaders who have constructed personality cults around themselves, Turkmenistan's self declared "President for Life" has erected massive monuments to himself; named streets, cities, regions, and even months of the year after both himself and his family; and forced all citizens (including those undergoing military training) to spend countless hours memorizing passages from the "Rukhnama" spiritual guide book that he authored.[77] In fact, knowledge of the Rukhnama is a prerequisite for admission to Turkmenistan's officer training institute.[78]

Despite Niyazov's declared desire to achieve economic autarky and defense self-sufficiency, Turkmenistan's strategic location and large natural gas reserves have allowed him (much like his counterparts throughout Central Asia) to court military assistance from multiple sources. In early 2005 Niyazov declared that modernization of the armed forces was a high priority, and that such modernization would include officer training by foreign forces.[79] The U.S. Coast Guard has reportedly trained Turkmen border guards inside the country.[80] Earlier Niyazov had announced that Turkmenistan would send military personnel to study abroad in NATO programs.[81]

The size of the active army has grown by almost 50 percent in the past year, and now stands at 21,000 troops—double the number in 1995. Like his counterparts across Central Asia, Niyazov continues to rely on Soviet-era

---

[75] He claims that active forces number from 100,000 to 120,000. See RIA Novosti, "Turkmenia's Army Marks 13th Birthday," January 27, 2005.

[76] Interfax/AVN Military News, "More Turkmen Conscripts to Be Offered Alternative Service," October 8, 2004 (as reported by the BBC news service).

[77] Tom Templeton, "He Renamed January After Himself and April After His Mother," *Observer Magazine*, October 10, 2004.

[78] Esger (Ashgabat), "Turkmen Military Institute Applicants to Be Tested in Ruhnama," March 17, 2005 (as reported by the BBC news service).

[79] Roger McDermott, "Turkmenistan Seeks Stronger Military," *Eurasia Daily Monitor* 2, no. 24 (February 3, 2005).

[80] "Americans Instruct Turkmen Border Guards," *Krasnaya Zvezda* (Moscow), November 18, 2004 (as reported by the Defense and Security [Russia] WPS news service).

[81] But only after first directing "republican law enforcement agencies [to] check ... their backgrounds ... [to] prevent any possible high treason on their part." See RIA Novosti, "Turkmenistan Cooperating with NATO More Actively," March 30, 2004.

equipment, including 702 T-72 battle tanks. The air force, numbering 3,000 personnel, has grown to a level commensurate with the army, but has only 89 planes in active service. Improved air defense is one of Niyazov's major military hardware concerns.[82] In gaining military equipment and supplies for Turkmenistan's forces, Niyazov has used Turkmenistan's natural gas supplies as a bargaining card. Georgia pays its own longstanding gas supply debt with Turkmenistan; Ukraine pays for current gas supplies by providing weapons, equipment, and repairs to Ashgabat.[83] Niyazov stated that in 2004 he had purchased a set of Kalkan-M patrol boats from the Morye OAO Feodosia Ship-Building company in Ukraine, and had ordered twenty large Grif and Kalkan multi-purpose boats.[84] Turkmenistan may thus preempt Kazakhstan in the race to create a functioning naval force in the Caspian, even though at present it has only five boats at a single minor base.

Other Soviet-era links are retained in the purchase of military vehicles from Russia and Belarus.[85] Niyazov has also met with Pakistani and American defense officials to discuss military-technical cooperation, but as of yet no equipment contracts appear to have been signed.[86]

Uzbekistan

Relative to the size of its territory, Uzbekistan has a large army and air force. Since 1995 personnel strength has almost doubled to the current levels of around 55,000. Tashkent continues to rely on Soviet-era military assets, having procured 70 T-72s in recent years to augment the army's battle tank forces. While Uzbekistan plays host to huge storage bases filled with Soviet transfer equipment—including 2,000 T-64 tanks, 1,200 armored command vehicles, and 750 artillery pieces, much of this has deteriorated. Despite having purchased only nine new combat aircraft in the past decade, Uzbekistan's air force—with 30 MiG-29s and 25 Su-27s—is on par with Kazakhstan's.

Military modernization has been a priority of the defense ministry for the past several years. As elsewhere in Central Asia, however, reform has moved at a glacial pace. Given Tashkent's fear of the IMU and other cross-

[82] "Americans Instruct Turkmen Border Guards," *Krasnaya Zvezda*.

[83] ITAR-TASS News Agency (Moscow), "Georgia Repairs 43 Military Aircraft, Eight Helicopters for Turkmen Army," December 23, 2004.

[84] RIA Novosti, "Turkmenia's Army Marks 13th Birthday."

[85] Turkmen TV First Channel (Ashgabat), "Turkmen Border Units Get Russian-Made Vehicles," December 15, 2004 (as reported by the BBC news service).

[86] Turkmen TV First Channel, "Turkmen President, Pakistani Armed Forces Chief Mull Fight Against Terrorism," August 6, 2004 (as reported by the BBC news service); and Anna Kurbanova, "U.S. General Calls Military Cooperation with Turkmenistan Promising," ITAR-TASS News Agency, July 30, 2004.

border Islamist insurgents, reform plans have focused on upgrading artillery, ammunition, and transport equipment for use by compact groups of highly mobile troops in mountain and desert warfare. Improved helicopters and night-vision and communication equipment for air strikes are also on Tashkent's wishlist.[87] Uzbek authorities have talked about improving military professionalism, and toward this end have begun to implement a contract-based recruitment system.[88] The May 2005 civil violence in the Ferghana Valley, however, seems to have prompted registration for general mobilization of the entire male population of service age.[89]

Uzbekistan left the CIS collective security arrangement before the CSTO was made official in 2002, although Tashkent still participates in the joint CIS air defense system and sends observers to CSTO exercises. Tashkent's ties to Moscow have not been as close as its ties to many of the other post-Soviet Central Asian states. Uzbekistan had initially appeared to throw in its lot wholeheartedly with the United States, especially after September 11. Karimov welcomed American troops at their K-2 base at Khanabad, and in 2002 signed a "Strategic Partnership" agreement that brought in large amounts of U.S. money to train and equip Uzbek troops for counterterrorism and counternarcotics operations. In 2004 Uzbekistan also reached out more broadly for military cooperation with NATO as a whole.[90]

Continuing U.S. concerns about Uzbek human rights violations, however, as well as U.S. support for the populist democratization movement in Georgia in 2003, may have dampened Karimov's enthusiasm for the United States. In June 2004 he signed a new Strategic Partnership Agreement with Russian President Vladimir Putin that provided for joint military aircraft production and Russian training of Uzbek officers.[91] In March 2005, as a revolt began to unfold in neighboring Kyrgyzstan, Uzbek and Russian officials announced plans for bilateral airborne force exercises on Uzbek territory to take place in September.[92] U.S. dismay regarding the Karimov regime's brutal suppression of demonstrators in May 2005 may further push Uzbekistan

---

[87] "Uzbek Deputy Defense Minister Outlines Plans for Re-equipping Forces," *Vatanparvar* (Tashkent), May 23, 2000 (as reported by the BBC news service, June 9, 2000).

[88] Valery Petrovsky, "Military Reform in Action," *Narodnoe Slovo* (Tashkent), February 24, 2004 (as reported by the Defense and Security [Russia] News Service, February 27, 2004).

[89] Ekho Moskvy Radio, "Uzbek Authorities Likely to Declare General Mobilization," May 16, 2005 (as reported by the BBC news service).

[90] Roger McDermott, "Uzbekistan's Search For Improved Security," *Eurasia Daily Monitor* 1, no. 94 (September 28, 2004).

[91] Vladimir Mukhin, "Uzbek Aircraft Become Russian," *Nezavisimaya Gazeta*, June 18, 2004 (as reported by the BBC news service, June 19, 2004).

[92] Interfax/AVN Military News Agency, "Plan of Russian, Uzbek Airborne Forces Exercise Approved," March 5, 2005 (as reported by the BBC news service).

toward Russia. Russian Foreign Minister Sergey Lavrov refused to join the international call for an investigation of those events, and repeatedly stated his belief that Taliban remnants, Chechen rebels, and the IMU were responsible for the unrest.[93] CSTO officials expect that Uzbekistan might apply for membership in that organization in the near future.

Afghanistan

Kabul remains dependent on the 18,000 U.S.-led OEF and 8,000 NATO-led International Security Assistance Forces (ISAF) forces for its security needs. OEF has focused on defeating Al Qaeda and the Taliban, deterring the re-emergence of terrorism in the region and carrying out combat and humanitarian missions. The OEF Coalition Joint Task Force (CJTF) assists with recruiting, training, and equipping the Afghan National Army (ANA) and mentoring it on domestic security missions, while the Office of Military Cooperation works on security sector reconstruction.

ISAF is under separate NATO command and lacks a U.S. component. Authorized by the United Nations Security Council to help the Afghan government stabilize the country, ISAF is involved with everything from disarmament, demobilization, and reintegration of militia forces to police reform and infrastructure reconstruction. While ISAF activities were initially limited to Kabul, these activities have now expanded outward throughout the northwestern region of Afghanistan. An announcement in February at the NATO summit in Nice revealed plans to merge OEF and ISAF into a common NATO command structure sometime soon.

In May 2005 a *Loya Jirga* (traditional grand council) consisting of 1,000 representatives from around Afghanistan reconfirmed the support of regional leaders for the U.S. military presence.[94] Because both militant Taliban forces and Al Qaeda had appeared to be in decline throughout Afghanistan, however, Washington—in an attempt to aid its current force overstretch problem—expressed a desire to significantly cut the number of U.S. military personnel in Afghanistan in the near future. Fears of a precipitous U.S. withdrawal were probably the motivating factor behind President Hamid Karzai's offer put forward the following month that the United States could establish permanent military bases on Afghan territory.[95]

---

[93] Interfax, "Chechen Rebels Involved in Uzbek Unrest," June 2, 2005 (as reported by the BBC news service).

[94] Carlotta Gall, "Afghan Delegates Agree on the Need for Foreign Troops," *New York Times*, May 9, 2005.

[95] Thom Shanker, "Afghan Leader to Propose Strategic Ties With the U.S.," *New York Times*, April 14, 2005.

Violence in southeastern Afghanistan in May, sparked by reports that U.S. military interrogators at Guantanamo Bay had desecrated the Quran, added to Washington's concern that U.S. troops not overstay their welcome. While the continuing U.S. presence in Afghanistan is not without controversy, it now appears that the May violence was pre-planned and politically motivated. Some reports indicated that Pakistani intelligence agents might have been involved.[96] The general sense remains that most Afghans continue to welcome the attention that the United States is paying to security and reconstruction in their country, and are not eager for a quick departure. In a visit to Washington in the same month, Karzai signed a new memorandum of understanding with U.S. President George W. Bush that affirmed the continuation of a strategic partnership between the two countries, but did not offer any clarity or details about how long the U.S. military presence on the ground would endure.

By June 2005 it was no longer clear that the Taliban had in fact been defeated; a resurgence appeared to be underway that targeted both foreign forces and Afghan civilians and political figures. In recent months, CJTF trainers have stepped up the operational activities of the new ANA. The CJTF has begun sending ANA companies and even battalions to outlying areas of the country in order to identify and tackle insurgents, while giving them new security responsibilities toward the local population.[97] As part of this effort, the ANA is receiving armored personnel carriers and command vehicles from the United States, and the South Carolina National Guard is carrying out equipment specific training.[98] U.S. air support continues to be an important backbone of these operations, however, and it is not clear how much the ANA could accomplish on its own without the presence of an implicit U.S. deterrent guarantee. Indeed, as the Taliban resurgence began, ANA desertion rates skyrocketed and doubts concerning the force's effectiveness re-emerged.[99]

Even if some modicum of stability is achieved, the United States still will retain military interests in Afghanistan, if for nothing more than the country's strategic location on the borders of Pakistan and Iran. But the most difficult security problems in Afghanistan are the ones left unsuccessfully addressed by the outside world. President Karzai does not really

[96] Wahidullah Amani, "'Foreign Elements' Blamed for Riots," Institute for War and Peace Reporting, *Afghan Recovery Report*, no. 173, May 20, 2005.

[97] Arman-e-Milli (Afghanistan), "Afghan Army Starts Relieving U.S. Forces" (as reported by the Institute of War and Peace Reporting's *Afghan Press Monitor*, no. 69, May 12, 2005).

[98] "Afghan Army Gets Armored Personnel Carriers," *Blackanthem.com* (Kabul), April 29, 2005 (as reported by the Moby Capital Updates news service).

[99] Tom Coghlan, "Afghans Flee Army over Taliban and Low Morale," *London Telegraph*, June 9, 2005.

exercise control of the country, and Afghanistan is in danger of becoming a narco-state that derives most of its national income from the illegal sale of opium poppies and heroin.[100] This drug trade is dominated by so-called warlords—local militia leaders left over from the civil war, who freely ignore Karzai's edicts and rule many areas with a brutal fist. The country's first parliamentary elections, delayed many times but now scheduled for September 2005, will likely be wracked with violence and intimidation.

Afghanistan's poppies create a major security threat for both Central Asia and its European neighbors (whose citizens are the primary consumers of Afghanistan's opium and heroin production). While military modernization efforts may make poppy field and drug lab eradication efforts easier, modernization alone cannot address the complex political realities of Afghanistan's drug-based economy. Instead, more resources must be committed and more creativity shown toward developing alternative livelihood options for Afghanistan's impoverished population.

Conclusion: Policy Implications for the United States

Military modernization in Central Asia is moving slowly, and efforts by these states to increase foreign military support have mixed motives.

The U.S. military presence in Central Asia is undoubtedly a stabilizing influence. It constrains the activity of potential Islamist insurgents and terrorists, and in turn helps prevent additional attacks on U.S. soil. By killing or capturing many Taliban, Al Qaeda, and IMU leaders, and by providing a continuing presence that deprives potential terrorists and insurgents of a training ground, OEF operations in Afghanistan have made the entire Central Asian region more secure. The fact that the United States is showing more attention to the political and financial problems of the region may also contribute to declining tensions among the Central Asian states. The U.S. base presence alone deters hostilities that might otherwise erupt. Thus U.S. involvement in Central Asia has direct mutual security benefits.

The continuing military interest shown by Russia and China in the region—alongside American distrust of neighboring Iran—will add to U.S. motives for staying engaged in Central Asia. Washington's desire to diversify the sources of U.S. and allied petroleum imports beyond the Persian Gulf will also steer the United States to make the region—and in particular Kazakhstan's Caspian oil fields—a high security priority. Yet U.S. policymakers should keep in mind that, for the purpose of garnering increased financial and political support, Central Asian leaders have a habit of playing outside

---

[100] Paul Watson, "Afghanistan: A Harvest of Despair," *Los Angeles Times*, May 29, 2005.

powers against each other. Requests for assistance do not always reflect the actual security needs of these countries.

Recent events in both Kyrgyzstan and Uzbekistan show that the United States must remain attuned to the politics underlying military assistance and other forms of security support in the region. This is especially true given the Bush administration's goal to aid the spread of democratization on a global level. All five post-Soviet Central Asian states appear headed in an anti-democratic direction and, despite its recent popular election, Kyrgyzstan's democratic trajectory remains in doubt. U.S. security support for authoritarian regimes, including both direct military assistance and other forms of partnership, can have unintended consequences. Such military assistance can financially and politically strengthen those regimes, and thus make them increasingly independent of their domestic audiences and potentially contribute to their lack of human rights accountability. Foreign military contracts can also become a pawn for domestic political battles between corrupt leadership factions, whose actions undermine democratic advancement.

The United States should be careful not to view the threat level of Islamist insurgency as the sole barometer of military support for Central Asian countries. Genuine popular discontent—a product of poverty and political desperation—is often miscast by the region's leaders as evidence of an Islamist threat in order to gain more sympathy abroad. In reality, discontent is more threatening to weak regimes than to U.S. security interests. In fact, should Washington ultimately be cast as a friend of dictators by those who oppose these corrupt regimes, military support that serves to buttress their authoritarian rule may create new threats to U.S. security interests. As the United States continues to support military modernization (in particular officer corps, NCO training, and professionalization) in Central Asia, Washington would do well to pay close attention to how military assistance is used by state leaders. Central Asia will remain a high geopolitical priority for the United States in the foreseeable future, and the long-term regional political consequences of U.S. security support are an important component of Washington's policy decisions.

Executive Summary

This chapter investigates how the security concerns and military modernization programs of India and Pakistan might alter regional security dynamics over the near term.

MAIN ARGUMENT:

- India's forces today are sufficient to defend against China beyond the near term, but do not guarantee a quick, decisive conventional victory over Pakistan. Qualitative changes in technology, doctrine, and military culture, however, could shift the calculus in India's favor in the next ten to fifteen years.

- While trying to cope with domestic instability and maintain promising economic growth, Pakistan will modernize its armed forces at the margins in order to keep pace with India; these modernization efforts will continue to be based on incremental hardware improvements rather than doctrinal changes.

POLICY IMPLICATIONS:

- Fundamental miscalculations regarding comparative force capabilities and terrorist violence remain the two most likely sparks for military confrontation. Stability could be fostered on the subcontinent if the nascent India-Pakistan dialogue can be reinforced, particularly in the institutionalization of conflict management measures.

- Pressing for an unambiguous end to militant infiltration into Indian Kashmir and for the dismantlement of terrorist infrastructure, as well as helping reconstruct Pakistani civil society and political institutions that neutralize extremist elements, could help reduce the threat to Pakistan's stability and regional peace posed by radical non-state groups.

- If New Delhi pursues an agenda of tailored modernization, including interoperability with U.S. and other foreign forces, then India will have the potential to become an important security provider in the region.

India and Pakistan: A Shift in the Military Calculus?

John H. Gill

Comparative military capabilities are a central theme in South Asian security affairs. They dominate the complex India-Pakistan security dynamic and inform all interactions between South Asia's two largest powers and the rest of the international community. Given that the India-Pakistan relationship could once again explode into armed confrontation under the nuclear shadow, the status and prospects of Indian and Pakistani modernization programs warrant particular attention.

The main findings of the chapter are as follows: India—whose military advantages are routinely overestimated—has been traditionally unable to translate its numerical superiority into a rapid battlefield victory over Pakistan. If it can overcome a set of significant obstacles, however, New Delhi may succeed in acquiring the hardware and doctrine necessary to shift the military calculus decisively in its favor by 2020. The military dimension is also central to Sino-Indian relations. India casts a wary eye over its Himalayan shoulder, carefully monitoring the progress of Chinese military modernization even as the two Asian giants slowly move toward more productive and cooperative ties. Barring a major change in China's modernization efforts, India will only seek to equip itself with defensive and deterrent capabilities to keep Beijing at bay. Looking beyond the possibility of regional confrontations, the ability of India and Pakistan to keep pace with international military developments will largely determine each country's respective utility

John H. Gill is a retired U.S. Army colonel on the faculty of the Near East-South Asia Center for Strategic Studies at the National Defense University. He has served as a South Asia specialist with the Joint Staff, the U.S. Pacific Command, and the Defense Intelligence Agency. He can be reached at <gillj@ndu.edu>.

The views expressed are solely those of the author and do not reflect the official policy or position of the National Defense University, the Department of Defense, or the United States government.

in counterterrorism operations, peacekeeping missions, and other cooperative international security enterprises. India, in particular, could become an important security provider along the sea lanes and littoral of the Indian Ocean. The speed, scope, and trajectory of military modernization in India and Pakistan are thus immediately relevant to the interests of the United States, Europe, and Asia.

This chapter is divided into two main sections that investigate India and Pakistan's responses to each country's respective security concerns. Each section first examines the military capabilities of India and Pakistan within the context of these countries' national strategies. An assessment looking at current and projected modernization programs then follows, before the chapter concludes with considerations into how these modernization programs might increase the options available to national leaders in coming years.

India

Consistent Goals, Expanded Strategies

As the modern avatar of an ancient civilization and heir to the British Empire's preeminence in the Indian Ocean, India believes that its overriding national security goal should be to establish "its rightful place in the emerging world order."[1] While the main thrust of Indian foreign policy has been consistent since independence, Indian grand strategy can be said to have slowly adjusted since the end of the Cold War. Having moved away from being a "permanent protestor" to assuming a more pragmatic role, India may now indeed be "on the verge of multiple breakthroughs."[2] Even if this assessment proves premature, New Delhi has successfully maintained the general contours of this new grand strategy amidst several changes of government since 1991 and is unlikely to make major alterations in the near future.

In practical terms, securing India's great power goals imposes two strategic requirements. The first of these is a sustained 5 to 6 percent economic growth rate.[3] Near-term growth will depend upon uninterrupted access to foreign sources of oil. Given the small contribution that nuclear power currently makes and the long lead time involved in significant expansion of such energy, the oil and natural gas components of energy security will occupy

---

[1] Indian Ministry of External Affairs, *Annual Report: 2003–04*, 1.

[2] Quotes from C. Raja Mohan, *Crossing the Rubicon* (New York: Palgrave Macmillan, 2004), 262; and C. Raja Mohan, "India's Diplomatic Spring," *Indian Express*, March 22, 2005.

[3] As measured in GDP in Dominic Wilson and Roopa Purushothaman, "Dreaming with the BRICs: The Path to 2050," Goldman Sachs Global Economics Paper, no. 99, October 1, 2003, 4.

a salient position in Indian strategic thinking. India's geographic position along the sea lines connecting the Persian Gulf with Asia's other growing economies reinforces India's potential to be a security provider along this crucial route. The need to secure access to these resources and unhindered foreign trade will have a clear impact on the direction of military development.

The second requirement is relative stability on the domestic front. With a persistent insurgency in Kashmir, continued unrest in the patchwork of northeastern states, and periodic outbreaks of leftist violence in the east, India's internal security situation is daunting. A multitude of police and paramilitary organizations are supposed to act as the principal line of defense against domestic turbulence, but the government has frequently turned to the army to cope with these ills. Such tactics distract regular troops from preparing for conventional conflict, absorb a portion of the military budget, and hinder the army's ability to recruit young officers. Efforts to replace regular army units with special counterinsurgency units under the control of the army (units known as "Rashtriya Rifles") have met with only partial success.[4] In a war situation, however, India would likely accept some risk on the domestic front in order to concentrate all available regular forces against the external foe.

Against this backdrop of economic exigencies and internal instability, New Delhi's strategic concerns can be envisaged as a set of expanding circles.[5] Within the immediate vicinity, Indian strategy must cope with three challenges: China, Pakistan, and its smaller neighbors—Nepal, Bhutan, Bangladesh, Burma, Sri Lanka, and the Maldives. The internal stability of these smaller states is a burgeoning concern for New Delhi, as any instability would call for increased border security and an *in extremis* ability to project regional force on short notice (as it did to quash a 1988 coup attempt in the Maldives). India's intervention in Sri Lanka in the late 1980s, however, was a chastening experience and, generally speaking, New Delhi today does not view these smaller states as arenas for active combat involvement.

China, on the other hand, constitutes one of India's most important relationships and plays a host of contradictory roles: economic competitor, potential military threat, increasingly important trading partner, occasional diplomatic collaborator, and ally and military supplier of rival Pakistan. Indian strategists are also concerned that Beijing's influence in Nepal, Ban-

---

[4] India has no trouble recruiting enlisted soldiers, but the exigencies of military service and the lure of a booming economy have left the army some 13,000 officers short of its authorized strength. See Rahul Bedi, "Gen. J. J. Singh Faced with Task of Revamping Force," *Deccan Herald*, February 5, 2005.

[5] Ashley J. Tellis, "South Asia," in *Strategic Asia 2001–02: Power and Purpose*, ed. Richard J. Ellings and Aaron L. Friedberg (Seattle: The National Bureau of Asian Research, 2001).

gladesh, Burma, and Sri Lanka may be inimical to Indian interests. Nevertheless, Sino-Indian relations have steadily improved over the past decade and the two Asian giants have achieved a notable *modus vivendi* along their contested frontier. New Delhi's recent approach has thus been to facilitate slow reconciliation, accentuate new opportunities, and downplay controversies. Nonetheless, the 1962 war still casts a shadow, and India cannot ignore Beijing's military modernization programs. India's military capabilities must therefore account for the potential danger posed by China's conventional and nuclear forces—despite the growing commercial and diplomatic ties between the two countries.

Though China is a security concern over the long term, Pakistan presents an immediate challenge. Whereas India and China have not experienced a serious crisis for almost twenty years and have not fought one another for more than forty, Indian-Pakistani relations have, since independence, been punctuated with conflict, including a significant armed clash in 1999, a near-war confrontation in 2002, routine artillery exchanges in Kashmir up until late 2003, and ongoing Pakistani support for a separatist militancy inside India.[6] Recognizing that unremitting confrontation with Pakistan mires Indian foreign policy in a subcontinental context, New Delhi generally follows an unstated containment approach in dealing with its western neighbor. Though expanding political, economic, and cultural ties with Pakistan, India also uses diplomatic maneuvers to isolate Pakistan internationally. In terms of defense, New Delhi must cope with the entire spectrum of conflict; from nuclear exchange and full-scale conventional war to counterinsurgency operations in Indian Kashmir. The requirements inherent in this strategy—credible nuclear deterrence, conventional superiority, and counterinsurgency capabilities—have been relatively constant and are unlikely to change significantly in the near term.

The next circle of policy concern for New Delhi includes the Persian Gulf, Central Asia, and Southeast Asia. With over 70 percent of India's oil drawn from the Gulf and an expectation that demand will rise dramatically in the coming decades, India has a vital interest in the maintenance of stability in Iran and the Arab Gulf states. Furthermore, an estimated 3.5 million Indians work in the Gulf, providing valuable remittances and obligating New Delhi to take their safety into consideration.[7] Iran is also important as a potential avenue for commercial access to Central Asia and Afghanistan. Good relations with all of these countries serve a security purpose by deny-

---

[6] For the 2002 crisis, see Stephen P. Cohen, "South Asia," in *Strategic Asia 2002–03: Asian Aftershocks*, ed. Richard J. Ellings and Aaron L. Friedberg (Seattle: The National Bureau of Asian Research, 2003).

[7] Indian Ministry of Defence, *Annual Report 2004–05*, 13.

ing Pakistan the illusion of "strategic depth" in its dealings with India. While maintaining favorable ties with the Middle Eastern states, New Delhi has also succeeded in building an extraordinary relationship with Tel Aviv, with Israel being a particularly important source for military technology.[8] Trade and security concerns also drive the expansion of India's commercial and strategic contacts with the Association of Southeast Asian Nations countries. New Delhi is keenly aware that India's geographic location allows it to provide security of shipping in the Indian Ocean, and believes that stability and counterterrorism constitute key common interests with India's Southeast Asian neighbors.[9]

The outermost circle of India's security interests encompasses global issues and interactions with more distant governments, chiefly the United States. In this arena, New Delhi recognizes that broad and deep ties with the world's sole superpower are central to India's continued economic success and to what Indian leaders see as the recovery of India's "due status in the world."[10] At the same time, India has not abandoned the ideal of strategic autonomy. Close relations with Russia, China, Japan, and the European Union serve India's economic needs and enhance its freedom of action vis-à-vis the United States. To advance its agenda at the global level, however, New Delhi believes that India must be militarily credible, internally stable, economically strong, and diplomatically savvy.

Although India does not publish a national security strategy, its armed forces clearly have an important role to play that spans several key dimensions of this broad strategy. First, the vast array of military and paramilitary organizations are central to New Delhi's approach to internal stability. Second, India's conventional and nuclear capabilities are essential to the wary engagement with China and Pakistan.[11] Third, India's growing energy needs will impose increasingly significant demands on the military (principally the navy) to provide security for unimpeded access to oil. At the same time, India's security interests in the immediate region necessitate at least a force projection capability along the Indian Ocean littoral. Fourth, India's armed forces (again, particularly the navy) have become important as adjuncts to New Delhi's diplomacy. A powerful military is one of the emblems of great power status, and New Delhi hopes to use military cooperation and

---

[8] After Russia, Israel is India's most important arms supplier, and Israeli technical expertise is critical to a broad range of India's weapons upgrade projects. See Sandeep Unnithan, "Getting a Boost," *India Today*, February 14, 2005.

[9] Indian Ministry of Defence, *Annual Report: 2004–05*, 14.

[10] Prime Minister Manmohan Singh, speech at *India Today* conclave, New Delhi, February 25, 2005.

[11] Indian Ministry of Defence, *Annual Report: 2004–05*, 8–13.

arms deals to expand its influence abroad.[12] Similarly, India has consistently contributed to United Nations peacekeeping operations, both from a moral commitment to the institution and from a desire to bolster its Security Council aspirations. While success in weapons sales has largely eluded India thus far, an expanding menu of international military interactions is raising India's profile as a major player in the region and on the global stage. The corollary is that interaction with foreign forces, especially those of the United States, offers the Indian military unique training opportunities and experience with new technologies.

The Armed Forces Today: Competencies and Conundrums

The force India maintains to support its grand strategy is one of the largest conventional military establishments in the world. India's one million man army is exceeded in number only by China's, its air force numbers more than 600 combat aircraft, and its navy is one of the ten largest in the world when measured by the number of principal surface combatants.[13] Many of the 650,000 paramilitary soldiers also have a role in directly supporting the regular forces. The bulk of India's military equipment is of Soviet/Russian origin, but much of this hardware is at or beyond the end of its expected service life and in urgent need of replacement.[14] The Indian Army is by far the dominant service, with the air force second in priority and the navy often underfunded and struggling for attention. All three services, however, exhibit high degrees of professionalism, training, and proficiency in fulfilling the demands the state has placed upon them.

Beyond these conventional capabilities, India possesses a growing nuclear force,[15] and nuclear considerations influence all of New Delhi's planning. A combination of aircraft and missiles are available as delivery means for nuclear weapons; India thus has the range to strike almost anywhere in Pakistan, but not yet to reach China's key population centers. Nuclear doctrine and force size continue to provoke lively debate, but Indian govern-

---

[12] Such as exercises with the French Navy and Air Force, training with Singapore, limited support to Iran's armed forces, and efforts to market arms in Southeast Asia and the Gulf.

[13] The number of aircraft does not include trainers or intelligence collectors. See International Institute for Strategic Studies, *The Military Balance 2004-2005* (London: Oxford University Press, 2004).

[14] See Vivek Raghuvanshi, "Indian Army Faces Tank Shortages," *Defense News*, May 23, 2005.

[15] Estimates of Indian nuclear warhead numbers vary from 30–150 plutonium fission warheads of 5–25 kiloton yield. Most estimates are well below 100. See the Carnegie Endowment for International Peace at http://www.carnegieendowment.org (which provides an estimate of 70), the Natural Resource Defense Council at http://www.nrdc.org (est. 30–35), the Arms Control Association at http://www.armscontrol.org (est. 45–95), and *Jane's Sentinel Security Assessment—South Asia: India*, April 27, 2005 (est. 60 to 150).

ments since 1998 have maintained a "no first use" policy and have viewed nuclear weapons as "not really useable."[16] India's nuclear arsenal thus remains as "force in being" with a second strike capability designed to deter enemy use of weapons of mass destruction, rather than a tool of tactical utility.[17]

Though able to sustain a satisfactory defensive posture in the unlikely event of a war against China, India has only limited force projection capabilities around the Indian Ocean littoral or in the adjoining sub-regions, and would encounter serious strategic deficits in a conflict with Pakistan.[18] The two full-scale India-Pakistan wars were short (two to three weeks in duration),[19] and strategic thinkers on both sides expect that another conflict would be similarly brief, with international pressure, nuclear threats, and/or nuclear exchange bringing combat to a swift conclusion.[20] Therefore, although a prolonged conflict would allow India to exploit its numerical superiority and could exhaust Pakistan's logistical stocks, Indian strategists believe that India must mobilize and win quickly.[21] Even in a purely conventional scenario, however, India's armed forces do not currently have the capabilities necessary to guarantee a decisive military victory against Pakistan within such a narrow time frame.

Although the Indian and Pakistani armies are generally equivalent in qualitative metrics such as training and leadership, India's numerical advantage is deceptive. The Indian quantitative superiority in personnel and equipment is relatively narrow in relation to Pakistan, and India's services are dogged by major deficiencies that reduce its advantages to near parity. In the first place, in any war with Pakistan a significant number of troops would have to be held on the border with China in order to make sure that Beijing did not assist its nominal ally. Second, India's acquisition of new hardware can give a misleading impression of its overall technological level—while important on the local battlefield, they may not transform overall Indian capabilities. Three hundred and ten T-90 tanks, for instance, represent less than ten percent of the Indian tank fleet, much of which is obsolete. More

---

[16] Quoted from Natwar Singh (address at the Conference on Emerging Proliferation Challenges, New Delhi, March 28, 2005), http://meaindia.nic.in.

[17] Ashley J. Tellis, *India's Emerging Nuclear Posture* (Santa Monica, CA: RAND, 2001); for India's doctrine, see "The Cabinet Committee on Security Reviews Operationalization of India's Nuclear Doctrine," January 4, 2003, http://meaindia.nic.in.

[18] Pravin Sawhney, "Evolving Nuclear Environment Moulds India's Military Strategy," *Jane's Intelligence Review*, August 2004.

[19] The 1947–48 war is not considered "full-scale" here because of the relatively small number of forces involved, the fact that it was confined to Kashmir, and the peculiar circumstances associated with the partition of India.

[20] *Indian Army Doctrine*, October 2004, http://www.indianarmy.mic.in; and Shaukat Qadir, "War Termination Strategy for Pakistan," *Daily Times*, December 13, 2003.

[21] Shaukat Qadir, "India's 'Cold Start' Strategy," *Daily Times*, May 8, 2004.

Figure 1. India-Pakistan Division and Brigade Comparison

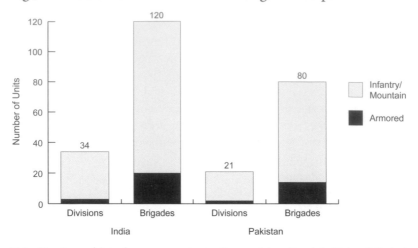

Note: Numbers of brigades are approximate. **Source:** International Institute of Strategic Studies, *The Military Balance 2004-2005*, London: Oxford University Press, 2004; *Jane's Sentinel Security Assessment – South Asia*.

important for the ground forces, however, are weaknesses in logistics and mobility, especially given the immature infrastructure along much of the India-Pakistan border. Only 20 of approximately 120 maneuver brigades in the Indian Army are fully mobile, for instance—the rest have only a limited capacity to transport their organic troops, weapons, and supplies simultaneously.[22] Other critical assets, such as self-propelled artillery, are also in short supply, and thus commanders are constrained from employing their few mobile troops in bold advances.[23] Instead, the bulk of the army's maneuver forces—some 84 percent of its brigades—rely on railroads, military trucks, and civilian hire transport to make any significant moves; their ability to conduct deep penetrations across the border is thus questionable. As a result, much of the Indian manpower advantage is almost irrelevant in a war of short duration. The army's conservative institutional culture is another hindrance militating against decisive offensive warfare.[24] Political constraints against losing any Indian territory and a lack of real-time intelligence would exponentially compound the challenges of moving large ground forces over

---

[22] The number of brigades is an estimate based on *The Military Balance 2004–2005*, and is probably low as some Indian infantry divisions have more than the normal three maneuver brigades.

[23] To equip just its three armored divisions and seven independent armored brigades with self-propelled artillery, the Indian Army would need at least 300 such guns. It has about 30 serviceable self-propelled guns and perhaps 150 more in storage.

[24] See V. K. Kapoor, "Indian Army: A Perspective on Future Challenges, Force Development and Doctrine," *Journal of the United Services Institution of India* 134, no. 557 (July–September 2004).

difficult desert and semi-desert terrain rapidly enough to achieve a decisive victory over Pakistan.[25]

India's real quantitative superiority over Pakistan in air and maritime forces is not currently sufficient to compensate for this near parity of ground force capabilities. Furthermore, doubts about the timeliness and accuracy of intelligence, the limited numbers of precision-guided munitions, and differences with the army over the merits of close air support all reduce the effectiveness of army-air force cooperation.[26] Historically, Indian joint operations have seldom proceeded smoothly; the air force, for instance, has not given much priority to the army's demands for on-call support for tactical targets.[27] Air force-navy cooperation has also been problematic.

All of these conventional force considerations are complicated by India's longstanding strategic conundrum: how to gauge when India is close to crossing one of Pakistan's intentionally ambiguous nuclear "red lines." New Delhi also faces a major challenge in defining its war aims and crafting suitable military operations to achieve them. What military actions will force Pakistan to cease support for militants in India? Will punitive strikes alter Pakistani behavior or merely start a cycle of escalation? Can escalation be controlled? These questions remain under debate, but the gap between Indian operational plans and probable war aims is likely quite large. The gap between those same plans and Pakistan's nuclear threshold, on the other hand, could be quite small. Assessing Pakistani perceptions of the shifting battlefield situation and calibrating the Indian response would be enormously challenging in the tension and confusion of combat. The scope for miscalculation is thus high and the problem is not amenable to technological solutions—that is, a new piece of equipment is not likely to offer much additional clarity for the decisionmaker in a future crisis.

Indian Modernization Programs: Enough Parts to Make a Whole?

India is looking to use military modernization as one means to exert influence and move closer to its grand strategic goals of building a regional force projection capability, keeping pace with China, and presenting a credible conventional threat to Pakistan despite the latter's nuclear arsenal. Moreover, many Indian military officers believe that modernization is imperative

---

[25] J. F. R. Jacob, "The Maginot Mentality," *Force*, April 2005.

[26] An overview of joint issues appears in Vijay Oberoi, "Air Power and Joint Operations: Doctrinal and Organisational Challenges," *Journal of the United Services Institution of India* 133, no. 551 (January-March 2003); Vinod Patney provides an IAF perspective in the same issue of this journal.

[27] Prasan Sengupta, "Air Warriors in the New Millennium," *Vayu Aerospace Review*, vol. 5 (2001).

to restoring the conventional superiority over Pakistan that has in many respects steadily diminished over the past three decades.[28]

The Army. Although the Indian government's national strategy is broad, the focus of army thinking is Pakistan. The two recent confrontations between India and Pakistan sharpened New Delhi's frustration at being unable to translate conventional superiority into an effective exercise of power in the face of what it perceives as incessant Pakistani sub-conventional provocation. Though this conundrum is not new, the 1999 Kargil war intensified the search for a "strategic space" in which India's conventional forces could operate beneath Pakistan's nuclear thresholds. Proponents referred to the conventional force answer as "limited war," a problematic strategy under which Indian forces could launch shallow attacks or "surgical strikes" into Pakistani-controlled territory without prompting a nuclear response.[29] Indian strategic thinkers refined the "limited war" concept in the wake of the 2002 confrontation.[30] Some Indians were convinced that their country had enjoyed a brief advantage over Pakistan during the first weeks of the crisis, but was unable to exploit this opportunity because the transition from peace to deployment (called Operation Parakram) unfolded too slowly, thereby giving the international community time to intervene.[31]

The Indian Army conducted a detailed review of Operation Parakram and announced a new service strategy in April 2004. Popularly called "Cold Start," this strategy calls for the creation of some eight "integrated battle groups" of army, air force and, where appropriate, navy forces.[32] The hope is that these battle groups, garrisoned near the border, will be able to mobilize rapidly, launching powerful attacks within days while reserves from the interior move to the front. The army intends to boost the effectiveness of its quantitative advantage through greater cooperation with the air force and better utilization of high-technology force multipliers such as intelligence assets, special forces, and command/control systems.[33] Whereas the old strategy aimed to divide Pakistan by seizing critical terrain through deep penetrations, the operational goal now seems to be to inflict severe damage

---

[28] See Vivek Raghuvanshi, "Indian Army: Our Edge is Slipping," *Defense News*, October 13, 2003.

[29] Jasjit Singh, "Exploring India's Options," *Indian Express*, May 16, 2002.

[30] For trenchant critiques, see V.R. Raghavan, "Limited War and Nuclear Escalation in South Asia," *Nonproliferation Review*, Fall-Winter 2001; and Suba Chandran, "Limited War with Pakistan: Will It Secure India's Interests?" (Champaign-Urbana: University of Illinois, 2004).

[31] See, for instance, "Cold Start to New War Doctrine," *Times of India*, April 14, 2004; and Anil Athale, "We Were Ready to Punish Pakistan," *Rediff.com*, Rediff Special, March 1, 2005.

[32] Pravin Sawhney, "Lean and Mean: New Command Boundaries against Pakistan Give Sharper Teeth to the Army," *Force*, March 2005.

[33] Vijay Mohan, "Shift in Army's War Strategy," *Tribune*, May 13, 2005.

on Pakistan's armed forces through the application of massive firepower.[34] Indian forces theoretically could remain on their own side of the border/line of control while launching stunning artillery and airpower assaults. Indian ground units could also make shallow incursions, forcing the Pakistanis to launch counterattacks and thereby allow India's artillery and air force to have their most punishing effect.[35] The army has already changed the command structure on the Pakistan border to accommodate "Cold Start" and, in an effort to promote new thinking, has released a new doctrine outlining a reinvigorated operational philosophy.[36]

This emphasis on firepower is reflected in recent and projected army moves: standardizing the caliber of medium artillery, purchasing more guns overall, and supplementing these guns with multiple rocket launchers and Prithvi short-range ballistic missiles (SRBM). The army has also let a contract for an automated artillery fire control system, tested laser designation systems and acquired upgraded artillery ammunition.[37] It is not clear, however, that any steps have been taken to modernize the logistical chain that will be needed in order to supply the enormous amounts of ammunition suggested by the new doctrine.

Simultaneously, the army is endeavoring to correct serious deficiencies in command/control and intelligence capabilities so that commanders, operating from "force multiplier command posts," will see the battlefield more clearly and respond more rapidly to changing operational situations.[38] Special forces are another area of increased army interest. Many Indian strategists see special forces as valuable assets not only against Pakistan, but also against China and in other regional force projection scenarios as well. The army chief has called for doubling the number of special forces battalions from five to ten by 2010.[39]

Though focused on the artillery arm at present, the army is also pursuing other modernization programs, such as replacing some of its aging

---

[34] Not all Indian strategic thinkers agree with this "shallow penetration" concept. For the views of a proponent of the "strike hard, strike deep" approach, see Brig. (ret.) Gurmeet Kanwal, "Pakistan's Nuclear Threshold and India's Options," Observer Research Foundation, January 18, 2005, http://www.observerindia.com.

[35] Shishir Gupta, "No Eyeball to Eyeball Any More in New War Doctrine," Indian Express, March 6, 2004; and Y. I. Patel, "Dig Vijay to Divya Astra: A Paradigm Shift in the India Army's Doctrine," Bharat Rakshak Monitor 6, no. 6 (July 2004).

[36] Vijay Mohan, "New Command 9 Corps Formed," Tribune, March 20, 2005.

[37] See, for instance, Dalip Singh, "New Toys on Show at War Games," Telegraph, March 2, 2004; Pravin Sawhney, "Artillery Goes on the Biggest Shopping Spree Ever," Force, November 2003; and Vivek Raghuvanshi, "ACCS Links Indian Army Artillery," Defense News, October 18, 2004.

[38] Ajit K. Dubey, "Gaming for War," Force, May 2005.

[39] Gurmeet Kanwal, "Indian Special Forces: Reorganising for an Expanding Role," Security Research Review 1, no. 2 (January 2005).

tank fleet with Russian T-90s and upgrading infantry equipment in select units.[40] Whereas the new doctrine and systems associated with the artillery, intelligence, and command/control are potentially transformative, however, these other cases merely represent product improvements or the replacement of outdated models with newer equipment.[41] Moreover, much of the Indian Army's success will be determined by how well it copes with a mundane problem: overcoming the distance many units have to travel from their home garrisons to their deployment areas near the border. *The Air Force.* Where the army's modernization efforts are focused on Pakistan, the Indian Air Force (IAF) is acquiring capabilities that will be applicable against China as well. Benefiting from steady growth in its share of the defense budget since 2001 (from 17.6 percent to 24.7 percent), the IAF is making important acquisitions. The most important addition to the combat aircraft fleet has been 40 SU-30MKIs—one of the most advanced multi-role fighters in the world—purchased from Russia with a license to produce an additional 140 aircraft in India.[42] For medium-range fighters, the IAF has announced its interest in purchasing 126 aircraft in the near future to replace many of its MiGs, while at the same time upgrading several older types.[43] The indigenous Light Combat Aircraft could also begin to enter service around 2012. Less glamorous, but equally important, is the conclusion of a deal to purchase 66 advanced jet trainers from the United Kingdom to address a glaring gap in the IAF's pilot training capacity. Despite these prospective acquisitions, the advanced age of many current airframes means that the IAF will struggle to keep its numerical strength at existing levels during the next five to ten years.[44]

The heart of IAF modernization is the acquisition of key force multipliers. Air-to-air tankers are already in service (extending loiter time and range for many of the fighter types), while Israeli Phalcon airborne early warning and control systems (AEW&C) will for the first time give India an aerial surveillance platform to track multiple threats and vector friendly fighters. These new capabilities—if melded with sophisticated air-to-air missiles, proposed aircraft self-protection systems, and the acquisition of preci-

---

[40] See interview with Gen. J. J. Singh, Chief of the Army Staff, in *India Today*, February 14, 2005.

[41] Enhanced capabilities for infantry units at the tactical level do contribute directly to the ongoing fight against infiltrators and insurgents in Kashmir and elsewhere. See P. K. Vasudeva, "Futuristic Weapons for the Army: But a War Doctrine Should Also Be Ready," *Tribune*, May 15, 2004.

[42] A. Suresh, "Indian Air Force: Enhancing Operational Capability," *Asian Defence Journal* 1, no. 2 (January-February 2005).

[43] Rahul Bedi, "India Paves Way for Arms Upgrade Package," *Jane's Defence Weekly,* April 6, 2005. This paragraph also draws from *Jane's Sentinel Security Assessment—South Asia: India*, April 27, 2005.

[44] Gulshan Luthra, "IAF Needs at Least 300 Aircraft," *Tribune*, August 18, 2004.

sion-guided munitions—could make a dramatic difference.[45] Indeed, these changes—along with a potentially major role for the air force in "limited war" punitive scenarios—argue for a comprehensive doctrinal review and close integration with the army; yet the IAF seems inclined to retain its traditional emphasis on air defense, interdiction, and strategic targets.[46]

The Navy. Of the three services, the Indian Navy's modernization efforts have the potential for the broadest strategic applicability. The navy's greatest concern is China, but New Delhi's maritime calculations also encompass such security issues as piracy, drug trafficking, and interdiction of terrorists.[47] Moreover, the maritime doctrine announced in 2004 specifically calls for the Indian Navy to serve as "an effective instrument of foreign policy," not only as a source of coercive military power, but also as a diplomatic link to other countries.[48] The extensive program of bilateral training exercises, port visits, and other events that the navy has developed thus supports important national strategic objectives in the Indian Ocean and beyond.

Although the navy's share of the defense budget has increased from 12.5 percent to 16.5 percent between 2001 and 2004, attaining the navy's blue water requirement will be difficult. Owing to the "lost decade" between 1985 and 1995 when very few new ships were ordered, India's admirals expect that the number of ships being decommissioned will outnumber new entrants until approximately 2012.[49] Ideally, the Indian Navy would be based around two carrier battle groups, a fleet of 24 conventional submarines, several nuclear-powered submarines, and as many as 30 long-range maritime patrol aircraft. The navy's plan to build a force of three carriers (necessary to support two carrier groups reliably) is underway due to both an agreement reached with Russia to purchase the refurbished *Admiral Gorshkov* with an air wing, and the decision to construct an "air defense ship" (actually a carrier of 37,000 tons). Achieving the three carrier goal in the mid-term (optimistically by 2012) will remain problematic, however, since the navy is supposed to retire its lone extant carrier upon the arrival of the *Gorshkov*.[50] The submarine arm

---

[45] R. K. Jasbir Singh, *Indian Defence Yearbook 2004* (Dehra Dun: Natraj, 2004), 334.

[46] Jasjit Singh, "The Indian Air Force: Meeting the 21st Century Challenge," *Vayu Aerospace Review,* September 2000; and A. Y. Tipnis, "Indian Air Force 2020," *Security Research Review* 1, no. 2 (January 2005).

[47] "New Naval Doctrine Stresses on Developing Nuclear Triad," *Outlook,* June 23, 2004. This section draws on *Jane's Fighting Ships* (updated April 29, 2005), http://www.4janes.com; and *Jane's Sentinel Security Assessment—South Asia: India,* April 27, 2005.

[48] Indian Navy, *Indian Maritime Doctrine* (2004), 102.

[49] See the interview with Admiral Arun Prakash in *Defense News,* March 28, 2005; and India Defence Consultants, "Indian Navy Update: It Requires Manpower," April 7, 2005, http://www.indiadefence. com.

[50] Ranjit Rai, "ADS Finally on Track," India Defence Consultants, July 4, 2004, http://www.indiadefence.com.

will diminish in the short term, but reconditioning programs for existing models as well as new acquisitions should restore its numbers sometime after 2010. Probably owing to extensive problems with its own nuclear submarine project, India is also reportedly considering the lease or purchase of one or two nuclear-powered attack submarines from Russia. The navy is unlikely to reach the desired 30 maritime patrol aircraft in the foreseeable future and has opted instead to upgrade existing airframes and perhaps purchase P-3C Orions from the United States. India is also interested in the purchase or lease of four nuclear-capable Tu-22 Backfire bombers, but the status of this possible deal is unclear.[51] On the other hand, some of the new ships and refurbished submarines include a capability to launch SS-N-27 Klub anti-ship cruise missiles, and the supersonic Indo-Russian BrahMos anti-ship cruise missile (290-kilometer range) could enter the naval arsenal during 2005; both missiles are also being developed for the land attack role.

Strategic Forces. India is also modernizing its strategic forces. On the hardware side, ballistic missile testing and production continues as the army expands the number of missile groups in its order of battle to accommodate the short-range Prithvi (150 to 250 kilometers) and medium-range Agni variants currently entering service.[52] The versions of the Agni thought to be in service have a maximum range of 700 to 2,500 kilometers and carry nuclear warheads. They can thus hit any target in Pakistan, but are of limited use against China. In order to increase India's ability to deter China, New Delhi is developing an Agni with a range greater than 3,000 kilometers.[53] At the same time, the navy's new doctrine urges development of a submarine-based "non-provocative strategic capability" as the best means of acquiring an assured nuclear second-strike platform.[54] In order to address some of the structural aspects of nuclear weapons ownership, India recently formed a tri-service Strategic Forces Command to manage operational employment. Details of how this command is to function, including authority over the delivery means owned by the services and the command's interface with the scientific community that controls the warheads, remain unclear. Among other complex issues, New Delhi will have to locate resources to support a nuclear command/control system with the concomitant communications, intelligence, and protection requirements.[55]

---

[51] Vivek Raghuvanshi, "India OKs Russian Royalty Demands," *Defense News*, May 9, 2005.

[52] Missile data compiled from *The Military Balance 2004–2005* and compared with the information in *Jane's Sentinel Security Assessment—South Asia: India*, April 27, 2005.

[53] "Govt to Testfire Agni III this Year," *Indian Express*, January 2, 2005.

[54] Quoted in Rahul Bedi, "A New Doctrine for the Navy," *Frontline* 21, no. 14 (July 3–16, 2004).

[55] Quoted in Vivek Raghuvanshi, "Indian Nuclear Command Plans Face Long Delay," *Defense News*, January 27, 2003.

While strengthening its deterrent posture through improvements in its offensive weapons, New Delhi is also exploring defensive options. India has already acquired several Green Pine radars from Israel, has expressed interest in the Arrow anti-tactical ballistic missile (ATBM) system affiliated with these radars, and may have already signed a deal with Russia for several ATBM suites. Additionally, missile defense has been a key component of the ongoing U.S.-Indian military-to-military dialogue.[56]

The effectiveness of military modernization. This overview of India's military modernization programs suggests that, if current trends maintain their general trajectories, the country's armed forces could acquire significant new capabilities over the coming decade. Some of these capabilities could be on hand as early as 2010, though 2015 is a more realistic time frame. By that time, the navy will have improved sea denial and power projection capabilities with a modernized submarine fleet and one, perhaps two, carrier battle groups equipped with updated aircraft. Cruise missiles will not only provide a major upgrade in combat power at sea but will also give the navy the ability to strike littoral targets with greater accuracy and lethality. Deficiencies in logistical support, reconnaissance aircraft, and command/control will, however, continue to hamper the navy's efforts to achieve a true blue water power projection status. The army, combining a potentially tremendous increase in firepower with greater agility and somewhat enhanced mobility, could have the capability to launch powerful, short-notice attacks to relatively shallow depths in Pakistan. Though the army will not be able to conduct and sustain deep penetration offensives, Indian officers now seem to consider operations of this nature unnecessary and too close to the Pakistani nuclear threshold. India will likely possess some medium-range ballistic missiles that, in combination with manned aircraft, may have sufficient range to threaten important Chinese targets, and may also have some limited missile defense capability around a few select locations. The most substantial and meaningful advances, however, are most likely to be manifested in the IAF. The continued introduction of advanced aircraft and the integration of critical force multipliers will boost the air force's capabilities against China and, if coupled with timely intelligence and adequate numbers of precision-guided munitions, could allow the air force to exploit its numerical superiority over Pakistan as never before.

At present, however, the defense budget does not seem adequate to support comprehensive modernization across the services. On the one hand, funds allotted to defense have risen steadily from $15.5 billion in Indian fiscal year 2002–03 to $19.1 billion in 2005–06 (the equivalent of between

---

[56] "New Framework for the U.S.-India Defense Relationship," June 28, 2005, http://newdelhi.usembassy.gov.

2.6 and 2.9 percent of GDP per year), thus giving India a greater capacity for modernization in comparison to Pakistan. On the other hand, Indians argue that these figures are insufficient to underwrite both the replacement of obsolescent equipment and the simultaneous introduction of new hardware in numbers sufficient to make a major difference on the battlefield. The training required to integrate these new doctrinal concepts is also both time consuming and costly. Moreover, the military may have to make major investments in personnel in order to compete with the private sector for skilled human capital. The cumbersome acquisition bureaucracy, including a new set of restrictive regulations, is an additional impediment to rapid, holistic modernization. For the past three years, for example, the Ministry of Defence has returned $1–2 billion per annum because it has been unable to commit these funds during the course of the fiscal year. A number of high-profile acquisition scandals have compounded the delay and uncertainty by inducing further caution in the bureaucracy.[57]

Even if budgetary and bureaucratic problems are mastered and all of the acquisition wishes of each service are fulfilled, the central question remains whether India's armed forces can successfully employ their new systems. Three key inhibiting factors must be considered. First, India, like many other countries, has been dogged by bitter interservice rivalry. Despite joint educational programs and field exercises, successful joint endeavors in the past have relied on personal interaction among senior officers rather than institutionalized coordination.[58] The second problem is the frequent disconnect between national security policy as formulated by the civilian leadership and the military's strategy, doctrine, and procurement decisions. Although national policy and military strategy are sometimes well synchronized during times of crisis, senior officers often deplore the absence of clear direction from their civilian leaders.[59] Third, a generally conservative institutional culture pervades all three services, dampening initiative and creativity.[60] There is also a question concerning how much new technology and doctrine the three services can absorb over the short term. In aggregate, therefore, the Indian military could bring on board several significant new capabilities during the next ten to twelve years, but will have to overcome daunting institutional barriers in order to realize the potential implied in these proposed hardware acquisitions and new doctrinal thinking. Failing

---

[57] Vijay Oberoi, ed., *Army 2020* (New Delhi: Knowledge World, 2005), 171–200; figures are from *The Military Balance 2004–2005*.

[58] See Government of India, "Recommendation of the Group of Ministers on Reforming the National Security System," February 2001.

[59] Pravin Sawhney, "Unity of Command," *The Pioneer*, May 2, 2004.

[60] Vijay Oberoi, "Army Drafts New War Doctrine," *The Hindu*, March 5, 2004.

to do so will limit the military options available to India's political leaders in any future confrontation with Pakistan, and will leave India struggling to keep pace with China beyond the short term.

Pakistan

A Strategy of Survival

From the time of its establishment as an independent state, Pakistan's worldview has been dominated by the perception that it faces an existential threat from its enormous eastern neighbor. This perception pervades all aspects of Pakistan government policy, and the fear of an India committed to "undoing" the 1947 partition of British India has meant that successive Pakistani governments have viewed national security almost exclusively through a distorted military lens—to the detriment of economic, political, judicial, and social considerations.[61] This emphasis on military security has contributed to the overwhelming influence of the armed forces, above all the army, in policy and governance through most of Pakistan's history.[62] In this presumably hostile environment, survival as a sovereign state has been the central national goal, and the military's narrow institutional interests have assumed an awkward prominence that is often manifested in Pakistan's international behavior.

Within this context, Pakistan's grand strategy has coalesced around three principal elements. First, Pakistan seeks to maintain sufficient conventional and nuclear strength to deter an Indian attack or, if deterrence fails, to prevent a catastrophic defeat long enough for the international community to intervene and halt the conflict.[63] Second, Pakistan relies on external allies to bolster its own defenses through arms supplies and diplomatic support, seeking to translate its geostrategic position into a claim on the resources and attentions of outside actors—especially the United States and China. Islamabad, however, has been unable to secure specific security guarantees against India. Third, Pakistan seeks to weaken India militarily by enmeshing Indian forces in domestic unrest while at the same time limiting New Delhi's access to foreign sources of diplomatic assistance, moral support, and weapons transfers. In the 1990s, some Pakistani leaders briefly added a fourth element: seeking "strategic depth" against India by establishing a

---

[61] Teresita C. Schaffer, "Pakistan's Future and U.S. Policy Options," Center for Strategic and International Studies, March 2004, 7.

[62] See Ayesha Siddiqa Agha, "Pakistan's Security: Problems of Linearity," *South Asian Journal*, no. 3 (January-March 2004).

[63] Pervez Musharraf, address to the National Security Workshop, National Defence College, Islamabad, February 12, 2004, http://www.presidentofpakistan.gov.

Pakistani sphere of influence in Afghanistan and Central Asia. It was never clear what real benefit was supposed to accrue to Pakistan from this notion, and it eventually foundered on the rocks of reality. Pakistan remains vitally concerned, however, with developments in Iran/Central Asia in general and Afghanistan in particular, as instability on its western border can have deeply dangerous repercussions inside Pakistan.

Pakistan's armed forces are the foundation of this grand strategy. The three services must provide conventional strength and competence adequate to persuade India that a rapid attack has little chance of producing substantial gains without triggering a nuclear response; Pakistani strategic forces, in turn, must be sufficiently numerous and reliable to make the nuclear deterrent credible. At the same time, the Pakistan Army aims to retain an offensive capability sufficient to tie down Indian forces, conduct counterattacks, and seize key bits of Indian terrain. This has led Islamabad to support "jihadi" insurgents operating in Indian Kashmir and elsewhere as a low-cost means of occupying and demoralizing Indian ground forces, reducing the likelihood that they will be capable of launching a major cross-border attack.[64] The jihadis, however, have come to threaten Pakistan itself, sowing instability and violence, frightening investors, and nearly provoking full-scale war with India. Since 2001, according to Pakistani accounts, Islamabad's military decisionmakers have thus been seeking to reduce the danger that these non-state groups pose to Pakistan, while at the same time retaining them as a strategic reserve to force New Delhi into negotiations on the status of Kashmir.[65]

The military will remain crucial to Pakistan's grand strategy for the foreseeable future, though there are indications that General Musharraf is trying to alter the fundamental strategic paradigm. Since early 2002, he has highlighted Pakistan's economic strength as a key aspect of national security equivalent, at least in theory, to military power.[66] Thanks in part to Pakistani policies and in part to copious international assistance, the economy has rebounded from its calamitous state several years ago and could see a growth rate of more than 8% for 2005.[67] Following the assassination attempts against

---

[64] Abdul Sattar, "Development of Pakistan's Foreign Policy," Pakistan Institute of Legislative Development and Transparency, Case Study, no. 2, April 2004; and Lt. Gen. (ret.) Farrakh Khan, "Air Support Requirements of Pakistan Army and the Role of Army Aviation," Centre for Aerospace Power Studies (Karachi), September 2002, http://www.caps.org.pk.

[65] Feroz Hassan Khan, "Pakistan's Challenges and the Need for a Balanced Solution," *Strategic Insights*, August 10, 2002; and Jay Solomon, Zahid Hussain, and Keith Johnson, "Despite U.S. Effort, Pakistan Remains Key Terror Hub," *Wall Street Journal*, July 22, 2005.

[66] Musharraf, address to the National Security Workshop; and Josh Meyer, "Terror Camps Scatter, Persist," *Los Angeles Times*, June 20, 2005.

[67] Asian Development Bank, "Pakistan Economic Update," April 21, 2005, http://www.adb.org. For a dose of skepticism, see Shahid Kardar, "Maintaining High Growth Rates," *Dawn*, April 18, 2005.

Musharraf and other leaders during 2003 and 2004, Pakistani officials also began stressing "enlightened moderation" and the dilution of extremism. They adopted this new tack in part due to the damage such extremism inflicted on the investment climate, but also because of the danger radical and violent political groups pose to both government and society.[68] This new attitude has led to substantial army operations against foreign fighters and other extremists in select areas along the Afghan border, and has resulted in the capture of several high profile terrorists during 2004–05. The extent to which Pakistan will continue these operations remains to be seen, but the recent emphasis on economic progress and domestic threats suggests that the Pakistani leadership's definition of national security is tentatively broadening beyond a purely military perspective. Despite this nascent trend, military considerations are likely to remain paramount in Pakistani security thinking for the near term, and the defense apparatus will continue to absorb between 4% and 5% of the nation's annual GDP.

Pakistan's Armed Forces Today: Military, State, and Society

The military forces available to support Pakistan's grand strategy are large, professional, and well-trained in their chosen tactics. With 550,000 men, the army is among the largest in the world and by far the most dominant service in the Pakistani armed forces. Strategically, the Pakistani military benefits from the locations of its main cantonments. While many of India's ground troops are based in the country's interior and require a minimum of seven to ten days to deploy to their battle positions, the bulk of the Pakistan Army, including all of its armored/mechanized formations, are stationed in the east where they can mobilize and move to their wartime locations in as little as 72 hours.[69] More than 300,000 paramilitary troops are available to supplement the army and some are routinely incorporated into regular units. The Pakistan Air Force (PAF), with some 320 combat aircraft, is only small relative to India and has always prided itself on its training and professional competence.[70] Whether this traditional self-perceived edge in training, experience, and spirit is still valid or whether it would provide a significant advantage in combat under 21st century circumstances are both debatable questions. The small Pakistan Navy, historically lowest on the priority list for resources, would have difficulty preventing Indian attacks on

---

[68] Jehangir Karamat, "Leadership in a Disturbed Region: The Case of India and Pakistan" (speech at Dickinson College, Pennsylvania, April 26, 2005), http://www.embassyofpakistan.org.

[69] Ashley J. Tellis, "The Air Balance in the Indian Subcontinent: Trends, Constants and Contexts," *Defense Analysis* 4, no. 2 (1986), 264.

[70] This figure (from the 2004–2005 *Military Balance*) does not include trainers or intelligence collection aircraft.

Karachi, but the high-quality boats and well-prepared crews of its submarine arm would present a significant threat to Indian surface ships.[71]

Conventional and nuclear deterrence. Pakistan's armed forces suffer from a number of critical deficiencies. Although the Indian numerical advantage is not as great as a superficial review of the raw data would suggest, the fact remains that Pakistan is outnumbered in terms of major combat formations as well as in almost every significant category of equipment.[72] Like the Indian Army, Pakistani ground forces have limited mobility, with armored or mechanized brigades representing only some 17.5% of the total available. There are also problems with much of the army's equipment. A large portion of the tank fleet is obsolete, air defenses are rudimentary, the mechanized infantry's vehicles are vulnerable, and communications gear has been generally inadequate. The army's command structure is also problematic since all nine corps are controlled directly from General Headquarters.[73] Training and education, though generally of high quality, suffer from the same institutional conservatism that afflicts India: an urgent search for "school solutions" that generates "careful but imitative" analysis rather than creative thinking beyond the tactical level.[74]

Joint operations constitute a major challenge for all three services. Despite the presence of a joint staff at the national level and discussion of interservice cooperation, the three services have traditionally trained and fought in near isolation from each other. For example, the lone PAF squadron dedicated to maritime strike missions presumably interacts closely with the navy, but the army and the air force disagree on priorities: the PAF is focused on air defense and deep strikes, while the army expects close air support for its tactical formations.

Pakistan's nuclear arsenal is central to its concept of deterrence. Although largely opaque, the Pakistani program seems to be very similar to India's in terms of actual weapons: 30–70 fission warheads in the 5–25 kiloton range, all of which use highly-enriched uranium.[75] Likewise, Islamabad's

---

[71] See *Jane's Sentinel Security Assessment—South Asia: Pakistan*, June 13, 2005.

[72] Commentators often note that Pakistan has more self-propelled artillery than India (240 Pakistani types to at most 30 Indian systems fielded). This is true, but the absence of self-propelled artillery is an isolated superiority with at best local impact, not a war-winning feature of the Pakistan Army.

[73] See *Jane's Sentinel Security Assessment—South Asia: Pakistan*, June 13, 2005.

[74] Stephen P. Cohen, *The Idea of Pakistan* (Washington D.C.: Brookings, 2004), 128; and Brian Cloughley, *A History of the Pakistan Army: Wars and Insurrections* (Karachi: Oxford University Press, 2000), 339–58.

[75] Estimates are drawn from the Carnegie Endowment for International Peace at http://www.carnegieendowment.org (est. 30–50 highly-enriched uranium warheads and 3–5 plutonium weapons), the Natural Resource Defense Council at http://www.nrdc.org (est. 48), the Arms Control Association at http://www.armscontrol.org (est. 30–50), and *Jane's Sentinel Security Assessment—South Asia: Pakistan*, April 27, 2005 (est. as many as 100).

stated goal is also "minimum credible deterrence," defined not as a function of India's inventory but rather based on Pakistan's own assessment of its needs. In other important respects, however, the Pakistani approach to nuclear capability is the opposite of India's. In the first place, where New Delhi looks north as well as west, Islamabad is focused solely on its eastern neighbor. Whether and how this traditional Pakistani view will change should Iran declare itself a nuclear power is unclear, but an overt Iranian nuclear capability is not likely to be welcome in Islamabad. Second, Pakistan's leaders believe that their planning "benefits from a degree of ambiguity" regarding the country's nuclear doctrine.[76] The government seems to view Pakistan's nuclear warheads as weapons of war, not just tools of deterrence, a stance that implies the option of first use in a conflict. There are no stated criteria for when Pakistan might resort to nuclear weapons. Pakistani officials and commentators, however, often emphasize that the threshold is low, a "one-rung nuclear escalation ladder," and express concerns that Indian modernization will drive the threshold still lower.[77] The four "red lines" that have undergone public scrutiny—significant loss of territory, significant damage to military forces, threat of economic strangulation, and threat to internal stability—are deliberately vague.[78] Even a cursory comparison between these unofficial thresholds and the Indian "limited war" concept, however, reveals much room for miscalculation by both sides. Third, Islamabad regards the army's missiles as "the core of Pakistan's nuclear weapons delivery systems."[79] PAF aircraft could also be used, but missiles offer advantages of range and reliability, and their employment would not detract from other PAF missions. The mainstays of the Pakistani missile force are the Hatf-III (Ghaznavi) and Hatf-IV (Shaheen) SRBMs with ranges up to 290 and 650 kilometers respectively. Reaching out to 1,300 kilometers, the Hatf-V (Ghauri) allows the Pakistan Army to target most key Indian cities and military garrisons; and the Hatf-VI (Shaheen II), tested for the first time in 2004 with an estimated range of 2,200 kilometers, will cover almost all of India.[80] Command and control is exercised from the National Command Authority through the Strategic Plans Division to Strategic Forces Commands in each service.

---

[76] Mahmud Ali Durrani, "Pakistan's Strategic Thinking and the Role of Nuclear Weapons," Cooperative Monitoring Center, Occasional Paper, no. 37, July 2004, 28, 31.

[77] Shireen Mazari, "Nature of Future Pakistan-India Wars," *Strategic Studies* 22, no. 2 (Summer 2002); and Rodney W. Jones, "Conventional Military Imbalance and Strategic Stability in South Asia," South Asia Strategic Stability Unit Research Report, University of Bradford, no. 1, March 2005.

[78] Paolo Cotta-Ramusino and Maurizio Martellini, "Nuclear Safety, Nuclear Stability and Nuclear Strategy in Pakistan," Landau Network-Centro Volta, February 11, 2002, http://www.mi.infn.it.

[79] Durrani, "Pakistan's Strategic Thinking," 20.

[80] Ibid.

The military in society. Though similar in many ways, two key characteristics differentiate the armed services of these South Asian rivals. The first is the Pakistan Army's role as the dominant political force in that country. While this condition has had a distorting effect on Pakistan's domestic and foreign policies, the army—given its preeminent political role—has the final say in the allocation of national resources and is accountable to no one but itself for decisions on equipment, doctrine, and strategy. This dominant role can also limit or exclude non-army inputs to national decisionmaking and reinforce military tendencies toward worst-case interpretations. Whether by actually governing or exercising a decisive influence behind the scenes, the army will almost certainly retain this paramount position through the remainder of the decade and probably well beyond.

Moreover, the infiltration of the Pakistan military (principally the army) into almost every other aspect of national life has accelerated since Musharraf assumed power in 1999. Approximately 1,000 active and retired officers have been placed in top political, commercial, and managerial positions under his tenure. On the one hand, such sinecures promote the military's institutional interests by giving senior officers a stake in the system and reducing incentives to dissent; on the other, they divert the military from its core functions, while providing endless opportunities for patronage, corruption, and friction with civil society. As such, this growing entrenchment weakens the country's tottering democratic institutions, taints the army's reputation, and angers many civilians.[81] The dominant position of Pakistanis from Punjab Province in the army (as in all government agencies) exacerbates these resentments in other parts of the country and leaves the army unrepresentative of the population at large.[82]

The second differentiating factor is the role of religion in Pakistan's armed forces. While utilizing Islamic ideals as motivational tools, the military has traditionally discouraged excessive religiosity; the modern Pakistani officer corps is generally pious but not extremist in its beliefs. Officers who demonstrate religious tendencies that might threaten the army's relatively secular institutional interests are reportedly weeded out at the midgrade level.[83] The military, however, also reflects the society from which it springs, and religion has become a more prominent dimension of Pakistan's socio-political landscape since the mid-1980s.[84] Although the majority of Pakistanis are, as Musharraf maintains, pious but moderate, it is similarly

---

[81] Among many reports on this trend, see Massoud Ansari, "The Militarisation of Pakistan," *Newsline*, October 2004.

[82] "Govt Focus on Balochistan Uplift," *The Nation*, February 10, 2005.

[83] Cohen, *Idea of Pakistan*, 108.

[84] Khan, "Pakistan's Challenges"; and Cohen, *Idea of Pakistan*, 107–8.

evident that extremist elements have gained in numbers and influence in recent years. Little is known for certain of the impact this broad shift has had on the military (especially on the junior officers and *jawans*, or common soldiers), but they could hardly be entirely immune.[85] Personnel who have been involved with radical "jihadis" could be particularly vulnerable to "reverse osmosis," whereby they absorb the violent views of their nominal clients.[86] Musharraf purged some officers from the military and the Inter-Services Intelligence Directorate following September 11 and has apparently taken additional measures in the wake of the December 2003 assassination attempts, which involved military personnel (albeit junior ones). The institutional culture of Pakistan's armed forces has a powerful normative effect, however, and the financial and social benefits available to both serving and retired military personnel provide a strong incentive to stay within the rules. A "colonel's coup" or similar disruption is therefore unlikely in the near term, but the attitudes of junior officers and the mid-term impact of extremist ideologies constitute important concerns for the country's senior commanders.[87] The threat of a coup may be small, but sympathy for or tolerance of such extremist jihadi attitudes, if left unchecked, could undermine military discipline, erode the leadership's ability to counter internal instability, and present a direct personal threat to individual senior officers.

Pakistan's Military: Modernization at the Margins

Pakistan's military modernization efforts are aimed at incorporating incremental improvements to existing hardware rather than developing new doctrine. Even prior to the announcement of the "Cold Start" approach, Pakistani observers discerned India's shift from a "space-oriented" to a "destruction-oriented" strategy, but the army so far sees no need to part with its "offensive-defense" or "riposte" strategy.[88] This operational concept calls for Pakistani ground forces to take the offensive, perhaps preemptively, across the border before India can mobilize its full might.[89] Seizing key terrain and unbalancing the enemy, the Pakistanis hope to blunt an Indian advance long enough to allow time for the international community to intervene. "We are very capable of an offensive defense," Musharraf told the press in 2002,

---

[85] Hasan Askari Rizvi, "Pakistan's Strategic Culture," in *South Asia in 2020: Future Strategic Balances and Alliances*, ed. Michael R. Chambers (Carlisle: U.S. Army War College, Strategic Studies Institute, 2002), 320.

[86] See Hasan Askari Rizvi, "Military and Islamic Militancy," *Daily Times*, May 31, 2004.

[87] John Lancaster, "Pakistan Struggles to Put Army on a Moderate Course," *Washington Post*, April 4, 2004.

[88] Khan, "Air Support Requirements of Pakistan Army."

[89] General Mirza Aslam Beg, "Deterrence, Defence and Development," *Defence Journal*, July 1999.

"We'll take the offensive into Indian territory."[90] Confident in this approach, Pakistan's military leaders have dismissed India's Cold Start concept. "Operating on interior lines in an offensive-defensive role," writes a retired brigadier, "the Pakistan Army can give a befitting reply to an invading force at any place and time."[91]

Given the army's role in governance and the dominance of security concerns in Pakistan's strategic thinking, the armed forces, especially the army, have an almost unquestioned claim on the state's resources (note, for instance, that Pakistan's defense expenditures were at least 4.5 percent of GDP in 2004). With a far smaller economy than India's, however, the announced budget for 2005 amounts to some $3.4 billion, a total that has grown each year since 2001. Combined with a $1.5 billion U.S. military assistance package over the next five years, this figure will allow some modernization at the margins, but will not support extensive revamping of the armed forces. Unlike India, actual Pakistani defense expenditure tends to exceed the budget by $100–$200 million every year.[92]

This confidence in its existing doctrine, combined with resource constraints, has left the army with a modernization program limited primarily to select pieces of hardware. The most important equipment acquisition in recent years has been improved tanks. The bulk of Pakistan's tank fleet is still composed of outdated Chinese models, but the purchase of 320 T-80UDs from the Ukraine has added enough relatively modern tanks to equip one armored division.[93] Upgrades for some older models and the introduction of a new tank, the Al-Khalid, means that slightly more than half of the army's first-line tanks will be fairly modern variants within the next five years. These measures will enhance current capabilities and reduce India's chances of gaining a local armor advantage—yet hardly represent a significant change beyond the tactical arena. Recent increases in the inventory of transport helicopters will assist in counterinsurgency operations, but would have no major impact in an India-Pakistan conflict. Other than additional anti-tank guided missiles, some Bell helicopters, and possibly some communications gear, it is not clear what other hardware the army may receive as a result of the restored defense supply relationship with the United States.

Modernization in the PAF was hobbled throughout the 1990s by U.S. sanctions, the high cost of European alternatives, and the inferiority of the

---

[90] Musharraf quoted in "India Sought to Weaken Me, Says Musharraf," *Daily Times*, May 28, 2002.

[91] Brig. (ret.) A. R. Siddiqi, "Indian War-Games: An Overview," *Dawn*, May 5, 2005.

[92] Figures from *The Military Balance 2004–2005*. Sherry Rehman has noted that the budget is practically opaque and allows for neither legislative debate nor detailed analysis, "Enigma of the Defence Budget," *Dawn*, June 16, 2005.

[93] In addition, the army manufactures another relatively up-to-date tank under license from China.

available Chinese planes. After several deals for new fighters fell through, the air force leadership resorted to stop-gap measures, but now hopes that the first of 150 modern, "medium-tech" Sino-Pakistani JF-17 Thunder fighters will be delivered in 2006. The air force is also working with China to develop its first beyond-visual-range air-to-air missile. The key question for the PAF, however, concerns the number and model of F-16s it hopes to receive from the United States. A batch of new F-16s with appropriate air-to-air missiles could represent a substantial increase in Pakistan's air combat and strike capabilities later in the decade. Pakistan is considering the purchase of either a Swedish or an American AEW&C aircraft that could enter into service between 2007 and 2010, and is also reported to have interest in the Chinese FT-2000 surface-to-air missile system, which would be used to counter Indian AEW&C platforms.[94] There seems to be little procurement activity, however, for less esoteric ground-based air defense weapons and sensors.[95]

The navy has another French Agosta 90B diesel submarine scheduled to arrive during 2005, bringing the number in this class to three and Pakistan's submarine force to nine. Pakistan will attempt to replace its older boats with more of the Agosta 90Bs over the coming decade. The surface fleet expects to receive four new Chinese frigates by 2008, raising the total number of frigates from six to ten; the naval air arm is slated to benefit from the U.S. military assistance package with the provision of up to eight P-3C Orion maritime patrol aircraft capable of carrying Harpoon missiles. In addition, should one of the AEW&C acquisitions come to fruition, the navy is in line to receive several of these aircraft.

Pakistan's strategic forces will continue to grow as its arsenal of ballistic missiles expands in both size and capability. As with Pakistan's other modernization programs, improvements in missiles, warheads, and command systems will be incremental, increasing the quantity and quality of Pakistan's military hardware rather than acquiring significant new capabilities. Furthermore, Pakistan must contend with serious impediments to modernization: budgetary restrictions, interservice rivalry, conservative military thinking, and limited absorptive capacity. Nonetheless, hardware modernization at the margins should suffice, for the near term, to sustain the minimum credible nuclear and conventional capabilities necessary to deter India. On the more dangerous internal security front, however, Pakistan will have to develop personnel policies that eliminate or neutralize any extremist sentiment within its armed forces and intelligence services. Moreover, Islamabad

---

[94] S. M. Hali, "Saab 2000 & Erieye AEW&C System," *Pakistan Observer*, July 18, 2004; and Barbara Opall-Rome, "U.S. Offers Pakistan Radar Planes," *Defense News*, December 6, 2004.

[95] Jamal Hussain, "PAF Begins to Narrow the Technological Gap Some," Centre for Aerospace Power Studies, Karachi, October 2004, http://www.caps.org.pk.

will also have to find ways to cope with the jihadis themselves. These radical elements are too dangerous and unpredictable to retain as weapons in the state's arsenal. Pakistan's leaders, especially those in uniform, will have to craft plans to defang these groups and return to a national military strategy that relies on a combination of conventional forces and nuclear weapons to preserve the country's security, all while strengthening the economy and building democratic political institutions.

Conclusions and Implications

This analysis suggests several sets of conclusions regarding the likely development of Indian and Pakistani armed forces over the next five to ten years.

The Near Term: Marginal and Symbolic Modernization

The first set of conclusions relates to India, specifically how modernization will support several aspects of New Delhi's grand strategy in the foreseeable future. On the domestic security front, enhancements in infantry equipment (particularly in night-vision devices) are already proving their worth in counterinfiltration and counterinsurgency operations in Kashmir. Given the importance of internal security and counterterrorism for India, this change is not inconsiderable. Yet military modernization can at best help only to contain militancy; long-term solutions require policies that address local grievances and restore legitimate avenues for political expression. Even from the security force perspective, there are limits to the value of technology; instead, sharper and sustained focus on training, improved discipline, and more modern small arms will offer the best return on investment. Further abroad, military modernization programs have an important symbolic content for India's foreign policy: technically advanced military forces will help undergird New Delhi's efforts to achieve a more prominent role in the world order of the 21st century.

New Delhi's modernization projects and enhanced combat capabilities are intertwined with India's evolving place in Asia. Although the Indian Army remains focused on the western border, India will, for instance, soon have a credible aircraft and missile delivery means for nuclear weapons aimed at some major Chinese targets. In the face of possible Chinese encroachment, the Indian Navy will also look to construct new means of exerting its influence in the Indian Ocean and beyond. Although many of its new ships, aircraft, and systems will not be available until the next decade (roughly sometime between 2010 and 2015), the PLA Navy is unlikely to present a substantial threat prior to that time frame.

The second set of conclusions concerns Pakistan's domestic problems. In addition to destabilizing violence between Sunni and Shia extremists, Pakistan faces difficult internal security problems along the entire Afghan border and, sporadically, in Sindh and Balochistan as well. Military modernization in the form of helicopters and improved infantry equipment will serve as useful tactical upgrades with immediate utility against terrorists and tribal troublemakers in these remote areas. The significance of technology, however, is limited, and the hardware improvements will only be effective if they are mated with low-technology basics such as training, leadership, and sustained attention to local grievances. Fighter aircraft, AEW&C platforms, submarines, and tanks have little relevance to these and other immediate internal threats, and Pakistan will need to allot domestic revenue and foreign assistance carefully in order to address the many pressing problems within its own borders.

Having examined each country separately, the third set of conclusions addresses the points where their modernization programs intersect. At the broadest level of analysis, the general "balance" that exists today will likely obtain for the near term. India will retain a numerical superiority sufficient to contain Pakistan in the conventional realm, but its ability to alter Pakistan's behavior, especially sub-conventional provocation, will likely be limited, for the next five years or so, to incremental improvements in conducting punitive strikes. India's quantitative advantage will not translate into the ability to inflict a rapid, convincing defeat on Pakistan. Instead, Pakistan's conventional forces will be able to impose sufficiently heavy costs in time, men, and equipment so as to dissuade India, in most cases, from attacking. At the same time, Pakistan's acknowledged nuclear capability and its ambiguous use criteria will induce caution in Indian thinking. India will thus have to overcome significant disincentives inherent in an attack on Pakistan, and will encounter serious problems in defining its war aims should New Delhi determine that an instance of provocation demands a military response. If war does break out, New Delhi may have to alter its initial aims in order to avoid a nuclear exchange.

The Mid Term: Possible Shift in the India-Pakistan Military Calculus?

Moving past the short term (i.e., looking seven to ten years ahead), the India-Pakistan situation could shift to India's advantage. This shift will proceed from qualitative rather than quantitative improvements in the Indian armed forces. While the gross numerical ratios between Indian and Pakistan will probably remain similar for the foreseeable future, India's ability to employ its armed forces in a synchronized, synergistic fashion could increase significantly in the coming decade. This is not an inevitable outcome, and progress will be slow. Nonetheless, if New Delhi can overcome budget constraints, bureaucratic impediments, interservice rivalry, and conservative military cultures, then the Indian armed forces could be in a position to deliver a swift and crippling blow against Pakistan's conventional forces during a short, intense conflict.

Examining the specific services, the Indian Navy will maintain and probably increase its substantial advantages over its Pakistani counterpart. Overall, however, the two navies are peripheral to the outcome of a short India-Pakistan war. Although Indian officers would hope to incapacitate Karachi, such a move would only have a psychological impact in a war lasting only two to three weeks.[96] A blockade might even work to India's detriment by pushing Pakistani leaders closer to nuclear use. Likewise, a successful attack against a major Indian surface combatant by a Pakistani submarine might provide a morale boost to Pakistan but would have little material effect on the outcome of the conflict.

In the ground war, the Indian Army has the potential to repair some of its key deficiencies and make Cold Start a realistic option. By combining a larger, more mobile, and more lethal artillery component with improved command/control and intelligence, the army should be able to apply devastating firepower in select tactical locations in order to seize and hold critical pieces of terrain, and all within a time period short enough to be acceptable to Indian planners. Mobility and logistics challenges suggest that deep, sustainable penetrations across the border will remain difficult to accomplish, but a series of shallow advances followed by intense engagements with Pakistani mobile reserves could be enough to incapacitate the Pakistan Army's offensive combat power.

Successful ground assaults will depend on close cooperation with the air force, and IAF capabilities could see the most dramatic changes over the next several years. By 2008 or so, the cumulative effect of AEW&C and air-to-air refueling capabilities, large numbers of first-rate multi-role fighters, enhanced avionics, and superior air-to-air missiles could in aggregate give India a decisive advantage over the Pakistani air force. The missing ingredients are timely targeting intelligence, precision-guided munitions, and emphasis on joint operations. On the other side of the border, Pakistani acquisition of an AEW&C capability, a significant number of new fighters, and improved air-to-air missiles will even the odds somewhat, but the IAF

---

[96] Rahul Bedi, "The Military Dynamics," *Frontline* 19, no. 12 (June 8–21, 2002).

would still hold the quantitative and qualitative capabilities necessary both to hold off the PAF and make a major contribution to the ground battle.

Strategic forces on both sides will continue to evolve at an incremental pace. Both will have more missiles and probably more nuclear warheads, but significant change will come only when one or both acquire a near-precision targeting capability and a suite of conventional warheads that will permit reliable destruction of targets such as bridges as well as airfields, supply depots, and other large sites. India may have a limited missile defense system, but this will do little to alter the nuclear dynamic in the subcontinent; the multiplicity of targets and the range of Pakistan's missiles means that the real impact would be marginal. Perceptions, however, could be important, and an extensive Indian missile defense system that appears to undermine Pakistan's ability to attack India could increase Islamabad's sense of insecurity.[97]

Implications for Regional Stability

Finally, the respective military modernization schemes highlight two important points and raise a troubling question. First, India's numerical advantage is deceptive. India does enjoy a considerable conventional superiority over Pakistan—a superiority that is quantitative in almost every category and qualitative in several key areas of air and naval combat. This advantage, however, has been subject to frequent exaggeration on the basis of simplistic quantitative comparisons. In reality, deficiencies in mobility, logistics, doctrine, and military culture have compromised India's ability to translate its many advantages in specific items of equipment or overall manpower into the capability to inflict a decisive defeat on Pakistan's armed forces within the short time frame of a conventional war. Pakistan suffers from many of the same weaknesses, but given that Islamabad is the power on the strategic defensive, the effect is less debilitating.

Second, India's plans to modernize hardware and doctrine, if executed as intended, could change the force calculus within the next ten years. This outcome is, however, subject to numerous critical uncertainties. To achieve a transformational military effect, the Indian services will need a concatenation of successes across a broad array of disparate hardware programs. Such success must be combined with fundamental shifts in operational concepts and organizational outlook. Breakdown in one or more key areas could undermine the entire process. Moreover, Pakistani modernization, even at the margins, might suffice to stave off a partially upgraded Indian military.

---

[97] Ashley J. Tellis, "The Impact of Missile Defence in Asia," *IISS Strategic Comments* 10, no. 6 (July 2004).

The question arising from the state of Indian-Pakistani military modernization programs revolves around perceptions—that is, how each side perceives its own capabilities as compared to the capabilities and intentions of the other. In the nuclear environment, an error in judgment by either government could have potentially devastating consequences. Indian strategists, for example, could overrate their own capabilities or underestimate Pakistan's progress in modernization and respond to a provocation with a "limited" military action that quickly spirals into an unpredictable escalatory cycle. Likewise Indian military commanders, assuming clear knowledge of Pakistan's nuclear thresholds and the ability to calibrate operations to avoid these, could find that their forces have inadvertently crossed a Pakistani nuclear "red line." On the other side of the border, Pakistan could easily miscalculate the likely Indian reaction to a provocative incident (as Islamabad did in 1965 and 1999). Contrary to common assumptions, the two sides do not necessarily understand each other as well as they think they do, and there exists broad scope for dangerous misinterpretation.

Furthermore, the security scene is complicated by the presence of non-state actors in the form of violent, jihadist groups. As happened twice during 2001–02, extremist groups pursuing their own agendas could conduct terrorist attacks that bring India and Pakistan into confrontation and possible war. Many Indians were dissatisfied with the results of New Delhi's "coercive diplomacy" during the 2001–02 crisis, and internal political pressures could prompt armed retaliation to a future provocation regardless of the state of military modernization. Although both countries have often shown remarkable restraint during previous confrontations, the dangers involved in misreading one another or in dismissing the threat of semi-independent jihadi groups are too great to ignore.

Considerations for the United States and Outside Powers

Although India and Pakistan ultimately bear responsibility for the resolution of their disputes, or at least for the management of bilateral crises, outside powers can contribute to South Asian stability in significant ways. Most important is sustained, nuanced, and imaginative support for the normalization of ties between India and Pakistan. The general trajectory of relations has been favorable since 2003, but ties are fragile and near-term resolution of the historically burdened issues that divide the two is unlikely. The "ugly stability" of the past fifteen years is thus likely to continue, and both New Delhi and Islamabad must be prepared to cope with sudden crises for the foreseeable future.[98] The United States and other outside actors can assist by helping to strengthen the limited set of existing confidence-building measures for conventional forces and by introducing new ones, especially in the area of nuclear risk reduction. The tenuous situation on the subcontinent also argues for extreme caution in arms sales by outside producers and a recognition of the long-term utility of many weapons systems and the psychological impact such deals can have on both sides of the border.

External powers should also seek ways to reduce the threat posed by radical non-state groups. This entails not only pressing for an unambiguous end to militant infiltration into Indian Kashmir and dismantling of the terrorist infrastructure, but also supporting both neutralization of the jihadis who threaten Pakistani society and assisting Islamabad in reconstruction of the civil institutions essential to stability and prosperity.[99] Finally, Afghanistan's success is vital for Pakistan's future. The two form a symbiotic pair and disturbances on one side of the border will quickly reverberate on the other. Conversely, success in reconstruction and governance in Afghanistan will ease pressures on Pakistan's fractured polity, contributing to Pakistan's stability and discouraging the extremists attempting to uproot both countries.

Beyond the challenge of averting India-Pakistan confrontations, military modernization in India can present opportunities for external actors. Washington's growing strategic partnership with New Delhi, for example, can form the foundation for mutually beneficial security cooperation in the broader Indian Ocean region. By building interoperability and accumulating operational familiarity, the United States can help streamline future multilateral military interaction with India in peacekeeping and humanitarian missions (such as the 2004 tsunami relief mission). The United States can also collaborate with New Delhi to strengthen India's military capacity so that India—by combating terrorism, piracy, proliferation, and other threats—becomes a key provider of security in the vital area between the Persian Gulf and the Straits of Malacca.

Indian and Pakistani military modernization aspirations, in many respects dependent on foreign involvement, thus present both challenges and opportunities for outside powers. Washington and other external actors, while avoiding costly and futile efforts to act as "balancers," can play a useful role in influencing the choices New Delhi and Islamabad make, and more importantly, help craft an environment conducive to normalization and crisis containment rather than one of recurrent confrontation and potential conflict.

---

[98] The term "ugly stability" is taken from Ashley J. Tellis, *Stability in South Asia* (Santa Monica: RAND, 1997), 5.

[99] Secretary of State Condoleezza Rice interview, March 16, 2005 at http://www.state.gov.

Executive Summary

This chapter examines the military and security capabilities as well as the strategies of the major Southeast Asian states—Indonesia, Malaysia, Thailand, the Philippines, Singapore, and Vietnam—and their security relations with the United States, China, Japan, India, and Australia.

MAIN ARGUMENT:

- The region's security concerns are more internal than external: separatism, ethnic and religious dissidents, and the smuggling of contraband, people, and arms.

- Most Southeast Asian armed forces are not purchasing state-of-the-art weapon systems but are rather developing air and naval capabilities to monitor nearby air and sea spaces.

- Although Southeast Asian states are concerned about transborder terrorism, military cooperation is mostly bilateral rather than multilateral.

- China is both building a naval presence in Southeast Asia and conducting diplomacy designed to reassure the region of Beijing's intentions.

- Southeast Asian states desire a continued U.S. presence to balance China. In the future they may also be willing to accept Indian and Japanese patrols designed to protect the sea lines of communication.

POLICY IMPLICATIONS:

- By maintaining an ongoing air and naval presence in the region, the United States can both assist Southeast Asian states with external balancing vis-à-vis China and support anti-piracy and anti-terrorism efforts.

- Southeast Asia's focus on internal security fits U.S. strategy to build capabilities in the region to cope with terrorist challenges.

- U.S. military assistance to facilitate more multilateral engagement will lead to such security benefits as the joint patrol of regional waters.

Southeast Asia's Defense Needs: Change or Continuity?

Sheldon W. Simon

The eleven states of Southeast Asia—Indonesia, Malaysia, Thailand, the Philippines, Singapore, Laos, Cambodia, Vietnam, Burma (Myanmar), East Timor, and Brunei—are small and medium players on the international stage. Strategic theorists have traditionally held that states in these categories are more sensitive to their environments than are larger, more powerful actors; Southeast Asian security policies are therefore more reactive than proactive, responding to major power policies that affect the region more than initiating actions. The other chief characteristic of Southeast Asia's strategic situation is that these states are more concerned with internal security than external defense.

Given extensive changes in the post-Cold War world order as well as the current fixation on the U.S. war on terrorism, this chapter addresses the manner in which several Southeast Asian states have attempted to reconcile security challenges that are essentially internal to the individual states—separatism, ethnic and religious unrest, and the smuggling of people and arms—with the growing presence and pressure from major external powers, particularly the United States and the People's Republic of China (PRC). The Southeast Asian states demonstrate a range of security policy preferences toward outsiders that reflect their differing interpretations about whether external actors can significantly add to local security capabilities

Sheldon W. Simon is Professor of Political Science and Faculty Affiliate of the Center for Asian Studies and Program in Southeast Asian Studies at Arizona State University, as well as Chairman of the Southeast Asian Studies Advisory Group and Senior Advisor to The National Bureau of Asian Research. He can be reached at <shells@asu.edu>.

The author wishes to thank Jessica Keough, Peter Mattis, Shannon Tow, and ASU Junior Fellow Suzanne Johnson for helpful comments and research support. He also wishes to extend appreciation for the constructive criticism of two anonymous reviewers.

(as in Singapore, the Philippines, and Thailand) or alternatively whether the military presence of great powers may challenge local sovereignties (as in Indonesia and Malaysia).

Superimposed upon these regional political concerns is the fact that Southeast Asian states are active participants in global commerce and therefore need to ensure that the sea lines of communication (SLOC) traversing Southeast Asian waters remain free. The navies of external powers have a significant role to play in sustaining freedom of the seas. This chapter argues that a tension exists between those Southeast Asian states concerned with internal security (of which counterterrorism is only one component) and the U.S. view of Southeast Asia as a prime counterterrorism venue. Given the varied security needs of the many Southeast Asian states, there can be no single overarching explanation for defense. Rather, this chapter assesses the changing defense capabilities and needs of the major Southeast Asian states and concludes with a somewhat pessimistic evaluation of the prospects for defense collaboration.

To examine the defense roles of external powers, the major Southeast Asian states, and the synergy of their interaction, this chapter begins with an overview of the impact that the agendas of the United States and China have had on the region. The second section then addresses the security issues that dominate the region's own agendas: the drug trade, illegal population movements, maritime disputes, and piracy. A third section then examines the grand strategies of several key Southeast Asian players—Singapore, the Philippines, Thailand, Indonesia, Malaysia, and Vietnam—and relates each country's military modernization plans to their grand strategies. The chapter then concludes with an evaluation of Southeast Asian military effectiveness in respect to local defense challenges; the role of the armed forces of Japan, Australia, and India in the region; and the future of Southeast Asian defense collaboration both among themselves and with external powers.

External Setting

Southeast Asia's external security setting consists primarily of the two great powers—the United States and China—whose intentions, capabilities, and activities in the region must be taken into account by its members. Of the two, the United States has the longest record of involvement, having been a colonial power in the Philippines, an ally of the Philippines and Thailand during the Cold War, an active military force during the second Indochina War (1965–75), and a major trade and investment partner over the past 30 years. China is a relative latecomer whose negative legacy of aiding Southeast Asian communist insurgencies from the 1950s through the 1970s has tarnished that country's image in the region. By the end of the 1990s, Beijing had gone a long way toward dispelling its negative image in Southeast Asia, and was seen as an important trading state for a region whose members are eager to diversify their economic relations.

The United States

Southeast Asia's salience to the United States is based on three strategic priorities: as a third front (after the Middle East and South Asia) in the war on terrorism, as a key transit region between the Persian Gulf and the Sea of Japan, and as a "lily pad" location for the U.S. Navy and Air Force where ships and aircraft can resupply and exercise with regional armed forces.

The U.S. antiterrorism effort in Southeast Asia began soon after September 11 when the United States convened a low-profile conference in November 2001 between senior American officials and those from the ten-member Association of Southeast Asia Nations (ASEAN). At the gathering, the United States announced that Southeast Asia had re-emerged as an important strategic area and a major front for the global war on terrorism. In fact the region's major *jihadi* organization, Jemaah Islamiyah (JI), had already perpetrated violence in the region by coordinating bombings in Jakarta and Manila in 2000.[1] The U.S. goal for ASEAN in the war on terrorism has been to convince the Southeast Asian states that they share a common interest in suppressing terrorist groups and related criminal activities. Washington has also offered logistical, intelligence, and law enforcement support as well as military aid. In return, the United States has asked ASEAN members to mount a coordinated attack against terrorist recruitment, terrorist financing, forged documents, and unmonitored movements across national borders.[2] While regional cooperation has been forthcoming with varying degrees of enthusiasm and effectiveness, Southeast Asians are concerned that the U.S. antiterrorism strategy legitimizes outside intervention in their domestic affairs.[3] In large part due to American prodding, the ASEAN states have signed a counterterrorism pact committing each member to freeze terrorist assets, strengthen intelligence sharing, and improve border patrols. Implementation has been spotty, however; Singapore and

---

[1] These events were seen at the time as unrelated. Only after Islamist militants were captured in 2002 and 2003 did regional authorities realize that a single terrorist group had been responsible. Renato Cruz de Castro, "U.S. War on Terror in East Asia: The Perils of Preemptive Defense in Waging a War in the Third World," *Asian Affairs: An American Review* (Winter 2005): 216–17.

[2] Ibid., 217.

[3] For an extended discussion of U.S.-Southeast Asian collaboration and difficulties in the war on terrorism, see Sheldon W. Simon, "Southeast Asia: Back to the Future?" in *Strategic Asia 2004–2005: Confronting Terrorism in the Pursuit of Power*, ed. Ashley Tellis and Michael Wills (Seattle: The National Bureau of Asian Research, 2004), 261–99.

Malaysia have been the most capable, while Indonesia, the Philippines, and Thailand—though improving—are still havens for terrorists and their activities. The United States is helping Singapore, Malaysia, and Indonesia develop a command, control, and communications infrastructure that will allow them to share maritime security information with both each other and the United States.[4]

Since the 1992 closure of U.S. bases in the Philippines, Singapore has hosted a naval logistics command center, accepted the regular deployment of U.S. combat aircraft for exercises, and in 2001 built the Changi naval base specifically so that U.S. aircraft carriers could berth there. An example that Singapore is closely cooperating with the United States in counterterrorism and WMD nonproliferation is the island state's participation in the U.S.-led Proliferation Security Initiative (PSI), which is aimed at interdicting illegal weapon cargoes over the oceans and through the air.[5] Moreover, Singapore's strategic location permits U.S. forces to move quickly either west into the Indian Ocean for a Middle East contingency or east and north through the South China Sea to the Sea of Japan.

Thailand has also become an important component in the U.S. "places not bases" strategy. A series of terrorist-related arrests that Thailand made in 2003 in cooperation with U.S. intelligence linked Bangkok to the U.S. war on terrorism; in recognition of those efforts the United States declared Thailand a "major non-NATO ally."[6] Thailand is also cooperating with the United States by reopening both the air base at U-Tapao and the naval base at Sattahip where the U.S. military has prepositioned supplies.

Even Malaysia, which is not a formal U.S. ally and has been openly critical of the war in Iraq, participates in the U.S. Container Security Initiative (CSI) that permits U.S. Customs officials to work with local authorities to ensure that maritime trade is secure from terrorists. Malaysian military officers train in the United States through the International Military Education and Training (IMET) program; Washington also extends military assistance to Malaysia via the Foreign Military Sales (FMS) program. Particularly significant with respect to the war on terrorism is a 2003 U.S.-Malaysian Extradition Treaty. Malaysia also hosts between fifteen and twenty U.S. Navy ship visits annually and provides U.S. Navy SEALs the opportunity to train twice a year in jungle warfare in the country. Similar to the agreements with

---

[4] Gopal Ratnam, "U.S. Asia Policy Faces Myriad Challenges," *Defense News*, June 13, 2005, 24.

[5] Evelyn Goh, "Contemporary Southeast Asian Regional Security Strategies and the Role of the United States," in *Policy Studies* (Washington, D.C.: The East-West Center, forthcoming 2005), 34.

[6] The Thaksin government also contributed forces to the U.S. occupation of Iraq, though these troops were withdrawn in late 2004.

Singapore and Indonesia, U.S. naval vessels can be repaired and supplied at Lumut dockyard in Perak.[7]

The U.S. Pacific Command signed a Mutual Logistics Support Agreement with the Philippines in late 2002, permitting U.S. forces to preposition supplies for bilateral exercises there. U.S. forces also engage in jungle warfare training in Luzon.

By 2005 the U.S. military had access rights as well as facility-use and repair and bunkering arrangements with the five original members of ASEAN (Indonesia, Malaysia, Singapore, Thailand, and Singapore). With respect to military relations, this cooperation means that counterterrorism components have now become regular features in exercises with Thailand and the Philippines. More broadly, U.S. intelligence and law enforcement—especially the Federal Bureau of Investigation (FBI)—are also cooperating with the original ASEAN-5. None of these arrangements requires a significant permanent U.S. presence in the region, but they do offer opportunities to use Southeast Asian facilities and establish a limited degree of interoperability with regional armed forces, intelligence, and law enforcement.

China

Though the primary target of China's military buildup over the past decade has been Taiwan, Southeast Asian states fear that the region's primary trade route—the South China Sea—could be next. China has followed a strategy of "creeping assertiveness." Beijing has been gradually consolidating its presence on the Paracel and Spratly islands at a pace that may provoke complaints from the Philippines and Vietnam but will not likely lead to a counterthrust from either ASEAN or the United States. The PRC has offered positive security incentives to Southeast Asia as well, including arms sales and a network of general bilateral agreements that include military exchanges. Thailand now refers to China as a "strategic partner"—though, of course, Bangkok has no claims in the South China Sea.[8] Cambodia will receive six coastal patrol boats from China. Thailand has purchased Chinese military vehicles in exchange for produce. The Philippines has been given $1.2 million in military aid and has agreed to annual security talks. Jakarta, too, is holding defense cooperation talks with Beijing. China is in effect creating a strategic partnership with the ASEAN states designed to reduce regional suspicion and help the PRC acquire a measure of legitimacy

---

[7] Pamela Sodhy, "U.S.-Malaysia Relations During the Bush Administration: The Political, Economic, and Security Aspects," *Contemporary Southeast Asia* 25, no. 3 (December 2003): 378–81.

[8] Shannon Tow, "Southeast Asia in the Sino-U.S. Strategic Balance," *Contemporary Southeast Asia* 26, no. 3 (December 2004): 446, 450–51.

within Southeast Asia. The ASEAN states have been wary of China's maritime capability which has been growing since the 1990s. The 1988 Sino-Vietnam clash over the Spratly islands and subsequent Chinese assertiveness in the early 1990s demonstrated Beijing's willingness to utilize the People's Liberation Army (PLA) to advance its claims. Moreover, the 1995 occupation of Mischief Reef and more recent Spratly incidents have constituted a direct challenge to ASEAN's 1992 Declaration on the South China Sea, which abjured the use of force. The PRC has been building its navy and shifting from a doctrine of coastal to offshore defense. As long as Beijing's primary military target remains Taiwan, however, Southeast Asians will not see China as an imminent military challenge. When and if Taiwan's political future is determined, however, Southeast Asia will begin to worry.

In the last half of the 1990s, Beijing demonstrated a new flexibility in its South China Sea diplomacy. China accepted the UN Law of the Sea as a basis for negotiations, achieved bilateral understandings with Malaysia and the Philippines, raised the prospect of joint development, and agreed to discuss the Spratlys with ASEAN multilaterally.[9] In the past five years, China signed both the ASEAN Declaration on the South China Sea and ASEAN's Treaty of Amity and Cooperation that commits its signatories to nonaggression. The PRC is also enhancing military relationships with its neighbors. The PLA Navy (PLAN) and its Vietnamese counterpart are engaged in both joint search-and-rescue missions and efforts to counter smuggling. A bilateral security dialogue has been initiated with Thailand. Within the ASEAN Regional Forum (ARF), China has proposed both regional military exchanges and an annual security policy conference that would discuss military strategies and doctrines. ASEAN accepted the proposal, and the ARF's first high-level meeting of military officers representing 24 countries convened in Beijing in November 2004.[10]

As for the PLAN's ability to dominate Southeast Asian waters, there are two schools of thought. The optimists believe that the PLA has made little progress in power projection. China has no plans for aircraft carrier battle groups and possesses few destroyers that can operate in the open ocean. The Chinese military has no military bases on foreign shores, no long range bombers, and no airborne early warning aircraft—though negotiations are under way with Russia for radar planes, and China may be constructing its own AWACs aircraft. The PLA Air Force (PLAAF) does not yet seem to have mastered in-flight refueling, making it difficult to provide air cover for the

[9] Alice Ba, "China and ASEAN: Renavigating Relations for a 21st Century Asia," *Asian Survey* 43, no. 4 (July-August 2003), 627–28, 633.

[10] David Shambaugh, "China Engages Asia: Reshaping the Regional Order," *International Security* 29, no. 3 (Winter 2004–05): 81, 87–88.

navy in the open ocean. Finally, PLA doctrine still emphasizes peripheral defense rather than force projection.[11]

Those less sanguine about China's intentions and capabilities point to its navy's acquisition of several *Sovremenny* destroyers from Russia, ships specifically designed to attack U.S. aircraft carriers. The PRC also seems to be courting Burma to gain access to the Indian Ocean. Burma depends on China for military hardware, financial assistance, industrial equipment, and diplomatic support. Since almost 75 percent of China's trade goes through the Malacca Straits, PLAN deployments into the Indian Ocean seem to be inevitable. Chinese ships have been engaged in magnetic resonance imaging of the seabed near the Andaman islands in the Indian Ocean, a precursor to submarine deployments. China may also be planning to upgrade ports near Rangoon (Yangon) as well as western Burma, Chittagong port in Bangladesh, and Sihanoukville in Cambodia. As Nayan Chanda suggests, these could be "part of an incremental effort to build a 'string of pearls' presence in the Indian Ocean rim," a goal that may still be a decade away from realization.[12]

Southeast Asia's "Problematiques"

Southeast Asia's "problematiques" refer to the persistent security problems that plague the region, problems for which there are no clearcut solutions. Finding ways to cope with and control these challenges are the tasks of each country's defense, intelligence, and law enforcement forces. The primary security concerns of ASEAN states (with the possible exception of Singapore) do not place global terrorism at the top of the list. Rather, a host of challenges emanating from within their societies and across their borders top the agenda. The problems of terrorism, porous borders, piracy, and maritime disputes are examined below.

Terrorism

In the spring of 2002 ASEAN adopted a Work Program on Terrorism as an addendum to its Action Plan to Combat Transnational Crime. The addendum covered all the problematiques enumerated above and introduced action plans for intelligence sharing, law enforcement cooperation, institutional capacity-building, and extra-regional cooperation. Unfortunately, implementation has been spotty and intermittent. This is due partly to an

---

[11] Shambaugh, "China Engages Asia," 85–86.

[12] Nayan Chanda, "Crouching Tiger, Swimming Dragon," *New York Times*, April 11, 2005.

inability among ASEAN members to achieve a common definition of terrorism. For example, violence perpetrated by ethnic-Malay Muslims in southern Thailand may be interpreted as terrorism in Bangkok but seen in Kuala Lumpur as self-protection for a persecuted minority.[13] Moreover, none of the plans to combat terrorism cooperatively include the use of military force. Indeed, ASEAN cooperation has seldom gone beyond bilateral arrangements. For the association as a whole, the measures are non-binding and unspecific.

Porous Borders

Indicative of the problems created by porous borders is the current tension between Thailand and Malaysia in which southern Thai Muslims of Malay ethnicity who have been involved in violence against local police, military, and schools have fled to northern Malaysia to escape arrest. Before the current cycle of violence (which began in January 2004 when southern Thai Muslim separatists escaped to Malaysia), these individuals were frequently apprehended and quietly returned to face trial in Thailand. In April 2004 at the Kreu Se mosque, however, the Thai army killed more than 100 of these young Muslims who had attacked army and police posts; in October 2004, 80 such Muslims were killed when they suffocated to death in army trucks. Since then, Malaysia has refused to extradite those who flee, fearing they would be extrajudicially executed.[14]

A more insidious result of porous borders has been the entry of JI recruits and trainers from Indonesia to the southern Philippines. This group has been working with radical Islamist separatists in the Moro Islamic Liberation Front (MILF) and Abu Sayyaf.[15] One Indonesian bombmaker confessed to training Abu Sayyaf for a series of Valentine's Day 2005 bombings in Manila and Mindanao that killed 8 and wounded more than 150. Philippine authorities claim the Indonesian explosives specialist was the JI liaison to Abu Sayyaf, and he himself had trained in the MILF's Camp Abubakar before it was overrun by Philippine forces in 2000.[16]

---

[13] Ralf Emmers, "ASEAN and the Securitization of Transnational Crime in Southeast Asia," *The Pacific Review* 16, no. 3 (2003): 426, 429–30.

[14] Peter Chalk, "Transnational Threats in Southeast Asia" (presentation, Arizona State University, February 17, 2005).

[15] For a discussion of the Indonesian-based transnational jihadist group, see Simon, "Southeast Asia: Back to the Future," 264–68.

[16] "Bomb Trainer of Abu Sayyaf Falls," *The Inquirer*, March 23, 2005.

Piracy and Maritime Disputes

Because Southeast Asia is a poorly patrolled maritime environment and piracy is rampant, regional authorities fear that terrorists and pirates could ultimately work together. Most ASEAN members refuse to prosecute pirates who find sanctuary in their territories after perpetrating maritime crimes either in international waters or in the jurisdictions of other states. In 2003 Singapore and Vietnam were the only ASEAN members to have ratified the 1988 Rome Convention on Maritime Crime empowering signatories to prosecute or extradite maritime criminals for crimes committed in the territorial waters of other countries.

As a preventive step, the three states that straddle the Malacca Straits (i.e., Indonesia, Malaysia, and Singapore) have mounted coordinated naval patrols and set up telephone hotlines to inform one another of pirate activities. The patrols are not, however, joint endeavors in that the ships of each navy may patrol only up to its maritime territory line, upon which they must hand off any pursuit to the neighboring jurisdiction. This constraint has been imposed by Kuala Lumpur and Jakarta, for whom terrorism and piracy are less important than the trafficking of people and drugs, the security of national fishing interests, and environmental pollution from ship discharges. Meanwhile, the cargo ships of heavy-user states—particularly the United States, Japan, China, and South Korea—steam through the Straits with minimal protection.[17]

Maritime disputes in Southeast Asia relate primarily either to claims on the Paracel and Spratly Islands in the South China Sea or, due to the two hundred nautical mile rule of the 1982 Law of the Sea, overlapping sea boundaries and economic zones. China is the most important actor with respect to the Paracels and Spratlys, having used force against Vietnam in 1974 to occupy the former and again in 1988 to seize some of the latter. By 1995 the PRC had occupied features on both the northern and southern extremes of the Spratlys, strengthening by military means Beijing's claim to the full archipelago (including the resources in its seabed and surrounding waters). In early 1999 the Philippines declared that Beijing had developed facilities for a small permanent presence on Mischief Reef.

Through most of the 1990s ASEAN claimants developed two differing approaches to the Spratlys' disposition. Malaysia bandwagoned with China, agreeing with Beijing that negotiations on the islands' future should be bilateral, not multilateral. At the same time Kuala Lumpur increased its military presence on the features it occupies and deployed a small number of forces

---

[17] Sam Bateman, "Straits Security: Not Straightforward," *Asia-Pacific Defence Reporter*, February 2005.

to two additional reefs. The Philippines, by contrast, tried external balancing. Manila first enlisted ASEAN support after the 1995 Chinese occupation of Mischief Reef. Turning once again to the United States, Manila signed a new Visiting Forces Agreement with Washington in 1998 that permits U.S. forces to use Philippine facilities and train Philippine soldiers.[18]

Simultaneously, a Declaration on the South China Sea was signed at the 2002 Phnom Penh ASEAN summit prohibiting the occupation of uninhabited features but not foreclosing the prospect of new structures on the islands or reefs already inhabited.[19]

The stalemate persisted until a breakthrough agreement was announced in March 2005 by the Philippines, China, and Vietnam that has facilitated a three-year period of "joint marine seismic work" in a 140,000 square kilometer space around the Spratly islands. Initiated by the Philippines, the agreement sets aside sovereignty claims and authorizes the first systematic seismic survey to determine whether oil and gas resources exist in the seabed and how significant they might be. Each country will bear one-third of the cost.[20] Postponing sovereignty claims does not, however, mean they have disappeared. The true test of this new cooperative spirit will occur when and if oil and gas in commercially feasible quantities are discovered.

Other maritime disputes simmering among the ASEAN states are engendered by fishermen crossing national maritime boundaries and being detained by neighboring coast guards. Though disputes over fishery violations are generally handled at a low level, the stakes increase when possible petroleum reserves are involved. In March 2005 Indonesian and Malaysian naval ships stalked each other over a maritime border dispute in the Sulawesi Sea off Indonesia's East Kalimantan and Malaysia's Sabah state. Malaysia had granted an exploration contract to Royal Dutch/Shell in the East Ambalat block, an area claimed by Indonesia and already under contract by Jakarta with Unocal since December 2004. Malaysia draws its boundary from the continental shelf, placing the East Ambalat block in its exclusive economic zone (EEZ), while Indonesia, basing its claim on the 200-mile rule of the UN Law of the Sea, insists that the block is in its own zone. As Indonesian ships and aircraft patrolled the contested area in early March, both sides increased nationalist rhetoric.

Malaysian-Indonesian relations have always been complicated. The two are economically interdependent, with labor-short Malaysia relying on

---

[18] Leszek Buszynski, "ASEAN, the Declaration on Conduct and the South China Sea," *Contemporary Southeast Asia* 25, no. 3 (December 2003): 352.

[19] Ibid., 355–57.

[20] Gil C. Cabacungan, Jr. and Abagail Ho, "RP, China, Vietnam Sign Joint Accord on Spratlys," *Philippine Daily Inquirer*, March 15, 2005.

Indonesian migrants and capital-short Indonesia depending on Malaysian investors. In late 2004 and 2005 Malaysia sent packing over one million illegal Indonesian and Philippine workers just as the devastating tsunami hit Sumatra. These actions and the new territorial dispute led to noisy public protests in Indonesia. Exacerbating the border dispute are Indonesian plans to build 25 lighthouses on islands bordering the Malaysian claim. Though ASEAN's Secretary General Ong Keng Yang has called for a peaceful settlement, he has stated that the association has no plans to become involved. As oil prices continue to rise and deep sea drilling technology improves, exploiting underwater assets in the South China Sea is becoming increasingly probable; when ownership is contested, navies and air forces will likely be mobilized.[21]

Grand Strategies of Selected Southeast Asian States

Southeast Asian states engage major external powers on political, economic, and even strategic dimensions in order to enhance their own maneuverability. All ASEAN states either tacitly or openly welcome a U.S. military presence along the East Asian littoral. The U.S. presence is beneficial in that it reduces Southeast Asia's responsibility to provide only regional security, and therefore permits each state to devote more resources to local defense and development. The U.S. presence plays a major—although by no means determinative—role when the ASEAN states form their grand strategies. This section examines the individual grand strategies of the Philippines, Thailand, Indonesia, Malaysia, and Vietnam.

The Philippines

For the Philippines, a combination of low budgets, corruption, an entrenched communist insurgency, and Muslim separatist activities in the south have led to Manila's 1999 reactivation of U.S. defense ties which had been frozen for the previous seven years. Joint military exercises emphasize American training for both Philippine infantry and special forces, and include a multi-year, multi-million dollar security assistance program, representing the largest U.S. military and economic aid commitment in the region. In return, regular military access to the Philippines provides the United States with a Southeast Asian location for counterterrorist training, which provides a boost to U.S. efforts to block possible Al Qaeda-related opera-

---

[21] "Indonesia and Malaysia: Border Disputes and Emerging Trends," *STRATFOR*, March 10, 2005.

tions.[22] Thus the Bush administration was able to extend its war on terrorism into Southeast Asia without involving significant numbers of U.S. forces in direct combat. It is noteworthy that the U.S. presence in the Philippines has nothing to do with external defense, protecting the SLOCs, or balancing China. The U.S. presence is focused exclusively on helping the Philippines to meet internal threats.

Although the Moro and communist insurgencies are independent of each other, the insurgents cooperate to the extent of providing one another sanctuary if pursued by the Philippine armed forces (AFP). The military has designated the communist New People's Army (NPA) the larger threat. Thus the AFP's strategy is to contain the various Moro challenges while pursuing the NPA. The AFP's external defense role has been reduced so that it can better cooperate with the National Police in counterinsurgency efforts. These combined forces of about 11,000 face an armed MILF of 8,000–10,000 and an NPA of about 12,000. The AFP needs basic equipment: rifles, tactical radios, small armored vehicles, and armored personnel carriers—all of which are included as part of the ongoing U.S. aid package.[23]

Manila has adopted carrot-and-stick tactics in order to cope with the insurgencies. Sporadic negotiations with the NPA are currently in abeyance due to recent military clashes. By contrast, negotiations are taking place in 2005 with the MILF, and an international monitoring team from Malaysia, Brunei, and Libya has been in Mindanao since November 2004 to observe an ostensible ceasefire.

Thailand

Thailand's grand strategy concentrates on maintaining close ties to the United States while strengthening relations with China. Bangkok's military agenda has focused on two main issues: one is the ongoing border conflicts with Burma and Laos over drugs and illegal population movements; the other is the escalating violence in southern Thailand from alienated Muslims. The major annual U.S.-Thailand joint exercise, Cobra Gold, contains counterterrorism and countercrime components; even before September 11, the two countries' intelligence services founded a Counter-Terrorism Intelligence Center. This center was instrumental in the August 2003 capture of the JI operations chief Riduan Isamuddin, popularly known as Hambali. Although

---

[22] Renato Cruz de Castro, "The Revitalized Philippine-U.S. Security Relations," *Asian Survey* 43, no. 6 (November-December 2003): 982–87; Robert Karniol, "Briefing: The Philippines—Internal Security Concerns," *Jane's Defence Weekly*, January 19, 2005, 26–27; and Sheldon W. Simon, "Theater Security Cooperation in the U.S. Pacific Command: An Assessment and Projection," *NBR Analysis* 14, no. 2, (August 2003): 33–40.

[23] Karniol, "Briefing: The Philippines," 26–27; and Simon, "Theater Security Cooperation," 33–40.

Thai Muslims opposed the U.S. invasions of Afghanistan and Iraq, Prime Minister Thaksin's government granted refueling rights to U.S. aircraft at U-Tapao naval base and allowed U.S. ships en route to the Middle East to visit Thai ports, though Bangkok once again refused to permit the United States to preposition supplies on U.S. ships in the Gulf of Thailand. By September 2003 Thailand had dispatched a force of several hundred engineers to Iraq (though they were withdrawn a year later). The original decision to send these engineers may have been made in the belief that cooperation with the United States would yield lucrative reconstruction contracts. In fact, no such contracts were ever offered.[24]

Counterterrorism is a dominant strategic interest for Bangkok. Thailand has border agreements on procedures for dealing with security incidents with all its neighbors except Laos. Thailand also has counterterrorism agreements with Australia and is party to the ASEAN-U.S. counterterrorism declaration. Bangkok hosts an interagency financial crimes group that tracks terrorist financing, and Thailand has promised to accede to twelve UN antiterrorism conventions.[25] The problems, however, are in Thailand's implementation of its commitments, and—with the growing southern insurgency—a military crackdown that egregiously tramples human rights.

Indonesia

As in the Philippines, the Indonesian military has been underfunded, undertrained, overpoliticized, and plagued by corruption. The country's grand strategy has emphasized independence from all outside powers—especially through both the creation of an autonomous capability to defend its sea and air approaches and a leadership role in ASEAN. Ever since the 1997–98 financial crisis that plunged Indonesia into economic free fall, the prospect for achieving these goals has receded. Therefore, Indonesia relies for the time being on the U.S. Navy for SLOC protection, continuing to focus its own armed forces—the Tentara Nasional Indonesia (TNI)—on internal security.

Jakarta is viewed by Washington as a crucial player in the war on terrorism. As the world's most populous Muslim country, one characterized by a predominantly moderate and tolerant version of Islam, it is also one

---

[24] Paul Chambers, "U.S.-Thai Relations After 9/11: A New Era of Cooperation?" *Contemporary Southeast Asia* 26, no. 3 (December 2004): 465–66. Washington had first requested the prepositioning of supplies in the mid-1990s, only to be rebuffed. Analysts stated that the Thai government believed permanent maritime-based U.S. military supplies off the Thai coast would provoke China. Also see Sheldon W. Simon, "Philippines Withdraws from Iraq and JI Strikes Again," *Comparative Connections* 6, no. 3 (October 2004): 6.

[25] Michael Tivayanond, "Counter-Terrorism in Thailand: A New Direction?" *Asia Insights*, no. 3 (September 2003): 13.

of Southeast Asia's newest democracies. Indonesia's own problems center, however, on homegrown Islamist extremists who are externally linked to Al Qaeda and JI. The United States has been somewhat hamstrung in aiding Indonesian counterterrorism actions because of the constraints Congress has placed on military relations (even though U.S. intelligence and law enforcement assistance has been ongoing).

Nevertheless, in the aftermath of the 2004 Indian Ocean tsunami, new opportunities for U.S.-Indonesian military relations have emerged. In its dealings with the TNI, the Bush administration took advantage of American sympathy for Indonesia's tsunami travails by expressing the hope that IMET could be restored. This program had been withdrawn in 1992 when the Indonesian military launched a bloody attack on pro-independence protesters in East Timor. The sanctions were further tightened in 1999 when the Indonesian army was accused of directing the killing of some 1,500 people in East Timor in an unsuccessful effort to prevent the territory's independence. The IMET ban was written into law by Congress in 2002 when lawmakers insisted that Indonesian generals were blocking an investigation into the killing of two American school teachers in Papua province.

Subsequently, Indonesian authorities have taken steps to improve cooperation with the FBI and brought charges against a member of a Papuan separatist group for the killings of the two Americans. This development coincided with President Bush's stress on the importance of strengthening counterterrorism cooperation with Indonesia. In a January 16, 2005 Jakarta joint press conference with then Deputy Defense Secretary Paul Wolfowitz (a former U.S. ambassador to Indonesia), Indonesian Defense Minister Sudarsono announced that "my job now is to try to reconfigure the Indonesian defense force ... so that it will be more accountable to democracy ... [T]here's no excuse for some of their alleged human rights abuses that have been taking place over the past 25 years." Sudarsono went on to ask the United States to improve TNI training, which is "a very important part of consolidating our democracy ...."[26]

By mid-February 2005, Secretary of State Condoleezza Rice had raised with Congress the issue of IMET's restoration. It appears that IMET will be restored for Indonesia—the allocation for 2005 being about $600,000. In fact, since September 11, Washington has spent several million dollars annually under a separate program to train Indonesian soldiers in counterterrorism, human rights, and civil-military relations. IMET, then, may be more symbolic of Indonesia's reinstatement into U.S. good graces rather than a significant addition to the military relationship. By the end of March 2005,

---

[26] Sheldon W. Simon, "Aid Burnishes U.S. Image, But Other Concerns Persist," *Comparative Connections*, January-March 2005.

the two countries announced a joint naval exercise off Madura Island in the Java Sea, the first such exercise in four years.[27]

Indonesia also hopes the restoration of military ties with the United States will lead to the resumption of the sale of spare parts and military equipment in addition to military aid. Indonesia's defense budget is one of ASEAN's lowest, covering only half of the TNI's expenditures—the rest comes from military-run enterprises and other, more nefarious, sources. In May 2005 Washington announced the renewal of non-lethal defense equipment sales to Indonesia, though such sales remain on hold until both TNI forces involved in human rights abuses are prosecuted and greater transparency exists in military financing.[28]

Malaysia

Malaysia's internal security situation is reasonably stable, although tensions exist both with Indonesia over illegal labor and with Thailand over ethnic-Malay Muslim insurgents who flee to northern Malaysia. Fortunately, however, none of these issues threatens Malaysia's prosperity or security. Kuala Lumpur's grand strategy can focus, therefore, on its primary concern—Malaysia's maritime environment. Piracy in the Malacca Straits is a significant concern. Lack of effective cooperation with Indonesia could lead to the presence of more powerful foreign navies, including that of the United States and India and possibly also of Japan and China. Indeed, the U.S. ambassador to Malaysia, Christopher J. LaFleur, stated that the U.S. Navy was capable of assisting the region's antipiracy actions if requested, but both the U.S. and Japan's offer to help patrol the straits in March 2005 were rejected.[29]

Vietnam

Of all the major Southeast Asian countries, Vietnam experienced the least strategic alteration after September 11. Because terrorism is not a major concern and since Hanoi's relations with Washington are limited, U.S.

---

[27] Jane Perlez, "Indonesia Welcomes U.S. Plan to Resume Training Its Military," *New York Times*, March 1, 2005; and "U.S., Indonesian Military Exercises: Tightening the Circle of Friends," *STRATFOR*, March 30, 2005.

[28] Munningar Sri Saravwati, "Indonesia Hopes Visit by United States Delegation Will Boost Military Ties," *Jakarta Post*, March 23, 2005; and Joshua Kucera, "U.S. Resumes Non-Lethal Defence Sales to Indonesia," *Jane's Defence Weekly*, June 1, 2005, 6.

[29] "Malaysia Wants Indonesia to Stress Anti-Piracy Fight, Fears Foreign Interference," *Bernama* (Kuala Lumpur), April 2, 2005; and "Making Southeast Asia Safer and More Secure," *New Straits Times*, March 19, 2005.

policy is not an important determinant.[30] Due to geographical proximity, China will always be Vietnam's primary strategic concern. The PRC's economic dynamism and growing military capabilities were increasingly forcing Vietnam to accommodate the PRC's needs. Thus, Hanoi agreed in March 2005 to joint energy exploration of a portion of the Spratly Islands' seabed with both the Philippines and China (discussed above), despite having been a major contender for sovereignty with both countries prior to this new undertaking.

External balancing against China is probably not an option for Vietnam.[31] Moreover, Hanoi remains suspicious of American motives, particularly the U.S. strategy of "peaceful evolution" that is designed to apply pressure on communist regimes to accept international human rights standards, political pluralism, and the depoliticization of the military. Vietnam has also been disappointed in ASEAN's role as an external balancer. The association has had little impact on the Spratlys dispute. Any Vietnamese hedging against China is done through its own military modernization effort.

Southeast Asia's Military Modernization

Prior to the 1997–98 Asian financial crisis, Southeast Asian armed forces, benefiting from the region's spectacular economic performance, had all begun to acquire modern arms designed for external defense. Internal insurgencies, which had been the primary security challenge to most Southeast Asian states from the 1960s through the 1980s, had for the most part been defeated, suppressed, or contained by the 1990s. Regional militaries were thus free to address external challenges. Modern combat aircraft were acquired by Malaysia, Thailand, Indonesia, and Singapore. These countries purchased frigates and submarines to upgrade their navies. Thailand even acquired a helicopter/short take-off and landing (STOL) carrier. A major justification for these acquisitions was the need to protect each state's EEZ attendant upon the 1982 UN Law of the Sea. Related to this extension of defense responsibilities was a growing concern over piracy, narcotics, weapons trafficking, and illegal population movements—all of which could be better interdicted with the proper equipment.

---

[30] Much of this Vietnam discussion is drawn from Goh, "Southeast Asian Regional Security," 24–30.

[31] Nevertheless, there have been three visits by U.S. ships to Vietnam since November 2003 as well as a number of high-level contacts between the Vietnam Ministry of Defense and the U.S. Defense Department. In June 2005, an agreement was concluded in Hanoi that provides IMET participation for Vietnamese officers. Initially, this program will focus on English-language training. The U.S. arms embargo will stay in place, however. See Robert Karniol, "U.S., Vietnam to Expand Links; Embargo Remains," *Jane's Defence Weekly*, July 6, 2005, 7.

The financial crisis derailed weapon modernization throughout Southeast Asia (Singapore excepted). Economic recovery began around 2000, and renewed defense purchases soon after that. Once again, with the exception of Singapore, none of the other Southeast Asian militaries are actually attempting to acquire the techniques and capabilities for a true revolution in military affairs (RMA). The RMA goes beyond acquiring modern weapons to create integrated logistics, joint force doctrine, and C4ISR capabilities.[32] These capacities are essential for effective power projection, but they are not required if a country's defense concerns are focused on internal security. The RMA is predicated on information technology, stealth technology, and precision-guided munitions. To embark on the path to RMA, armed forces must also fundamentally change doctrine, logistics, and internal organization. Of the Southeast Asian states, only Singapore is involved in all three. Malaysia has expressed interest in RMA but so far has not made much progress because of interservice rivalries and budget constraints.[33]

The primary external focus of almost all ASEAN states is the protection of economic resources, for which maritime and air capabilities are essential to monitor 200-mile EEZs and to patrol SLOCs vital for each country's international trade. Navies are therefore emphasizing littoral security through the acquisition of maritime patrol aircraft and offshore patrol vessels. These systems are also employed to defend maritime boundaries, protect fishing fleets, and apprehend illegal immigrants and contraband.[34]

For Indonesia and the Philippines, archipelagic security is related to both internal rebellions on their peripheries as well as land-based insurgencies. In these states and southern Thailand, infantries dominate strategy, while for Singapore and Malaysia, air and maritime enhancement propels defense budgets. An examination of selected important Southeast Asian armed forces follows.

Indonesia

Indonesia's primary concern has been the counterinsurgency of and low intensity operations against Free Aceh Movement (GAM) in Aceh as well as separatists in Papua province. The army has also been involved in suppressing Christian-Muslim violence in the Moluccas. Indonesia is a far-flung archipelago that requires ships and aircraft to patrol vast waterways and sea-

---

[32] C4ISR refers to the integration of command, control, communications, computers, intelligence, surveillance, and reconnaissance.

[33] Andrew Tan, *Force Modernization Trends in Southeast Asia*, (Singapore: Institute of Defence and Strategic Studies, January 2004), 26.

[34] Ibid., 30–31.

lanes. Because of the U.S. weapons embargo, Indonesia has turned to Russia for modern combat aircraft, acquiring two Su-20 and Su-27 fighter bombers and two Mi-35 combat helicopters. Long-term plans include three Sukoi squadrons and Polish-built maritime patrol aircraft for the navy by the end of the decade. The navy is also requesting new offshore patrol vessels, two new submarines, four destroyers, and two minesweepers by 2011; the source of funding for these acquisitions, however, remains unknown.[35] Although the United States has restored many components of IMET, Washington has not lifted its lethal arms embargo, with the exception of spare parts for Indonesia's C-130 transport aircraft which can deliver supplies to tsunami-devastated Aceh.

The air force claims to have not only less than half the aircraft needed to safeguard Indonesian air space, but also that its radar stations are unable to cover the eastern region of the country. The air force also contends that the sources of most violations of Indonesian airspace are planes from U.S. carriers. The service has asked for an additional $2.7 billion to lift its capabilities from 30–40 percent readiness to 70–80 percent readiness by the end of the decade.[36] The purchase of Russian Sukois, currently on hold because of tsunami reconstruction costs, is particularly attractive because the Russians have been willing to accept countertrade in palm oil to cover most of the payment (a practice the United States does not follow). Even the North Koreans are interested in selling arms to Indonesia, offering to sell radar systems and submarines. Other countries already exporting arms to Indonesia include South Korea, Singapore, the Czech Republic, and the Netherlands.[37]

President Yudhoyono has proposed a $538 million budget increase for 2005–06, the bulk of which would go to the army for the establishment of 22 new territorial commands. Critics of this plan, including human rights advocates, point out that expanded territorial commands would reverse the military reform process.[38]

The U.S. Department of State's Diplomatic Security Service has even trained an assault element within the police called Detachment 88. This is a group comparable to a military special operations force, and consists of 144

---

[35] Tan, *Force Modernization Trends in Southeast Asia*, 17; and International Institute of Strategic Studies, *The Military Balance 2004–2005* (London: Oxford University Press, 2004), 164–65.

[36] "R.I. Air Force Needs $2.7 Billion to Improve Armament," *Antara* (Jakarta), February 23, 2005.

[37] "Indonesia Mulls DPRK on Weapons Offer," *Asian Export Control Observer*, no. 6, February-March 2005, 3; John Haseman, "Arms Salesmen Woo Jakarta," *Asia-Pacific Defence Reporter*, December-January 2004–05; and John Haseman, "Indonesia Casts Wider Procurement Net," *Asia-Pacific Defence Reporter*, March-April 2004, 54–55.

[38] This process has included the reduction in these commands as well as the military's role in local governance. See "Indonesia Army to Have 22 Additional Territorial Commands," *Media Indonesia*, March 23, 2005; and Tiama Siboro, "Critics Caution Over Rise in Military Spending," *Jakarta Post*, April 5, 2005.

officers. The training costs for Detachment 88 have approached $20 million. Australia has committed $27.7 million over five years for the establishment of a Jakarta Center for Law Enforcement that is staffed by a bi-national contingent of Indonesian and Australian lawyers and intelligence officers. The center assists Detachment 88 with intelligence.[39]

Singapore

Singapore's military development has been continuous and sustained. It is the only regional armed force with a serious commitment to RMA, particularly with respect to command and control (C2). Superior intelligence collection and dissemination is designed to provide situational awareness in the sea and land spaces adjacent to the city-state. C2 is integrated with precision-guided weapons and demonstrated in advanced defense electronics, communications, sensors, and unmanned vehicles. The Singapore Armed Forces Training Institute (SAFTI) is the most advanced in the region and emphasizes the integration of technology across the services. Nonetheless, SAFTI's commandant admits that while joint operations exist, they are not yet fully integrated.[40]

Defense spending in Singapore is scheduled to increase by 7.4% for 2006 to $5.8 billion, accounting for over 31% of the national budget, representing the biggest share of spending among government ministries. While all other ministries took a 3% cut from the preceding year, the defense ministry continues to grow.[41] The Singapore Air Force (SAF) is the best equipped and trained armed force in Southeast Asia. In addition to 42 F-16C-D fighters in the air force, Singapore has twenty more on order. The city-state has also expressed interest in the U.S. Joint Strike Fighter as a next-generation replacement for the F-16. With six DCN Lafayette "stealth" frigates and three ex-Swedish navy submarines, Singapore is also developing a regional maritime force capable of deploying beyond the Malacca Straits.[42] Still, the Singapore Strait itself is the responsibility of the island's coast guard, which possesses the most modern patrol craft along the littoral. If permitted, Singapore will be able to augment Indonesian and Malaysian antipiracy efforts along the

---

[39] Tasking the police with a combat role risks compromising their relationship with the community, but leaving counterinsurgency to the military dredges up past human rights abuses. See International Crisis Group, *Indonesia: Rethinking Internal Security Strategy* (Jakarta: International Crisis Group, 2004), 20–22.

[40] Richard Bitzinger, "Defense Transformation and the Asia-Pacific: Implications for Regional Militaries," *Asia-Pacific Security Studies* 3, no. 7 (October 2004): 3; and interview with Brig. General Eric Tan Huck Gim, Commandant of Singapore's SAFTI, *Jane's Defence Weekly*, March 9, 2005, 34.

[41] Agence France-Presse, "Singapore Increases Defense Budget by 7.4 percent," February 18, 2005.

[42] Tan, *Force Modernization Trends in Southeast Asia*, 6–7.

entire Malacca Strait; however, the sensitive politics of trilateral relation-ships prohibit such genuinely joint actions.

Malaysia

Malaysia's armed forces have a wide variety of skills, including extensive experience in counterinsurgency warfare going back to the 1960s, participa-tion in two decades of international peacekeeping, the world's best jungle warfare school located in Johor, and a capable regional navy and air force able to monitor the country's exceptionally long coastlines and oil and gas fields. With two submarines on order, Malaysia's navy currently consists of frigates, missile corvettes, and missile boats. The air force has seventeen Mig-29 and eight F-18D jet fighters, among other aircraft. Kuala Lumpur is purchasing eight more F-18s and a variety of helicopters for both the air force and navy, and is planning to buy maritime patrol aircraft in future years. Already on order are eighteen Sukoi-30s, Russia's most up-to-date combat jet.[43]

While partly designed to balance Singapore's capabilities, Malaysia's ac-quisitions are more broadly a commitment to sustain and improve a well-balanced conventional force that could be used to cooperate with, or to bal-ance against, neighbors. Enhanced maritime security and regional power projection, undertaken in cooperation with Singapore and Indonesia, are important components for maintaining security in the Malacca Straits. In March 2005 Malaysia's new Maritime Enforcement Agency (MEA), respon-sible for law enforcement in Malaysia's territorial waters and EEZ, became operational. The MEA pools assets from the Marine Police, Navy, and the Fisheries Customs and Marine Department. With over 4,000 personnel, six helicopters, and a number of fixed wing aircraft, and 82 small and medium size vessels, the MEA frees up larger navy ships to move beyond the Straits to the South China Sea islands; the smaller ships provided to the MEA are, however, probably insufficient in number and endurance for the tasks they have been given.[44]

A similar problem exists for Malaysia's Air Force. Because purchases have focused on combat aircraft rather than C4ISR and Airborne Early Warning and Control (AEW&C) planes, air defense coverage is inefficient. Six to eight AEW aircraft are needed for east and west Malaysia, but only two to four platforms are budgeted, and these may not enter service until

---

[43] Tan, *Force Modernization Trends in Southeast Asia*, 8–10; and IISS, *The Military Balance 2004–2005*, 166.

[44] Dzirhan Mahadzir, "New Maritime Agency Steps Up," *Asia-Pacific Defence Reporter*, February 2005, 26–27.

2010. Moreover, airlift capability is minimal, as the air force is unable to transport a fully-equipped battalion.[45]

Thailand

Over the past decade, Thailand has begun to pay increasing attention to improving its weakest service, the navy. The acquisition of a STOL carrier from Spain in 1997 was indicative of Thailand's hopes to develop a blue water navy capable of patrolling the country's Indian Ocean seaboard as well as the Gulf of Thailand. Thailand is acquiring helicopters for its army and navy to be used along its contentious borders, taking delivery in mid-2004 of 30 refurbished Hueys. Both attacks in Thailand's volatile south by ethnic Malay Muslims and the military's use of lethal force have led to difficulties in obtaining new recruits for the army. By April 2005, fewer than 10,000 had volunteered—well below the 30,000–40,000 recruits signed up in each of the past four years.[46]

The Philippines

Of the five founding ASEAN members, the Philippines is the only member whose dominant security concern has always been internal insurgencies stemming from the Philippine communist party and the Moro rebellions in the south. Externally, Manila's South China Sea claims require an effective navy and air force, but the resources have never been available to create such a force. The Philippine military's only source of modernization is surplus U.S. equipment available under the Excess Defense Articles program, which has provided the Philippine armed forces with Huey and Blackhawk helicopters and some coastal patrol vessels.[47]

Manila had planned in the mid-1990s to entrust counterinsurgency operations against the communists to the National Police. By the end of the decade, however, the government concluded that due to a doubling in size of the communists' military arm to 12,000 troops, the army would also have to become involved.

Beginning in 1999, when the United States and the Philippines ratified a new Visiting Forces Agreement, the two countries initiated a Joint Defense Assessment (JDA) through which Washington and Manila negotiated

---

[45] Dzirhan Mahadzir, "Malaysia Covering Capability Gaps," *Asia-Pacific Defence Reporter*, March-April 2004, 18–19.

[46] IISS, *The Military Balance 2004–2005*, 166; "Thailand Accepts Super Lynx 300 Multirole Helicopters," *Jane's Defence Weekly*, February 16, 2005, 15; and Wassona Nanaman, "Fewer Young Men Now Volunteering for Draft," *Bangkok Post*, April 7, 2005.

[47] Tan, *Force Modernization Trends in Southeast Asia*, 23–24.

equipment transfers and training designed primarily for counterinsurgency. The JDA is linked to the Philippines' own defense reform program, which began in 2004 and will cost an estimated $357 million over ten years. In its first year, the United States contributed $7 million to this effort. Beyond this allocation, the United States also provided $248.8 million in military aid to the Philippines between 2002 and 2004. Force modernization is directed to internal threats, particularly basic equipment. The navy and air force, too, are acquiring systems to support ground force needs. Since 2002, the United States has provided a C-130B transport aircraft, 3 coastal patrol vessels, and 28 Huey helicopters. The navy is also acquiring a landing ship in order to transport ground forces more effectively.[48]

In 2004, the Philippine Air Force (PAF) improved its operational readiness from 58 to 70 percent, largely because of U.S. training in maintenance. Australia has also provided assistance, and Thailand has gifted the PAF with eight used OV-10C Bronco counterinsurgency aircraft.[49]

Vietnam

Of all the significant Southeast Asian armed forces, only Vietnam has not engaged in systematic military modernization or expansion during the 1990s. Hanoi is aware of Vietnam's military deficiencies and is attempting to redress them, especially with respect to defending the country's maritime resources. Vietnam is thus acquiring new missile boats, corvettes, and Sukoi-27 fighter bombers. The boats are to be delivered in the course of this decade and the corvettes, ordered from Russia, will be equipped with surface-to-surface missiles.[50]

Vietnam spends 2.5 percent of its GDP on defense, and has cut its armed forces to 484,000.[51] The reduction in uniformed personnel is part of a plan to professionalize the services. Hanoi published a defense white paper in December 2004, emphasizing preparation "for self-defense against any action encroaching upon its territory, airspace, and territorial waters" but also insisting that "Vietnam is always ready to enter into peaceful negotiations to find reasonable and sensible solutions …." The white paper specifically des-

---

[48] Robert Karniol, "The Philippines: Internal Security Concerns," *Jane's Defence Weekly*, January 19, 2005, 25–29.

[49] Ibid., 29.

[50] Tan, *Force Modernization Trends in Southeast Asia*, 20–21.

[51] "Vietnam Publishes National Defense White Paper," *Asia Pulse*, December 13, 2004. This is a two-thirds reduction in force size since the end of the Second Indochina War in the mid-1970s.

ignated the Spratly islands in this regard and stressed the necessity of "reaching an agreement on the 'Code of Conduct' pending the final solution."[52]

In 2005 Vietnam purchased from Poland eighteen maritime surveillance aircraft with command and control modules that should enhance Hanoi's ability to monitor its 2,000 kilometer coast. Poland is also supplying 150 tanks to the army and 40 second-hand Sukoi-22 fighter bombers. These sales make Poland Vietnam's most important external military supplier.[53]

Effectiveness of Southeast Asian Militaries

How prepared are Southeast Asian armed forces to cope with the challenges of the early 21st century? Moreover, how effectively do these forces cooperate internationally to enhance regional security? Recall that ASEAN states must deal with three sets of security problems: internal threats, transnational threats, and balancing with external powers. Specifically, if security (against terrorism, transnational crime, and piracy), boundary disputes, and economic zone conflicts dominate the regional agenda, then how effectively do militaries, police forces, and intelligence organizations interact? The United States in particular has urged Southeast Asian states to cooperate more closely on counterterrorism, with the goal being to mount an "across-the-board attack" on terrorist recruitment, forged documents, and illegal cross-border movements and financial transactions.[54]

The closest ASEAN has come to attempting to integrate the security components previously listed is found in the 2003 action plan conceived by Indonesia. The Declaration of ASEAN Concord 2, popularly known as the Bali Concord 2, is an ambitious, multifaceted plan for the creation of ASEAN Economic and Social Communities as well as a Security Community. The latter entails the construction of an ASEAN Peacekeeping Force to be established by 2012. It also envisages a regional peacekeeping training center, an ASEAN counterterrorism center, and possibly even an ASEAN maritime surveillance center. By mid-2004, objections from Vietnam and Singapore led ASEAN to drop the regional peacekeeping force, though Indonesia promises to revisit the issue in future ASEAN discussions.[55] The ASEAN

---

[52] Ibid.

[53] Grzegorz Holdanowica, "Vietnam's $150 Million Deal with Poland," *Jane's Defence Weekly*, March 2, 2005, 16.

[54] Renato Cruz de Castro, "Addressing International Terrorism in Southeast Asia: A Matter of Strategic or Functional Approach?" *Contemporary Southeast Asia* 26, no. 2 (August 2004): 199.

[55] R. James Ferguson, "ASEAN Concord II: Policy Prospects for Participant Regional 'Development,'" *Contemporary Southeast Asia* 26, no. 3 (December 2004): 402.

Security Community also called for an association-wide extradition treaty and a human rights commission.

While there is some intelligence exchange within ASEAN (especially among the founding five members), the most effective counterterrorist activities seem to be conducted with outsiders, especially the United States and Australia. The Central Intelligence Agency (CIA) and FBI as well as the Australian Federal Police have funded new counterterrorism units and centers in Indonesia, Thailand, and Malaysia. Although separate entities, each focuses primarily on internal terrorist activities. Australian and U.S. intelligence and law enforcement representatives are involved in Indonesia and Thailand, while the United States funds the center in Malaysia.

The ASEAN armed forces have, however, been unable to meet the challenges of transnational terrorists. The Indonesian "Security Community" concept attempted to address this deficiency. Army Chief Ryanizord Ryacudu insisted that ASEAN must hold military exercises. Others urged that association members permit cross-border pursuits and establish consistent counterterrorism legal frameworks. In practice, however, the most specific intelligence input comes not from the region itself but from the United States and Australia. Western security analysts who have examined ASEAN counterterrorism efforts conclude that national activities are too piecemeal, and governments are still wary of sharing information with neighbors. Those agents most likely to come into contact with terrorists—customs, immigration, and border security personnel—are also insufficiently trained. Moreover, there is a belief among some analysts that Indonesian and northern Malaysian security services have been infiltrated by fundamentalists who, though probably not terrorists themselves, may be willing to turn a blind eye to those engaged in regional violence.[56]

Indonesian intelligence and law enforcement, though having succeeded in capturing 200–300 alleged JI terrorism suspects, nonetheless reveal significant deficiencies. The two prime perpetrators of the Marriott hotel and Australian embassy bombings, explosives expert Azahari Husin and top JI recruiter Mohammad Noordin Top, have—despite a regionwide manhunt—managed to elude authorities for over two years. Neither the police nor Indonesian intelligence have been able to penetrate JI, and the army's territorial presence down to the village level has been equally unsuccessful in finding the two bombers.[57] Meanwhile, extradition agreements with neighboring countries remain in limbo. A good example of the difficulty in negotiating such agreements can be found in the different goals Indonesia

---

[56] For an excellent review of the failures in Southeast Asian security cooperation, see Alan Boyd, "Jakarta Blast, A Sign of What's to Come," *Asia Times Online*, September 11, 2004.

[57] John Haseman, "JI Remains a Threat," *Asia-Pacific Defence Reporter*, November 2004, 20.

and Singapore set in their extradition negotiations. Singapore wants a treaty that provides for the extradition of terrorist suspects who could be tried in the city-state's justice system. Indonesia, on the other hand, is more interested in having Singapore return those Indonesians who fled to the island because of financial crimes (usually ethnic Chinese). Jakarta hesitates to agree to Singapore's criteria for terrorist extradition for fear of an Islamic backlash, while Singapore believes that a number of Indonesian Chinese in the city-state fled in order to escape the anti-Chinese pogroms attendant upon the 1997–98 financial crisis and Suharto's loss of the presidency.[58]

Despite the escalation of violence in the Thai south, there is no evidence as yet of foreign involvement or links to either JI or Al Qaeda among the ethnic Malay Muslims. Neither suicide bombings nor claims of credit—both typical of Al Qaeda and JI operations—have occurred. Nor have Westerners, or the locations that they tend to congregate, been targeted.[59] The Thai government has also insisted that it does not require foreign assistance to deal with the insurgency.

By contrast, since October 2004 a small international monitoring team composed of armed forces from Malaysia and Brunei has been in the southern Philippines acting as ceasefire observers between the MILF and AFP. Peace talks between the two forces began in May 2005 in Kuala Lumpur. Despite the presence of these observers, armed engagements between AFP and MILF combatants have continued. The Malaysian navy has captured a major JI leader, Zulfikar Mohamad Shariff (Zulfiki), who was in charge of its Philippine operations. Detained in Malaysia, he has so far not been extradited. The southern Philippines has become a JI training ground for Moro insurgents affiliated with the Abu Sayyaf and the breakaway factions of the MILF and the Moro National Liberation Front (MNLF). In April 2004 the U.S. embassy in Malaysia expressed concern that the Mindanao region was becoming "the new 'Mecca' for terrorism and, if not controlled, the next Afghanistan."[60] Finally, it should be noted that Southeast Asian armed forces often confront as well as collaborate with each other. Throughout 2005 Malaysian and Indonesian ships and aircraft have had run-ins over disputed territorial waters in the Sulawesi Sea where each country has offered drilling contracts to separate petroleum companies. There was even a brief collision

---

[58] For articles on the difficulties of negotiating an Indonesian-Singapore extradition treaty, see *Jakarta Post*, February 11, 2005 and March 14, 2005.

[59] For an excellent analysis of the Thai southern insurgency, see Joseph Liow, "Observations on Islamic Radicalism in Thailand: Separating Fact from Fiction" (paper prepared for The National Bureau of Asian Research, March 2005); and B. Raman, "Thai Militants Turn Savvy," *Asia Times Online*, April 6, 2005.

[60] Kit Collier, "Precarious Peace in Mindanao," *Asia-Pacific Defence Reporter*, December–January 2004–05, 16–17.

at sea, followed by heated public rhetoric from both capitals before military leaders met to defuse the situation.[61]

Exercises between the United States and some Southeast Asian services have been ongoing for some time. For instance, Singapore and Thailand have trained with U.S. forces in disaster relief and humanitarian intervention in the annual Cobra Gold exercise. Indonesian tsunami relief, however, was not a joint and coordinated effort. Singapore and Malaysia provided assistance in Aceh that was separate from that of the U.S. Navy. There was cooperation in the division of tasks but not in the delivery of relief supplies and services; collaboration took place at the command level but not in the field. Because the United State's navy is much more technologically proficient than that of other states and its supplies were massive, the U.S. presence worked independently of other relief efforts.

Other External Armed Forces and Southeast Asia

Japan dispatched peacekeepers to Cambodia and East Timor in the 1990s, and sent over 1,000 Japanese Self-Defense Force (JSDF) personnel to provide Indonesia tsunami relief in January 2005. That such dispatches took place demonstrates the receptiveness of the region to the presence of Japanese peacekeepers. Whether these peacekeepers have paved the way for Japan to adopt a more proactive defense role in Southeast Asia, however, remains to be seen. These are, however, initial indicators that the region would accept a Japanese naval deployment in Southeast Asian waters that is aimed at antipiracy efforts: the Japanese Coast Guard (JCG) has conducted joint training exercises with six ASEAN states and Japanese aid programs have been provided to coastal defense forces along the Southeast Asian littoral.[62]

Security of the seas is paramount to Japan because seaborne trade provides Japan with 20 percent of its food imports, nearly all of its petroleum imports, and 99 percent of its product exports.[63] The Malacca Strait alone carries 80 percent of Japan's petroleum imports. Japan's Maritime Self Defense Force (MSDF) has the capability to protect these sea lanes, but Article 9 of Japan's Constitution prohibits collective defense and appears to prohibit direct naval cooperation with other states. Nevertheless, since 1999

---

[61] Mohammed Haikal and Mohammed Isa, "Navy Chiefs Pledge No Repeat of Sulawesi Sea Ships Incident," *Bernama* (Kuala Lumpur), April 16, 2005.

[62] Jian Yang, "Sino-Japanese Relations: Implications for Southeast Asia," *Contemporary Southeast Asia* 25, no. 2 (August 2003): 318; John H. Bradford, "Japanese Anti-Piracy Initiatives in Southeast Asia: Policy Formulation and Coastal State Responses," *Contemporary Southeast Asia* 26, no. 3 (December 2004): 481; and Brad Glosserman, "Japan Seizes the Moment," *PacNet2A*, January 13, 2005.

[63] Simon, "Aid Burnishes U.S. Image, But Other Concerns Persist."

Japanese prime ministers have proposed antipiracy initiatives for Southeast Asia. Only China has openly opposed Japanese participation in joint coast guard patrols and multilateral antipiracy activities in Southeast Asia.[64]

In a visit to states bordering the Straits of Malacca in January 2005, Tokyo's Defense Minister Yoshinori Ono urged ASEAN members to increase antipiracy surveillance. Japan is particularly concerned with loopholes in the current arrangements that prohibit pursuit across territorial waters. By late 2004 hijacking of tugs and kidnapping were a weekly occurrence. Though wreaking havoc on the pirates who operated out of Aceh, the tsunami also radically altered the channels through which ships travel in the straits. Although two U.S. Navy ships are resurveying the seabed, until new charts are drawn, ships going through the Malacca Straits are forced to steam at low speeds and are thus even more vulnerable to pirate attacks.[65]

In two separate events in mid-March 2005, pirates attacked a gas tanker and a Japanese tug boat in the same area of the Malacca Strait. The well-armed pirates kidnapped the captain and chief engineer, and demanded a ransom. In response, Japan offered to send coast guard ships but was turned down by Indonesia and Malaysia. Singapore was willing to accept the Japanese offer, with the city-state's Ministry of Defense stating that "These incidents highlight the need to find more ways by which enforcement agencies can cooperate to take action to enhance the security of regional waters ...."[66] In June 2005 the JCG dispatched an armed patrol boat to the Malacca Strait to carry out an anti-piracy "drill" with the Indonesian Navy.[67]

A new legal regime lobbying for security in the Malacca Straits might be one way of sharing responsibilities between the littoral and user states. Article 43 of the 1982 UN Law of the Sea treaty provides for cooperation between coastal and user states. Indeed, Japan already contributes funds for navigational aids and hydrographic surveys in the Malacca Strait. New arrangements would be justified under the UN treaty if all states involved could agree both to the escort of vulnerable vessels by user states and/or littoral states, as well as to contingency plans that would permit coastal and/or user states to board and search suspect vessels. To date, however, neither Malaysia nor Indonesia has expressed interest in this possibility.[68]

On the other hand, there are indications that greater maritime cooperation may be in the works. Indonesia and Singapore launched a new maritime

---

[64] Bradford, "Japanese Anti-Piracy Initiatives," 488, 491.

[65] Niall Chorney, "Call For Protection Against Piracy," *Jane's Defence Weekly*, January 26, 2005.

[66] Agence France-Presse, "Singapore Says Attempted Attack on Japanese Tanker Was in Indonesian Waters," April 7, 2005.

[67] "Japanese Patrol Boat Heads to Malacca Strait to Fight Piracy," *Jakarta Post*, June 7, 2005.

[68] Bateman, "Straits Security: Not Straightforward," 5–7.

surveillance system in June 2005 that will permit their two navies to share a common real-time picture of the Singapore Strait. The Indonesian and Thai Navies have also agreed to enhance cooperation. Though both navies have agreed to share information, they are still not allowed to enter each other's waters. Particularly interesting is Singapore's hosting of a multinational exercise in August 2005 designed to train participating units in procedures to stop WMD shipments. This is the first rationalization, standardization, and interoperability (RSI) exercise to be held in Southeast Asia.[69]

Given the reticence of the littoral states to collaborate in joint patrols, the private sector may be stepping in. Background Asia Risk Solutions, a private security firm based in Singapore, employs former members of elite military units, has its own armored boat, and offers to accompany vessels anywhere between Sri Lanka and the South China Sea for about $50,000 per mission.[70] Neither Indonesia nor Singapore has commented on this arrangement, though in April 2005 Malaysia announced that it will place armed guards on tugboats and barges in the waterway. Kuala Lumpur also rejected the idea of mercenaries functioning as armed escorts, warning that any such escorts entering Malaysian waters would be detained. Nevertheless, in June Malaysia softened its objection, saying that it would "reluctantly" allow armed escorts as long as they stay out of—or at least receive advanced permission to enter—Malaysia's territorial waters.[71]

India is another regional power with an interest in Southeast Asian security. Seeking closer ties with Burma in order to counter China's influence, India has also conducted antipiracy naval patrols in the Malacca Strait. India has acquired the 44,000-ton Russian aircraft carrier *Admiral Gorshkov*, which is replacing an aged carrier, the *Viraat*. Moreover, starting in 2005 New Delhi plans to build its own carrier with an operating range of 7,500 nautical miles, the first step in a plan for a three carrier navy.

Always interested in inviting outside powers to assist in protecting the SLOCs, Singapore has held discussions with the Indian Navy about joint patrols. Singapore is also seeking training access for its army and air force in India. New Delhi has hosted defense cooperation discussions with Kuala Lumpur and Bangkok dealing with counterterrorism, drugs, and antipiracy. India is also servicing and upgrading Vietnam's Soviet-made aircraft.[72]

---

[69] Richard Scott, "Surveillance System Strengthens Vision on Monitoring Singapore Strait," *Jane's Defence Weekly*, June 22, 2005, 16.

[70] Agence France-Presse, "Armed Escorts for Hire on Pirate-Infested Southeast Asian Waters," April 8, 2005.

[71] Agence France-Presse, "Armed Escort Vessels Can Sail in Malaysian Waters: Minister," June 6, 2005.

[72] Satu Limaye, "India 2004: A Year of Living Actively," *Comparative Connections*, July-September 2004, 5–9.

On the political-security front, India is now a full ASEAN dialogue partner, has endorsed ASEAN's Nuclear Weapons Free Zone, and in 2003 adhered to the Association's Treaty of Amity and Cooperation. Naval exercises, with a focus on search and rescue as well as antipiracy, began with Singapore and now involve other ASEAN members. India's many exercises with the U.S. Navy and its growing maritime activities with ASEAN navies may lead to easier interoperability among them all.[73]

Australia's continued concern for Southeast Asian stability is seen in Canberra's leadership of the UN Transitional Authority in Cambodia (1992) and its leading role in the UN Transitional Authority in East Timor (1999). There is also a long standing security tie to Malaysia and Singapore through the Five Power Defense Arrangement, which includes annual military exercises. In 2003 Prime Minister John Howard announced a bilateral counterterrorism assistance package for the Philippines that included training for Philippine officers in Australia. Australian police have also collaborated with Philippine authorities in covert operations to crush Muslim extremist networks, particularly after Manila asked for Canberra's help in investigating the February 2004 Manila Bay ferry bombing that killed more than one hundred people. Australian experts found links between the Abu Sayyaf kidnapping gang, JI, and a new group known as Rajas Sulaiman. These efforts reportedly thwarted a plot to carry out a Madrid style train bombing in Manila.[74]

Unfortunately, Australia's security diplomacy has sometimes seemed maladroit. In September 2004 Howard declared that Australia reserved the right to launch preemptive attacks against those countries from which threats to Australia emanated. This statement elicited outrage from Southeast Asia, needlessly setting back political relations. In December of the same year the Prime Minister announced a one thousand nautical mile-security zone around Australia to protect shipping, ports, and oil rigs. In response Malaysia, Indonesia, and even New Zealand all accused Australia of violating their sovereignty.[75] These tensions probably could have been avoided if Howard had consulted his neighbors about Canberra's security concerns and plans before announcing policies regarding externally based terrorist threats and the establishment of a security zone. These declarations stem

---

[73] Manjeet S. Pardesi, "Deepening Singapore-Indian Strategic Ties," *IDSS Commentaries*, March 22, 2005, 1–3.

[74] See Rommel C. Banlaoi, "Broadening Philippine-Australian Defense Relations in the Post 9/11 Era: Issues and Prospects," *Contemporary Southeast Asia* 25, no. 3 (December 2003): 475–79, 485.

[75] Agence France-Presse, "Australia Boosts Anti-Terror Defenses With New Maritime Security Zone," December 15, 2004; "Malaysia Slams Anti-Terror Plans," *The Australian*, December 18, 2004; and "Malaysia: Minister Says Australia's Maritime Security Plan Shows 'Arrogance'," *Bernama*, December 18, 2004.

from Australia's February 2003 Strategic Review, which emphasizes that threats to Australia are no longer state-based but rather originate in states unable to suppress terrorists.[76]

On a more positive note, exercises involving Australia under the Five Power Defense Arrangement for the first time included a maritime antiterrorist scenario in September 2004. The exercise—which involved Australia, New Zealand, the United Kingdom, Singapore and Malaysia—included 3,500 personnel, 31 ships, 2 submarines, and 60 aircraft that tracked and recovered a vessel "hijacked" by terrorists. Canberra also announced plans for a counterterrorist school for regional intelligence officers that would be located in the Australian capital and would work with the Australian-funded Jakarta Center for Law Enforcement.[77] These are all examples of how Australia promotes security cooperation at the regional level. More could be done if the Indonesian, Malaysian, and Thai maritime police would be willing to accept training and equipment from the Australian Navy and Coast Guard. So far, however, that prospect has not materialized.

Finally, in June 2005 U.S. and Australian forces launched their largest joint exercise in four years off the Queensland coast. Involving 11,000 U.S. and 6,000 Australian service personnel, exercise *Talisman Saber* was billed as the largest bilateral exercise ever undertaken by the U.S. military. Australia's commander, Major General Mark Kelly, noted that future Australian Defense Forces (ADF) war-fighting operations are likely to be conducted as part of a coalition.[78]

The Future of Southeast Asian Defense Collaboration

Despite the Treaty of Amity and Cooperation, Southeast Asian armed forces still cast a wary eye toward one another. Military modernization as a balancing act remains a primary preoccupation of Southeast Asian states. Collaborative efforts can, however, also be found. Asia-Pacific Economic Cooperation (APEC) meetings issue security declarations on counterterrorism and non-proliferation. In July 2004 the ASEAN Regional Forum convened its first meeting of senior-level defense officials. This initial gathering of Asia-Pacific defense officials discussed how their armed forces

---

[76] Rod Lyon, "Australia's Security and the Threat of Islamic Terrorism in Southeast Asia," *Cambridge Review of International Affairs* 16, no. 3 (October 2003): 458; see also "Country Briefing: Australia," *Jane's Defence Weekly*, November 2, 2003, 25–30.

[77] Agence France-Presse, "FPDA Exercises will Feature First Anti-Terror Sea Drill," September 10, 2004; and "Australia's Plans for Counterterrorism Cooperation," *STRATFOR*, October 8, 2004.

[78] Agence France-Presse (Sydney), "U.S., Australia to Stage Military Exercise Off Queensland," June 7, 2005.

could cooperate in dealing with such non-traditional security threats as terrorism, drug smuggling, money laundering, and illegal arms trafficking.[79] Multilateral discussions in a conference setting do not, however, necessarily translate into multilateral actions on land, sea, and air. Once again, rhetoric exceeded reality for Southeast Asian states.

In fact, there are no true multilateral defense arrangements among Southeast Asian states. That is, there are no ongoing exercises or patrols involving the armed forces of three or more Southeast Asian states that either cross national boundaries or operate on the high seas or in international air space. Indonesia has proposed a standing ASEAN peacekeeping force that could help settle disputes in places such as Aceh and the southern Philippines; these proposals have not yielded any action so far, though ASEAN will be sending observers to Aceh to monitor the Indonesia-GAM ceasefire.[80] The closest to a genuine multinational arrangement is tripartite cooperation among Singapore, Malaysia, and Indonesia in the Malacca Strait. Singapore was prepared for full joint patrols through the national waters of all three states, as well as inviting the participation of more effective navies (particularly that of the United States and India); however, Malaysia and Indonesia flatly refused. Instead, Singapore and Malaysia are separately escorting certain high value ships through the Strait on their own. Because of Indonesian-based pirate attacks on Thai fishing boats, even Thailand has offered to participate in policing the Strait.[81]

Mutual suspicion among ASEAN states is reflected in the fact that the country with which most bilateral and multilateral exercises are held is the United States. The United States has training arrangements with Malaysia, Thailand, and the Philippines as well as repair and maintenance agreements with Malaysia, Singapore, and Indonesia. For the past decade, U.S. forces have held annual bilateral exercises involving all three services with Malaysia, Singapore, the Philippines, Thailand, Indonesia, and Brunei. The most elaborate bilateral exercises are the annual Balikatan exercises, which train Philippine forces in counterinsurgency. These exercises also include a civic action component in Mindanao through which U.S. medics and engineers treat local villagers and build such infrastructure as schools, roads, and wells.

---

[79] Ralph Cossa and Jane Skanderup, "Tsunami Brings Us Together: Provides Perspective," *Comparative Connections*, January 2005, 9–10.

[80] "Indonesia Proposes Southeast Asian Peacekeeping Force," *Utusan Malaysia* (Kuala Lumpur), February 21, 2004.

[81] "Better Defense in the Strait," *Bangkok Post*, March 8, 2005; Agence France-Presse, "Singapore Navy to Escort Passing Merchant Ships," February 28, 2005; and Muninggar Sri Sarawati and Adianto P. Simamora, "Thailand Offers to Help To Secure Malacca Strait," *Jakarta Post*, May 4, 2005.

The best known multilateral exercise is Cobra Gold, which has been held in Thailand since 1982. The May 2005 exercise included for the first time 25 JSDF personnel. They joined 2,655 personnel from Thailand, 3,614 from the United States, and 76 from Singapore, in addition to observers from a number of Asian armed forces. Singapore and Japan only participated in the command post portion of the exercise, indicating that the field exercise was essentially bilateral.

Although not a central feature of this chapter, some mention of Burma is warranted. A perennial problem for ASEAN solidarity and regional security, the Burmese military junta's security and economic relations with China have raised anxiety levels in other ASEAN states, especially regarding the potential PLAN acquisition of port facilities on Burma's coast. Rangoon's egregious human rights record is an embarrassment to ASEAN and created a split in the organization over the implications of Rangoon's scheduled chairmanship in 2006. Yielding to pressure from member states and wishing to avoid controversy, Burma publicly renounced its turn for chairmanship of ASEAN in July 2005. Further complicating Burma's position in the region are periodic military skirmishes along the Thai border. Also problematic is the existence of methamphetamine laboratories in Burma, from which millions of pills are illegally sold in Thailand—a serious national security and public health problem for Bangkok.

None of the Southeast Asian states possesses the military capabilities to challenge such big powers as the United States, China, or Japan. Nor can ASEAN armed forces (again excepting Singapore) effectively interoperate with these global players. Moreover, the armed forces of ASEAN countries are conservative, risk averse, and concerned primarily with maintaining capabilities they acquired from the 1980s and 1990s; thus gradual modernization is the watchword, a strategy which is probably sufficient to meet both internal security and external defense requirements.[82]

Southeast Asia's focus on internal security is also compatible with post-September 11 U.S. strategic doctrine, which emphasizes preemption, intervention, and irregular warfare. In Southeast Asia, enhancing the capabilities of friendly and allied countries to deal with internal challenges is the best way for the United States to assist in suppressing indigenous terrorism before it burgeons into an international problem.[83] U.S. doctrine implicitly acknowledges that local authorities possess more legitimacy in defeating terrorist groups than do outsiders. U.S. aid to Philippine, Indonesian, and

---

[82] Richard Bitzinger, "Challenges to Transforming Asian-Pacific Militaries," *Asia-Pacific Security Studies* 3, no. 8 (October 2004): 1–4.

[83] This point is made in the 2005 National Defense Strategy document summarized by Joshua Kucera, "U.S. Strategy Emphasizes Irregular Warfare," *Jane's Defence Weekly*, March 30, 2005, 5.

Thai police, intelligence, and armed forces is a useful model to follow in the rest of Southeast Asia, as opposed to the direct intervention in Afghanistan and Iraq. Nevertheless, excessive reliance on the use of force to suppress terrorists and secessionists in Aceh, the Moluccas, Papua province, Mindanao, and southern Thailand are at best incomplete strategies that have led to continuing violence and human rights violations. Promoting economic development, social justice, and political participation are additional tasks of governance that must be met in order to achieve truly effective national security. These tasks require time, considerable economic resources, patience, education, and a commitment to pluralism. The U.S. Agency for International Development (USAID) could provide planning expertise and financial support for this kind of nation-building, but the primary responsibility rests with each government.

For the time being, China is emphasizing diplomacy rather than force in its relations with Southeast Asia. This approach is best epitomized by China's March 2005 agreement with Vietnam and the Philippines for joint exploration of the petroleum potential around their competing Spratly islands claims. Though seemingly providing a peaceful means for the economic exploitation of the Spratlys seabed, the agreement isolates the remaining Spratlys claimants—Malaysia, Brunei, and Taiwan—and ends any potential united ASEAN front on the future of the Spratlys. Moreover, there is no doubt that the PLAN is developing global reach to protect its far-flung shipping interests. In turn, the Pentagon and CIA both perceive China as a peer competitor—not necessarily an adversary—in Southeast Asia over the next ten to twenty years. If this competition is devoted to helping ASEAN members build their own defense and security capabilities, the rivalry could be benign. However, if China seeks to replace the United States as the region's external security guarantor, Southeast Asian security diplomacy will confront its greatest challenge since the Vietnam War. China's growing naval presence, the reticence of ASEAN states to collaborate militarily in their security domains, and America's focus on the Middle East and South Asia in the war on terrorism all suggest that while a U.S. role in Southeast Asian security is still essential, such a role will be confined to military sales, training, and roving air and naval forces. This is essentially a continuation of current practice—more of the same rather than significant defense change.

STRATEGIC ASIA 2005–06

SPECIAL STUDIES

Executive Summary

This chapter explores the development of Australian strategic policy and defense capabilities since the end of the Vietnam War.

MAIN ARGUMENT:

The 2000 White Paper broadened the focus of Australia's strategic policy beyond a narrow emphasis on the defense of the continent to a conception that includes U.S. support for preserving a stable power balance in Asia.

This shift in strategic policy carries two main implications for the Australian Defence Force: (1) an increase in land force capabilities for regional operations and (2) sustained investment in high-tech air and naval capabilities.

Three factors have influenced Australian defense policy since 2000:

- The war on terrorism, particularly operations in Iraq, has raised questions about the balance between size and weight in Australia's land forces.

- Instability in the region has increased demands to develop the capacity to mount stability operations in places such as the Solomon Islands.

- As new economic and political opportunities overshadow traditional strategic anxieties, shifting Australian attitudes regarding China raise questions over the future alignment of U.S. and Australian objectives.

POLICY IMPLICATIONS:

- Whether the U.S. and Australia can agree on the region's future strategic architecture will depend in part on the extent to which the U.S. is willing to concede legitimacy to China's growing leadership role in Asia.

- The U.S. can ensure Australia's help in maintaining regional stability by (1) supporting Australia in retaining superior Pacific air and naval capabilities and (2) continuing to allow Canberra access to sophisticated U.S. military technologies and systems.

- By offering a clear assessment of which Australian capabilities could aid future coalition operations, the U.S. can help clarify confusion in Australia's current policy debates.

Australian Strategic Policy

Hugh White

Australia is one of the United State's oldest and closest allies. During the later stages of the Cold War, although continuing to commit to the United States and the Western alliance in general, Australia increasingly began to focus defense efforts within its own neighborhood. Ever since the end of the Cold War, Canberra has recognized the need to take a broader view of Australia's strategic interests and defense needs, in large part because Australia is situated on the front line of many of today's key strategic issues: the war on terrorism, failing states, and the rise of China. Nearby Indonesia is a fledgling democracy home to the world's largest Muslim population and the site of a number of terrorist attacks (including those against Australians). Other close neighbors include Papua New Guinea, East Timor, the Solomon Islands, and Vanuatu, all of which are among the most weak and vulnerable states in the world. Furthermore, Australia's fastest-growing economic and political relationship is with China, and Beijing is clearly seeking to draw Canberra into its growing sphere of influence.

This chapter examines how Australia's strategic posture and defense policy is adapting to these challenges, and suggests implications for the future of the U.S.-Australian alliance. The findings are as follows: Australia sustains an active and engaged strategic posture that clearly supports U.S. interests in Asia and beyond. In addition to defending its own continent, Australia contributes to stability in its nearer region and in the wider Asia-Pacific, and offers modest support to the global war on terrorism. Canberra meets these responsibilities with small but high-quality land forces and air and naval capabilities that are significant in regional terms. Demands to support the United States globally and help stabilize its neighborhood are, however,

Hugh White is Professor of Strategic Studies at the Australian National University and a Visiting Fellow at the Lowy Institute for International Policy. He can be reached at <Hugh.White@anu.edu. au>.

raising questions about the relative priority of a larger versus more heavily equipped army. Meanwhile, the challenge of sustaining air and naval forces at levels comparable with Chinese and other forces will put major strain on Australia's defense funding and management. Differences over how best to respond to China's rise could, moreover, undermine cooperation between Canberra and Washington on this critical issue. The United States can help by maintaining Australia's access to high technology, clarify how its ally can best contribute to coalition operations, and above all foster closer dialogue on the question of China.

The first section of this chapter traces the origins of Australia's current strategic alignment to the aftermath of the Vietnam War, and explores how the continent-oriented defense policies put in place during that era were affected by post-Cold War developments in the 1990s. The second section explains the new defense policies that were adopted in 2000 to meet the demands of the post-Cold War world. The third section outlines the current capabilities and development plans of the Australian Defence Force (ADF). The fourth section explores developments since 2000, including the war on terrorism, increasing engagement in Australia's near neighborhood, and the rise of China. A conclusion sums up the main arguments and examines how U.S. policy can strengthen the alliance with Australia.

Foundations—The 1990s

Australia's unique historical and geostrategic settings have shaped its strategic policy for over a century. Ever since British maritime supremacy began to wane in the late 19th century, Australians have been uncomfortably aware of their country's position as an isolated Western outpost on the margins of Asia. Canberra's security concerns have long focused on the need to help preserve stability in the politically and ethnographically complex archipelago situated to its immediate north, and to guard against the rise of potentially powerful and hostile forces from among the emerging great powers of Asia. The United Kingdom's failure to provide effective protection for Australia after the fall of Singapore in 1942 left Australians more conscious than ever of their potential vulnerability, and embedded a strong instinct for defense self-reliance. Nonetheless, when decolonization transformed Australia's strategic environment following World War II, Australia established a policy of "forward defense" that emphasized close cooperation with British and U.S. forces in Asia. As Britain withdrew from Asia in the late 1960s and the Guam Doctrine foreshadowed limits on future U.S. strategic commitments in the region, Australian policy became focused on building forces capable of defending Australia's own territory without relying on combat support from the United States.[1] In 1986 a government-sponsored review established clear force-structure priorities to underpin the new defense posture.[2]

Forces for Change

By the time Canberra had worked out the details of this new defense posture, changes were well underway that would overturn some of its premises. Throughout the 1990s five developments placed pressure on Australia's post-Guam/post-Vietnam defense policy.

First, much like other countries, Australia found that after years of scarce military operations, demands on its armed forces had suddenly increased. Throughout the 1990s Australia deployed substantial forces on a range of operations in Namibia, the Persian Gulf (including *Operation Desert Storm*), Cambodia, Somalia, Rwanda, Western Sahara, Papua New Guinea, East Timor, and numerous other smaller operations.[3]

Second, this global trend was sharpened by developments in Australia's own backyard. Two coups in Fiji in 1987 and a protracted separatist conflict on the Papua New Guinea island of Bougainville beginning in 1989 demonstrated the potential for instability among the small island nations in Australia's immediate neighborhood. The Asian financial crisis of 1997–98 and the consequent fall of President Suharto in Indonesia raised questions about the stability of Australia's large neighbor. In 1999 the crisis in East Timor spurred Australia to initiate and then lead INTERFET, the international force in East Timor sanctioned by the United Nations (UN). This experience established beyond doubt the need for Australia to develop forces capable of maintaining stability on its own doorstep.[4]

Third, Australian strategic policymakers recognized from the early 1990s that the combined effect of the end of the Cold War along with China's economic growth had raised important new questions concerning the long-term balance of power in Asia. As Cold War restraints relaxed, the future roles of and relationships between Japan, the United States, India, and especially China became uncertain.[5]

---

[1] Department of Defence, *Australian Defence* (Canberra: Department of Defence, 1976).

[2] Paul Dibb, *Review of Australia's Defence Capabilities* (Canberra: Department of Defence, 1986).

[3] Australian Strategic Policy Institute, *Defence Almanac* (Canberra: Australian Strategic Policy Institute, 2004), 81.

[4] Department of Defence, *Australia's Strategic Policy* (Canberra: Department of Defence, 1997), 20.

[5] Department of Defence, *Defending Australia: Defence White Paper 1994* (Canberra: Department of Defence, 1994), 10–11, 15.

Fourth, in the years leading up to the Asian financial crisis it became increasingly clear that economic growth in Asia and the concomitant growth in military capabilities (especially air and naval capabilities), both in Southeast Asia and in the wider Asia-Pacific region, were steadily undermining key Australian strategic assumptions. Not only did Australia lose its local monopoly over technologies such as beyond-visual-range air combat capabilities, modern anti-ship missiles, and stealthy submarines, but consistent differences in rates of economic growth also suggested that Australia's relative strategic weight in its immediate neighborhood was in gradual decline.[6]

Fifth, in the 1990s Australian military planners—like their counterparts elsewhere—were forced to wrestle with the implications of the information and communications technology revolution on the conduct of military operations. In particular, sustaining interoperability and increasing network capabilities with the United States in the aftermath of *Operation Desert Storm* became an important issue.[7]

The U.S.-Australian Alliance in the 1990s

The above developments led to a serious reconsideration of many aspects of Australian defense policy, including the U.S. alliance. Although never fearing that the United States would quickly withdraw from Asia after the Cold War, Australian policymakers did at least expect significant changes and possibly a long-term erosion of U.S. strategic engagement in the Western Pacific. As Canberra's 1994 defense white paper stated "The United States will remain a major contributor to security in the region over the next fifteen years, but it will neither seek nor accept primary responsibility for maintaining peace and stability in the region."[8] Canberra viewed continued U.S. engagement as critical to maintaining a stable balance of power in Asia. In particular, U.S. engagement forestalled both China's emergence as a regional hegemon and the almost equally unpalatable alternative of direct and acute strategic competition between China and Japan. If Australia wanted the United States to stay engaged, then it would need to take active steps to support and encourage that engagement, and to persuade others in the region to do the same.

This engagement became a key priority both for Australia's energetic multilateral diplomacy (especially in the promotion of APEC and the ASEAN Regional Forum [ARF] in the early 1990s) and for bilateral alliance

---

[6] Although these concerns eased temporarily after the 1997 financial crisis slashed defense spending in some Southeast Asian countries, the deeper trend remained. See *Australia's Strategic Policy*, 5.

[7] Ibid., 56.

[8] *Defence White Paper 1994*, 8.

diplomacy with the United States. Canberra increasingly came to understand that the prime value the U.S.-Australian alliance held for Australia was the role it played in ensuring a stable regional balance of power by supporting sustained U.S. strategic engagement in Asia.[9] Canberra also recognized Australia's role in the alliance chiefly as a modest contribution supporting U.S. global engagement that was critical to stability in more distant places like the Middle East—where Australian interests were engaged—and, more broadly, to the post-Cold War global order.

The U.S.-Australian alliance in the post-Cold War period began to take on a rather different form from that which had been embedded in Australia's defense policies of the 1980s. Australia was now keenly focused on working to maintain a stable strategic balance among Asia's great powers. At the strategic level, Canberra saw the alliance primarily as a contribution to this balance, and recognized that the alliance may well require Australia to support the United States militarily in order to maintain such a balance of power. On the other hand, the experience of East Timor in 1999 affirmed both that Australia's neighbors would likely require continuing security attention and that Australia needed to be able to respond to these needs independently.

The 2000 Defense White Paper

All of these factors came to bear in a new defense white paper published in 2000. *Defence 2000* was the first major attempt to overhaul Australia's defense policies in order to meet the new demands of the post-Cold War era. Though the demands of the East Timor crisis in late 1999 made the issuance of a white paper imperative, the real driver of the review process was fiscal. A decade and a half had passed since the Dibb Review had codified Australia's post-Vietnam defense policy,[10] and in that time Australia's defense spending had remained stable in real terms. But the buying power of the defense budget had eroded as costs—especially per capita personnel costs—had increased relentlessly in real terms. Despite major reductions in personnel numbers partially offsetting this increase in per capita costs, the scope for further cuts had been exhausted. Ministers were persuaded

---

[9] *Australia's Strategic Policy*, 19. For an earlier reflection of the same idea, see *Defence White Paper 1994*, 95: "Increasingly as we seek security in and with Asia, we will value our alliance with the United States not just for the contribution it makes to Australia's own defence, but also for its broader contribution to regional security."

[10] Paul Dibb, *Review of Australia's Defence Capabilities* (Canberra: Department of Defence, 1986). The Dibb Review, commissioned by then Defence Minister Kim Beazley, drew the strands of Australian defense thinking together into a coherent policy and provided the foundation for a major white paper, *The Defence of Australia*, published in 1987.

that the Australian government would either have to vote long-term real increases in the defense budget or cut capabilities.

Canberra's review of Australia's strategic interests and objectives in the 1990s resulted in a much broader conception of the foundations of Australian defense policy.[11] Though the core defense priority remained the defense of the continent, Canberra also explicitly identified four additional sets of strategic interests and objectives.

First, in terms of fostering the stability, integrity, and cohesion of countries in Australia's immediate neighborhood, *Defence 2000* stated that Australia would be concerned with all major internal challenges to the stability of any of Australia's nearer neighbors, as well as any threat of outside aggression toward them. This new emphasis means that Australia has a vested interest in preventing foreign force positioning in neighboring states that might be used to attack Australia. Elsewhere the white paper explicitly mentions Australia's commitment to providing forces to help resist external aggression against Papua New Guinea or other Southwest Pacific Islands.[12]

Second, regarding the promotion of stability and cooperation in Southeast Asia, *Defence 2000* stated that Australia has a key interest in helping to maintain a resilient regional community in Southeast Asia that can cooperate to prevent the intrusion of potentially hostile powers into the region.

The third strategic interest focused on supporting strategic stability in the wider Asia-Pacific region, the white paper noted Australia's interest both in precluding the emergence of a security environment in the Asia-Pacific region dominated by any one power with strategic interests possibly inimical to Australia's, and in preventing destabilizing strategic competition between the region's major powers.[13]

Finally, *Defence 2000* articulated the need to "support global security." This would particularly include the UN's role in upholding global norms against interstate aggression and the role of the United States in maintaining and strengthening global security. This latter objective includes the maintenance of an international order that effectively deters aggression, combats specific global security challenges such as terrorism and WMD proliferation, and supports international efforts to respond to humanitarian crises around the world.[14]

---

[11] Department of Defence, *Defence 2000: Our Future Defence Force* (Canberra: Department of Defence, 2000), ch. 4.

[12] *Defence 2000: Our Future Defence Force*, 43–44.

[13] Ibid., 31.

[14] *Australia's Strategic Policy*, 32.

This new, broader conception of Australia's strategic interests carries significant implications for the Australian Defence Force (ADF). First, in order to buttress security in Australia's immediate neighborhood—a need clearly evident after East Timor—the ADF must be capable of both undertaking substantial independent operations as well as leading regional coalitions. Such ambitions will require an increased capability to deploy and sustain relatively light land forces for stabilization operations. To meet this need, the white paper broke with previous policy by stating that land force capabilities would in the future be developed specifically to meet the demands of deployments on Australia's doorstep.[15]

Second, if Canberra desires to support the wider regional strategic balance, then Australia would need to consider more carefully the kinds of capabilities necessary in the event of a conflict involving Asia's great powers—in particular China. Canberra recognizes that any significant Australian contribution to a U.S.-led coalition would utilize Australia's air and maritime capabilities. In order to operate effectively within U.S.-led coalitions against the more sophisticated air and naval forces that China and other regional great powers could potentially deploy, Canberra would have to make heavy investments in Australia's own such forces.

Canberra thus faced two options in 2000. First, Australia could expand its light land forces in order to ensure an enhanced capacity for operations in the immediate neighborhood. Alternatively, Canberra could sustain long-term investment in air and naval capabilities, thereby ensuring that Australian forces could both operate effectively against China and other regional powers as well as interoperate with those of the United States. Due to a strong economy, robust public support for higher defense spending, the continued deployment of major forces in East Timor, and a growing awareness of the complex and demanding strategic future the region faced, the government of Prime Minister John Howard decided both to significantly upgrade Australia's air and naval forces and to expand upon the army's capability to undertake sustained offshore deployments in lower level operations in the region surrounding Australia. In order to achieve these objectives, the Howard administration developed a detailed Defence Capability Plan (DCP) and made a commitment to increase defense spending by an average of 3 percent in real terms annually from 2001–11.

---

[15] *Defence 2000: Our Future Defence Force*, 79.

The Australian Defence Force: Current Capabilities and Future Plans

The implementation of the Canberra's DCP is providing Australia with significant modern defense capabilities. Australia's land forces are small but of high quality, and air and naval forces as well as information systems are comparable in quality to those being developed by larger regional powers like China. Current investment plans should allow Australia to remain the most capable maritime power south of China and east of India. The following sections outline the current and future development of the ADF in the areas of land, naval, and air forces, as well as information systems.

Land Forces

The 2000 White Paper obliges Australia's land forces to retain the capabilities to deploy and sustain a brigade as part of any operation in its nearer neighborhood while simultaneously maintaining a battalion ready to undertake a second operation upon short notice.[16] In order to achieve this goal, the army maintains six battalions prepared to deploy at less than 90 days notice, with most ready within 30 days. These include a parachute battalion, two light infantry air-mobile battalions, a motorized battalion, a mechanized battalion and a commando battalion. A special air service (SAS) regiment of around seven hundred personnel is also held at high readiness. These forces are organized into a Special Operations Group, a mechanized brigade, a light infantry brigade, and a motorized infantry brigade.[17] A part-time citizens reserve force of around 16,000 personnel is intended to sustain these forces. Artillery, aviation, air defense, logistics, and other units support the infantry battalions, and some 360 refurbished M113 armored personnel carriers, 250 DDGM light-armored vehicles (LAV), and around 300 Australian-designed Bushmaster protected trucks provide mobility. The aviation inventory consists of 36 Blackhawk, 25 UH1H, 6 Chinook, and 42 Kiowa helicopters, while orders have been placed for 12 Eurocopter NH-90 transport helicopters and a fleet of 22 Eurocopter Tiger fire support helicopters. Fixed-wing air transport is provided by 24 C-130, including 12 new J models and 14 Caribou.[18]

This type of force is clearly optimized for relatively small-scale, light operations most likely to occur in the immediate vicinity surrounding

---

[16] *Defence 2000: Our Future Defence Force*, 80.

[17] *Defence Almanac*, 17.

[18] Ibid., 21–22.

Australia, rather than for the large-scale heavier conflicts likely to occur in mainland Asia or in the Middle East. This should come as no surprise; in the 2000 White Paper the government explicitly rejected the development of heavier land forces:

> We have ... decided against the development of heavily armored forces suitable for contributions to coalition forces in high-intensity conflicts. These forces would be expensive, and are most unlikely to be needed in the defence of Australia or in our immediate region.[19]

Since 2000, however, army leadership has campaigned for what it calls the Hardened and Networked Army program, which is intended to develop land forces that are both harder-hitting and harder to hit, as well as exploit networking opportunities that will increase combat effectiveness.[20] What this means in practice is still unclear, but the trend in recent years has been to make the army heavier. In 2003 the government approved a proposal by the army to replace its fleet of 100 Leopard 1 tanks with about 60 M1A1 Abrams. The defense minister argued that, because they are needed to protect Australian soldiers engaged in operations within Australia's immediate neighborhood, the purchase of these tanks is consistent with current strategic priorities.[21] Equally likely, however, is that the purchase of these tanks reflects a desire by army leaders to develop heavier hardware capable of contributing to U.S.-led coalitions in higher-level operations. Canberra also plans to enhance Australia's amphibious capabilities by replacing two 8,500-ton amphibious transports (LPA) and one 5,800-ton landing ship with two amphibious assault ships (LHD) of over 20,000 tons and a roll-on/roll-off transport ship of comparable size.

Canberra has not clearly delineated the strategic rationale for these proposals, and in the absence of a clear explanation it would appear that these decisions are being taken in an ad hoc fashion. The greater issue revolves, however, around an unresolved debate between a view that land forces should continue to focus on independent operations capable of maintaining stability in Australia's immediate neighborhood, and a view that heavier forces need to be developed so as to provide new options for contributing to U.S. led coalitions beyond that neighborhood. Proponents of the first view argue that the army's chief deficiency is not that its inventory is too light, but that it is too small. With total full-time personnel numbering around

---

[19] *Defence 2000: Our Future Defence Force*, 79.

[20] Lt. Gen. Peter Leahy, "Address to CDSS," March 23, 2005, http://www.defence.gov.au/army/PUBS/CAspeeches/CA%20CDSS%2023%20Mar%2005%20(Final).pdf.

[21] Senator Robert Hill, "M1 Abrams Chosen as Australian Army's Replacement Tank," March 10, 2004, http://www.minister.defence.gov.au/Hilltpl.cfm?CurrentId=3643.

26,000,[22] the army struggles to meet the benchmark set in the 2000 White Paper. This severely limits the scale of forces that Australia can responsibly commit to more distant theaters of conflict.

Naval Forces

Australia's naval combat force consists of twelve small surface combatants and six modern diesel-electric submarines. According to current plans, the surface fleet over the next few years will consist of four U.S.-designed *Oliver Hazard Perry* guided-missile frigates (4,100 tons) and eight German-designed *Anzac*-class frigates (3,600 tons). Both classes have the ability to operate naval helicopters, and are undergoing combat system upgrades that will improve offensive and defensive capabilities. They are supported by an auxiliary tanker and an afloat replenishment ship. This is a capable fleet of small warships by regional standards, and one that can operate independently in a low- to medium-threat environment. This fleet has, for instance, made a useful contribution to U.S.-led coalition operations in the Persian Gulf, but would still have limited capacity for operations against more capable regional powers, especially within range of land-based air or capable submarine forces—such as in a Taiwan Strait conflict.[23] Canberra is, however, planning to build three Aegis-capable air warfare destroyers. Due to enter service around 2014–15, these destroyers would increase Australia's ability to contribute surface ships to major coalition operations in higher-level conflicts.[24]

Australia's six *Collins*-class submarines are large, long-range boats with a submerged displacement of 3,350 tons. After initial problems in several areas, these are now very capable boats that can operate effectively against any regional adversary. Their Mk 48 torpedoes are being replaced by the new ADCAP torpedo, and the submarine is also able to fire Harpoon anti-ship missiles (ASM). This fleet provides an effective deterrent against hostile naval operations in Australia's neighborhood, and would be well-suited to contribute to coalition naval operations in medium to high levels of conflict against any regional adversary.

The navy's surface and submarine capabilities are supplemented by the Royal Australian Air Force's (RAAF) 19 P-3C Orion long-range maritime patrol aircraft. These capabilities are now being upgraded with highly-capa-

---

[22] *Defence Almanac*, 41.

[23] Ibid., 15–16.

[24] Though whether they are a cost-effective investment for Australia remains subject to debate. See Hugh White, *Buying Air Warfare Destroyers: A Strategic Decision* (Sydney: Lowy Institute for International Policy, 2005).

ble surface-search radar and upgraded anti-submarine warfare (ASW) capabilities that, when combined with Harpoon missiles and Mk 46 torpedoes, provide a strong anti-surface and anti-submarine capability for operations against any regional adversary. In addition, Australia has a significant anti-ship strike capability via its F/A-18 and F-111 fleets, all of which are fitted for Harpoon missiles.

Air Forces

The 2000 White Paper describes air combat as the single most important factor in the defense of Australia.[25] Australia's core air combat capability today lies in its 71 F/A-18 Hornet multi-role fighters. Though the Hornets are older A/B models, they are undergoing an extensive upgrade program in order to fit new APG-73 radar, improved electronic warfare systems and cockpit displays, and new weapons.[26] These aircraft also carry Harpoon ASMs as well as conventional and laser-guided bombs.[27]

The Hornets will also be supported by six new and highly-capable Airborne Early Warning and Control (AEW&C) aircraft, with a 400 km-range phased-array radar and other sensors, all mounted on a B737 airframe (due to enter service later in the decade), as well as by a fleet of five Airbus 330 air-to-air refueling aircraft (which will replace three old B707 tankers around 2009).[28]

Australia has also traditionally placed a high priority on long-range land strike capabilities, and the 2000 White Paper made clear that the current administration intends to retain such capabilities. The new goal is to be able to mount sustained strike campaigns at reasonable risk against military targets "within a wide radius of Australia," and to be able to contribute to regional coalitions in the face of more capable adversaries."[29] In addition to the strike capability of the F/A-18s, which flew many successful strike missions in *Operation Iraqi Freedom* (OIF) in 2003, Australia operates F-111 long-range strike aircraft. The current operational fleet of around 21 aircraft is armed with laser-guided bombs and Harpoon ASMs. The F-111s have

---

[25] *Defence 2000: Our Future Defence Force*, 84.

[26] New weapons include the AIM 120 Advanced Medium Range Air to Air Missile and the AIM-132 Advanced Short Range Air to Air Missile, and later in the decade a new stand-off air to surface missile.

[27] Australian Strategic Policy Institute, *The Cost of Defence: ASPI Defence Budget Brief 2005–2006* (Canberra: Australian Strategic Policy Institute, 2005), 153–55.

[28] Ibid., 151–52.

[29] *Defence 2000: Our Future Defence Force*, 92.

been upgraded in various ways over recent years, and are now being fitted with AGM-142 ASMs.[30]

Over the next decade Australia plans to purchase up to one hundred F-35 Joint Strike Fighter (JSF) aircraft to replace both the F/A-18s and F-111s.[31] The possibility of price increases and delivery delays on the JSF raises significant doubts concerning whether the current fleets can be supported with adequate capabilities until the new JSFs arrive, and whether there will be enough money to buy one hundred of the new aircraft within an investment budget squeezed by other major projects (such as the air warfare destroyers).[32] Cuts to the fighter program are apparently being considered. Nonetheless, it is clear that Australia intends to retain and enhance its capacity to both defend its own air approaches against any regional adversary, as well as to join coalition air combat and strike operations in high-intensity conflicts. In recent years more attention has been given to developing air-combat and strike deployment capabilities offshore for the purpose of joining coalition operations away from Australia.

Information Systems

Canberra is undertaking substantial investments in information systems to support military operations, including a comprehensive "over the horizon" radar system covering Australia's northern air and sea approaches out to several thousand nautical miles. An additional area of investment is in satellite communication systems, including dedicated communications payloads on commercial satellites. Yet another focus is command support systems. Intelligence collection and processing has long been a high priority; as part of worldwide intelligence cooperation arrangements with the United States and other close allies, Australia takes special responsibility for its own neighborhood and retains a focus on key issues in the wider Asia-Pacific. Most attention in recent years has focused on the development of intelligence coverage of potential terrorist groups and operations, but Australia also continues to give high priority to broader strategic and operational intelligence questions in its region.

Australia's defense organization has been highly focused on the revolution in military affairs (RMA) and the emergence of network-centric warfare (NCW). Canberra has produced several broad policy documents that,

---

[30] *The Cost of Defence*, 155.

[31] For a full account of this major initiative, see Australian Strategic Policy Institute, *A Big Deal: Australia's Future Air Combat Capability* (Canberra: Australian Strategic Policy Institute, 2004).

[32] Hugh White, *Buying Air Warfare Destroyers: A Strategic Decision* (Sydney: Lowy Institute for International Policy, 2005).

drawing heavily on RMA concepts, offer visions for the way in which the ADF will be transformed over coming years; a program has already been set for their realization.[33] Though little tangible success has been achieved in translating these concepts into genuinely new approaches to the development and use of military capabilities, heavy investment in a wide range of information systems is slowly but surely leading to a more networked approach to warfare.

In these and other decisions about future ADF capabilities, interoperability with U.S. forces has been a key consideration. A history of cooperation—including frequent training, exercising, and service in coalition operations—means that Australian and U.S. forces have high levels of interoperability. The ADF is conscious, however, of the demands of sustaining those levels of interoperability. This is especially so in air and naval operations, as U.S. forces become increasingly sophisticated and networked. In order to maximize interoperability with U.S. forces, Australia has over recent years been increasingly prepared to overlook non-U.S. suppliers of critical systems. For instance, interoperability has been a key factor in decisions to seek U.S. solutions for submarine and surface ship combat systems and the JSF.

Since 2000

Events since the publication of *Defence 2000* have spurred an active public debate about the extent to which the policies of the white paper remain appropriate to Australia's future strategic situation. Canberra continues to reaffirm that this document remains the basis of Australia's strategic and defense policies, but the debate has not yet played itself out.[34] Major developments since the end of 2000 have affected Australia's perceptions of its strategic interests, objectives, and capabilities. Three sets of developments predominate: the global war on terrorism, new policies of engagement in Australia's immediate neighborhood, and the rising political and strategic influence of China.

---

[33] See for example, Commonwealth of Australia, *Defence 2020* (Canberra: Department of Defence 2003), http://www.defence.gov.au/publications/f2020.pdf; *Future Warfighting Concept* (Canberra: Department of Defence 2003), http://www.defence.gov.au/publications/fwc.pdf; and Senator Robert Hill, Minister for Defence, "Network Centric Warfare: Address to the ADF Network Centric Warfare Conference," May 20, 2003, http://www.minister.defence.gov.au/HillSpeechtpl.cfm?CurrentId=2770.

[34] Geoffrey Barker, "Score One for the Army," *Australian Financial Review*, April 18, 2005, 62.

The War on Terrorism

In the months since the inauguration of U.S. President George W. Bush, Howard seems to have moved Australia closer to the United States. Even before September 11, Howard was looking to put his own stamp on Australia's relationship with the United States, which, despite five years of coalition government, still conformed to the basic outlines set by his Labor predecessors. While in Washington, Howard aimed to promote a bilateral U.S.-Australia Free Trade Agreement that he hoped would transform the relationship and invigorate Australia's economy by integrating it with the world's most dynamic engine of innovation.[35]

After September 11, of course, Howard's hopes for a redefined U.S.-Australia relationship instantly refocused on the new security agenda of the war on terrorism. Howard followed European leaders in symbolically invoking the Australia-New Zealand-United States (ANZUS) Treaty in the first days after the attack, and committed Australia to wholeheartedly support its ally in the war on terrorism. Australia offered a range of combat capabilities for *Operation Enduring Freedom* in Afghanistan; along with other contributions, a company-size contingent of the SAS that fought alongside U.S. and British colleagues in the overthrow of the Taliban. Howard made clear from the beginning, however, that Australia would not provide forces for peacekeeping and reconstruction once the Taliban had been toppled.

By the time of this transition, the war on terrorism had started to take on a distinctly local and regional tinge for Australia. Evidence found in Al Qaeda camps suggested that active Al Qaeda affiliates in Southeast Asia were planning attacks on Western (including Australian) targets; it quickly became evident that Australia's periphery—in particular Indonesia—was home to active, effective, well-funded, and operationally capable Al Qaeda offshoots. On October 12, 2002 these affiliates struck in Bali, killing several hundred people, including over 80 Australian nationals. Henceforth, while continuing to recognize terrorism as a global problem, Canberra has turned its attention to the war on terrorism closer to home. Australia has been reasonably effective in fostering close cooperation on counterterrorism measures with Indonesia and other Southeast Asian neighbors, and has significantly increased intelligence and police cooperation.[36]

Australia's revised focus on the regional war on terrorism influenced Canberra's response to U.S. pressure on Iraq in 2002 and 2003. Early in 2002, perhaps buoyed by the strong domestic support for operations in

---

[35] White, "The U.S. and Australia in the Age of Terror."

[36] Commonwealth of Australia, *Transnational Terrorism: The Threat to Australia* (Canberra: Department of Foreign Affairs and Trade, 2004), http://www.dfat.gov.au/publications/terrorism/.

Afghanistan, Howard and his ministers indicated that they would be willing to join the United States should Washington launch military operations against Iraq. But as the year progressed, it became clear that Canberra was not prepared to make a large or sustained force commitment so far from home. Even before the Bali bombing, Howard said that any commitment of forces to Iraq would not come at the expense of the ADF's ability to respond to regional contingencies, and that any forces committed would be withdrawn quickly once Saddam Hussein had been removed. Australia eventually committed a small number of special forces, F/A-18 aircraft, naval ships, and other units—a total of around 2,000 personnel—to the opening phases of OIF. These forces made a useful contribution to the initial invasion: Australian special forces penetrated deep into Iraq in the early days of the operation and F/A-18s contributed to the strike campaign. Howard's contribution to Bush's small "coalition of the willing" was, however, important more for its political symbolism than its military impact. Moreover, most of Australia's forces were rapidly withdrawn after the fall of Baghdad. Only persistent pressure from Washington succeeded in persuading Canberra to send significant forces back to Iraq in early 2005, and back to Afghanistan in mid-2005.

Competing strategic priorities closer to home have not been the only reason for Australia's modest contribution in Iraq. John Howard has probably also attempted to limit his political liabilities. In this he has succeeded—many Australians have been uneasy about involvement in Iraq, but Howard's own standing has been damaged much less than British Prime Minister Tony Blair's. Nonetheless, the U.S.-led invasion of Iraq and the strategic doctrines that motivated the war have not been popular in Australia. As elsewhere, the spontaneous sympathy and support of late 2001 has been replaced by public debate about the future of the alliance.[37]

This disquiet is not only limited to what would in America be called liberals. Paul Kelly, Australia's preeminent political commentator and a robust supporter of the U.S.-Australian alliance, wrote in 2003 that:

> Australia prefers an America that values partnerships and coalitions, that utilizes soft as well as hard power, that emphasizes political methods as well as military ones. It is idle to suppose that any lurch to an American unilateralism would not erode the domestic political support within Australia for the alliance.[38]

---

[37] See, for example, William Tow, "Deputy Sheriff or Independent Ally? Evolving Australian American Ties in an Ambiguous World Order," *Pacific Review* 17, no. 2 (June 2004): 271–90.

[38] Paul Kelly, "Australian for Alliance," *National Interest*, no. 71 (Spring 2003): 92–93.

Howard has drawn criticism in Australia and Southeast Asia for appearing to have adopted some aspects of Bush's policies as his own. For example, he has pointedly kept open the option of preemptive military action in Australia's own region should that be necessary to forestall terrorist threats against Australia.

Controversy over Iraq has made the management of the alliance a matter of partisan politics in Australia for the first time in decades. Labor opposed Australia's support for OIF, and in early 2004 a new and inexperienced party leader, Mark Latham, committed his party to an early withdrawal of Australia's tiny remaining forces should Labor win the election later that year. Latham lost the election and was subsequently replaced by the experienced Kim Beazley, a former defense minister and highly articulate supporter of the U.S. alliance. Iraq, however, still remains a contentious issue between government and opposition. The past few years have clearly been difficult ones for alliance management in Australia; polls show that Australian voters have consistent doubts about U.S. policy under Bush, though they do remain strongly committed to the alliance itself.[39]

New Commitments in Australia's Immediate Neighborhood

In fact, the most visible change to Australia's broader strategic policy since the white paper of 2000 has not been in response to the terrorist attacks of September 11, but rather in the long-term erosion of effective government among Australia's small Pacific island neighbors. *Defence 2000* and other policy documents have consistently emphasized Australia's strong interests in the stability and viability of these countries. Fears of accepting open-ended commitments and being seen in a neo-colonialist light have, however, constrained Canberra's response to such concerns. In 2003, however, the government announced a reversal of previous policy on the long-running crisis in the Solomon Islands. Australia joined with other countries in the region (including New Zealand) in a major initiative to restore law and order in the Solomon Islands and undertake an ambitious ten-year program of political, social, and economic reconstruction in the country.[40]

Australia also began to adopt similar approaches elsewhere, especially in Papua New Guinea, its much larger and more deeply troubled former colony. In 2004 Canberra initiated a major program to support law and or-

---

[39] Ivan Cook, *Australians Speak: Public Opinion and Foreign Policy 2005* (Sydney: Lowy Institute for International Policy, 2005).

[40] The Solomon Islands, a former British Colony, was pushed to the brink of state failure by a low-level but persistent armed conflict between ethnic groups operating around Honiara, the capital. For details, see Elsina Wainwright, *Our Failing Neighbor—Australia and the Future of Solomon Islands* (Canberra: Australian Strategic Policy Institute, 2004).

der and improve financial management in Papua New Guinea. Though this "Enhanced Cooperation Program" has now run into significant political and legal issues, Australia is determined to commit resources and political capital to supporting effective government in its own backyard. Helping Papua New Guinea will require major commitments of resources and attention that will inevitably affect Australia's ability to engage elsewhere.

At home, Canberra has justified its new South Pacific activism partly on the grounds that, after September 11, allowing failed states on its doorstep raises the risk of terrorist attacks in Australia. Skeptics have suggested that the new policy reflects Howard's own version of some of the more interventionist elements of President Bush's policies. Concern over terrorism may have been a factor behind the new policy direction, but was hardly a key motive, since the risk of the South Pacific islands becoming a haven for terrorists is far from acute. The real imperatives to a more activist policy lie in the enduring interest that Australia has in stability in the South Pacific and in the growing legitimacy of more interventionist policies in the post-Cold War world. In many ways, Australia's large, if inadvertent, role in East Timor's transition to independence during and after 1999 was probably the more important signpost to this new policy direction.

Australia's new South Pacific engagement has so far not placed any exacting demands on its military. In the Solomon Islands, ADF elements provided logistic support and tactical backup in the early stages of deployment, but Australian police led security operations in both the Solomon Islands and Papua New Guinea. Canberra has raised the capacity of the Australian Federal Police force to undertake these and other international operations. The decision to place increasing responsibility for nation-building security operations into the hands of specially trained and organized civil police is one of the most interesting adaptations of Australia's security capabilities to the new demands of the post-Cold War era. The above mentioned trend toward heavier capabilities in the land force suggests that the ADF is, if anything, placing lower priority on this new engagement.

Australia's increasing commitments in its own immediate neighborhood have important implications for its alliance with the United States. Washington has welcomed Canberra's willingness to undertake independent action to stabilize its own neighborhood. At the same time, however, these commitments reduce Australia's capacity to assist the United States in other strategic theaters.

China

The third dynamic factor in Australia's strategic situation over the past five years has been China. Beijing's success in converting economic growth and booming trade into political influence and strategic weight has changed Australia's view of China in ways that run contrary to enduring elements of Australia's strategic outlook; such changes, in turn, have important implications for the U.S.-Australian alliance. Since Japan defeated Russia at Tsushima a century ago, Australians have been anxious about the emergence of an Asian power that could dominate the Western Pacific, and have looked to the United States to forestall that outcome by containing rising Asian powers.[41] This was the lens through which Australia first viewed the rise of China. Canberra recognized from the early 1990s that, as China grew, Beijing would seek to expand its influence throughout Asia, and perhaps aspire to hegemonic preeminence.[42] This prospect did not appeal to Canberra. In 1994 Australia's strongly Asian-oriented Prime Minister Paul Keating posed the question: "Do we want to be in the Chinese orbit? No, of course we don't...."[43] In 1997 an official Strategic Policy Review identified as one of Australia's enduring strategic threats the prevention of "the emergence in the Asia-Pacific region of a security environment dominated by any power(s) whose strategic interests might be inimical to those of Australia."[44] The drafters of this language had China principally in mind. They went on to write:

> It would not be in Australia's interests for China's growing power to result in a diminution of U.S. strategic influence, or to stimulate damaging strategic competition between China and other regional powers.... China will need to work hard to convince the rest of the region that its national objectives and the means it uses to achieve them will be consistent with the basic interests of its neighbors.[45]

These concerns regarding China amplified Australia's already strong desire to see the United States stay actively engaged in the Western Pacific.[46] Canberra recognized that this would require Australia to offer support for U.S. policy positions aimed at countering China's rise. The Howard administration faced this question during its first weeks in office, which also hap-

---

[41] Neville Meaney, *The Search for Security in the Pacific 1901–1914* (Sydney: Sydney University Press, 1976), 120–75.

[42] *Defending Australia: Defence White Paper 1994*, 9.

[43] Greg Sheridan, *Tigers: Leaders of the Asia-Pacific* (Sydney: Allen and Unwin, 1998), 137.

[44] *Australia's Strategic Policy*, 8.

[45] Ibid., 14–15.

[46] Ibid., 19. For an earlier reflection of the same idea, see *Defending Australia: Defence White Paper 1994*, 95.

pened to coincide with the Taiwan Strait crisis in early 1996. His new government gave strong and unqualified support to Washington; the Australian endorsement of the deployment of U.S. aircraft carriers to the vicinity of Taiwan particularly angered Beijing. Moreover, during the 1990s China began to loom larger in Australia's defense planning, and was a key factor in Canberra's decision to sustain relatively high investment in air and naval capability in the 2000 defense white paper. Ministers accepted that Australia needed air and naval forces capable of qualitatively matching China's emerging capabilities. Such considerations strongly influenced the pivotal decision in the white paper to fund large numbers of fifth-generation combat aircraft to replace the F/A 18s and F-111s.[47]

At the same time, however, China's economic growth has long been recognized as a key economic opportunity for Australia. The development of strong bilateral ties with China has been a broadly-shared objective across the Australian political spectrum ever since the initial opening of diplomatic ties in the 1970s. The bilateral trade relationship has never attracted the kind of domestic controversy so characteristic of U.S. policy toward China over the same period. Former Prime Ministers Bob Hawke and Paul Keating both worked hard to build trade ties with China, but John Howard has perhaps done more than any of his predecessors to place this issue at the center of Australia's foreign policy. Trade with China has consistently topped Howard's long-term policy priority list in Asia, and is his second-highest priority overall after the U.S. alliance. Howard's efforts have been amply repaid. Two-way merchandise trade between Australia and China has quadrupled in the past decade, and Australia's merchandise exports to China have grown by an average of 20 percent per year since 1998.[48] Recent growth in key mineral exports has been especially dramatic; the value of iron ore exports, for instance, has more than tripled between 2001 and 2004.[49] Australia's vision of its future prosperity is closely tied to hopes of ever-growing exports of raw materials to China's manufacturing juggernaut. An agreement to commence negotiations for a free trade agreement between the two countries, announced in 2005, has symbolized the promise of the relationship.

China's appeal to Australia extends beyond economics. Beijing's active diplomacy over the past few years has helped to foster a new and deeper sense of East Asian regionalism that positions China at the center. Australia

[47] Some reflection of the thinking on this issue can be found in Hugh White, "Australian Defence Policy and the Possibility of War," *Australian Journal of International Affairs* 56, no. 2 (2002): 253–64.

[48] Mark Vaile, Minister for Trade, speech, "Engaging China 2005" conference, June 8, 2005, http://www.trademinister.gov.au/speeches/2005/050608_engaging_china_2005_conference.html.

[49] Department of Foreign Affairs and Trade, *Australia-China Free Trade Agreement: Joint Feasibility Study* (Canberra: Department of Foreign Affairs and Trade, 2005), 14.

does not want to be excluded from the new dynamic, prosperous, Sino-centric Asia that seems to be emerging. Hence Canberra has made a major diplomatic and political investment by accepting an invitation to the inaugural East Asian Summit in Kuala Lumpur in November 2005—a meeting that will not include the United States. Canberra realizes that, if it wants to engage effectively with Asia in future, then Australia will have to accept the reality of Chinese political leadership in the region. Indeed, Australians are learning to view China in optimistic and pragmatic terms. They tend not to see China's growth—even its growing military capabilities—as a threat.[50] Despite occasional concerns regarding human rights, Australians generally accept the system of government in Beijing as legitimate, and China as a country with which they can do business. Little wonder then, that in a recent poll for the Lowy Institute for International Policy in Sydney, 69 percent of Australians said they had positive views of China, compared to 58 percent who said they had positive views of the United States.[51]

Australia's increasing acceptance of China's growing power and influence obviously raises issues for Canberra's strategic relationship with Washington. John Howard has understandably sought to downplay the likelihood of tension between Australia's relationship with China and the alliance with the United States.[52] Having obvious short-term appeal as a diplomatic and political gambit, this posture cannot mask the tough strategic choices that Australia is already being called upon to consider. Beijing has made clear that, in return for booming trade relations and a place in the political structures of a new China-led Asia, Canberra will need to pay more attention to Chinese interests on political and strategic questions. In particular, China apparently hopes to dilute U.S. influence over Australia's strategic policy and to secure Australian acknowledgement of China's regional leadership. In recent years this policy has been pursued quite deftly. China has largely abandoned earlier strident criticisms of Australia's alliance with the United States, and has instead focused its diplomacy on establishing China's place in Canberra's policy hierarchy.

Australia has responded to this pressure from China. One powerful symbol of the shift in relative weight accorded to China and the United States in Australia's international policy was provided in October 2003 when Howard agreed to simultaneous but separate visits to Australia by Presidents Bush and Hu Jintao. The two leaders were invited to address joint sittings of Australia's Parliament on consecutive days. Whereas this was routine proto-

---

[50] Ian McAllister, *Representative Views: Mass and Elite Opinion on Australian Security* (Canberra: Australian Strategic Policy Institute, 2005).

[51] Cook, *Public Opinion and Foreign Policy 2005*, 7.

[52] Howard, "Australia in the World," March 31, 2005.

col for a U.S. president, Hu's address marked the first time that any other foreign leader had been honored in this way. Hu's reception in Parliament, and his generally successful visit overall, conveyed an impression of symbolic parity between the two relationships in Australia's foreign-policy priorities. The impression of a new balance in Australia's relations with the two powers was amplified in Howard's words of welcome to Hu. He conjured an image of Australia as a country that would not take sides in disputes between the United States and China:

> Our aim is to see calm and constructive dialogue between the United States and China on those issues which might potentially cause tension between them, and it will be Australia's aim as a nation which has close but nonetheless different relationships with both of those nations to promote that constructive and calm dialogue.[53]

Howard reiterated this stance in a major policy speech to the Lowy Institute in March 2005: "we see ourselves as having a role in continually identifying, and advocating to each, the shared strategic interests these great powers have in regional peace and prosperity."[54] For the conservative, pro-U.S. leader of a country that describes itself as Washington's closest ally in Asia to portray his government as even-handed and neutral on issues of possible dispute between the United States and its major potential strategic competitor is both an important development and a major political victory for China.

On specific issues, Canberra has even shown itself willing to take the side of Beijing. In early 2005, for example, Australia pointedly declined to join the United States and Japan in pressing the European Union (EU) not to relax its arms embargo on China.[55] Later in the year, Australia's defense minister declined to follow U.S. Defense Secretary Donald Rumsfeld in questioning the rationale for China's military buildup.[56] Australia's long-serving foreign minister, Alexander Downer, likewise raised concerns in Washington by suggesting during a trip to Beijing that a U.S.-China conflict over Taiwan would fall outside the scope of the U.S.-Australian alliance, and that Australian military support for the United States in a war with China

---

[53] Howard, "Address to Joint Sitting of the Houses of Parliament."

[54] John Howard, "Australia in the World," address to the Lowy Institute for International Policy, Sydney, March 31, 2005, http://www.pm.gov.au/news/speeches/speech1290.html.

[55] Greg Sheridan, "PM Defies Bush Over China Arms," *The Australian*, February 12, 2005, 1.

[56] In June 2005, Senator Hill responded to questions in Beijing concerning Rumsfeld's earlier characterization of China's military buildup as unnecessary by stating that, "we accept that it is perfectly legitimate that China modernise its defence force..." See Stephen Wyatt, "Hill Shows His Moderate Side to a Bristling China," *Australian Financial Review*, June 17, 2005, 28.

over Taiwan was by no means a matter of course—a view clearly at odds with U.S. expectations.[57]

Interpreting these statements solely at face value, however, would probably be a mistake. The roots of public support for the United States in Australia go very deep, and Australia remains a close and dependable U.S. ally. Recent appearances to the contrary could be more the results of wishful thinking and inept diplomacy than of any deliberate and fundamental strategic realignment. In the long run, Canberra will continue to value and support the U.S. presence in Asia, both as a safeguard against the possibility that China's regional ambitions will expand from influence to hegemony, and to forestall the emergence of the kind of direct strategic competition between Japan and China that could destabilize and impoverish the entire region.

Even so, there remain important underlying differences between U.S. and Australian attitudes toward China. As long as China follows the broad approaches of recent years, Canberra will not support U.S. policies that presuppose or promote an adversarial relationship with China, and will encourage the United States to accept greater Chinese influence in Asia. Canberra will look to both Washington and Beijing to fashion a *modus vivendi* that accords China a reasonable level of increased influence commensurate with its growing power. Washington may not so readily accept such changes, however. Regardless, unless China suddenly pursues a drastic shift in policy, Australia will not support a U.S. approach that forces its allies to choose between the United States and China.

Competing Visions

Against the background of these three new influences on Australia's strategic policy, the past few years have witnessed an active debate concerning the conceptual foundations of Australia's defense policy and the kinds of capabilities that should be developed in the future. The issue of China, though probably the most momentous of the dynamic forces acting on Australia at present, has played little part in this debate. The key starting point has been the global security environment after September 11 and a discussion regarding the degree to which Australia's strategic and defense policies as set out in *Defence 2000* need to be revised in light of the terrorist attacks in New York and Washington. The main debate has evolved around the extent to which the war on terrorism would change the long-term roles

---

[57] Alexander Downer, media conference, Beijing, August 17, 2004, http://www.foreignminister.gov. au/ transcripts/2004/040817_ds_beijing.html.

required of the ADF.[58] This debate has merged with a long-running tussle concerning the appropriate balance between the land and maritime elements of Australia's defense posture.

Advocates of a higher priority for land forces have naturally adduced the war on terrorism as supportive of their case. They argue that in the post-Cold War era, and especially in the post-September 11 era, the risk of conventional state-to-state conflict had receded and the demands of sub-state and transnational security issues had significantly increased.[59] This approach would mean that Australia should spend less on high-cost air and naval forces suited to conventional inter-state conflict in the Asia-Pacific, and more on the kind of land forces suited to the complex wars of the postmodern era—wars in which adversaries are more likely to be non-state actors. This position has found support in the argument that—the terrorist threat in Australia's own region notwithstanding—the global war on terrorism demands a globalized response, and Australia should therefore focus less on its own region and invest more in capacities to join U.S.-led coalition operations beyond the Asia-Pacific.

The debate has pitted the established orthodoxy in Australian defense policy against a fresher approach more in tune with post-Cold War and post-September 11 realities. The traditionalist position, personified by Paul Dibb, gives primacy to developing forces designed for the direct defense of Australia from conventional attack. The reformist position, which emphasizes capabilities for global engagement in post-modern conflicts, has received wide support among academic and journalistic commentators, including conservative commentators who look to maximize Australia's capacity to support the United States in the war on terrorism. Within the Australian government, Defense Minister Senator Robert Hill was also in support of such arguments.[60] The *Defence Update* paper published in February 2003 made clear, however, that, for the time being at least, Australia's policy would broadly retain the strategic and defense priorities of the 2000 white paper. Some concessions were made to Australia's support for the "Bush doctrine" and what was then an imminent commitment to Iraq, but the new document made clear that Howard's government would limit its contributions to

---

[58] The ADF's capacity to respond to terrorist threats within Australia was quickly boosted with additional tactical assault and chemical and biological response capabilities, but these were changes at the margins and did not affect major capability priorities.

[59] Alan Dupont, *Transformation or Stagnation?: Rethinking Australia's Defence*, SDSC Working Paper, no. 374 (Canberra: Australian National University, 2003).

[60] Senator Robert Hill, "Beyond the White Paper: Strategic Directions for Defence," speech, Australian Defence College, Canberra, June 18, 2002, http://www.minister.defence.gov.au/HillSpeechtpl.cfm? CurrentId=1605.

any coalition efforts far from Australia's shores. The *Defence Update* stated specifically that:

> ADF involvement in coalition operations further afield is somewhat more likely than in the recent past. But involvement in coalition operations is likely to be of the type witnessed in Afghanistan, and which the Government has considered in Iraq if necessary—that is, limited to the provision of important niche capabilities.[61]

The *Defence Update* went on to explain that new circumstances indicate a need for some rebalancing of capabilities and priorities in order to take account of the new strategic environment—but did not elaborate on what that might mean in practice. Canberra has now announced that a new update paper will be published in late 2005, but has suggested that there will be no major revisions of the current policy. Moreover, Canberra apparently does not intend to review the long-term affordability of the current defense posture. Australia now spends a little under 2 percent of GDP on defense. Defense spending has grown steadily over the past five years and will most likely continue to grow by 3 percent annually (in real terms) through 2011.[62] After that, the outlook is less certain; there have been hints that the government would like to extend its funding growth commitment through around 2015.[63]

Given budget constraints, a review of long-term defense funding will become imperative soon. In order to restore a robust foundation for setting priorities, the conceptual debate between traditionalists and post-modern reformers will no doubt first need to be resolved. Confusion over the basic objectives of defense policy has led to a serious loss of coherence in force development decisions in recent years. A thorough review would likely begin by recognizing that, contrary to the arguments of the reformers, the 2000 white paper had already departed significantly from traditional defense policy by explicitly identifying a range of interests and objectives beyond the defense of Australia that the ADF would need to address.[64] The government will also have to recognize the demands that might be placed on the ADF not only by the war on terrorism and the need to support stability among Australia's small and fragile neighbors, but also by the rise of China.

---

[61] Department of Defence, *Australia's National Security: A Defence Update* (Canberra: Department of Defence, 2003), 24.

[62] Australian Strategic Policy Institute, *ASPI Budget Brief 2005-6* (Canberra: Australian Strategic Policy Institute, 2005), vi.

[63] Lincoln Wright, "Costello's Asian Arms Race," *Sunday Sun Herald*, May 1, 2005, 4.

[64] Graeme Cheeseman, "Facing an Uncertain Future: Defence and Security under the Howard Government," in *The National Interest in the Global Era: Australia in World Affairs 1996–2000*, ed. James Cotton and John Ravenhill (Melbourne: Oxford University Press, 2001), 207.

Conclusion

Over the next five to ten years, Australia will seek to maintain a strategic posture that combines active integration in the economic, political, and security affairs of an increasingly dynamic and integrated Asian region along with a solid U.S.-Australian alliance. To promote this strategic posture, Australia will need a defense force that can fulfill three roles. First, Australia will need forces that can contribute to wider national and international efforts to stabilize and support weak states in Australia's neighborhood. Military capabilities will more often than not play only relatively minor supporting roles in such efforts, but Australia must be ready to undertake and lead significant interventions that will place heavy demands on its defense capabilities. Second, Australia will need forces that can contribute to the stability of the wider Asia-Pacific region and can help protect Australia from any significant regional conflict. Finally, Australia will need forces that can contribute to international coalitions (especially those led by the United States) so as to address global threats beyond the Asia-Pacific region.

Maintaining armed forces capable of meeting this range of tasks will not be easy for a country of 20 million people—even if Australia's recent strong pattern of economic growth can be sustained. The country will need to make investments in two key areas. The first area is in enhancing air and naval capabilities. As an island continent in the maritime-dominated theater of the Western Pacific, air and naval forces are crucial. These two services allow Australia to make a serious contribution to regional coalition operations that are designed to maintain a stable strategic balance among the nations of Asia. They also increase Australia's ability to defend its own borders. Acquiring platforms and systems that can keep up with improvements in capabilities elsewhere in the region will require not only sustained increases in defense spending, but also highly disciplined and effective force development, acquisition, and support processes. It is not clear that today's Department of Defence organization can meet these challenges. Recent experience is not encouraging. Plans for major investments in large amphibious ships and air warfare destroyers have not been subjected to rigorous scrutiny, and may divert money and technical resources away from higher-priority capabilities such as submarines and combat aircraft. Critical programs, including one for combat aircraft upgrade, have been mismanaged. Convoluted procurement processes have caused delays in critical capabilities, particularly in the information and communications area.

Second, Australia will need to increase the size of its land forces. Six high-readiness battalions cannot provide adequate strength both to fulfill Australia's responsibilities in its immediate neighborhood and to provide sufficient forces capable of making substantial and sustained contributions to U.S.-led operations in places like Iraq and Afghanistan. The likelihood that peacekeeping and intervention operations will remain a high priority in the future suggests that the focus of development for Australia's army should be on numbers rather than weight. An upgrade to nine high-readiness battalions would be a step in the right direction.

By meeting these challenges, Australia can retain the capacity to be an effective strategic partner for the United States, can take the lead in managing problems and promoting shared interests in its own neighborhood, and can make useful contributions to U.S.-led coalition operations in a wide range of scenarios. Australia and the United States will likely retain close and effective cooperation in a wide range of regional and global security issues. The health of the alliance, and its strategic value to the United States, will depend, however, on the extent to which the United States and Australia can sustain compatible understanding of mutual interests and objectives. If, contrary to current indications, the United States returns to the more radical strategic policies of President Bush's first term, Australian support for the U.S. global posture would come under some strain. Moreover, if the United States adopts a confrontational approach to China's growing power in Asia, the alliance with Australia would be weakened.

This in turn suggests three ways by which the United States can strengthen its alliance relationship with Australia:

First, the United States can support Australia's goal to retain, over the longer term, air and naval capabilities that are a qualitative match to those of other militaries in the Western Pacific. The United States has long been generous in allowing Australia access to sophisticated and sensitive military technologies and systems. By maintaining and, if possible, even improving upon this access, U.S. interests can benefit by ensuring that Australian forces can pull their weight in maintaining regional stability.

Second, the United States can help clarify the confusion in Australia's current defense policy debate by offering clear and realistic assessments of what kind of capabilities Australia might best be able to contribute to future coalition operations. Current heavy investments in amphibious capabilities, for example, in part reflect a view that such forces would be welcome additions to U.S. capabilities. The United States, however, may prefer that higher priority be given to light infantry forces better suited to stabilization operations in places such as Afghanistan.

Third, both the United States and Australia would benefit from a comprehensive and frank exchange of views concerning their respective approaches both to China and to the broader evolution of Asia's strategic balance over the coming years. On this key issue the alliance risks becoming a victim of its own success. After many decades of easily attained consensus on key strategic issues, the alliance now lacks the habits of close and open dialogue on contentious issues. Canberra and Washington are not accustomed to discussing differences and finding ways to resolve them. As the junior partner, it is Canberra's responsibility to open this dialogue, but it is equally in Washington's interests to ensure that the dialogue is initiated as soon as possible.

Executive Summary

This paper analyzes the current security climate in Asia with regard to nuclear weapons, incentives for their acquisition, and different contingencies that may prompt nuclear proliferation.

MAIN ARGUMENT:
Powerful incentives exist in Asia for countries to acquire nuclear weapons, including desires to alleviate insecurity and increase international status. The U.S. will likely remain the key actor in preventing nuclear proliferation in the region but such efforts will require significant time and resources.

POLICY IMPLICATIONS:
- In order to prevent nuclear proliferation in Asia, Washington can enhance its security assurances to friends and allies and respond to proliferation pressures in a manner that does not aggravate U.S. relations with these countries, provoke the very proliferation pressures Washington seeks to curtail, or diminish U.S. stature and standing in the region. This task will grow increasingly difficult due to such factors as the phasing out of traditional instruments of U.S. credibility, a greater U.S. focus on the Middle East, and North Korea's nuclear weapons ambitions.

- The U.S. can retain its influence and standing in Asia by adopting a broader, more strategic approach that emphasizes less the war on terrorism and more the local needs and interests of countries in the region (such as free trade and economic development). A good place to start would be the creation of new multilateral arrangements that address transnational challenges such as energy insecurity, health pandemics, and narco-trafficking.

- The prospects for nonproliferation success in Asia rely on good governance, regional stability, and world order. A multi-pronged approach would include providing more support and resources to reinvigorate international efforts that manage nonproliferation, such as the IAEA, NPT, and the U.S. Cooperative Threat Reduction (Nunn-Lugar) program.

Prospects for Nuclear Proliferation in Asia

Mitchell B. Reiss

Asia is clearly transitioning into a position of world leadership. Asian governments, industries, and militaries are assuming roles and missions outside of their traditional domains, and the region is increasingly characterized by representative rather than authoritarian governments. As these countries develop domestically, they are concurrently improving commercial relations between and among each other. Protectionist barriers are being lowered, and cross-border trade and financial investment flows are proceeding smoothly. Asians are coordinating currency swaps through the Chiang Mai initiative. Bilateral free trade agreements are being negotiated; China and Japan have each offered free trade agreements to the Association of Southeast Asian Nations (ASEAN). It is only a matter of time, according to some analysts, until there are sub-regional and regional free trade zones.

Stability in the region has often seemed precarious, however. In spring 1996 tensions between the United States and China increased alarmingly over Taiwan; although conflict was averted, Beijing has subsequently engaged in a determined military effort to ensure it has more options should another crisis arise. In 1998, India and Pakistan each conducted a series of nuclear tests. Delhi and Islamabad have since continued to refine their nuclear capabilities, as well as develop more advanced missile systems. The neuralgic issue of Kashmir has defied resolution. Despite the 1994 Agreed Framework, North Korea has continued to pursue nuclear weapons in violation of its international treaty obligations. Since October 2002, Pyongyang has expelled international inspectors, withdrawn from the Treaty on the

Mitchell B. Reiss is Vice Provost for International Affairs at the College of William & Mary, and holds teaching positions both at the Law School and in the Government Department. He has served in a number of government positions, most recently as Director of Policy Planning at the State Department. He can be reached at <Reiss@wm.edu>.

Non-Proliferation of Nuclear Weapons (NPT), admitted to having a "nuclear deterrent," and declared that North Korea will continue to build nuclear weapons.

Long simmering historical animosities have resurfaced throughout Asia, often erupting into spasms of chauvinistic nationalism and boycotts of foreign products. Almost every country in the region has some unresolved territorial claim against a neighbor. Home-grown insurgencies throughout the region not only have exacted their deadly toll on civilians, but also have weakened efforts to embed democracy. Terrorism is on the rise, especially in Southeast Asia. Piracy, narcotics trafficking, and other criminal activities are rampant. Environmental degradation, energy scarcity, and health scares such as SARS and avian influenza present additional structural challenges to regional stability and prosperity. The dark side of China's remarkable economic growth—endemic corruption, a failing banking system, and uncontrolled mass migration from rural to urban areas—has raised doubts both about the country's economic health and even future stability.

In the past, affluent, technologically competent societies located in unstable regions and untethered to alliance networks have often considered nuclear weapons to be a possible solution to their security dilemmas. Will this pattern hold true for Asia? If so, for which Asian countries? What U.S. response could prevent or delay this prospect? What hedging or coping strategies might Washington adopt if prevention fails?

This chapter will briefly outline the traditional factors that have influenced the spread of nuclear weapons, both those that have inhibited proliferation and those that have fueled it. It will then examine particular proliferation "drivers" in Asia—those local, regional and international factors that will directly impact a country's decision to acquire or abstain from nuclear weapons. Finally, the chapter will analyze policy implications for the United States should additional Asian states acquire nuclear weapons, devoting special attention to Washington's ability to maintain its alliances and preserve its preeminent position in the region.

Nuclear Weapons: Incentives and Disincentives

Powerful incentives have always existed for countries to acquire nuclear weapons. The catalog of motivations has been well known, if not always well understood. These motivations differ from country to country, and all countries can claim more than one motive for their pursuit of the bomb.[1]

---

[1] An excellent overview can be found in Scott Sagan, "Rethinking Nuclear Proliferation: Three Models in Search of a Bomb," in *The Coming Crisis: Nuclear Proliferation, U.S. Interests, and World Order*, ed. Victor Utgoff (Cambridge, MA: MIT Press, 2000), 17–50.

The most common motive is the desire to alleviate insecurity. This insecurity could be rooted in a generalized fear of systemic threats. The demise of the bipolar security architecture with the end of the Soviet Union, the rise of terrorism, the dissemination of weapons of mass destruction (WMD), and the inability of the nonproliferation regime to deal adequately with the nuclear weapons ambitions of North Korea and Iran have injected greater uncertainties into the international system, thereby elevating the prospects for nuclear weapons acquisition.

Insecurity could arise in response to a specific, tangible challenge to a country or its interests. For example, nuclear arms have traditionally been viewed as useful for deterring aggressive behavior or actions by a more powerful rival, or a coalition of antagonistic countries. North Korea has openly cited this motivation in recent years, accusing the United States of harboring "hostile intent" toward it. Conversely, nuclear weapons may be viewed as a means to enhance security through coercion or intimidation of rival states. The mere threat to use such weapons could compel other countries to accommodate the nuclear power.

The perceived ability of nuclear weapons to confer status and prestige on the holder has also been part of the mix of incentives. Since the days of the Manhattan Project, splitting the atom has been considered an exceptional accomplishment, validating a country's indigenous scientific, engineering, and technical competence and symbolizing its modernity. In addition, important domestic constituencies and powerful bureaucratic forces have influenced the acquisition of nuclear weapons.[2] For example, nuclear weapons "champions" such as Homi Bhabha in India and A.J.A. Roux in South Africa skillfully used their influence to acquire the budgets, talent, and infrastructure for nuclear weapons projects.

Other factors may influence a country's thinking about the bomb Although not an incentive in the traditional sense, the increased opportunity to acquire nuclear technology, materials, and expertise may alter some countries' calculations. The infrastructure required to make the bomb—precision machine tools, advanced computing, and engineering competence—is far more widely available today than ever before. The activities of A.Q. Khan, the Johnny Appleseed of nuclear proliferation, exposed the flourishing in ternational black market in nuclear technology. Although this network has been curbed, others are still in business. Similarly, there have been numerous documented cases of attempted smuggling of nuclear materials from the

---

[2] There has been increasing awareness of this motivation in recent literature. See, for example, George Perkovich, *India's Nuclear Bomb: The Impact on Global Proliferation* (Berkeley, CA: University of California Press, 1999).

former Soviet Union; some of which may even have succeeded.[3] In addition, thousands of nuclear scientists, engineers, and technicians with specialized knowledge have been laid off in the former Soviet Union; some have already been recruited by North Korea and perhaps other nuclear aspirants. To cite one particular nightmare scenario, the collapse of centralized control in Pakistan could lead to the rapid dissemination of nuclear technology, fissile material, and bomb-making expertise around the world.

Matched against this array of incentives has been a set of proliferation disincentives. Foremost have been bilateral and multilateral security guarantees to come to the defense of a non-nuclear weapons state. In a multilateral context, the North Atlantic Treaty Organization (NATO) remains the preeminent example. Bilateral security guarantees, such as those between the United States and Japan and between the United States and South Korea, have similarly reassured some countries that there is little need to acquire nuclear weapons. Other countries lacking formal alliances or bilateral security relationships nonetheless fell under the penumbra of a nuclear power and thus felt less urgency to acquire an independent nuclear weapons capability. This thinking formed part of Sweden's strategic planning in the late 1950s when it examined its nuclear options.[4]

The technical difficulty of manufacturing nuclear weapons may act as an impediment, particularly the challenge of enriching uranium or separating plutonium for bombs; the costs associated with these facilities are also significant. A strategy of technology denial through export controls by the nuclear-armed states and advanced industrialized countries has been another disincentive to proliferation. In the early 1970s, the group of existing nuclear-armed states formed the Zangger Committee to restrict trade in sensitive nuclear or dual-use technologies.[5] These efforts were subsequently expanded in the mid-1970s by the Nuclear Suppliers Group, which continues to meet and regulate states' nuclear exports. Though having prevented countries from building nuclear weapons in few cases, technology denial, however, has been widely credited with raising the costs and extending the amount of time needed for counties to realize their nuclear ambitions.

Domestic opposition to nuclear weapons, whether by broad-based popular opinion or by the consciences of nuclear scientists, has rarely influ-

---

[3] See Graham Allison, *Nuclear Terrorism: The Ultimate Preventable Catastrophe* (New York: Henry Holt, 2004); and Matthew Bunn and Anthony Weir, "The Seven Myths of Nuclear Terrorism," *Current History*, April 2005, 153–61.

[4] Mitchell Reiss, *Without the Bomb: The Politics of Nuclear Nonproliferation* (New York: Columbia University Press, 1988), 37–77.

[5] The Zangger Committee was originally intended to assist countries in interpreting the NPT's Article 3(2). See David Fischer, *Towards 1995: The Prospects for Ending the Proliferation of Nuclear Weapons* (Aldershot, UK: UNIDIR/Dartmouth, 1993), 98–99.

enced decisionmaking. The best-known exception to this general rule has been Japan, where a strong anti-nuclear taboo has permeated society since the atomic bombings of Hiroshima and Nagasaki. Of greater consequence to proliferation decisionmaking has been the reluctance of states to alienate key allies and neighbors. The possibility that security assurances will be withheld or punitive economic and commercial sanctions will be imposed has acted as a key deterrent for some countries. This has been the case because the long lead time between making the decision to acquire a nuclear arsenal and actually having operational nuclear weapons could expose a country to months, or potentially years, of acute vulnerability.

Finally, a set of global nonproliferation agreements and arrangements has acted as a further legal and normative barrier to weapons acquisition. These agreements and arrangements—centered on the NPT and the International Atomic Energy Agency's (IAEA) safeguards system—largely codify a previous political decision and thus advertise to other states a signatory's determination not to pursue nuclear weapons. They are best seen as offering a form of public reassurance.

By the early part of the 21st century, there was widespread concern that the calculus of incentives and disincentives for proliferation had shifted during the 1990s, with incentives increasing and disincentives declining. No one event was determinative; rather, the cumulative effect of nuclear testing by India and Pakistan, the nuclear ambitions of North Korea and Iran, the inability of the IAEA to detect nuclear cheating—much less enforce compliance—and the unwillingness of the international community to halt or roll back these developments, all contributed to this shift. In addition, the growth of terrorist groups, the diffusion of bomb design information, and poorly secured or unaccounted for nuclear material in the former Soviet Union have further heightened anxieties. As George Tenet, then Director of Central Intelligence, testified in 2003, "The desire for nuclear weapons is on the upsurge. Additional countries may decide to seek nuclear weapons as it becomes clear their neighbors and regional rivals are already doing so. The 'domino theory' of the 21st century may well be nuclear."[6]

Proliferation "Drivers"

Will Asia be the site where this new domino theory plays out? Proliferation never takes place in the abstract, but rather occurs in specific countries that respond to local and regional factors, and in reaction to pat-

---

[6] Senate Select Intelligence Committee, *Current and Projected National Security Threats to the United States*, S. Hrg. 108–161, 108th Cong., 1st sess., February 11, 2003.

terns and trends in the general strategic environment. Even if one judges that North Korea is already a member of the nuclear club, there are—at least for the foreseeable future—actually a relatively small number of Asian dominoes. The three leading candidates for future proliferation in Asia are Japan, South Korea, and Taiwan.[7] Some "second-tier" candidates may also be interested in acquiring nuclear weapons, but this interest and any mature nuclear weapons capability would occur over a much longer time period.[8]

When looking at Asia, a number of factors, or proliferation "drivers," may increase the chances that these countries will develop an independent nuclear capability. These drivers are not mutually exclusive, and play out over different time frames. The first two are best categorized as prompt, or potentially prompt, drivers, while the others would grow in influence over a longer time period. Drivers also operate in different realms—within countries, throughout regions, and upon international institutions. Significantly, all types of drivers could overlap and interact synergistically in ways that would accelerate a country's strategic imperative to acquire a nuclear arsenal and thus spur proliferation throughout Asia.

A Nuclear-Armed North Korea

North Korea's continued investment in its nuclear weapons programs will critically influence the proliferation landscape of Asia in the near term. In July 2005, for example, the U.S. intelligence community asserted that North Korea possessed one or two nuclear weapons and enough separated plutonium for at least six more, has clandestinely pursued a uranium enrichment capability since the late 1990s, has repeatedly tested the conventional explosives package for an implosion device, and continues to produce plutonium at its Yongbyon reactor. For its part, Pyongyang admitted in February 2005 that North Korea possessed nuclear weapons. Furthermore, Pyongyang condemned President Bush and his administration in the strongest terms, and revealed in June 2005 that North Korea is continuing to build nuclear bombs.

A diplomatic solution to end Pyongyang's nuclear weapons program seemed possible when North Korea returned to the negotiating table in Beijing in late July 2005 for another round of Six-Party Talks. Still, obstacles to a lasting nuclear deal remain formidable. North Korea refuses to acknowledge that it has secretly acquired uranium enrichment technology, the

---

[7] See Kurt M. Campbell, Robert J. Einhorn and Mitchell B. Reiss, eds., *The Nuclear Tipping Point: Why States Reconsider Their Nuclear Choices* (Washington, D.C.: Brookings Institution, 2004).

[8] See Chaim Braun and Christopher F. Chyba, "Proliferation Rings: New Challenges to the Nuclear Nonproliferation Regime," *International Security* 29, no. 2 (Fall 2004): 5–49.

elimination of which would be an essential element of any comprehensive solution. Pyongyang must also give a complete accounting of its plutonium stores, some of which can be used for producing nuclear bombs, and verification measures would have to be implemented in order to ensure that Pyongyang abided by any deal it signed. Given the secretive nature of the North Korean regime and its past history of cheating on agreements, any inspection regime would need to be comprehensive and highly intrusive.

North Korea has made some of its interests clear, too. First and foremost, Pyongyang would like to be assured that the United States does not harbor "hostile intent" against the North Korean regime; in short, North Korean leaders would like assurances that the United States does not intend to bring about regime change. Second, Pyongyang would welcome greater financial assistance and infrastructure support to boost the moribund North Korean economy. Finally, Pyongyang wants eventually to normalize diplomatic relations with the United States, Japan, and South Korea.

Should the Six-Party Talks fail and North Korea retain its nuclear weapon program, all of the countries in the region would face increasing danger, although the nature and severity of the threat for any particular country would depend on that country's geographic proximity to, and political relationship with, Pyongyang. Reaction by countries in the region would also depend on the circumstances under which Pyongyang pursued its nuclear ambitions. For example, if North Korea had a recessed nuclear weapons program—with no tests or formal declarations of capability—other countries could choose to ignore the reality of North Korea's nuclear capabilities. In the short term, there would be less political pressure for those countries to respond by developing a similar capability, although a policy of "reality denial" would not likely be sustainable in the long term. On the other hand, if North Korea conducted a series of nuclear tests; further developed its missile delivery systems; preserved its present social, political, and economic structures; and did not temper its xenophobia, neighbors could consider North Korea a far more immediate security threat and even be compelled to acquire their own nuclear deterrent.[9]

Over time, a North Korea with any nuclear weapons, recessed or not, would have a significant impact on the region. Such a development would signal the impotence of the other members of the Six-Party Talks (the

---

[9] Although a North Korean nuclear test would make international headlines, more worrisome than the confirmation of a pre-existing technical capability would be the suggestion that North Korea had a sufficient inventory of fissile material to conduct such a test. For recent studies of North Korea's nuclear programs, see Joel S. Wit, Daniel B. Poneman, and Robert L. Gallucci, *Going Critical: The First North Korean Nuclear Crisis* (Washington, D.C.: Brookings Institution, 2004); and International Crisis Group, "North Korea: A Phased Negotiating Strategy," Special Report, no. 61, August 1, 2003.

United States, China, Russia, Japan, and South Korea)—the major Northeast Asian powers that publicly and repeatedly declared such a result "unacceptable"—to adequately address a core security threat and shape the strategic environment in Northeast Asia. Allowing such a situation would further expose the weaknesses of the international nonproliferation regime, specifically the IAEA and the NPT. Under such circumstances, Japan, South Korea, and Taiwan would all likely reconsider their earlier decisions to abstain from development of a nuclear weapons program.[10]

A Crisis over Taiwan

A crisis in the Taiwan Strait could have important proliferation consequences under a variety of scenarios. Such a confrontation would signal failure at multiple levels: the miscalculation of independence-minded leaders on Taiwan as to how far they could push China, Beijing's failure to reach out to moderate voices on the island, the People's Liberation Army's provocative modernization efforts aimed at Taiwan, and Washington's inability to restrain Taipei and jointly manage the issue with Beijing. Pointedly, the attractiveness of nuclear weapons to countries in Asia could be enhanced regardless of how the United States responds to a crisis over Taiwan.

The reactions of the key regional players, and the lessons other countries would draw from their response, would be sensitive to the particular circumstances. Naked aggression by China and an outright declaration of independence by Taipei are perhaps the least likely ways in which a crisis would start. Most likely is a series of smaller steps by either side aimed at modifying the status quo unilaterally, each move provocative but none constituting the actual spark that would ignite a military conflict. In this situation, the other party would feel compelled to respond or risk both alienating important domestic constituencies and suffering the loss of longstanding foreign policy goals. The forces of China, Taiwan, and the United States would be placed on alert and on patrol, thereby increasing the chances for miscalculation and reducing the ability of the political leadership to exercise control in a timely manner. Escalating tensions could spill over into an open military conflict. In such a scenario, the United States would almost certainly fulfill its legal commitment under the Taiwan Relations Act and come to the defense of Taiwan.

In the weeks or days of mounting tensions across the Taiwan Strait, Asian allies of the United States would face a stark choice between backing the United States or China. Washington would demand that allies provide, or be prepared to provide, bases, logistical and operational support, and per-

---

[10] See the chapters on Japan, South Korea, and Taiwan in *The Nuclear Tipping Point.*

haps even ships and troops. Assuming a positive response to Washington's request and a successful rebuff of China's attempt to alter the status quo through military force, the United States would send strong signals both to the region and international community that it was a staunch ally, willing to place its own forces at risk in defense of its friends, and the leader of a robust alliance network. U.S. credibility would be enhanced; the incentive for independent nuclear forces would decline.

Alternatively, Washington's allies could choose to slow roll or renege on their alliance commitments and remain on the sidelines. U.S. alliances in Asia are unlikely to survive long if U.S. allies stand on the sidelines, leaving the United States to defend Taiwan on its own. Washington would rightly question the continued utility of such alliances; under such circumstances, the United States might renounce its responsibility as the primary security provider for its Asian allies. Over time, these countries would seek alternative sources of security, including, perhaps, the security provided by a nuclear weapons capability.

The United States might also choose not to pursue a military response to Chinese aggression against Taiwan. Much would depend on how the crisis unfolded and whether Taipei was viewed as the provocateur, which could diminish sympathy and public support in the United States for Taiwan's defense. Despite differing perceptions of Taipei's culpability, U.S. abandonment of its longstanding ally would inevitably raise questions about whether Washington could be trusted to keep its security commitments. If the United States would not come to the aid of Taiwan, even if Taiwan had behaved irresponsibly, what guarantee could any country have that the United States would assist them in their moment of need? With diminished U.S. credibility, an independent nuclear arsenal could be considered an insurance policy in an uncertain world.

A Rising China, Retreating America, and Rearming Japan

A rising China, even if peaceful, may trigger insecurities in East Asia that could influence decisions on nuclear weapon acquisition.[11] Most worrisome from the standpoint of proliferation would be if such a rise occurred concomitantly with a U.S. retreat from Asia, which would create a security deficit that traditional U.S. allies such as Japan might seek to fill through the acquisition of nuclear weaponry.

---

[11] For a recent U.S. government analysis of China's rise, see Department of Defense, "The Military Power of the People's Republic of China, 2005," annual report to Congress, http://www.defenselink. mil.news/Jul2005/d20050719china.pdf.

A rising China. For the past decade, China's economy has grown at a remarkable clip, averaging 9 percent per year. China has been the engine powering development throughout much of Asia, especially in the aftermath of the 1997–98 Asian financial crisis. More recently, Beijing has placed this economic strength, with currency reserves in excess of $600 billion, in service to an increasingly sophisticated diplomatic strategy.

China has apparently assimilated Joseph Nye's lessons about the uses of "soft power" as a means to enhance its position in Asia.[12] In the words of one expert on Asia, "China's extraordinary economic dynamism has accelerated the process of integration and accommodation with nearly all its neighbors…"[13] Bilaterally, Beijing has engaged in joint ventures with other countries in the region (especially in Southeast Asia), invested commercially in these countries, signed free trade agreements with ASEAN, and opened its markets—including its agricultural market—to its neighbors.

Beijing has also used this "soft" approach to enhance China's security position in the region.[14] Multilaterally, Beijing has shaped the regional economic and security architecture in order to maximize China's influence. Beijing co-founded the Shanghai Cooperation Organization (which operates in the post-Soviet space), plays a leading role in ASEAN+3, has formalized annual trilateral foreign ministerial meetings with Japan and South Korea, and has recently been pushing a new mechanism, the East Asian Summit, which Beijing is expected to shape and lead. This astute diplomacy has been spearheaded by a new generation of talented, engaging, and highly effective foreign service officers.

One of the results of these diplomatic efforts has been to marginalize the United States. Washington is not a party to any of the regional institutions that China promotes and which are now setting the future Asian agenda. To be sure, the United States does not have to belong to every international organization, but China is defining multilateralism for the region in ways that specifically exclude the United States.[15] The larger pattern seems clear: Beijing is trying to push Washington off the continent and out of Asia.

---

[12] See Joseph S. Nye, *The Paradox of American Power: Why the World's Only Superpower Can't Go It Alone* (New York: Oxford University Press, 2002); and Joseph S. Nye, *Soft Power: The Means to Success in World Politics* (New York: Public Affairs, 2004).

[13] Jonathan D. Pollack, "The Bush Administration and East Asia: Does the United States Need a New Strategy?" in *George W. Bush and East Asia—A First Term Assessment*, ed. Robert M. Hathaway and Wilson Lee (Washington, D.C.: Woodrow Wilson International Center for Scholars, 2005), 99–116.

[14] See, for example, "China and Indonesia Seal Strategic Pact," *International Herald Tribune*, April 25, 2005; "Korea Steps Up Military Cooperation with China," *Chosun Ilbo*, April 4, 2005; and "Philippines, China Agree to Explore Possible Military Ties," *Defense News*, April 27, 2005.

[15] I am indebted to Evan Feigenbaum for this point.

Will China always be viewed as the benign and benevolent neighbor? As China continues to rise, will countries in the region acquiesce to China or will they seek to qualify and balance against its power? At what point does China's influence become dominance in the eyes of its Asian partners? Already, one can detect the beginnings of a backlash in Japan and, to a lesser extent, in South Korea.

Still, fear of a rising China by itself may not be sufficient to propel countries in the region to build nuclear weapons, at least in the short term. Over time, however, these calculations could change if combined with other proliferation drivers.

A retreating America. Lack of confidence in the United States as a security provider could be one such driver. According to a veteran scholar of Asia, "The trend is away from the role of the United States as a patron, the dominating force in alliances and regional affairs..."[16] At the same time that China is playing a sophisticated long-term game, there is the prospect that the U.S. role in Asia may diminish over the coming decades.

There is ample precedent for a U.S. disengagement from Asia, particularly from the Korean Peninsula. The Bush administration's decision to remove 12,500 troops from South Korea over the next few years as part of a larger force relocation effort is only the latest effort by Washington to reduce the U.S. military presence in Asia. Under President George H.W. Bush in 1991, the White House announced the removal of all land, sea, and air-launched nuclear weapons from South Korea. Earlier, in July 1977 President Jimmy Carter announced plans to withdraw all remaining U.S. troops from Korea during the next four to five years. Moreover, in July 1969, after only six months in office, President Richard Nixon announced the "Guam doctrine," which called on Washington's Asian allies to become more self-reliant in their own defense in order to compensate for Washington's growing commitment to the war in Indochina. Over the next three and a half years, the United States withdrew 24,000 troops from the Republic of Korea (ROK).

In addition to the historical record of the United States pulling back from Korea, there is the increasing likelihood that Seoul could push Washington away. A "push-pull" dynamic has already begun to develop, with strong voices in both societies wanting to redefine the alliance in ways that have already strained, and perhaps could end, the relationship. One source of tension has centered on the type of incidents that occur wherever U.S. forces are stationed overseas, such as disputes over the status of forces agreement, base

---

[16] Robert A. Scalapino, "America's Role in Asia—the Evolution Required," in *The Newly Emerging Asian Order and the Korean Peninsula*, Korea Economic Institute, Joint U.S.-Korea Academic Studies, vol. 15, 2005, 216, http://www.keia.com/2-Publications/2-3-Monograph/Monograph2005/Scalapino.pdf.

relocations, perceived lack of adequate consultations, and the tragic deaths of two young school girls by a U.S. armored personnel carrier in June 2002.

Another source of tension involves differing approaches to North Korea. Increasingly, U.S. and ROK officials question whether they share the same strategic assumptions concerning the nature of the North Korean regime and the threats Pyongyang poses to regional and international security. Beginning with the Kim Dae-jung administration's "sunshine" policy and accelerating under President Roh Moo-hyun's "peace and prosperity" policy, Seoul has apparently determined that broad engagement with Pyongyang, as opposed to isolation, would best produce a softening of North Korea's hard-line stance, albeit over time. In South Korea, the near-term threats posed by North Korea's conventional forces, ballistic missiles, and nuclear weapons has either been minimized or dismissed altogether.[17] Washington, on the other hand, views North Korea in more Manichean terms, with Kim Jong Il as an illegitimate tyrant who starves his own people and threatens international security with ballistic missiles and WMD.

Deeper, structural fault lines in the U.S.-ROK relationship are also present. Historical memories of U.S. heroism and sacrifice during the Korean War are fading, along with gratitude for the economic assistance that fueled South Korea's rise to economic prosperity. For many South Koreans, especially the younger generation, the United States—not North Korea—is considered the greatest threat to South Korean security. The so-called 386 generation—those currently in their thirties, educated in the 1980s, and born in the 1960s—instead associates the United States with the 1980 Kwangju massacre, remembers U.S. support for South Korea's military regimes, and evinces greater confidence about Seoul charting its own future.[18]

The Blue House recently stated its desire to chart a more independent future, though the details remain vague. President Roh declared that the ROK military should be independent of the United States[19] and that South Korea should play a "balancing" role in Northeast Asia: "We will safeguard peace in the region as an important balancing factor in Northeast Asia,"

---

[17] For example, in a major speech in Los Angeles immediately after President Bush's reelection, President Roh indicated that Seoul would not support either military or economic pressure to shape Pyongyang's behavior. Roh Moo-hyun, "The U.S.-Republic of Korea Alliance and the Situation on the Korean Peninsula," speech, Los Angeles World Affairs Council, November 12, 2004.

[18] Recent public opinion polls indicate a marked split in attitudes toward the United States between those Koreans over 45 and those younger than 45. See James Marshall, "South Koreans See Two Faces of America," U.S. Department of State, Office of Research Opinion Analysis, October 17, 2002.

[19] Roh first publicly stated the goal of ROK military independence within a ten-year time period on August 15, 2003. See also *Joongang Ilbo*, "Ministry Seeks Independence for Military," April 28, 2005.

adding that "Within ten years we should be able to develop our military into one with full command of operations."[20]

Even if these statements are best viewed as aspirational rather than operational (note that current ROK defense budgets are robust but inadequate to implement Roh's vision), they nonetheless raise questions concerning the future of the alliance. As U.S. forces are downsized on the Korean Peninsula, Seoul will begin to better understand what a future without any U.S. military presence would be like. No longer anchored to the United States, but still situated in a dangerous region with three nuclear-armed neighbors, Seoul might view nuclear weapons as necessary for South Korea's long-term independence and survival.[21]

A rearming Japan. Another likely consequence of a rising China and a retreating United States would be a rearming Japan. For many years, Japan has boasted one of the world's largest defense budgets, but its effectiveness as a fighting force was qualified by self-imposed constraints. In the past few years, however, Japanese leaders have lifted many of these constraints. As Japan has become a more "normal" state in security terms, Tokyo has taken a number of steps many thought unthinkable. Most strikingly, Japan dispatched its Self-Defense Forces to Iraq and even though they remained in a non-combat role, this was the first time that the Japanese military was dispatched to a combat zone since the end of World War II.[22] Japan has also integrated its planning and programs more closely with the United States on ballistic missile defense, the potential defense of Taiwan, and counter proliferation efforts (by joining the Proliferation Security Initiative [PSI]). In February 2005 the defense and foreign secretaries from the United States and Japan codified this relationship by signing a joint statement on common regional and global strategic objectives.[23]

The emergence of an increasingly robust Japanese military is set against a backdrop of concerns in Japan regarding the international nonproliferation regime, the North Korean nuclear and ballistic missile threats, the rise

---

[20] Roh Moo-hyun, address, 53rd Commencement and Commissioning Ceremony of the Korea Air Force Academy, March 8, 2005, http://www.cheongwadae.go.kr; and Roh Moo-hyun, address, 40th Commencement and Commissioning Ceremony of the Korea Third Military Academy, March 22, 2005, http://www.cheongwadae.go.kr.

[21] During the U.S. withdrawal from Vietnam, South Korea—doubting the U.S. security commitment—tried to acquire nuclear weapons. See Jonathan D. Pollack and Mitchell B. Reiss, "South Korea: The Tyranny of Geography and the Vexations of History," in *The Nuclear Tipping Point*, 254–92.

[22] In addition, the Japan Maritime Self-Defense Force participated in tsunami relief efforts in late 2004 and early 2005 in Southeast Asia, and Tokyo participated in the annual *Cobra Gold* military exercises in Thailand in May 2005 for the first time.

[23] See U.S. Department of State, "Joint Statement of the U.S.-Japan Security Consultative Committee," February 19, 2005, http://www.state.gov/r/pa/prs/ps/2005/42590.htm.

of China, and overall concerns regarding Washington's ability to manage the regional security environment in a manner that safeguards Japan's interests.

From Japan's perspective, recent developments have eroded the underpinnings of the nonproliferation regime. In May 1998 India and Pakistan each conducted a series of nuclear tests; subsequent international sanctions were ineffective in penalizing the two South Asian powers. A few months later, North Korea test-launched a Taepodong-1 ballistic missile over Japan's Honshu Island. Combined with the demise of the 1994 Agreed Framework and the inability of the nonproliferation regime or international community to enforce Pyongyang's compliance with its non-nuclear commitments, North Korea has subsequently loomed larger as a strategic threat to Japan.

China's ongoing military modernization has also compounded Japanese anxieties of a new regional rivalry. A 2003 Japan Defense Agency white paper questioned whether China's military modernization plans exceeded what was necessary for the defense of China.[24] A newly aggressive China, for example, has repeatedly sent its vessels into Japanese waters to assert territorial claims.

All of these anxieties have existed previously in some form and have proven manageable. In the past, U.S. leadership has been a constant; now Japan increasingly views it as a variable.

Some Japanese officials question the shift in U.S. strategy from addressing known threats, such as North Korea, to preparing for prospective threats and unknown contingencies anywhere in Asia. It is unclear whether Tokyo sufficiently understands the roles Washington expects Japan to play in some of these other contingencies, such as a crisis in the Taiwan Strait. Further, despite differences with Seoul, Tokyo likely fears the erosion of the U.S.-ROK alliance and possible implications for the long-term basing of U.S. forces on the Korean Peninsula. Should the United States withdraw from South Korea, Tokyo may find it hard to justify the continued maintenance of U.S. bases in Japan to a domestic audience.

Perhaps most importantly, Washington's handling of the North Korea problem worries Tokyo. Over the past four years, North Korea has increased its nuclear capability significantly, thus also increasing the risk it poses to Japan and others. The inability of the Bush administration, as of July 2005, to successfully address this core security threat presented by a charter member of the "axis of evil" has damaged U.S. standing in both Japan and the rest of Asia.

There is a great distance between a militarily resurgent Japan and a Japan that seeks nuclear weapons. Indeed, even without a perceptible U.S. retreat

---

[24] Note that fears of China rising have been exacerbated by concerns of "Japan passing" due to its "lost decade" of stagnant economic growth.

from East Asia, Japan has been steadily improving its defense capabilities and more boldly defending its national security interests.[25] Yet the deterioration of the nonproliferation regime, the increased North Korean nuclear and ballistic missile threat, the longer-term challenge posed by China, and emerging doubts regarding U.S. strategy and leadership all have bearing on Tokyo's military posture. In recent years, Japanese politicians have publicly discussed the nuclear option, a once-taboo subject.[26] Should these trends continue, Tokyo may seriously consider acquiring nuclear weapons.

Changes in U.S. Security Strategy

Changes in U.S. security strategy may also influence proliferation decisions in Asia. The National Security Strategy of the United States (NSS), issued in September 2002, indicated that the United States would respond preemptively and, if need be, unilaterally, to the threats posed by the union of terrorists and WMD. The NSS stated:

> The greater the threat, the greater is the risk of inaction, and the more compelling the case for taking anticipatory action to defend ourselves, even if uncertainty remains as to the time and place of the enemy's attack. To forestall or prevent such hostile acts by our adversaries, the United States will, if necessary, act preemptively.[27]

Issued a few months prior to the start of the Iraq war, this language closely associated preemption with the looming war in Iraq and appeared to elevate a military option available to every U.S. president to the level of a "new" doctrine for meeting the threats of the 21st century. The NSS raised questions as to where and when Washington would find militarily preemption acceptable, but the Bush administration has done little to clarify the parameters or the finer points of the NSS's emphasis on preemption, or even how this concept might trespass analytically into preventive war.[28] For a number of reasons, there is concern that the United States will now place greater emphasis on using military rather than diplomatic means to resolve disputes: the willingness of the United States to use military force in Afghanistan and Iraq, confrontational statements made by senior U.S. offi-

---

[25] See, for example, "Japan's Defense Chief Given Power to Shoot Down Missiles," *New York Times*, July 23, 2005.

[26] See Kurt M. Campbell and Tsuyoshi Sunohara, "Japan: Thinking the Unthinkable," in *The Nuclear Tipping Point*, 238–39.

[27] The White House, "The National Security Strategy of the United States of America," 10, http:// whitehouse.gov/nsc/nss.html.

[28] For two useful discussions of preemption, see Robert S. Litwak, "The New Calculus of Preemption," *Survival* 44, no. 4 (December 2002); and M. Elaine Bunn, "Preemptive Action: When, How and to What Effect?" *Strategic Forum*, no. 200 (July 2003), http://www.ndu.edu/nduspeeches/bunn.htm.

cials to both allies and adversaries, the overwhelming power of U.S. conventional forces, and the subjective nature of determining when threats might mature to the point where they are deemed imminent and thus subject to preemptive attack (made even more problematical by erroneous estimates of an Iraqi WMD capability before the war).

In the wake of the NSS and the Iraq war, some countries may feel increasingly threatened by the United States, and see themselves as no match for the weight and sophistication of U.S. conventional forces. The leadership of those countries, hence, may conclude that only a nuclear deterrent could equalize Washington's conventional superiority and prevent the United States from seeking regime change. Indeed, this was the lesson some strategists took away from the first Gulf War, arguing that the United States would not have fought Iraq in 1991 if Saddam had possessed nuclear weapons.[29] Current administration critics hold that in the Asian context, President Bush's naming of North Korea as an "axis of evil" member in his January 2002 State of the Union Address has led to an acceleration of Pyongyang's drive toward improved nuclear capabilities.

A strategic shift by the United States away from East Asia could also influence nuclear decisionmaking in the region. In the past few years, the majority of U.S. time, effort, and attention has focused on the greater Middle East, sometimes referred to as the arc of instability, which stretches from northern Africa to southwest Asia. The United States has identified this region as the primary focus for its post-September 11 foreign policy. Post-war stabilization efforts in Afghanistan and Iraq, the nuclear threat posed by the Islamic Republic of Iran, and the task of helping democratize the entire region all pose long-term challenges for the United States.

East Asia could be relatively shortchanged by this new emphasis. According to one analyst, "Without question, the Bush Administration's open-ended preoccupations with Iraq and Islamic [sic] terrorism have deferred or delayed full attention to regional strategy."[30] A United States that is seen as neglecting its responsibilities as a stabilizing force in East Asia—the provider of security "oxygen" for development—could cause countries to question U.S. interest and credibility, and could be another factor that spurs those countries to assume a greater responsibility for their own defense, one that might eventually include the pursuit of nuclear weapons.

---

[29] For a thoughtful treatment of this subject, see Stephen Peter Rosen, "Nuclear Proliferation and Alliance Relations," in *The Coming Crisis*, 126–56.

[30] Pollack, "The Bush Administration and East Asia."

Changes in U.S. Nuclear Strategy

The U.S. reliance on nuclear weapons is sometimes cited as a reason why other countries acquire nuclear weapons. This correlation is questionable at best and spurious at worst. U.S. possession of nuclear weapons not only plays an important role in deterring threats and aggression against the United States, but formal and informal agreements with U.S. friends and allies around the globe also reduce proliferation motivations by offering extended deterrence. As long as these countries feel they can rely on the United States for security, they have less reason to develop independent nuclear capabilities.

As for other countries not under the U.S. nuclear umbrella, the size and orientation of the U.S. nuclear stockpile alone are likely to come far down the list of factors influencing the decision to build nuclear weapons. As two experts with extensive government experience recently observed:

> Bush administration policies to continue improving the US nuclear arsenal will have little or no *direct* effect on the nuclear choices of others—either to stimulate them to acquire nuclear weapons or to discourage them from doing so. Furthermore...the allegation that the United States has not sufficiently reduced its vast stockpiles of nuclear weapons and therefore failed to live up to its NPT "bargain" is also judged to have little immediate relevance to in the complex decision-making surrounding those choices.[31]

Examinations of countries that have considered yet rejected the acquisition of nuclear weapons have likewise found that the U.S. nuclear arsenal had little or no influence on these decisions.[32]

This calculus could change, however, were the United States to resume nuclear testing as part of a dedicated program to develop new nuclear warheads. Although there is no indication that the Bush administration is interested in resuming nuclear testing, the administration has shown interest in researching new types of nuclear weapons to target hardened, underground targets and biological and chemical stockpiles. While such research programs are still budgeted modestly by Department of Defense standards, these programs suggest to some critics an ongoing interest in new weapon designs and, eventually, nuclear tests. If the United States were to resume testing (note that Washington is not a party to the Comprehensive Test Ban Treaty), Russia and China might feel compelled to match the United States with tests of their own. Moreover, India, Pakistan, or North Korea would

---

[31] Campbell and Einhorn, "Concluding Observations," in *The Nuclear Tipping Point*, 323 (emphasis in original).

[32] See Reiss, *Without the Bomb*; and Reiss, *Bridled Ambition*.

certainly pay a lower political price if they tested nuclear weapons in this environment. The same would be true for new entrants to the nuclear club.

The Erosion of the International Nonproliferation Regime

Events at the 2005 NPT Review Conference reinforced growing concerns about the erosion of the international nonproliferation regime. The regime's efforts to handle the tough cases like North Korea and Iran—by expanding the IAEA's verification mandate, generating a consensus on enforcement measures, and punishing those who do not comply with their treaty commitments—have all failed, at least so far. If the regime's inability to fulfill its mandate persists, it may signal the death knell for global efforts to stem the tide of nuclear proliferation. There are also worrying changes on the supply side, such as the potential revival of A.Q. Khan's black market network (or its facsimile) in nuclear and ballistic missile technologies, and the possibility of instability in Pakistan turning the country into a WMD supermarket. Taken together, these developments cause many to fear that proliferation could easily spin out of control, causing a general breakdown of the international system. A new member of the nuclear club, the actual use of nuclear weapons by a state or terrorist group, and a return to nuclear testing would challenge world order and stability. In such a Hobbesian environment, countries could view nuclear weapons as essential for preserving their national security.

Policy Implications for the United States

What are the policy implications for the United States of proliferation trends in Asia? How can Washington anticipate and counter these proliferation drivers?[33]

For the past sixty years, the United States has been a stabilizing influence in Asia. If Washington is no longer able or willing to play that role in the coming decades, chances for combating the spread of nuclear weapons will diminish. The challenge for the United States is to respond to these proliferation trends in a manner that does not aggravate U.S. relations with key friends and allies, does not provoke the very proliferation forces Washington seeks to curtail, and does not diminish U.S. stature and standing in the region.

---

[33] I am assuming that the United States would not want to encourage even selective proliferation in Asia, although the argument is sometimes made that the nuclear arming of U.S. allies in the region would serve U.S. interests. Without addressing this argument in detail here, it should be recalled that the United States has *never* initially supported the acquisition of nuclear weapons, even by our allies in World War II.

Preventing the spread of nuclear weapons in Asia will require skill and patience, and the collaboration of likeminded countries in the region. Despite Washington's best efforts, proliferation may nonetheless occur, but the following four policy options may ameliorate the worst of these trends and retard, if not prevent, the spread of nuclear weapons. As with proliferation drivers, no single policy prescription is likely to be determinative. Rather, success will be cumulative. Victories in one area will likely lead to successes in other areas. The same will be true with defeats.

North Korea

It may already be too late to persuade North Korea to reverse course and comprehensively and verifiably abandon its nuclear weapons programs. Should the United States deem that a diplomatic solution is beyond its reach, then Washington would need to consider alternative strategies.

One possibility is military strikes. President Bush has repeatedly stated that "all options are on the table." There is, moreover, little doubt that the United States has the capability to eliminate the Kim Jong Il regime, although the costs of doing so would be high. Even a limited attack on North Korea's nuclear facilities, however, raises daunting challenges. First, U.S. military planners may not know for certain the location of all of North Korea's critical nuclear infrastructure, especially any separated plutonium; how can you hit what you can't find? Second, the United States might not be able to prevent North Korea from retaliating massively; Seoul, a city of 12 million people, would be particularly vulnerable. Ensuring intrawar deterrence— i.e., signaling to Pyongyang that our military objectives were limited to the elimination of its nuclear weapons program and not the elimination of the regime—may be impossible. Would Washington signal such intentions to Pyongyang in advance? If so, would Kim Jong Il find such assurances credible? Could he even distinguish between a limited and all-out military campaign?[34] Third, our South Korean ally would not likely be willing to risk a re-run of the first Korean war; South Korea would not support any decision to strike North Korea in the absence of large-scale, overt North Korean aggression. Although Washington could design an operational plan that does not involve South Korea, what would the execution of such a plan mean for the U.S.-ROK alliance? How would other friends and allies in the region react to this unilateral use of military power by the United States? These

---

[34] As an added complication, uncertain intelligence could lead the United States to strike a broader array of targets, some of which may include facilities unrelated to North Korea's nuclear weapons complex.

are just a few of the challenges that even a limited military strike on North Korea would entail.

If a diplomatic solution is not possible, and if military options have priced themselves out of the market under all but the most extreme scenarios, then the United States needs to develop a strategy for managing a nuclear-armed North Korea. This means that should the Six-Party Talks fail, then Pyongyang—not Washington—must be seen as the source of the failure by the other parties to the talks and the larger international community. Other members of these talks, however, have publicly and privately criticized the United States for poisoning the atmosphere by personally insulting Kim Jong Il and for being inflexible during negotiations.[35] Winning the support in particular of China and South Korea, the only two countries with the ability to apply coercive pressure short of war against North Korea, is essential if the United States is to have any chance of reversing Pyongyang's nuclear ambitions. Should this issue move to the UN Security Council, Chinese support (or at least acquiescence) will be essential to ensure that Beijing does not veto any resolutions calling for economic sanctions or other punitive measures.

Quite apart from the negotiations, managing a nuclear-armed North Korea would present a range of challenges, few of which the United States could address on its own. The first step would be for the United States to coordinate with ROK military leaders to ensure that deterrence remained robust on the Korean Peninsula.[36] Economically, Washington would want to keep Pyongyang isolated so that the North Korean regime could not fund greater conventional, ballistic missile, or nuclear forces. Yet there are few additional economic or commercial tools that Washington can mobilize, given that the United States has already subjected North Korea to a plethora of sanctions and embargoes. One promising possibility, however, would be to expand the scope of the Illicit Activities Initiative, a little-known but highly effective Bush administration program aimed at choking off the revenue that Pyongyang derives from its sale of narcotics, counterfeit cigarettes, and fake U.S. currency. The income from these activities is estimated to run into the hundreds of millions of dollars annually.

---

[35] See, for example, "China Says U.S. Impeded North Korea Talks," *New York Times*, May 13, 2005, A6.

[36] At a joint press conference with the French foreign minister on May 2, 2005, Secretary of State Condoleezza Rice declared that "the United States maintains significant—and I want to underline significant—deterrent capability of all kinds in the Asia-Pacific region. So I don't think there should be any doubt about our ability to deter whatever the North Koreans are up to." U.S. Department of State, "Remarks With French Foreign Minister Michel Barnier After Meeting," May 2, 2005, http://www.state.gov/secretary/rm/2005/45484.htm.

If military operations are unappealing, then placing a *cordon sanitaire* around North Korea to prevent the export of nuclear technology and materials would be impractical. Although the PSI can be used under certain circumstances to board vessels, it is not well-suited to emplace a permanent naval quarantine. (Notably, neither China nor South Korea is a PSI member.) Even if the United States could mobilize the intelligence capabilities and air- and sea-borne assets to sustain permanently some interdiction capability in the region, Pyongyang has land and air routes by which it could smuggle nuclear materials. The unhappy reality is that North Korea now has the ability to provide fissile material to other countries or terrorist groups. In the near term, Washington's optimal policy response under these circumstances is to communicate unequivocally to Pyongyang the consequences if the regime should choose to spread such materials. In the longer term, the United States can only plan, or at least hope, for the end of the Kim Jong Il regime.

Deterrence, Reassurance, and Alliance Management

Should North Korea retain its nuclear weapons, the United States and its allies in Asia will be faced with important challenges to both the continued viability of extended deterrence and the credibility of U.S. security commitments. How well Washington responds to these challenges in the coming decades will determine both the continued viability of the U.S. alliance network and the U.S. ability to stem nuclear proliferation in Asia.

During the Cold War, U.S. support for South Korea vis-à-vis the North was part of the larger calculus of the U.S.-Soviet competition. Military aggression by the clients of one side had to be resisted and countered before they resulted in gains at the other's expense or escalated from the regional to the global level, thereby embroiling the two superpowers in a potential nuclear conflict. Today, in the absence of this Cold War context, there is far less need for the United States to come to the aid of its allies, especially those faced with a nuclear-armed regional adversary. Stephen Peter Rosen has written that

> Hostile regional nuclear powers are, therefore, in a good position to deter U.S. military intervention against them, and so may be in a better position to threaten the allies of the United States that do not have nuclear weapons and are within reach of the non-nuclear forces of the aggressive power.[37]

A nuclear-armed North Korea will increasingly strain alliance ties as doubts in Seoul and Tokyo loom larger about the U.S. security commit-

---

[37] Rosen, "Nuclear Proliferation and Alliance Relations," in *The Coming Crisis*, 127.

ment to the defense of South Korea and Japan. These doubts will grow as Pyongyang increases its nuclear weapons stockpile and long-range ballistic missile capabilities. If faced with the possibility of a nuclear attack from North Korea on a U.S. city, would Washington automatically come to the defense of its Asian allies? During the Cold War, questions over U.S. credibility and commitment to the defense of Western Europe—despite deep historical ties, multiple legal agreements, the stationing of U.S. nuclear weapons, and the presence of U.S. troops—were a constant theme of the transatlantic debate. Even so, Western Europeans were unsure whether the United States would risk Boston for Bonn. The ties that bind Washington to Seoul and Tokyo are less tightly woven, making it even harder to persuade these countries that the U.S. commitment is firm. Distilled to its essence, would the U.S. be willing to risk Seattle for Seoul?[38]

Related to the question of how, or how well, extended deterrence would operate with a regional nuclear power is the question of how Washington might promote stability in this type of regional environment. During the Cold War, Washington's European allies also worried that the United States might provoke a conflict with the Soviet Union that would be fought on their territory; they repeatedly demanded assurances that Washington would behave prudently. Given the Bush administration's public hostility towards Kim Jong Il, Seoul and Tokyo may have similar worries. Would the United States be a prudent guardian of the regional order? Or would Washington destabilize that order by attempting to overturn the Pyongyang regime? Do Asian allies have confidence that the United States would refrain from measures that could cause North Korea to lash out militarily?

To complicate matters further, U.S. efforts to reassure South Korea and Japan of its security commitment may raise their own problems. U.S. signals of a robust defense commitment—via declaratory policy, contingency planning, force deployments, and training exercises—could be interpreted by Seoul and Tokyo (and, needless to say, by Pyongyang as well) as a harbinger of regime change and thus as overly provocative. Even if Washington's credibility was unassailable, its judgment could still be questioned. Washington would have to walk a fine line between a posture that both deters and reassures on the one hand, and one that is not seen as overly confrontational on the other. Further shaping perceptions is that a debate over U.S. stewardship of the regional order would take place only after the United States had already proven itself incapable of deterring or preventing North Korea from acquiring nuclear weapons in the first place.

---

[38] For a discussion of extended deterrence on the Korean Peninsula, see Marc Dean Millot, Roger Molander, and Peter A. Wilson, "*The Day After ...*" *Study: Nuclear Proliferation in the Post-Cold War World*, vol. 2 (Santa Monica, CA: RAND, 1993), 73–110.

If South Korea and Japan determine that the United States was no longer automatically committed to their defense and cannot be relied upon to maintain stability in Northeast Asia, they may respond in one of three ways: by (1) capitulating to North Korea; (2) aligning themselves more closely to the lead regional power, China; or (3) developing their own nuclear deterrent.

It is unlikely, however, that either South Korea or Japan would view their choices in such stark terms. A hedging strategy that retains alliance relations with the United States and combines elements of all three paths, however, is possible for South Korea. The ROK already goes out of its way not to publicly criticize or antagonize North Korea. In recent years, relations between Seoul and Beijing have warmed; in August 2003 China surpassed the United States as the ROK's leading export market. Younger South Koreans are increasingly matriculating at Chinese universities rather than those in the United States. With respect to building nuclear weapons, the ROK has long had the technical capability in, and has recently demonstrated a covert interest in the more sensitive aspects of, the nuclear fuel cycle.[39]

Japan, however, is unlikely to appease North Korea, even if the U.S. commitment is questioned. In addition, Tokyo's desire for regional leadership will limit how much it is willing to defer to Beijing. More realistic is that Tokyo would explore more aggressively the steps needed to develop a nuclear arsenal. Japan already has a more impressive nuclear infrastructure than South Korea, including hundreds of tons of separated plutonium that could be fashioned into nuclear warheads. Estimates of the time it would take Japan to construct nuclear weapons range from "a few months" to "a year's time."[40] A hedging strategy for Japan would involve maintaining the U.S.-Japan security relationship while simultaneously increasing Japan's nuclear capability so that Tokyo could construct nuclear weapons on short notice if it decided it could no longer rely on the United States.

It is contrary to U.S. strategic interests that Washington's credibility be questioned by any of its Asian allies. Yet preserving this credibility will become increasingly difficult. The traditional totems of Washington's security commitments—U.S. troops and nuclear weapons stationed on foreign soil—are largely relics of the Cold War. Large concentrations of U.S. "boots on the ground" are being downsized and redeployed as part of the Pentagon's revolution in military affairs (RMA), which seeks the creation of leaner, lighter fighting units that can respond more nimbly to a variety of contingencies. In

---

[39] See "South Korea's Nuclear Experiments," IISS *Strategic Comments* 10, no. 8 (October 2004).

[40] The shorter estimate is cited by the Federation of American Scientists. See http://www.fas.org/nuke/guide/japan/nuke (February 2004). The longer estimate is Ariel E. Levite, "Never Say Never Again: Nuclear Reversal Revisted," *International Security* 27, no. 3 (Winter 2002–03): 69.

short, U.S. troops will be a less visible presence in South Korea and Japan in the years to come.

U.S. nuclear weapons were withdrawn from South Korea in the early 1990s and, according to the U.S. government, were never officially present in Japan. It is unlikely these decisions will be reversed anytime soon. This means that Washington will need to place greater weight on other aspects of U.S. security commitments. These could include joint policy statements, such as the February 2005 "2+2" summit of U.S. and Japanese foreign and defense ministers; strategic dialogues, such as the Trilateral Coordination and Oversight Group (TCOG); and stepped-up joint military planning and operational exercises. In day-to-day diplomacy, moreover, Washington will need to exhibit greater sensitivity to the concerns of regional allies. How well these steps will substitute for more tangible, traditional forms of reassurance is unknown. It is clear, however, that the United States will have to invest more time and effort in alliance management in the future.

A New Regional Strategy for Asia

The fundamentals of Washington's strategy are unlikely to change anytime soon. All U.S. presidents have had the option of using military force preemptively or preventively, and none is likely to surrender this prerogative lightly. The war on terrorism and the greater Middle East will occupy the time and attention of senior U.S. officials for many years to come.

Washington's preponderance of military power is a necessary but not sufficient condition for continued U.S. influence in Asia. U.S. policymakers need to adopt a broader, more strategic approach that is more closely attuned to the needs and interests of friends and allies in the region. Much could be gained by a simple change in tone, downplaying some of the more bellicose rhetoric and emphasizing instead the traditional U.S. policies of trade liberalization and economic development.

Even better would be the promotion of a more positive, attractive vision for the region to replace the current emphasis on (1) the fight against terrorism, which is not as high on the agenda of many Asian nations as it is on the U.S. agenda, and (2) the portrayal of China as a regional military threat, which is neither entirely credible nor relevant to many of China's neighbors. A revised vision would better address some of the transnational challenges that bedevil many of the countries in the region. These issues include energy insecurity, environmental degradation, transnational security threats, and such health scares as SARS and the avian flu.

No one country can deal effectively with these new threats; collective action and cooperative policies are required. One way to foster collective action is through the formation of a new organization comprised of five members of the Six-Party Talks (excluding North Korea, at least for the time being). Such an organization would include the world's largest trade and financial actors, key currencies, greatest energy producers and consumers, and main sources of environmental pollution. This "Northeast Asian Forum" could build on existing cooperation and personal relationships established during the Six-Party Talks. The organization could even be expanded over time to enlist countries in South and Southeast Asia that have an important stake in addressing these challenges. Form would follow function.

With respect to energy issues, transnational cooperation is necessary to lay oil and natural gas pipelines, to coordinate on strategic petroleum reserves to prevent volatility in world oil prices, to compare practices on nuclear power safety and spent fuel management, and to explore the potential of new technologies such as carbon sequestration and the international thermonuclear experimental reactor (ITER). With respect to security threats, collective action is needed to address piracy, narcotics trafficking, maritime safety, and other criminal activities. Similarly, no one country is equipped to deal with the challenges of climate change, clean water, yellow dust, brown fog, and the need for early warning systems to detect infectious diseases before they spread.

U.S. leadership is essential if this new type of Asian architecture is to flourish. By being deeply embedded in this organization, Washington would anchor itself more firmly to many of the most important and daunting challenges confronting Asia. Such leadership would also undercut China's attempts to marginalize the U.S. role in Asia.

Reviving the Nonproliferation Regime

The sources of proliferation concern lie in the conduct of "evil doers" (in President Bush's memorable phrase), repressive regimes, and the competitive nature of international politics.[41] Expressed differently, prospects for nonproliferation success will depend on good governance, regional stability, and world order. Any effective strategy must address all three sources.

Reversing the nuclear ambitions of North Korea and Iran must lie at the heart of such a strategy. Although it may be too late to persuade Pyongyang to surrender its nuclear programs and weapons, North Korea must not be allowed to benefit from its new status. There are some indications that Pyongyang would like to follow the same path forged by India after its 1998 tests: a brief period of international censure, followed by gradual re-engage-

---

[41] This template was first articulated by Kenneth N. Waltz, *Man, the State and War* (New York: Columbia University Press, 1954).

ment and eventual full acceptance of its new standing. This should not be allowed to happen. Ensuring that Pyongyang remains isolated and unable to participate in the dynamism of Northeast Asia would send a clear signal to other would-be proliferators of the long-term costs involved in acquiring nuclear weapons.

There is a greater chance of success with Iran. Tehran's nuclear program is not nearly as advanced as Pyongyang's: senior officials in the U.S. intelligence community have assessed that Iran will not be able to construct nuclear weapons until the early part of the next decade.[42] This may make it relatively easy to dismantle facilities—such as uranium enrichment and plutonium separation facilities—that present the greatest proliferation risks. In short, in Iran's case there is time for diplomacy to work.

IAEA safeguards to verify that countries adhere to their commitments to abstain from using nuclear fuel and technologies for nuclear weapons purposes have long constituted the foundation of the nonproliferation regime. Yet as nuclear technologies are disseminated and ways to deceive inspectors become more sophisticated, there is a greater need to strengthen the IAEA's inspection capabilities. One such improvement effort is the "Additional Protocol," which improves the IAEA's capability to address the problem of undeclared nuclear material and activities in a state. The Additional Protocol is an important new tool for the IAEA, even if its ultimate effectiveness has

---

[42] Director of Central Intelligence Porter Goss, "Global Intelligence Challenges 2005: Meeting Long-term Challenges with Long-term Strategy," testimony to the United States Senate Select Committee on Intelligence, February, 16, 2005, http://intelligence.senate.gov/0502hrg/050216/goss.pdf; Director of the Defense Intelligence Agency Adm. Lowell E. Jacoby, "Current and Projected National Security Threats to the United States," testimony to the United States Senate Select Committee on Intelligence, February, 16, 2005, http://intelligence.senate.gov/0502hrg/050216/jacoby.pdf; and Bunn and Wier, "The Seven Myths of Nuclear Terrorism." See also, Dafna Linzer, "Iran Judged 10 Years from Nuclear Bomb; U.S. Intellience Review Contrasts with Administration Statements," *Washington Post*, August 2, 2005; but see also Gary Milhollin, "Don't Underestimate the Mullahs," *New York Times*, August 23, 2005. One reason Tehran has offered for its pursuit of the entire nuclear fuel cycle is Iran's need for energy independence from foreign suppliers. By developing an indigenous uranium enrichment capability, Iran argues that it would not have to worry about being cut off from fuel for its nuclear power reactors. Countries with substantial civilian nuclear power programs understandably want energy independence from foreign suppliers of nuclear fuel, even if such a desire is not justified in Iran's case because of Iran's extensive oil and natural gas reserves. Ultimately, however, any further proliferation of uranium enrichment and reprocessing technologies are simply too risky in the 21st century, given the danger of nuclear smuggling networks and the elevation of the terrorist threat. Both the director general of the IAEA and President Bush have endorsed the concept of ensuring reliable access to fuel for civilian reactors. Using the IAEA as a global fuel bank, for example, could both satisfy states desirous of ensuring a reliable fuel supply and limit the spread of sensitive nuclear technologies. This was actually one of the IAEA's original missions. In the 1950s, the United States and the Soviet Union provided nuclear fuel to the IAEA, which then leased it to other countries for their nuclear programs. A reinvigorated "back to the future" initiative along these lines, perhaps with the added sweetener of subsidizing the cost of the fuel, would assure a reliable (and apolitical) fuel supply and eliminate the perceived need of some countries to build their own enrichment and reprocessing facilities. See Mohamed el Baredei, "Towards a Safer World," *Economist*, October 16, 2003; and George W. Bush, "Remarks at the National Defense University," Washington, D.C., February 11, 2004, http://www.whitehouse.gov/news/releases/2004/02/print/20040211-4.html.

yet to be fully demonstrated in the field. As of mid-2005, the Additional Protocol has entered into force for only 67 countries. The Bush administration needs to press hold-outs to ratify this protocol as soon as possible.

Existing nonproliferation programs need to be reinvigorated. As a first step, the United States and Russia need to resolve their current differences over liability for U.S. workers and access to sites that are limiting the effectiveness of the U.S. Cooperative Threat Reduction (Nunn-Lugar) program.[43] In addition, at the 2002 G-8 summit at Kananaskis, Canada, the United States, and the other G-8 countries announced a global partnership against the spread of weapons and materials of mass destruction. President Bush and his colleagues agreed to raise $20 billion over the next ten years for projects pertaining to disarmament, nonproliferation, counterterrorism, and nuclear safety. The United States pledged to provide half of the total funding. Yet three years later, momentum has lagged and the original pledges have not been fulfilled. There is no doubt that additional resources could accomplish more. Securing research facilities and nuclear stockpiles in the former Soviet Union is also unfinished business, and, although the A.Q. Khan network has been exposed, other clandestine networks still operate in a nuclear black market.

Conclusion

Numerous pressures will stimulate the desire for nuclear weapons in Asia over the coming years. These include a nuclear-armed North Korea, possible conflict over Taiwan, a rising China, a rearming Japan, and a United States that will increasingly focus on the greater Middle East. Yet this does not mean that proliferation is inevitable. Although some pressures will make nuclear weapons more attractive to some countries in the region in the coming decades, the policies that other countries—particularly the United States—adopt can diminish this attractiveness while raising the costs to new nuclear aspirants.

The United States will play the key role in preventing further proliferation in the region for the foreseeable future. With U.S. power has come unprecedented responsibilities, especially in the realm of nonproliferation. If Washington does not help deliver greater security and prosperity to the countries of Asia, they will look for leadership elsewhere. In the past decade, China has filled many of these needs for some countries, and appears to have

---

[43] By mid-2005, the United States and Russia had reached agreement in principle on a liability protocol for plutonium disposition; it is hoped that this agreement will serve as the model for extending the Cooperative Threat Reduction agreement. As of mid-July 2005, however, negotiations on this agreement had not begun.

every intention of continuing to do so. Alternatively, countries that are wary of China's embrace or simply wish to hedge their bets may rely on self-help, with some believing that nuclear weapons could resolve their insecurities. Which future unfolds will depend in large measure on whether other countries view the United States as promoting a narrow post-September 11 agenda or a more positive vision that enhances stability for the entire region.

EXECUTIVE SUMMARY

This chapter examines whether China will be able to sustain high rates of economic growth over the coming decades and draws implications for the Chinese defense budget.

MAIN ARGUMENT:
- Numerous weaknesses in the Chinese economy include a banking system with non-performing loans, serious environmental challenges, and the need to accommodate 300–500 million rural-to-urban migrants over the next two decades.

- Barring war in the Taiwan Strait, however, high rates of economic growth are likely to continue in China for at least the next decade. Both China's high rate of investment and the rapid expansion in the education level of its workforce are likely to continue. The large pool of underemployed rural labor can also be shifted to higher productivity urban jobs.

- During the first half of the reform period, military expenditures did not seem to increase at all in real terms. Since 1996, however, defense expenditures have been rising more rapidly than the growth rate of GDP.

POLICY IMPLICATIONS:
- Sustained high rates of growth help China to remain politically stable, which is in the best interests of the U.S.

- By contrast, protectionist trade measures directed at China will make little real difference to unemployment levels in the U.S. or the size of the U.S. current account deficit, but could hurt Chinese growth and certainly increase tension between the two nations.

- China's defense expenditure will continue to rise. The U.S. is not in a position to stop this growth, but there is likewise little reason for the U.S. (or the European Union) to try to facilitate this growth, either through direct sales of advanced weaponry or by cooperation in research that has clear military applications.

China's Economic Growth: Implications for the Defense Budget

Dwight Perkins

China's rapid economic growth and the need to sustain this high growth rate well into the future have, for the past two decades, driven Chinese policy decisions not only in the economic sphere but also in the political and foreign policy arenas. Economic considerations are likely to be equally central in both China's domestic and foreign policies for the coming decade. Though most policy choices are shaped by economic considerations, the need to sustain high levels of growth will not override what Chinese leaders feel to be fundamental challenges either to Chinese sovereignty (e.g., if Taiwan were to declare independence) or to the rule of the Chinese Communist Party (CCP).

Sustained, rapid economic growth is desirable not only because it will raise the standard of living of the Chinese people, but also because it is essential if the government is to maintain political stability. The CCP bases its continued legitimacy on the fact that Party rule has brought unprecedented prosperity to a large portion of the Chinese people, particularly those in urban areas. Communist ideology, by contrast, plays very little role in maintaining popular support for the CCP-led government or in providing the cement that holds the Party itself together. Rapid economic growth over the past quarter century has also fueled feelings of nationalism brought on by pride in China's rising strength on the international stage.

It thus does not take much imagination to see how a failure to sustain high economic growth rates could lead to both domestic and international crises. The demands of economic efficiency have already led to large-scale

Dwight Perkins is the H.H. Burbank Professor of Political Economy at Harvard University and was Director of the University's Asia Center from 2002 to 2005. He can be reached at <dhperkin@fas.harvard.edu>.

unemployment (particularly in northeastern China), and slower growth would both produce fewer jobs for urban residents and slow or halt increases in their still overall low standard of living. More importantly, a vast store of underemployed labor remains in the countryside; this massive workforce could move to the cities without any significant decline in farm output. If, over the next two decades, China follows the pattern laid down by neighboring countries such as Japan and South Korea, roughly 300–500 million workers and their families will migrate to urban areas and take up non-agricultural employment. If the economy is not able to supply the additional jobs required by this massive infusion of labor, these migrants will either remain underemployed in large urban slums or languish in the countryside and resent the better life of registered urban residents. Either way, discontent among the citizenry will rise and the government will resort to non-economic means—such as strident appeals to Chinese nationalism—in order to try to maintain control. Such appeals would no doubt have a strong anti-foreign element and would thus impact China's international relations.

If China does manage to sustain high economic growth rates, not only will such growth strengthen political stability, but Beijing would also find it easier to expand China's military expenditures. Over the long term, China will likely strive to become a world military power commensurate with the country's size, population, and role in world history.[1] Slow growth will not necessarily stop this military expansion (Beijing can to some degree raise the share of GDP allocated to the military), but would certainly make this expansion much more difficult. Attempts to forecast China's future economic growth rate, therefore, are not simply exercises designed to provide information to investors on the Shanghai and Shenzhen stock exchanges. Having a reasonably reliable estimate of China's future economic growth prospects is also essential for any informed discussion of China's future domestic stability and the likelihood of continued international stability in Asia more broadly.

In the analysis that follows, therefore, the first section tackles the issue of whether China can in fact sustain the high rates of economic growth that it has achieved over the past two decades. This question will be divided into two parts. The first will look at whether China can maintain high rates of investment and high rates of growth in the labor force (particularly the highly

---

[1] There is no authoritative way of establishing that this is China's long-term goal. Statements by government officials or members of the military (even those not meant for public consumption) are not a very good guide to China's long term ambitions. There is considerable evidence that Chinese leaders, together with the internationally aware population at large in China, want to see China take its place in the world alongside the great powers as a major player in the political, economic, and military arenas. The same can also no doubt be said of several other large countries, such as Russia and India, that do not now play a role in international affairs commensurate with their potential importance in the future.

educated part of the labor force). The second explores whether China, given some of the enormous problems that exist, can maintain the relatively high productivity growth of recent decades. These problems include the reform of a very weak financial sector and the need to accommodate the migration of hundreds of millions of workers and their families from the rural areas to the cities.

The second section of the chapter then attempts to explore the implications of continued high growth for the size of the Chinese military budget. Building upon the work of others that suggests that the real Chinese military budget is double (or more) the size of the published official budget, this section attempts to convert that budget into real terms (i.e., stripped of the impact of rising prices). The argument is that the budget in real terms probably stagnated in absolute numbers until the mid-1990s, and actually declined significantly as a share of GDP. From the mid-1990s onward, however, that budget has risen rapidly in real terms both in absolute size and to some de gree as a percentage of GDP. The chapter concludes with a summary of the basic argument and outlines implications for U.S. policy.

Prospects for Sustained High Growth

Any attempt to forecast China's future economic growth must begin with an understanding of what has driven the high growth rates of the past quarter century. With the changes over the past two decades as background, one can then ask whether the conditions that brought about such high growth in the past will remain in place in the future or will be replaced by other equally supportive conditions.

The Fundamentals of Growth

An understanding of past and future high growth rates can be approached on three different levels. The first level is based on the fundamental components of high economic growth anywhere in the world. These components include a high rate of investment or capital formation, a rapidly growing labor force, a rapid rise in the education level of that labor force, and the efficiency with which these increases in capital and labor are being used. China today has an extraordinarily high rate of investment—gross capital formation as a share of GDP has been above 35% in every year since 1985 and even reached 42.3% in 2003.[2] With that level of investment, China's economic policymakers can make quite a few mistakes and yet the economy

---

[2] National Bureau of Statistics, *China Statistical Yearbook, 2004*, 65.

will still continue to grow. Such a high rate of investment is fueled by China's equally high rate of savings. This high rate is partially explained by the lack of adequate retirement support from public programs, by what appears to be an East Asian cultural preference for high savings, and, most of all, by China's current low dependency ratio (the number of young and old outside the labor force relative to the number in the labor force).[3] This low dependency ratio will gradually disappear due mostly to the long-term effects of the one-child policy and the increasing life expectancy of the Chinese population; this withering away will not, however, happen in the next decade or even the next two decades. China's savings and investment rates are thus likely to remain very high for some time into the future.

The education level of China's labor force is also rising rapidly; this trend will, regardless of the overall growth rate, likely continue over the next decade and beyond. Although the government has supported rapid expansion of education at the secondary and tertiary levels, private demand has outstripped the public supply and has led to the creation of private educational institutions, particularly at the tertiary level. For example, in 2003 secondary schools enrolled 96 million students out of a relevant age group pool of approximately 100 million. This is in contrast to 62 million in 1995 and 51 million in 1985.[4] By any standard, this is a rapid increase for a two-decade period, although universal education is compulsory for only the first eight grades, with some poorer rural areas not yet even complying with that standard. There were 11 million students enrolled at the university level in 2003, up from 2.9 million in 1995 and 1.7 million in 1985. This rise is even more rapid, though still translates into only about 10% of the relevant age cohort attending post-secondary institutions.[5]

Educated labor and human capital, of course, are not the only inputs into growth. Due to China's current level of per capita income, there is also a very large demand for unskilled labor. Though the one-child policy is slowing down growth in the total Chinese labor force, this is an irrelevant figure for understanding the sources of GDP growth. A more telling statistic is the rate of increase in the labor force in the modern non-agricultural sectors. Due to migration from low productivity jobs in the countryside, this rate of

---

[3] The underlying theory behind the connection between the dependency ratio and the savings rate is based on the life-cycle savings model as developed by Franco Modigliani. The basic idea is that families have lower savings when their children are young and at home, save at high levels during their most productive years after their children are grown, and then dissave when they retire. Thus the more people there are who are not in the labor force (because they are too young or too old), the lower savings will be.

[4] The size of the age cohort is the author's estimate based on census data. The data on secondary enrollment are from The National Bureau of Statistics, *China Statistical Yearbook, 2004*, 779.

[5] Ibid. The statement that poorer rural areas often do not fully comply with the compulsory education standard is based on direct observation by the author and by many others.

increase will remain high well beyond the coming decade. During the past several years employment growth in urban areas has been slow, largely because of all of the layoffs in the state sector made necessary by the policies of overemployment in state firms in earlier years. Urban employment growth between 2000 and 2003, for example, was around 3.5% per year, but with continued rapid growth in output and large-scale migration from the countryside, the urban labor force and employment could grow at a faster rate.[6]

Maintaining High-Productivity Growth

The inputs required for growth in China are thus likely to continue growing rapidly over the next decade and beyond. Inputs, however, are only a little more than half of the story. The other half involves the efficiency with which these inputs are used: the rate of growth of productivity (or to use the technical term, total factor productivity). Productivity growth in China since reforms began in 1979 can be understood largely as the result of a series of specific reforms that led to significant leaps in productivity growth in particular sectors. These increases occurred in first one sector and then another, but in all cases the jump in productivity petered out over time and productivity growth had to be sustained by a new reform that accelerated growth in another sector.

The first sector to experience an increase in productivity was agriculture, a change that was brought about between 1979 and 1985 as a result of the return to household farming and the freeing up of rural markets. After 1985, however, agricultural and productivity growth slowed markedly. The second sector to experience a leap in productivity was the township and village enterprise (TVE) sector, which benefited from the freeing up of industrial and other inputs for purchase on the market instead of allocation through the central plan. This TVE boom began in 1985 and continued, after a brief slowdown in 1989–90, into the 1990s, after which the sector began a much more significant slowdown. The third sector to experience a boom was foreign direct investment (FDI) enterprises, which took off in 1992 or 1993, and have continued to grow at a high level ever since. The FDI growth rate has, however, also slowed down largely due to the finite amount of capital available for investment in developing countries in general and China in

---

[6] These estimates of the urban employment growth rate are more problematic than many of the other figures used in this essay. The Chinese government reports figures for employment in industry and services in the *China Statistical Yearbook 2004*, and I have assumed that these figures are a rough estimate of the growth rate of urban employment—even though some of industry and services employment has not taken place in the urban areas. Moreover, these figures probably do not accurately reflect the employment of many of the unregistered migrants to the cities from the rural areas. The 3.5% figure, therefore, should be seen as a conservative estimate of the growth of urban employment. See The National Bureau of Statistics, *China Statistical Yearbook, 2004*, 120.

particular. FDI will no doubt continue to grow, but the boom that whisked FDI from a few billion dollars a year to the current $60 billion a year will not be able to continue at such a heated pace.[7]

Two other reforms have helped bring about these sector jumps in growth and productivity that existed throughout the 1980s and '90s. One key reform has been the expansion of foreign trade from the relatively miniscule level of $26.4 billion in 1978 to $1,154.8 billion (imports plus exports) in 2004. With export earnings of $593.4 billion and FDI of another $60.6 billion (in 2004), China has enough foreign exchange to import virtually anything that the country needs—but is unable to produce more efficiently at home—for urban sector development. No longer do Chinese industrial firms have to rely on inferior domestic parts and machinery simply because of a lack of foreign exchange to import those items from Japan, the United States, or Germany. Nor do industrial firms have to endure the bottlenecks that were usually so prevalent in the planning period, when key inputs were simply not available for long periods of time due to lack of foresight in the central plan.

There is a second way in which the opening up to foreign trade has boosted Chinese growth, particularly in recent years. In 2003 and 2004 exports grew at an average rate of 35% per year. That very large expansion in exports (well over $100 billion a year in each of these two years) played an important role in maintaining growth in the demand for Chinese output.[8] By contrast, consumer demand in China grew more slowly than the GDP (the downside of the high and rising rate of savings). China will not, however, be likely to sustain exports of this magnitude—or even half of this magnitude in percentage terms—for many more years. At 91% of GDP (Exports+Imports/GDP), China's foreign trade ratio in comparative terms is already extraordinarily high for a large country.[9] Continued increases in exports of over $100 billion a year will inevitably lead to resistance from countries that buy Chinese goods, many of whom feel they are being forced to adjust too quickly. This has already occurred, when in 2005 receiving countries slapped high

---

[7] The foreign direct investment into China that is actually utilized is regularly reported in the annual statistical yearbooks. The 2004 figure of $60.6 billion is from The National Bureau of Statistics, *China Monthly Economic Indicators, 2005.2*, vol. 59, 43.

[8] Ibid., 35. To be more precise, total Chinese exports in 2004 grew by $154 billion over total exports in 2003, and the growth rate of exports in the first half of 2005 has slowed only slightly in percentage terms from the export growth rate of 2004. See also Chris Buckley, "China's Economy Grows Despite Effort to Slow It," *International Herald Tribune*, July 21, 2005, 11.

[9] One of the basic findings of Nobel Laureate Simon Kuznets was that the ratio of foreign trade to GDP tends to decline in more populous countries. The ratio of exports+imports/GDP for the United States, for example, was 19% in 2001, and 18% for Japan. In terms of population China is the largest country in the world, yet its trade ratio is five times that of two of the other large trading nations. See The World Bank, *World Development Report 2003: Sustainable Development in a Dynamic World* (Washington, D.C.: The World Bank, 2003), 238–41.

tariffs on certain Chinese textile exports that had rapidly expanded in the wake of the termination of the international fiber agreement. Thus in the future China cannot rely as much on the growth stimulus of rapid increases in demand for Chinese exports. China will instead have to find ways of stimulating a more rapid rise in domestic consumer demand.

The real challenge in this area for both China and its trading partners is to keep trade disputes from escalating into sustained vitriolic confrontations based more on domestic politics than on any consideration of actual national interest. In this regard China's July 2005 decision to revalue its currency—even if only by a miniscule 2%—was a step in the right direction. The hope is that this initial revaluation will be followed by additional revaluations in the not-too-distant future. Hopefully trade disputes can be kept as much as possible within the technical framework of the World Trade Organization (WTO) dispute mechanism. That may be wishful thinking, but trade disputes that escalate into political confrontations and undermine security cooperation are not in the interests of any country.

The other change underlying growth in all of China's economic sectors has been the steady expansion of the role of the market to the point where most goods and services today are sold on the market. The market first expanded most rapidly in the rural areas but then began expanding for industrial inputs in late 1984, with a portion of those inputs being made available on the market at market prices. By the end of the 1990s virtually all industrial inputs were being distributed through the market at market prices. Thus China today has as much of a market economy as most other developing (and many developed) countries.[10] China's market economy is highly imperfect, however, lacking many of the strong institutions of market economies in high-income countries.

Maintaining high productivity growth over the next decade and beyond will depend critically on China's ability to steadily improve market-supporting institutions. As the above analysis has indicated, all of the other sources of high productivity growth over the past quarter century appear to have run out of steam. The past decades have basically involved correcting major weaknesses caused by the centrally planned command system. For the most part, these structural weaknesses no longer exist. The market still needs to function much more efficiently, however. This effort must involve improving corporate governance by making enterprises and their management truly independent of the government and the CCP, as well as subject to boards

---

[10] This statement will seem controversial to some since both the United States and the European Union have not been willing to grant China market economy status for trade purposes. Goods and services in China, however, are overwhelmingly allocated through the market, and even imports are not as subject to various quantitative quotas as is common in many developing countries.

of directors whose sole function is to ensure the success of the enterprise. There will also need to be a steady improvement in the quality and independence of the judiciary in order to enable commercial disputes in a wide variety of areas (including bankruptcies and mergers) to be handled without intervention from the executive branch of the government. The challenge for China will be to build these and other related institutions in a way that supports rapid, stable, and sustained growth. There are also specific sectors that are particularly weak and in need of reform.

Potential Economic Crises

The weaknesses in many of China's economic institutions are apparent to even the most casual observer of the Chinese economy. The best known example is the Chinese financial system. China's banks have been burdened with large portfolios of non-performing loans virtually from the moment the government first stopped financing state enterprise investment directly from the government budget and entrusted that task to the banks. Some have implied that the weakness of these banks, which would all be formally bankrupt if their loan portfolios were properly classified by international standards, could bring down the Chinese economy in a financial crisis similar to what occurred in Asia in 1997–98. That particular crisis, however, occurred in countries that engaged in heavy short-term borrowing from abroad in dollar- or yen-denominated debt and had very low and declining foreign exchange reserves (in part because of overvalued exchange rates). China has massive foreign exchange reserves ($610 billion at the end of 2004)[11] and a still undervalued exchange rate (despite the recent revaluation). Chinese public and private borrowing from foreign sources has been mostly long term, and debt service-to-export ratios in China was and remains low.

Any financial crisis in China would occur for different reasons. The banking system could collapse under a massive run on Chinese banks prompted by depositors at last aware of how weak these institutions really are. This is not, however, a very realistic scenario. For both economic and political reasons, the government cannot afford to let state banks fail: antagonizing hundreds of millions of depositors is a formula for political suicide. If refinancing the banks with bonds is not possible, the government could always simply print the money required by the banks. This step might be inflationary, but given that China today does not have a serious inflation problem, some increase in inflation would be economically tolerable.

The real danger from the weak banking system is more long term in nature. If sustaining high rates of growth requires China to make its mar-

---

[11] National Bureau of Statistics, *China Monthly Economic Indicators, 2005.2*, vol. 59, 51.

ket economy steadily more efficient, then one of the areas most in need of attention is the banking system (and the financial system more generally). The Chinese stock market, to take only one example, is plagued by insider trading and company reporting requirements that are far from adequate. Beijing has been trying to reform China's banks for nearly a decade now, and in recent years there has been some evidence of progress. The share of non-performing loans in bank portfolios has been falling and the range of bank services and technical capacity has been improving. Pressure from foreign banks entering China under the new WTO rules will lead to further improvements in bank performance. The largest single remaining problem is that bank loans are still heavily influenced by local politicians; thus many of these loans go bad because they are often lent to the chronically loss-making state enterprises. This politicization makes it harder to reduce the non-performing portion of their portfolios. China could end up in a system similar to Japan, where the banking sector is so conservative that it does not lend to the most dynamic entrepreneurs in the economy. Conservative in the Chinese context means loaning mainly to state enterprises and the government (i.e., by buying government bonds) and lending little to the private sector.

The proclivity of the state banks to lend mainly to state enterprises is illustrative of a related problem that goes beyond the problems of the banks and financial markets themselves. A high percentage of Chinese investment in general is carried out by the state, with state investment in China having commonly been subject to high levels of waste (including corruption). If China is to enhance the overall productivity of its investment, more of that investment needs to be carried out by private firms operating in response to market forces without state subsidies. In particular, investment by many of the state enterprises has involved little more than propping up firms that have grim prospects of ever becoming competitive. The solution to many of these problems is to close the chronic loss-makers and privatize those with a chance of survival. This seems to be happening: note that most TVEs, for example, have been privatized in one way or another. The central government has also made clear that Beijing will no longer subsidize most of the state enterprises. The localities will have either to privatize these firms (though the word privatization is seldom used) or to find a way to subsidize them should they continue to make losses. The key remaining question is not whether most state enterprises will eventually be privatized, but whether the pace of privatization will be fast enough to maintain high rates of growth in productivity. Beijing is, however, walking a tightrope between the need to accelerate the devolution of state firms to private owners, and the implications for political stability inherent in creating the inevitable high rates of unemployment among older state enterprise workers. Though some critics suggest that the pace of devolution has been too slow, China has laid off more than 30 million urban workers from the formerly bloated payrolls of closed, reorganized, and privatized state enterprises.

A second danger for the Chinese economy is that current efforts to rein in growth may lead to what many refer to as a "hard landing." Though often times not clearly articulated, presumably the idea behind this term is that efforts to control inflation will misfire and cause a recession. An analogous situation in the United States would be a recession generated by too-high interest rates imposed by Federal Reserve policies rather than underlying fundamental problems with the economy. Certainly such a policy-generated recession is possible (even though the current stewardship of China's central bank is in the ablest hands in Chinese history). Such a recession would, however, consist of only a year or two of slow or negative growth, and not necessarily indicate a fundamental downturn in the long-term growth trend. Recessions of this sort can also be generated by external shocks of various kinds. Given China's increasing dependence on imports of energy and minerals, a sharp rise in energy and other raw material prices, for instance, could trigger a recession in China. If private investment were to experience a sharp downturn (as happens in all advanced market economies), then that could also generate a one- or two-year recession. Short-term political turmoil is another possibility. In short, there are many ways in which China could experience a year or two of very slow or negative growth, but none of these "hard landing" scenarios have much long-term significance.

A problem of greater long-term significance is the impact of environmental degradation on Chinese economic growth. For a variety of reasons China is experiencing major problems of environmental degradation at a much earlier stage of growth than the nations of Europe, North America, and even Japan.[12] Beijing is increasingly cognizant of the fact that, if the health of the population is not to suffer, substantial sums will have to be spent on controlling certain environmental hazards. In particular, urban air pollution requires immediate action and expenditures.

From a budgetary point of view, the acute shortage of water in much of northern China is also an alarming problem. The water table in the region is falling to ever greater depths as water is consumed at a rate greater than that which can be replenished by natural flows.[13] If this situation continues, economic growth in many of the northern cities would not be sustainable, and

---

[12] Presumably the main reason is that, although China's total geographic area is quite large, most of the country's 1.3 billion people are concentrated in the eastern half of the country. As a result, Chinese population centers are much more crowded than in North America or Europe.

[13] Evidence that the water is being mined is based on the fact that tube wells in the rural areas and elsewhere are being dug deeper and deeper to find water.

northern farmers would have to depend entirely on the weather for a successful harvest. To combat this dire prospect, China is currently spending tens of billions of dollars to divert water from the Yangtze River in the south to the parched northern regions. Three routes are being developed precisely for this purpose, each involving the transport of large amounts of water over long distances (not unlike the diversion of the Colorado River in the United States). For all of this expense, however, it is difficult to see how this or any other environmental problem will stop Chinese growth. Though several tens of billions of dollars is a large sum, China's annual level of gross investment in 2004 alone was over $600-700 billion (after conversion of Chinese data into dollars at the official exchange rate).[14]

Another worry is that a shortage of key resources will create bottlenecks in the economy. The most likely scenario would be a severe shortage of energy, but shortages of food are also plausible. China today is rapidly increasing its petroleum imports and will no doubt be importing large quantities of natural gas in the future. Chinese investors are scouring the world for opportunities to secure energy supplies for the future. The most recent attempt was the effort by the China National Offshore Oil Company (CNOOC) to purchase Unocal, a company with large oil and natural gas fields (many of which are in Asia). In 2004 China imported 122 million tons of crude petroleum (roughly 2.7 million barrels a day). China's consumption of petroleum over the past decade has grown at just over 6% per year, while domestic production of petroleum has grown at only 1.6% per year.[15] If these trends continue over the next decade, the gap between consumption and domestic production will continue to widen, and Chinese petroleum imports could reach over 350 million tons (or around 7 million barrels) per day.[16] Yet 7 million barrels a day at $50 per barrel is $128 billion a year, the equivalent of 21% of China's foreign exchange earnings from exports in 2004. At $70 per barrel, these figures rise to $179 billion and 30% respectively. Though these are large sums, Chinese export earnings within the next decade are likely to go well past $1 trillion. There is no reason to suppose that imports of this

---

[14] China's GDP in 2004 in Chinese currency was RMB13,615.5 billion, around 40% of which went into gross capital formation for a total investment of RMB5,446 billion (which converts into $672 billion at the new official exchange rate of US$1 = RMB8.1). By applying purchasing power parity estimates of GDP and investment, the investment figure in dollars would be significantly higher.

[15] Petroleum consumption and production data, as well as energy consumption and production data, are given in a number of sources. See The National Statistical Office, *China Statistical Yearbook, 2004*, 275.

[16] A more refined forecast of future Chinese petroleum demand would require a much more elaborate formal econometric model that would take into account shifts between high and low energy-using sectors, assumptions about improvements in the efficiency of energy use, and much else. Such refined forecasts, however, are not likely to be substantially different from these straight-line projections into the future.

magnitude will cripple growth in any substantial way. Only an oil embargo on China could seriously restrict China's growth prospects and, barring a major war involving China, such an embargo is highly unlikely.

Social and Political Challenges to Sustainable Growth

China also faces challenges in the social sphere. In China today, roughly half of the work force of 760 million people is employed in agriculture.[17] The other half has already shifted to industry and services mainly in the cities but also on the urban fringe. During the two decades after reaching this point in their structural transformation, Japan and South Korea experienced a shift out of agriculture where the percentage of workers in agriculture fell to 10% of the total work force. If something similar occurs in China (and in a very real sense this is already well underway), 250 million or more workers will shift out of agriculture and into urban and suburban areas over the next two decades. Over the coming decade alone, approximately 100 million new workers are likely to join the 100 million recent rural migrant workers that have come into the cities over the past two decades.[18] If these workers bring their families with them, Chinese cities will have to accommodate around 200 million new migrants per decade.

This massive migration—the largest rural to urban migration in history over such a short period of time—will present both an opportunity and a challenge for China. Such migration could generate a large, sustained building boom to house these migrants and their families, and provide them with adequate urban infrastructure. For migrants from the poorer and more remote areas, this influx into urban areas will present an opportunity to provide their children with access to a far better education than anything they could have received in their home villages. This assumes, however, that the migrants are accompanied by their families and that the cities do provide the necessary housing, infrastructure, and education. None of this is occurring on a substantial scale at present, as the migrants are being treated as temporary residents who have no rights to any urban services. If this situation persists into the next decade, China's cities are likely to have very large populations of poor young men and women who are separated from the stable environment of their families. The potential for urban unrest, crime, and the

---

[17] To be more precise, 49.1% of the labor force is in the primary sector, which is mainly made up of agriculture but also includes mining. The percentage in agriculture would thus be several percentage points less than the percentage for the primary sector as a whole. See The National Statistical Office, *China Statistical Yearbook, 2004*, 120.

[18] There is no officially published figure for the number of rural migrants currently in the cities, but there have been a variety of informal statements by officials and others suggesting that the total was probably somewhere in the vicinity of 100 million.

spread of deadly diseases such as HIV/AIDS is substantial. Such problems could easily have an unwanted impact on the political stability so essential for sustained rapid growth.

Though improper management of this massive migration may constitute a potential threat to political and social stability, there are other serious threats as well. Essays elsewhere in this volume deal with the possible political changes that may occur in China. Here we will only deal with the implications of two of the greatest potential threats to continued stability. The implication easiest to understand stems from the consequences of a war in the Taiwan Strait. If such an outbreak of hostilities were prolonged and drew in the United States and others (as seems quite possible), then there would be little prospect of continued rapid growth in China. Many of China's export markets would be closed, and the United States and others would move to place an embargo on all manner of strategic sales to China—including oil. Foreign investors, even those sympathetic of the Chinese position in the dispute, would pull out. Though it is possible that growth might continue at a much slower pace, China would more likely be driven into a deep recession.

Whether and when China will make a transition to a more pluralistic political system—one involving the active participation of the Chinese population as a whole in major national decisions—is the second political issue of relevance. There is no way of knowing when or if such a change will occur, and if so whether the transition would be gradual and peaceful or abrupt and violent. The most that can be said is that, given China's rapidly growing educated and urban populations, the Chinese citizenry is not likely to tolerate indefinitely rule by a self-selected group of leaders, regardless of how capable that leadership might be in a technical sense. That said, however, China still has a large rural and poor population that is no doubt more interested in greater economic benefits than in political participation—unless they come to see the latter as essential to the former. Thus the most plausible estimate is that this transition will occur beyond the time frame of the one decade that is the focus of this essay. An earlier and violent transition would obviously disrupt growth, but the duration of such a disruption would depend on the nature and length of the violence. South Korea went through two somewhat violent transitions: the assassination of President Park in 1979 that was followed by a coup in 1980, and the 1987 student demonstrations-riots over the contested direct election of the president. The former contributed to only a one-year downturn in the economy and the latter had little economic impact. China will chart its own transition with consequences that cannot be predicted with confidence.

The Likely Range of GDP Growth over the Coming Decade

How do the above considerations translate into concrete economic fore-casts for the next decade? Since the beginning of economic reforms in 1978, the official GDP growth rate has been slightly over 9% per year. Since 1995 the GDP growth rate has averaged over 8% per year. Some outside observers argue that China's GDP growth rate may be somewhat overstated. During the early 1990s, for example, there was some evidence that the value added of TVEs was included in GDP in current prices that did not adjust for infla-tion. There are also questions about China's GDP at the height of the Asian financial crisis in 1997–98, when the official growth rate remained above 7% despite the severe decline in output in much of the rest of East and Southeast Asia.[19] On the other hand, there are also questions about whether Chinese GDP growth properly measures the rapid improvement in quality occurring in a wide variety of manufactured products. Measuring quality improve-ments properly has been difficult even in advanced economies; the tendency in most such estimates (probably including China's) is to understate the pace of quality enhancement. Thus China's actual growth rate for many years may even be higher than the official estimates.

Fifty years ago a growth rate of 9% or even 8% per year would have been considered a "miracle," and many observers use that term today to de-scribe what has been happening in China. Prior to the 1950s and 1960s, the fastest GDP growth rates in the world averaged less that 4% or 5% per year. Growth rates of 7% to over 9% became common is Asia, however, in the 1950s through the early 1990s, beginning in Japan and then spreading to South Korea, Taiwan, Singapore, and even to Thailand and Indonesia.[20] Basically any developing country that adopted the proper policies could take advantage of the large backlog of unexploited technologies and begin to catch up with the high-income countries. Economies regulated under sound policies often tend to converge or catch up over time with the countries with the highest per capita income.

Thus China has, over the past twenty-six years, been gradually converg-ing to the levels of per capita income of the high income countries, yet still

---

[19] The official data for GDP growth are put out regularly by the National Statistical Office and re-ported in the annual statistical yearbooks cited above. The argument that the GDP growth rate figures for 1997 and 1998 may be overstated is based on work by such analysts as Thomas Rawski at the University of Pittsburgh that argues that the official figures are not consistent with certain other statistical indicators that normally are correlated with GDP growth. Though this latter view is controversial, whether it is correct or not applies mainly only to the late 1990s. There is little doubt among most foreign analysts that GDP growth in China since the year 2000 has been very rapid, and some analysis even suggests that the real growth rate could be higher than the official rate. Delving into these statistical issues is well beyond the scope of this essay.

[20] Data on the growth rate of these other Asian nations can be found in many sources. See The World Bank's annual *World Development Reports*.

has a long way to go. In 2004 Chinese per capita GDP in U.S. dollars (converted using the official exchange rate at that time) was still only $1,270. The Chinese exchange rate—much like the exchange rates of South Korea and Japan during the early phases of their rapid growth—is widely perceived to be undervalued, however. If China's exchange rate is still undervalued by 25% (even after the July revaluation of 2%), then China's exchange rate-converted per capita GDP would be roughly $1,600, still a low figure. The purchasing power parity (PPP) figure most often quoted for China in recent years is over $4,000 per capita.

China is thus very much still a relatively poor developing country. As such, assuming China adopts the proper policies as outlined above and maintains high productivity growth, the economy should continue to grow at an accelerated rate. As per capita income rises toward levels currently seen in economies such as South Korea and Taiwan, that growth rate will come down. The higher a country's income and the more complex and advanced its modern industrial and service sectors, the harder it is to achieve sustained rapid growth in the 7–9% range. The GDP growth rate in South Korea and Taiwan over the past decade has been around 5% per year. Rather than reflecting problems with their economies, these lower growth rates simply demonstrate the fact that these two economies can no longer simply follow along a well-trodden path laid down by the more advanced economies. The same situation occurred in Japan in the 1970s, when near double-digit growth rates came to an abrupt end. All of these economies have had to rely increasingly on their own research and development efforts in order to sustain high growth rates; growth at the frontiers of new technologies is a much slower process.

China, however, will not catch up to the current per capita income levels of South Korea or Taiwan for at least two decades—and will only do so if it grows on average at over 7% per capita or around 8% overall for the next 20 years. Can China sustain such high growth rates? As argued at the beginning of this essay, there is no clear reason for presuming China cannot achieve sustained growth rates of this magnitude, though there are also clearly many unknowns (such as unanticipated external shocks) that could upset growth for a time. Uncertainty also hovers over whether or not China can create efficient market institutions fast enough to sustain high productivity growth. Thus a conservative estimate of the growth prospects for China would be below 8% per year. This essay assumes a growth rate of 6–8% per year over the next decade. If growth is situated within this range over the coming decade, Chinese GDP in 2015 will be about double what it is today. Should growth at these rates be maintained for two decades, GDP will be around four times the current level.

China's Defense Budget Growth

China's rapid GDP growth has facilitated an even more rapid growth of the Chinese defense budget, at least over the past decade. At the beginning of the reform period in 1978, however, the officially reported Chinese defense budget was a much higher share of GDP (4.3%) than it is today. That percentage declined steadily throughout the 1980s and into the 1990s, bottoming out at just under 1.1% of GDP in 1996. By 2003, the official share of defense spending in GDP had risen to 1.6%.

It is well known, however, that the official defense budget does not include many items that would normally appear in the defense budgets of the United States or the nations of Europe. Certain expenditures, for example, are supported by funds from local, county, municipal, and provincial governments and are not formally part of the defense budget. One particularly murky area for almost two decades were the funds derived from the profits of industrial and commercial enterprises. Chinese leaders issued a directive in 1998 ordering the Chinese military to withdraw from the management of non-military businesses. Moreover, items known to be excluded from the official defense budget include certain major purchases of weapons from abroad; a portion of the budget for military-related research, development, testing and evaluation; and the funds for the People's Armed Police (*Wujing*), a paramilitary force.[21]

Estimates regarding the size of the expenditures that are not included in the formal budget vary widely but, for the purposes of this study, a figure roughly double the official defense budget will be used since something in that range is similar to the estimates of many prominent sources of defense expertise.[22] The figures for the official defense budget and the estimated (doubled) budget are presented in **Table 1**. Two straightforward conclusions can be drawn from the data. Accelerated Chinese growth has enabled Beijing to expand China's military budget very rapidly at least in nominal terms. However, China has—at least until the mid-1990s—actually chosen to steadily reduce defense expenditures as a share of GDP.

One can speculate as to why the Chinese government steadily reduced the share of GDP spent on defense, but one plausible reason is that the perceived external military threat from the Soviet Union began to recede

---

[21] This brief discussion is based on David Shambaugh, "Calculating China's Military Expenditure" (report prepared for the Council on Foreign Relations, Task Force on Chinese Military Power, June 25, 2002).

[22] A figure of roughly double the official defense budget is preferred in ibid. See also Office of the Secretary of Defense, "Annual Report of the Military Power of the People's Republic of China, 2004," May 2004; and International Institute of Strategic Studies, *The Military Balance, 2004–2005* (London: Oxford University Press, 2004).

steadily in the 1980s (from a high point in the 1970s). A second reason is that most Chinese weapons (such as aircraft and tanks) were obsolete, and China did not yet have the technological capacity to significantly upgrade these weapons. Simply expanding purchases of obsolete weapons and re-cruiting more infantry soldiers would do little to enhance China's military capacity. China's homeland defense efforts in the 1970s and early 1980s were based on what the Chinese called "peoples' war," a strategy which utilized a vast militia trained in the use of infantry weapons. Such a militia could not stop an armored invasion from the Soviet Union or other adversary, but could make life miserable for any invading army trying to occupy and govern any significant amount of populated territory.

By the mid-1990s, in contrast, China had begun to establish its research and development capacity in a wide variety of areas of advanced technology, including some areas of military technology. Furthermore, as mentioned above, China had acquired the capacity to earn large amounts of foreign exchange, making purchases of military equipment from abroad easily af-fordable. With foreign exchange earnings of over $600 billion per year (ex-ports plus foreign direct investment), China can afford purchases of foreign military equipment totaling in the tens of billions of dollars per year. Beijing has, however, chosen to purchase far less than this, presumably because it does not want to become dependent on foreign sources of military equip-ment. Beijing is also deterred by the fact that U.S. and European military equipment is not available for purchase.

Before speculating on how large the Chinese military budget might be-come over the next five to ten years, it is useful to try to understand what such a budget (measured either in Chinese currency or in U.S. dollars) in-dicates regarding China's military capacity. Roughly one-third of China's official military budget is allotted for expenditures on personnel, whether in the form of salaries or the direct provision of benefits such as housing and healthcare. With the rise of the market economy and the elimination of labor allocation policies (which had determined where a person could work), China's military has had to compete for skilled personnel by offer-ing increasingly competitive wages. Wages in the Chinese military have thus risen rapidly in recent years, a change that has been reflected in the military budget.

The cost of military equipment and of maintenance services has no doubt also risen over time, but we do not have an appropriate deflator for military equipment. Table 1, for lack of a better deflator, uses the index for ex-factory prices of industrial products. For personnel costs, the state sec-tor's average wage change stands as a plausible estimate for the change in the average salary of all military personnel. The use of this wage index to

Table 1. China's Official and Estimated Defense Budget

	Official Budget (bn yuan, current prices)	Defense expenditures (as share of GDP)	Estimated defense budget (official budget x 2; bn yuan, current prices)	"Real" national defense expenditures (bn yuan, 2003 prices)
1978	16.8	0.046	33.6	...
1980	19.4	0.043	38.8	...
1985	19.2	0.021	38.3	113.7
1990	29.0	0.016	58.1	97.2
1991	33.0	0.015	66.1	102.8
1992	37.8	0.014	75.6	104.6
1993	42.6	0.012	85.2	95.6
1994	55.1	0.012	110.1	96.0
1995	63.7	0.011	127.3	95.5
1996	72.0	0.011	144.0	100.3
1997	81.3	0.011	162.5	109.1
1998	93.5	0.012	186.9	120.0
1999	107.6	0.013	215.3	133.1
2000	120.8	0.013	241.5	140.0
2001	144.2	0.015	288.4	157.9
2002	170.8	0.016	341.6	180.0
2003	190.8	0.016	381.6	190.8

... = data not available for price deflation

Methodology: The official national defense budget in current prices is taken from the year-books of the National Statistical Office. The share of that budget in GDP is obtained by dividing the official Chinese GDP in current prices by the official military budget. The estimated total defense budget was obtained by multiplying the official budget by two. Many attempts to estimate the true size of the defense budget come up with figures double that of the official budget, but there are somewhat lower estimates and some much higher estimates of the true figure. The total defense budget in 2003 prices was calculated by first assuming that one third of defense expenditures were for personnel (this is the figure sometimes given in Chinese sources although it is unknown whether it would apply to total defense expenditures including items excluded from the official defense budget) and two-thirds for non-personnel expenditures such as military equipment. The personnel budget in current prices was then converted into 2003 prices using the index of wages in the state sector as the assumed deflator for personnel wages. The non-personnel expenditures were converted into 2003 prices using the ex-factory price index. The personnel and non-personnel figures so obtained were then added together and that is the figure presented in this table. This methodology, it needs to be emphasized, is only a very crude indicator of the real changes in defense expenditures over the period covered because a variety of plausible assumptions subject to a considerable margin of error had to be made in making these calculations.

convert Chinese military personnel expenditures into constant year 2000 prices probably understates the growth in actual military personnel budget since these prices assume no improvement in personnel quality over time. Because the quality of both military and civilian personnel has certainly improved since the 1990s, Chinese military capacity in real terms grew somewhat faster (though by an unknown amount) than the deflated figures in Table 1.

The above exercise provides imperfect measure of the real increase in Chinese military expenditures, but does not indicate the size of the Chinese military budget relative to that of other countries. To make that comparison, the data must first be converted from Chinese renminbi into a common currency such as U.S. dollars. The usual practice is to use the official exchange rate between the Chinese yuan and the U.S. dollar, as has been done in Table 1. Exchange rate conversions are, however, notoriously unreliable measures of the difference in standards of living between countries that have widely varying per capita incomes. For similar although not identical reasons, exchange rate conversion comparisons are also an unreliable basis for comparing military capacities between countries with very different levels of per capita income. The preferred method for trying to attain a reliable comparison of living standards between developed and developing coun tries is PPP—although this method poses its own theoretical problems. The question that should now be posed is: what is the equivalent to the method in the military sphere?

A direct application of the PPP method to Chinese military expenditures would involve revaluing each item in the budget at international prices (usually in U.S. dollars). For the Chinese military budget, this would mean an erroneous increase in the personnel expenditures. Chinese military personnel are no doubt less well-trained and less skilled than those in the U.S. military, but the difference in fighting abilities (ignoring, for now, the quality of equipment) hardly approaches the salary differential. By contrast, weapons are, at least in principle, traded goods with similar prices on the world market. China can and does purchase military aircraft and other weapons from abroad at international prices. Because China places a premium on the ability to produce its own military equipment, however, it is no doubt more expensive for China to produce high technology military hardware than it is for the United States to produce similar hardware. On the flipside, China can certainly produce standard infantry weapons at a lower cost than can the United States.

Plausible PPP estimates of Chinese military expenditures suggest that the figure would be at least double current total defense expenditure estimates (which are themselves double the official defense budgets).[23] Does this supposed PPP figure imply, however, that China's true military capacity is twice that of Western estimates of four times the official published figure for China's true defense expenditures? Any answer to such a question depends on what kind of war this military would be expected to fight.

A war in defense of the Chinese homeland would presumably make use of China's vast reserves of manpower, including, but not limited to, the regular military, the peoples' armed police, and the militias. Such a force would be difficult to defeat by any measure. Thus it is reasonable to calculate China's military capacity as being far greater than even a PPP figure four times the official defense expenditure. On the other hand, should a military engagement take place far from the Chinese mainland, involve large naval and air force capacities, and be dominated by high-tech weapons, then the exchange rate conversion of the Chinese military budget would be a better measure of the country's true military capacity. Manpower and infantry weapons would be largely ineffective in such a conflict.

When contrasting military capacity with military expenditure, therefore, the Chinese budget is not a very reliable guide. True analysis of China's military capacity needs to take into account, in addition to many other factors, the quality of specific weapons and the training and motivation of personnel; even then, the measure of capacity would depend on the situation. Such a calculation is beyond the scope of this paper. All that can be attempted here are a few projections concerning the Chinese military budget likely to occur under realistic circumstances, keeping in mind, of course, the limitations of budgetary figures and the true capacity of the Chinese military in specific situations.

How large could the Chinese military budget become over the next five to ten years? The most plausible range of scenarios encompasses a China largely at peace with the rest of the world and hesitant to settle the Taiwan issue through military means. A more extreme scenario would include a China determined to settle the Taiwan issue militarily—even at the cost of an extended confrontation with the United States. Under the former scenario, one could anticipate Chinese defense expenditures rising slowly from the current roughly 3% of GDP to perhaps 3.5% over the next five to ten years. If, as suggested above, GDP growth is 6% to 8% a year (or, to simplify

---

[23] A plausible exercise is to revalue the wages of the 2 million personnel in the armed forces at the U.S. minimum wage rate (a rate that applies to the least skilled workers in the U.S. labor market). This assumption probably understates the true worth of the Chinese soldier, but even this rate leads to Chinese expenditures on military personnel of 172 billion yuan (5x40x52x8.28x2,000,000=172 billion yuan). This figure is almost as large as the total official defense expenditures in the 2003–04 period. If the percentage of personnel costs in the unofficial parts of the defense budget estimates is similar to that in the official budget, then the PPP figure for personnel alone would double the unofficial defense budget (which is in turn double the official defense budget).

the calculations, 7%), then GDP would rise by 40% in five years and would double in ten years. In that case, defense expenditures would rise to around $80 billion in 2010 to nearly $140 billion in 2015. These figures assume that the Chinese yuan-U.S. dollar exchange rate remains similar to what it was after the July revaluation (which seems unlikely). If, for instance, the Chinese exchange rate is revalued to RMB7=US$1, then defense figures for 2010 and 2015 would be $95 billion and $164 billion respectively (in 2004 prices). In the more pessimistic scenario, China could easily expand defense expenditures to 5% or 6% of GDP, with resulting defense expenditures of $135–160 billion in 2010 and $230–280 billion in 2015.[24]

Though the specific figures in these projections are not of great significance, they do make one important point. If China's leadership so demands, then the country will soon have the capacity to support a very large military budget. A budget of even 5% or 6% of GDP could be sustained for quite some time without cutting into the overall rate of economic growth. If, for example, the increase in military expenditure came out of the investment total currently at around 40% of GDP, that investment rate would fall to 37% or 38% of GDP, which is still an extraordinarily high figure. If a reduction in the rate of investment led to an increase in the efficiency of the remaining investment (since the investment cut out was largely the least productive public sector investment), then the GDP growth rate might not fall at all.

Although these higher projections suggest that Chinese defense spending is at levels four times the current projections, it is important to reiterate that this does not necessarily mean that China's military capacity will similarly increase fourfold as well. The main constraint on China's military capacity at present is not the country's inability to fund an expanding military. The real constraint is China's inability to rapidly improve its military technology to a point where the Chinese military can effectively engage in conflicts some distance from the Chinese mainland. Chinese technological capacities are clearly improving at a quick pace, but whether or not that pace is also rapidly catching up with the technological capacities of potential adversaries is an issue beyond the scope of this chapter.

Conclusion

Since the beginning of the reform period in 1978, China's rapid growth has impacted China, the region, and the world in ways that extend well beyond economics. With the notable exception of the Tiananmen Square tragedy, this sustained growth has been a prime factor contributing to the most

---

[24] These figures also assume an exchange rate of RMB7=US$1.

prolonged period of political stability in China in the past century. Such growth has also enabled China to become a major international power influencing both the economic and political sphere. The question for the future is whether this high economic growth can sustain itself.

As the above analysis has indicated, China is likely to accumulate both physical and human capital at an accelerated rate for at least the next decade (and probably longer). The real challenge for China's economy will be to maintain a high rate of growth in the efficiency with which those inputs of capital and labor are being used. Many of the productivity gains to date have been one-shot affairs, and China needs to find a way of sustaining high productivity growth. That goal will involve a steady and determined effort to improve institutions such as corporate governance and the legal and financial system. Beijing is trying to accomplish precisely this, in part through the steady expansion of the private sector and in part through the curtailment of the share of the state-owned industrial and service sectors. The only real question concerns whether or not the Chinese leadership is doing so with sufficient determination and speed to obtain the desired results.

This chapter has argued that, if Beijing can avoid a major domestic political upheaval or international conflict, then China is very likely to sustain high rates of economic growth over the next decade and beyond. Rapid growth in and of itself will help to maintain political stability in the short term. Over the long term, however, rapid economic growth will create a more prosperous and better-educated population that will demand greater participation in the political arena. The transition to a more pluralistic political system, however, is likely beyond the single decade framework of the forecasts in this essay.

In addition to facilitating a rapid rise in the standard of living of most of the Chinese people, rapid economic growth will also make possible a steady rise in the Chinese military budget. Having the ability to increase the military budget, of course, is not equivalent to actually expanding military expenditures to match or surpass the growth rate of GDP. Even in a peaceful environment, however, China will eventually desire major world power status in military as well as economic terms. The Chinese military already has a formidable capacity for defense of the homeland. With continued enhancement of its military technological capacity, China will no doubt at some point possess a major military capacity extending beyond its borders, but this is probably unattainable within the coming decade.

All of these rapid-growth forecasts could, of course, come to a grinding halt should China suffer a sustained period of domestic political instability or become involved in major military confrontations with other world powers. A slowly growing China that stumbles from crisis to crisis would, however, probably be of more danger to the outside world than it is today, or is likely to be if high growth continues. Chinese military technology would continue to improve and the military budget could become a much larger share of GDP. Most importantly, the world would have to deal with a Chinese leadership desperate to use whatever means possible to retain power. Such a leadership would be far more difficult to deal with than one which works in the context of an increasingly prosperous economy. The best hope for the long-term future, therefore, is that China continues to enjoy high rates of economic growth and increasing integration of its economy into the world economic system.

The United States can draw two primary conclusions from the above discussion. First, China's continued rapid growth, combined with the steady integration of China's economy into the global economic system is, from Washington's perspective, the most ideal scenario. Conversely, a slow-growing China lumbering from crisis to crisis would have far graver implications for the United States, particularly in the security sphere. This situation does not preclude the United States from taking whatever measures it deems necessary to support domestic industries facing inappropriate forms of competition from China. It does, however, preclude the United States from pushing for across-the-board protectionist measures certain to do real harm to the Chinese economy, particularly if similar measures were introduced by the European Union. Such measures would, of course, also undermine the global economic system in general, given China's large and growing role in that system—a system that the United States has spent decades trying to build and strengthen.

Second, there is little Washington can do to significantly slow the growth of Chinese military expenditures or of Chinese domestic research and development efforts in the military sphere. That said, U.S. and European Union long-term interests are clearly not served through advanced weapon sales to Beijing or research assistance with clear military applications.

Executive Summary

This chapter discusses the security environment of the Republic of China (ROC, also known as Taiwan) and Taipei's qualitative and quantitative efforts to modernize its military in the face of growing threats from China.

Main Arguments:

- Taiwan's military is clearly modernizing (and will improve in the near- to mid-term). A reorientation away from an army-centric focus has led to such improvements as joint warfighting capability among branches of the military and improvements in missile defense systems, front-line military units, and naval defense capabilities.

- Progress has been slow, however, and characterized by a number of deficiencies, including inadequate funding levels, an absence of strategic clarity, often misplaced priorities, and unaddressed vulnerabilities.

- Deficiencies in Taiwan's military modernization in large part reflect the influence of Taiwan's highly dynamic and divisive domestic political, bureaucratic, and social environment; a historical legacy of military-oriented rule; and the vagaries of U.S. political and military assistance.

Policy Implications:

- Glaring shortcomings in Taiwan's military modernization efforts could lead to miscalculations both in China and on Taiwan regarding the cross-Strait military balance, resulting in either side undertaking dangerous or destabilizing actions.

- Taipei and Washington must balance a mutual desire to modernize Taiwan's military for deterrence purposes against the need to avoid an escalation of tension with the mainland.

- Washington could benefit by further improving Taiwan's ability to "hold on" in the initial stage of a cross-Strait conflict, the period of greatest military and political risk for Taiwan.

Military Modernization in Taiwan

Michael D. Swaine and Roy D. Kamphausen

Taiwan's current and future military capabilities, military modernization and reform program, and underlying national security strategy pose
major implications for stability and prosperity in East Asia. This is largely
because the security and political status of Taiwan are a major source of tension and dispute between Asia's two dominant nuclear powers: the United
States and the People's Republic of China (PRC). The United States seeks to
use political and military means to deter China from employing any form of
coercion or force against Taiwan that is aimed at either preventing independence or attaining national unification. China seeks to deter both Taiwan
and the United States from employing political or military means to achieve
de jure independence for the island or to close off the option of eventual reunification. Taiwan's evolving military capacity, security policy, and defense
relationship with the United States directly affect both of these sets of U.S.
and PRC deterrence calculations. In addition, Taiwan's military capabilities—or lack thereof—as well as its defense policies and relationships also
influence the calculations of Taiwan's political leadership as Taipei strives to
strengthen both the island's security and status in the international arena.

In terms of Chinese calculations, there is little doubt that significant
changes in the composition, size, and doctrinal or strategic underpinnings of
Taiwan's military and the island's defense relationship with the United States

Michael D. Swaine, Senior Associate in the China Program at the Carnegie Endowment for
International Peace, has testified to Congress and served as a consultant to the U.S. government. He
can be reached at <mswaine@carnegieendowment.org>.

Roy Kamphausen, Director of National Security Affairs at The National Bureau of Asian Research, is
a retired U.S. Army China Foreign Area Officer. He can be reached at <rkamphausen@nbr.org>.

Some of the information presented in this chapter was derived from interviews with government
officials, defense planners, and strategists based in both the United States and Taiwan. These interviews
were conducted on a confidential basis. The authors would like to thank John Kemmer and Peter
Mattis for providing invaluable assistance in the research and writing of this paper.

can significantly influence a range of key factors relating to Beijing's threat assessment, military posture, and overall strategy regarding triangular relations. Such factors include: China's assessment of the capability and willingness of Taipei to press for greater levels of autonomy (or, conversely, to enter into meaningful negotiations over unification), China's ability to prevail in coercing or defeating Taiwan, and Chinese perceptions of Washington's political and military stance toward the island, including potential U.S. support for Taiwan independence. As for U.S. calculations, the evolution of Taiwan's military deterrence and warfighting capabilities as well as Taipei's security strategy clearly have a significant influence on Washington's confidence in its overall ability to work with Taipei to deter or defeat Chinese aggression; these calculations include a basic assessment of China's willingness and ability to employ force against the island. Finally, Taipei's military and strategic features—and their implications for U.S. political and military support—can greatly influence the willingness of the Taiwan government to pursue (or resist) political negotiations with Beijing, to seek additional sources of political and military support beyond the United States, and to undertake indigenous efforts to strengthen the Taiwan military.

The first section of this chapter examines Taiwan's national security objectives and resulting foreign and defense policies, and identifies several major ongoing policy debates and political/social tensions relevant to military modernization. The second section describes the most important functional elements of Taiwan's force structure and military modernization program, identifies the significance of each element to Taiwan's defense capabilities, and assesses the progress achieved thus far. The third section evaluates the likely capacity of the Taiwan military to cope with several possible conflict scenarios that might occur over the next five years. The conclusion examines the implications of the preceding for the overall ability of Taiwan to defend itself and suggests how the island's military modernization effort might be improved over the near to medium term.

This chapter argues that Taiwan has acquired significant military capabilities that will help the island cope with the growing PRC threat. Taiwan's program of military modernization has not, however, developed in as focused, deliberate, and determined a manner as one might expect given the daunting challenges the island faces; advances have been sporadic, and have been marked by inadequate levels of funding, an absence of strategic clarity, often misplaced priorities, and persistent unaddressed vulnerabilities.

Such deficiencies in large part reflect the influence of Taiwan's highly dynamic and divisive domestic political, bureaucratic, and social environment; a historical legacy of military-oriented rule; and the vagaries (and pressures) of U.S. political and military assistance. Overall, given the nature of the increasing threat and Taiwan's importance to Asian stability and U.S. interests, the implications of the current scope and composition of Taiwan's military modernization program are ominous. Though increasing levels of U.S. assistance are enabling Taipei to address these problems to some degree, it remains unclear how successful this effort will be in maintaining deterrence and sustaining Taiwan's ability to defend itself against a growing Chinese threat. Washington should consider focusing more closely on improving Taiwan's ability to "hold on" in the initial stage of a conflict—the period of greatest military and political risk for Taiwan.

Taiwan's National Objectives and Resulting Foreign and Defense Policies

National Objectives

Taiwan has four broad national objectives that together shape the island's overall national security strategy and foreign and defense policies:

- To sustain popular confidence in the ability of the government to protect Taiwan's physical security and to ensure Taiwan's continued economic prosperity and political freedom in the face of a growing Chinese threat[1]

- To maximize all possible political and diplomatic assistance (including recognition) provided by the international community, particularly that provided by the United States

- To ensure Taiwan's continued access to overseas markets and sources of materials and technologies necessary both to sustain Taiwan's growth and security and to enhance the island's international influence

- To create and sustain an indigenous military capability and to receive military assistance and support from the United States and other Western powers sufficient to deter China from attacking Taiwan and, if deterrence fails, to prevent China from subjugating the island

China poses a significant threat to Taiwan both because of the PRC's claim to sovereignty over the island as well as because of Beijing's steadfast

---

[1] This objective requires the Taiwan government to walk a fine line between ensuring the strength, dignity, and de facto independence of the island and its populace while avoiding any provocation of the PRC regime that could result in a potentially disastrous attack.

commitment to preventing Taiwan from achieving *de jure* independence, by force if necessary. While clearly preferring to resolve the status of Taiwan by peaceful means, the Chinese leadership nonetheless fears that the emergence of an increasingly separate Taiwanese identity (as a consequence of the island's ongoing democratization and increasing levels of U.S. political and military support) could eventually result in an attempt by Taiwan's leaders to achieve a position of permanent separation as a *de jure* independent state recognized by the major world powers. As a result, since the mid- to late-1990s, the People's Liberation Army (PLA) has accelerated its military modernization efforts in response to central leadership directives to develop military options to deter such an outcome, or, should deterrence fail, to prevail in a military conflict over the island.[2] Under current circumstances, China's leaders would almost certainly utilize force against Taiwan if they were to conclude that a peaceful resolution of the issue had become a virtual impossibility.

The ability of mainland China to threaten Taiwan has increased significantly since the early 1990s. In particular, high economic growth rates and increasing involvement in the international community have permitted China to acquire greater military capabilities, significantly increased Beijing's access to and influence within the international community, and increased the desire of other countries to maintain good relations with China and to support Beijing's position regarding the status of Taiwan.[3] Moreover, as a result of the rapid emergence and deepening of a broad range of economic and financial ties between the island and the mainland, Beijing's ability to influence—if not coerce—Taipei has arguably increased significantly over the past decade or more.[4]

In meeting the Chinese threat, Taiwan remains heavily dependent on support provided by the United States. President George W. Bush has clearly conveyed a high level of commitment to assist the island if it is attacked by the mainland. Yet U.S. support and assistance for Taiwan are not founded on an explicit security alliance or any formal security guarantees, nor are they based on a formal diplomatic relationship. Moreover, U.S. strategy and tactics in upholding its commitments to Taiwan are heavily influenced by Washington's larger strategic, economic, and political interests in Asia—and China in particular. These interests include the desire to prevent the Taiwan

---

[2] U.S. Department of Defense, "The Military Power of the People's Republic of China, 2005," annual report to Congress, ii, at http://www.defenselink.mil/news/Jul2005/d20050719china.pdf.

[3] For details of recent acquisitions of the People's Liberation Army (PLA), see David Shambaugh's chapter on China in this volume; and David Shambaugh, *Modernizing China's Military: Progress, Problems, and Prospects* (Berkeley, CA: University of California Press, 2002), chs. 3, 4, 6.

[4] This paragraph is drawn from Michael D. Swaine and James Mulvenon, *Taiwan's Foreign and Defense Policies: Features and Determinants* (Santa Monica, CA: RAND, 2001), 5–6.

issue from fundamentally destabilizing Sino-U.S. relations.[5] Thus, while Taiwan is highly reliant on U.S. support and enjoys an enhanced security commitment from the current U.S. administration, Taipei should not assume that the United States can (or will) guarantee Taiwan's security and provide unconditional support.[6]

Taiwan's vulnerability is accentuated by its high level of dependence on overseas markets, products, and technology for continued economic growth and prosperity. In other words, Taiwan is a trading state and hence must maintain access to regional and global resources and markets in order to survive. At the same time, so long as the level and scope of Taiwan's foreign economic power remain high, economic links with the Asia-Pacific and beyond provide Taipei with an important potential source of political influence. Outside of the United States, however, international political support for Taiwan remains highly limited. No major nations—and only a relatively small number of minor nations—recognize Taiwan as a sovereign, independent state.[7]

Finally, Taiwan's interactions with China also clearly influence the island's overall foreign and defense policy objectives. Taipei strives to expand and improve its economic, social, and cultural contacts with China in order both to assist Taiwan's development and to lower tensions that could lead to a cross-Strait conflict. On the other hand, Taipei also desires to avoid being placed in a position whereby Beijing can use the mainland's growing links with the island either to pressure Taipei to accept its approach to reunification or otherwise increase pressure on Taiwan to come to terms with China in a manner that compromises Taiwan's interests.[8]

---

[5] The latter interest has become especially important ever since the emergence of the global war on terrorism and the war in Iraq, which together make it imperative for Washington to avoid any new crises with major states such as China. Indeed, the need to maintain cooperation with China on issues such as the North Korean nuclear program has grown markedly since those events. See Michael Swaine, "China: Exploiting a Strategic Opening," in *Strategic Asia 2004–05: Confronting Terrorism in the Pursuit of Power*, ed. Ashley Tellis and Michael Wills (Seattle: The National Bureau of Asian Research, 2004), 67–101; and Swaine and Mulvenon, *Taiwan's Foreign and Defense Policies*, 6–7.

[6] The Taiwan Relations Act merely indicates that any use of force against Taiwan by the PRC would be viewed with "grave concern" by Washington, and that, if mainland China poses a military threat to Taiwan's security, the U.S. president should consult with Congress as to how to respond. For the full text of the TRA, see Paul H. Tai, ed., *United States, China, and Taiwan: Bridges for a New Millennium* (Carbondale, IL.: Public Policy Institute, Southern Illinois University, 1999), 237–51.

[7] This paragraph was drawn primarily from Swaine and Mulvenon, *Taiwan's Foreign and Defense Policies*, 7.

[8] Ibid., 10.

Foreign Policy

Taiwan's foreign policy strives to maintain and, if possible, expand Taiwan's political, diplomatic, and economic relationship with the international community. This has required a rather unconventional approach to conducting foreign relations. Such an approach is based upon a rejection of the past, narrow "zero-sum" China-Taiwan competition over diplomatic recognition and participation in international bodies in favor of a highly flexible and pragmatic "positive-sum" approach that tolerates a wide variety of international contacts. This new effort centers on the pursuit of a de facto "dual recognition" or "two Chinas" strategy that is marked by a willingness to use a variety of enticements (mostly economic) that will enable Taipei to establish diplomatic relations with states irrespective of their existing relations with Beijing. Taipei's strategy also includes a general emphasis on the establishment and expansion of a wide range of both official and unofficial, non-diplomatic "substantive" political, cultural, and economic ties with other states and international bodies as well as efforts to facilitate the expansion of Taiwan's access to overseas markets, technology, and resources. ROC leaders hope to accomplish these goals by using a variety of formulations and mechanisms.

Taipei's overriding foreign policy objective is to strengthen the U.S. commitment to Taiwan's security and prosperity without increasing tension or provoking a major conflict with mainland China. Taiwan seeks a continued U.S. commitment to both the Taiwan Relations Act and to the "six assurances,"[9] which together provide the basis of U.S. political and military support for Taiwan. This objective, in turn, implies a desire to expand the degree of support for Taiwan provided by U.S. political and economic elites, especially members of Congress and important business leaders. Taipei hopes that such support would improve the level and type of U.S. military assistance provided to Taiwan, both for the sake of strengthening Taiwan's military capabilities with respect to China as well as conveying an impression of a heightened U.S. commitment to the security of Taiwan and to the peaceful resolution of the China-Taiwan imbroglio. Although rarely openly acknowledged, Taiwan's policy toward the United States also includes efforts to prevent Washington from either improving relations with Beijing

---

[9] The six assurances were six points proposed by the ROC government to the U.S. government in 1982 as guidelines for the latter to use in conducting U.S.-Taiwan relations; they state that: (1) the United States will not set a date for termination of arms sales to Taiwan, (2) the United States will not alter the terms of the Taiwan Relations Act, (3) the United States will not consult with China in advance before making decisions about U.S. arms sales to Taiwan, (4) the United States will not mediate between Taiwan and China, (5) the United States will not alter its position regarding the sovereignty of Taiwan and would not pressure Taiwan to enter into negotiations with China, and (6) the United States will not formally recognize Chinese sovereignty over Taiwan. See Tai, *United States, China, and Taiwan*, 260–61.

at Taipei's expense or explicitly striking a deal with Beijing that might compromise Taiwan's interests. This foreign policy objective is clearly reflected in the six assurances.[10]

Defense Policy and Military Strategy

Taiwan's defense policy and military strategy seek to maintain a credible deterrent or otherwise adequate countermeasures against all likely future PRC military threats. This is to be achieved through the formulation of an appropriate military doctrine and related operational guidelines for the Taiwan military as well as the maintenance of a comparably capable force structure and C4I/logistics infrastructure.[11]

In the early 1990s, when Taipei formally abolished its longstanding goal to retake the Chinese mainland, Taiwan's military doctrine shifted from an emphasis on unified offensive-defensive operations (*gongshou yiti*) to a purely defensive-oriented concept (*shoushi fangyu*) that excludes provocative or preemptive military actions.[12] Taiwan's current defensive posture contains two strategic notions: "resolute defense" (*fangwei gushou*) and "effective deterrence" (*youxiao hezu*). The former concept is largely political and defensive, and connotes the determination of the Taiwan military to defend all the areas directly under its control without ceding any territory. The latter concept is more active and forward-oriented, and connotes a commitment to the development and maintenance of a military capability sufficient to severely punish any threatening or invading force and to deny such a force the attainment of its objectives. In other words, Taiwan's defense strategy focuses on survival, not on "winning" *per se*.[13]

Despite their arguably limited objectives, the implementation of the above defense concepts presents enormous challenges for Taiwan for several reasons. First, China is a very large potential adversary in possession of significant resources. Second, while serving as a defensive barrier against ground assault, the Taiwan Strait is only 100 nautical miles wide and thus in close proximity to the Chinese mainland. Third, Taiwan is a long, narrow

---

[10] These two paragraphs were largely drawn from Swaine and Mulvenon, *Taiwan's Foreign and Defense Policies*, 98–99.

[11] Much of the following description of Taiwan's defense doctrine and related military policies is excerpted from Michael D. Swaine, *Taiwan's National Security, Defense Policy, and Weapons Procurement Processes* (Santa Monica, CA: RAND, 1999), 51–61.

[12] Alexander Chieh-cheng Huang, "Taiwan's View of Military Balance and the Challenge It Presents," in *Crisis in the Taiwan Strait*, ed. James R. Lilley and Chuck Downs (Washington, D.C.: National Defense University Press, September 1997), 282–83.

[13] The preceding two paragraphs were largely derived from Swaine and Mulvenon, *Taiwan's Foreign and Defense Policies*, 11.

island that provides little opportunity for maneuver and defense-in-depth.[14] These factors suggest that the Taiwan military must possess a military strategy that is highly efficient in the use of limited resources, effectively integrates early warning and rapid response capabilities, maximizes the application of military countermeasures against the most likely and potent threats from the PLA, does not inadvertently provoke a PLA attack during a crisis or unnecessarily escalate an existing conflict, and reinforces to the maximum extent possible any assistance that the United States might provide in a crisis or conflict.[15]

As a result of these requirements and conditions, Taiwan's defense planners have for many years maintained a four-layer defense-in-depth strategy that consists of (1) a front line that encompasses the defense of ROC territory lying in close proximity to the Chinese mainland (including the highly fortified islands of Quemoy and Matsu); (2) the middle line of the Taiwan Strait, which has served for over forty years as an unofficial but mutually understood "boundary" separating PRC and ROC air and naval forces; (3) Taiwan's coastline, which must be successfully defended to ensure the defeat of any invasion force; and (4) the western plain of Taiwan, the successful defense of which would prevent any invading forces from securing Taiwan's north-south Chungshan highway and thereby gain rapid access to the entire island.[16]

Until recently, this approach has translated into a relatively simple defense doctrine of air-to-air, naval-to-naval, and ground-to-ground force interdiction marked by almost no operational interactions between the services; weak levels of both intra- and inter-service command, control, and communication; the maintenance of very sizeable ground forces; and an emphasis on retaining significant forces in reserve in order to stave off a PRC invasion until U.S. assistance arrives.[17]

Since at least the late 1990s, Taiwan's military leaders and defense planners, along with their U.S. advisors, have clearly recognized the need to improve this strategic approach as part of a larger effort to reform and strengthen the Taiwan military to cope with a growing Chinese threat. Specifically,

---

[14] For a detailed analysis on geographical issues, see Yuan Lin, "The Taiwan Strait is No Longer a Natural Barrier—PLA Strategies for Attacking Taiwan," *Kuang Chiao Ching*, April 16, 1996.

[15] Much of this paragraph is derived from Michael D. Swaine, "Deterring Conflict in the Taiwan Strait," Carnegie Paper, no. 46, July 2004, 12.

[16] This paragraph was derived from Swaine and Mulvenon, *Taiwan's Foreign and Defense Policies*, 12.

[17] Specifically, Taiwan's military forces were given three largely independent missions: (1) air superiority (*zhikong*) for the air force; (2) sea denial (*zhihai*) for the navy; and (3) anti-landing warfare (*fandenglu*) for the army. Each of these missions was generally viewed by each service as constituting a relatively separate and distinct task. In recent years, however, a greater emphasis has been placed on developing joint operations capabilities, as discussed in some detail below.

these leaders realize that the Taiwan military must streamline, restructure, and strengthen the organization and combat effectiveness of its forces and sharpen their strategic focus. In the former area, primary emphasis is on the creation of a more integrated, joint, and balanced military in possession of more mobile ground units, greatly improved naval and air capabilities, better surveillance and battle management systems, quicker response times, increased survivability (including both passive and active forms of defense against missile and air attack), and enhanced deterrence capabilities.[18]

In the latter area, the emphasis is on developing both a more comprehensive, integrated national security concept as well as a strategic planning system. These improvements are viewed as necessary to link growing threat perceptions to strategic priorities, military missions, operational doctrine, and force structure requirements in a way that will maximize the capacity of Taiwan's scarce military assets to protect vital national interests.[19] A series of organizational and procedural reforms are also viewed as necessary to ensure more effective civilian control over the armed forces, to more effectively integrate defense planning within the larger priorities of the government's national security policies (and within U.S. defense planning), and to eliminate waste, corruption, and inefficiency in military procurement and readiness. This ambitious set of objectives is in turn seen to require more concerted efforts to augment Taiwan's limited indigenous military systems through the procurement of critical weapons, support infrastructure, and military technology and training from outside sources, in particular the United States military.[20]

Taiwan has made some significant progress in recent years in attaining these highly ambitious objectives. During the past five years, Taipei passed two major defense reform laws that were designed to strengthen civilian control over the military and to streamline decision-making between the professional military command and Taiwan's political leaders.[21] Taipei is also

---

[18] Swaine, "Deterring Conflict in the Taiwan Strait," 7.

[19] Equally important, a more transparent, systematic, pragmatic, and institutionalized national security and military strategic planning process would permit the Taiwan government to deliver more convincing arguments regarding its weapons requirements to the United States, the Legislative Yuan, and other interested and influential players; to adjudicate disputes among the armed services more effectively; and to reduce the level of arbitrary or personal influence exerted over the entire process.

[20] Swaine and Mulvenon, *Taiwan's Foreign and Defense Policies*, 13–14.

[21] These two laws were the National Defense Law (NDL) and the Ministry of National Defense Organization Law (sometimes referred to collectively as the "Two Defense Laws"), which after ratification by the Legislative Yuan, were promulgated by the ROC president in January 2000 and subsequently went into effect on March 1, 2002. See Ministry of Defense, "2002 National Defense Report, Republic of China," July 2002, 164, 227, 230–32, http://www.mnd.gov.tw/report/index.htm; John Pomfret, "Also on Taipei's Radar: Reform," *Washington Post*, April 25, 2001; and Michael Tsai, "Organizational Reinvention and Defense Reform," *Taiwan Defense Affairs* 2, no. 3 (Spring 2003).

reportedly on the verge of promulgating a first-ever National Security Report (NSR). Developed primarily by the president's National Security Council (NSC), the NSR purportedly will present the first-ever integrated, detailed national security strategy for Taiwan and identify the role each agency will play in carrying out this strategy.[22]

In addition, Taipei has been attempting—with extensive U.S. assistance—to modernize and improve many aspects of Taiwan's force structure and operational doctrine (discussed in detail in the next section). Finally, according to at least one knowledgeable expert, Taiwan is putting much thought into strategies for greater indigenous defense industrial production and the use of offsets. The Executive Yuan has set up a commission to examine this issue, and an association akin to the National Defense Industrial Association in the United States already exists in Taiwan.[23]

Nonetheless, a host of factors continues to complicate the process of organizational reform, strategic revision, and force modernization. These include the influence of parochial senior leadership interests and views (in particular those of the president and the chief of staff of the military), vested military service interests (in which the ground forces continue to hold a privileged position), general political and bureaucratic rivalries, financial limitations, and differing political and social views over the urgency of the Chinese threat posed to Taiwan and the most likely type of military assault the PLA would launch against the island. Such divisions and differences have generated much conceptual debate and political tension relevant to various aspects of force modernization: defense spending; arms acquisitions; the utility of developing an offensive strike capability against China; and the relative size and importance of air, naval, and ground forces.[24]

Political/Social Tensions and Key Debates
Relevant to Military Modernization

The sharply divisive, zero-sum nature of Taiwan politics and the existence of fundamental societal differences over the island's identity and relations with mainland China have produced exceedingly high levels of political manipulation, obstructionism, and policy deadlock within Taiwan's political system. Indeed, despite President Chen Shui-bian's comments in his May 2004 inaugural address, in which he proclaimed Taiwan's demo-

---

[22] Huang Tai-lin, "Expectations Grow for National Security Report," *Taipei Times*, July 6, 2005, http://www.taipeitimes.com/News/taiwan/archives/2005/07/06/2003262399.

[23] The authors would like to thank an anonymous reviewer of the draft of this chapter for this information.

[24] Swaine, "Deterring Conflict in the Taiwan Strait," 13–14.

cratic development an "exemplary success," much remains to be done to enhance and consolidate Taiwan's democracy.[25] Such tasks include, among others, furthering constitutional reform, strengthening and improving the Legislative Yuan and—perhaps most importantly—eliminating vestiges of a KMT-dominated political system.[26] The apparent willingness of Taiwan's opposition parties to resort to extra-legal means to oppose the 2004 presidential election results and President Chen's attempt to push constitutional reform through popular referendum demonstrate "the fragility of some political elites' commitment to democratic procedures and norms."[27] These and other actions have not only further polarized Taiwan politics between the KMT-led pan-Blue and the DPP-led pan-Green coalitions but have also poisoned attempts to push forward with needed government reforms and democratic restructuring.[28]

The highly divisive nature of Taiwan politics and society is reflected in various aspects of civil-military relations. Many members of the ruling Democratic Progressive Party (DPP) and their political allies remain highly suspicious of large segments of Taiwan's senior officer corps—and in particular the army, which they regard as a bastion of pro-mainlander and pro-KMT influence.[29] Moreover, many politicians and a significant segment of the public view the military leadership as excessively secretive and prone to corruption and insider dealings with foreign and domestic defense corporations. For their part, many senior military officers regard the DPP as a disruptive, potentially dangerous political force that threatens to weaken the solidarity and effectiveness of the armed forces through often misguided attempts at excessively rapid and far-reaching reform. These officers also feel that the DPP risks a war with China by the party's steadfast pursuit of de jure independence. Civil-military relations have improved notably since 1990, when then Premier and former Chief of the General Staff Hau Pei-tsun stated that the army would not stand idly by should civilian authorities declare independence. However, many high-ranking officers reportedly remain intensely bitter toward what they see as efforts by the DPP and other

---

[25] See Chen Shui-bian's May 20, 2004 inaugural address, http://www.gio.gov.tw/taiwan-website/4-oa/20040520/2004052001.html

[26] For a good description of the challenges facing Taiwan's democratic development, see Shelley Rigger, *Politics in Taiwan: Voting for Democracy* (London: Routledge, 1999), 178–93; and Yun-han Chu, "Democratic Consolidation in the Post-KMT Era: The Challenge of Governance," in *Taiwan's Presidential Politics: Democratization and Cross-Strait Relations in the Twenty-First Century*, ed. Muthiah Alagappa (Armonk: M.E. Sharpe, 2001), 90–112.

[27] Shelley Rigger, "The Unfinished Business of Taiwanese Democratization," in *Dangerous Strait: The U.S.-Taiwan-China Crisis*, ed. Nancy Tucker (New York: Columbia University Press, 2005), 26.

[28] Ibid.

[29] For more on the lingering problem of military influence in politics, see Yun-Han Chu, "Democratic Consolidation," 94.

political forces to create a new Taiwan identity that rejects any future political association with mainland China.[30]

These political and social tensions significantly undermine efforts to reform and modernize the Taiwan military. In particular, they greatly complicate the already contentious process involved in the approval of arms purchases, allocation of defense spending, and downsizing of the military. For example, many opposition politicians and large portions of the public oppose major arms purchases (such as the unprecedented arms package approved for sale by the Bush administration in April 2001),[31] arguing that such purchases are overpriced, unnecessary (given Washington's supposed virtual "security guarantee" to Taiwan), unaffordable (given the faltering state of Taiwan's economy), and excessively provocative to Beijing.[32] Similarly, efforts to increase defense spending—currently at historically low levels—face protracted debates and politically-driven opposition. Even if approved, however, the proposed special budget would not cause the overall defense budget to exceed 3 percent of GDP.[33] Moreover, the efforts of the Chen administration to reduce the size of the army and strengthen civilian controls have encountered significant resistance from within the military. At the same time, the Chen administration has decided, apparently for financial and political reasons, to further reduce the period of mandatory military service while failing to provide incentives to increase the level of volunteerism.

---

[30] M. Taylor Fravel, "Towards Civilian Supremacy: Civil-Military Relations in Taiwan's Democratization," *Armed Forces and Society* 29, no. 1 (Fall 2002): 63–66.

[31] The April 2001 arms package approved by the United States included 12 P-3C anti-submarine and reconnaissance planes, six batteries of PAC-III ballistic missile defense systems, and an offer to assist Taiwan in acquiring eight diesel submarines. The total cost of the package has been estimated at approximately $16–18 billion. The Chen administration has proposed a special budget to supplement the annual defense budget in order to cover the cost of these systems. On the U.S. decision, see Steven Mufson and Thomas Ricks, "Dispute May Take Toll on Relations; Taiwan Arms Sales May Receive Boost," *Washington Post*, April 12, 2001; and Bill Gertz, "Bush Ponders Sale of Enhanced Arms Systems to Iran," *Washington Times*, March 31, 2001.

[32] For further details, see Swaine, *Taiwan's National Security, Defense Policy*, 45–47; and Swaine and Mulvenon, *Taiwan's Foreign and Defense Policies*, 65, 87–88. For a discussion of public attitudes regarding defense spending, see Swaine and Mulvenon, *Taiwan's Foreign and Defense Policies*, 74–75.

[33] An MND official has claimed that Taiwan's defense budget and special budget combined would be 2.85% of GDP; the regular defense budget alone comprises 2.54% of GDP; see, S.C. Chang, "Defense and Arms Purchase Budget Won't Top 2.85% of GDP: Official," *Central News Agency*, July 13, 2005. Taiwan recently toyed with the idea of increasing defense spending to 3% of GDP; see "TSU Backs Raising Defense Spending to 3% of GDP," *Taipei Times*, June 5, 2005, 3. However, an MND official said Taiwan can't afford a budget of this size; see Rich Chang, "Nation's Defense Budget Can't Be Expanded," *Taipei Times*, May 25, 2005, 3. For a general discussion of sustained Taiwan defense budget decline over the past decade, see Michael S. Chase, "Defense Reform in Taiwan," *Asian Survey* 45, no. 3 (May-June 2005): 372–73.

Such factors influence several related strategic debates over Taiwan's force structure and defense doctrine.[34] In the former debate, the dominant school of thought holds that Taiwan must develop a military strategy centered on the development of truly potent air and naval forces. The belief is that without such capabilities, Taiwan would be unable to deter or defeat the most likely types of PLA attack, such as an air and missile barrage, a naval blockade, or an amphibious assault—all of which require air and naval superiority for success. Moreover, according to proponents, air and naval forces would be especially important in any attempts to deflect a rapid, intense PLA strike against military, communication, infrastructure, and political centers in Taiwan. Some analysts view such a decapitation-centered *fait accompli* strike as the most likely type of attack, and one that is liable to occur before U.S. forces could appear on the scene. Proponents argue that the continued maintenance of large, costly ground forces mostly diverts scarce resources and energies away from the development of far more important air and naval capabilities. To support such capabilities, Taiwan should develop small, light, and highly mobile ground forces capable of responding quickly to limited PLA ground assaults.[35] As suggested above, proponents of this view—including senior naval and air force officers, as well as many U.S. military advisors and experts—largely shape current efforts to restructure the Taiwan military. In addition, some members of the pan-Green alliance reportedly support such a strategy as a means of reducing the influence of the army.

The opposing minority viewpoint believes that Taiwan must, for both military and political reasons, retain sizeable ground forces. This viewpoint holds that, from a military perspective, such forces are absolutely vital to prevent the PLA from achieving any final victory through seizure of the island of Taiwan. Without such a seizure, any military strategy the PLA might adopt would fall short of success. Moreover, proponents of this view argue that Taiwan's air and naval forces will never be able to attain the size and capability necessary to repel a massive PLA air and naval attack. They believe that the PLA would be quite willing to sacrifice large numbers of inferior aircraft and ships so as to deplete Taiwan's capabilities in a rapid conflict of attrition—in effect leaving the island defenseless, especially if the army were heavily reduced in size. For these advocates, the only sure guarantor of Taiwan's survival—presumably until U.S. forces arrive on the scene—are sizeable ground forces.

---

[34] The following paragraphs on these debates are primarily drawn from Swaine, "Deterring Conflict in the Taiwan Strait," 19–21.

[35] Author interviews, Washington and Taipei, spring and summer 2003.

From a political perspective, a sizeable ground force presence would also serve, for some observers, as a vital source of leverage for Taipei during any negotiations that might ensue in the aftermath of a conflict with China. Some proponents of this view are concerned that Beijing and Washington (or Washington alone) might attempt to coerce Taipei into accepting terms for resolving a conflict that do not serve Taiwan's interests. They believe that, without substantial ground forces Taiwan will have little ability to resist such pressure.

Because it is supported by significant numbers of influential senior army officers as well as some Taiwan strategists and scholars, this minority argument in favor of ground forces persists within the strategic debate. This support only reinforces efforts to resist major reductions in the size of the ground forces.[36] Moreover, this debate reportedly continues despite the fact that the army is downsizing and acquiring new roles, including leadership of an integrated counterterrorism/homeland security task force directed by the Executive Yuan.[37]

The defense doctrine debate largely focuses on the utility of offensive weapons, and has sharpened in recent years. Two basic schools of thought exist among proponents. One group argues that the acquisition of an offensive conventional counterforce capability is necessary to deter China from launching a conventional attack against Taiwan and, if deterrence fails, to effect a significant degradation of China's ability to sustain such an attack against Taiwan. These forces would have enhanced offensive information warfare capabilities and would essentially consist of several hundred short-range ballistic missiles (SRBM), land-attack cruise missiles (LACM), and air assets armed with standoff attack weapons capable of striking China's ports, theater command, control, and communication nodes, and missile launch sites.[38] Some advocates even argue that such capabilities might be used pre-emptively to derail a PLA strike before it is launched.[39] The second group argues that Taiwan must focus on acquiring offensive strategic countervalue capabilities to threaten major cities in central and southern China, such as Shanghai, Nanjing, Guangzhou, and even Hong Kong. These would mostly consist of a relatively small number of intermediate-range ballistic missiles (IRBM) or medium-range ballistic missiles (MRBM) armed with large con-

---

[36] Author interviews, Taipei, spring and summer 2003.

[37] One well-informed anonymous reviewer provided this information.

[38] See, for example, Richard D. Fisher, "Taiwan Considers Active Defense," Jamestown Foundation, *China Brief* 3, no. 2 (January 28, 2003).

[39] Defense Minister Tang Yiau-ming made this assertion; see "ROC Military Doesn't Rule Out Pre-emptive Attack on Mainland: Tang," *China News Agency*, October 8, 2003.

ventional (or perhaps even nuclear) or biological warheads, and would serve purely as a deterrent against an all-out Chinese assault on Taiwan.[40]

Political leaders of both the pan-Blue and the pan-Green coalitions have at times seemed to support, or at the very least express sympathy for, one or both of these arguments. When Chen was running for president, for instance, he advocated what many observers regarded as an offensive-oriented policy that explicitly called for a change in Taiwan's defense strategy from "pure defense" to "offensive defense" (*gongshi fangyu*). This formulation abandoned the "old concept of attrition warfare" in favor of an emphasis on "paralyzing the enemy's warfighting capability" and "keeping the war away from Taiwan as far as possible."[41] A key principle of Chen's platform was the "decisive offshore campaign" or "decisive campaign beyond boundaries" (*jingwai juezhan*), which called for Taiwan's military to "actively build up capability that can strike against the source of the threat" by using enhanced naval and air forces as well as joint operations and information warfare.[42] Advocates of an offensive strike capability also include individuals who are concerned both about the high cost of acquiring more sophisticated defensive weaponry from the United States during hard economic times, as well as Taiwan's failure to keep up with advances in China's offensive capabilities. They view offensive weapons such as ballistic missiles as a more cost effective means of deterring China. This group also includes some army officers who view the deployment of such weapons as a means of avoiding the acquisition of more sophisticated and costly air and naval forces—and thus a convenient rationale for maintaining large ground forces.[43]

There are many who oppose the acquisition of either type of offensive capability, however. These individuals point out that Taiwan could not develop a large enough offensive counterforce capability credible enough to threaten the extensive number of potential mainland military targets. Moreover, they argue that locating and destroying China's large and growing number of mobile SRBMs (a key priority for proponents of offensive capabilities) would prove extraordinarily difficult; on the other hand, Taiwan's relatively small missile force and infrastructure would be a top priority target for Chinese missile, air, and special forces attacks. In addition, an offensive countervalue capability would be of very limited value, opponents argue,

---

[40] Author interviews, Taipei, summer 2003; and Swaine and Mulvenon, *Taiwan's Foreign and Defense Policies*, 66–67.

[41] Chen Shui-bian, *Xinshiji xinchulu: Chen Shui-bian guojia lantu—diyice: Guojia anquan* [New Century, New Future: Chen Shui-bian's Blueprint for the Nation—Volume I: National Security] (Taipei: Chen Shui-bian Presidential Campaign Headquarters, 1999), 50–51.

[42] Ibid.

[43] Author interviews, Taipei, spring and summer 2003.

because the Chinese would not only likely remain undeterred if Taiwan were only capable of threatening central and southern cities and not Beijing, but any type of credible countervalue capability would also almost certainly require warheads equipped with weapons of mass destruction (WMD), which the United States would oppose. An offensive countervalue capability would thus likely prove inadequate and ultimately exacerbate U.S.-Taiwan relations. Moreover, such capabilities might also provoke a massive preemptive Chinese strike, or at the very least a devastating Chinese counterstrike.[44]

Opponents of an offensive deterrent include significant numbers of scholars, military strategists, and even many individuals within the United States government. A significant number of knowledgeable U.S. observers believe that Taiwan would waste considerable time, effort, and resources in any bid to acquire a genuine counterforce offensive capability.[45] In addition, from the perspective of some U.S. observers, the possession of significant offensive weapons by Taiwan would inject a potential element of unwanted instability into the equation. In a political-military crisis, Taiwan might use such weapons to retaliate against the mainland without the consent of the United States. Such an attack might be mistaken by China as a U.S. strike, and would thus invite retaliation against the U.S. mainland or otherwise result in a major escalation. All in all, many U.S. observers believe that Taiwan seems to be developing offensive systems without a clear sense of how they will be used.[46]

The Modernization of Taiwan's Force Structure and Weapons Systems

The following section describes the six most important elements of Taiwan's military modernization program—C4ISR, air and missile defense, anti-submarine warfare, joint warfighting capability, air offensive capability, and counter-landing/surface defense capability—and assesses the significance of each category of capabilities as well as progress attained thus far.

The first element, C4ISR (command, control, communications, computers, intelligence, surveillance, and reconnaissance), is the critical inte-

---

[44] Swaine and Mulvenon, *Taiwan's Foreign and Defense Policies*, 67.

[45] "Pentagon Reviews Taiwan Ties," *Taiwan Defense Review*, January 18, 2003. The article states that U.S. opposition emanates "mainly from the State Department," but the author has heard similar views expressed by senior U.S. military officers.

[46] Unfortunately, to date there has been scant discussion between the United States and Taiwan of these and other related dangers, apparently because of an unwillingness by both sides to discuss their respective warfighting plans. On the U.S. side, this is due in part to a deep concern that such U.S. plans would be leaked to China. On the Taiwan side, it is due to a fear that the U.S. might somehow utilize its war plans in ways that do not serve Taiwan's interests.

grating component of modern warfare. The central tasks of any capable C4ISR system include the abilities to detect enemy forces or capabilities, cue friendly response capabilities, and then manage the process of integrating both maneuvering and firing operations against the enemy. Such a system will be particularly crucial in a potential cross-Strait scenario, where a premium would be placed on the intelligent coordination of air, naval, and ground forces, as well as on effective communication with any supporting U.S. forces.[47]

Command, Control, Communications, and Computer Systems (C4)

The development, with extensive U.S. assistance, of the command and control portion of a more sophisticated C4ISR system (codenamed Po-Sheng) has been a major priority of Taiwan's modernization program for several years. Owing to funding difficulties, implementation challenges, and service-level opposition, however (note for instance that the C4ISR architecture only began in 2005), progress has been slow. On the other hand, Taiwan's military has made important strides at the operational and functional level, despite system integration problems. For example, the recent Han Kuang No. 21 exercise witnessed the implementation of a joint theater-level simulation system (JTLS), which the United States had introduced in 2004. Though designed as an exercise management system, the JTLS can also serve as a bridging C4ISR structure through its capability to remotely link up to the island's main military commands, and thus distribute command center elements away from the Hengshan Command center.[48] The JTLS reportedly will also enable Taiwan to link up with the U.S. Pacific Command.[49] The future development of this system aims to link 14 command centers, 8 Mirage fighters, at least 24 F-16 fighters, all 4 Kidd-class destroyers, 2 Cheng Kung-class frigates, and 2 Kang Ding-class frigates.[50]

Implications. More modern command and control systems can significantly enhance the effectiveness of Taiwan's military forces. Without such systems, the chances of both catastrophic failure and significant friendly casualties in a military conflict would be great. In addition, such systems—if integrated with U.S.-led coalition systems—would be critical to the attainment of interoperability with U.S. forces. If Taiwan is to perform all these functions effectively under attack, however, Taipei must do more to

---

[47] Because C4ISR is defined via the integration of its two main constituent parts, the following analysis will treat C4 and ISR separately.

[48] Rich Chang, "MND Says Admiral Blair Will Attend War Exercises, Taipei Times, April 19, 2005, 1.

[49] Chang, "Admiral Blair Will Attend War Exercises," 1.

[50] Bernard D. Cole, Taiwan's Security: History and Prospects (London: Routledge Press, 2006), 4.

increase the survivability of its primary command and control infrastructures. Equally important, Washington should carefully consider the positive and negative strategic implications of establishing greater interoperability between U.S. and Taiwan forces. On the one hand, U.S.-Taiwan combat interoperability might better dissuade the PRC from the use of force against Taiwan, largely because of the more certain (and likely more effectual) U.S. response that would result from such a capability. On the other hand, interoperability might also create expectations of an alliance partnership that could prove destabilizing to regional security due to possible adverse reaction from China.

Intelligence, Surveillance, and Early Warning (ISR)

Improved intelligence-gathering and analysis capabilities, of which early warning is an important component, are essential elements of an upgraded C4ISR capability—and therefore critical to Taiwan's defense. Obtaining, assessing, and conveying accurate intelligence enables Taiwan to monitor China's force posture and will enhance Taipei's ability to anticipate a PRC attack. Given Beijing's increasing focus on developing a preemptive, anti-access strategy to attain PLA objectives vis-à-vis Taiwan prior to the arrival of U.S. forces, such intelligence would prove crucial to Taiwan's defense. The following analysis briefly addresses three ISR components that have the ability to "see deep" into China and thereby improve early warning of a PRC attack.

Space-based intelligence. Washington has encouraged Taipei to invest in space intelligence assets, including a Synthetic Aperture Radar (SAR) satellite, which could provide early notice of large PLA vehicle convoys moving toward staging areas as well as the massing of ships in Chinese ports. In June 2004 Taiwan launched a ROCSAT-2 satellite capable of taking remote photographs of the earth with a 2-meter resolution.[51]

Human intelligence. Taiwan's cultural and linguistic similarities with China increase the chances for success of Taiwan's human intelligence operations, which, it is hoped, would provide firsthand observations of impending Chinese military operations against Taiwan. Conversely, PRC penetration of Taiwan's intelligence services is already a threat. Indeed, Taiwan's apprehension of seventeen ROC military officers and civilians in May 2005 on suspicion of passing secrets to the PRC underlines the importance to Taiwan's defense of effective counterintelligence.[52]

---

[51] Jacky Hsu, "Island's Satellite Sends Back First Pictures," *South China Morning Post*, June 10, 2004, 5.

[52] Chris Hogg, "Taiwan Rounds Up Suspected Spies," *BBC News*, May 11, 2005.

Early Warning and Surveillance Radar Program. Ever since the United States agreed in principle in 1999 to sell a long-range, early warning radar system capable of providing advance notice to Taiwan of a Chinese missile attack, the issue of whether to purchase the system has been hotly debated in Taiwan.[53] Despite continued concerns in Taiwan over costs and other issues, in late June 2005 the Raytheon Corporation won a U.S. Air Force contract worth up to $752 million to supply an early warning surveillance radar system to Taiwan by September 2009.[54] The system will provide ballistic missile warning and warning of air breathing threats (including aircraft and cruise missiles) as well as a potential maritime ship tracking capability. This radar could also potentially cue PAC-III systems for the possible targeting of inbound missiles.

Implications. The importance of being able to receive unambiguous early warning of a PRC attack is critical to Taiwan's ability to prepare for and sustain the island in a military crisis or conflict. Not surprisingly, Taipei has sought, with some success, to gain access to existing U.S. national intelligence capabilities and systems in an effort to further improve Taiwan's early warning capabilities. A U.S.-Taiwan intelligence cooperation relationship would, however, probably prove less provocative to China than would the achievement of interoperability between U.S. and Taiwan combat units, especially since the United States enjoys close intelligence relationships with many other non-allies. Such cooperation raises other considerations, including counterintelligence security implications and the question of whether Taiwan-supplied information—in particular human intelligence—would exert a disproportionate influence on U.S. analyses of PLA capabilities.

Air and Missile Defense

The PRC missile build-up and growing deployment of fourth-generation fighters (such as Su-27s, Su-30s, and F-10s) constitute an increasingly lethal threat to Taiwan's air and missile defense systems—especially if such weapons were launched as part of a concentrated and sustained cruise and ballistic missile barrage. Although Taiwan has historically enjoyed a qualitative advantage over the PRC in terms of pilot proficiency and aircraft performance, this advantage is now eroding due to the increasing numbers of advanced PRC fighters and the overall numerical superiority of China's air

---

[53] Philip Shenon, "U.S. Approves Deal for Taiwan to Buy Radar to Monitor China," *New York Times,* April 30, 1999, 1.

[54] For more on the awarding of the contract, see Jim Wolf, "Taiwan to Get U.S. Early Warning Radar," Reuters, June 24, 2005, http://taiwansecurity.org/Reu/2005/Reuters-240605.html.

forces.[55] What follows is an assessment of Taiwan's most important air and missile defense capabilities.

Air Force counter-air capability. Taiwan's inventory of fighter jets consists, in part, of F-16s that can be armed with "fire-and-forget" AIM-120 advanced medium-range air-to-air missiles (AMRAAM). In 2004 the United States delivered 120 AMRAAMs to Taiwan following the People's Liberation Army Air Force's (PLAAF) successful testing of the similarly capable AA-12 missile.[56] The rest of Taiwan's Air Force counter-air capability is comprised of French-manufactured Mirage 2000 fighters and Taiwan's own Indigenous Defense Fighters (IDF). The Taiwan Air Force has also been working toward procuring a new generation fighter. Options include the F-35 Joint Strike Fighter, F-18 Hornet, or an upgrading of its existing F-16 fleet.[57]

Despite such strengths and improvements, Taiwan's counter-air capability continues to display some severe deficiencies. The air force contains a serious shortage of air-to-air missiles. According to one knowledgeable observer, in addition to the limited number of AMRAAM, Taiwan has only 600 AIM-7 sparrow and 900 AIM-9 sidewinder missiles for its F-16s and F-5s, or about one-third what the Taiwan air force would require in order to mount an effective counter-air capability. Taiwan faces a similar shortage of missiles for its Mirage 2000 aircraft.[58] Moreover, despite the high quality of Taiwan's pilots, the ratio of pilots to aircraft is dangerously low for sustained combat operations.[59] Taiwan's political and military leadership have not adequately addressed these major deficiencies.

Air and missile defense systems. Taiwan's air defense missile inventory currently consists of three Patriot Modified Air Defense System missile batteries that are comprised of PAC-III ground units and PAC-II missiles,[60] Sky Bow I and II missile batteries, Sky Sword I and II missiles, U.S.-designed Hawk missiles, Skyguard and Chapparal short-range missiles, and more than 70 mobile Avenger systems (vehicle-mounted modified Stinger mis-

---

[55] In a speech given at the U.S.-Taiwan Defense Industry Conference in February 2003, then-Deputy Assistant Secretary of Defense (now Deputy Under Secretary of Defense) Richard Lawless emphasized the seriousness of the PRC missile threat and the imperative for Taiwan to develop effective countermeasures. See Richard Lawless, "Remarks to the U.S.-Taiwan Defense Industry Conference," San Antonio, Texas, February 13, 2003, 3, http://www.us-taiwan.org/reports/lawless_speech_feb13_2003.pdf. Later in 2003, the United States reportedly urged Taiwan to procure a more effective missile defense system. See William Foreman, "China Accuses Washington of Sending Military Delegation to Taiwan," Associated Press, March 15, 2003, http://taiwansecurity.org/AP/2003/AP-031503.htm.

[56] "Nation's Defenses Strengthened with New U.S. Missiles," *Taipei Times*, September 23, 2004, 2.

[57] U.S.-Taiwan Business Council, "Defense and Security Report," 1st quarter 2005, 9.

[58] Wendell Minnick, "Taiwan's Military Will Fire Blanks," *Taipei Times*, May 25, 2005.

[59] Cole, *Taiwan's Security*, 11–13.

[60] John P. McLaren, "U.S. Arms Sales to Taiwan," *Asian Survey* 40, no. 4 (July 2000): 622.

sile systems).[61] Due to a Legislative Yuan debate over the special budget (of which the PAC-III system is a part), however, procurement of an additional six PAC-III missile batteries has been stalled.

Taiwan's four *Kidd*-class destroyers—reportedly to be delivered in full by the end of 2006—will provide an effective missile defense and anti-air warfare (AAW) capability.[62] In the future, Taiwan's anti-air and anti-missile capability might also include even more advanced Aegis-equipped destroyers armed with highly effective SM-3 missiles. Many in Washington believe, however, that—in order for the United States to seriously consider the approval of Aegis equipped destroyers—Taipei should first prove that the Taiwan military is not only capable of operating the *Kidd* destroyers, it is also willing and able to acquire and deploy most if not all of the advanced weapons systems included in the special budget.[63]

Implications. Even if the PLA missile threat could not be completely neutralized, a truly effective missile defense force could significantly undercut the PRC's coercive capabilities. For Taiwan, however, a capable air and missile defense would require both the deployment of adequate numbers of effective PAC-III batteries as well as the successful integration of both existing and future systems. For example, PAC-III missile defense batteries—in combination with Aegis destroyers and existing air force counter-air assets—might significantly improve Taiwan's ability to withstand a sudden PRC attack. Progress in missile and air defense has, however, been slow and uncertain. Moreover, even if approved into budget by the Legislative Yuan, it remains unclear whether PAC-III batteries will prove effective against relatively sophisticated Chinese SRBMs and IRBMs. Even if PAC-III proves to be effective, Taiwan may not purchase missile interceptors in sufficient numbers to counter the large and growing PLA ballistic missile force deployed along the Taiwan Strait. Reports of the ROC military's admission that Taiwan cannot defend against a PLA surprise missile attack do not inspire confidence.[64] Finally, military aspects aside, any effective missile defense would require Taipei to prepare the Taiwan public psychologically for a large-scale ballistic missile attack; the government has, however, thus far done nothing in this regard.

---

[61] Shirley Kan, "Taiwan: Major U.S. Arms Sales Since 1990," CRS Report for Congress, March 21, 2005, 31.

[62] Cole, *Taiwan's Security*, 18.

[63] Other concerns also exist regarding the sale of Aegis-equipped destroyers to the Taiwan Navy, including whether an effective strategy exists that will maximize their use.

[64] Lawrence Cheng, "Taiwan 'Cannot Ward Off Surprise Missile Attack,'" *Straits Times*, March 22, 2005, http://taiwansecurity.org/ST/2005/ST-220305.htm.

Indeed, a kinetic, active defense response alone is inadequate. Taiwan must also strengthen its passive and "soft" defenses against PLA missiles. Toward that end, Taipei has undertaken—at Washington's behest—a Critical Infrastructure Protection program, which is currently in the early stages of implementation.[65] Other passive protection efforts—such as rapid runway repair, the use of highways as secondary airfields following missile strikes, the hardening of government facilities and command posts, and increased security measures—have all seen greater progress.

Given the clear need to provide both military countermeasures as well as some level of psychological reassurance to the public, Taipei's inability to procure a more competent active and passive missile defense system in a timely manner casts doubt on the Taiwan government's understanding of the threat and its willingness to take action to protect and reassure its own people.

Anti-Submarine Warfare (ASW)

Another credible threat to Taiwan's security concerns China's growing capability to deploy quiet submarines to critical chokepoints around Taiwan ports and important sea lines of communication (SLOC)—a capability that Taiwan has apparently ceded unchallenged. Taiwan must improve its ability to observe and detect the deployment of these subs from their homeports, track their location as they move, and, if necessary, destroy detected subs. To be most effective, Taiwan's ASW capability must integrate air, surface, and subsurface assets. Such integration will be difficult to achieve.

Air-based ASW. Taiwan's current air-based ASW capability is extremely limited. The Taiwan navy has 20 S-70C anti-submarine helicopters equipped with air and surface search radars, electronic data link capability, a dipping sonar, sonobuoys, and torpedoes. Though the navy has additional air-based ASW platforms, these are outmoded and nearly ineffective. In April 2001 the United States approved the sale of 12 P-3C anti-submarine and recon-naissance planes to Taiwan; all were subsequently included in Taiwan's special budget. The acquisition and deployment of these aircraft would significantly enhance Taiwan's ASW effectiveness. As with the other special budget items now under consideration in the Legislative Yuan, however, the status of these aircraft remains uncertain.

---

[65] In a speech to the 2004 U.S.-Taiwan Defense Business Industry Conference, Deputy Undersecretary of Defense Richard Lawless noted that "safeguarding telecommunications, fiber optics, energy supplies, and major transportation arteries are areas where U.S. and Taiwan industry can work in concert to strengthen Taiwan's commercial, civil, and military infrastructure." For the text of the speech, see Nuclear Threat Initiative, http://www.nti.org/db/china/engdocs/lawless_100404.pdf, 4.

Surface-based ASW. Taiwan is continuing to improve its surface-based ASW capability. In addition to possessing highly effective AAW capabilities, the four *Kidd*-class destroyers, once fully deployed, will significantly boost Taiwan's ASW capability. Taiwan also possesses a fleet of 22 frigates—together comprising the *Chi Yang, Cheng Kung,* and *Kang Ding* classes, with effective ASW capabilities (although this varies according to class).[66]

Subsurface-based ASW. Taiwan currently lacks a subsurface ASW capability. Taiwan's four subs—two former U.S. *Guppy*-class and two Dutch-built *Zwaardis*-class—would be no match in a conflict with the People's Liberation Army Navy (PLAN) submarine fleet. In April 2001 the United States offered to assist Taiwan in the acquisition of eight diesel submarines. According to one observer, the subs would "provide an asymmetrical means to put PRC surface assets at risk" and—if part of an integrated ASW architecture (including some type of undersea surveillance system)—would be effective against the PLAN's submarine force.[67] Legislative Yuan debates concerning the cost and desirability of these subs (which are included in the special budget) and uncertainties regarding who will build them and how adequately they will be manned, continue to delay their procurement, however.[68]

Implications. In addition to enhancing Taiwan's ASW capability, successful acquisition and integration of diesel subs would also present an inherent deterrent capability. Despite the potential operational value of these types of capabilities, however, significant obstacles remain. As indicated above, it is unclear whether and when Taiwan would acquire these expensive and sophisticated platforms. Furthermore, even if Taipei were to procure and integrate some of the ASW capabilities included in the special budget, Taipei would still face a steadily improving PLAN submarine force.[69] Some observers argue that, in light of such a prospect, the acquisition of even eight submarines would be inadequate to cope with the mounting threat, and would likewise require a significant amount of time to manufacture and deploy (i.e., perhaps 8–10 years). For many such critics, the large amount of funds that would be required to build, deploy, and maintain such a relatively small number of submarines would be better spent elsewhere. Finally,

---

[66] For more on the ASW capability of Taiwan's frigates, see Cole, *Taiwan's Security,* 13–16.

[67] Author interview with LTC Mark Stokes, U.S. Air Force (ret.), published in "Arms Procurement Necessary for the Nation's Survival," *Taipei Times,* April 24, 2005, 3, http://www.taipeitimes.com/News/archives/ 2005/04/24/2003251743.

[68] For a good discussion of the sub issue, see Mac William Bishop, "The Troubles Over Sub Deals Are More Political than Financial," *Taipei Times,* July 23, 2004, 9; "Delegation Gives Thumbs Down to Purchase of Subs," *Taipei Times,* June 24, 2004, 3; and Jim Mann, "U.S. Promised Subs to Taiwan It Doesn't Have," *Los Angeles Times,* July 15, 2001, http://taiwansecurity.org/News/2001/LAT-071501.htm

[69] See Lyle Goldstein and William Murray, "Undersea Dragons: China's Maturing Submarine Force," *International Security* 28, no. 4 (Spring 2004): 161–96.

should Taiwan employ its submarines offensively against the mainland (e.g., to blockade PRC ports), there is the risk that—given China's disproportionate ability to respond in overwhelming ways—Taipei and Washington would lose the ability to control escalation.

Joint Warfighting Capability

The ability to conduct joint warfare, at least as exemplified by the U.S. military, has become the hallmark of a modern military. Since the late 1990s U.S. assistance has allowed Taiwan to make efforts toward achieving this critical capacity. This has in large part been brought about through the formulation of more sophisticated operational doctrines—such as "defensive counter-strike"—that employ greater jointness.[70]

As suggested above, developing C4ISR infrastructure is important for enabling a joint warfighting capacity. Completion of the *Po-Sheng* program will provide Taiwan with a modern command and control system that will link communications among the Taiwan army, navy, and air force. Taiwan began testing new joint operations procedures during the *Han Kuang No. 18* exercises held in 2002; with the process accelerating since then.[71] For its part, the Pentagon has played a critical role in assessing Taiwan's C4ISR systems, and is providing mobile training teams and other assistance packages in specific areas such as battle management/C4ISR joint operations and joint air defense doctrine.[72] Moreover, in an effort to advance further Taiwan's joint warfighting capability, the U.S. military has observed Taiwan's annual *Han Kuang* exercises.[73] Retired U.S. general and flag officers with experience in the Asia-Pacific—including a retired former U.S. Commander of the Hawaii-based Pacific Command—have assumed roles in these exercises that have been critical in promoting jointness among Taiwan's military leaders.

Implications. Although Taiwan has made substantive and important improvements in its joint warfighting capacity, challenges remain, particularly at the service level. For example, even though the Taiwan army has created more than 30 joint branch brigades,[74] joint training and planning with the

---

[70] Michael D. Swaine, "Deterring Conflict in the Taiwan Strait," 12–13.

[71] Brian Hsu, "Hankuang No. 19 to Test Operations-Mechanism Again," *Taipei Times*, March 13, 2003, 2, http://www.taipeitimes.com/News/taiwan/archives/2003/03/13/197808.

[72] Swaine, "Deterring Conflict in the Taiwan Strait," 8–9.

[73] U.S. observation of these exercises began during the *Han Kuang No. 18* exercises in 2002. See Ching Cheong, "China-Taiwan Arms Race Heating Up; Jane's Says Beijing is Getting Subs with Ultra-quiet Missile Systems from Russia While Taipei Has a Big Arms Deal with U.S.," *Straits Times*, June 14, 2002.

[74] Cole, *Taiwan's Security*, 5.

air force and navy is minimal.[75] Efforts by Taiwan's navy to promote jointness have been disappointing. Furthermore, as one knowledgeable observer
points out, annual exercises have only a limited ability to create the true joint
service culture necessary for the navy to be able to make maximized, synergistic contributions to Taiwan's defense.[76] According to this observer, greater
jointness in operations and planning would be beneficial.

The legacy of Taiwan's army-dominated military also continues to impede the development of jointness. One example is Chen's desire to merge
the three service colleges into one academy. Originally proposed partly in
the hope that such a merger would improve jointness in Taiwan's military
forces, the measure instead has provoked fierce opposition from those who
view the initiative as an affront to the ROC military's traditional emphasis
on ground forces as well as to the belief that Taiwan is a part of China.[77]

Finally, the issue of joint operations is closely tied to an important debate
within the U.S. policymaking community on whether to break the ban on
sending active duty general officers to the island to help mentor the Taiwan
military. Although recently retired U.S. senior officers are providing valuable assistance (as noted above), some in defense circles believe that only
active-duty general officers with joint operations experience can adequately
perform this function for Taiwan.[78]

Air Offensive Capability

Although Taiwan's overall defense posture is premised upon an "effective deterrence, resolute defense" doctrine, there are active elements within
this posture that are worthy of examination. Indeed, many of Taiwan's defensive weapons could easily be utilized for offensive purposes. This is especially true in the area of air capabilities.

Supplementing a highly capable fleet of F-16's, Mirage fighters, and
IDF's (in all totaling approximately 340 aircraft) is Taiwan's improving missile force. Taiwan currently possesses U.S.-made Harpoon anti-ship cruise
missiles, and in late 2004 reportedly successfully test-fired the Hsiung Feng
III anti-ship missile.[79] Taiwan also recently test-fired the Hsiung Feng II-E

---

[75] Ibid., 24.

[76] Ibid., 22.

[77] John Pomfret and Philip P. Pan, "U.S. Hits Obstacles in Helping Taiwan Guard Against China,"
Washington Post, October 30, 2003, A1.

[78] We are indebted to one of our three anonymous reviewers for this point.

[79] "CSIST 'Successful' in Firing Supersonic Anti-Ship Missile," *Taipei Times*, January 8, 2005.

land attack cruise missile (which is similar to the U.S. Tomahawk).[80] The Hsiung Feng II-E is capable of reaching targets as far away as Shanghai. Taiwan has also deployed the Sky Spear, a short-range (i.e., less than 1,000 km), surface-to-surface ballistic missile. There are also reports that Taiwan is developing a longer-range ballistic missile, although Taipei has not authoritatively confirmed the existence of such a weapon. In May 2005 Taiwan Minister of Defense Lee Jye hinted for the first time that Taiwan was developing missiles for offensive purposes (though he did not specify what type of missile). He made a distinction between Taiwan's "tactical" and "strategic" missiles, and said that the Missile Defense Command would be disbanded, and then reconstituted and restructured once a "strategic" missile capability was achieved.[81]

Implications. Taiwan has long held the qualitative edge over China in air combat capability. This advantage is due both to the number of deployed advanced fighter jets as well as the extensive training received by Taiwan air force pilots overseas. Moreover, the development of ballistic and cruise missiles enhances Taiwan's capability to strike the mainland. As indicated above, however, this qualitative advantage is eroding in the face of both improving PLAAF weapons/platforms and training as well as the PLAAF's numerical advantage in many of these areas. In addition, as also discussed earlier in this chapter, the apparent absence of a clear and convincing strategy for the application of Taiwan's air and missile assets in an offensive manner makes the acquisition of such capabilities increasingly risky and dangerous.

Practical limitations also inhibit Taiwan's ability to develop offensive capabilities. For example, striking mainland targets requires an extensive system of sensors and integrated command and control facilities capable of vectoring the strike aircraft to the target; Taiwan currently lacks this technology. Indeed, a mainland strike capability is not a substitute for expensive C4ISR and missile defense systems, which are essential to carrying out such a mission effectively.

Despite these significant drawbacks, pressure will likely mount for Taiwan to attain such capabilities, especially if Washington does not unambiguously object.

---

[80] See Richard Fisher, Jr., "Turn Missile Buildup Against China," *Taipei Times*, June 11, 2005, 8; and Associated Press, "Report: Taiwan Test-Fires Cruise Missile," June 5, 2005, http://www.washingtonpost.com/wp-dyn/content/article/2005/06/05/ AR2005060500385_pf.html.

[81] Rich Chang, "Military Talks About Missile Program," *Taipei Times*, May 3, 2005, 1.

Counter-Landing/Surface Defense Capability

Taiwan recognizes that its military forces must neutralize any PLA amphibious and merchant fleet before they reach Taiwan's shores, and Taipei is thus developing such a focused capability. In addition to superb AAW and ASW capability, Taiwan's four *Kidd*-class destroyers will greatly enhance the island's counter-landing/surface defense capability. In addition, although not currently on offer to Taiwan, destroyers equipped with the Aegis AAW system would present a highly effective supplement to the island's counter-landing and surface defense capability (assuming they were utilized effectively). The Aegis system possesses the potential to serve as a coordinating node for the integration of sea-based and land-based command, control, intelligence, surveillance, and reconnaissance systems.[82]

Of similar significance is Taiwan's stock of fast-attack missile boats. These boats allow Taiwan forces to approach larger PLA capital, merchant, and even amphibious ships. Taiwan currently possesses 50 aging *Seagull* class fast-attack boats, which are each equipped with two Hsiung Feng I anti-ship missiles.[83] Progress in building the newer four-missile *Kuanghua VI* craft has, however, progressed slowly.

Because the Taiwan army continues to view itself as the last line of defense against an attempted PLA occupation of the main island, the army is therefore attempting to add to the island's counter-landing capability. As part of this effort, the army has developed a new mission for attack helicopters. Rather than acquiring a medium lift capability that could transport rapid reaction troops around the island to counter PLA paratroop or special operations forces (SOF), the army is instead seeking to employ Apache (or improved Super Cobra) helicopters[84] in over-water missions against PRC merchant shipping. This program is valued at approximately $2.7 billion. Funds were originally slated for inclusion in the 2005 budget, with deliveries to begin in 2008.[85] The attack helicopter modernization program is on hold, however, awaiting possible inclusion in the 2006 defense budget.[86]

The army has also considered the acquisition of M1A1 tanks, but their 68-ton weight almost certainly exceeds the capacity of many of Taiwan's highways and bridges.[87] An alternative is to develop a lighter armored vehi-

---

[82] Cole, *Taiwan's Security*, 12.

[83] Brian Hsu, "Navy Shows Off Its Missile Boats with Simulated Assault," *Taipei Times*, January 14, 2004, 3.

[84] Cole, *Taiwan's Security*, 15–16.

[85] Ibid., 16.

[86] Ibid.

[87] Ibid., 11.

cle, such as the U.S. wheeled Stryker vehicle, that would offer greater maneuverability and accessibility with respect to Taiwan's road system. The slow shift away from heavy armor systems is likely to continue, largely due to an increasing emphasis on air and naval modernization.

Implications. Kidd-class destroyers and modern, highly-mobile missile boats will doubtless strengthen Taiwan's counter-landing and surface defense capabilities. As mentioned above, however, Taiwan's construction and acquisition of *Kuanghua VI* fast-attack missile boats is only in its nascent stages, and thus will not add significantly to Taiwan's counter-landing and surface defense needs in the short- to mid-term. For the time being, the considerably older and less capable *Seagull*-class boats will have to suffice.

The decline in the Taiwan army's modernization program is likely to continue. A tightening defense budget coupled with a steady shift away from the past emphasis on ground forces suggest that the army's efforts to acquire many, if not all, of the above-mentioned systems will prove difficult. The army is instead likely to continue to feel pressure to transform itself into a lighter, more maneuverable force with a greater capability both to repel a PRC assault before it reaches Taiwan's shores and to react quickly to sudden landings by PLA amphibious and paratroop/SOF units. For many observers in both Taiwan and the United States, this would not necessarily constitute an unwelcome development, however, given China's increasing ability to carry out a rapid decapitation strike (as discussed in the next section).

Conflict Scenarios

The previous section described the major dimensions of Taiwan's military modernization effort. This section now turns to an assessment of Taiwan's prospects to withstand a PRC attack over the next five years.[88] The assessment will consider the likelihood for successful defense against a combined assault on the main island of Taiwan, the attempted seizure of an off-shore island, an attempted naval blockade/sea denial, and a decapitating

---

[88] This timeframe allows for integration of new weapons systems already slated for delivery to Taiwan, including the *Kidd*-class destroyers, and for significant improvements in C4ISR, but does not include as of yet unfunded missile defense as well as ASW capabilities contained in the special budget. This timeframe also encompasses the sensitive period leading up to and following the 2008 Olympic Games scheduled for Beijing.

strike that includes ground-to-ground and air-to-ground missile and bomb strikes, fifth column elements, and information warfare (IW).[89]

Combined Assault on the Main Island

The Taiwan military's ability to defend against a large-scale combined assault on the main island will depend on a number of factors. First, adequate intelligence and early warning mechanisms will be necessary to inform Taipei of an impending strike. Given the modern intelligence capabilities of both the United States and Taiwan, the strong sharing relationship between the two, and the fact that any PRC combined assault would require the amassing of troops and equipment opposite Taiwan, the likelihood of Taiwan being caught unawares by a PRC combined assault is small. Even if such an assault were disguised as simply a military exercise, U.S. and Taiwan surveillance and intelligence capabilities would likely detect the differences in size, scale, and movement indicative of a genuine attack. This would give the United States ample time to deploy forces against the PLA.

Taiwan's ability to achieve air superiority is a second factor that impacts Taiwan's defense capability. Taiwan's skilled pilots and modern aircraft—marginally supported at close range by the army's short-range, shoulder-fired, ground-to-air missiles—would likely enable Taiwan to achieve air supremacy for a short period of time. Taiwan's ultimate capacity to maintain air superiority would depend in large part, however, upon the survivability of command and control facilities, runways, and hangars in the face of a PRC missile attack aimed at "softening up" Taiwan prior to the main assault. Moreover, sheer attrition of Taiwan's more capable but numerically limited fighters would eventually turn the tide toward the PRC. If heavy air combat is ongoing and Taiwan cannot effectively disrupt PLA air bases and the large number of missile launch sites, the air advantage could shift to the PRC

---

[89] A number of caveats must accompany this section. First, since most military analysts doubt Taiwan's ability to stave off single-handedly a PRC attack indefinitely, the definition of "successful defense" is as follows: Taiwan's ability to absorb or repel an assault long enough to ensure the arrival of U.S. air and naval forces while simultaneously sustaining Taiwan's independent political decision making ability; this would require "holding on" for up to two weeks. Second, the following scenarios assume an *unprovoked* PRC assault. If Taiwan were to aggravate the PRC and incite a military strike, the willingness of the United States to intervene would likely be drastically reduced. Third, the goal here is not to predict the most likely PRC course of action (which is beyond the scope of this chapter) but rather to assess Taiwan's defense capabilities as measured against a range of PRC threats. Fourth, a conflict scenario in the Taiwan Strait, regardless of the form it takes, will certainly meld political and military considerations—it will not simply be a military conflict. For the purposes of this chapter, however, the sole focus is on Taiwan's military capability to respond and defend against a set of particular PRC military threats.

perhaps within a week. This places a premium on timely U.S. assistance.[90] In addition, the ROC Air Force's (ROCAF) small number of AMRAAM, Sparrow, and Sidewinder air-to-air missiles will curtail Taiwan's ability to dominate the air.

A third factor concerns Taiwan's missile defense capabilities. Given Taiwan's modest capabilities in this area both at present and over the foreseeable future, a sustained PLA missile attack would severely disrupt the ability of the ROCAF to maintain air superiority, even if over a relatively short period of time (i.e., 5–7 days). Improvements in bolstering critical infrastructure, however, would likely ensure that a sufficient number of ROC aircraft could take flight.

Finally, effective coordination of Taiwan's assets would depend on a robust command and control system, the development of which is still ongoing. In general, a capable command and control system would aim to stifle a PRC attack as far from Taiwan's shores as possible.

On balance, if confronted over the next five years by a determined Chinese combined assault involving large numbers of air, missile, naval, and amphibious/paratroop units, Taiwan would probably be hard pressed to hold out for longer than a week without significant U.S. intervention. On the other hand, over this future time period, the United States will likely have warning of a full-scale assault early enough in order to respond within 7–10 days with a force sufficient to deflect a large-scale PLA assault.

This scenario elicits some important and intriguing questions. For example, given both the intelligence capabilities of Taiwan and the United States and their likely ability to ascertain PRC mobilization, and despite the repeated assertion of the Taiwan government that it would absorb a first strike before responding to any attack, would Taipei be willing to launch pre-emptive strikes on the mainland in order to reduce the effectiveness of PLA air and missile attacks? Similarly, if Taiwan gained intelligence on PRC mobilization prior to the United States, would Taipei launch a pre-emptive attack without notifying Washington? This in turn poses challenges for Washington. Would the United States assist Taiwan in launching a pre-emptive attack? If so, would the United States come to the aid of Taiwan in the event of an almost certain PRC counterattack? Alternatively, does Taiwan have the targeting, battle damage assessment, and offensive strike capabili-

---

[90] A 2000 RAND modeling of an outright PRC air and amphibious invasion of Taiwan found that, although the ROCAF would fare well in most cases against the PRC, attrition rates on both sides would still be high (e.g., a median loss rate after four days of fighting of 75 and 45 percent for the PRC and Taiwan, respectively). The authors concluded, however, that a modest commitment of U.S. forces from Okinawa would greatly enhance the ROCAF's chances of repelling a PRC air attack. See David A. Shlapak, David T. Orletsky, and Barry A. Wilson, *Dire Strait? Military Aspects of the China-Taiwan Confrontation and Options for U.S. Policy* (Santa Monica, CA: RAND, 2000).

ties to launch retaliatory strikes against bases and missile launchers on the mainland while simultaneously attempting to maintain air superiority over the Strait? This latter possibility seems doubtful.

Seizure of an Off-Shore Island

At first glance, it appears that, should the PRC launch an attack against Taiwan, one or more of Taiwan's off-shore islands could be seized with relative ease, especially given these islands' short distance from the mainland. PRC deficiencies in sea-lift capacity, Taiwan's current qualitative edge in air warfare, and the level of fortification of these islands, however, make it clear that any attempt to occupy the islands would prove extremely costly and difficult. Moreover, the limited battlespace could work to Taipei's advantage, enabling Taiwan's military forces to target amassed PLAN amphibious ships much more easily. Quite apart from these military obstacles to success, though, the PRC would also likely confront negative international repercussions in the aftermath of an attempted seizure of an off-shore island. By signaling to outside observers that China was more inclined to use force to resolve the issue, such an action could greatly intensify U.S. (and larger international) political and military support for Taiwan.

Nevertheless, most military experts believe that, without steady resupply and air cover, the offshore islands would eventually succumb to a determined PLA assault. Beijing has in the past demonstrated that China is willing to sustain heavy casualties in order to achieve a limited, high-value objective. In addition, China would likely have the capacity to prevent Taipei from resupplying and providing air support over several weeks, especially if Taiwan sought to hold the bulk of its air and naval forces in reserve to protect against a possible attack on the main island. Moreover, from Beijing's perspective, this sort of limited action—short of further aggressive action—would have a much smaller chance of escalating into a broader conflict with the United States. In short, attacking an off-shore island would allow Beijing to demonstrate the use of force, avoid conflict with the United States, and maintain control over escalation.

On the other hand, the seizure of all off-shore islands would eliminate a major territorial link between the island of Taiwan and mainland China, thereby removing any tangible expression of Taipei's association with the "one China" concept. This association alone makes such a scenario rather unlikely. Nonetheless, because it at least affords Beijing the opportunity of conducting a relatively low risk coercive or "demonstration" military strike, the option remains on the table.

Naval Blockade/Sea Control

From a military perspective, Taiwan would find it difficult to break a determined PLA naval blockade without outside help. Taiwan's lackluster ASW capabilities, weak submarine capability, and failure to procure P-3C ASW aircraft and an array of necessary support systems could enable PRC submarines and surface vessels to operate long enough to wreak havoc on Taiwan's maritime trade. This would likely be the case even though PLAN surface combatants (e.g., destroyers, frigates, etc.) would be at risk from Taiwan's capable missile force.

In the absence of an accompanying assault on the island, however, Taiwan's political leadership and populace could likely withstand the pressures of a blockade long enough for U.S. naval forces to arrive on the scene. Indeed, U.S. fighters based at Kadena Air Base are less than an hour's flight time away. Moreover, their stand-off attack capability would probably force the PLA to attempt a blockade that would somehow avoid providing the United States with a pretext to respond with force—an extremely difficult task. Also, even though currently displaying limitations in ASW, the U.S. Navy would nonetheless stand a much better chance of breaking a blockade than would the Taiwan navy alone. In addition to such military factors, Taiwan's willingness to withstand a naval blockade would also allow more time for international opposition against China to grow, thus further complicating Beijing's strategy. Finally, a failed attempt at a naval blockade would likely produce some highly unpalatable alternatives for Beijing, including an escalation of military pressure in the presence of significant (and probably growing) U.S. forces or a humiliating retreat and the acceptance, at least over the near term, of both a much closer U.S.-Taiwan military and political relationship and a highly antagonistic Sino-U.S. relationship. Thus, despite clear weaknesses in Taiwan's ability to cope with a blockade, Beijing is unlikely to embark on such a course of action. The possibility cannot, however, be entirely discounted.

Decapitating Strike

A rapid SRBM and aircraft strike aimed at key command and control centers and government facilities, and possibly combined with fifth column and SOF attacks, arguably presents the greatest threat to Taiwan over the next five years. A missile and air strike alone could be carried out as part of a limited coercive strategy designed to compel Taipei's acceptance of certain Chinese demands (e.g., regarding political negotiations). Such a strike would almost certainly provoke a major U.S. response, however, and would likely lead to further escalation. Alternatively, such strikes might be carried out as one component of a much larger *fait accompli*-type attack designed to decapitate Taiwan's political and military leadership and create a level of panic and disarray on the island that compels Taipei to capitulate or open negotiations with Beijing before the United States can intervene. Taiwan's ability to withstand such a rapid, intense set of strikes is largely dependent on the extent to which critical infrastructure nodes and leadership facilities are hardened and defended. Such a strong "survival capability" would not only make possible a robust military response but would also send a clear signal to Washington that the island remained viable and hence capable of receiving U.S. assistance. As indicated above, Taiwan has made some progress in its preparations to resist a rapid, intense attack, but needs to do much more in order to provide security for its political leaders, communications facilities, and key energy and transportation sites. A successful defense will also depend on an improved Taiwan missile defense capability, for which the acquisition of the additional six PAC-III missile batteries is an integral element.

Conclusions and Implications

There is little doubt that Taiwan's military capability is increasing overall. The size, configuration, and orientation of the armed forces continue to adjust to the challenges posed by a more complex and expanding Chinese threat. In particular, the capability and readiness of several front-line military units is improving, a limited but notable level of joint warfighting capability is emerging among the services; advances are taking place in missile defense, including improved rapid runway repair and hardening capabilities and the establishment of a new Missile Defense Command; a joint ASW center has been created; and Taiwan's defense strategy is gradually being reoriented away from an army-centric focus on the counter-landing mission to an air force and naval offshore engagement strategy.[91] As part of this effort, important programs such as C4ISR, the acquisition of *Kidd*-class destroyers, and more robust training and exercise regimens are all moving forward.

Yet despite such advances, many problems and concerns remain that when taken together cast serious doubt on the ability and willingness of Taipei to create a truly credible set of deterrence and defense capabilities against the most likely Chinese threats, even in the context of continued U.S. support—and likely U.S. military intervention—in the event of a conflict. First, the pace of change remains excessively slow in many areas, which raises questions about how committed Taiwan's leadership and political parties

---

[91] Swaine, "Deterring Conflict in the Taiwan Strait," 22.

are to those measures necessary to enhance Taiwan's self-defense capability. Taiwan's normal annual level of defense spending for procurement, operations, training, and personnel has fallen by over 50 percent (in constant currency terms) since 1993, and Taipei continues to drag its feet in allocating even a portion of the special budget. Taipei has also reduced the period of military service and failed to encourage volunteerism. As a result, some U.S. observers fear that Taiwan will not have available the financial and human resources necessary both to attain requisite levels of readiness for its existing forces as well as to acquire, deploy, and operationalize future weapons systems.

The second concern regards Taiwan's military modernization and reform efforts, which are being stymied to some extent by an intense focus on the special budget as the "solution" to Taiwan's defense problems. The capabilities represented in a significant portion of the special budget (i.e., missile defense and ASW) represent an effort to redress the most pressing PRC challenges faced by Taiwan. Even if they can be effectively integrated into Taiwan's force structure, they do not offer, however, a cure-all for dealing with the increasingly sophisticated threats posed by the PLA. Moreover, should sophisticated weapons systems such as PAC-III, P-3C aircraft, and advanced diesel submarines eventually receive funding via special budget or some other procedure,[92] the length of time required to field at least some of these weapons calls into question their ultimate utility, particularly if the PRC were to conduct an operation against Taiwan within the next five to seven years.[93]

Third, to the extent Taiwan's military is modernizing, efforts are not sufficiently focused on the most likely PRC threats. Taiwan has certainly improved its ability to withstand a PRC full-scale invasion, naval blockade, or attempted seizure of an off-shore island. Yet a decapitating strike on Taiwan's political and military leadership—believed by many to be the most likely option—continues to present a significant challenge to Taipei, given the ROC military's current inadequate missile defense capability and level of passive defenses (i.e., hardening of critical military and civilian infrastructure, etc.). Moreover, Taipei apparently refuses to acquire adequate numbers of criti-

---

[92] For further details on the impasse, see, for example, Jimmy Chuang, "Pan-Blues Shoot Down Weapons Budget—Again," *Taipei Times*, December 15, 2004, 3; "Parties Striving to Break Impasse on Arms Budget," *China Post*, January 3, 2005; Central News Agency, "Pan-Party Talks Needed in New Legislature on U.S. Arms Sale," February 24, 2005; Central News Agency, "Arms Package Needed to Maintain Military Balance: Defense Minister," March 11, 2005; "Pan-Blues Kill Arms Bill Again," *Taipei Times*, March 23, 2005, 3; "Retired U.S. Air Force Lieutenant Colonel Mark Stokes During an Interview," *Taipei Times*, April 24, 2005, 3; and "Cabinet Rejects Lien Letter's Allegations," *Taipei Times*, June 22, 2005, 3.

[93] This is especially true for the submarines.

cal munitions (such as AMRAAMs) that would enable Taiwan to cope with various scenarios, including a decapitation strike.

Several conclusions can be drawn regarding the possible implications of Taiwan's military modernization. First and foremost, the possible emergence (or further growth) of specific vulnerabilities in the Taiwan military could lead to an increase in China's confidence to undertake specific types of military contingencies, including, but not limited to, a rapid decapitation strike. In the event of a major erosion in Sino-U.S. and/or China-Taiwan relations, such vulnerabilities could prove highly dangerous. Second, increasing U.S. concerns over Taiwan's military vulnerabilities could lead to both qualitative and quantitative increases in U.S. military assistance to, and involvement with, Taiwan's defense. This in turn could spark an acceleration of the PLA buildup, and a greater sense of Chinese fatalism regarding the use of force. Third, significant increases in the level of U.S. support for Taiwan, or significant improvements in Taiwan's own military capabilities, could lead to a greater willingness on Taipei's part to take risks in the pursuit of permanent political separation from the mainland, and could possibly even lead to *de jure* independence.

In sum, although Taiwan's military continues to modernize, the ROC must do much more in a relatively short period of time to create a military capable of withstanding if only for one to two weeks—a determined and rapid PRC attack.[94] In the final analysis, however, Taiwan's military limitations and problems in military modernization cannot be evaluated and addressed solely on the basis of military criteria alone. China's military threat to Taiwan and Taiwan's attempts to meet that threat are heavily influenced by a range of political considerations: Taiwan's strong need for continued U.S. support, Taipei's internal political and social dynamics and the implications these dynamics pose for Taiwan's movement toward independence, China's assessment of Washington's willingness to resist such movement, and the overall value to both Washington and Beijing of maintaining reasonably cooperative bilateral relations. Seen within this context, a purely military approach to Taiwan's military modernization deficiencies could increase, rather than decrease, the chance of conflict. Without the proper reassurances, for instance, China might conclude that significant increases in Taiwan's military capabilities were intended to protect Taipei as it moves toward *de jure* independence.

---

[94] In March 2005, Taiwan's Minister of National Defense Lee Jye testified to the Legislative Yuan and noted that Taiwan's defense capability may not allow the island to repel sustained attacks by the PLA after 2006. See "Defense Chief Sees Mainland Attack in 5 to 10 Years' Time," *China Post*, March 10, 2005.

Thus, although little doubt remains that Taiwan must strengthen its military significantly in order to deal with an arguably more ominous PLA threat, the resulting increase in Taipei's deterrent and warfighting capabilities must be balanced by an equally savvy and effective political effort by Washington. At one level, this entails a consistent reminder that force must never be used to resolve the situation in the Taiwan Strait. Beijing's continued willingness to employ force—albeit apparently to deter Taiwan independence rather than to achieve unification[95]—has itself created a military component to an essentially political problem. Washington must also communicate to Beijing that helping Taipei resist Beijing's coercive efforts is a far cry from endorsing or shielding a move toward permanent or full independence. Ultimately, this balancing act between military deterrence and political dissuasion necessitates a much clearer understanding by both Washington and Taipei of the requirements and limitations of their mutual effort to carry out defense reform and modernization in Taiwan.

For the United States, reaching such an understanding should necessitate a closer examination of the specific purposes and consequences of current efforts to strengthen Taiwan's military in a wide variety of areas. Washington must ensure that U.S. assistance to Taiwan is utilized specifically for the development of those military capabilities that will prolong the island's ability to resist submission during the initial stages of an attack, while constantly gauging the political ramifications of such assistance (and Taiwan's resulting increased capabilities) both in Taipei and in Beijing. Although requiring a labor-intensive diplomatic effort, there is no alternative to this continual hands-on approach.

For its part, Taiwan must work to demonstrate a trans-party domestic political commitment to national defense that in and of itself would enhance Taiwan's overall deterrence capabilities. Beijing's military threats have contributed, in no small measure, to political disunity on Taiwan. Recognition of this reality, along with focused military reform and modernization of the kind described above, will go a long way toward ensuring the viability of Taiwan for the foreseeable future.

---

[95] For example, it is notable that the PRC's Anti-Secession Law was not labeled a "Reunification Law" (although the goal of "peaceful reunification" is emphasized several times in the text). See http://english.people.com.cn/200503/14/eng20050314_176746.html; and Hu Jintao's "Four Point Guideline on Cross-Strait Relations," which discusses peaceful unification. For the complete text, see http://english1.people.com.cn/200503/05/eng20050305_175645.html.

STRATEGIC ASIA 2005–06

INDICATORS

Strategic Asia
by the Numbers

The following eighteen pages contain tables and figures drawn from NBR's Strategic Asia database and its sources. The appendix consists of 21 tables covering: economic growth, trade and foreign investment, population size and growth; politics and international relations; energy consumption and oil supplies; and armed forces, defense expenditures, conventional military capabilities, and weapons of mass destruction. The data sets presented herein summarize the critical trends in the region and changes underway in the balance of power in Asia.

The Strategic Asia database contains additional data for all 37 countries in Strategic Asia. Hosted on the program's website (http://strategic-asia.nbr.org), the database is a repository for authoritative data for the years 1990 to 2004, and is continually updated. The 70 indicators are arranged in 10 broad thematic areas: economy, finance, trade and investment, government spending, population, energy and environment, communications and transportation, armed forces, weapons of mass destruction, and politics and international relations. The Strategic Asia database was developed with .NET, Microsoft's XML-based platform, which allows users to dynamically link to all or part of the Strategic Asia Program's data set and facilitates easy data sharing. The database also includes additional links that allow users to seamlessly access related online resources.

The information for *Strategic Asia by the Numbers* was compiled by Strategic Asia graduate research fellows Peter Mattis and Evan Morrisey.

Economies

Strong domestic demand and high levels of investment have led to strong growth in Asia. The GDP growth rates of Strategic Asia's economies continue to outpace the rest of the world, driven in large part by China. In 2004, China's GDP growth was 9.1%, Northeast Asia's (excluding China) average GDP growth was 5.5%; Southeast Asia's average was 5.4%; and GDP growth in South Asia averaged 5.1%.

- China's economy continues to diversify and expand from labor-intensive production to more high-technology/heavy manufacturing sectors.
- Japan appears to be nearing the end of its decade-long stagnation, but South Korea's reliance on export-led growth appears to be slowing its economy recovery.
- While China pursues an economic modernization policy focused on manufacturing, India is instead pursuing service sector related growth.
- Southeast Asia is finally recovering from the financial crisis of 1997–98, with GDP and investment levels returning to previous highs.

1. Gross Domestic Product

	GDP (constant 2000 $ billion)				Rank	
	1990	1995	2000	2003	1990	2003
United States	7,055.0	7,972.8	9,764.8	10,343.0	1	1
Japan	4,107.8	4,428.5	4,746.1	4,876.1	2	2
China	412.7	726.9	1,080.7	1,375.2	4	3
Canada	535.0	582.3	713.8	766.1	3	4
South Korea	283.7	413.2	511.9	586.1	6	5
India	268.0	345.4	457.4	543.7	8	6
Australia	274.4	322.0	389.1	431.2	7	7
Russia	385.9	239.7	259.7	306.7	5	8
Taiwan*	...	...	309.5	286.0	...	9
Hong Kong	106.2	139.4	165.4	174.7	9	10
Indonesia	99.3	145.1	150.2	167.7	10	11
Thailand	79.4	120.0	122.7	141.1	11	12
Malaysia	45.5	71.5	90.3	99.4	15	13
Singapore	43.9	67.5	91.5	93.2	16	14
Philippines	56.2	62.6	75.9	85.3	12	15

Sources: World Bank, *World Development Indicators*, 2005. Data for Taiwan is from Central Bank of China, *Financial Statistics*, 2005.

Note: Figures are calculated using the average exchange rate of corresponding year. Ellipses indicate that no data is available.

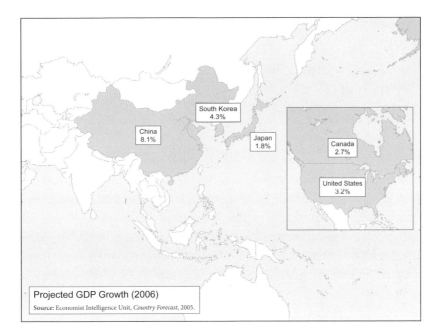

Projected GDP Growth (2006)

Source: Economist Intelligence Unit, *Country Forecast*, 2005.

2. GDP Growth and Inflation

	GDP growth (%)			Inflation rate (%)		
	1990–94	1995–99	2000–04	1990–94	1995–99	2000–04
United States	1.9	3.3	3.0	3.6	2.3	2.5
Japan	2.4	0.5	1.3	2.1	0.4	-0.5
China	9.8	8.7	8.4	2.5	1.6	2.9
Canada	1.5	2.7	3.0	33.2	8.0	2.3
South Korea	7.5	5.0	5.7	6.6	4.5	3.0
India	4.0	5.6	5.7	10.4	9.7	5.0
Australia	3.0	3.8	3.9	2.9	2.3	2.1
Russia	-11.0	-2.3	5.7	29.0	40.6	15.9
Taiwan	5.8	5.8	3.4	4.2	2.1	0.6
Hong Kong	4.6	2.4	4.6	10.5	4.2	-0.1
Indonesia	6.2	1.0	4.1	9.6	28.9	9.1
Thailand	8.2	2.1	4.7	5.4	4.8	1.8
Malaysia	8.7	4.6	5.0	8.2	3.6	-1.5
Singapore	8.1	5.6	3.8	3.0	0.9	1.0
Philippines	1.8	3.6	4.2	10.8	7.6	4.5

Source: Central Intelligence Agency, *The World Factbook*, 1991–2005.

Note: Data for some countries is partial for 1990–1994.

Trade

Trade continues to be a major factor in the economic growth of Strategic Asia, particularly in the rising economies of East and Southeast Asia. However, poorer areas of Central, South, and Southeast Asia remain largely unequipped to compete in global trade markets. Asian states are aggressively promoting free trade; since 1999, Asian states have established or proposed 100 bilateral and multilateral free trade agreements.

- China's trade flows are growing rapidly with indications that they will soon surpass those of Japan.

- Over one quarter of the United States' record trade deficit is with China, prompting recent calls for trade protection against Chinese goods.

- The recent dissolution of quotas on textiles under the WTO has led to trade disputes between the United States, the EU, and China.

- Indian exports are expected to double to around $150 billion by 2009, yet for the past three years, *volume of growth* in Chinese trade has exceeded *total* Indian trade.

3. Trade

	Trade flow (constant 2000 $ billion)				Rank	
	1990	1995	2000	2003	1990	2003
United States*	1,159.6	1,627.3	2,572.1	2,498.9	1	1
Japan	647.4	757.7	957.6	1,048.4	2	2
China	...	...	530.2	944.6	...	3
Canada*	296.3	414.3	616.7	593.5	4	4
Hong Kong	197.3	380.7	475.3	567.7	5	5
South Korea	118.0	235.5	401.8	499.9	6	6
Taiwan	...	...	...	...	...	...
Singapore	...	...	...	...	...	...
Russia	305.9	157.0	176.8	250.2	3	7
Malaysia	67.0	150.0	206.7	211.8	9	8
Australia*	88.2	127.9	178.0	190.7	7	9
Thailand	68.3	131.9	153.3	176.6	8	10
India	38.4	81.0	130.5	172.3	13	11
Indonesia	64.6	115.9	114.7	121.4	10	12
Philippines	43.0	67.9	82.7	92.1	11	13

Source: World Bank, *World Development Indicators*, 2005.

Note: Data is for U.S., Canada, and Australia is for 2002 rather than 2003. Data for some countries over certain periods is partial. Ellipses indicate that no data is available.

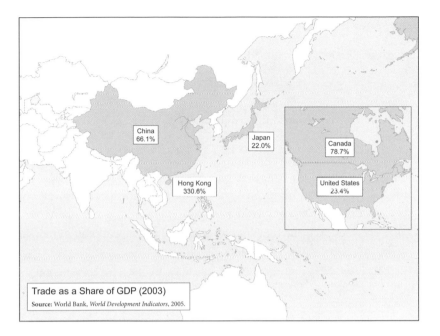

China
66.1%

Japan
22.0%

Canada
78.7%

Hong Kong
330.6%

United States
23.4%

Trade as a Share of GDP (2003)

Source: World Bank, *World Development Indicators*, 2005.

4. Export Partners

	Exports ($bn) 2004	Export destinations (top three partners in 2004 with percentage share of total exports)
United States	795.0	Canada (23%), Mexico (14%), Japan (7%)
China	583.1	U.S. (23%), Hong Kong (17%), Japan (12%)
Japan	538.8	U.S. (23%), China (13%), South Korea (8%)
Canada	315.6	U.S. (85%), Japan (2%), UK (2%)
Hong Kong	268.1	China (44%), U.S. (17%), Japan (5%)
South Korea	250.6	China (22%), U.S. (18%), Japan (8%)

Source: Central Intelligence Agency, *The World Factbook*, 2005.

5. Import Partners

	Imports ($bn) 2004	Import origins (top three partners in 2004 with percentage share of total imports)
United States	1,476.0	Canada (17%), China (14%), Mexico (10%)
China	552.4	Japan (16%), Taiwan (11%), South Korea (10%)
Japan	401.8	China (21%), U.S. (14%), South Korea (4.9%)
Hong Kong	275.9	China (44%), Japan (12%), Taiwan (7%)
Canada	256.1	U.S. (59%), China (7%), Mexico (4%)
South Korea	214.2	Japan (22%), U.S. (13%), China (12%)

Source: Central Intelligence Agency, *The World Factbook*, 2005.

Investment

Although global investment slowed significantly after September 11, it is now showing signs of recovery and is increasing across Asia, particularly in Northeast and Southeast Asia. The increase of investment in China does not appear to have significantly reduced FDI to other Asian countries and has in fact often encouraged it as a means of supporting Asian supply chains, primarily in Southeast Asia.

- Foreign direct investment in China increased from less than $4 billion in 1990 to more than $40 billion in 2003. Manufacturing continues to attract the largest share, but investment is expanding to information technology, high-tech, and the retail and wholesale sectors.

- Foreign investment in Japan surpassed Japanese investment abroad in 2004 for the first time in fifty years.

- FDI to Russia has increased significantly in the past four years, nearly quadrupling since 2001. This investment has, however, been overwhelmingly concentrated in the oil and natural gas sectors.

6. Foreign Direct Investment

	FDI inflows ($ billion)				Rank	
	1990	1995	2000	2003	1990	2003
China	3.5	35.8	38.4	47.1	5	1
United States	48.5	57.8	321.3	39.9	1	2
Hong Kong	...	...	61.9	13.6	...	3
Singapore	5.6	11.6	17.2	11.4	4	4
Russia	...	2.1	2.7	8.0	...	5
Australia	8.1	12.0	13.6	7.0	2	6
Canada	7.6	9.3	66.1	6.3	3	7
Japan	1.8	0.0	8.2	6.2	8	8
India	...	2.1	3.6	4.6	...	9
South Korea	0.8	1.8	9.3	3.2	10	10
Malaysia	2.3	4.2	3.8	2.5	7	11
New Zealand	1.7	3.7	3.4	2.4	9	12
Kazakhstan	...	1.0	1.3	2.1	...	13
Thailand	2.4	2.1	3.4	1.9	6	14
Pakistan	0.2	0.7	0.3	0.5	11	15

Sources: International Monetary Fund, *International Financial Statistics*, 2005. Data for Taiwan is from Central Bank of China, *Financial Statistics*, 2005.

Note: Ellipses indicate that no data is available.

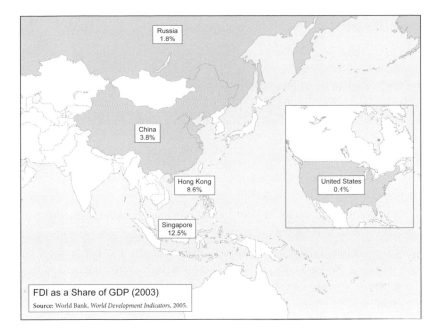

FDI as a Share of GDP (2003)
Source: World Bank, *World Development Indicators*, 2005.

7. Origins of FDI

	Origins of FDI (leading countries of origin for inward investment in 2003)
China	Hong Kong, U.S., Japan
United States*	UK, France, Netherlands
Hong Kong*	China , Bermuda, Netherlands
Singapore	U.S., Japan, EU
Russia	Germany, Britain, Cyprus
Australia	U.S., UK, Japan
Canada*	U.S., EU, Japan
Japan	U.S., Netherlands, France
India	Mauritius, U.S., Netherlands
South Korea	U.S., EU, Japan,
Malaysia	U.S., Singapore, Japan
New Zealand	Australia, UK, U.S.
Kazakhstan	U.S., Switzerland, Netherlands
Thailand	Japan, Germany, U.S.
Pakistan	Switzerland, U.S., United Arab Emirates

Sources: U.S. Department of Commerce, *U.S. Country Commercial Guides*, 2004 and 2005; and Economist Intelligence Unit, *World Investment Prospects*, 2005.

Note: Data for the United States, Hong Kong, and Canada is for 2002. Since data for FDI by country is not reported in a consistent form and varies across sources, this table shows only the main countries of origin for FDI and omits the values and percentage share.

Population

Asia comprises over 60 percent of the world's population and average population growth rates are higher than in the rest of the world. Although population growth in China and India continues to slow, their large populations impose a huge burden on state and natural resources. Cultural preferences for males, particularly in China and South Asia, are greatly distorting natural sex ratios, creating potential social, economic, and security problems in the near future.

- China faces a major problem with its "floating population"—the estimated 100–150 million migrant workers moving from rural to urban areas.
- Many Asian nations, such as Japan and China, are aging rapidly, with implications for workforce productivity, pensions and benefit systems.
- Lack of decent health infrastructure, unawareness, and cultural beliefs continue to prevent effective HIV/AIDS education and treatment in much of Asia. According to some analysts, HIV/AIDS threatens to escalate to severe proportions in China, Russia, and India.

8. Population

	Population (in millions)				Rank	
	1990	1995	2000	2003	1990	2003
China	1,135.2	1,204.9	1,262.6	1,288.4	1	1
India	849.5	932.2	1,015.9	1,064.4	2	2
United States	249.6	266.3	282.2	290.8	3	3
Indonesia	178.2	192.8	206.3	214.7	4	4
Pakistan	108.0	122.4	138.1	148.4	8	5
Russia	148.3	148.1	145.6	143.4	5	6
Bangladesh	110.0	120.1	131.1	138.1	7	7
Japan	123.5	125.4	126.9	127.6	6	8
Philippines	61.0	68.3	76.6	81.5	10	9
Vietnam	66.2	73.0	78.5	81.3	9	10
Thailand	55.6	58.6	60.7	62.0	11	11
Burma	40.5	44.1	47.6	49.4	13	12
South Korea	42.9	45.1	47.0	47.9	12	13
Canada	27.8	29.4	30.8	31.6	14	14
Uzbekistan	20.5	22.8	24.7	25.6	16	15

Sources: World Bank, *World Development Indicators*, 2005. Data for Taiwan is from Central Intelligence Agency, *The World Factbook*, 1990–2004.

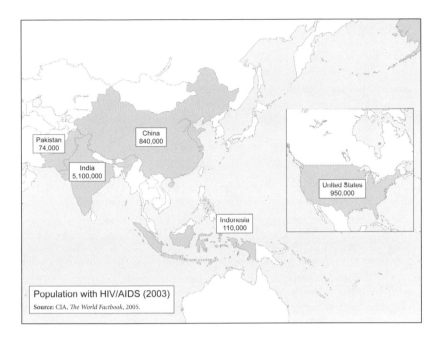

Pakistan
74,000

China
840,000

India
5,100,000

United States
950,000

Indonesia
110,000

Population with HIV/AIDS (2003)
Source: CIA, *The World Factbook*, 2005.

9. Population Growth and Life Expectancy

	Population growth (annual %)			Life expectancy at birth (yrs)		
	1990	2000	2003	1990	2000	2004
China	1.5	0.7	0.6	69	71	72
India	2.0	1.7	1.5	57	63	64
United States	1.1	1.1	0.8	...	77	77
Indonesia	1.8	1.3	1.3	62	68	69
Pakistan	2.5	2.4	2.4	57	61	63
Russia	0.4	-0.5	-0.4	69	65	67
Bangladesh	2.4	1.7	1.7	53	60	62
Japan	0.3	0.2	0.1	79	81	81
Philippines	2.3	2.3	1.9	64	68	70
Vietnam	2.2	1.3	1.1	66	69	70
Thailand	1.8	0.8	0.6	68	70	72
Burma	1.7	1.4	1.2	58	59	60
South Korea	1.1	0.8	0.6	71	76	77
Canada	1.5	0.9	0.9	78	79	80
Uzbekistan	2.1	1.0	1.3	67	64	64

Sources: World Bank, *World Development Indicators*, 2005. Data for Banglasdesh is from Central Intelligence Agency, *The World Factbook*, 1990–2004. Ellipses indicate that no data is available.

Politics and International Relations

Democratization characterizes one of the most significant trends in Asian politics, and authoritarian regimes are under increasing pressure to introduce democratic reforms. Although U.S. relations with many Asian countries are better than ever, there have been efforts to exclude the United States from regional organizations and fora.

- Nationalism in Asia is on the rise. Historical grievances have played a prominent role in recent state-to-state relations, particularly among China, South Korea, and Japan.

- The ASEAN+3 process is a prime example of regional agreements that exclude the United States. Although ASEAN is primarily an economic organization, this development is a significant step toward greater Asian political leadership in regional affairs.

- The recently formed Shanghai Cooperation Organization, headed by China and Russia, has demanded a timetable for the exit of U.S. forces in Central Asia.

10. Politics

	Political leadership	Date took office	Next election
Australia	Prime Minister John Howard	March 1996	2008
Canada	Prime Minister Paul Martin	December 2003	2009
China	President Hu Jintao	March 2003	...
India	Prime Minister Manmohan Singh	May 2004	2009
Indonesia	President Susilo Bambang Yudhoyono	October 2004	2009
Japan	Prime Minister Junichiro Koizumi	April 2001	2005
Kazakhstan	President Nursultan A.Nazarbayev	December 1991	2006
Malaysia	Prime Minister Abdullah bin Ahmad Badawi	October 2003	2006
Pakistan	President Pervez Musharraf	June 2001	2007
Philippines	President Gloria Macapagal-Arroyo	January 2001	2010
Russia	President Vladimir Putin	May 2000	2008
South Korea	President Roh Moo-hyun	February 2003	2007
Taiwan	President Chen Shui-bian	May 2000	2008
Thailand	Prime Minister Thaksin Shinawatra	February 2001	2009
United States	President George W. Bush	January 2001	2008

Source: Central Intelligence Agency, *The World Factbook*, 2005.

Note: Ellipses indicate that no data is available. Table shows next election year in which the given leader may lose or retain his/her position.

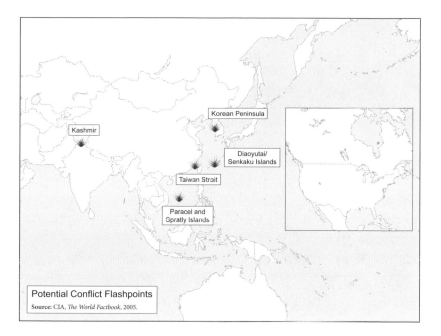

Potential Conflict Flashpoints
Source: CIA, *The World Factbook*, 2005.

11. Political Rankings

	Political rights score*		Corruption score*		Globalization index*	
	2000	2004	2000	2004	2001	2004
Australia	1	1	8.3	8.8	23	13
Canada	1	1	9.2	8.5	10	6
China	7	7	3.1	3.4	47	57
India	2	2	2.8	2.8	48	61
Indonesia	3	3	1.7	2.0	38	59
Japan	1	1	6.4	6.9	29	29
Kazakhstan	6	6	3.0	2.2	...	...
Malaysia	5	4	4.8	5.0	20	20
Pakistan	6	6		2.1	...	46
Philippines	2	2	2.8	2.6	33	33
Russia	5	6	2.1	2.8	44	44
South Korea	2	1	4.0	4.5	31	32
Taiwan	1	2	5.5	5.6	...	36
Thailand	2	2	3.2	3.6	30	48
United States	1	1	7.8	7.5	12	7

Sources: Freedom House, *Freedom in the World*, 2001 and 2004; Transparency International, *Corruption Perception Score*, 2001 and 2004; and AT Kearney/Foreign Policy, *Globalization Index*, 2001 and 2005.

Note: Political rights = ability to participate freely in the political process (1 = most free/7 = least free). Corruption = degree to which public official corruption is perceived to exist (1 = most corrupt). The globalization index tracks changes in economic integration, technological connectivity, personal contact, and political engagement (rank of 62 countries, 1 = most globalized). Ellipses indicate that no data is available.

Energy

Increasing demand for energy in Asia is one of the drivers for recent rises in world oil and gas prices. Yet insufficient and inefficient energy infrastructures are struggling to keep up with demand and could hamper economic growth in the region, particularly in India and China. Blackouts are increasingly common in many Asian countries.

- China has surpassed Japan as the world's second largest oil consumer behind the United States. It is estimated that in the next 20 years, oil consumption in China will match that of the United States.
- Tensions between China, Japan, South Korea, and Southeast Asia remain high over islands in the East and South China Seas which are believed to hold oil and natural gas reserves.
- Central Asia is rapidly developing oil production infrastructure.
- The greatest use and future growth of nuclear energy is in Asia. There are currently over 100 nuclear power reactors in operation, and plans to build a further 20 to 40 in the region.

12. Energy Consumption

	Energy consumption (quadrillion Btu)				Rank	
	1990	1995	2000	2003	1990	2003
United States	84.6	91.2	98.9	98.8	1	1
China	27.0	35.2	38.9	45.5	2	2
Russia	...	27.9	27.2	29.1	...	3
Japan	18.3	20.9	21.9	22.4	3	4
India	8.0	11.5	13.5	14.0	5	5
Canada	11.1	12.1	12.9	13.5	4	6
South Korea	3.8	6.6	7.8	8.6	6	7
Australia	3.7	4.1	4.9	5.1	7	8
Indonesia	2.3	3.3	4.0	4.7	8	9
Taiwan	2.0	2.9	3.8	4.2	9	10
Thailand	1.3	2.2	2.8	3.1	11	11
Malaysia	1.0	1.5	1.9	2.3	13	12
Uzbekistan	...	1.9	1.9	2.1	...	13
Kazakhstan	...	1.8	1.9	2.1	...	14
Pakistan	1.2	1.6	1.9	1.9	12	15

Source: U.S. Department of Energy, *Energy Information Administration*, 2005.

Note: Table shows energy consumption of petroleum, natural gas, coal, hydroelectric, nuclear, geothermal, solar, wind, and wood and waste power. Data for some countries is for 2001, 2002, and 2004. Ellipses indicate that no data is available.

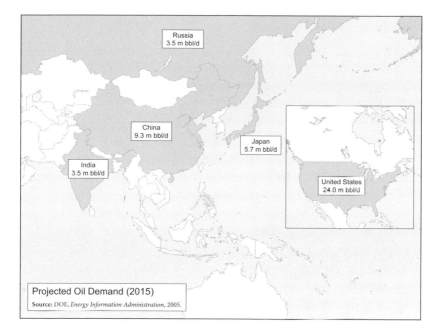

Projected Oil Demand (2015)

Source: DOE, *Energy Information Administration*, 2005.

13. Oil Supplies and Reserves

	Oil supply in 2003 (m bbl/d)			Proven oil reserves in 2003 (bn barrels and main fields)	
	Product.	Consum.	Imports		
United States	7.8	20.0	11.2	21.9	(Gulf of Mexico, Alaska)
China	3.5	5.6	2.0	18.3	(Daqing, Shengli)
Russia	9.3	2.6	-6.7	60.0	(Samotlor, Romashkin)
Japan	0.1	5.6	5.5	<0.1	
India	0.8	2.2	1.4	5.4	(Mumbai, Upper Assam)
Canada^	3.1	2.3	-0.8	178.8	(Alberta, British Columbia)
South Korea*	<0.1	2.1	0.7	...	
Australia	0.6	0.9	0.2	3.5	(Bass Strait, Carnarvon Bas.)
Indonesia	1.3	1.1	-0.1	4.7	(Duri, Minas)
Taiwan	<0.1	0.9	0.9	<0.1	
Thailand	0.3	0.9	0.6	0.6	(Gulf of Thailand)
Malaysia*	0.9	0.5	-0.3	3.0	(Peninsular Malaysia)
Uzbekistan†	0.2	0.2	<0.1	0.6	(Kokdumalask, Shurtan)
Kazakhstan*	1.2	0.2	-0.9	9–17.6	(Tengiz, Karachaganak)
Pakistan	0.1	0.4	0.3	0.3	(Potwar Plateau, Sindh prov.)

Source: U.S. Department of Energy, *Energy Information Administration*, 2005.

Note: Oil production data for Canada, South Korea, Malaysia, and Kazakhstan is for 2004. Production data for Uzbekistan is for 2001. Ellipses indicate that no data is available.

Defense Spending

Defense expenditures continue to rise across Asia, although the defense burdens (spending as a share of GDP) are generally decreasing. The increasing budgets should augment the efficiency and modernization efforts begun during the late 1990s. The region is wary of China's defense modernization program, but there is no indication of an arms race yet.

- China's official defense budget increased 12.6 percent to $29.9 billion, continuing a 15-year trend of double-digit percentage increases. U.S. government and other analysts put the actual defense expenditure between 1.5 and 3 times greater than official Chinese figures.

- Japan and Taiwan warily eye China's military buildup, but have not yet made corresponding changes in their defense budgets.

- While India's defense planning focuses on Pakistan, it is increasingly watching China, which appears to be driving India's aircraft purchases.

- Russia's defense spending is rising, but without reforms, the military will not be able to deal with most regional challenges.

14. Total Defense Expenditure

	Expenditure ($ billion)				Rank	
	1990	1995	2000	2003	1990	2003
United States	293.0	267.9	300.5	404.9	1	1
Russia	...	82.0	60.0	65.2	...	2
China*	11.3	33.0	42.0	55.9	3	3
Japan	28.7	50.2	45.6	42.8	2	4
India	10.1	10.0	14.7	15.5	6	5
South Korea	10.6	14.2	12.8	14.6	4	6
Australia	7.3	8.4	7.1	11.8	8	7
Canada	10.3	9.1	8.1	10.1	5	8
Taiwan	8.7	13.1	17.6	6.6	7	9
Indonesia	1.6	4.4	1.5	6.4	13	10
Burma	0.9	1.9	2.1	6.3	15	11
North Korea*	...	5.2	2.1	5.5	...	12
Singapore	1.7	4.0	4.8	4.7	11	13
Pakistan	2.9	3.6	3.7	3.1	9	14
Vietnam	...	0.9	1.0	2.9	...	15

Source: International Institute of Strategic Studies, *The Military Balance*, 2005.

Note: Estimates for China and North Korea vary widely. Ellipses indicate that no data is available.

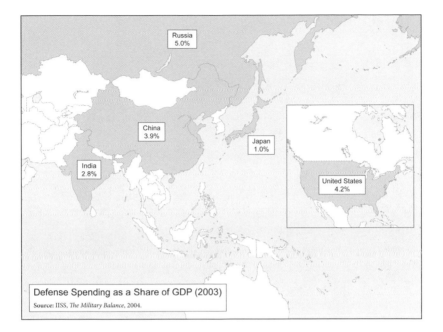

Defense Spending as a Share of GDP (2003)
Source: IISS, *The Military Balance*, 2004.

15. Defense Expenditure

	Def. exp. as a share of GDP (%)			Def. exp. as a share of CGE (%)		
	1990–94	1995–99	2000–03	1990–94	1995–99	2000–03
United States	4.9	3.4	3.3	20.6	16.3	...
Russia	9.7	6.0	4.6	29.7	24.0	...
China	4.8	5.6	3.9	31.3	25.3	...
Japan	1.0	1.0	1.0	7.8	7.0	...
India	2.8	3.1	2.8	...	...	...
South Korea	3.7	3.2	2.8	19.7	14.0	...
Australia	2.5	2.2	2.1	9.5	8.6	...
Canada	1.9	1.3	1.2	6.6	6.0	...
Taiwan	5.0	4.9	3.4	31.8	27.7	...
Indonesia	1.7	1.6	2.4	12.8	14.4	...
Burma	4.2	6.3	8.1	71.7	122.3	...
North Korea	25.5	21.6	21.9	28.5	...	...
Singapore	4.9	5.2	5.1	24.4	19.3	...
Pakistan	7.3	6.1	4.3	27.6	26.2	...
Vietnam	9.6	3.8	7.2	11.1	11.5	...

Sources: International Institute of Strategic Studies, *The Military Balance*, (various editions); and Department of State, *World Military Expenditures and Arms Transfers*, 2003.

Note: No data available for defense spending as a share of central government expenditures in 2000–03. Ellipses indicate that no data is available.

Conventional Military Capabilities

The war on terrorism has challenged traditional security concerns, but the modernization efforts underway in Asia suggest that traditional concepts of security are far from obsolete. China's rise increasingly influences defense considerations in neighboring countries. Maritime disputes across East Asia, coupled with assertive efforts to stake national claims, have fueled greater naval spending in the region.

- Australia and Japan have both strengthened their alliance commitments to ensure a continued U.S. security presence in the region.

- Changes in defense posture are unlikely to substantially affect the U.S. role in Asia. The United States has bolstered forces in Japan and Guam to compensate for troop reductions in South Korea.

- China continues to deploy ballistic missiles opposite Taiwan, casting doubt on Beijing's willingness to peacefully resolve the Taiwan question.

- Southeast Asia remains focused on internal unrest, which has declined in Indonesia and the Philippines, but is worsening in southern Thailand.

16. Manpower

	Armed forces (thousands)				Rank	
	1990	1995	2000	2004	1990	2004
China	3,030	2,930	2,470	2,255	2	1
United States	2,118	1,547	1,366	1,434	3	2
India	1,262	1,145	1,303	1,325	4	3
Russia	3,988*	1,520	1,004	1,213	1	4
North Korea	1,111	1,128	1,082	1,106	5	5
South Korea	750	633	683	688	7	6
Pakistan	550	587	612	619	8	7
Burma	230	286	344	485	13	8
Vietnam	1,052	572	484	484	6	9
Thailand	283	259	301	307	10	10
Indonesia	283	275	297	302	10	11
Taiwan	370	376	370	290	9	12
Japan	249	240	237	240	12	13
Sri Lanka	65	125	....	151	19	14
Bangladesh	103	116	137	126	16	15

Source: International Institute of Strategic Studies, *The Military Balance*, 1991–2005.

Note: Active duty and military personnel only. Data value for Russia in 1990 includes all territories of the Soviet Union. Ellipses indicate that no data is available.

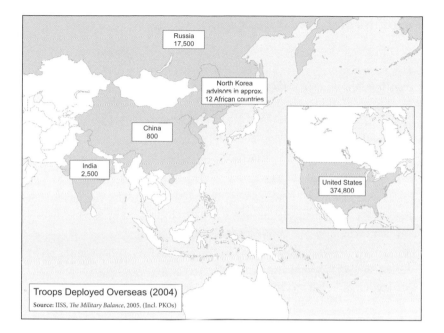

Troops Deployed Overseas (2004)

Russia
17,500

North Korea
advisors in approx.
12 African countries

China
800

India
2,500

United States
374,800

Source: IISS, *The Military Balance*, 2005. (Incl. PKOs)

17. Conventional Warfare Capabilities

	Conventional warfare capabilities (2003)			
	Tanks, APCs/ LAVs, artillery	Fixed-wing aircraft	Principal surface combatants	Submarines
China	29,680	2,600	63	69
United States	26,984	5,991	118	72
India	12,874	714	25	16
Russia	78,005	2,002	27	51
North Korea	16,400	584	3	26
South Korea	8,514	554	39	20
Pakistan	2,576	421	7	11
Burma	783	125	0	0
Vietnam	5,735	195	6	2
Thailand	1,740	234	13	0
Indonesia	541	94	16	2
Taiwan	3,641	511	32	4
Japan	2,550	360	54	16
Sri Lanka	366	22	0	0
Bangladesh	500	83	5	0

Source: International Institute of Strategic Studies, *The Military Balance*, 2004.

Note: Some data is for 2004.

Weapons of Mass Destruction

While the NPT Review Conference and the Proliferation Security Initiative have moved export controls forward, they have achieved few tangible results in addressing new security concerns. India, Pakistan, and North Korea continue to modernize their ballistic missile forces. Despite the breakup of the A.Q. Khan proliferation network, new evidence suggests a greater government role than previously thought.

- North Korea maintains that it has several nuclear weapons, but this has not been independently or demonstrably confirmed.

- India made significant progress in 2004–2005 on a wide range of ballistic and cruise missile capabilities that will help strengthen Indian naval modernization and power projection capabilities.

- Pakistan successfully tested a medium-range ballistic missile and a short-range surface-to-surface missile, effectively giving Pakistan a nuclear-strike capability on any Indian target.

18. Nuclear Weapons

	Nuclear weapons possession				Warheads
	1990	1995	2000	2004	2004
Russia	√	√	√	√	~16,000
United States	√	√	√	√	~10,300
China	√	√	√	√	410
India	√	√	√	√	70–110
Pakistan	...	...	√	√	50–110
North Korea	?	?	?	prob	~5–10

Sources: Carnegie Endowment for International Peace; and Monterey Institute for International Studies.

Note: Table shows confirmed (√), probable (prob), and unknown (?) possession of nuclear weapons. Ellipses indicate that no data is available.

19. Intercontinental Ballistic Missiles

	Number of ICBMs			
	1990	1995	2000	2004
Russia	1,398	930	776	635
United States	1,000	580	550	550
China	8	17+	20+	30+
North Korea	...	...	...	?
India	...	...	...	...
Pakistan	...	...	...	...

Source: International Institute of Strategic Studies, *The Military Balance*, 1991–2005.

Note: Ellipses indicate that no data is available. Question mark indicates unknown possession of ICBMs.

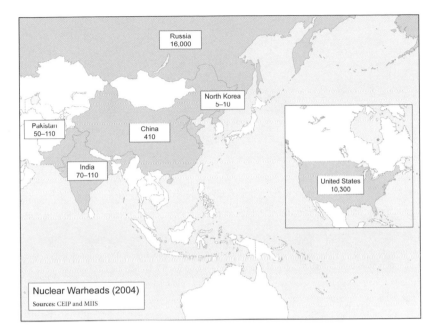

Nuclear Warheads (2004)

Sources: CEIP and MIIS

20. Non-Proliferation Commitments

	NPT	IAEA Additional Protocol	CTBT	CWC	BTWC
Russia	Ratified	Signatory	Ratified	Ratified	Ratified
U.S.	Ratified	Signatory	Signatory	Ratified	Ratified
China	Ratified	Ratified	Signatory	Ratified	Ratified
India	...	...	...	Ratified	Ratified
Pakistan	...	...	...	Ratified	Ratified
North Korea	Withdrew in 2003	...	...	...	Acceded

Source: Nuclear Threat Initiative, Monterey Institute for International Studies.

Note: NPT= Non-proliferation Treaty, CTBT = Comprehensive Test Ban Treaty, CWC = Chemical Weapons Convention, and BTWC = Biological and Toxic Weapons Convention. Ellipses indicate non-participation.

21. WMD Export Control Regimes

	Nuclear Suppliers Group	Australia Group	Wassenaar Arrangement	Zangger Committee	Missile Technology Control Regime
Russia	Member	...	Member	Member	Member
U.S.	Member	Member	Member	Member	Member
China	Member	...	...	Member	...
India	...	...	...	...	...
Pakistan	...	...	...	...	...
North Korea	...	...	...	...	...

Source: Nuclear Threat Initiative, Monterey Institute for International Studies.

Note: Ellipses indicate non-participation.

Index

About the Authors

Stephen J. Blank (Ph.D. University of Chicago) is Professor of Russian National Security Studies at the Strategic Studies Institute of the U.S. Army War College. Dr. Blank has been an Associate Professor of National Security Affairs at the Strategic Studies Institute since 1989. From 1998 to 2001, he was Douglas MacArthur Professor of Research at the U.S. Army War College, and prior to that was Associate Professor for Soviet Studies at the Center for Aerospace Doctrine, Research, and Education at Air University, Maxwell Air Force Base. He has published over 380 articles and monographs on Soviet/Russian military and foreign policies. His most recent book is *Imperial Decline: Russia's Changing Role in Asia* (1997, co-edited with Alvin Rubinstein). His other notable works include *The Sorcerer as Apprentice: Stalin's Commissariat of Nationalities* (1994) and *The Soviet Military and the Future* (1992, co-editor).

Richard J. Ellings (Ph.D. University of Washington) is President and Co-founder of The National Bureau of Asian Research (NBR). He is also Affiliate Professor of International Studies at the Henry M. Jackson School of International Studies, University of Washington. Prior to serving with NBR, from 1986–89, he was Assistant Director and on the faculty of the Jackson School, where he received the Distinguished Teaching Award. He served as Legislative Assistant in the United States Senate, office of Senator Slade Gorton, in 1984 and 1985. Dr. Ellings is the author of *Embargoes and World Power: Lessons from American Foreign Policy* (1985), co-author of *Private Property and National Security* (1991); co-editor (with Aaron Friedberg) of *Fragility and Crisis* (2003), *Asian Aftershocks* (2002), and *Power and Purpose* (2001); co-editor of *Korea's Future and the Great Powers* (2001, with Nicholas Eberstadt) and *Southeast Asian Security in the New Millennium* (1996, with Sheldon Simon); and the founding editor of the *NBR Analysis* publication series. He also established the Strategic Asia Program and AccessAsia, the national clearinghouse that tracks specialists and their research on Asia.

John H. Gill is a retired U.S. Army colonel on the faculty of the Near East-South Asia Center for Strategic Studies at the National Defense University. He has served as Special Assistant for India/Pakistan to the Joint Staff and, from 2001–02, as Military Advisor to the U.S. envoy to the Afghan opposition forces. From August 2003 to January 2004, he served in Islamabad as U.S. liaison officer to the Pakistan Army. He has been analyzing South Asia in positions with the Joint Staff, U.S. Pacific Command, and the Defense Intelligence Agency since the mid-1980s. His recent publications include *An Atlas of the 1971 India-Pakistan War* (2003) and chapters on India and Pakistan in *Strategic Asia 2003–04: Fragility and Crisis* (2003). He is also an internationally recognized military historian and has authored several books and numerous papers on the Napoleonic era.

Christopher W. Hughes (Ph.D. University of Sheffield) is Senior Research Fellow and Deputy Director at the Centre for the Study of Globalisation and Regionalisation, University of Warwick. Formerly he was Visiting Professor with the Faculty of Law at the University of Tokyo and Research Fellow at Hiroshima University. Dr. Hughes' research interests include Japanese security policy, Japanese international political economy, regionalism in East Asia, and North Korea's foreign relations. He is the author of *Japan's International Relations: Politics, Economics and Security* (2005, co-author), "Japan's Re-emergence as a 'Normal Military' Power" (2004), *Japan's Security Agenda: Military, Economic and Environmental Dimensions* (2004), and *Japan's Economic Power and Security: Japan and North Korea* (1999). He is a joint editor of the journal *The Pacific Review* and co-editor of *New Regionalisms in the Global Political Economy* (2002).

Roy D. Kamphausen is Director of National Security Affairs at The National Bureau of Asian Research. Prior to his retirement from the military, he was Country Director for China-Taiwan-Mongolia Affairs in the Office of the Secretary of Defense. Lt. Col. Kamphausen also worked for the last three Chairman of the Joint Chiefs of Staff as an intelligence analyst and later as China Branch Chief in the Joint Staff Directorate for Strategic Plans and Policy. As an Army Foreign Area Officer, he served two tours at the U.S. Embassy in the People's Republic of China Defense Attaché Office. He holds a Master's degree in International Affairs from Columbia University in New York.

Kimberly Marten (Ph.D. Stanford University) is Associate Professor of Political Science at Barnard College, Columbia University, and also teaches at Columbia's School of International and Public Affairs. She is the author of *Enforcing the Peace: Learning from the Imperial Past* (2004), *Weapons, Culture, and Self-Interest: Soviet Defense Managers in the New Russia* (1997), and *Engaging the Enemy: Organization Theory and Soviet Military Innovation* (1993), which received the Marshall Shulman Prize. She has also completed two projects for the Office of the Secretary of Defense: "Emerging Threats in Post-Soviet Central Asia and the Caspian" (2004) and "The Russian Military in 2025: Alternative Futures" (2001). Dr. Marten is a member of the Council on Foreign Relations and the Program on New Approaches to Russian Security at the Center for the Strategic and International Studies.

Michael O'Hanlon (Ph.D. Princeton University) is Senior Fellow in Foreign Policy Studies at the Brookings Institution where he specializes in U.S. defense strategy and budgeting, homeland security, and U.S. foreign policy. He is a visiting lecturer at Princeton University, and a member of the International Institute for Strategic Studies and the Council on Foreign Relations. Prior to joining Brookings, Dr. O'Hanlon held positions with the Congressional Budget Office and the Institute for Defense Analyses. He is the author of many books, including *Defense Strategy for the Post-Saddam Era* (2005), *The Future of Arms Control* (2005, co-authored with Michael Levi), *Neither Star Wars nor Sanctuary: Constraining the Military Uses of Space* (2004), *Crisis on the Korean Peninsula* (2003, co-authored with Mike Mochizuki), and *Expanding Global Military Capacity for Humanitarian Intervention* (2003).

Dwight Perkins (Ph.D. Harvard University) is H.H. Burbank Professor of Political Economy at Harvard University and is Director of Harvard's Asia Center. He has served as an advisor or consultant on economic policy and reform to the governments of China, Korea, Malaysia, Vietnam, and Indonesia. He has also been a long-term consultant to the World Bank, the Ford Foundation, various private corporations, and agencies of the U.S. government. Dr. Perkins has authored or edited twelve books and over one hundred articles on economic history and economic development, with special references to the economies of China, Korea, Vietnam, and other nations of East and Southeast Asia. He is a member of the American Philosophical Society and of various professional organizations in the fields of economics and Asian Studies.

Jonathan D. Pollack (Ph. D. University of Michigan) is Professor of Asian and Pacific Studies and Chairman of the Asia-Pacific Studies Group at the U.S. Naval War College. From 2000 to 2004, he also served as Chairman of the Strategic Research Department at the Naval War College. Prior to this, he worked for the RAND Corporation, and has taught at Brandeis University, the RAND Graduate School of Policy Studies, and UCLA. Dr. Pollack has published extensively on the international relations of East Asia, U.S. policy in the Asia-Pacific, Korean politics and foreign policy, nuclear weapons and Asian security, and East Asian technological and military development. His recent publications include *Strategic Surprise? U.S.-China Relations in the Early 21st Century* (2004). He is a member of the International Institute for Strategic Studies, the Council on Foreign Relations, and the National Academy of Sciences.

Mitchell B. Reiss is Vice Provost for International Affairs at the College of William & Mary, and holds teaching positions both at the Law School and in the Government Department. From July 2003 to February 2005, he served as Director of Policy Planning at the U.S. Department of State. In January 2004, he was appointed as the President's Special Envoy to the Northern Ireland Peace Process, a position he continues to hold. From 1995 to 1999, Dr. Reiss was the Assistant Executive Director and Chief Negotiator for the Korean Peninsula Energy Development Organization. He has served in a number of government positions, including as a consultant to the U.S. Department of State, as well as Los Alamos and Livermore National laboratories. Dr. Reiss is the author of numerous books and articles on nonproliferation, arms control, and American foreign policy, and has lectured widely in the United States and overseas.

David Shambaugh (Ph.D. University of Michigan) is Professor of Political Science and International Affairs, Director of the China Policy Program in the Elliott School of International Affairs at The George Washington University (since 1996), and Nonresident Senior Fellow in the Foreign Policy Studies Program at the Brookings Institution (since 1998). Before joining The George Washington University, he taught for eight years at the University of London's School of Oriental and African Studies, where he also served as Editor of the *China Quarterly* from 1991 to 1996. Dr. Shambaugh has been a visiting scholar in Asia, the former Soviet Union, and Europe. He has published widely—having authored or edited sixteen books, about one hundred articles and book chapters. He sits on the editorial boards of several scholarly journals, and serves as a consultant to several governments, research institutes, and private corporations.

Sheldon W. Simon (Ph.D. University of Minnesota) is Professor of Political Science and Faculty Affiliate of the Center for Asian Studies and Program in Southeast Asian Studies at Arizona State University where he has been a faculty member for 30 years. Dr. Simon is also Chairman of the Southeast

Asian Studies Advisory Group and Senior Advisor to The National Bureau of Asian Research. Dr. Simon is a consultant to the U.S. Departments of State and Defense on Asian security. He has contributed more than one hundred scholarly articles to various academic journals, and is the author or editor of nine books, including most recently *The Many Faces of Asian Security* (2001). He is a frequent contributor to the *NBR Analysis* series and has authored chapters on Southeast Asia for all of the previous *Strategic Asia* volumes. In recent years, Dr. Simon has held research grants from the U.S. Pacific Command, the W. Alton Jones Foundation, and the United States Institute of Peace.

Michael D. Swaine (Ph.D. Harvard University) is Senior Associate and Co-director of the China Program at the Carnegie Endowment for International Peace. He previously worked as a Senior Political Scientist in International Studies and Research Director at the RAND Corporation's Center for Asia-Pacific Policy. Prior to joining RAND, Dr. Swaine was a consultant with a private sector firm; a postdoctoral fellow at the Center for Chinese Studies at UC Berkeley; and a research associate at Harvard University. He has testified to Congress and served as a consultant to the U.S. government. Among his many publications, he contributed a chapter on China to *Strategic Asia 2004–05: Confronting Terrorism in the Pursuit of Power* (2004), and authored "*Deterring Conflict in the Taiwan Strait*" (2004) and "*Trouble in Taiwan*" (2004). Dr. Swaine is also the co-author of *Ballistic Missiles and Missile Defense in Asia* for *NBR Analysis* (2002) and a RAND report entitled *The Role of the Chinese Military in National Security Policymaking* (1998).

Ashley J. Tellis (Ph.D. University of Chicago) is Senior Associate at the Carnegie Endowment for International Peace and a leading policy researcher in international security, defense, and South Asian policy studies. He is Research Director of the Strategic Asia Program at NBR and co-editor of *Strategic Asia 2004–05: Confronting Terrorism in the Pursuit of Power*. He has served in the U.S. Department of State as Senior Advisor to the Ambassador at the U.S. Embassy in New Delhi, and then briefly on the National Security Council staff as Special Assistant to the President and Senior Director for Strategic Planning and Southwest Asia. Prior to his government service, Dr. Tellis was Senior Policy Analyst at the RAND Corporation and Professor of Policy Analysis at the RAND Graduate School. He is the author of *India's Emerging Nuclear Posture* (2001) and co-author of *Interpreting China's Grand Strategy: Past, Present, and Future* (2000, with Michael Swaine). His academic publications have appeared in many edited volumes and journals including the *Journal of Strategic Studies, Asian Survey, Orbis, Comparative*

Strategy, Naval War College Review, Security Studies, and the *NBR Analysis* series.

Hugh White is Professor of Strategic Studies at the Australian National University and a Visiting Fellow at the Lowy Institute for International Policy. From 2001 to 2004, Professor White was the first Director of the Australian Strategic Policy Institute. Prior to that, he served as an intelligence analyst with the Office of National Assessments, as a journalist with the *Sydney Morning Herald,* as a Senior Adviser on the staffs of Australian Defense Minister Kim Beazley and Prime Minister Bob Hawke, and as a senior official in the Australian Department of Defense, where from 1995 to 2000 he was Deputy Secretary for Strategy and Intelligence.

Michael Wills is Director of the Southeast Asia Studies Program and the Strategic Asia Program at The National Bureau of Asian Research. He is co-editor of *Strategic Asia 2004–05: Confronting Terrorism in the Pursuit of Power,* a contributing editor to *Strategic Asia 2003–04: Fragility and Crisis* and *Strategic Asia 2002–03: Asian Aftershocks,* and has served as technical editor on numerous books and articles, including *Strategic Asia 2001–02: Power and Purpose and The Many Faces of Asian Security.* Before joining NBR, Mr. Wills worked at the Cambodia Development Resource Institute in Phnom Penh, and prior to that with the international political and security risk management firm Control Risks Group in London. He holds a B.A. (Honors) in Chinese Studies from the University of Oxford.

About Strategic Asia

The **Strategic Asia Program** at The National Bureau of Asian Research (NBR) is a major ongoing research initiative that draws together top Asia studies specialists and international relations experts to assess the changing strategic environment in the Asia-Pacific. The Strategic Asia Program transcends traditional estimates of military balance by incorporating economic, political, and demographic data and by focusing on the strategies and perceptions that drive policy in the region.

The program's integrated set of products and activities includes an annual edited volume written by leading specialists, an executive summary tailored for public and private sector decisionmakers and strategic planners, an online database that tracks key strategic indicators, and briefings and presentations for government, business, and academe. Special briefings are held for key committees of Congress and the executive branch, other government agencies, and the intelligence community. The principal audiences for the program's research findings are the U.S. policymaking and research communities, the media, the business community, and academe.

The program's database contains an unprecedented selection of strategic indicators—economic, financial, military, technological, energy, political, and demographic—for all of the countries in the Asia Pacific region. The database, as well as previous volumes and executive summaries, are hosted on the Strategic Asia website at http://strategicasia.nbr.org.

Research and Management Team

The Strategic Asia research team consists of leading international relations and security specialists from universities and research institutions across the United States. A new research team is selected each year. The research team for 2005 is led by Ashley J. Tellis (Carnegie Endowment for International Peace). General John Shalikashvili (former Chairman of the Joint Chiefs of Staff), Aaron Friedberg (Princeton University, and Strategic

Asia's founding research director), and Richard Ellings (The National Bureau of Asian Research, and founding program director) serve as Senior Advisors. Advising the program is the executive committee, composed of Thomas Christensen (Princeton University), Herbert Ellison (University of Washington), Donald Emmerson (Stanford University), Francine Frankel (University of Pennsylvania), Mark Hamilton (University of Alaska), Kenneth Pyle (University of Washington), Richard Samuels (Massachusetts Institute of Technology), Robert Scalapino (University of California-Berkeley), Enders Wimbush (Hudson Institute), and William Wohlforth (Dartmouth College).

The Strategic Asia Program depends on a diverse funding base of foundations, government, and corporations, supplemented by income from publication sales. Support for the program in 2005 comes from the Department of Energy, the GE Foundation, the Henry M. Jackson Foundation, and the Lynde and Harry Bradley Foundation.

Attribution

Readers of Strategic Asia reports and visitors to the Strategic Asia website may use data, charts, graphs, and quotes from these sources without requesting permission from The National Bureau of Asian Research on the condition that they cite NBR *and* the appropriate primary source in any published work. No report, chapter, separate study, or extensive text, or any other substantial part of the Strategic Asia Program's products may be reproduced without the written permission of The National Bureau of Asian Research. To request permission, please write to:

The NBR Editor
The National Bureau of Asian Research
4518 University Way NE, Suite 300
Seattle, WA 98105
nbr@nbr.org

The National Bureau of Asian Research

The National Bureau of Asian Research is a nonprofit, nonpartisan research institution dedicated to informing and strengthening policy in the Asia-Pacific. NBR conducts advanced independent research on strategic, political, economic, globalization, health, and energy issues affecting U.S. relations with Asia. Drawing upon an extensive network of the world's leading specialists and leveraging the latest technology, NBR bridges the academic, business, and policy arenas. The institution disseminates its research through briefings, publications, conferences, Congressional testimony, and email forums, and by collaborating with leading institutions worldwide. NBR also provides exceptional internship opportunities to graduate and undergraduate students for the purpose of attracting and training the next generation of Asia specialists.